Table of Contents

Prologue   xviii
    Mormonism: a Scriptural Community, xviii
    The Scriptural Base of the Community, xx
    Mormonism: An Introduction, xxi

Chapter 1. The *Book of Mormon* in Its Historical Setting   1
    The Sons of Noah 1
    Who Are the Indians? 1
    Cromwell and Manasseh ben Israel 2
    Thomas Thorowgood: Jews in America 3
    John Eliot, "Apostle to the Indians" 5
    The Idea of Hebrew Indians Continues and Strengthens 6
    Constantine Samuel Rafinesque 12
    The Latter Days and Second Coming 14
    Jonathan Edwards: America and the Isles of the Sea 15

Chapter 2. History, Archaeology and the *Book of Mormon*   17
    Archaeology: Quest for the Nephites 17
    The Archaeological BOM Item List 17
    The Sound of Silence: Nephite History in a Vacuum 33
    The Archaeology Cultures List 36-41

Chapter 3. Mapping the *Book of Mormon* Setting   43
    The Abstract Approach 44
    The South America Approach 45
    The Central America Approach 47
    The Quest for an Alternative Setting 49
    Mapping the *Book of Mormon* 53
    The Map 69
    Where Did All the Cities Go? 71
    Crucifixion Cataclysm: A Research Perspective 73

Chapter 4. Demographic Issues   76
    Nephites Maximized: Demographic Improbabilities 76
    Record-Keeper Recording Time and Nephite Generations 82
    Jaredite Chronology 86
    Nephite Life Expectancy 87
    Millennial Population Growth 87

Chapter 5. The Bible versus the *Book of Mormon*   90
    The Brass Plates of Laban 90
    Lehi's Jerusalem: Bible vs. *Book of Mormon* 91
    The Age of Scientific Discovery, and the Bible 94
    Isaiah 95
    John and the Book of Revelations 97
    Biblical Variant Readings in the *Book of Mormon* 99
    BOM Isaiah and the King James Mistranslations 117
    New Testament Intrusions 126

Chapter 6. Nephite-Lamanite Intangible Culture: Religion   129
    The Religion of the Nephites 129
    The Religion of the Lamanites 137
    The Case of the Missing Nephite Christians 139

Chapter 7. Nephite-Lamanite Intangible Culture: Language   145
    The Brass Plates of Laban: Establishing the Language Base 145
    Approaches to the Study of BOM Language Issues 150

Chapter 8. The Post-Biblical Euro-Christian Text   169
    Unsustainable Biblical Interpretation 170
    Freemasonry 176
    Influences from Hymns 180
    Theological Euro-Christian Phrases 189
    Addressing Modern Issues 205

Chapter 9. Restoring and Supplementing Biblical Texts   210
    The Book of Abraham 210
    Reformed Egyptian Exists 210
    Joseph Smith's Notion/Rational for Reformed Egyptian 211
    Facsimile No. 1. The Lion Couch Scene 219
    The Egyptians Never Occupied Ur of Chaldea 228
    Facsimile No. 2. The Hypocephalus 232
    Facsimile No. 3 237
    The Book of Ether 238
    The Book of Moses 239
    The Doctrine and Covenants 242

Chapter 10. Lehi: A History to Convert the Lamanites   246
    "For This Very Purpose Are These Plates Preserved" 246
    The Book of Lehi: The More Particular Record 247
    The Devils in the Details: The First Centuries in the New World 247
    The Devils in the Details: "Our Proceedings in the Wilderness" 248

The Ministry Material 256
The Isaiah Package 257
The Life of Lehi 261
The Genealogy Quagmire 262
Outlining the Book of Lehi 262

Chapter 11. The Book of Lehi: Its Genesis and Exodus   264

Joseph Smith's 1826 Pretrial Examination 264
An Angel by Any Other Name… 267
The Ordeal of Getting the Plates 270
The Weighty Issue of a Gold Bible 272
How About Brass Plates? 276
The Production of the Book of Lehi 277
Martin Harris: A Doubting Thomas? Or A Scout? 278
The Fate of the Purloined Pages 282
Lucy Smith on the Purloined Pages 286
Joseph Smith on the Purloined Pages 287
Baseless Fears, or Lame Explanation? 288
Demise of Lehi, Birth of a Bible and Confederates All 289

Chapter 12. BOM Authorship: From Drafts to Ms ⊙   293
From Drafts to Ms ⊙ 294
The Page Headings: A Nonissue? 295
Book Summaries & the Division of the Book of Nephi Draft 301

Chapter 13. BOM Authorship: The Spalding-Rigdon Theory   304
The Spalding-Rigdon Theory 304
Hurlbut: The Syllogism's Minor Premise & Conclusion 305
The Oberlin Manuscript 318
Sidney Rigdon 319
Multiple-Contingency Hypothesis: Beware the Weakest Link 325

Chapter 14. BOM Authorship: One Author or More?   328

The War of the Statisticians 328
Wordprinting Egyptian? 333
BOM Segmentation: A Facilitator for Division of Labor 333

Chapter 15. BOM Authorship: Interfacing Nephi & Mosiah   337

The Great Mosiah Mystery 337
Mosiah Restored 339
Issue of Mosiah Priority: D&C 10 343

Issue of Mosiah Priority: The Gathering Folds   345
Issue of Mosiah Priority: The Problem of the Retained Pages   347
Issue of Mosiah Priority: Words of Mormon   349
Metcalfe's Style Shift: *Wherefore/Therefore* & Mosiah Priority   351

Chapter 16. BOM Authorship: Sequential or Collaborative?   358

Distribution of Distinctive and/or Thematic Words & Phrases   359
The Distribution of Strategies & Habits of English Usage   362
The Distribution of Superfluous *That* Phrases   364
The Distribution of *That* Clauses   365
The Distribution of Participial, Infinitive & Gerund Phrases   374
Nephi-Mosiah Simultaneity?   378

Chapter 17. Project Completion: Smith's A Team & Their Milieu   381

Predispositions in early 19th-Century New England   382
Perspective: Pseudepigrapha and Other Deceptions   383
The Necromancer's Magic Book and the Rodsman's Hazel   386
The Heritage and Family of Joseph Smith   388
Joseph Smith Sr. (1771-1840)   391
Joseph Smith Jr. Begins His Mission   393
Joseph Smith's First Vision   398
Hyrum Smith: Elder Brother, Confidant & Collaborator   401
Joseph Smith Sr. Seizes the Moment   402
Enter Oliver Cowdery   405
The Witnesses   411
The Witnesses: Demise and Apostasy   418
Any Confessions?   419
Lucy Smith: Devoted Mother, Biographer & Propagandist   420
Oliver Cowdery: You Can Run, but You Cannot Hide   421
Martin Harris: The Disgruntled Investor   422
David Whitmer: Waiting in the Wings   423

Chapter 18. Project Completion: Getting to Mormon, & Moroni   426

From Initial Drafts to Completed Drafts, to Ms *O*, to Ms *P*   429
Cousin Rivalry: Oliver Cowdery's Revelation   434
The Moroni Addition   439
Getting the Job Done   444

Chapter 19. Church, Power and the Promised Land   447

Proselytism: Mormonism on the Rise   450
Security, Persecution and Slander   451
Creating a Church: Organization and Control   452
Hierarchy, Incipient Theocracy, Opposition, and Resolution   463

Creating a Church: Ritual   465
Creating a Church: Theology   476
Worship   480
Are Mormons Christians?   482
Financial Foundations   483
Theocracy and the Power to Coerce   487
Joseph Smith & Criminal Justice in Missouri   492
Security & Enforcement in Nauvoo   494
Security & Enforcement in Brigham Young's Utah Territory   495
Joseph Smith: Loose Cannon, or Mission Accomplished?   496

Chapter 20. Private Initiatives to Develop a Mormon Culture   501
Dimensions of Insulation   501
Demography and Economy   502
State/Secular Education   503
Mormon Education to Enable Orthodox & Reverent Learning   505
LDS Publishing   510
Private Publishing   510
The Relief Society   510
The LDS Welfare Program   511
The LDS Primary Organization   512
The LDS Fast Offerings Program   512
Mutual Improvement Association   512
The Mormon Tabernacle Choir   514
Theater in Zion   514

Chapter 21. Secular Issues and LDS Apologetics   519
Secular Progress in Knowledge Relevant to LDS Claims   519
Mormon Apologetics   522
A Bible in Search of a Geographical Setting   527
Archaeology: Just Horsing Around?   530
Hugh Nibley, Apologist in Chief   531
In Search of a Hebrew BOM Text   534
Chiasmus, *Parallelismus Membrorum*, *Māshal*, & Poetry   549
Lehi's Arabia   558

Chapter 22. Fragmentation and Consequent Conflict   561
Churches That Separated in Joseph Smith's Lifetime   561
Churches Resulting from Bids to Succeed Joseph Smith   562
Churches That Split over the Suspension of Polygamy   564
Schismatic Secularism: the Godbeites   567
Schisms and Lifestyle: the Gay Mormons   568
Mormon-Related Crime   570
Church-related Incidents of Violence in the Utah Territory   574

Assassination & Murder in & among Mormon Splinter Groups   575
Rape under Religious Cover   578
Incest & Inbreeding in Mormon Communities   580

Chapter 23. Quest for Exaltation in a Secular Society   **583**
Socialization into the LDS Community: From Cradle to Temple   585
The Appeal of LDS Theology   591
The Anguish of Apostasy   592
Thou Shalt Be Happy   594
The Plight of Willful Women   595
Where Have All the Apostates Gone?   598
Cultural Mormons   598
A Scriptural Community Like No Other   602

Tables
Table 1. Archaeology and the *Book of Mormon* Item List   18
Table 2. Pre-Columbian Cultures   36
Table 3. Max Nephite Population & Significant Events   78
Table 4. Plates Transmission & Record-keeper Recording Time   83
Table 5. Jaredite Begats (From the Tower of Babel to 600 BCE)   86
Table 6. A Hypothetical BOM Demography, 88
Table 7. Distribution of *Book of Mormon* Variants   102
Table 8. The Longer *Book of Mormon* Variants   112
Table 9. Mistranslation in the King James Version of Isaiah   119
Table 10. Some Pre-Christian NT Passages in the *Book of Mormon*   127
Table 11. Distribution of Nephite/Lamanite Names   151
Table 12. 118 Personal Names Borne by Only 1 Individual in the OT   154
Table 13. BOM Name Recurrence   155
Table 14. Names Ending in *hor*   156
Table 15. Evil vs. Good: Gad and Gid Names   156-57
Table 16. Name Elements in Biblical Hebrew   158-59
Table 17. Names & Aliases after *Book of Mormon* Publication   162-163
Table 18. Names with "Interpreted" Semitic or Egyptian Content   164
Table 19. BOM Place Names & Locations in the New York Area   167-168
Table 20. Middle Egyptian and Coptic Pronouns Compared   211
Table 21. Examples of Smith's Egyptian Alphabet and Grammar   214-115
Table 22. Smith's BOA Translation from the Abraham Papyrus   224-226
Table 23. Weight of the Plates (Various Metals Compared)   273
Table 24. Page Content Headings & Book Synopses in Mss *O* & P   295-99
Table 25. Solomon Spalding (also Spaulding)   305
Table 26. Doctor Philastus Hurlbut   306
Table 27. Hurlbut's Statements re Spalding's Ms (1833)   309-310
Table 28. Sidney Rigdon   320-21
Table 29. Distribution of Thematic Words and Expressions   360-361

Table 30. Grammatical Element Distribution   366-367
Table 31. The Paternal Line of Joseph Smith Jr.   388-389
Table 32. The Maternal Line of Joseph Smith Jr.   389
Table 33. The Birth Family of Joseph Smith Jr.   390-391
Table 34. Heritage and Family of Oliver Cowdery   405-406
Table 35. Claims of Persons Purported to Be Witnesses   416-417
Table 36. Death and Apostasy among the Witnesses   418
Table 37. The *Book of Mormon* Remake: Events and Dates   426-419
Table 38. Religion Statistics Profile of Salt Lake County, Utah   502
Table 39. Utah Employment by Industry Sector, 2014   502-503
Table 40. Utah Performing Arts, 2016-17   516
Table 41. Initiators of Institutions in the Mormon Heartland   517
Table 42. Decipherment of Mayan Writing   520-522
Table 43. Summary of BOM Cartography Efforts   527
Table 44. Assertion that BOM Names Occur in Hebrew Inscriptions   538
Table 45. Assertion that Egyptian Names Occur in the BOM   545-546

Figures
Figure 1. Distribution of *Book of Mormon* Variants   103
Figure 2. Does Egyptian Have a More Compact Script?   213
Figure 3. Copy Made from the Anthon Transcript   216
Figure 4. Facsimile No. 1 (*The Book of Abraham*)   219
Figure 5. Egyptologist Bell's Proposed Reconstruction   220
Figure 6. The Papyrus used for a part of *The Book of Abraham*   221
Figure 7. Smith's Modified Papyrus for Facsimile No. 1   221
Figure 8. The Passage to the Left of the Lion Couch Scene   223
Figure 9. Texts Used to Produce Abraham & the Hypocephalus   223
Figure 10. BOA Facsimile No. 2: Smith's Hypocephalus Fabrication   233
Figure 11. Facsimile No. 2: Scribe's Copy Showing Missing Sections   233
Figure 12. Papyrus JS IV: Smith's Source for the Boat Insert   235
Figure 13. How to Customize a Hypocephalus   236-237
Figure 14. Book of Abraham facsimile No. 3   237
Figure 15. Computer-Enhanced Oberlin Ms Wrapper   317
Figure 16. Distribution of *Therefore & Wherefore*   354
Figure 17. Distribution of *Whoso, Whosoever* and *He That*   355
Figure 18. Distribution of Phrases with Superfluous *That*   364
Figure 19. Distribution of Adverbial & Direct Object *That* Clauses   369
Figure 20. Distribution of *Relative, Redundant and Insomuch That*   370
Figure 21. Distribution of *Would That, Suffer That & Cause That*   371
Figure 22. Distribution of *Suppose That, See That & Know That*   372
Figure 23. Distribution of *Command That* and *That Thereby*   373
Figure 24. Distribution of *Unto & Like Unto*   374
Figure 25. Distribution of Infinitive and Participial Phrases   376
Figure 26. Distribution of *Behold, Begin* (Plus Infinitive) & *for to*   377

Figure 27. Apologetics in the *Improvement Era* and *Ensign*   525
Figure 28. The Temple of the Panels of Reliefs: Hunter vs. Others   530

Maps
Map 1. Topography of Columbia & Neighbors   21
Map 2. The Great Lakes BOM Setting (without Details)   50
Map 3. The Americas and the Principal Nephite Territory   55
Map 4. 1820's School-Book Map of Central America   56
Map 5. The Lands of the Nephites and Lamanites   70
Map 6. The 8th Campaign of Thutmose III   230
Map 7. Jerusalem to the Red Sea   250
Map 8. Arabian Trade Routes   251

Appendices
Appendix 1. Additional Analysis of BOM-KJ Variants   606
Appendix 2. Mistranslation in the King James Version of Isaiah   610
Appendix 3. Scribe Details as Per Manuscript Page of Ms 𝒪   624
Appendix 4. Apologetics in the Improvement Era & Ensign   629
Appendix 5. Documents Prior to 1830   631

Bibliographies
Bibliography 1. Biblical Materials (Annotated)   634
Bibliography 2. Lexical and Linguistic Resources   646
Bibliography 3. *Book of Mormon* Cartography   647
Bibliography 4. General References   650

Index   658

Acknowledgments

MAGNA CUM GRATIA

My research began in 1967 when I was a graduate student at Harvard in the Semitic languages. I had shared with a fellow graduate student some of the claims made by LDS scholars regarding the Isaiah variant readings in the *Book of Mormon*. He responded, "Have you checked these claims yourself?" With no little embarrassment, I admitted that I had not. He then simply said, "Well Chris, with your background in Classics and Semitic, you could couldn't you?" Enough said. I set about scouring the collections at Harvard Library and Harvard Andover Library, to supplement the critical editions of the Old and New Testaments, having no idea what I would find.

By 1972 this work was completed in agonizing detail. I then found myself back at the University of Utah working on a second MA It was there that I first met Michael Marquardt. Even at that early date, we recognized that we were pilgrim scholars on the same quest. We occasionally communicated over the decades, and I followed his extensive research, up to when I retired in Hawaii, which some might say is as close to Paradise as I am likely to get. A visit from Michael and his wife Dorothy reawakened my interest in my own Mormon research. From that moment on, I found Michael to be supremely generous with his time. He has been an unerring touchstone for whatever I came up with. When my draft had reached a nearly complete state, he volunteered to read it, and provided me with numerous corrections and valuable suggestions.

It was through Michael that I met Dale Broadhurst, whose invaluable websites are well known to serious scholars and students interested in Mormon studies. We began a series of discussion lunches where ideas flowed while pouring only modest libations to our muses. He typically would urge me down a path that I was unaware of and would never have taken without him.

A review of my footnotes readily reveals that the present study is deeply indebted as well to the work of many other scholars in Mormon studies. I hasten to add that my expression of gratitude is not intended to imply that any of those who have helped me is in full agreement with all of my interpretations of information in this very challenging field.

Prologue

Mormonism: A Scriptural Community

A scriptural community is a community of believers who share a common faith in a foundational scripture that is in some way unique to them. The creation of a scriptural community presupposes the prior creation of such a scripture. Examples usually cited are the Jews and their *Torah*, the Christians and their *New Testament*, and the Muslims and their *Qur'an*. The second task, is to develop the rites of the faith. The third of course, is to attract adherents to the faith that centers itself on this scripture. And fourth, the community must succeed in maintaining this faith. In the case of the Mormons (the Church of Jesus Christ of Latter-day Saints, i.e. the LDS), and the Community of Christ (formerly the Reorganized Church of Jesus Christ of Latter Day Saints, i.e. the RLDS), the principal founding scripture is the *Book of Mormon*.

The rise of the Mormons in the nineteenth century resulted in what is arguably the first scriptural community of note since Muhammad. With the rise also of the age of reason, so called, and modern science, the scriptures of all such communities have been subjected to serious scrutiny, including the Bible and the Qur'an. The scriptures that provide the basis of identity of the members of the LDS Church are no exception, i.e. primarily the books of Mormon, Abraham and Moses. These three, plus Smith's personal revelations, contain the basis for LDS polytheist Christianity.

These three can be exposed to scientific scrutiny of a totally higher order than the Bible and Qur'an, since the extra-Biblical works of the LDS canon are based on assertions upon which their authenticity rests, and which are potentially amenable to the strict canons of empirical testing. The efforts to do so have a checkered history, but have produced serious problems for many of the more intellectual and educated members of the community, and some concern that a significant number are losing their faith, especially among the intelligentsia and youth. Being almost totally a lay church, the LDS establishment has developed a unique form of pastoral care to instill and preserve the faith of the Latter-day Saints from cradle to temple. It has also responded with large and well-funded institutions to defend the faith: LDS apologetics.

The present work commences with a study of the development of cultural and theological beliefs, from Columbus to the early nineteenth century, that shaped the development of LDS scripture, including, especially, the assertion that the Native Americans descend from an ancient migration of Hebrews (or Israelites) to the Americas. It proceeds to delineate the development of the LDS Church, and ultimately the later institutions that characterize today's Mormon scriptural community, which has come to be respected, and to some degree admired, even outside Mormon circles. These latter, it will be shown, were largely developed by the faith and efforts of extraordinary nonclerical believers.

Within this context, this work presents a significant number of empirical tests of the three canonical works that claim ancient origin, and in particular the *Book of Mormon*, and the results of these tests. Some of these are newly developed by the author, and others have been expanded and/or updated. Every effort has been made to present them in sufficiently clear and documented terms to enable the reader to evaluate and replicate them. Those which have been around for some time have met with criticism from the community of LDS scholars. Their work is also examined, in this context, and beyond, extending to their own efforts to find proofs for the authenticity of LDS scriptures. This scope of work can be described succinctly by an alternative title for this book: Mormonism, the Creation *and Maintenance* of a Scriptural Community.

Due to the radical departure of Mormon theology from the traditional theology of the various Christian groups that came from Europe to the New World, Mormonism has attracted considerable attention from other Christian leaders, at times antagonistic to the Mormons, to say the least, as well as from scholars of the historical and comparative study of religion. Although various "churches" arising in the Americas have differed in theological details, they have all been based on cardinal articles of belief based on the Nicene Creed agreed in the Council of Nicaea in 325 CE. LDS theology is at odds with it. As a result, specialists in the history of religion have referred to Mormonism as being the American religion, a theologically new development in the United States, rather than a reinterpretation of the theology brought from Europe. By contrast, groups, such as the Seventh Day Adventists and Jehovah Witnesses, still do adhere to the basic tenets of the Nicene Creed.

The Scriptural Base of the Community

The career of Joseph Smith traditionally begins with his *First Vision*. There are three written versions of this account; and actually, from a totally empirical perspective, it cannot be proved that any one is truly what he might have experienced. The date of the described event is also in dispute. It is generally said to have been c. 1822. The earliest version is dated 1832. The third version was published in a Mormon collection of scripture called the *Pearl of Great Price*, and was originally dictated by Joseph Smith in 1838. This has become the Church's official version. In it, Smith recounts:

> When the light rested upon me I saw two personages... One of them spake unto me calling me by name and said, pointing to the other— *This is my beloved Son, Hear him!* ... I asked the personages who stood above me in the light, which of all the sects was right—and which I should join. I was answered that I must join none of them, for they were all wrong; and the Personage who addressed me said that all their Creeds were an abomination in his sight... (Smith 2:17-19)

The Joseph Smith story, with this version of the vision, has ever since been a part of the *Pearl of Great Price*, and is treated as scripture. Apart from being the experience *princeps*, this third account seems to be an inchoate expression of what would later become the heart of Mormon Christian polytheism, i.e., that God the Father and God the Son (Jesus Christ) are two separate anthropomorphic deities. The LDS godhead consists of these plus the Holy Ghost, all separate deities.

The second important account is that in which Joseph Smith describes his acquisition of the gold plates through the agency of an angel, Moroni (the ancient New-World son of Mormon), who had hidden them to come forth in the latter days. In 1830, Smith published the text that he claimed to have translated from the plates by the power of God. This text purports that the account therein is a fifth-century CE abridgment made by Mormon of the records of a civilization of Israelite origin, just before the total destruction of his people (hence the title, the *Book of Mormon*, and the nickname given the believers in the book, the Mormons).

Although the process of canonization happened over time, and possibly continues, by the date of the murder of Joseph Smith at Carthage Jail, Illinois, in 1844, the corpus of scriptures in the Mormon canon was complete as it existed from 1860 to the second half of the twentieth century, including:

The Old Testament (OT, usually the King James Version, KJV)
The New Testament (NT, usually the King James Version)
The Book of Mormon (BOM)
The Book of Moses (Moses, first book of the *Pearl of Great Price*)
The Book of Abraham (BOA, second book of the *Pearl of Great Price*)
Writings of Joseph Smith (Smith, third book of the *Pearl of Great Price*, later called *Joseph Smith–History*)
The Doctrine and Covenants (D&C, originally, the *Book of Commandments*, BC, Joseph Smith's revelations)

This corpus, then, but especially the *Book of Mormon*, became the core of the shared belief of the Mormon scriptural community.

Mormonism: An Introduction

Among the general public, Mormonism is often associated with polygamy, Joseph Smith, gold plates and some notion of a Mormon Bible. Few are aware of Mormon polytheism. Few have any idea of what the *Book of Mormon* is. Actually, even many Latter-day Saints have not been adequately grounded in their own religion. Hence this introduction.

Mormons believe that the two American continents were kept apart from the rest of the world as part of a divine plan. The BOM identifies these as being two of the "isles of the sea" that Isaiah associates with the Israelite diaspora (24:15 & 60:9). They were to be given as an inheritance to two migrations. The first migration, the Jaredites, was led to the New World at the time of the Tower of Babel, by a prophet called the brother of Jared. They also brought animals to reintroduce them after Noah's flood. The Jaredites eventually fell into ungodly and sinful ways, and their internecine wars resulted in their total annihilation by around 600 BCE. It is generally held that only one survived to make a relatively brief contact with the second group, who, like the first, were given the land for their exclusive occupation, as a promised land.

Around 600 BCE, another prophet, Lehi, was called in Jerusalem and given the mission of leading an Israelite group to the New World. He led his family east of Jerusalem into Arabia. His sons were then commanded to return to Jerusalem twice, once to get the family of Ishmael, which had daughters, so that the sons of Lehi could marry. The second time was to obtain the Bible to take with them, such as it existed at that time. This contained the works from Exodus, through Isaiah, and even part of Jeremiah, who at that time was still issuing revelations from his prison cell. The BOM description of this body of scripture is that it had already been collected as a single volume, and had been inscribed on brass plates in an Egyptian translation, for reasons not explained. They were in the possession of a wealthy Judean warrior and elder named Laban, who had to be killed to get the plates. In the *Book of Mormon*, they are referred to as the Brass Plates of Laban.

After eight years, this group arrived at the shore of the Indian Ocean, where they built a ship and sailed to the Americas, landing on the west coast of South America. The younger son, Nephi, had emerged as the spiritual leader and the man who could get things done, which stirred up resentment in the hearts of the oldest of Lehi's sons, Laman, and his brother Lemuel. These revolted and formed their own group. Nephi was commanded to depart into the wilderness with his faithful followers, who accepted the teachings of the Gospel of Jesus Christ. Somewhere south of the Isthmus of Panama they established a new city, called Nephi, the center of a land called the land of Nephi. These became the Nephites, who for most of their history were largely faithful to the gospel. The followers of Laman came to be called the Lamanites, were cursed by God with a "dark and loathsome" skin, and are described as being bloodthirsty, savage and indolent.

A second group was also commanded by God to leave Jerusalem, led by Mulek (not mentioned in the OT), a righteous son of the unfortunate king Zedekiah. These made landfall north of the Isthmus of Panama, and eventually founded their city, Zarahemla. Several centuries after their first landfall (over one century BCE), the rising power of the evil Lamanites forced the Nephites to relocate to the north and join with the Mulekites in Zarahemla. Thus this city became the capital of the Nephites, while the city of Nephi became the capital of the Lamanites.

When Jesus was crucified, the wrath of God rained down on both of these groups, who had become sinful, and only the righteous among them were spared. After his resurrection, Jesus spent some time with them, called twelve disciples, and organized his Church. After his departure, the Twelve succeeded in converting all the land to Christianity and the true Church prospered in the land for about two centuries, the Christian era of pre-Columbian America. Then, however, a great apostasy arose in the land, and the Lamanite-Nephite division emerged again. Around 421 CE, the Lamanites succeeded in totally annihilating the Nephites. The Lamanites became the "savages" (native Americans), fallen Israelites, found in the New World when the Europeans arrived, albeit with a promise that if they convert to Mormonism (the restored gospel of Christ), they will become white and delightsome.

For reasons to be explained later, Nephi had been commanded to keep two records, engraved on metallic plates, one focusing on historical detail, and the other on the teachings of the gospel of Christ. A line of successors continued the record, eventually producing a variety of records. The last great Nephite general, Mormon, abridged the records of the Nephites on gold plates, writing in reformed Egyptian, with the explanation that he did not have enough gold to write them in Hebrew. His son, Moroni, buried the plates in a hill, Cumorah, in upstate New York, and appeared later as an angel to Joseph Smith to deliver the plates to him. These were translated by divine power, and published as the *Book of Mormon* in 1830.

The Mormons initially concentrated in Kirtland, Ohio, where they built their first temple. They then began gathering to Jackson County, Missouri, which Joseph Smith revealed was the site of the Garden of Eden. Persecution in Kirtland contributed to this move. Conflict arising from Mormon settlement and aspirations in Missouri resulted in what Missouri historians have dubbed the Mormon war. In 1839 they moved to Commerce, Illinois, which they purchased, and then established a new city, which they renamed Nauvoo. The Church established a War Department, with General (Prophet) Smith as its head. By the time Joseph Smith was murdered (27 June 1844), the texts that would become the Mormon canon had been completed, as well as their ritual practices, including temple rituals partly derived from Freemasonry but attributed to the temple of Solomon. Their migration from Illinois to the Utah Territory, under the iron-fisted leadership of their new Prophet, Seer and Revelator, Brigham Young, brought them to a state of splendid isolation, where for many decades, indeed effectively for a whole century, they could develop their society and culture without significant outside (gentile) interference. The Mormons were becoming a people. Although they believe that their church is always headed by a prophet of God, no subsequent prophet has added to the Mormon canon. Eventually, in the second half of the twentieth century, Mormonism found its isolation increasingly penetrated, on various fronts. The LDS establishment responded by developing institutions to shield its members from non-Mormon influences, and to mount a vigorous apologetic capability to counter faith-disrupting information.

Chapter 1

The *Book of Mormon* in Its Historical Setting

The Sons of Noah

In the early centuries of the period of history we now refer to as the Common Era (CE, rather than AD), two scriptural communities, the Jews and the Christians, overlapped in their belief in certain books later incorporated into what the Christians came to call the Old Testament. In those days, even the most erudite of their scholars believed that Noah's flood had actually happened, and that a wrathful deity had destroyed every man, woman and child from the face of the earth, with the exception of the family of Noah in the Ark. Partly to define how they should relate to the peoples of the earth, but also to make their belief in this tale more credible, they set about constructing a global family tree. They had become aware of the existence of numerous large, well-peopled and even ancient civilizations in Europe, Africa and Asia, all of which had to somehow be descended from the family of Noah. Various branches of the tree were more favored by God, and others even cursed. This established some concept of a racial ranking of the nations.

The earliest and most influential effort to define the global family tree was that of Flavius Josephus (1st century CE), in his book *Antiquities of the Jews*. Christian efforts built on the work of Josephus, such as the works of Hippolytus of Rome (c. 234 CE), Saint Jerome (c. 390 CE) in his work *Hebrew Questions on Genesis*, and Isidore of Seville (c. 600 CE) in his *Etymologiae*. As Christians became more aware of other civilizations than their own, and even some other significant civilizations, it became necessary to rethink the family tree. The entire enterprise suffered a bit of a shock, when in 1492, Columbus discovered the New World, replete with yet other extensive and even rich civilizations.

Who are the Indians?

Although most Europeans who actually went to the Americas spontaneously recognized that the inhabitants native to these new lands were actually human beings, strange views of these people began to circulate back home. Europe already had many tales of wild men, monstrous races and fabulous creatures. Lewis Hanke, in his work *Aristotle and the American Indians*, provides many details of Europe's first theories to explain these peoples. "A 1498 edition of John of Holywood's *Sphaera Mundi* describes the inhabitants of the New World as being 'blue in colour and with square heads.'"[1] In Wilberforce Eames' "Description of a Wood Engraving, Illustrating the South American Indians (1505)," we read

> They go naked, both men and women; they have well-shaped bodies, and in colour nearly red; they bore holes in their cheeks, lips, noses and ears, and stuff these holes with blue stones, crystals, marble and alabaster, very fine and beautiful. This custom is followed alone by the men. They have no personal property, but all things are in common. They all live together without a king and without a government, and every one is his own master. They take for wives whom they first meet, and in all this they have no rule. And they eat one another, and those they slay are eaten, for human flesh is a common food. In the houses salted human flesh is hung up to dry. They live to be a hundred and fifty years old, and are seldom sick.[2]

Already in the sixteenth century, we find notions that the Americas had become the home of giants, of Gog and Magog, and even of remnants of the Lost Tribes of Israel.

Cromwell and Manasseh ben Israel

In addition to establishing the Church of England, King Henry the Eighth (1491-1547) began the foundations for the British navy, which would eventually "rule the waves" in an empire upon which the sun never set. The Jews had not had any significant presence in England prior to the Normand conquest, and were expulsed from England at the time of the defeat of the Normand occupation. Oliver Cromwell (1599-1658), who ruled England as Lord Protector (1653-58), undertook an economic policy of mercantilism, to promote the expansion of British trade abroad. He saw that by allowing a Jewish commercial presence, he could expand England's international economic reach, almost with the stroke of a pen.

---

[1] Lewis Hanke, *Aristotle and the Americdan Indians. A Study in Race Prejudice in the Modern World* (Mishawaka, IN: Better World Books, 1970).
[2] *Ibid*, 5.

To do this, he would have to overcome opposition in Parliament, where deep prejudices existed against Jews, based on the religious prejudice that branded them as "Christ killers."

Manasseh ben Israel (1604-1657), a leading rabbi in Amsterdam, undertook a mission of Christian-Jewish reconciliation, and worked to secure the resettlement of Jews in England. In his famous book, *Spes Israelis* (*The Hope of Israel*), published in Latin, Spanish and English in 1650, he presented an elaborate argument that the Tribes of Israel had been dispersed to every corner of the world, including the Americas. If prophecy makes it clear that the Jews are to be scattered to every corner, and every isle of the earth, then their absence in England must be holding up the End of Times. But Manasseh knew well that Cromwell had other than religious interests in this issue. He wrote a booklet to the Lord Protector titled *How Profitable the Nations of the Jewes Are*. When he arrived at Whitehall in the fall of 1655, his petition in hand, he was not admitted to the Council of State. Cromwell had taken the matter into hand personally, and had met with fierce opposition. Even though the petition was never actually accepted, Manasseh's efforts are deemed a success, as the presence and commercial activities of the Jews in England soon began to prosper, and some already there took off their Christian masks. The theological dimension remained important. "The 'Hope of Israel'–the Messiah–could not come until the Jews were dispersed to the ends of the Earth. Since they had been found even in America, and since the oppressions accompanying the 'Coming' were apparent, it became more and more vital to return the Jews to England."[3] England was holding up the Second Coming.

Thomas Thorowgood: Jews in America

In the same year that Manasseh published *Spes Israelis*, Thomas Thorowgood (1600-1669) published in England his *Jews in America, or Probabilities That the Americans Are of That Race*, in which he quotes

---

[3] Lee Eldridge Huddleston, *Origins of the American Indians. European Concepts, 1492-1729* (Austin: The University of Texas Press, 1967), 132. The Hebrew original of *Spes Israelis* apparently claimed that the Indians did not descend from the Ten Tribes, although Israelites had gone to America. See Henry Méchoulan & Gérard Nahon, "Introduction," in Menasseh ben Israel, *The Hope of Israel. The English Translation by Moses Wall, 1652* (Oxford: Oxford University Press, 1987), 63 & 89.

from *Spes Israelis*. His work is an investigation into the evidence that the native Americans are descended from the Israelites, a condemnation of the treatment that the Indians have suffered at the hands of the Conquistadors, and, at the same time, concern regarding the religious neglect they have suffered at the hands of the English. Although he began his career as a priest in the Anglican Church, he joined the Puritans in 1640.

In 1550, a century before these works were being published and read in England, the king of Spain, Charles V, summoned the Council of the Fourteen to sit in Valladolid, to judge the issues regarding what the relationship should be between the Spanish and the Indians, to wit: "is it lawful for the king of Spain to wage war on the Indians before preaching the faith to them in order to subject them to his rule, so that afterwards they may be more easily instructed in the faith?"[4] Sepulveda argued that the use of force was both lawful and expedient as a preliminary to conversion, while Bartolomé de Las Casas took the opposite view. Thorowgood echoes this debate when he writes: "Athanasius never committed any man to a Gaoler, saith hee himselfe in his Apology; and againe, the truth is not preached with swords, and darts and Armies, but by reason and Arguments..." The first of the four requirements he lists to this end is language, the need to approach the Indians in their own tongue, and, presumably, to translate the scriptures. He urges that

> a stock of money must be remembered, which in some sense, is as it were the soule of this worke ...If we meane the Indians shall be Gospellized, they must first be civilized... The Spanish books relate strange things of their zeale in this kinde, and one whom we may credit tells us, that America hath foure Arch-Bishops, thirty Bishops, and many other houses as they call them of Religion, and if it be said their lot fell into the golden part of that world, and out of their superfluities they might well spare vey much, tis very much indeed, and yet tis somewhat more that the same writer observeth how the King of Spain maintaines the lists and bonds of Missionaries, Priests, Fryers and Jesuits, that are continually transported into America, hee provides for every of them ten yeeres, and that to this day.[5]

---

[4] Hanke, *Aristotle and the Indians*, 38.
[5] Thomas Thorowgood, *Jews in America, or Probabilities That the Americans Are of That Race* (London: W.H. for Thomas Slater, 1650), 70, 94-95.

Since reports back to England on the progress of "gospellizing" the Indians is urged, it is noteworthy that his book contains such a report, published anonymously (by Thomas Shepard?), titled *The Day-Breaking, if not the Sun-rising of the Gospell* (sic) *with the Indians in New England* (London, 1647), usually included as one of the Eliot tracts).

There was of course an awareness that there were many Indian languages, although people tended to refer to the language of the Indians. The need to be able to communicate with these people was felt also by Roger Williams, founder of Providence, who published *A Key into the Language of America* in 1643. His was the first book on an Indian language in English. He made some reference to a comparison with the Hebrews, and though he found some words similar to Hebrew, he wrote, "Yet againe, I have found a greater Affinity of their Language with the Greek Tongue."[6]

A point of interest is Thorowgood's consideration, and ultimate rejection of the idea that the Indians had been Christianized c. 150 CE:

> ...all are not of the mind that the Indians have not heard of the Gospell: for Osiander speaking of Vilagagno, and his planting there in Brasil, writes confidently, without doubt those people received the Gospel of Christ by the preaching of the Apostles 1500 years since, but they lost it againe by their unthankfulnesse; and Malvenda allegeth some conjectures that Christianity might have been among them..[7]

John Eliot, "Apostle to the Indians"

John Eliot, a Puritan minister at the church in Roxbury (Massachusetts Bay Colony), immigrated to New England in 1631. Although he held no high position in the colony, or in the church, his influence was considerable, to the point that he was considered by his contemporaries (and ever since) as the Apostle to the Indians, a sort of New England Paul. Already in the colonies there were not only the Native Americans who were not Christian, but a growing number of settlers, born in frontier areas, who had no church affiliation, and had never been baptized. This situation gave rise to The Great Awakening (or The First Great Awakening), oriented both to the conversion of the Indians, and

---

[6] Roger Williams, "To the Reader," in *A Key into the Language of America* (Bedford MA: Applewood Books reprint, 1936). First published in 1643.
[7] Thorowgood, *Jews in America*, 24.

relatively heathen Gentiles alike. Eliot authored various tracts, mostly to raise funds in England for the missions to the Indians, and his key role in this regard made him, posthumously, a central figure in the Second Great Awakening, in the first few decades of the nineteenth century. His view that the Indians were descended from the Israelites continued to attract attention in the revival movements in New England. In pursuit of his mission, he published in 1666 *The Indian Grammar Begun, or an Essay to bring the Indian Language into Rules*. He set up the Christian Indian town of Natick for the Nonantum, Neponset, and Musketaquid Indians, in an effort to prepare them for the reign of Christ. "The Lord Jesus is about to set up his blessed kingdom among these poor Indians" (first letter to Winslow). "In September 1651, he installed the millennial civil polity at Natick up through a single ruler of one hundred,"[8] and in that same year he published his translation of the New Testament into the Indian tongue, and his translation of the Old Testament two years later. This was the first Bible printed in America. Eliot remained almost a revivalist rock-star; in 1822, Martin Moore published the *Memoirs of the Life and Character of Rev. John Eliot* (Boston), and a steady flow of books and pamphlets about John Eliot has continued to this day.

The Idea of Hebrew Indians Continues and Strengthens

> And the Lord shall scatter thee among all people, from the one end of the earth even unto the other; and there thou shalt serve other gods, which neither thou nor thy fathers have known, even wood and stone. (Deuteronomy 28:64)

In 1775, James Adair, "A Trader with the Indians, and Resident in their country for Forty Years," published *The History of the American Indians*, which is largely a marshaling of what he considered to be evidence for a Hebrew origin of the Indians. He wrote, "From the most exact observations I could make in the long time I traded among the Indian Americans, I was forced to believe them lineally descended from the Israelites, either while they were a maritime power, or soon after the

---

[8] Richard W. Cogley, *John Eliot's Mission to the Indians before King Philip's War* (Cambridge: Harvard University Press, 1999), 92.

general captivity; the latter however being the most probable."⁹ Contrary to his information, Israel had never been a maritime power. The Hebrews had generally not inhabited the coastal regions of the Land of Canaan, and the fleet of Solomon was built for him by Hiram, King of the Canaanites (Phoenicians), at Tyre/Sidon.

Another writer speculating on the origin of the American Indians was Daniel Gookin, who had ties to Rev. John Elliot Sr., Apostle to the Indians, by the marriage of his daughter to Elliot's son. In his *Historical Collections of the Indians in New England* (1674), he presented various theories, including that of derivation from the Israelites. He refers to "those inhabiting Peru and Mexico, who were most populous, and had great cities and wealth..." Of the Israelite theory, he says it is "perhaps not so improbable, as many learned men think."¹⁰

In 1816, Elias Boudinot published his *Star in the West; or, a Humble Attempt to Discover the Long Lost Ten Tribes of Israel, Preparatory to their Return to their Beloved City, Jerusalem.* In this work, a sense of national mission emerges. "Who knows but God has raised up these United States in these latter days, for the very purpose of accomplishing his will in bringing his beloved people to their own land."¹¹

In 1801, Charles Crawford published the second edition of *An Essay on the Propagation of the Gospel; in which there are numerous facts and arguments adduced to prove that many of the Indians in America are descended from the Ten Tribes*. He refers to the work of Adair, among others, to make his arguments. He writes that William Penn (General Description of Pennsylvania) said of the natives of Pennsylvania, "For their original I am ready to believe them of the Jewish race, I mean of the stock of the Ten Tribes; and that for the following reasons: First, they

---

⁹ James Adair, *The History of the American Indians*, edited and with an introduction and annotations by Kathryn E. Holland Braund (Tuscaloosa: University of Alabama Press, 2005), 74. First published in 1775,
¹⁰ Daniel Gookin, *Historical Collections of the Indians in New England* (Boston: At the Apollo Press, by Belknan & Hall, 1792), 145. The copy cited is an exact replica from Book Renaisance.
¹¹ Elias Boudinot, *Star in the West or a Humble Attempt to Discover the Long Lost Ten Tribes of Israel Preparatory to Their Return to Their Beloved City Jerusalem* (Trenton, NJ: George Sherman, Printer, for D. Fenton, S. Hutchinson and J. Dunham, 1816), 297.

were to go to a land not planted or known, which to be sure Asia and Africa were, if not Europe."[12]

In 1823, Ethan Smith (no relation to Joseph Smith), a Congregational pastor in Poultney, Vermont, published *View of the Hebrews* asserting that the Indians are the descendants of Israel, and in 1825, he published an expanded edition, *View of the Hebrews; or The Tribes of Israel in America*. He wrote

> It inevitably follows, that the ten tribes of Israel must now have, somewhere on earth, a distinct existence in an *outcast* state. And we justly infer, that God *would* in his holy providence provide some suitable place for their safe keeping, *as his outcast tribes*, though long unknown to men as such…If God will restore them at last as his Israel, and as having been '*outcast*' from the nations of the civilized world for 2500 years; he surely must have provided a place for their safe keeping, as a distinct people, in some part of the world during that long period.[13]

Quoting from 2 Ezra (13:40-44, called the Fourth Book of Ezra, an apocryphal work, in a Latin text, thought to be originally in Greek, composed c. 100 CE), he writes:

> Those are the ten tribes which were carried away prisoners out of their own land, in the time of Osea, the king, whom Salmanezer, the king of Assyria, led away captive; and he carried them over the waters, and so came they into another land…But they took this counsel among themselves, that they would leave the multitude of the heathen, and go forth into a further country, where never man dwelt; that they might there keep their statues (sic) which they never kept in their own land.—There was a great way to go, namely , of a year and a half.[14]

---

[12] Charles Crawford, *An Essay on the Propagation of the Gospel in Which There Are Numerous Facts and Arguments Adduced to Prove That Many of the Indians in America Are Descended from the Ten Tribes* (Philadelphia: James Humphreys, 1801), 12.

[13] Ethan Smith, *View of the Hebrews, Exhibiting the Destruction of Jerusalem…* (Poultney, VT: Smith & Shute, 1823). Ethan Smith, *View of the Hebrews; or the Tribes of Israel in America. Second edition, improved and enlarged* (Poultney, VT: Smith & Shute, 1825). The edition cited is: (Salt Lake City: Bookcraft for the Religious Studies Center at Brigham Young University, 1996), 50.

[14] See Ethan Smith, *View of the Hebrews* (1825), 51.

In 1824, John V. Yates and Joseph W. Moulton listed many prominent finds of the early inhabitants of the Americas, in their *History of the State of New York*. They wondered at the remains:

> In the valley of the Mississippi, the monuments of buried nations are unsurpassed in magnitude and melancholy grandeur by any in North America. Here cities have been traced similar to those of ancient Mexico, once containing hundreds of thousands of souls. Here are to be seen thousands of tumuli, some a hundred feet high, others many hundred feet in circumference, the place of their sepulchers, their worship, and perhaps of their defence [sic]. Similar mounds are scattered throughout the continent, from the shores of the Pacific into the interior of our state, as far as Black river, and from the lakes to South America.
>
> There is one class of antiquities which present themselves on digging from thirty to fifty feet below the surface of the ground. They occur in the form of firebrands, split wood, ashes, coals, and occasionally tools and utensils, buried to these depths by the alluvion.[15]

Their work sounds very modern, although lacking the information available today. After stating that "not one authentic record remains of even the name of any of these populous and powerful nations,"[16] they review many writers, with as many theories, including the possibility that the Indians descend from the Tartars, and that they in turn descend from the lost tribes of Israel. They also suggest that a number of Old World nations might have made contact with the New World prior to Columbus.

In 1828, Israel Worsley published his book, sold by the author at Plymouth, *A View of the American Indians, their General Character, Customs, Language, Public Festivals, Religious Rites and Traditions: Shewing them to be the Descendants of the Ten Tribes of Israel. The Language of Prophecy concerning them, and the course by which they travelled from Media into America.* He quotes from 2 Ezra, the same passage quoted by Ethan Smith above. By his estimation, they crossed by "Bhering's Straits" near a copper island, and reached this continent through the Northeast Passage.[17]

---

[15] John V. N. Yates and Joseph W. Moulton, *History of the State of New York*, vol. I, part I (New York: A. T. Goodrich, 1824), 20.

[16] *Ibid*, 22.

[17] Israel Worsley, *A View of the American Indians* (Plymouth: W. W. Arliss, 1828); edition cited (New York: Arno Press reprint, 1971), 132-34.

In 1826, Josiah Priest published *The Wonders of Nature and Providence Displayed*, a collection of very disparate accounts of natural and human phenomena. It includes two accounts of North American Indians, and one of sacrifices to idols in Mexico. One of the former is titled "Proofs that the Indians of North America are lineally descended from the ancient Hebrews."[18] In 1833, he published three editions of his *American Antiquities*.[19] The fifth edition of this work advertises that 22,000 copies had been sold to subscribers only. In 1829, Barbara Anne Simon published *Hope of Israel. Presumptive Evidence that the Aborigines of the Western Hemisphere are Descended from the Ten Missing Tribes of Israel*.[20] After 1830, some authors sought to buttress this view by referencing *Antiquities of America* by Edward King.[21] By 1836 Simon's sequel bore a more assertive title.[22]

Many of these accounts attempt the precarious task of describing the Hebraic character of the American Indians, while admitting that they are now in a savage or degraded condition. The work of Ethan Smith is significant, not just that it asserts an Israelite origin of the Indians, but that it argues that the land had been set aside for the lost tribes to be kept distinct and apart. This is also the view in the *Book of Mormon*, 2 Nephi 1:8, "And behold, it is wisdom that this land should be kept as yet from

---

[18] Josiah Priest, *The Wonders of Nature and Providence Displayed* (Albany: published by the author, 1826). It includes "Proofs that the Indians of North America Are Lineally Descended from the Ancient Hebrews," 372; "An Account of Festivals in Honour of Idols among the Ancient Mexicans," illustrated with a lithograph, 173; and "Narrative of the Travels and Adventures of Mr. Ker, through the Wilderness from New-Orleans, toward New-Mexico, as far as the Macedus, or Welch Indians—Also his account of several other Tribes, of Mines, Wild Bests, &c.," 472.

[19] Josiah Priest, *American Antiquities and Discoveries in the West being an Exhibition of the Evidence that an ancient population of partially civilized nations, differing entirely from those of the present Indians, peopled America, many centuries before its discovery by Columbus, and inquiries into their origin* (Albany, NY: Hoffman and White, 1833)

[20] Barbara Anne Simon, *Hope of Israel. Presumptive Evidence that the Aborigines of the Western Hemisphere are Descended from the Ten Missing Tribes of Israel* (London: R. B. Seeley, 1829).

[21] Edward King (Lord Kingsborough), *Antiquities of Mexico* (London: A. Aglio, 1830-48).

[22] Barbara Anne Simon, *The Ten Tribes of Israel Historically Identified with the Aborigines of the Western Hemisphere* (London: R. B. Seeley, 1836).

the knowledge of other nations; for behold, many nations would overrun the land, that there would be no place for an inheritance."

One might think that the Americans in the first half of the nineteenth century would be surprised to read in the *Book of Mormon* that pre-Columbian America had been Christianized in antiquity. But some already considered this obvious. Note, for example, the argument of Samuel Mather published in 1773. "Then there must be above two hundred and fifty Brethren, besides the twelve Apostles and the Seventy Disciples, who had seen CHRIST, and could attest to the Truth and Certainty of his Resurrection, and so to the Divinity of his Religion: And a considerable Number of these might come to our Western World. And so America must have been filled up with the Gospel, according to our Apostle's Expression."[23] In the minds of the BOM authors, the visit of Jesus himself to the new world would be an equally obvious deduction from the verse "And other sheep I have, which are not of this fold: them also I must bring, and they shall hear my voice; and there shall be one fold, and one shepherd." (John 10:16)

The American Jewish community had their own vision of the near future, which grew into the Zionist movement. A prominent example almost in Joseph Smith's backyard was the effort of Mordecai Manuel Noah (1785-1851). "In 1825, Noah helped purchase a tract of land on Grand Island in the Niagara River near Buffalo, where he envisioned a Jewish colony to be called Ararat."[24] "Noah's city of refuge became a nationwide *cause célèbre* in the weeks and months that followed his 'Proclamation for the Jews' at the dedication and the elaborate speech he gave the following day."[25] "To accommodate the large inaugural crowd, Noah rented a Buffalo church. Cannoneers fired a salute and Seneca Chief Red Jacket arrived by boat (Noah was convinced that America's

---

[23] Samuel Mather, *An Attempt to Shew that America Must Be Known to the Ancients* (Boston: J. Kneeland, 1773), 23-24.
[24] "Mordecai Manuel Noah," in the Jewish Virtual Library, accessed 24/03/2017.
[25] Eran Shalev, "'Revive, Renew, and Reestablish': Mordecai Noah's Ararat and the Limits of Biblical Imagination in the Early American Republic," posted on http//:www.americanjewisharchives.org (downloaded 25/03/2017).

Indians were the Ten Lost Tribes of Israel)."[26] The Smiths, Cowderys and Whitmers could hardly have been unaware of this extravaganza.

Constantine Samuel Rafinesque

These days, it seems that everyone wants to lay claim to getting to the Americas before Columbus. One begins to wonder, "Who didn't discover America?" The two claims that seem to have real evidence are those for the Vikings and for the Polynesians. Prior to 1825 the list was much shorter, and sometimes literary rather than literal.

Lest we give the impression that in the 1820's everyone was tracing the Amerindians to the Israelites, we must make mention of the work of the polymath Professor Rafinesque. He was an indefatigable reader and field worker, who identified and published quite a number of American species, some of which still bear the names he gave them. Natural history was his main field, but he included human history in that rubric. He assembled a huge collection of actual and legendary names of people, peoples and clans, worldwide, and attempted to arrive at a history of the dispersion of the postdiluvian peoples across Eurasia and Africa, and then the Americas. The earliest arrivals included migrations and more casual contacts from Europe to North America, including from the Atlantans of Plato, which he thought had occupied an island complex in the eastern Atlantic, near the Canary Islands. A second migration came from Central Asia and Siberia, across the Behring Straits.[27] This is an example where he was able to apply his impressive imagination to a mass of details, and arrive at an important core of truth, albeit couched in a tremendous amount of legendary chaff. The migration from Asia is now well established, and the migration from Europe is not yet a dead theory, although very skimpily evidenced. Along the way, he presented a description of the evolution of the species, without a knowledge of the

---

[26] "Mordecai Manuel Noah," http//:www.myjewishlearning.com (downloaded 25/03/2007).
[27] C. S. Rafinesque, *Ancient History, or Annals of Kentucky; with a Survey of the Ancient Monuments of North America; and a Tabular View of the Principal Languages and Primitive Nations of the Whole Earth* (Frankfort, KY: printed by the author, 1824); see also *Atlantic Journal and Friend of Knowledge* (1832-33).

mechanisms later supplied by Darwin.[28] Mayanists respect him for identifying the elementary principles of how the Mayans represented their counting system, generally considered to be the first correct step anyone every made towards deciphering Mayan texts.[29] It is notable that, unlike so many others, when giving the names of so many peoples and clans that figured in the settlement of the Americas, he never included the Israelites. Indeed, he maintained "that many nations came to America before and after the flood; but no Jews ever came there before Columbus."[30]

Another alternate of note is the 1807 epic poem written by Robert Southey, published in two volumes in London. According to Welsh folklore, Madoc, or Madog ab Owain Gwynedd, sailed to America in 1170. In Southey's treatment of the legend, he makes a dangerous voyage to the west, and at long last:

> When, like a cloud, the distant land arose
> Grey from the ocean... when we left the ship,
> And cleft, with rapid oars, the shallow wave,
> And stood triumphant on another world!

Madoc witnesses Aztec human sacrifice and recruits the assistance of a local tribe to subdue the Aztecs and put an end to this practice. On a return voyage, he finds that the Aztecs had reverted to the practice.

A more famous work in Mormon studies is that of Solomon Spalding (Spaulding), who died in 1816. He wrote a historical romance based on a landing of Romans headed to England, but blown off course. We will examine this work in greater detail within the context of the Spalding-Rigdon theory of BOM authorship.

---

[28] C. S. Rafinesque, "Extract of a letter to Dr. J. Torrey of New York dated 1st Dec. 1832," in Charles Boewe, ed., *Rafinesque Anthology* (Jefferson, NC: McFarland & Company, 2005), 242-48.

[29] This was published in a letter to the editor of the *Saturday Evening Post*.

[30] C. S. Rafinesque, "Letter of Professor Rafinesque, of Philadelphia, to Mr. Josiah Priest, of Albany, on *American Antiquities*," dated 5 January 1835, in Boewe, *Rafinesque Anthology*, 16.

The Latter Days and Second Coming

A central rationale of the *Book of Mormon* is that the gold plates will be dug up as part of the restoration of all things, and to gather the part of Israel in the New World in the Last Days. This is stressed early in the text (1 Nephi 25-27), and near the end. In Mormon 5:15 we find that "this people shall be scattered, and shall become a dark, a filthy, and a loathsome people." But "out of the earth shall they [the plates] come in a day when it shall be said that miracles are done away..." (Mormon 8:26) "Behold, the Lord hath shown unto me great and marvelous things concerning that which must shortly come, at the day when these things shall come forth among you." (Mormon 8:35) "Behold, will ye believe in the day of your visitation—behold, when the Lord shall come..." (Mormon 9:2)

This reflects the belief among many during much of the nineteenth century, that the Second Coming was imminent. Heightened expectations of millennialism and Adventism began in the First Great Awakening of the eighteenth century, were revived in the Second Great Awakening, and produced a number of notable movements in the nineteenth century. In 1758, millennialism was spelled out in Joseph Bellamy's *The Millennium*, his "immensely popular sermon."[31] He said:

> But when shall the son of David reign, and the church have rest? ... Perhaps the very time was designed to be shadowed forth in the law of Moses, in the institution of their holy days. The *seventh day*, said God, who always had this glorious season of rest in view, 'the seventh day shall be a Sabbath of rest, the seventh month shall be full of holy days, the seventh year shall be a year of rest' so, perhaps, after *six thousand* years are spent in labour and sorrow by the church of God, the *seven thousandth* shall be a season of spiritual rest and joy, an holy Sabbath to the Lord.[32]

> Surely it is infinitely unbecoming the followers of Him who is King of kings and Lord of lords, to turn aside to earthly pursuits, or to sink down into unmanly discouragements, or to give way to sloth and effeminacy, when there is so much to be done, and the glorious day is coming on.[33]

---

[31] Alan Heimert and Perry Miller, eds., *The Great Awakening* (Indianapolis and New York: The Bobbs-Merrill Company, Inc., 1967), 610.
[32] Heimert and Miller, *The Great Awakening*, 617.
[33] Heimert and Miller, *The Great Awakening*, 634.

In Pennsylvania, communal millennialism was promoted by the Rappists (Harmonites), and the Harmony Society founded by Johann Georg Rapp. Their center was at first at Harmony, Butler Co., Pennsylvania, then Harmony, Indiana, and at the time of the Second Great Awakening at Economy (Ambridge), Pennsylvania. The Shakers (originally, the United Society of Believers in Christ's Second Appearing) also formed millennialist communal settlements, centered in New Lebanon, New York (southeast of Albany). The popularity of the millennialist doctrine is seen in Josiah Priest's 1828 work, *A View of the expected Christian Millenium* (sic), *which is promised in the Holy Scriptures, and is believed to be nigh; its commencement, and must transpire before the Conflagration of the Heavens and the Earth, Embellished with a chart, of the Dispensations from Abraham to the end of time.* (Albany: Published for subscribers, Loomis' Press, 1828)

Jonathan Edwards: America and the Isles of the Sea

"The Latter-day Glory Is Probably to Begin in America"

Few American writers on religion were as influential as Jonathan Edwards. He is often considered to be the greatest American theologian. When he fell out of favor with the religious establishment in his district, he could have had a parish in Scotland, or alternatively a Virginia church. Declining both, in 1751 he became pastor of the church in Stockbridge, Massachusetts and a missionary to the Housatonic Indians. He boldly defended their interests, successfully attacking the whites who were using their official positions among them for self enrichment. His view that the work of God in the Latter-day glory will most likely begin in America is consistent with the rise of the view of America as the modern Zion. He writes:

> And there are many things that make it probable that this work will begin in America.—It is signified that it shall begin in some very remote part of the world, with which other parts have no communication but by navigation, in Isa. lx. 9. "Surely the isles shall wait for me, and the ships of Tarshish first, to bring my sons from far." It is exceeding manifest that this chapter is a prophecy of the prosperity of the church, in its most glorious state on earth, in the latter days; and I cannot think that any thing else can

be here intended but America by the isles that are far off, from whence the first-born sons of that glorious day shall be brought.[34]

In the late eighteenth and early nineteenth centuries, assertions that the Indians were descended from the tribes, or a tribe, of Israel had become commonplace, both in books and in some newspapers. No doubt this theme had also made its way into the sermons preached from the pulpits and in the less formal tent revivals of the Second Great Awakening. It was believed by many that the gathering of these "fallen Israelites" was needed in preparation for the imminent arrival of the millennium of Christ's rule on earth. It followed that they must have been taken to an isolated place far from other nations in order to keep their race pure. The most influential theologian of the time, Jonathan Edwards, argued that this place must be in the Americas, which he identified with the islands of the sea referred to by Isaiah. These popular views of the Hebrews in the New World had swelled to become a significant wave, and the *Book of Mormon* would prove that it could ride it well.

---

[34] Jonathan Edwards, "The latter-day glory, is probably to begin in America," in *Some Thoughts Concerning the Revival of Religion in New England*, Part II, Sect. II, (Boston: Printed and sold by S. Kneeland and T. Green in Queen-street, 1742). The edition cited is in *The Works of Jonathan Edwards* (Edinburgh: The Banner of Truth Trust, 1990), 381.

Chapter 2

History, Archaeology and the *Book of Mormon*

Archaeology: Quest for the Nephites

In the nineteenth century, what developed into the school of Higher Criticism undertook to find and apply rational and scientific methods for the study of history, and perhaps especially of the Bible, with seminal works by Julius Wellhousen, Friedrich Schleiermacher, David Friedrich Strauss, Ludwig Feuerbach, Ernest Renan and Rudolf Bultmann. By the end of the twentieth century a number of scholars in Mormon studies had done some similar work, which has laid the foundation for a Higher Criticism of the *Book of Mormon*.

Initially, critics of the *Book of Mormon* were virtually all self-declared foes of this new bible. Their work was built on faded memory, hearsay, rumor and at times deliberate calumny. A century later, pre-Columbian archaeology began providing a scientific basis for a school of Higher Criticism to address BOM issues. Some major civilizations sometimes cover only a few centuries. Classical Greece lasted about three. The Mormon bible asserted that for a millennium after 600 BCE pre-Columbian America had been occupied exclusively by what eventually became millions of Israelites, and gave extensive details of the material culture, geography, cities and villages. We should expect to find scientifically dated remains of items mentioned in the BOM, including fortifications, cities, tools, furnishings, clothing, weapons, and the crops and animals used for food, wool and work.

The Archaeological BOM Item List

To systematize this inquiry in an efficient manner, an item table has been prepared of items mentioned in the BOM narrative, with indications of what has and has not been found.

Table 1. Archaeology and the *Book of Mormon* Item List

Item in the BOM	Found in Pre-Columbian Archaeological Sites?
Hebrew Texts	none, in either book or inscriptional format
reformed Egyptian Texts	none, in either book or inscriptional format
City walls	yes, but associated with other cultures only
High places, temples	yes, but associated with known Mayan, Olmec, Aztec (etc.) cultures
Iron works	no smelted iron has been dated to this time frame (although cold hammered iron objects have been found in the Pacific Northwest)
Steel works	no evidence of steel smelting in this time frame
Brass	no evidence of brass in the New World, but bronze existed in South America
Copper	yes, especially in South America (including smelting)
Gold	yes, but it spread rather late into Mesoamerica
Silver	yes, but it spread rather late into Mesoamerica
Ziff	none (See discussion below)
Chains	none, with the possible exception of gold jewelry
Swords of metal, esp. steel	none
Breastplates of metal	none found
Cement houses	none (only adobe, of late production, and plaster)
Plowshares	none
Wheeled vehicles	none (toys, but no vehicles, there being no draft animals)
Chariots	none
Roads	paved roads for processions and to enable teams of men to carry heave tax/tribute bundles through rainforests and other difficult terrain
Machinery	See below
Gold & silver coins	No coinage has been found in the New World. (Note: The BOM does not use the word "coin" but "pieces" of silver & gold, each with a different name, which it refers to as "money." The chapter heading used to say "Nephite coins and measures," up to the 1960's, but now says "Nephite coinage")
Horses	none found by the Europeans, and no bones have been found of horses dated to within the last 7,000 years
Cattle, bull, calf, ox	no cattle found by the Europeans, nor any bones of cattle
Sheep	no sheep found by the Europeans, nor any bones of sheep
Goats	no goats found by the Europeans, nor any bones of goats (apart from mountain goats)

(Table 1 continued)

Ass	not found
Swine	not found
Flocks, herds	none for any of the above animals
Elephants (Jaredites)	not found (or even mammoths, in the last 7,000 years, nor bones in this period)
Barley	none found, nor barley pollen
Wheat	none found, nor wheat pollen
Corn (maize)	found
Grapes	no *vitis vinifera* (wine grapes), but other species did exist
Figs	none
Silk	none
Linen	none
Crucifixion cataclysm	see discussion below
Israelite DNA	not found (see discussion below)

Ziff is found in Mosiah 11:3 in a list of metals, which are, in the order found in the text: gold, silver, ziff, copper, brass and iron. The use of a Nephite word should indicate that it is a material for which there was no equivalent in the English language of the 1820's. There is no evidence of a metal in pre-Columbian America that was unknown to English speakers when the *Book of Mormon* was being prepared.

There is no way to know what is meant by "machinery" in Jarom 1:8. Noah Webster, in 1828, defined it as:

> A complicated work, or combination of mechanical powers in a work, designed to increase, regulate or apply motion and force as the machinery of a watch or other chronometer.[35]

In this context, one can suggest that minimally it refers to laborsaving and/or task-enabling devices with at least one moving part, based on the principle of the lever, and/or the wheel. Examples of early machinery include the water-driven mill, ox-driven or man-driven mills, weight lifting devices, including the lever (beam on a fulcrum), simple cranes and pulleys, water lifting devices (the simple *shādūf*, in the Middle East by 1500 BCE, and the larger and more complex noria water wheel, developed in Egypt possibly 300 BCE) and simple cog-wheels (using pegs as cogs). The reference is important because it implies an advanced

---

[35] Noah Webster, *An American Dictionary of the English Language* (New Haven: S. Converse, 1828).

agricultural economy that benefits from devices developed by urban-based artisan specialists, such as one might possibly expect to some degree of the Maya or Olmec civilizations. In any case, if they were in use anywhere, these are items that should have left discoverable remains.

It is clear from this list that nineteenth-century authors replicated their New England farm and town life in the *Book of Mormon*, with an item list that is largely just not found in the pre-Columbian New World.

Pre-Columbian DNA

The result here is quite definitive. It has been best presented in the Mormon context by Simon G. Southerton, an accomplished research scientist, and former Mormon, who served two years as an LDS missionary, and two years as a bishop. His study discusses the scientific findings in detail. His conclusions are succinctly stated as follows:

> The ancestors of Native Americans were Asians who unknowingly became the first Americans as they walked across Beringia over 14,000 years ago. The ancestors of the Polynesians were Asians who honed their considerable nautical skills among the islands of Southeast Asia before sailing out into the Pacific during the last 3,000 years. Regardless of coincidental cultural, linguistic or morphological parallels with the Old World, the peoples of the Pacific Rim who met Columbus and Cook were not Israelites. They were descendants of a far more ancient branch of the human family tree that had existed thousands of years before the Israelite branch sprouted into existence.[36]

It is worth noting here, too, that the languages of the pre-Columbian peoples are in no way similar to the Semitic family or to Egyptian. The Polynesian language group has been identified as being most closely linked to the pre-Chinese people of Taiwan, as well as their DNA.

Grain & Climate

According to the BOM narrative, Lehi's party landed on the west coast of South America. The military and missionary campaigns in and to the Land of Nephi (ultimately occupied mostly by the Lamanites) indicate that it was not far from the Nephites in Central America (see Chapter 3).

---

[36] Simon G. Southerton, *Losing a Lost Tribe. Native Americans, DNA and the Mormon Church* (Salt Lake City: Signature Books, 2004), 130.

This would place the landing most probably in Columbia or Ecuador. This is as tropical as it gets. Furthermore, the land rises abruptly from the sea to the heights of the Andes mountain chain. The elevation of Quito, capital of Ecuador, is 9,350 feet, the highest capital in the world. Yet it is only about 125 miles from the sea, and lies almost exactly on the equator. Medellin, Columbia, is lower, only 5,000 feet, and also about 125 miles from the sea. Further to the south, Pasto, Columbia, is 8,299 feet above the sea. The rise is so abrupt and rugged that going very far inland would not have been a realistic proposition. These Israelite settlers would have been confined to a relatively narrow equatorial coastal plain (v. Map 1).

When strife among them produced a split, Nephi's flight with his followers, a group of families, with their possessions, planting seed and flocks, can only have been up the coastal plain, to the lowlands south or southeast of the Isthmus of Panama. An idea of the totally tropical climate on the west coast can be had by noting that of Buenaventura, Columbia, which has an average high temperature in the nineties, 247 inches of rain annually and average humidity in the mid to high eighties. What a change for a band of Jerusalemites.

Map 1. Topography of Columbia & Neighbors

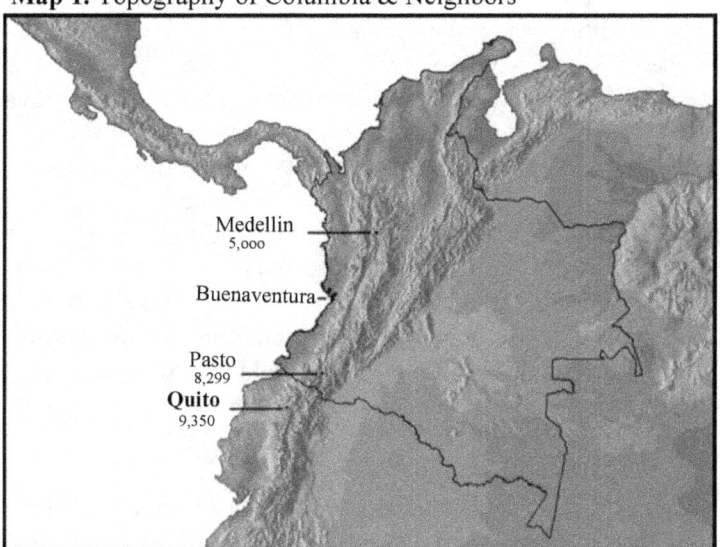

Based on a copyright-free map from Wikimedia Commons

Wheat is a temperate climate crop, and prefers moderate rainfall. One wonders if the Middle Eastern grains would have survived at all; certainly their yield and quality would have been miserable.

Grain Detection in Archaeology

This is a hypothetical discussion. There is no evidence that wheat or barley ever were cultivated in pre-Columbian America. Every modern excavation takes systematic soil samples for laboratory examination. A good example is the excavations at Shanidar Cave in northern Iraq, dating 35,000 to 60,000 years ago. There, Ralph and Rose Solecki discovered a burial, next to the Neanderthal cave that they excavated. They took routine soil samples to be analyzed and were informed that the layer of earth associated with the skeletal remains bore a very large concentration of pollen from flowering plants. The conclusion was that these Neanderthals had sufficiently developed feelings for their dearly departed and burial traditions that they had gathered a large number of flowers to throw in on top of the body before covering it with earth. For us, this is a good illustration of the extreme durability of pollen. Wheat and barley culture, during a millennium of Nephite-Lamanite occupation of large parts of the Americas must have produced settlement areas with soil saturated with wheat and barley pollen.

Another way of knowing what plants ancient peoples exploited, either as cultivars, or wild plants, comes to us from the excavation at Sandy Hill, Mashantucket, Connecticut. There, archaeologists analyzed stone tools for traces of starchy grains, dated to the ninth millennium BP (before present). They found some, including cyperus esculentus (a sedge) that is suitable as a food source. Indications are that one of the tools was used to process it. Due to the damp ecology, of the 23,000+ bone fragments collected, only white tailed deer could be identified with confidence.[37] Modern archaeology has come to closely resemble CSI forensics. Just as CSI might use sophisticated technology to analyze traces of blood, or explosive residue, archaeology uses similar and

---

[37] Thomas C. Hart & Timothy H. Ives, "Preliminary Starch Grain Evidence of Ancient Stone Tool Use at the Early Archaic (9,000 B.P.) Site of Sandy Hill, Mashantucket, Connecticut," in *Ethnobiology Letters* (http//:www.ethnobiology.org/ publications/ethnobiology-letters, Vol. 4:87-95, accessed 02 Sept 2013).

equally high-tech methods to analyze trace evidence on ancient tools. This technology would also detect other cultivars in addition to grain.

Horses, Chariots and Roads

These three are interlinked, although there is no skeletal evidence of horses in Pre-Columbian America since they had gone extinct in the Americas. When they were reintroduced by the Spanish, they began to spread from tribe to tribe. By collecting the oral history on this subject from the tribes, Francis Haines has traced their dispersion in North America from what emerged as the point of introduction.[38] The modern horse had evolved from the *eohippus* (by between 45 to 55 million years ago), to the *mesohippus* (by 32 to 37 million years ago), to the modern horse by c. five million years ago, all in the New World. For reasons poorly understood, the modern horse became extinct in the Americas by 10,000 to 7,000 years ago. Wild horses are of two types, the feral horse, once domesticated but later ranging free, such as the mustang (originally brought by the Spanish), and two species of the true wild horse, Przewalski's horse (or Mongolian horse) in Asia, and the tarpan (European wild horse, found in Europe and much of Asia up to c. 1900). Some LDS scholars have suggested that in a pocket or two in the Americas, the modern horse may have survived extinction at least into the BOM Nephite period. To bring this theoretical hypothesis into the realm of empirical reality, one must find and date skeletal remains.

Roads and Wheeled Vehicles

The absence of draft animals in Pre-Columbian America has implications for the probability of chariots. Although a model of a crude wheeled vehicle has been found, this is thought to have been a child's toy, showing that the concept of the wheel existed. So who knows? Even without draft animals, was a king ever moved about with a sort of rickshaw? Not impossible, but more pertinent would be to find remains of a chariot. Such remains have been found in the Old World. In the Champagne district of France an ancient chariot has been found in a tomb. A 4,000 year-old burial in Georgia (Eastern Europe) has preserved

---

[38] Francis Haines, "Where Did the Plains Indians Get their Horses?" *American Anthropologist*, new series, 1938, 40:112-137.

chariot remains. In Bulgaria, a Thracian chariot and two horses were buried, apparently upright. The remains of a beautifully decorated Thracian chariot were also found near a tumulus (burial) in Serbia.[39] In England, a 2,500 year-old chariot has been found with wheels, their iron rims intact,.[40] Also in England, Iron-Age ornate bronze remains of chariot fittings, and what possibly could be equestrian tools have been found at the fort at Burrough Hill.[41] In China, a Zhou dynasty burial yielded several intact wooden chariots with the complete skeletal remains of four horses, dated as early as 700 BCE, showing how wood can survive if buried.[42] Roman chariots have been found in Greece and Thrace.[43] The archaeological remains of chariots survive.

Finally, it is argued that since the Maya built roads (*sacbeob*, singular *sacbe*), they must have had wheeled vehicles. Indeed, the *sacbe* was a very sophisticated road, often quite narrow, but at times very wide. The majority are intrasite, meaning they were short procession ways connecting buildings inside the city. But others connected cities, and a few were quite long. The Cobá-Yaxuna *sacbe* was 100 kilometers long. In addition to ceremonial functions, these intercity *sacbeob* were used for commerce, bringing in tribute on the backs of slaves and possibly even for moving troops. The *sacbe* was often an elevated road, in places elevated to as much as one, or even up to three meters. They were essential for human foot travel through rugged land, especially land that is overgrown with forest and dense brush. In swampy areas, the elevated *sacbeob* kept the marchers above the flood level. Ancient Roman roads have deep ruts from the passage of wheeled vehicles. No evidence of this nature is associated with the *sacbeob*. Given the great utility of the roads for processions and foot travel, there is no reason to assume that they were used for wheeled vehicles.

---

[39] April Holloway, "4,000-year-old Thracian Chariot Unearthed in Serbia," (http//:www.ancient-origins.net, accessed 8/12/2013).
[40] *Deseret News*, 4/12/2003.
[41] "Stunning Discovery of Ancient Chariot Parts, Equestrian Tools", http//:www. Horsetalk.co.nz, accessed 14 Oct, 2014. "Burrough Hill Archaeologists Find Iron Age Chariot Remains", BBC News, accessed 14/10/2014.
[42] "Trip to the Zhou: Remains of horses and chariots unearthed from tomb dating back to 3,000-year-old Chinese dynasty" (http//:www.dailymail.com, accessed 2/09/2011).
[43] "Roman chariot burial site found [Greece]," with a subtitle "More Roman carts in Thrace" (http//:www.romanhideout.com, 15/02/2003).

Weapons

Relevant to the above are the remains of swords. Those with blades are found mostly in burials or river beds, since both environments are inimical to oxidation (rusting). Even if fully rusted, a sword that for any reason came to be covered with soil, or river or flood silt, would not disappear. Iron oxide is itself a stable compound, retaining every iron atom that went into the formation of the rust. Such a blade would have a bloated form, but would retain a recognizable blade shape. Together with a hilt, the weapon's identity would be certain.

In 2015, hikers in Norway found a Viking sword dated to c. 750 CE. This is a complete steel blade, rusted, but treatable.[44] Of more than a hundred Viking blades found, only around sixteen are swords, apparently because they were very expensive. At least 166 iron swords were found in La Tène at the northern edge of Lake Neuchatel. It is thought that the majority, but not all, of the Celtic swords found in lake beds were votive offerings. Finds have been made in various sites in Britain, such as the Williams and Thames Rivers, Llyn Cerrig Bach, Llyn Fawr, Flag Fen, Blackburn Mill and Carlingwark (Scotland).[45] Two Etrurian swords have been found, one in 7th century BCE Vetulonia and another in 4th century BCE Chiusia. The former was made of five strips of steel of varying carbon content, while the latter was made of a single ferrous bloom. A Roman sword has been found in a drainage system in Jerusalem, possibly dating to c. 66 CE. Another Roman sword has been found in Thrace (Bulgaria). The remains of Roman swords have been found in the excavations of the site of the famous battle of Teutoburg Forest, where the Germans slaughtered three legions led by Publius Quintilius Varus in 9 CE. Several Roman swords have been found in Pompeii. These are just a few of the steel swords that have been found. The reader needs only to visit online dealers specializing in ancient weapons to see images of many others, although the place and details of the find are often not given. Much more common are the sword hilts and scabbards that resist the ravages of time more successfully. Throughout Old World archaeology, one also finds the telltale evidence of sword cuts in the bones of human skeletal remains. Bronze and other copper alloy swords

---

[44] "1,200-year-old Viking sword discovered by hiker," cnn.com, 22 Oct 2015.
[45] Patrick Hunt, "Celtic Iron Age Sword Deposits and Arthur's Lady of the Lake," (Archaeolog, http//:www.traumwerk.stanford.edu/archaeolog/2008/02/celtic_swords_and_arthurs_lady.html, accessed 10 Feb 2016).

have been found of even earlier date. Given the massive exterminations in the BOM narrative, if they happened, similar finds would be inevitable, professionally dated to the pre-6th-century Americas.

Although our focus is on Pre-Columbian America, it is worth noting that the steel bow of Nephi (1 Nephi 16:18) is highly improbable. Actually, steel bows have existed for perhaps as much as two thousand years. During thirty years in the Semitic Middle East, I systematically collected premodern ethnographic artifacts, which eventually came to be my personal very focused museum of same, now on display in my home in Hawaii. I have an antique steel bow, made of spring steel with a silver layer on the front side of the bow and small inlaid gold nuggets. An almost identical one is on display in the museum in Riyadh, Saudi Arabia, dated to the nineteenth century. Although this may have been a ceremonial bow, early steel bows were used in hunting and warfare. The earliest development of steel bows appears to have been in India. There is indirect evidence that Indian metallurgists were experimenting with them perhaps as early as the third century BCE.[46] Such a bow constructed in the seventh century BCE is extremely unlikely. In an intriguing verse (1 Nephi 16:21) Nephi says that his brothers' bows had "lost their springs." This appears to be a double misconception, first of how an ancient bow might have been constructed, and second, the date of the emergence of spring steel. The existence of Steel swords in that century, such as the sword of Laban, has to be addressed cautiously. Some sort of sword made of iron is attested perhaps as early as the sixth century BCE. Could a ferrous bow have been made eighty years earlier? We cannot rule this out. Furthermore, since early forms of steel existed, the best might be called "most precious steel" at the time, even if it would be called mediocre at best today. The steel bow found in Wyoming, now in the Jim Gatchell Museum in Buffalo, is in perfect unrusted condition and considered to have been blacksmith-forged in the nineteenth century.[47]

---

[46] D. Elmy, "Steel Bows in India," *Journal of the Society of Archer-Antiquaries*, vol. 12, 1969.
[47] Benjamin Storrow, "Mystery Aiming for Answers. Historic Wyoming Steel Bow's Origins Confound Researchers," *Star-Tribune*, 8 September 2013.

Construction: Can the Absence of BOM Cities Be Finessed?

Even though stone construction was dominant in the parts of the Americas with high civilization, and the construction tradition of Judea was with stone where wood was somewhat scarce, some have argued that BOM civilization built exclusively with wood, and it all decayed, becoming soil, conveniently leaving nothing behind, nothing to find. There are a number of references in the BOM of buildings of wood. We also find references to "cities both of wood and cement" in the land northward. This gives rise to the observation that the BOM authors confused adobe with cement. (Helaman 3:7-11) When Nephi builds his temple, he describes it in glowing terms (2 Nephi 5):

> 14. And I, Nephi, did take the sword of Laban, and after the manner of it did make many swords, lest by any means the people who were now called Lamanites should come upon us and destroy us; for I knew their hatred towards me and my children and those who were called my people.
> 15. And I did teach my people to build buildings, and to work in all manner of wood, and of iron, and of copper, and of brass, and of steel, and of gold, and of silver, and of precious ores, which were in great abundance.
> 16. And I, Nephi, did build a temple; and I did construct it after the manner of the temple of Solomon save it were not built of so many precious things; for they were not to be found upon the land, wherefore, it could not be built like unto Solomon's temple. But the manner of the construction was like unto the temple of Solomon; and the workmanship thereof was exceedingly fine.

In addition to the main construction, there are other mentions of spacious buildings and fine materials used to ornament the walls (Mosiah 11):

> 8. And it came to pass that king Noah built many elegant and spacious buildings; and he ornamented them with fine work of wood, and of all manner of precious things, of gold, and of silver, and of iron, and of brass, and of ziff, and of copper;
> 9. And he also built him a spacious palace, and a throne in the midst thereof, all of which was of fine wood and was ornamented with gold and silver and with precious things.
> 10. And he also caused that his workmen should work all manner of fine work within the walls of the temple, of fine wood, and of copper, and of brass.

11. And the seats which were set apart for the high priests, which were above all the other seats, he did ornament with pure gold; and he caused a breastwork to be built before them, that they might rest their bodies and their arms upon while they should speak lying and vain words to his people.
12. And it came to pass that he built a tower near the temple; yea, a very high tower, even so high that he could stand upon the top thereof and overlook the land of Shilom, and also the land of Shemlon, which was possessed by the Lamanites; and he could even look over all the land round about.
13. And it came to pass that he caused many buildings to be built in the land Shilom; and he caused a great tower to be built on the hill north of the land Shilom, which had been a resort for the children of Nephi at the time they fled out of the land; and thus he did do with the riches which he obtained by the taxation of his people.

In archaeological fact, much has remained of wood-built sites, even without the wood. These include earthen mounds or walls, and sometimes with stone city walls. In China, earthen walls and other remains have been preserved at Dongzhao, from various ancient periods (Prehistory, Shang and Zhou dynasties). Just in 2014, complete dragon kilns were found at Yueyan, a mining site cluster at Dazhuangke and burials and cemeteries at Zunyi (Guizhou), Guojiamiao cemetery (Zaoyang, Hubei), Dabona cemetery (west Yunnan, Chu vthag cemetery (Ngari, Tibet) and Yihenaoer cemetery (Inner Mongolia). In Spain, a range of remains were found at Los Millares, possibly the largest city in Europe in its day. A mass of information has been collected from the Durrington camp of the builders of Stonehenge. Note too the mound builders in North America. It is clear that even if we limit BOM construction to that which the BOM authors knew best in New England, the cities should be found.

The ancient cities of Babylonia provide us with a striking example of urban survival. In the plain where the Tigris and Euphrates flow, there is precious little wood and almost no stone. Although some use was made of fired brick, and even rarely glazed brick, most construction was done with sun-baked brick which over time, covered by the accumulation of a tel, slowly returned to soil. Archaeologists work very carefully to locate the remaining outline of walls, which are almost indistinguishable from the soil that now encases them. When located, they slowly remove the soil on both sides of a wall, sifting every ounce in search of the tiniest object or fragment for analysis. This leaves the wall with a few inches of soil on both sides. When removing it, as the wall surface is approached, one uses a brush to gently remove the soil, and little by little a clear outline of bricks emerges. Unless coated over with plaster before the end of a dig season, or roofed over, these walls become mounds of mud in the winter rains, and only the archaeological photos remain. Even so, with careful painstaking work, the walls and foundations of the city emerge. The objects found are used to identify the use of each structure to the extent possible.

Many Mormons have generally believed that BOM architecture also involved some stone monumental structures. Surprisingly, some seek a way out by asserting that the Nephites were early Olmecs, or early Mayans. David A. Palmer flirted with the idea that the Olmecs relate to the Jaredites.[48] E. L. Peay believed that "the ancient Maya and the Nephites are the same people."[49] A good overview of assertions made regarding connections between the Olmecs, Maya and Aztecs, and the *Book of Mormon* peoples, can be found in the *magnum opus* of John L. Sorenson.[50] As writers become more aware of the wealth of archaeological and written information, this strategy has been losing steam. The sites are decorated with deities that are now well known, and with Mayan inscriptions that we can now read.[51]

BOM Fortification

There are many mentions of fortified cities, some with earthen circumvallation, and others with defensive stone walls:

---

[48] David A. Palmer, *In Search of Cumorah, New Evidences for the* Book of Mormon *from Ancient Mexico* (Bountiful, UT: Horizon Publishers, 1981), 125.
[49] E. L. Peay, *Lands of Zarahemla, A* Book of Mormon *Commentary* (Salt Lake City: Northern Publishing Inc., 1993), vi.
[50] John L. Sorenson, *An Ancient American Setting for the* Book of Mormon (Salt Lake City: Deseret Book Company, 1985), 96-137. See also John L. Sorenson, *Mormon's Codex, an Ancient American Book* (Salt Lake City: Deseret Books, 2013).
[51] Michael Coe, *Breaking the Mayan Code* (London: Thames & Hudson, 1999). See also the DVD documentary *Breaking the Mayan Code*, which shows step by step how Mayan was deciphered.

> Yea, he had been strengthening the armies of the Nephites, and erecting small forts, or places of resort; throwing up banks of earth round about to enclose his armies, and also building walls of stone to encircle them about, round about their cities and the borders of their lands; yea, all round about the land. (Alma 48:8)

Here, we have both city walls, and border walls of stone. This is massive. So this being the case, is it conceivable that no stone was used in the construction of monumental buildings, of temples and palaces?

Furthermore, earthen berms or packed earth walls were so high that "the Lamanites could not cast their stones and their arrows at them that they might take effect..." (Alma 49:4) The Nephites "encircled the city of Bountiful round about with a strong wall of timbers and earth, to an exceeding height." (Alma 53:4) Defensive walls were such that one needed "strong cords and ladders, to be let down from the top of the wall into the inner part of the wall." (Alma 62:21) Far from constructions that could have easily disappeared, we read of massive walls of earth and wood, and stone walls, not just around cities, but round about the borders of the land.

The use of berm-and-ditch fortification is noted in Alma 49:

> 13. For they knew not that Moroni had fortified, or had built forts of security, for every city in all the land round about.
> 18. Now behold, the Lamanites could not get into their forts of security by any other way save by the entrance, because of the highness of the bank which had been thrown up, and the depth of the ditch which had been dug round about, save it were by the entrance.

The use of berms to enclose an area is ancient. Especially on flat ground the berm is associated with a ditch, not just because of its defensive value, but because the ditch is the source of the soil to raise up a berm. The circumference of a berm is less than that of the ditch, and the soil is less packed than the native soil of the ditch, thereby producing a berm higher than one might expect compared to the depth of the ditch.

The first point to note here is that fortified cities of this nature survive extremely well. In England there are from two to three thousand hill forts, built in this manner.[52] Some were constructed in the Bronze

---

[52] About 3,300 are listed in A. H. A. Hogg, "British Hill-forts: An Index" (Oxford: BAR Brit. Ser. 62, 1979). See also "Hillforts in Britain" (Wikipedia,

Age, but the majority were built in the Iron Age, falling out of favor by the 2nd century BCE. The berm or berm-and-ditch structure is very well preserved in many of them. Originally thought to be nothing more than forts, some are now seen to have been or doubled as fortified towns.

When the early colonists arrived in New England, they noted the existence of raised earthen defense structures, which they attributed to a people prior to the Indians they encountered. Some still survive, but many have been plowed or bulldozed away. In the 1820's, more were in evidence to New England residents than can be visited today. They have been considered by some archaeologists to have been constructed under the influence of the mound builders to the west. Josiah Priest provides us with a description: "They [the fortifications at Marietta, Ohio] consist of walls, and mounds of earth, running in straight lines, from six to ten feet high, and nearly forty broad at their base. There is also, at this place, one fort, of this ancient description, which encloses nearly fifty acres of land."[53]

Although the BOM authors could have known about these earthen fortifications, it might be more probable that they had knowledge of those thrown up by their countrymen in the Revolutionary War and the War of 1812, for this construction persisted into the 19th century. An example is Fort Winchester on the Maumee River in Ohio, but closer to home is Fort George on the Niagara River.[54] A cursory reading of the BOM narrative reveals that its authors had more than a passing interest in military affairs, a trait that manifested itself later in Smith's formation of Zion's Camp and the Nauvoo Legion, which he commanded.

Great Expectations

If the *Book of Mormon* were an authentic history, the first thing that one would expect to find is the massive and extensive defensive stone walls and earthen berms. The latter have been found even in bronze-age forts and towns in England, and both were found at Los Millares, 5,000 years old. The BOM makes it clear that fortified walled cities existed in considerable number among the Nephites and Lamanites. Once found,

---

accessed 08/12/16); and D. W. Harding, *Iron Age Hillforts in Britain and Beyond* (Oxford: Oxford University Press, 2012).
[53] Josiah Priest, *American Antiquities*, 40.
[54] Ronald J. Dale, "Fort George National Historic Site" (http://www.eighteentwelve.ca/?q=eng/Topic/37, accessed 9 January 2016).

the area enclosed would be investigated for foundations of buildings. Usually one does not find massive ancient temples, apart from Egypt and, of course, Central America. Often there is some sort of a promontory that would have been taken over for the palace or chief temple, an acropolis. The elevation achieved would befit the position and prestige of the ruler or governor, and would enhance its other role as a last redoubt, against invaders, or one's own people. The BOM describes large and impressive buildings. These would have had adequate foundations. At least the thresholds and other recognizable construction elements would have been of stone, and the floors a sort of burnished clay, lime plaster, stone or bricks. Principal buildings would include a palace, one or more temples or other shrines or places of worship, storage buildings for tribute in kind (crops), etc. In other sites, ancient wood structures are clearly delineated by the large post holes for the large beams. These have been found in many parts of the world. It is the case, for example, of a temple in predynastic Hierakonpolis in Egypt, and at Woodhenge (once paired with Stonehenge) in England.

The site would have no signage. Every little thing found and its location would be photographed, *in situ* when possible, labeled, stored and studied in a dig house, and catalogued. Frequently, buildings are identified by what is found in association with them. Apart from all this, four data sources are potentially very rich. First, the site would typically be littered with pot shards. Some pieces would be distinctive enough to identify the culture, i.e., the people of the site. It is also possible that some otherwise unremarkable shards will bear some writing, a votive text on an offering jar, or graffiti, a curse against the king, a message passed between lovers, or simply, "Jonathan was here," or "made by Jacob". A second source of data would be the findings at a butcher or sacrificial site, where bones of animals would be found. A third, and very rich site would be the rubbish mound, which would be stratified to a degree, with dating possibilities. Finally, a fourth site would be that for the burials. Both Hebrews and Egyptians honored their dead, and took pains to bury them properly. There may be humble burials, richer burials of the notables, and more impressive burials of the rulers. Here one would expect to find grave goods appropriate to the culture, possibly bone boxes, and commemorative and blessing inscriptions.

2. History, Archaeology and the *Book of Mormon*

Agricultural activity, food production, preservation, storage and preparation all leave signs, even artifacts. Fields yield valuable information regarding crops. Soil analysis would allow the examination of pollen, which is extremely durable, revealing the crops grown. Wheat is processed at long-term, even ancestral threshing floors, which should be found, and yield pollen and other trace evidence. Then it is taken to winnowing sites. Bread ovens should remain (maize is not suitable for bread). Wheat straw is used for basketry, fodder and dung fuel. Bran is used to fill cushions. One could not just run over to a grocery store like today. Families would have grain storage jars or clay bins, while grain dealers, temples and palaces would have large grain storage buildings sufficient to keep out rain and pests, and pay their retainers. Wine not only implies the existence of a suitable species of grape, but also wine presses. Wine storage skins or jars would still bear trace evidence.

Every site would have its own history, and ecological/historical vicissitudes. Some may be partially or largely covered over by soil and vegetation. Others may be wind-swept. Lucky sites might have had a mountain (mud slide?) fall on them, or volcanic ash. A site at the bottom of the sea would be in a cold and oxygen-starved environment. Ancient wood ships have been recovered from the sea in good repair, and Viking burials in wood ships fare well under the ground. Pompeii was protected by volcanic ash. They would also vary with respect to pillage. Earthquakes might cause objects to be covered up, including coinage, if it exists. Surprisingly, coins are almost always found. Islamic coins have been found as far away as Scandinavia. Then there are treasure troves, hidden in response to invaders, or the Gadianton robber threat, at various times, but especially in the last years of the Nephites: "And these Gadianton robbers, which were among the Lamanites, did infest the land, insomuch that the inhabitants thereof began to hide up their treasures in the earth." (Mormon 1:18)

If the Nephite/Lamanite civilization ever existed, all of the items in this study would be found. Most would be collocated in the same find, a whole city.

The Sound of Silence: Nephite History in a Vacuum

Apologists focus primarily on Middle Eastern and Biblical topics, rather than the archaeology of pre-Columbian North, Central and South America. Undoubtedly they have found the Americas to be unproductive turf for their objectives. Yet even the average Mormon has heard of problems, such as the consensus among archaeologists, paleontologists and other experts, that horses did not exist in the New World during the past several millennia, in agreement with the eye-witness reports of the first Europeans arriving in the New World, *to wit*, that they found no horses. Indeed, this is just the very tip of the iceberg. Its massive body includes such things as horses, cows, sheep, goats, wheat, barley, iron smelting, steel making, written materials in Nephite Hebrew and reformed Egyptian, and the list goes on.

For many, this is enough to conclude that the *Book of Mormon* is a nineteenth century historical fiction. But the faithful for their part base hopes on the view that the remains of Jaredite, Nephite and Lamanite cities might lie in some remote valley, yet to be discovered, or have simply vanished.

And yet, it is what the *Book of Mormon* does not say that provides the ultimate test, and the most ineluctable conclusion.

The *Book of Mormon* makes it clear that upon the arrival of the families of Lehi and Ishmael, and the band of Mulek, all leaving Jerusalem during the reign of Zedekiah (c. 597-590 BCE), the new land of their inheritance was empty. It was theirs alone, to preserve a branch of Israel in its purity, to be gathered to Christ in the latter days. Note, in 2 Nephi 1:

> 8. And behold, it is wisdom that this land should be kept as yet from the knowledge of other nations: for behold, many nations would overrun the land, that there would be no place for an inheritance.
> 9. Wherefore, I, Lehi, have obtained a promise that inasmuch as they which the Lord God shall bring out of the land of Jerusalem shall keep his commandments, they shall prosper upon the face of this land; and they shall be kept from all other nations, that they may possess this land unto themselves.

The BOM had to go to atrocious lengths to make this happen, since the non-Israelite Jaredites and their civilization were there first, also led there by God, but from the tower of Babel. What to do? Note this statement in Ether 11:

> 20. many prophets... prophesied... and cried repentance unto the people, and except they should repent, the Lord God would execute judgment against them to their utter destruction;

21. and that the Lord God would send or bring forth another people to possess the land.

The Jaredites too had divided into two branches. Initially one was more righteous than the decidedly wicked other group, but eventually both became very iniquitous. Warfare between the two ultimately led both leaders to gather their forces to – where else? – Upstate New York. These were men of might, Coriantumr, leader of the formerly more righteous group, and Shiz, leader of the wicked group. They commanded great masses of people: "the people began to flock together in armies, throughout all the face of the land." (Ether 14:19) In their initial battles, Coriantumr "saw that there had been slain by the sword already nearly two millions of his people ... there had been slain two millions of mighty men, and also their wives and their children." (Ether 15:2 2) So these mighty men, plus wives and children, should total perhaps four million, just on one side. One can assume that the casualties among the wicked group were no less. So the grand total would possibly reach eight million dead in the initial encounters alone. This makes every known historical battle a back-alley brawl. At this point, the two leaders realized that this was a fight to the extermination of one group or the other. So they took four·years to gather every living human being from throughout the Americas, to have available to them the fighting potential of every man, woman and child. (Ether 15:12-14) While doing this, apparently others fabricated armor and weapons for every man, woman and child: "both men, women and children being armed with weapons of war, having shields, and breastplates, and head-plates, and being clothed after the manner of war." (Ether 15:15) Then, the preparations made, they all fought to the end, to their mutual total extermination. We are left to imagine the horrific scene of child slaughtering child. Only the two leaders were left standing, the classic duel of the chiefs. Coriantumr killed Shiz, and eventually made contact with the successor Nephite-Mulekite group, spending the last nine months of his life in Zarahemla. Thus the promise was kept, and the Israelite group entered into the land of their inheritance, purged of prior inhabitants, and totally reserved just for them. Splendid isolation.

The *Book of Mormon* text reinforces this assertion in its historical narrative. There is no single mention of any people or group that is not descended from Lehi, Ishmael, Zoram or Mulek's group. Realistically, upon their arrival they would have found the land full of occupants. Like the arriving European explorers and settlers (and even the Vikings), they would have found all the best lands taken. In addition to accounts of negotiation and cooperation, there would be accounts of conflict and warfare with these other peoples. The fierce Vikings could not hold out, and the lost colony of Roanoke is famous. Even the Jaredite account makes no mention of other peoples in the New World.

The test based on the omissions in the *Book of Mormon* is more final than that of the commissions, because in the case of the omissions, the data set is fixed. We will not wake up one morning and suddenly find in our BOM copy mentions of numerous other peoples, and wonder, "how did I not notice this before?" Improvements in the table below will only add more peoples that should have been mentioned. In stark contrast with the BOM, the Hebrew Bible is replete with mentions of many other peoples, both near and far.

The Archaeology Cultures List

The many important Pre-Columbian cultures and cities that existed during the timeframe of the BOM narrative cannot be fully represented here. Table 2 lists some of the salient ones, and details of interest to the present study.

Table 2. Pre-Columbian Cultures

A. Cultures before or during the BOM Jaredite Period	
Culture	Dates and Details
Clovis	C. 13,000 BCE to 10,000 BCE, a Paleo-Indian population, noted for its arrow heads. They are considered to be the ancestors of most of the indigenous cultures of the Americas. Clovis tips are found in most of North & Central America. A boy preserved in a Clovis culture grave, dubbed Anzick-1, yielded DNA related to the modern Amerindians and the DNA found in eastern Asia.
Folsom	Ca. 9000 BCE, perhaps the principal tradition that replaced the Clovis culture, and appears to have grown out of it. They are more common in the Rocky Mountains and Great Plains, but not as rare east of the Mississippi as once thought.
Las Vegas	8000-4600 BCE (Holocene), 31 sites, primarily hunting, gathering, fish/shell fish, & primitive agriculture, near the Ecuador coast.
Valdivia culture	3500-1800 BCE, impressive ceramic finds (earliest in the Americas), cotton textiles, maize & vegetable cultivation, near the west coast of Ecuador. Used rafts with sails along the coast.

(Table 2 continued)

Norte Chile (Caral)	3,500-1,800 BCE, Peru, largest city of ancient Americas; large pyramids (contemporary with ancient Egypt); temple complex.
Monagrillo	2500-1200 BCE, Panama, early ceramic site; hearths, post holes, pits, shell, bone, pottery, stone tools, early maize culture.
Chavin de Huantar	1,500 (up to 400) BCE, Peru, largely a pan-regional ritual center (possibly a religious cult), temples, agricultural economy, gold soldering in jewelry.
Ancon	10,000 BCE to end of Incan period, a principal center, vast necropolis with thousands of burials.
Acre (Amazon)	In eastern Acre, the westernmost division of the state of Rondônia, and the southern part of the state of Amazonas, ca. 300 geometric earthwork structures have been registered. They represent a regional cultural institution related to ritual and/or sociopolitical institutions, in use from 1200 BCE to the 14th century CE.
B. Cultures Overlapping BOM Jaredite & Nephite Periods ⸸ designates some of those with pagan items in the BOM Christian Period	
Olmecs	1600—400 BCE, produced a developed writing system, and invented the concept of zero. It is considered to be the first major civilization in Mesoamerica.
San Lorenzo	1200—900 BCE, center of early Olmec culture with temples, plazas and royal residences. There are ten colossal stone heads, apparently of rulers.
La Venta	c. 900—c. 400 BCE—followed San Lorenzo as the most important Olmec center. The Great Pyramid was the largest Mesoamerican structure of its time. Even today, after 2500 years of erosion, it rises 34 m (112 ft.) above the naturally flat landscape. Buried deep within La Venta, lay opulent, labor-intensive "offerings" – 1000 tons of smooth serpentine blocks, large mosaic pavements, and at least 48 separate deposits of polished jade celts, pottery, figurines, and hematite mirrors.
Tres Zapotes	Pre-1000 BCE, & flourishing c. 900-800 BCE, the third major Olmec site. It continued after 400 BCE, but gradually transformed into post-Olmec (Epi-Olmec) culture.
Maya	2000 BCE—1697 CE (fall of the last Mayan city). Hieroglyphic writing was in use by the 3rd century BCE. By 500 BCE monumental architecture existed. 400 BCE—250 CE, late preclassic period. 250—900 CE, classical period, with Mayan sites at their height
Calakmul	Preclassic through late classic; a major site by the late preclassic period, and competitor of Tikal. Check out the Calakmul mask!
El Mirador	500 BCE—150 CE, a massive Mayan site and political center with a huge pyramid, other stone architecture, and preclassic glyphs.
Paso del Macho	600-500 BCE, situated in the Yucatan with a find of cocoa used as a condiment.

(Table 2 continued)

	Tikal	250-400 CE, the largest Maya dam ever found, 260' long and 33' high. It experienced a cultural florescence in the first century CE. In the 3rd century CE dynastic kingship was established. ☥ Its Mundo Perdido ceremonial complex, with a pyramid and three temples, was active in the late preclassic and on. Rich burials have been dated to the first century CE.
	Kaminaljuyu	1500 BCE-1200 CE, major site with large population by 700 BCE. ☥ A complex pantheon of deities by the middle preclassic period. ☥ 400 BCE—250 CE, late preclassic period, with a Principal Bird Deity, the maize god & a jaguar deity merged with the ruler.
	Piedras Negras	7th c. BCE-850 CE, the first population peak being about 200 BCE, and the dynasty list beginning c. 297 CE.
	Early Mayan writing	Slowly, a significant corpus of texts is emerging dating within the period from c. 100 BCE to c. 150 CE, i.e., the late preclassic period. See Ch. 6 by J. Kathryn Josserand, and Ch. 7 by Martha J. Macri, in Michael Love & Jonathan Kaplan, eds., *The Southern Maya in the Late Preclassic* (Boulder, CO: University Press of Colorado, 2011).
	Lamanai	4th c. BCE thru the classic period, a major site from the 4th century BCE through the 1st century CE, declining but persisting thereafter. It was a major copper center. ☥ *Lamanai* is Yucatec Maya meaning "Submerged Crocodile" and a temple features individuals wearing crocodile headdresses.
	El Baúl	A center known for obsidian production, with a stele bearing a long count date: 36 CE. Volcanic ash was deposited from nearby volcano.
	El Zotz	350-400 CE, Temple of the Night Sun, with ornate painted stucco inside and out. It has *wahob* figures (harmful spirits in animal form).
	Xno'ha	400 BCE—600 CE, elite residential complex, with pottery dated to this period, and an early classic tomb.
	Tak'alik Ab'aj	700-400 BCE, tomb of a ruler wearing a vulture-headed figure. ☥ Stele 5 bears two long count dates, the latest being 126 CE. It commemorates a transition of power, and exhibits the serpent.
	Chan Chich	770 BCE-850 CE, a midden and neighboring sites being excavated in this much looted Maya site, Belize.
	Plan de Ayutla	250-550 CE, a theater, in the palace on top of the acropolis.
Izapa		600 BCE—100 CE, the period within which the site reached its apogee. The site is not clearly Mayan nor Olmec, having elements of both, and purely local elements. ☥ It leads other sites in the number of sculptures, featuring *vucub caquix* (a powerful bird deity), a long-lipped deity (of lightening and rain?), a club-wielding deity with serpents as legs, and a scene of violence among deities with a decapitated god. ☥ A monolithic jaguar was found in 2012 dated to c. 100 CE, the 84th monolith found at the site.

2. History, Archaeology and the *Book of Mormon* 39

(Table 2 continued)

El Tajin	1st century-1200 CE, part of the Classic Veracruz culture. ☥ It was a center of the worship of the god Quetzalcoatl. Monumental architecture began in the 1st century CE. The ball court depicts human sacrifice.
Monte Alban	c. 500 BCE-1000 CE—A major site, considered Zapotec, that reached a population of over 5,000 by 300 BCE and over 17,000 by 100 BCE. During 200-500CE it was a regional capital with colonies. ☥ Over 300 tortured sacrificed war victims are depicted. The Zapotec language was one of the first written (with a syllabic script). ☥ The rain god Cocijo was important.
Teotihuacan	100 BCE thru 7th century CE, a major site in the Basin of Mexico, with major constructions from 100 BCE to 250 CE, but growing to its apogee at c. 450 CE. Its largest pyramid, Pyramid of the Son, was largely completed by 100 CE and finished by 200 CE. ☥ Its deities include the Storm God, Great Goddess, Feathered Serpent, Old God, War Serpent, Netted Jaguar, Pulque God and Fat God. Many of these are modern names given to them. ☥ Hundreds of human sacrifice remains have been found beneath and around the Pyramid of the Feathered Serpent (Quetzalcoatl), which was built from 150 to 200 CE.
La Mosquitia	A non-Maya culture in Honduras, not yet adequately dated, but notable for a stone head that appears to be a jaguar, or even a were-jaguar (possibly emblematic of a shaman).
Copán	An early Honduran site (across the border from Guatemala), with stone architecture by around 9th century BCE, that grew to importance, but was refounded by a Maya people in the 6th century CE. It is the principal Maya site in a largely non-Maya region.
Los Naranjos	An archaeological region in western Honduras, settled more or less continually from c. 800 BCE and notable for its ceramics, and in particular the highly decorated Yde vessel. The region has two earthen ditches of the BCE period, of unclear use.
Playa de los Muertos	An archaeological zone on the north Honduran coast known from its burials and ceramics, being as ancient as any Mesoamerican region. It has an extensive excavation history.
Talgua Caves	A cave ossuary in northeastern Honduras with numerous burials dated to c. 1000 BCE, possibly indicative of a notable degree of social development.
Yarumela	A major trade center c. 60 kilometers south of Los Naranjos, dating between 1000 BCE to 200 CE, with important mounds. (Honduras)
Sitio Barriles	4600-2300 BCE, the Tropical Forest Archaic period, rock shelter sites in Panama. 300 BCE—400 CE, Conception stage, first pottery 400-900 CE, Aguas Buenas period, featuring large villages & small farmsteads
Sitio Conte	450-900 CE, Panama, primarily a necropolis with ceramic remains. The iconography depicts animals, humans and animal-human beings.

(Table 2 continued)

Sitio Sierra	c. 250 CE to the conquest, a significant site in Panama, with periods poorly defined. Sites span 350 BCE to 750 CE.
Chorrera (Ecuador)	1300-300 BCE, noted for its advanced ceramic tradition, particularly hollow figurines.
Moche	100-800 CE, particularly noted for their elaborately painted ceramics, metallurgy, monumental constructions (huacas) and irrigation systems
Muisca	C. 500 BCE-present, an agrarian culture in the Andean highlands of the Columbian Eastern Range. Antecedent cultures go back to 5000 BCE. The Muisca were organized in an extensive confederation. They had large quantities of gold. The chief upon accession covered his body with gold dust. They are famous for the gold Muisca raft, dating between 600-800 CE, & other gold creations.
Nazca	100 BCE-800 CE, located in the southern coastal region of Peru, the Nazca were noted for textiles and ceramics. ☥ Their religion focused on powerful nature deities. The shaman cult used hallucinatory drugs. Their so-called trophy heads were either trophies from war, or ritual objects. The Nazca are known for their partial burials, of just parts of a body, or of decapitated bodies with a jar painted as a head. The little-understood Nazca lines include zoomorphic and phytomorphic figures, possibly to propitiate some corresponding celestial beings or forces.
Paracas	800-200 BCE, also in the southern coastal region of Peru, the Paracas culture is noted for its knowledge of irrigation and contributions to the textile arts. Their distinctive ceramics use incised polychrome and negative resist decoration. It appears that in some cases the heads of their deceased were used in rituals.
Recuay	200 BCE-600 CE, a Peruvian highland culture with highly elaborate pottery and impressive fabrics. Their iconography featured the so-called 'moon animal,' a fox-like or feline animal.
Tiwanaku	300 BCE-1000 CE, a precursor to the Incan culture, the ritual and administrative capital of a major state power for approximately five-hundred years. The ruins of the ancient city state are near the south-eastern shore of Lake Titicaca in Bolivia.
Chachapoyas	600 CE, in the Amazonas region of northern Peru. It is possible that they built a settlement called Gran Pajáten where some ceramics have been dated to 200 BC.
Tulor	380 BCE—1200 CE, a village complex in Chile (most surviving structures are post 800 CE). Boreholes were dug for groundwater.
Lagoa Santa	The center of Brazilian paleontology, a cave with 15 human skeletons and mega fauna. The oldest human fossil in Brazil, 11,000+ years old.
Pedra Furada	Circa 11,000 BCE Lithic art, possibly prior to the Clovis culture.
Acre	0-700 CE, Brazil Amazonian site, with many massive earthworks, apparently geoglyphs.

(Table 2 continued)

Basket Weaver	1500 BCE-500 CE, a people in the U.S. Southwest, with well-preserved mummies.
Phoenix/Tuscan	From 1,500 BCE on developed irrigation systems were in use in the Phoenix and Tuscan basins. Ancient footprints, c. 1,500 BCE, of what appears to be two adults, two children and a dog, appear to be a family at work opening & closing channel head gates.
Mound Builders	c. 3,400 BCE to the 16th century, a collection of cultures. The Hopewell culture spanned c. 100 to 700 CE. Burial mounds of the Middle Woodland period range from 100 BCE to 400 CE. ✧ There are many theories about their religion, but most believe that sun worship was a central element.
Woodlands Culture	c. 1,000 BCE—1,000 CE, in the eastern North America. c. 1,000 BCE—1 BCE, early woodlands period 1 CE—500 CE, middle woodland period, including the Hopewell culture sites, with burial mounds, evidence of hunting and gathering, pottery and some horticulture. Extensive trade system involving exotic items and materials. Sites with Hopewell traits are found in both New York and Ontario (cf. the Saugeen complex). Post-500 CE, introduction of the cultivation of maize, beans and squash. The Adena culture (c. 1000-200 BCE) built many mounds, including Criel mound, a burial site where many skeletons and grave goods (weapons and jewelry). The effigy mounds (350-1300 CE) were shaped like stylized animals, each having one, two or three people buried but almost totally without grave goods.

Conclusions

The claim of the *Book of Mormon* narrative to be a translation of an ancient record of the history and religious affairs of the pre-Columbian peoples of the Americas has been compared with the empirical findings of the archaeological records overlapping the relevant period.

1. The Archaeological BOM Item List was drawn up from the text of the BOM narrative to enable a focused comparison with the archaeological findings. The overwhelming majority of these items have been found to be unevidenced. For all but the most faith-bound, the conclusion is totally disconfirmatory to the BOM authenticity claim.

2. The Archaeological Cultures List was drawn up from a survey of pre-Columbian archaeology to provide an empirical test of the claim that the lands of the proposed Nephite/Lamanite territories had been kept away from the knowledge of all other peoples of the earth, a claim that the

BOM narrative states explicitly and examples clearly by its total lack of any reference to any people other than those descended from the Jaredites, the party of Lehi and the party of Mulek. In fact, we have found that the Americas have been fully populated by numerous cultures. A major civilization, with forty named cities and many unnamed others, covering a period of 1,000 years, must have had important and recurrent contact with the historical cultures of pre-Columbian America.

Highly committed, well-educated and intelligent LDS scholars laboring at this Gordian knot have produced creative research based on analyses of the BOM text and/or Middle Eastern cultural materials. The unstated premise that all such research is based on is that the *Book of Mormon* is the unquestionably best source for knowledge of pre-Columbian America, and therefore the pre-Columbian archaeological record cannot be totally disconfirmatory. The results from the analysis in this chapter make it clear that this premise is totally untenable, and that no amount of BOM textual or Middle-East cultural or literary analysis can overcome the clear facts on the ground in the New World.

This is the archaeological verdict.

Chapter 3

Mapping the *Book of Mormon* Setting

Pre-Columbian archaeological research brings an essential question unavoidably to the fore. Where in the New World is the setting for the events in the BOM narrative?

The *Book of Mormon* is a continuation of the long history of speculation regarding the origins of the Indians. Many members of its target audience were predisposed to believe in its central premise. In its pages, readers found a record of relations between various peoples of Israelite origin located somewhere in the Americas, including wars between well-fortified cities, and descriptions of concrete aspects of the material culture of the Nephites and Lamanites.

Who has not heard of Egyptian archaeology? Of Biblical archaeology? Of the excavations of Rome, Greece, Persia, India and China. But who has heard of *Book of Mormon* archaeology? What museum has a Nephite-Lamanite wing for artifacts identified and dated *in situ*? What *Book of Mormon* city has ever been discovered, and excavated, with dig reports, visitable ruins and findings on display in museums?

Once it was established as the founding scripture of a new religion, the believers began to want to see it like the Bible they were familiar with. It should be bound like a Bible, perhaps have gilded pages like a Bible, with a Concordance, and an index. Christians are accustomed to finding in their Bible a map of the Holy Land, and of the travels of the Apostles. So might not the *Book of Mormon* also be similarly equipped, with maps of the lands of the Nephites and Lamanites, showing the cities, rivers and routes of military and missionary campaigns? In 1901 Benjamin Cluff, president of Brigham Young Academy, the forerunner of BYU, conducted an expedition to South and Central America to identify the Land of Zarahemla. In 1921 a General Authority *Book of Mormon* Committee held a hearing of those who had views on the subject of BOM geography. No official conclusions were reached, and since then the LDS establishment has kept aloof from such research. In this absence of enthusiasm, private scholars have taken up

The quest for the Book of Mormon setting.

The Abstract Approach

One sort of LDS BOM cartography is both useful and straightforward. It is essentially a reader's guide. The typical map is in the shape of an hourglass, with no features that relate to actual geography. The shape is due to a key passage in Alma 22:32:

> And now, it was only the distance of a day and a half's journey for a Nephite, on the line Bountiful and the land Desolation, from the east to the west sea; and thus the land of Nephi and the land of Zarahemla were nearly surrounded by water, there being a small neck of land between the land northward and the land southward.

A straightforward reading of this passage indicates a land to the north, a land to the south, and a narrow neck of land connecting the two, such that it was a short journey between the east and west seas. Thus "the land of Nephi [south of the narrow neck of land] and the land of Zarahemla [north of the narrow neck of land] were nearly surrounded by water... [i.e. two continents]." (Alma 22:32)

This makes a geographical configuration in the shape of an hourglass. We find an example in *Geography of the Book of Mormon* by Fletcher B. Hammond.[55] The top and bottom lobes are effectively North and South America, as LDS cartographers sometimes map them out. Harold K. Nielsen follows a similar hourglass approach in his *Mapping the Action Found in the Book of Mormon* (1987).[56] These maps are provided as aids to the reader to follow the sometimes confusing movement of persons and armies in the *Book of Mormon*, similar to the ever-popular maps of Middle Earth in Tolkien's *Lord of the Rings*.

The works of J. Nile Washburn are a bit of a composite. The map is drawn to look a lot like one placing the BOM setting in Central America. But he adheres to the principle that "we do not really know" and perhaps "cannot know." While admitting that the narrow neck of land is the key feature, his position waffles as follows:

---

[55] Fletcher B. Hammond, *Geography of the* Book of Mormon (Salt Lake City: Utah Printing Company, 1959).
[56] Harold K. Nielsen, *Mapping the Action Found in the* Book of Mormon (Springville, UT: Cedar Fort, 1987).

We must not look too closely for it, however, in terms of modern coastlines. Too much has happened through the centuries. It ought to be noted, in relation to this matter of changes of geographical configurations, that the narrow neck was still a guiding feature of the landscape hundreds of years after the crucifixion of Christ, clear down to the days of Mormon.[57]

So for him, the narrow neck of land endured for possibly two millennia of Jaredite and Nephite history, and even through the Crucifixion Cataclysm, but possibly not through the centuries following 421 CE. Washburn admits the limits of his knowledge, but seems also to have decided not to decide. Paul R. Cheesman also urges caution regarding associating an abstract (internal) map with current maps of the Americas.[58]

The South America Approach

Finding a BOM setting in South America was given some legitimacy by Orson Pratt as early as 1872.[59] George Reynolds followed his lead in 1888.[60] These deal with the South America that we know.

By contrast, a very different approach is found in *The Book and the Map, New Insights into Book of Mormon Geography* by Venice Priddis (1975),[61] who also attempts to relate BOM cartography to the real world. This map is loosely based on the current elevation contour map of South America. It asserts that the entire continent was thousands of feet lower

---

[57] J. Nile Washburn, Book of Mormon *Lands and Times* (Bountiful, UT: Horizon Publishers, 1974), 207. See also J. A. Washburn and J. N. Washburn, *An Approach to the Study of the* Book of Mormon (Provo, Utah: New Era Publishing Company, 1939), 194-99.
[58] Paul R. Cheesman, *Early America and the* Book of Mormon, *A photographic Essay of Ancient America* (Salt Lake City: Deseret Book Company, 1972). His view ultimately favors a Central America setting. See also Paul R. Cheesman, *These Early Americans* (Salt Lake City: Deseret Book Company, 1974) and *The World of the* Book of Mormon (Salt Lake City: Deseret Book Co., 1978).
[59] Orson Pratt, "Nephite America—The Day of God's Power—The Shepherd of Israel" in *Journal of Discourses* (February 11, 1872), 14:324-31.
[60] George Reynolds, *The Story of the* Book of Mormon (Salt Lake City: J. H. Parry, 1888).
[61] Venice Priddis, *The Book and the Map, New Insights into* Book of Mormon *Geography* (Salt Lake City: Bookcraft, 1975).

up to the time of Christ's crucifixion, so that the northern end of the continent, a large swath of the west coast, and nearly all of Brazil and Venezuela were under water. Only the Andean backbone of the continent was above water. It, again, is configured like an elongated hourglass (p. 17). Then came the Crucifixion Cataclysm. Chapter ten is titled "The Land Changed." This is based on 3 Nephi 8:12, which depicts a terrible God who again destroys cities, men, women and children, in his righteous wrath: "For behold, the whole face of the land was changed because of the tempest and the whirlwinds and the thunderings and the lightnings, and the exceeding great quaking of the whole earth." Priddis finds it possible to write "Geological evidences such as the heaving upward of lower Chile from the ocean's bottom, the rising of Tiahuanaco to about 3,400 feet above its previous level, and the possible rising of the 150-mile 'Darien Gap' at Panama show this to be true. Apparently all the geological changes took place within the space of three hours."[62] (See 3 Nephi 8:19.)

Those who propose a setting in South America have some scenario for expansion into North America, and on to Cumorah, where the gold plates were deposited. A good example of this is the setting proposed by Orson Pratt in 1872. See also the geographical comments in Alvin Knisley's dictionary of the *Book of Mormon* (1901), especially under the entry for Zarahemla,[63] as well as the work of Cecil George Le Poidevin.[64]

The assertion that there was a great cataclysm at the time of the crucifixion does not hold up. Archaeologists have excavated numerous sites that straddle this timeframe. Flood layers, lava or volcanic ash deposition, seismic shifts in the strata, leveled structures and burn levels are all indications of some sort of a disaster. If these things are found in the same time period, and at all or at least most of the sites in a region, then one can talk about a major cataclysm. No such thing is evidenced.

Surprisingly, a problem in *Book of Mormon* cartography has arisen from efforts to locate a Hill Cumorah in Mesoamerica, although Joseph Smith claimed to have gotten the Golden Plates at the Hill Cumorah in upstate New York. Riley L. Dixon, in his book *Just One Cumorah*, makes a revealing comment about his methodology: "No external

---

[62] Priddis, *The Book and the Map*, 149.
[63] Alvin Knisley, *Dictionary of All Proper Names in the* Book of Mormon (Independence, MO: Ensign Publishing House, 1909).
[64] Cecil George Le Poidevin, *Zion, Land of Promise. An Atlas Study of* Book of Mormon *Geography* (N.P., by author, 1977).

evidence will be used that does not harmonize with the *Book of Mormon*, for that book is the only authentic and divine record that we have of Ancient America."[65] Thus unconstrained by real-world evidence, he locates the land of Nephi in the lands of Bolivia, Peru, Ecuador and the northern half of Chile, with the City of Zarahemla and its environs south of the Isthmus of Panama in the central part of that area, and the land of Desolation stretched out to include the northern reaches of Mexico and the southwestern part of the United States.[66] Thomas Stuart Ferguson's investigation of scriptural references came to the conclusion that Cumorah was exclusively in Central America, as well as the Nephite civilization.[67]

The Central America Approach

From 1900 to the 1980's, most cartography efforts eventually placed the *Book of Mormon* events, towns, cities, bodies of water and other natural features in an area somewhere between the equator and the Rio Grande. Either both the Land of Nephi (Lamanite territory) and the Land of Zarahemla (Nephite territory) were placed in Central America, or the latter was there, while the former was placed roughly in the northern part of present-day Columbia. These settings also possibly enjoyed the support of Joseph Smith. In 1842, while he was editor of the *Times and Seasons*, it began publishing selections from a book by non-Mormon John Stephens that reported on his travels in Central America.[68] An editorial comment possibly approved by Smith, says:

> Since our 'Extract' was published from Mr. Stephens' 'Incidents of Travel,' &c., we have found another important fact relating to the truth of the *Book of Mormon*. Central America, or Guatemala, is situated north of the Isthmus of Darien and once embraced several hundred miles of territory from north to south.–The city of Zarahemla, burnt at the crucifixion of the Savior, and rebuilt afterwards, stood upon this land as

---

[65] Riley L. Dixon, *Just One Cumorah* (Salt Lake city: Bookcraft, 1958), 12-14. Dixon also locates the principal Lamanite/Nephite territories in South America.
[66] Dixon, *Just One Cumorah*, 46, 65 & 78.
[67] Thomas Stuart Ferguson, *Cumorah—Where?* (Independence, MO: Press of Zion's Printing and Publishing, 1947), 14 & 55.
[68] John Lloyd Stephens, *Incidents of Travel in Central America, Chiapas and Yucatan* (New York: Harper, 1841).

will be seen from the following words in the Book of Alma:– 'And now it was only the distance of a day and half's journey for a Nephite, on the line Bountiful, and the land Desolation, from the east to the west sea; and thus the land of Nephi, and the land of Zarahemla was nearly surrounded by water: there being a small neck of land between the land northward and the land southward.'[69]

It is to be noted that over the course of his career, a variety of comments have been attributed to Smith that many have found to be a bit puzzling in this regard. For Mormons, an LDS prophet has every right to his personal views, which can change over time, and the faithful are not bound by a prophet's opinions, in the absence of a revelation to support it. Still, Smith's connection with this view can be expected to carry some weight.

The BOM setting began to be redirected to Central America (including Central America plus Columbia) by the report of Benjamin Cluff's expedition. He announced that the land of the Nephites was most probably in Central America.[70] This setting became dominant from 1900 to the 1980's. Two of the earliest works are Holmes (1903)[71] and Palfrey (1903)[72], followed by Shook (1910)[73], Hills (1917),[74], Farnsworth (1947),[75] Ferguson (1947)[76] and many others (Table 43 and Bibliography 3).

---

[69] *Times and Seasons*, 3:23 (1 October 1842).
[70] Joseph Lovell Allen and Blake Joseph Allen, *Exploring the Lands of the* Book of Mormon, 2nd ed. (Orem, UT: *Book of Mormon* Tours and Research Institute, Inc., 2008), 382-83.
[71] Robert Holmes, *Geographical Sketches of the* Book of Mormon (LDS Historian's Office).
[72] Louise Palfrey, *The Divinity of the* Book of Mormon *Proven by Archaeology* (Lamoni, IA: Zion's Religio-Literary Society, Herald Publishing House, 1903).
[73] Chas. A. Shook, *Cumorah Revisited* (Cincinnati: Standard Publishing Company, 1910).
[74] Louis Edward Hills, *Geography of Mexico and Central America from 2234 BC to 421 AD* (Independence MO: 1917).
[75] Dewey Farnsworth, *The Americas before Columbus* (El Paso, TX: Farnsworth Publishing Co., 1947), and Dewey Farnsworth and Edith Wood Farnsworth, Book of Mormon *Evidences* (Salt Lake City: Deseret Book Company, 1953).
[76] Thomas Stuart Ferguson, *Cumorah—Where?* (Independence, MO: Zion's Printing and Publishing, 1947).

The Quest for an Alternative Setting

By around 1980, considerable scientific archaeological research had been done in Mesoamerica, and Mayan texts were being confidently translated, including king dynasty lists, the names of the Mayan cities with their dominant vs. tributary relationships, and religious beliefs. This heralded a new era in LDS cartography, marked by a growing concern that it might no longer be tenable to superimpose the Nephite/Lamanite territories on top of the Mayan and Olmec regions. An alternative *Book of Mormon* setting was needed.

This turn of events was described in the work of Duane R. Aston (1998 & 2003). He writes that early in 1990 "...I learned that a Latter-day Saint author had spent nearly 25 years studying and researching *Book of Mormon* archaeology related to Central America, but that he had lost his faith in the authenticity of the *Book of Mormon* [reference must be to Thomas Stuart Ferguson]. It seems that this man had come to the conclusion that there was nothing to be found in the Central American setting that convinced him that the *Book of Mormon* belonged there.... Of course one should not expect to find any external evidence obtained from archaeology that would 'prove' the authenticity of the *Book of Mormon*... Then if *Book of Mormon* lands were not located in Central America, then where might they belong? The only reasonable possible solution that came to my mind was New York."[77]

Beginning in the 1980's, the relocation of the BOM setting to the Great Lakes region has grown and is striving for greater respectability, resulting in the works of Holley (1983),[78] Curtis (1988),[79] Aston (1998),[80] Olive (2000)[81] and Coon (2009)[82].

---

[77] Duane R. Aston, *Return to Cumorah* (Sacramento, CA: American River Publications, 1998/2003).
[78] Vernal Holley, Book of Mormon *Authorship. A Closer Look* (Ogden UT: Zenos Publications, 1983).
[79] Delbert W. Curtis, *The Land of the Nephites* (Orem, UT: self-published, 1988).
[80] Aston, *Return to Cumorah*.
[81] Phyllis Carol Olive, *The Lost Lands of the* Book of Mormon (Springville, UT: Bonneville Books, 2000).
[82] W. Vincent Coon, *Choice above All Other Lands.* Book of Mormon *Covenant Lands According to the Best Sources* (Salt Lake City: Brit Publishing, 2009).

The Great Lakes setting pays at least some deference to the various mentions of the narrow neck of land, by defining it to be the Erie-Ontario isthmus. To gain access to this area, proponents assert that Nephi sailed from the Arabian coast of the Indian Ocean around the southern tip of Africa, and up to the St. Lawrence River. One has to ask if it would not have been easier to spend eight years getting to Gibraltar to set sail, rather than crossing the wilderness of Arabia.

Map 2. The Great Lakes BOM Setting (without Details)

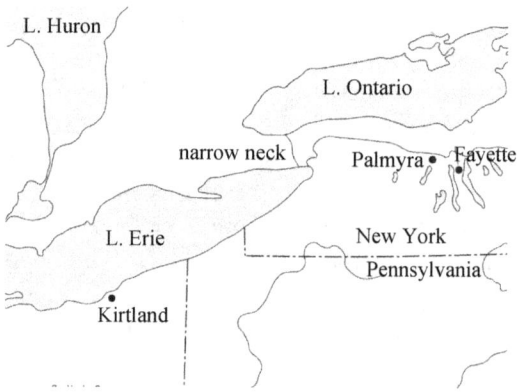

The place where both Lehi and Mulek disembarked is clearly stated in Helaman 6:10: "Now the land south was called Lehi and the land north was called Mulek, which was after the son of Zedekiah; for the Lord did bring Mulek into the land north, and Lehi into the land south." Presumably Mulek landed on the north shore of Lake Ontario, and Lehi on the New York shore. Niagara falls would have stopped them from sailing into Lake Erie. As we shall see, Mulek and his descendants remained in the land northward. This should be the location of Zarahemla, and therefore the land of the Nephites, in Ontario, while the Lamanites should be in New York. The Great Lakes setting usually has the Mulekites traveling south into New York, so that both the Nephites and Lamanites are there.

The principal problem with this approach is the location itself. It confuses the sea to the west and the sea to the east with the land with "large bodies of water and many rivers" in Helaman 3:4, speaking of some who had traveled away from Zarahemla: "And they did travel to an exceedingly great distance, insomuch that they came to large bodies of water and many rivers." This is usually associated with the Great Lakes region. Since the normal term to indicate distance is "many days," this passage stresses the distance much more. The Great Lakes approach, cannot have its cake and eat it too. If the Great Lakes are the east, west, north and south seas, then where are the great bodies of water associated with Cumorah? If they are the lakes in the Cumorah region, then where are these four seas? If the narrow neck of land is the Erie-Ontario Isthmus, then the Nephites should be in the land northward, in Ontario.

A second problem is perhaps equally telling. It arises from the voyages of a shipbuilder named Hagoth (Alma 63):

> 5. And it came to pass that Hagoth, he being an exceedingly curious man, therefore he went forth and built him an exceedingly large ship, on the borders of the land Bountiful, by the land Desolation, and launched it forth into the west sea, by the narrow neck which led into the land northward.
> 6. And behold, there were many of the Nephites who did enter therein and did sail forth with much provisions, and also many women and children; and they took their course northward. And thus ended the thirty and seventh year.
> 7. And in the thirty and eighth year, this man built other ships. And the first ship did also return, and many more people did enter into it; and they also took much provisions, and set out again to the land northward.

The site for embarkation is "on the borders of the land Bountiful, by the land Desolation," where Hagoth launched his ship "forth into the west sea, by the narrow neck which led into the land northward." In the Great Lakes approach, this site must be at the northernmost tip of Lake Erie (called the west sea in this theory), near the Erie-Ontario Isthmus. Launching from this site, the entire "west sea" lies to the south. It is not possible to take one's course to the north, and sail to the land northward.

A third problem is the location of Cumorah, which is fixed by the Joseph Smith story. The BOM narrative clearly locates Cumorah in the land northward (see below), but this setting places it in the land southward, in upstate New York. Furthermore, the Erie-Ontario isthmus is crossed by the Niagara River, and is dominated by the amazing Niagara Falls. The BOM narrative does not mention these.

Fourth, if Zarahemla is placed in the land northward, Lake Ontario can be to the east, but Lake Erie is to the south. If it is placed in the land southward, Zarahemla can be situated with lake Erie to the west, but Lake Ontario is to the north. As we shall see, in the BOM narrative the sea to the east and the sea to the west are located to the east and west of Zarahemla, respectively.

Finally, this relocation does nothing to facilitate dealing with the archaeological verdict.

Even though the Great Lakes proposal patently cannot be reconciled with the BOM narrative, the fact that a number of geographies have been based on it since the 1980's is important. It provides evidence that many LDS scholars are becoming seized of the fact that superimposing the Lamanite/Nephite territories on the Maya and Olmec region presents serious problems.

Related to the Great Lakes Model are other approaches that locate the BOM setting in the familiar areas of Mormon settlement prior to the move to Utah, particularly Missouri and Illinois, partly associated with the Great Lakes. These are usually only loosely based on BOM geographical references, or proceed by very creative or imaginative interpretations of only a few of those passages.[83] An example is the setting of Rod Meldrum. He proposes the American Heartland Model, which nestles the Nephite setting within the lands of the Ohio, Illinois, Mississippi, and Missouri rivers, largely from the confluence of the Ohio and Mississippi up to Lake Michigan. Even more than the foregoing, his model essentially ignores the narrow neck of land. It makes Lake Michigan the Sea West, Lake Superior the Sea North, Lake Erie the Sea South, and Lake Ontario the Sea East. It is very difficult to imagine a narrow neck of land separating Lake Michigan from Lake Ontario. For these models, selected and liberally reinterpreted quotations attributed to Joseph Smith and early Church leaders clearly trump the BOM text.[84]

---

[83] One such approach is that to which the website http//:www.bookofmormongeography is dedicated.

[84] Rod L. Meldrum, *Exploring the* Book of Mormon *Heartland Photobook* (New York: Digital Legend Press, 2011). An online map copyrighted by Meldrum was accessed from "Heartland Model" on 22/01/2016 at http//:www.josephsmithacademy.org, Inspira Wiki. See also J. A. Benson, "How Manifest Destiny Destroyed *Book of Mormon* Evidence" (http//:www.millennialstar.org, posted 12/02/2015).

Mapping the *Book of Mormon*

All who undertake BOM cartography have to deal with certain real-world features, including: 1) The Nephite and Jaredite narratives took place in the Americas. 2) The Nephite Cumorah and the Jaredite Ramah are one and the same, and are the Hill Cumorah near Palmyra in upstate New York, where Smith Jr. claimed to have found the gold plates. 3) There are four seas of note, these being primarily the sea to the east and the sea to the west, and secondarily, the sea to the north and the sea to the south (to all of which eventually people spread). 4) There are two land masses separated by a "narrow neck of land" that could be traversed at some point by a Nephite in a day and a half.

The elements that will compose the map must be placed in a manner that accommodates these key real-world features. Apart from that, the LDS cartographer tries to do this while locating other map elements in such a way that the action in the narratives (travels, military campaigns) is at least plausible in terms of the distances separating the features. By contrast, the secular cartographer attempts to give primary weight to the geographical information in the BOM narrative without feeling totally constrained by all of the BOM event logistics. He does not have to make the BOM narrative work in every respect. The principal source of knowledge regarding the geography of Mesoamerica probably was a small elementary map for school children (Map 4, *infra*), which only provided a distance scale in units of 1,000 miles. It is not even clear that the BOM authors were systematically mindful of the distance issue.

The Isthmus of Panama and North and South America

The key beginning point and operational kingpin for scholars willing to accept the *Book of Mormon* as their foundation, both LDS and secular cartographers alike, is the "small neck of land" (Alma 22:32) or "narrow neck of land" (Alma 63:5, Ether 10:20 & cf. Alma 50:11). This feature separates the land northward from the land southward, and at a point where one can cross east to west, from sea to sea, in a day and a half (Alma 22:32). The only reasonable region for this feature is the Isthmus of Panama. The distance from Panama City to Colón is 45 miles. The distance from David, Panama, to Chiriqui Grande is 70 miles. Power walking is from 4.5 to 5.5 mph, the Roman army is estimated to have marched about 3 mph fully laden, doing 15 miles a day, and the American pioneers usually traveled around twenty miles a day with all their possessions. These distances, using Google Maps, already take into consideration the need to vary one's course to go around obstacles. The need to contend with very rough terrain, rugged hills, thickets, briars and even jungles can be obviated by supposing there was a path for coast-to-coast trade in Alma's day. Three miles an hour might be optimistic; although a serious challenge for us, perhaps it was not for a Nephite. At five miles an hour, the crossing at Panama City would take ten hours. At a more believable pace, say 2.5 miles an hour, the crossing could be 28 hours at the David crossing, or very close to a day and a half (allowing for sleep). The crossing at Panama City could be done in one day. Actually, a later passage refers to a fortified line taking only one day (Helaman 4:7-8). Assuming that this is not a BOM contradiction, we can take the crossing at David to be the line Bountiful/Desolation, and the crossing at Panama City to be the shorter one chosen for fortification. Note that on the map most probably available to the BOM authors, it is not altogether clear which of these two points is the narrowest.

Other crossing points that have been considered for this feature take far too long. A crossing from present-day Coatzacoalcos, across the Isthmus of Tehuantepec, would take about four days, traveling 17 hours per day (based on Google Maps). A crossing from Puerto Barrios is even further off the mark. These crossing points involve superimposing Nephite and Lamanite lands on top of the Olmecs and Mayans. If we are to take the *Book of Mormon* at its own word, and certainly LDS researchers should be the first to insist on it, then a Panama crossing is the only viable candidate. Needless to say, geological evidence for any major change in coastlines between Columbia and Central Mexico does not exist.

The passage quoted above (Alma 22:32) clearly defines two land masses, the land northward and the land southward, divided by the narrow neck of land. But at times these phrases are purely directional, "up north" or "down south." The Lamanites came to occupy the land southward, called the land of Nephi, and the Nephites occupied the land northward, particularly in the land of Zarahemla. These two were nearly surrounded by water, which is to say that for the Nephites, but for the narrow neck of land, the land northward and the land southward would have been two separate isles of the sea. Zarahemla refers to the capital city of the Nephites, originally founded by the Mulekites, while the land of Zarahemla refers to the hinterland of that city, originally, but later to all the Nephite territories that belong to it. The city of Nephi was founded by Nephi, and its hinterland was the land of Nephi. The Lamanites took it over, making Nephi their capital, after the Nephites were driven to the land northward, to the city and land of Zarahemla. The land of Nephi acquired the meaning of all of the Lamanite territories under the control of their capital. (Alma 50:8) Thus the land of Zarahemla can refer to the part of the land northward primarily under Nephite occupation or political control, while the land of Nephi refers to the land southward under Lamanite occupation or political control. They were alternatively called after the leader of the group who had first made landfall, Lehi in the south and Mulek in the north (Helaman 6:10).

Map 3. The Americas and the Principal Nephite Territory

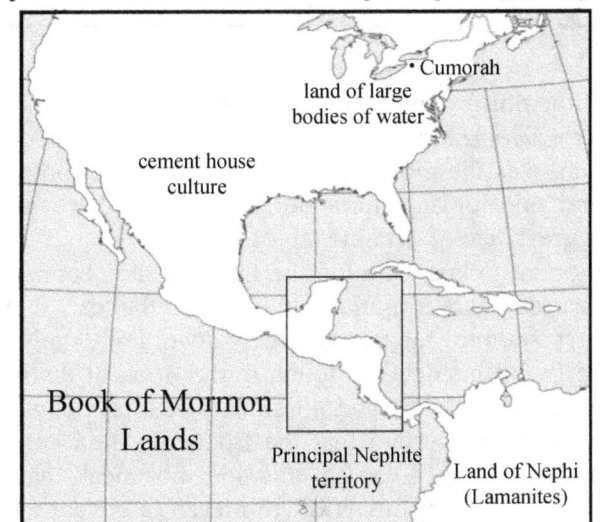

When Nephites occupied the wilderness Bountiful, only a narrow strip of wilderness separated the two lands. After five and one half centuries in the New World, the BOM peoples covered both continents:

> And it came to pass that they did multiply and spread, and did go forth from the land southward to the land northward, and did spread insomuch that they began to cover the face of the whole earth, from the sea south to the sea north, from the sea west to the sea east. (Helaman 3:8)

Map 4. 1820's School-Book Map of Central America

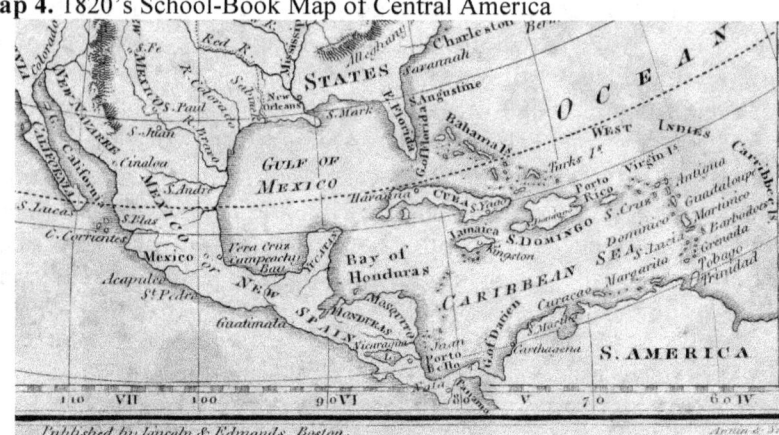

The map that the Smiths and Cowdery must have had available is *School Atlas to Adams Geography*,[85] which appeared every year or two in the relevant period, was the most popular atlas for school boys in the New York area, and sold for an affordable price. It is rather small, and does not provide a great deal of detail (Map 4).

It is important to bear in mind the fact that the geographical details of the BOM narrative are irregularly scattered in the text. As we shall see, at least the first fourth of the text is largely devoid of detail by design. In fact, the majority of this detail is found in the Book of Alma, apparently because the accounts of wars and missionary journeys could not be told without it. It is almost certain that the Book of Alma required a prior drafting of a simple map. Even so, this does not mean that the account was always told with a serious effort to present a cogent and consistent geography. Reference to the map developed here (Map 5) will help to follow the analysis of the main BOM geographical features.

The City and Land of Nephi. A couple of decades after Lehi's arrival, having made landfall on the west coast of the land south (South America), when his group had gotten a good start settling in with hunting and gathering, crops and flocks, Nephi was warned by the Lord to flee into the wilderness with those who would follow him, i.e. those who accepted his teaching about Christian gospel. They traveled for "the space of many days" and pitched their tents where they established what

---

[85] Daniel Adams, with H. (Hazen) Morse, engraver, *School Atlas to Adams Geography* (Boston: Lincoln and Edmonds, 1825).

became a new city, Nephi, and its territory the Land of Nephi (2 Nephi 5:1-9). The Nephites retained a historical memory of this land, referring to it as "the land of our first inheritance." (Mosiah 9:1; Alma 22:28)

Zarahemla. The group from Jerusalem led by Mulek made landfall in the land north (Helaman 6:10):

> Now the land south was called Lehi and the land north was called Mulek, which was after the son of Zedekiah; for the Lord did bring Mulek into the land north, and Lehi into the land south

The Mulekites dwelt there "from that time forth," where they built the great city Zarahemla (Omni 1):

> 15. Behold, it came to pass that Mosiah discovered that the people of Zarahemla came out from Jerusalem at the time that Zedekiah, king of Judah, was carried away captive into Babylon.
> 16. And they [Mulek, et al.] journeyed in the wilderness [that would be east of Jerusalem], and were brought by the hand of the Lord across the great waters, into the land where Mosiah discovered them [the land north]; and they had dwelt there from that time forth.

Here we have a clear syllogism: (A) Mulek was brought to his landfall in the land north; (B) Mulek was brought across the great waters to the land where Mosiah discovered them (i.e. Zarahemla), and "they had dwelt there from that time forth;" and (C) therefore, Zarahemla was in the land north. To repeat, it is said of the land to which the Lord brought them that "they had dwelt there from that time forth." There is no mention of Zarahemla leading a major migration with the Mulekites, traveling south, across the narrow neck of land, into the land southward. Clearly, Zarahemla was established in the land north of the narrow neck of land.

Its location is further clarified by this passage (Alma 50:11):

> And thus he [general Moroni] cut off all the strongholds of the Lamanites in the east wilderness, yea, and also on the west, fortifying the line between the Nephites and the Lamanites, between the land of Zarahemla and the land of Nephi, from the west sea, running by the head of the river Sidon— the Nephites possessing all the land northward, yea, even all the land which was northward of the land Bountiful, according to their pleasure.

We learn here that a line separating the Nephites and the Lamanites also separates the land of Zarahemla and the land of Nephi, and thus the Nephites possessed "all the land northward, yea, even all the land ... northward of the land Bountiful." As we shall see, Bountiful was the wilderness at the entry to the narrow neck of land extending up to the line Bountiful/Desolation. So once again, Zarahemla has to have been north of that isthmus.

This is further indicated in the following verses (Helaman 4):

> 7. And there they did fortify against the Lamanites, from the west sea, even unto the east; it being a day's journey for a Nephite, on the line which they had fortified and stationed their armies to defend their north country.
> 8. And thus those dissenters of the Nephites, with the help of a numerous army of the Lamanites, had obtained all the possession of the Nephites which was in the land southward.

At various times, the Nephites held territories in the land southward, but at this point they had lost those territories, and held only their land northward. This passage gives the time to cross as being only a day, which is consistent with a line of fortification at Panama City, as clarified above. In any case, again we are dealing with the isthmus, and the Nephites north of it, with their capital Zarahemla. The key references for this in the BOM narrative are consistent on this point.

It is possible to know too that Zarahemla was located inland:

> the Lamanites ... had come into the center of the land, and had taken the capital city which was the city of Zarahemla (Helaman 1:27)
> Now, the more idle part of the Lamanites lived in the wilderness, and dwelt in tents; and they were spread through the wilderness on the west, in the land of Nephi; yea, and also on the west of the land of Zarahemla, in the borders by the seashore (Alma 22:28)
> Now the Zoramites had gathered themselves together in a land which they called Antionum, which was east of the land of Zarahemla, which lay nearly bordering upon the seashore (Alma 31:3)

From Zarahemla one must cross the wilderness to get to the land of Nephi. (Alma 17:8, 22:27, 27:14) The wilderness wraps north and south around to the west of Zarahemla and in the west of the land of Nephi. (Alma 22:28). The wilderness also lay east of Zarahemla, having wrapped around up both the east and west coasts. (Alma 50:9) A land (unnamed) lay between Zarahemla and the land of Bountiful (3 Nephi 3:23):

> And the land which was appointed was the land of Zarahemla, and the land which was between the land Zarahemla and the land Bountiful, yea, to the line which was between the land Bountiful and the land Desolation.

In spite of all of this information, the difficulty of locating Zarahemla more specifically is due to the considerable stretch of land consisting of what is now the countries of Panama and Costa Rica, neither being a likely location. Nicaragua and Honduras are the first current locations that could qualify, with Panama and Costa Rica constituting the narrow neck of land.

Furthermore, in the BOM narrative we find "the city of Zarahemla," "the Land of Zarahemla" and just plain "Zarahemla." The land of Zarahemla began as the immediate hinterland of that city, but eventually referred to all the land under its control, much as Rome began as a city plus its hinterland, but came to refer to its empire. When it controlled some lands in the northern reaches of the land southward, especially the wilderness Bountiful, Zarahemla was separated from the Lamanite land of Nephi only by a narrow strip of wilderness.

Wilderness. The term "wilderness" refers to lands that are not inhabited or otherwise exploited by a human population. In Ether 2:5, a wilderness is described as being "that quarter where there never had man been." In much of the *Book of Mormon*, it is inhabited only by the lowest of the Lamanites, living off of hunting. In accordance with Biblical usage, when Lehi leaves Jerusalem, crosses Wadi Arabah and travels into the Arabian Peninsula, he journeys in the wilderness, largely desert and rocky scrubland. So, in the New World, we should not think that it refers exclusively to rainforests, rugged mountains or deserts. Presumably, much of what was wilderness for Nephi when he fled from the first settlement was no longer wilderness after the Lamanites had taken over the land south and filled it with their own cities and farms. It is distinguished from mountains: "...let us go up upon the mountains and into the wilderness..." (3 Nephi 3:20)

References to wilderness are to "the wilderness," a "narrow strip of wilderness," "the wilderness Bountiful," a wilderness "called Hermounts" (Alma 2:37), the "south wilderness" and the "east wilderness." The key reference is in Alma 22:

27. And it came to pass that the king [of the Lamanites] sent a proclamation throughout all the land, amongst all his people who were in all his land, who were in all the regions round about, which was bordering even to the sea, on the east and on the west, and which was divided from the land of Zarahemla by a narrow strip of wilderness, which ran from the sea east even to the sea west, and round about on the borders of the seashore, and the borders of the wilderness which was on the north by the land of Zarahemla, through the borders of Manti, by the head of the river Sidon, running from the east towards the west—and thus were the Lamanites and the Nephites divided.

28. Now, the more idle part of the Lamanites lived in the wilderness, and dwelt in tents; and they were spread through the wilderness on the west, in the land of Nephi; yea, and also on the west of the land of Zarahemla, in the borders by the seashore, and on the west in the land of Nephi, in the place of their fathers' first inheritance, and thus bordering along by the seashore.

29. And also there were many Lamanites on the east by the seashore, whither the Nephites had driven them. And thus the Nephites were nearly surrounded by the Lamanites; nevertheless the Nephites had taken possession of all the northern parts of the land bordering on the wilderness, at the head of the river Sidon, from the east to the west, round about on the wilderness side; on the north, even until they came to the land which they called Bountiful.

30. And it bordered upon the land which they called Desolation, it being so far northward that it came into the land which had been peopled and been destroyed, of whose bones we have spoken, which was discovered by the people of Zarahemla, it being the place of their [the Jaredites] first landing.

31. And they [the Jaredites] came from there up into the south wilderness. Thus the land on the northward was called Desolation, and the land on the southward was called Bountiful, it being the wilderness which is filled with all manner of wild animals of every kind, a part of which had come from the land northward for food.

32. And now, it was only the distance of a day and a half's journey for a Nephite, on the line Bountiful and the land Desolation, from the east to the west sea; and thus the land of Nephi and the land of Zarahemla were nearly surrounded by water, there being a small neck of land between the land northward and the land southward.

33. And it came to pass that the Nephites had inhabited the land Bountiful [by c. 90 BCE], even from the east unto the west sea, and thus the Nephites in their wisdom, with their guards and their armies, had hemmed in the Lamanites on the south, that thereby they should have no more possession on the north, that they might not overrun the land northward.

34. Therefore the Lamanites could have no more possessions only in the land of Nephi, and the wilderness round about. Now this was wisdom in the Nephites—as the Lamanites were an enemy to them, they would not suffer their afflictions on every hand, and also that they might have a country whither they might flee, according to their desires.

Since the Nephites at this time occupied the wilderness Bountiful, the narrow strip of wilderness separating them from the Lamanites ran along the southern side of Bountiful. We must avoid thinking that the narrow neck of land runs north-south, just because it connects North and South America. In fact, it and its wilderness run largely east-west, leaving Columbia at the eighth parallel, arching north, and descending south again to the eighth parallel. It rises again entering Nicaragua from the south, roughly at the point of the BOM city Manti on the west coast. There the wilderness occupies a portion of the land along the south of the land of Zarahemla called the south wilderness. Traversing from east (the Panama-Columbia border) to west (the land of Zarahemla), the total expanse of wilderness was considerable, beginning with this narrow strip, followed by the wilderness Bountiful, and then to and including the south wilderness. As for the distance just to arrive at the land of Zarahemla (not Zarahemla city proper), note that traveling from lands that the Lamanites had taken (Shemlon, Shilom and Amulon), Alma spent a day getting to the valley of Alma, and then twelve days in the wilderness to get to the land of Zarahemla. (Mosiah 24:1:25) This journey would have only been from a point just short of the border of Columbia to the line Bountiful/Desolation, since the land of Zarahemla effectively extended that far south at the time (Alma 22:32). For comparison, the distance from David, Panama, to El Real near the border with Columbia is 452 miles. To traverse this distance in 13 days they would have had to do 35 miles a day to get to the land of Zarahemla. For authors who thought that Lehi could get from Jerusalem to the Red Sea in just three days, this is close enough. (See also Mosiah 22:13)

The narrow strip of wilderness, angling north by northeast, extends not only from the sea east to the sea west, but down the coastline on both sides of the land of Nephi. But it is more than just a line of wilderness spanning those two points. It also extends up the coastline on both sides of the land of Zarahemla. It is not clear if the wilderness also wrapped completely around the northern side of the land of Zarahemla, but since the wilderness was inhabited by the more idle part of the Lamanites, so that "the Nephites were nearly surrounded by the Lamanites," it appears that this was nearly the case.

Accounts of events in the land of Nephi refer primarily to "the wilderness." Note those involving king Limhi. (Mosiah 7:9-29:44) There, it is never called the "south wilderness" but can refer to the "wilderness east." Whenever mentions are made of travels from the land of Zarahemla to the land of Nephi, or the reverse, the reference is usually to "the wilderness." That this is not limited to Bountiful or the narrow strip of wilderness in the land of Nephi is made clear in Alma 16:7: "And it came to pass that Zoram and his sons crossed over the river Sidon, with their armies, and marched away beyond the borders of Manti into the south wilderness, which was on the east side of the river Sidon." This refers to the entire extent of wilderness south of the land of Zarahemla, touching on the head of the Sidon on the north, and Antionum on the south.

Because all useful geographical references give one place in reference to one or more others, it is essential to establish beginning points. One such group is the wilderness Bountiful (land of Bountiful), Jershon and Antionum. The key references are in Alma:

> 27:22. the land of Jershon... on the east by the sea... joins the land Bountiful... on the south of the land Bountiful
> 31:33. a land called Antionum... east of the land of Zarahemla... nearly bordering upon the seashore... south of the land of Jershon... also bordered upon the wilderness south

The best axis to locate these is a three-corner point at the innermost part of the Gulf of Darien. The land of Jershon stretches northward from this point along the east shore of the gulf. The southeast part of the land of Antionum lies south of that point and stretches along the west shore of the Gulf of Darien and up to the line Bountiful-Desolation, where it borders the wilderness south. At that point, it lies east of the land of Zarahemla, and entirely so when Zarahemla had added Bountiful to its territory. (Map 5).

Similarly, the east wilderness refers to that branch of the narrow strip of wilderness along the east coastline of the land of Nephi (Alma 25:5), mentioned above (Alma 22:27). Although gathering all of this together is a bit complicated, the actual layout, seen in Map 5, is rather simple. The draft map of the BOM authors would have been equally simple, and easy to use to draft the text.

The Land of Bountiful. First of all, the Land Bountiful is a wilderness, or a part of the wilderness south of the land of Zarahemla, but east of the narrowest point on the narrow neck of land (Alma 22:31):

> the land on the southward was called Bountiful, it being the wilderness which is filled with all manner of wild animals of every kind

So "Bountiful" does not refer to a bounty of waving fields of grain, but to a bounty of game in a wilderness. It finds its corresponding designation in the Jaredite narrative (Ether 10):

> 19. And it came to pass that Lib also did that which was good in the sight of the Lord. And in the days of Lib the poisonous serpents were destroyed. Wherefore they did go into the land southward, to hunt food for the people of the land, for the land was covered with animals of the forest. And Lib also himself became a great hunter.
> 20. And they built a great city by the narrow neck of land, by the place where the sea divides the land.
> 21. And they did preserve the land southward for a wilderness, to get game.

The entry to the land southward is filled with game, just as is the land of Bountiful, in the same location, on the east side of the line Boutiful-Desolation. It is bordered after entering South America by a narrow strip of wilderness that does not support a bounty of game.

The Land of Desolation. This is another designation that seems to have been misunderstood by some, perhaps stemming from a misunderstanding of the meaning in English. It does not refer to land of low economic or agricultural value; it is not an arid land or desert at all. "To desolate" is defined as "To rid of or deprive of inhabitants. To lay waste; devastate." [86] The primary meaning in BOM geographical references is the lands formerly occupied by the Jaredites, which, when found by the Nephites, were devastated, full of ruins, devoid of their inhabitants. When Nephites first ventured north of the line Bountiful-Desolation, the land of desolation referred to the entire land northward. Since a great city was founded by the Jaredites near the narrow neck of

---

[86] *The American Heritage College Dictionary of the English Language*, Fifth Edition (Boston & New York: Houghton Mifflin Harcourt Publishing Company, 2011).

land (Ether 10:20), its ruins must have been the first site they found when Mosiah led them out of the land of Nephi. A similar description is given of the destruction found much further north, in the land of Cumorah. Even in Alma 22, most of the land northward, from the narrow neck of land to Cumorah, is the land of desolation, or any part of it if the context refers to a region of that larger territory. Other lands, such as the land of Zarahemla, are located within a part of it, just as Egypt is located within and is a part of the Sahara desert.

A key passage regarding these ruins follows (Mosiah 21):

> 8:8. And they were lost in the wilderness for the space of many days, yet they were diligent, and found not the land of Zarahemla but returned to this land, having traveled in a land among many waters, having discovered a land which was covered with bones of men, and of beasts, and was also covered with ruins of buildings of every kind...
> 21:25. Now king Limhi had sent, previous to the coming of Ammon, a small number of men to search for the land of Zarahemla; but they could not find it, and they were lost in the wilderness.
> 21:26. Nevertheless, they did find a land which had been peopled; yea, a land which was covered with dry bones; yea, a land which had been peopled and which had been destroyed; and they, having supposed it to be the land of Zarahemla, returned to the land of Nephi, having arrived in the borders of the land not many days before the coming of Ammon.

This expedition departed from the land of Nephi in search of Zarahemla, got lost in the wilderness, and found a land covered with dry bones and ruins, which they thought was Zarahemla. This most likely refers to the great city that the Jaredites established near the narrow neck of land, the furthest south they had spread to. The BOM phrase "many waters" usually refers to a large body of water such an ocean or great lake, such as Lake Nicaragua and Lake Managua (maps 4 and 5). The expedition cannot have traveled all the way from the land southward to the region of Cumorah (in upstate New York), and mistaken the ruins for Zarahemla.

The Line Bountiful and the Land Desolation. Without doubt, the key passage for BOM cartography is Alma 22:32:

> And now, it was only the distance of a day and a half's journey for a Nephite, on the line Bountiful and the land Desolation, from the east to the west sea; and thus the land of Nephi and the land of Zarahemla were nearly surrounded by water, there being a small neck of land between the land northward and the land southward.

A principal argument of the BOM narrative is that the Americas are included among the isles of the sea referred to in Isaiah (24:15 & 60:9), to which Israelites have been scattered (1 Nephi 19-22 and 2 Nephi 10:20). It was important therefore to stress that the land northward and land southward are each almost totally surrounded by water, but for a narrow neck of land. Hence they can be aptly called isles of the sea. Early in the BOM narrative, Nephi exclaims: "the Lord has made the sea our path, and we are upon an isle of the sea [South America]." (2 Nephi 10:20)

In the same vein, we read that "the Nephites possessing all the land northward, yea, even all the land which was northward of the land Bountiful, according to their pleasure," (Alma 50:11) and: "he [Lamanite Amalickiah] was marching forth with his numerous army that he might take possession of the land Bountiful, and also the land northward." (Alma 51:30) Taking the land Bountiful was preliminary to marching into the land northward. Apparently Bountiful was then under Nephite control.

The Narrow Passage. This is another feature associated with the small (narrow) neck of land: the narrow pass (passage) leading to the land northward (or southward). This passage is a choke point at one of the two narrowest parts of the Isthmus of Panama: "And it came to pass that they [Moroni and his troops] did not head them [off; i.e. the Lamanites] until they had come to the borders of the land Desolation [the line Bountiful/Desolation]; and there they did head them, by the narrow pass which led by the sea into the land northward, yea, by the sea, on the west and on the east." (Alma 50:34) This is also made clear in Mormon 2:29: "And the Lamanites did give unto us the land northward, yea, even to the narrow passage which led into the land southward. And we did give unto the Lamanites all the land southward." The narrow passage lies "by" the sea, both on the east and on the west. This passage is a choke point where one could head off the Lamanite army, and a specific location point on the narrow neck of land, where the land southward and the land northward are divided. Rather than being where a Nephite could cross in a day and a half, it may be where the crossing took only a day, the point that the Nephites fortified in Helaman 4:7. This is a natural point of defense.

The narrow neck of land is, after all, a neck, actually a long neck, not to be confused with the line of the shortest distance from the sea on the east to the sea on the west. Such a feature is the land stretching from South America roughly to the southern border of Nicaragua. Map 4 above is from the most popular, cheap and small booklet of maps for school children, in publication before and through the 1820's.[87] Note that although the sea to the east is north of the Isthmus of Panama, it is due east of Nicaragua, Honduras and the Yucatan Peninsula.

The River Sidon. A curious aspect of BOM cartography is the fact that only one river is mentioned, apart from unnamed rivers in the region of Cumorah. This is in contrast with the OT, which mentions the important rivers of the Middle East, from Egypt to Babylon. Every directional reference to the Sidon speaks of the west or east side of the river, indicating that it flowed in a direction within the range of due north-south and up to a forty-five degree angle off of due north-south, dumping into the Caribbean. Its headwaters are near the territory of Manti near the west coast (as opposed to the city proper), which is near the south wilderness, meaning within the southern extremity of the land of Zarahemla. Since it flowed near the city Zarahemla, it must have flowed from the highlands on the west side to spill into the sea on the east. This agrees with those of Map 4, from the Yucatan to Panama, flowing from the west to the Caribbean. The land of Melek was on the west of the borders of the wilderness, and on the west of the Sidon (Alma 8:3). From the city of Zarahemla, Alma went "over upon the east of the river Sidon, into the valley of Gideon" (Alma 6:7). Thus with Gideon to the east of the river, we read in Alma 2:

> 2:26 . And it came to pass that the people of Nephi took their tents, and departed out of the valley of Gideon towards their city, which was the city of Zarahemla.
> 2:27 . And behold, as they were crossing the river Sidon, the Lamanites and the Amlicites, being as numerous almost, as it were, as the sands of the sea, came upon them to destroy them.

It seems clear from these passages that the Sidon flowed near to and on the east side of the city Zarahemla.

---

[87] Adams, *School Atlas*. Shown is a detail of the map of North America.

Looking at rivers that exist today, there is no exact candidate for the Sidon in Panama or Nicaragua. Those wishing to find a real-world river may consider the Ulúa River in Honduras, used for Map 5, but elongated towards Manti. On the other hand, the Sidon may be better understood as an effort to recreate the Holy Land in the land of Zarahemla. It is especially referred to as a place for baptism, and for the BOM authors it may have been their equivalent to the River Jordan, rather than being based on any actual river.

The Land of Lakes and Rivers and the Adobe Culture. Speaking of people who went northward, beyond the land of Zarahemla, the BOM states, "And they did travel to an exceedingly great distance, insomuch that they came to large bodies of water and many rivers." (Helaman 3:4; cf. Alma 50:29) Cumorah, the site where Smith claimed to have found the gold plates, in upstate New York, and the site of the last Lamanite-Nephite battles, is described as follows "we did pitch our tents around about the hill Cumorah; and it was in a land of many waters, rivers, and fountains; and here we had hope to gain advantage over the Lamanites." (Mormon 6:4) This is most consistent with the region of the Great Lakes, the Finger Lakes in New York and rivers throughout the area.

Not so far north is another location that can be identified with considerable probability, a semiarid land that lacked sufficient trees for wood construction. Of it we read, "And there being but little timber upon the face of the land, nevertheless the people who went forth became exceedingly expert in the working of cement; therefore they did build houses of cement, in the which they did dwell." (Helaman 3:7) This appears to arise from the BOM authors' awareness and misunderstanding of adobe construction in the U.S. four-corner region. Current dating places the beginning of the Pueblo civilization in around the eighth century CE.

We read also of this land: "And it came to pass as timber was exceedingly scarce in the land northward, they did send forth much by the way of shipping." (Helaman 3:10) So this arid land was north of Zarahemla. Imagine the logistics and transportation nightmare given their limitations. How then did they transport the timber from the coast to the land of cement houses?

Cumorah. Cumorah is where Joseph Smith claimed to have found the gold plates in upstate New York (cf. D&C128:20, 1842; & Cowdery's letters to Phelps, 1835).[88] It is also where Mormon hid the Nephite records "save it were these few plates which I gave unto my son Moroni" (Mormon 6:6). The BOM text does not say where Moroni hid the plates. Even so, Cumorah is "a land of many waters, rivers, and fountains" (Mormon 6:4). So too is the hill where Smith claimed to have gotten his plates, in walking distance from his home, and in the region of the Great Lakes and Finger Lakes, as well as many rivers. If Mormon gave him only the plates of Nephi, then the relics (the sword and breastplate of Laban, and the interpreters) must have been hidden also at Cumorah. These and the plates of Nephi would have been rejoined when Moroni hid the plates of Nephi. Smith's hill and Mormon's Cumorah are located in the same region and seem to be one and the same.

First, it is clearly north of the narrow neck of land. The Jaredite narrative in the Book of Ether indicates this, where it is said that the Jaredites "built a great city by the narrow neck of land, by the place where the sea divides the land. And they did preserve the land southward for a wilderness, to get game. And the whole face of the land northward was covered with inhabitants." (Ether 10:20-21) The hill Cumorah is identified as being the Jaredite Ramah, both peoples having been annihilated there. "And it came to pass that the army of Coriantumr did pitch their tents by the hill Ramah; and it was that same hill where my father Mormon did hide up the records unto the Lord, which were sacred." (Ether 15:11) Mormon states that he buried all the plates entrusted to him "save it were these few plates which I gave unto my son Moroni." (Mormon 6:6) It is generally assumed that Moroni hid those plates in the same hill, because Joseph Smith called it also the hill Cumorah. This is not specified by Moroni. (Mormon 8:14) Since the Jaredites did not penetrate south of the narrow neck of land except to hunt game, Ramah, and therefore Cumorah, are located in the land northward.

Accordingly, at the beginning of General Mormon's final campaigns leading to the Nephite total defeat at Cumorah, he says, "And the Lamanites did give unto us the land northward, yea, even to the narrow passage which led into the land southward. And we did give unto the Lamanites all the land southward." (Mormon 2:29) The final struggle

---

[88] Oliver Cowdery to W. W. Phelps dated July 1835, in Dan Vogel, *Early Mormon Documents* (Salt Lake City: Signature Books, 2007), II:446-50; Oliver Cowdery to W. W. Phelps dated October 1835, *Ibid*, II:455-63

began "at the land Desolation, to a city which was in the borders, by the narrow pass which led into the land southward." (Mormon 3:5) The Nephites were driven from there to the city Angola, then the land of David, then to the land of Joshua, then to the city Boaz, and then to the city Jordan. These are all places not figuring in the history of the Nephites in their heartland, and must be on the way northward. When they arrived at Cumorah, it is described as being "in a land of many waters, rivers, and fountains" (Mormon 6:4), which is an apt description of the Great Lakes region and the Finger Lakes in upstate New York. In all of this account, there is no mention of any city south of the narrow neck of land, nor either the land or city of Nephi (Lamanite territory in the land southward).

Note too that Mormon, at age 10, was charged by Ammaron to go to the hill Shim when he was 24 years old to collect the Nephite records he had hid there. Apparently, at ten years of age, Mormon was familiar with Shim, in the Land Antum. A year later, at age eleven, he is taken "into the land southward" to Zarahemla, i.e., southward of the hill Shim in the north. (Mormon 1:2-6) This indicates that Mormon's family lived north of Zarahemla. During the Nephite's retreat, when they got to the land and city of Jashon (not mentioned elsewhere), Mormon went to the hill Shim for the plates. At this point he is near where he was before his father took him south to Zarahemla. The Nephite armies were being pushed further and further northward. Mormon took command around 327 CE and gathered the Nephites at the land of Cumorah in about 385 CE. So the time for the long retreat was about fifty-eight years. This seems to be an adequate period to arrive so far away.

The Map

Every effort has been made to base Map 5 on specific references in the BOM narrative. This map locates most of the Nephite homeland in Nicaragua and Honduras, relatively near the narrow neck of land and outside the lands of the Olmec and Maya. BOM cartography will never achieve consensus on the exact location of many BOM place names. Even so, Map 5 tends to agree with the Central American location preferred by most LDS scholars, although they have tended to locate the BOM setting in the region of the Olmec and Maya (Table 43).

Map 5. The Lands of the Nephites and Lamanites

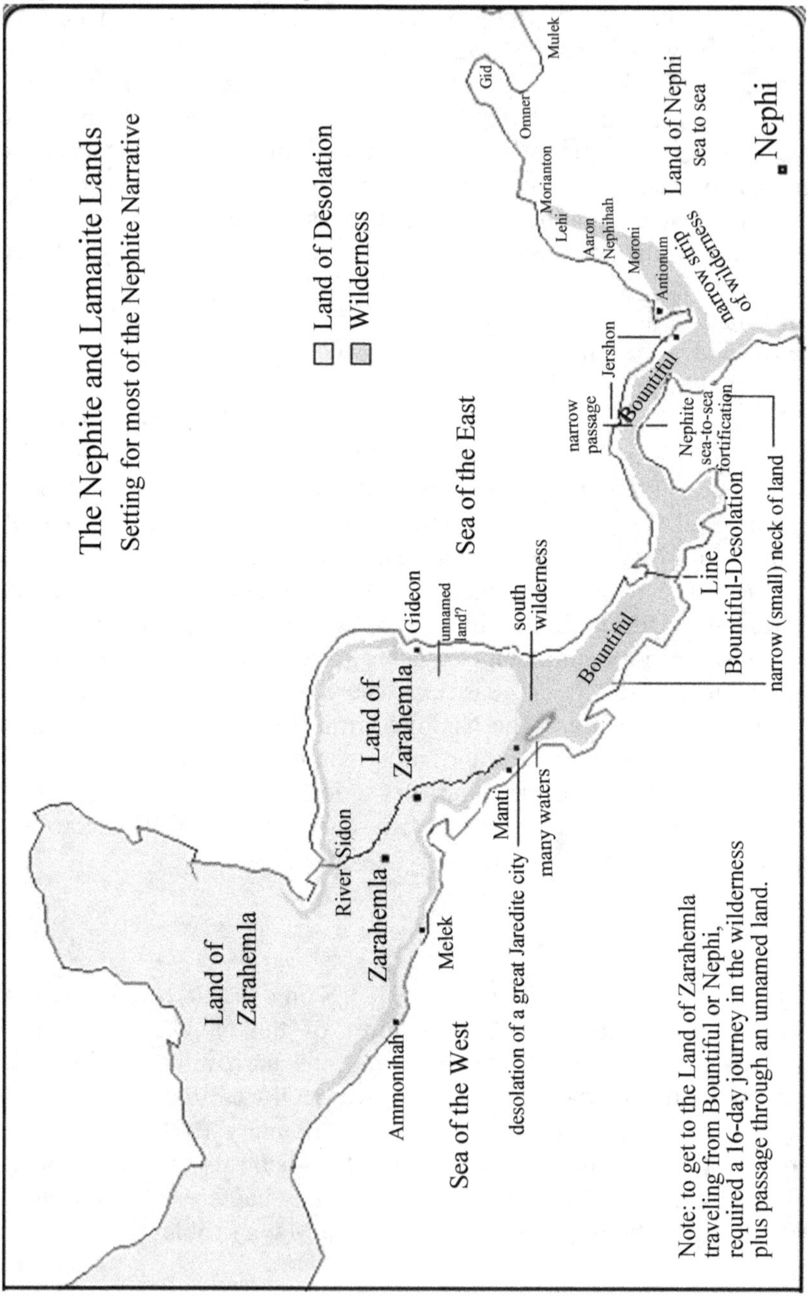

The Nephite and Lamanite Lands
Setting for most of the Nephite Narrative

- Land of Desolation
- Wilderness

Land of Zarahemla

Sea of the West

Ammonihah

Melek

Zarahemla

River Sidon

Land of Zarahemla

Gideon

unnamed land?

Manti

desolation of a great Jaredite city

many waters

south wilderness

Sea of the East

Bountiful

narrow passage

Jershon

Bountiful

Nephite sea-to-sea fortification

Line Bountiful-Desolation

narrow (small) neck of land

Mulek

Gid

Omner

Morianton

Lehi

Aaron

Nephihah

Moroni

Antionum

narrow strip of wilderness

Land of Nephi
sea to sea

Nephi

Note: to get to the Land of Zarahemla traveling from Bountiful or Nephi, required a 16-day journey in the wilderness plus passage through an unnamed land.

Locating the crossing point and the fortification point in the narrow neck of land is based on the observation that the crossing time in Alma 22:32 is fifty percent greater than the time in Helaman 4:7. This is considerable, and some say it is an internal BOM discrepancy. It is possible, some would say preferable, to colocate them, making the line Bountiful/Desolation, the narrow passage choke point and the Nephite fortification from sea-to-sea all at the Panama City crossing. Avoiding the internal discrepancy allegation, Map 5 places the first of these at the David crossing and the other two at Panama City.

NOTE: The BOM geographical references are very largely internally consistent. This can only have been realized if the authors used the student map (Map 4), or some equivalent, to produce their own map of the Nephites to use as a guide.[89]

Where Did All the Cities Go?

The *Book of Mormon* mentions at least 40 cities by name, including only one Jaredite city. These are clearly distinguished from villages, such as Ani-Anti, and many others. (Mosiah 27:6; Alma 8:7 & 23:14 & Mormon 4:22 & 5:5) The fact that this civilization, its cities, inscriptions and artifacts have never been found anywhere in the Americas, has driven some to the assumption that the great Crucifixion Cataclysm at the time of Christ's crucifixion had vaporized everything. Venice Priddis and Arthur J. Kocherhans have made the most extravagant argument, *to wit*, that South America was largely below sea level until the crucifixion. The land that had been above sea level was the land of the *Book of Mormon*.

---

[89] Many are based on specific verses, as follows. However, in some cases, the full import of the verse is context-dependent.
Aaron (Alma 50:14), Ammonihah (Alma 8:6); Antionum (Alma 27:22 & 31:3), Bountiful (Alma 22:31, 52:9), Bountiful-Desolation Line (Alma 22:30-33), City Desolation (Mormon 3:5, 3:7, 4:3; at or near the Jaredite "great city"?), desolation of a Great Jaredite city (Ether 10:20), Gid (Alma 51:26), Gideon (Alma 6:7), Head of the River Sidon (Alma 43:22), Hill Shim (Mormon 1:3) near Jashon (Mormon 2:17), Jershon (Alma 27:22 & 31:3), Land of Nephi (Alma 50:8), Lehi (Alma 51:26), Manti (Alma 43:32-42), Melek (Alma 8:3), Morianton (Alma 51:26), Moroni (Alma 50:13), Mulek (Alma 51:26), Nephihah (Alma 50:14), Omner (Alma 51:26) Shilom (Mosiah 9:6, 14), unnamed land (3 Nephi 3:23) & Zarahemla (Helaman 1:27).

At the time of the crucifixion, South America rose up thousands of feet in about three hours. Still, this leaves the locations prior to that event in the Andes highlands as candidates for exploration, where everything on the item list should be discoverable, in an ideal state of dry highland low-oxygen preservation. To save the day, her cataclysm should not have been just a sudden emergence from the deep, but also a kerplop, a turning over of the whole continent like a pancake, so that everything would wind up at the bottom. A sci-fi kerplop, or vaporization?[90]

Well, this is a lot of fun, but on a more serious note, and to be fair, most *Book of Mormon* cartographers minimize the effect of the cataclysm. After all, only some cities were destroyed, sixteen mentioned by name. (3 Nephi 8:15) Six were burned, five sunk into the earth, one sunk in the sea, three were flooded and one was covered by a mountain. When a city burns, it is still available for archaeology. The fire will just leave a burn level in the stratigraphy. A couple of major cities are said to have been rebuilt, including Zarahemla. This was followed by another four centuries of Nephite-Lamanite urban history, with cities and a material culture. Mormon around 322 CE observed, "The whole face of the land had become covered with buildings, and the people were as numerous almost, as it were the sand of the sea." (Mormon 1:7) Furthermore, the Jaredites also built many cities. (Ether 9:23 & 10:12)

When a city undergoes a major cataclysm, this fact can be observed in the archaeological record. Slipping into the sea leaves a large debris field, and a ready candidate for marine archaeology. Fire leaves a burn level in the stratigraphy. Collapsed buildings not only leave their own debris, but often skeletons and artifacts under it.

It is important to note that north of the Rio Grande cities developed rather late. When they did, these were in the Mississippian region, with the largest city being Cahokia, which existed from about 700 to 1250 CE. Another urban civilization was the Pueblo culture, and particularly Chaco Canyon, where the term Anasazi is often used for the people and culture. Beginning c. 700 CE, it had its golden age from c. 900 CE to 1130 CE, when a 300-year drought brought about its decline. Cities in the BOM Nephite period have not been discovered in North America.

---

[90] Priddis, *The Book and the Map*. Arthur J. Kocherhans, *Lehi's Isle of Promise* (Fullerton, CA: Et Cetera Graphics and Printing, 1989).

3. Mapping the *Book of Mormon* Setting

The last battles of both civilizations should have left behind a mass of steel swords, breastplates and helmets. In the Jaredite final conflict, millions of combatants fell to the sword, equipped with these items. In the end-of-days scenario for the Nephites, each of twenty-four commanders commanded 10,000 combatants, similarly equipped, resulting in 240,000 dead, and at least as many Lamanites. Both final confrontations happened in upstate New York. What a field day for weekenders wielding metal detectors.

Crucifixion Cataclysm: A Research Perspective

In the *Book of Mormon*, at the time of the crucifixion of Jesus, the whole land was convulsed and swept with terrible destruction. This great cataclysm was clearly intended to obscure the geography, so as to provide a way to evade the issue of the missing cities, and for many this has been its function in their faith. Such a major cataclysm, on a regional if not a bicontinental level, at a time not so long ago in geological time, would have left very obvious consequences. There are four areas of major investigation, any one of which should have found at least some evidence of this event, over a relatively broad territory and at the same point in time. Indeed, such a discovery would have been front-page news.

First, the Panama Canal involved massive earth moving over a long distance, creating a huge geological cross section. A special team of paleogeologists, paleontologists and archaeologists worked feverishly between the creation of the cross-section and the canal construction, to document everything of geological, paleontological and archaeological interest. At present, for the new expansion of the canal, the Smithsonian in collaboration with other institutions is taking advantage of this more recent massive earth excavation, to document geological and paleontological information.

Second, there has been extensive geological research, on land and offshore, in the whole area of the Chicxulub asteroid impact that wiped out the dinosaurs, on the coast of the Yucatan Peninsula. The same area had been extensively investigated by petroleum prospectors who obtained numerous core samples. These were inspected by those studying the asteroid impact. There has also been marine seabed research and investigation into the pattern and formation of the cenotes in relation to this impact. Cenote and other Mesoamerican cave exploration would also reveal the effects of such a cataclysm on the often fragile structures (stalagmites, stalactites, etc.), datable by the subsequent formation of calcite deposits. Mexico is the site of some of the most outstanding and intricate caverns on the planet.

Third, there have been numerous archaeological excavations covering the first-century timeframe, that have done painstaking stratigraphy research, often with spoons and small brushes, sifting everything, and comparing the strata within and across sites, that would have detected such a disruption. At many sites, continuous occupation straddles the first centuries BCE and CE.

Fourth, there is all the modern development activity in what has become highly populated countries, including geological surveys in search of resources, highway construction and excavations for buildings, all of which have a history of discovering paleogeological and archaeological elements that were not within the original scope of work.

By the normal standards of secular research, given all of this, it is safe to say that the cataclysm story borders on tales inspired by smoking wacky tabaki.

Observations

This study has been assiduously based on the geographical references in the BOM narrative. Each of these consists of mentions of a feature in connection with one or more other features. The approach has tried to follow a strictly literal reading of each passage. Three salient observations should be noted:

1) BOM geography is relatively complex, at least to the extent that it cannot be the result of casual composition or extemporaneous dictation. It is highly probable that a Nephite/Lamanite setting map was drawn up, most probably based on the school boys map (Map 4), with which teachers, such as Joseph Smith Sr. and Oliver Cowdery must have been familiar.

2) One is hard-pressed to find significant and clear-cut contradictions in the geographical references. This reflects a studied effort. Even the geographical references in the Jaredite record are consistent with those in the Nephite record, such as Cumorah/Ramah, the narrow neck of land separating two lands, a large Jaredite city near it probably being the ruins

found by the Nephite party sent out by King Limhi, and a region bountiful in game, at the entrance from the narrow neck of land into the land south.

By locating the BOM setting largely in Nicaragua and Honduras, a map has been arrived at that provides itinerary distances roughly within the realm of the possible, while removing the BOM setting from the Maya-Olmec region.

Chapter 4

Demographic Issues

Nephites Maximized: Demographic Improbabilities

When the Lehi party arrived from Jerusalem to the New World, they began the process of populating empty continents kept for them as what is called "the land of our inheritance," to preserve an intact branch of Israel to be gathered to Christ prior to the Second Coming. Initially they numbered no more than 29 individuals, including children born in the wilderness of Arabia (Jacob and Joseph are mentioned). Their population size is important, since population can be viewed both as a limiting factor, and an enabling factor. During the first five decades in their new environment, we find projects that require a population of an adequate size, and events, concerns and comments that only make sense when the population has reached a certain level.

The BOM narrative does not provide detailed population data. But for our purpose, this is no obstacle. A population growth model can be constructed with assumptions that yield maximum population growth well beyond what one can reasonably entertain, thereby producing figures that lean very heavily in favor of the BOM narrative.

1) The beginning point is what we are told about the initial party. Lehi sets out in the wilderness with his family. Just before his death he gives his sons their individual blessings. They number six: Laman, Lemuel, Sam, Nephi, Jacob and Joseph. There is a mention of his daughters, but, in keeping with the nearly total male dominance in the account, there is no mention of their names. We will assume that they too number six, giving Lehi twelve children, a goodly patriarchal number. Once in the desert, Lehi sends back to Jerusalem for the family of Ishmael, whom we will assume to have had twelve children as well, six sons and six daughters. Although there is a mention of Ishmael having five daughters upon leaving Jerusalem, we will assume that another was born in the wilderness. His family was needed so that Lehi's sons might be able to marry. (1 Nephi 7:1-5) The servant of Laban, Zoram, joined this hypothetical twenty-eight. The members who were of eligible age were married up shortly after leaving Jerusalem, in a place that the BOM

4. Demographic Issues 77

calls the Valley of Lemuel. The group that came over with Mulek were not encountered until long after the period of this study.

2. Rough age estimates are possible for Jacob and Joseph, who were born in the wilderness, meaning that they were sufficiently young that they did not marry immediately upon their arrival. In this study, in order to maximize population growth, we will assume that the generation span was short, i.e. that the average age of marriage was fifteen, with some marrying as early as fourteen, and others at sixteen. Outliers, beyond either side of this range, would have been rare, and would have offset each other.

3. The model further assumes that each couple also had twelve children, throughout.

4. Ishmael dies in the wilderness, and eventually Lehi, Sariah and Ishmael's wife die. Apart from these, the model assumes that there was no mortality, at least among the Nephites, for the first six decades; no infant mortality, nor death in childbirth, nor due to disease. Even though warfare occurs in this time frame, it is assumed that no Nephites were killed.

There is no population on earth with such an idyllic growth rate.

Our approach will be highly detailed. Every two years, an actual population chart has been constructed, listing all individuals existing at that time, and their relationship to the others. Initially, we have Lehi, Sariah, Laman, Lemuel, Sam, Nephi, Jacob, Joseph, LD1 (first daughter of Lehi), LD2, LD3, LD4, LD5, LD6, Ishmael, Iwife (Ishmael's wife), IS1 (first son of Ishmael), IS2, IS3, IS4, IS5, IS6, ID1 (first daughter of Ishmael), ID2, ID3, ID4, ID5, ID6 and Zoram. The *Book of Mormon* states that Jesus would come 600 years after their departure from Jerusalem, making that date 600 BCE. The fact that the first year of Zedekiah has been dated two or three years later is not of importance, since BOM dating initially is in years after their departure (ALJ, after leaving Jerusalem). When Nephi marries a daughter of Ishmael, whom we will designate as being his fifth daughter, the two are no longer recorded individually, but as a couple, Nephi/ID5. Of course in population counts, they are counted as two. Their son is recorded as S(Nephi/ID5), and no numbers are used to distinguish one son from another as this is irrelevant. As we progress through time, with a new chart every two years, updated for new marriages and children born, the designations become cumbersome. Thus, in the year 550 we have a daughter whose designation is:

D (S(S[IS3/LD3]/D[Jacob/ID6]) / (D[S[Jacob/ID6]/D[IS5/LD5]])

Here, the forward slash represents a marriage. This is: the daughter of a son from the marriage of a son from the marriage [IS3/LD3] and a daughter of the marriage [Jacob/ID6]), and from a daughter from the marriage of a son from the marriage [Jacob/ID6] and a daughter from the marriage [IS5/LD5]. At journey's end, this project had produced sixty-five pages of charts, one chart every second year from 598 through 546 ALJ, all organized in birth-year groups. As cumbersome as this is, all relationships were kept straight, and each chart was a clear picture of all persons alive in that year, with their marital status, age and descent. Although a hypothetical construct, the assumptions are such that each chart gives the maximum figures that one can possibly expect in that year.

In practice, each chart was copied and pasted to a new page to carry it over to the next chart two years hence, the ages were adjusted by two years, all eligibles were married up, and all couples who had not yet produced twelve children were given an additional child, with gender alternating, producing a 50/50 gender ratio.

Using this data, the following summary was made, including important events at their approximate times.

Table 3. Maximized Nephite Population & Significant Events

Date	Total Population	Elderly	Married	Unmarried (under 14)	Married (no children over 4)	Under Ten Years Old
2 ALJ (c. 598 BCE)	35	4	18	13	18	11
592	67	3	20	44	0	39
Arrival in the New World after eight years in the wilderness, and the oceanic crossing.						
590	77	3	20	54	0	40
580	143	3	48	92	26	55
c. 578-574	Nephi took his people to a new location, which they called the land of Nephi, and they took upon them the name Nephites. Nephi taught his brethren smelting and alloying metals, working in iron, copper, brass, gold and silver.					

(Table 3 continued)

	Nephi made many swords to arm Nephites against Lamanites. Construction of the temple. Nephi's brethren sought to make him king, but he refused. The followers of Laman were cursed with a skin of blackness, and made loathsome to the Nephites.					
576 total	198	3	64	131	24	87
From this point, only Nephites were reported, although Lamanites were still being charted.						
576	114	3	34	77	10	50
570	162	1	58	103	26	82
564	244	1	90	153	34	101
c. 574-560	Nephite-Lamanite wars and contentions					
	From this point on, only the Nephites were charted.					
560	328	8	114	206	46	144
550	657	14	214	429	80	273
546	824	14	260	550	120	358
c. 55 ALJ (c. 545 BCE)	Nephi dies, most probably in his seventies.					

Without the extravagant assumptions to maximize Nephites, and without the three sons of Ishmael and their families included with the Nephites, the figures in the table would be no more than half.

At some point between 580 and 570 BCE, Nephi leads his people to a new land, separate from the Lamanites, and the account focuses largely on the Nephites. At this early date, we are not dealing with individuals, but with a group of nuclear families, possibly living together as extended families. A large proportion was children or very young adults, i.e. no more than twenty years old. The BOM narrative indicates that the families of Nephi, Sam, Jacob, Joseph and even Zoram were among the Nephites. Three of Ishmael's sons were assigned to the Nephites and three to the Lamanites, even though most or all of his sons may have joined the Lamanites. By 400 BCE the Lamanites were more numerous than the Nephites (Jarom 1:6). Later in the BOM, the Ishmaelites are usually numbered among the Lamanites. If this 50/50 division inflates the Nephite count, then it too leans in favor of the BOM narrative. After this separation, the population charts were done only for the Nephites, since it is their events that loom large in this study. And in any case, any assumption that enhances the size of the Nephite population in the first several decades favors the credibility of the *Book of Mormon* narrative within the context of the present inquiry.

The following observations can be made from the charts and this table: 1) Initially, there was considerable inbreeding; 2) the population was very young; 3) the women were either pregnant or recovering from childbirth up to their late thirties, and raising young children up to age fifty; and 4) with so many children, and even with only three elders, the population in the New World had a very high dependency ratio.

When Lehi's party left the Old World, they brought "all manner of seeds of every kind, both of grain of every kind, and also of the seeds of fruit of every kind" (1 Nephi 8:1). Upon their arrival they found "beasts in the forests of every kind, both the cow and the ox, and the ass and the horse, and the goat and the wild goat, and all manner of wild animals, which were for the use of men." (1 Nephi 18:25) Numbering no more than 67, and with only about a dozen able-bodied men, they set about clearing the land and establishing farmsteads, supplemented by hunting and gathering. Then, only after about 17 years in the "land of their inheritance," the settlers, already warring among themselves, divided into two groups, and Nephi led his group off to a new land, which they named the land of Nephi (2 Nephi 5:8). There they worked hard and "did prosper exceedingly; for we did sow seed, and we did reap again in abundance. And we began to raise flocks, and herds, and animals of every kind." (2 Nephi 5:11) This they did, starting anew, with a population of only about 114, including only eighteen males aged 15 and above. In just a few years, they also established metallurgy, smelting iron, copper, gold and silver, and clearly also tin, to alloy it with copper to produce brass. They made steel adequate for sword blades: "I, Nephi, did take the sword of Laban, and after the manner of it did make many swords." (2 Nephi 5:14) The construction of buildings rounded out their production: "And I did teach my people to build buildings, and to work in all manner of wood, and of iron, and of copper, and of brass, and of steel, and of gold, and of silver, and of precious ores, which were in great abundance." (2 Nephi 5:15)

Even more remarkable, Nephi proceeded to build a temple (2 Nephi 5:16): "And I, Nephi, did build a temple; and I did construct it after the manner of the temple of Solomon save it were not built of so many precious things; for they were not to be found upon the land, wherefore, it could not be built like unto Solomon's temple. But the manner of the construction was like unto the temple of Solomon; and the workmanship thereof was exceedingly fine." To put this into perspective, the Israelites in their thousands were unable to build the temple of Solomon. Hundreds of years after the victories of Joshua, and after the establishment of the Davidic Empire, with the influx of slaves, booty and taxes, the Israelites were unable to build Solomon's temple. They contracted with the Canaanite Hiram, King of Tyre, to build it. Yet this tiny band, while establishing their farmsteads, and engaged in warfare with the Lamanites, were able to build a temple like unto that of Solomon, with exceedingly fine workmanship. Incredible.

At the time, one did not go to a lumber yard to buy boards and nails. The construction projects would have required felling trees, splitting logs, cutting wood to required lengths, hewing boards, one after another, probably with an adze, and drilling holes for pegs, or making one's own nails. All this was done while farming and hunting to put food on the table, and fending off the Lamanites.

These events are dated by the comment of Nephi, once his group had become thus well established in the new land, "And thirty years had passed away from the time we left Jerusalem." (2 Nephi 5:28)

It is not knowable what is meant by the assertion that already the two groups had been engaged in warfare: "And it sufficeth me to say that forty years had passed away, and we had already had wars and contentions with our brethren." (2 Nephi 5:34) In the fortieth year (660 BCE) the Nephite men over fifteen numbered only 57, and the Lamanites about the same. Most must have been at work in the fields. Warfare? "Fighting" would perhaps be a more appropriate term.

The BOM narrative uses the word "people" to imply a larger population than could have existed. When they establish the land of Nephi, we read in 2 Nephi 5:

> 8. And my people would that we should call the name of the place Nephi; wherefore, we did call it Nephi.
> 9. And all those who were with me did take upon them to call themselves the people of Nephi.
> 14. And I, Nephi, did take the sword of Laban, and after the manner of it did make many swords, lest by any means the people who were now called Lamanites should come upon us and destroy us; for I knew their hatred towards me and my children and those who were called my people. (Cf. 2 Nephi 5:15, *supra*, and vs. 17-33)

In this context, we read in 2 Nephi 5:

17. And it came to pass that I, Nephi, did cause my people to be industrious, and to labor with their hands.
18. And it came to pass that they would that I should be their king. But I, Nephi, was desirous that they should have no king; nevertheless, I did for them according to that which was in my power.

It is totally incongruous that this "people" should ask Nephi to be their king, when they are no more than his brothers, Sam, Jacob and Joseph, their wives, and in-laws (a son or two of Ishmael, married to granddaughters of Lehi), and their children (many still minors), and their children (all quite young). This is a handful of extended families, hardly even a clan. The BOM authors are getting ahead of their story.

One is also surprised to read Jacob's condemnations of the people of Nephi not so long after the death of Nephi, accusing the rich of neglecting the needs of the poor, and of having concubines and many wives. Nephi died c. 55 ALJ (545 BCE), and in the year 546 BCE the Nephites numbered only 824, with 260 adults, all closely related, cousins, second cousins, etc. At the time of Jacob's condemnation, perhaps a decade later, the demography would not have been seriously different. Socioeconomic stratification, severe divisions between the rich and the poor, excesses of concubinage and polygyny, are all characteristics of societies of considerably larger scale. In the case of plural wives in tribal society, each tribe exists in relationship with many other tribes, and the second wife usually comes from a different tribe, often of lower status, a situation that is hard to imagine in Jacob's day. The Nephites then constituted, at best, a small village of blood relatives.

This demographic analysis indicates that the BOM authors themselves probably had little awareness of the population they were penning, its size, composition and capabilities.

Record-Keeper Recording Time and Nephite Generations

The *Book of Mormon* records the handing down of the records from which Mormon's abridgment would be made on the gold plates. This information is sufficiently detailed to enable us to study record-keeping periods (how long each record-keeper recorded on the plates). By simple examination, one notes the difference between the time span 600-0 BCE and 0-400 CE. Not counting brothers, who are contemporary with the previous record-keeper and recorded only a few years, we have 14 recorder-keepers in the first period, up to when Nephi son of Helaman passes the plates to his son. There are five in the second period, going up to when Moroni gets the records from Mormon. The average record-keeper time of service in the first period is 42.86 years, which has been rounded up to 43 in the table (third column from the left). The average record-keeping time of service in the second group is 80 years. These have been accumulated in the column "Summing Average Time in Service," to see how well the averages track the actual passage of time. Note that in the column "Time Keeping Record," when the date of the passing of the records is not recorded, averages have been used from the previous to the next known date.

Table 4. Plates Transmission & Record-keeper Recording Time

				ALJ: After Leaving Jerusalem
				YOJ: Year of the Reign of the Judges
				YOS: Year Since the Sign (birth of Jesus)
				Summing Averages: accumulation of average record-keeping times
				    (*italics*=43-year intervals)
				    (**bold**=80-year intervals)
				Note: unknown dates resulted in averaging two or more record-keeping spans

Record Keeper #	Time Keeping Record	Summing average time in service	date (ALJ)	Event/Transmission of Plates
			0	Departure from Jerusalem.
			4	Approximate birth of Jacob, brother of Nephi.
			8 c. 10	After 8 years in the wilderness. (1 Nephi 17:4) Nephi makes the plates.
1	45	*43*	55	**Approximate death of Nephi.** Nephi gives plates to Jacob, his brother, born in the wilderness. (Jacob 1:-21)
2	c. 62	86	?	**Plates passed from Jacob** to Enos son of Jacob.
3	c. 62	*129*	179	**Approximate death of Enos** Jarom, son of Enos, receives plates.
4	59	*172*	238	**Approximate death of Jarom.** Omni son of Jarom receives plates.
5	44	*215*	282	**Approximate death of Omni.** Passed plates to Amaron son of Omni
6	38	*258*	320	**Approximate death of Amaron.** Plates passed to his brother, Chemish.
no calculation for a brother				**Chemish passes plates** to his son Abinadom.
7	c. 52	*301*	?	**Abinadom passes plates** to his son Amaleki.

(Table 4 continued)

8	c. 52	*344*	?	Having no heir, **Amaleki passes to King Benjamin**.
9	c.52	*387*		Birth of Mosiah (446)
			476	Mosiah reigns in his father's stead, at age 30. **King Benjamin passes plates** passed to Mosiah.
			479	King Benjamin dies.
10	c. 33	*430*	509	**King Mosiah passes plates to Alma** his son, Alma the Younger. (Mosiah 28:20) King Mosiah dies in 33rd year of his reign, age 63. Alma is appointed the first Chief Judge. Alma's father dies, age 82.
			518	Years of the Reign of the Judges begin (YOJ). 9th year of the reign of the judges, Alma delivers judgment seat to Nephiha. Moroni at 25 appointed Chief Captain over the Nephites.
11	19	*473*	528	**Alma the Younger** passes plates to Helaman the Elder, and departs (19 YOJ).
12	16	*516*	544	**Helaman the Elder dies** in 35th year of judges
no calculation for a brother			545	Shiblon brother of Helaman takes possession of plates in 36th year of judges (from Helaman).
			548	Shiblon dies in 39th year of judges. Delivers plates to **Helaman the Younger.** Helaman (younger, son of Helaman) appointed to
			551	the judgment seat, 42nd year of judges.
13	18	*559*	562	**Helaman the Younger** dies, leaving the plates to son Nephi, in 53rd year of judges.
			571	Nephi delivers judgment seat to Cezoram, in the 62nd year of judges.
			575	Cezoram murdered, then his son is murdered, in the 66th year of judges.
14	38	*602*	600	Lachoneus is chief judge, in 91st year of judges (date given: 91 YOJ = 600 ALJ; see 3 Nephi 1:1). **Nephi, son of Helaman, passes plates** to his son, Nephi, son of Nephi (600 AlJ; 3 Nephi 1:2). Years after the Sign (birth of Jesus) begin.
			609	Equals 100th year of the judges (3 Nephi 2:5-6). Equals also 9 years since the sign of the coming of Christ.
			630	Lachoneus son of Lachoneus becomes governor (30th year of the sign). Chief judge is murdered.
			634	A great storm, 34th year, 1st month, 4th day of the
			634	sign. "Age of man" defined by Christ as "72 years."

(Table 4 continued)

17	84	682	684	**Nephi, son of Nephi**, dies, having kept the record 84 years (4 Nephi 1:19-20). Plates passed to his son **Amos**.
			710	110 years after the sign equals first generation since Christ (age c. 76, i.e. 110-34)
18	111	762	794	194 years after birth of Christ (after the sign), Amos dies and passing plates to his son, **Amos son of Amos**.
			710	.
			801	Dissension begins in 201st year of the sign (or since birth of Christ).
			810	Many churches & schisms 210 years after the sign. Nephite/Lamanite division reestablished, 231st year
			831	after the sign.
19	111	842	905	**Amos son of Amos dies** and his brother Ammaron gets the records, in year 305'
			910	Mormon is born'
			922	Ammaron hides records in 322 after the birth of Christ' Mormon (c. 10) receives instructions from Ammaron.
20	40	922	921	Mormon accompanies father to Zarahemla. Nephite/Lamanite warring begins.
			926	Mormon is sixteen in 326 after Christ.
			945	**Mormon** gets the records & begins keeping the record.
21	36	1002	984	Nephites gather at Cumorah.
			c. 985	Mormon hides all records except those given to **Moroni** in the Hill Cumorah.
			1,000	**Mormon is killed**. Nephites destroyed; no more Christians (400 CE).
			1,021	Moroni seals the plates (c. 421 CE).

The records in Egyptian were passed mostly from father to son, along a line of descent of four families, from Nephi through Amaleki, then Benjamin and his son Mosiah, then from Alma through Ammaron, and finally Mormon and Moroni. It was a sequence mostly of prophets, who were spiritual, and sometimes political elites. Apart from these plates, there were plates kept by Mormon the disciple of Christ, and the plates of the kings: "Amaleki had delivered up these plates into the hands of king Benjamin, he took them and put them with the other plates, which contained records which had been handed down by the kings, from generation to generation until the days of king Benjamin." (Mormon 1:10)

As we shall see, the period after Christ occupies very few pages in the narrative for a four-hundred-year period. There are few new city and personal names. Everything indicates that once the story had been told of Jesus in the New World, they needed only to record the establishment of the church, the apostasy and the destruction of the Nephites. At this point the BOM authors were anxious just to conclude the *Book of Mormon* and get on with the establishment of their new church.

The longer record-keeping times have generational implications. Amos son of Nephi received the plates in 684 ALJ, and died in in 794. If he was only 20 when he got the plates, his age at death was 120. Amos son of Amos died in 905, having kept the record 111 years. If he received the plates at age twenty as well, then he died at age 131. But that would mean the Amos son of Nephi sired him at age 100.

Jaredite Chronology

Although the Jaredite narrative does not say so, one might assume that all Jaredites were Methuselahs. But even if all the progenitors in the begat list in Ether 1:6-32 lived to 900, this is not important for the calculation of the length of their account, from the Tower of Babel and their arrival in the New World to when Coriantumr wandered into Zarahemla. What is really important is the generation span. When a woman lives to 115 or beyond, in our day and age, she still goes into menopause at around age 50. Even when an aging patriarch is matched with a young bride, he rarely procreates beyond the age of seventy. We are not interested in the age of the progenitors listed in Table 5, but their age when the next one in line in the table was born. The table assumes that on average each one's procreative power expired at age sixty. One can make different calculations based on other virility expiration dates.

Table 5. Jaredite Begats (From the Tower of Babel to 600 BCE)

progenitor	years	progenitor	years	progenitor	years
1. Jared		11. Riplakish	600	21. Amnigaddah	1200
2. Orihah	60	12. Morianton	660	22. Coriantum	1260
3. Kib	120	13. Kim	720	23. Com	1320
4. Shule	180	14. Levi	780	24. Shiblon	1380
5. Omer	240	15. Corom	840	25. Seth	1440
6. Emer	300	16. Kish	900	26. Ahah	1500
7. Coriantum	360	17. Lib	960	27. Ethem	1560
8. Com	420	18. Hearthom	1020	28. Moron	1620
9. Heth	480	19. Heth	1080	29. Coriantor	1680

(Table 5 continued)

10. Shez	540	20. Aaron	1140	30. Ether	1740
Note: the phrase "descendant of" is used instead of "son of" three times in the list. In the text, we find that in fact, Ether was the son of Coriantor, and Aaron was the son of Heth. Morianton may not have been the son of Riplakish, but he carried on the fighting after Morianton was killed, and so is not a distant descendant.					

Although we do not know how long Coriantumr wandered before arriving at Zarahemla, let us say it was 70 years. We might be safe in assuming that he was not over sixty when he "smote off the head of Shiz," thereby becoming the last Jaredite warrior. So, based on the hypothetical used in this table, the period of time from the Tower of Babel to 600 BCE could be around 1,800 years, placing that much-storied event around 2,400 BCE. At this time, the Sumerian, Babylonian and Egyptian languages were already being written. Proto-writing had developed in China. The peoples of the planet had spread to every continent. The arrival of mankind to Australia was more than 40,000 years ago, while evidence of agriculture in South America dates to before 14,000 BCE. Presumably all these people actually did speak, and not all the same pure Adamic language, long before any Babel date.

Nephite Life Expectancy

As seen in the plates transmission list, death dates are usually stated, but birth dates are not. Since the lives of father and son overlap, and since it is not certain how old an individual was when receiving the plates, it is not possible to determine how long individuals lived with accuracy. On the other hand, Alma the Elder died at age 82 and Mosiah died at age 63. When Jesus asked his disciples what they wished, we read (3 Nephi 28):

> 2. And they all spake, save it were three, saying: We desire that after we have lived unto the age of man, that our ministry, wherein thou hast called us, may have an end, that we may speedily come unto thee in thy kingdom.
> 3. And he said unto them: Blessed are ye because ye desired this thing of me; therefore, after that ye are seventy and two years old ye shall come unto me in my kingdom; and with me ye shall find rest.

So, in this passage, the "age of man" is apparently 72 years.

Millennial Population Growth

One might wonder if demographic realities allow the BOM history to even be possible. In the preindustrial period, global population growth was extremely slow. For the Lehi and Mulek parties, we might assume that their combined initial number was 60. If we further assume that they were all perfectly healthy, carrying no disease, and arrived in a rich but empty land, where no diseases had evolved to prey on humans and food was plentiful, we might compare the situation with some third-world populations after the introduction of modern medicine and agriculture, resulting in a population explosion. Even though some have achieved a doubling rate of less than twenty years, for a while, let us assume a doubling rate of twenty years. In this case, on average, every generation would leave behind four offspring that survive to produce a new generation of the same size, and the population would double five times in a century. If this were sustained, then by the time of Christ, the population of the New World would be in the billions, which is totally ridiculous.

Let us make the same initial assumption, but assume that the population growth rate levels off, even with generous help from divine Providence, such that it has five doublings in the first century, four in the next, three in the next, two in the next two, one in the next three, and then is stable. The results are in the following table.

Table 6. A Hypothetical BOM Demography

Date After Leaving Jerusalem	Doublings per Century	Population
100	5	1,920
200	4	30,720
300	3	254,760
400	2	1,019,040
500	2	4,076,160
600	1	8,152,320
700	1	16,304,640
800	1	32,609,280
900	0	32,609,280
1000	0	32,609,280

Admittedly, population-doubling analysis is a rather crude demographic technique, and is in this case, totally hypothetical and intended to be heuristic. A skeptic might argue that this is unrealistic. But we do not know what could have happened if such idyllic circumstances had existed, especially with the operation of divine Providence. For comparison, note that Europe is estimated to have had a population of only fifty-six million in the year 1,000 CE, and only ninety million in 1500 CE. According to the estimate above, by 400 CE, the BOM New World population would have been over 16 million per continent.

The foregoing analyses allow the role of divine Providence a free hand. John C. Kunich, by contrast, has marshaled data to make a real-world analysis of BOM demographic issues. He argues, among other things, that given the observed growth rates of other preindustrial populations, especially with the limitations on population growth imposed by a hunter-gatherer economy (usually prevalent among the Lamanite majority), and the high level of war casualties, Jaredite and Nephite-Lamanite history and societies could not have developed as described in the BOM narrative.[91]

---

[91] John C. Kunich, "Multiply Exceedingly: *Book of Mormon* Population Sizes," in Metcalfe, ed., *New Approaches to the* Book of Mormon. *Explorations in Critical Methodology* (Salt Lake City: Signature Books, 1993), 231-267.

Chapter 5

The Bible Versus the *Book of Mormon*

When the project of composing a New World bible was undertaken, it was natural to use the existing Bible, the King James Version, Old Testament and New, as the model. A deep awareness must have existed that there would be opposition to any new bible, and deep suspicion regarding its contents. This was to be at least partly overcome by inserting a number of large Biblical inclusions.

The Brass Plates of Laban

One of the more astounding claims of the *Book of Mormon* is that a collection of Israelite scriptural works inscribed on brass plates and translated into the Egyptian language existed at the close of the seventh century BCE. According to Talmud tradition, the *tanakh* (Hebrew Bible) was established in c. 450 BCE by the Men of the Great Assembly. Modern scholars vary, dating it as early as the Hasmonean Dynasty, perhaps as early as 130 BCE, or as late as the the 2nd century CE, or even later. Among the Dead Sea scrolls, the books attested are found as individual scrolls, not collected into a complete *tanakh*. The authors of the *Book of Mormon* knew that the Bible had, in their day, been translated into many languages. Bible students are aware also that at an early date, the Old Testament existed in translations: Aramaic (called the *Targumim* [sg. *targum*], being *Targum Onkelos*, *Targum Yerushalmi* [Jerusalemite], Targum Yonathan [Jonathan] and Targum Neofiti), into Greek (the Septuagint), Latin (Italic and Vulgate), classical Ethiopic (Geez), Coptic and even Arabic. But, all of these translations were done at least a century after the Hebrew language was no longer spoken. They were done to meet a need, so that worshippers would have access to the Sacred Scriptures. We have no example of Hebrew Scriptures being translated into a Gentile language before the demise of Hebrew.

The claim that Israelite religious leaders had translated their scriptures into Egyptian is surprising. Egypt was seen as a land of the Israelites' bondage, a land of pagan idolatry, a symbols of evil and but land of refuge. Moreover, such a translation would have had to have been done by one or more individuals trained as an Egyptian scribe, to write it in the very complex Egyptian writing system.

Furthermore, there is such a huge wealth of Egyptian documentary and other artifact evidence that Egyptian museums often are forced to double as warehouses. And yet, there is no clear evidence even of the Israelite captivity in Egypt. The one clear case of a Jewish settlement in Egypt prior to 300 BCE is that uncovered on Elephantine Island, in Southern (Upper) Egypt. Although this sixth-century BCE community, possibly of mercenaries, had embraced some pagan influences, they had a temple, and left behind a trove of legal documents and letters. Significantly, these were written in Aramaic. Clearly they had not adopted the Egyptian language for their written documents, and there is no trace of their use of written Egyptian.

When the Rabbinical philosopher and exegete Sa'adiah ben Yosef Gaon (birth in Egypt and death in Baghdad, ninth to tenth century CE) translated the Pentateuch (the five so-called Books of Moses) into Arabic, he not only wrote it using the Hebrew alphabet, but used the Arabic passive participle *ma'bûd* (the one who is worshipped) to translate God, rather than Allah, which is the normal Arabic word for God not only in the Qur'an, but also in the New Testament. This is the extent to which he attempted to cling to at least some Hebrew in his translation, and avoid any hint of non-Israelite religious tainting.

Lehi's Jerusalem: Bible vs. *Book of Mormon*

The destruction of Jerusalem at the hands of Nebuchadnezzar, the destruction of the Temple of Solomon, Solomon's Palace and the walls of Jerusalem, are all events of epic proportion, and figure prominently in Judeo-Christian Biblical commentary and sermonology. There would seemingly be no better time to guide Lehi and his group out of Jerusalem to a new land, reserved just for them, to preserve a branch of Israel to be gathered in the Last Days, than shortly prior to this destruction, when, traditionally, Israel was carried off into Babylon.

Actually, there were two disasters of epic proportion: 1) the sack of Jerusalem including the captivity, and 2) the destruction of the temple, palace and walls. The sack of Jerusalem ended the reign of Jehoiachin, whose brief time on the throne (only a few months) followed that of his father, Jehoiakim. The sack is described as follows:

> And he [Nebuchadnezzar] carried out thence all the treasures of the king's house and cut in pieces all the vessels of gold which Solomon king of Israel had made in the temple of the Lord, as the Lord had said. And he carried away all Jerusalem, and all the princes, and all the mighty men of valour, even ten thousand captives, and all the craftsmen and smiths: none remained, save the poorest sort of the people of the land. (2 Kings 24: 13-14; Esther 2:5-6; Jeremiah 24:1-8; 27:19-22; 27:20; 29:1)

Effectively, this was by far the greater disaster. For a detailed analysis of this deportation, and its composition, see Smith-Christopher (2000).[92]

Nebuchadnezzar enthroned Jehoiakin's uncle, Mattaniah, and changed his name to Zedekiah (his throne name). He rebelled against Babylon, and in his ninth year Nebuchadnezzar attacked Jerusalem again, slew the sons of Zedekiah before his eyes, poked out his eyes, took him into captivity, and destroyed the temple, the palace and the walls. There is no mention of a son (Mulek) escaping. (2 Kings 24:20 & 25:1-21) The OT gives us little information regarding the second deportation (of the remnants of the first deportation), focusing mostly on the destruction of Solomon's Temple, which was symbolically the greater disaster.

The account in the *Book of Mormon* of Lehi's vision and departure from Jerusalem, in the first year of the reign of Zedekiah, gives curious details:

> For it came to pass in the commencement of the first year of Zedekiah, king of Judah, (my father Lehi having dwelt at Jerusalem in all his days); and in that same year there came many prophets prophesying unto the people that they must repent, or the great city of Jerusalem must be destroyed. (1 Nephi 1:4)

Actually, the most remarkable prophet to warn Jerusalem was Jeremiah, who dictated his vision/warning in his prison cell to Baruch to read it in the House of the Lord, and to the Judeans, which he did. Yehoiakim ordered that the scroll be brought to him, and hearing part of it, he burned it. When Jeremiah was released from prison is unclear, but Zedekiah again imprisoned him.

---

[92] Daniel L. Smith-Christopher, "Exile," in *Eerdmans Dictionary of the Bible* (Grand Rapids: Eerdmans Publishing Company, 2000), 439-40.

5. The Bible Versus the *Book of Mormon*

Lehi's family must have resided with him in Jerusalem for much if not most of their life. That Lehi was a man of great means is indicated by his possessions outside Jerusalem. In order to have the means needed to purchase the Brass Plates from their owner, Laban, Nephi says, "therefore let us go down to the land of our father's inheritance, for behold he left gold and silver, and all manner of riches." (1 Nephi 3:16) It is clear from this that Lehi and his household would have been carried off to Babylon in the sack of Jerusalem, prior to the enthronement of Zedekiah.

Laban meets two of the criteria to be deported as well: he was wealthy, and a military leader in Jerusalem. Nephi takes from him his breastplate (which he inexplicably was wearing at a drinking party) and his sword: "the hilt thereof was of pure gold, and the workmanship thereof was exceeding fine, and I saw that the blade thereof was of the most precious steel." (1 Nephi 4:9) Of his power, Nephi says, "he [the Lord] is mightier than all the earth, then why not mightier than Laban and his fifty, yea, or even than his tens of thousands." A servant, Zoram, has a key to Laban's treasury, where the Brass Plates were kept. Certainly no such wealthy and mighty elite would have remained in Jerusalem after its sack.

Zoram "spake unto me concerning the elders of the Jews, he knowing that his master, Laban, had been out by night among them." (1 Nephi 4:22) In the sack, just prior to the elevation of Zedekiah to the throne, the elders of the Jews had been carried off to Babylon.

There is an OT reference to Jeremiah being in prison, without the time being specified. But since it is probable that he had been released during the sack of Jerusalem, one might expect some reference to that fact.

The total chaos and destitution in that period, following the sac of Jerusalem, and just days prior to the elevation of Zedekiah to the throne, must have made it very difficult to outfit a caravan for two families to travel all the way across or around Arabia to the Indian Ocean. Such a party would constitute a very large caravan, with mounts, most probably camels, canopied sedans for the women, and as many camels to carry the tents, food, and of course the precious water. The sack of Jerusalem and these challenges were worth at least a mention. On the contrary, the *Book of Mormon* is altogether unaware of it. Only months after the sack of Jerusalem, Laman and Lemuel, the two rebellious sons of Lehi, murmured against their father: "Neither did they believe that Jerusalem, that great city, could be destroyed..." (1 Nephi 2:13) The BOM authors erroneously thought the destruction in the ninth year of Zedekiah included the sack of Jerusalem before he was made a tributary king.

The Age of Scientific Discovery, and the Bible

A list of works considered sacred by the rabbis, may have been drawn up as early as 450 BCE, but probably centuries later, the Hebrew OT (*tanakh*, from *t* for torah, *n* for *nevi'im* [prophets] and *k* for *ketuvim* [writings]). Even as late as the mid-third century CE, there was no Christian scriptural canon, no "bible" in the modern sense. Even when the works included in the earliest canon were selected, and copied into the first manuscript "edition," they were referred to as the sacred *biblia*, which is the plural of *biblion*, meaning little book, booklet. The manuscript was called the sacred books, not the Bible.

Long before the Christian era, the Judeans had begun the process of developing what became Judaism out of earlier Israelite religion or religions. They began the process of identifying various compositions as sacred. Evidence indicates that in many cases, some of these works were edited and augmented over time, arriving at their final form roughly perhaps a century before the time of the Qumran community and the now famous Dead Sea Scrolls.

During these first couple of centuries of Christian history, theology played a major role in determining what works would be selected. Although there are traces of at least some gnostic thinking in the canonic gospels, the gnostic compositions, discovered in Egypt, written in Coptic, were roundly rejected. Early scholars in theology developed their views of the works they accepted, and their authorship.

The nineteenth century witnessed a new age of critical and scientific reevaluation of almost everything. Scholars specializing in ancient literature were not immune to this broader movement. They found themselves confronted by numerous manuscript sources for the same composition, but with differences, variant readings. They had to produce critical editions in an attempt to arrive at the original text, while providing in their footnotes (the critical apparatus) the other manuscript readings that they had rejected, so that other scholars could check their work, and choose for themselves. Issues of authorship had to be addressed, and the historical development of a work. This effort focused on the classical works of the Greeks and Romans, Homer, Hesiod,

Herodotus, the dramatists, Plato and Aristotle. Over time, the methods they developed were extended, even to include the study of Hammurabi's Code, and the development of the compositions that collectively comprise the so-called Egyptian Book of the Dead. As religious hesitations were overcome, the works of the Bible were also subjected to the same sort of scrutiny, using techniques developed over centuries.

This work has implications for the *Book of Mormon* with respect to two ancient works, the Book of Isaiah and the Book of Revelations.

Isaiah

Isaiah was especially important to the BOM authors because it was initially the primary OT work that was interpreted to show that the ancient Israelite prophets were aware that a branch of Israel would be taken off by the Lord to distant lands across the sea, and later be reunited with the other branches of Israel in the last days. It provided the basis for the *Book of Mormon* to present its argument for itself. It claims that a seventh-century BCE "bible" inscribed on brass plates in ancient Egyptian contained all of the sacred books of the Hebrews up to King Zedekiah, including Isaiah, and was brought to the New World by Lehi and Nephi. It quotes long passages, including chapters 2-14, 48-49, and 50-51. Nephi makes it clear that he read these passages from the Brass Plates:

> *Isaiah 2-14*:
> 2 Nephi 11:8. And now I write some of the words of Isaiah
> 2 Nephi 25:1. Now I, Nephi, do speak somewhat concerning the words which I have written, which have been spoken by the mouth of Isaiah.
> *Isaiah 48-49*:
> 1 Nephi 19:23. And I did read many things unto them which were written in the books of Moses; but that I might more fully persuade them to believe in the Lord their Redeemer I did read unto them that which was written by the prophet Isaiah
> 1 Nephi 22:1. And now it came to pass that after I, Nephi, had read these things which were engraven upon the plates of brass
> *Isaiah 50-51*:
> 2 Nephi 6:5. And now, the words which I shall read are they which Isaiah spake concerning all the house of Israel
> 2 Nephi 9:1. And now, my beloved brethren, I have read these things that ye might know concerning the covenants of the Lord

The BOM is very clear that Nephi is reading from the Brass Plates, and writing the words of Isaiah onto his plates. His own commentary follows the quotation. This is clear in reading the text, but specified in 2 Nephi 25:1: "Now I, Nephi, do speak somewhat concerning the words which I have written."

Isaiah lived between 750-700 BCE. Even in medieval times, some Jewish scholars already held that certain sections of Isaiah were not authored by the prophet, most notably Abraham ibn Ezra in his 1167 commentary.[93] There has been a large amount of excellent research on the received Hebrew text. It analyzes the content, the occurrence of words, terms and syntax, comparison with well-documented historical events and comparison with other books of the OT. The results that enjoy a high degree of consensus among leading scholars are: 1) Isaiah wrote, or dictated to be written, passages of varying length at various times in his life, in response to events and his situation, usually in his capacity as a sort of advisor to each of four different kings. 2) At an early date, these documents were collected by followers of his mission, and edited together. There are passages that were added by these editors, probably sincerely believing that their additions were consistent with and supportive to the materials from Isaiah himself. 3) The initial compilation included chapters 1-39, which preserve the material done by Isaiah himself, plus some additions to tie them together. It was mostly completed prior to c. 600, i.e., the captivity of the leading Judeans during the short reign of Jehoiachin. 4) Chapters 40-55 are a later product, under Isaiah's name, either done during the exile in Babylon, or shortly after. 5) Chapters 56-66 are of even later composition, clearly postexilic. 6) Editing chapters 1-39 continued into or possibly even after the exile, and consequently they contain some later material as well. All of this is contrary to the position of the *Book of Mormon*. Although it is not clear that it asserts that all of chapters 1-66 were contained on the Brass Plates of Laban, minimally, chapters 2-14, 29, 48-51 and 53 are claimed to have been on the plates.

Although these divisions remain the dominant view, the analysis of the Dead Sea material has suggested a different division. In the Great Isaiah Scroll, the best preserved of the Dead Sea Scrolls, there is no

---

[93] George A. Buttrick, *The Interpreter's Bible* (New York: Abingdon Press, 1956), 382.

break between Isaiah 39 and 40, but there is a large vacant space between Isaiah 33 and 34. Perhaps more significant, other Isaiah texts included in the find contained portions of Isaiah 1-33, or 33-66, but not both. These pre-Christian manuscripts provide evidence in support of current analysis, differing only on the point of division.[94].

Consequently, having been composed decades after Zedekiah, Isaiah 48-49, 50-51, 53 & 54 could not have been on the Brass Plates of Laban, and were not even written by Isaiah.

John and the Book of Revelations

The *Book of Mormon* relies heavily on the Book of Revelations for the language that condemns all churches existing throughout most of the Christian era, as being the work of Satan. 1 Nephi 14 is explicit:

> 8. And it came to pass that when the angel had spoken these words, he said unto me: Rememberest thou the covenants of the Father unto the house of Israel? I said unto him, Yea.
> 9. And it came to pass that he said unto me: Look, and behold that great and abominable church, which is the mother of abominations, whose founder is the devil.
> 10. And he said unto me: Behold there are save two churches only; the one is the church of the Lamb of God, and the other is the church of the devil; wherefore, whoso belongeth not to the church of the Lamb of God belongeth to that great church, which is the mother of abominations; and she is the whore of all the earth.
> 11. And it came to pass that I looked and beheld the whore of all the earth, and she sat upon many waters; and she had dominion over all the earth, among all nations, kindreds, tongues, and people.

The attribution that provides the link to the Book of Revelations is in verses 20-22 and 27:

> 20. And the angel said unto me: Behold one of the twelve apostles of the Lamb.

---

[94] See Marvin A. Sweeney, *Isaiah 1–39: with an introduction to prophetic literature* (Grand Rapids, MI: Eerdmans, 1996); & Marvin A. Sweeney, "The Latter Prophets," in Steven L. McKenzie and M. Patrick Graham, *The Hebrew Bible Today: An Introduction to Critical Issues* (Westminster: John Knox Press, 1998).

21. Behold, he shall see and write the remainder of these things; yea, and also many things which have been.
22. And he shall also write concerning the end of the world.
27. And I, Nephi, heard and bear record, that the name of the apostle of the Lamb was John, according to the word of the angel.

Although this is clear enough, it is important to remember that the *Book of Mormon* does not use the title "apostle" loosely. When Jesus visits the New World and chooses a similar body of twelve, he calls them the Twelve Disciples, not apostles.

Traditionally, the so-called Johannine works (the Gospel according to John, the first, second and third epistles of John and Revelations) were thought to have been authored by John the Apostle. It is now generally agreed that even the gospel bearing the name of John was written after the apostle's death. Indeed, the majority view is that all four gospels were written by others, possibly by students of the apostles. Note that each is traditionally called the Gospel *according to...* (Mathew, Mark, Luke or John), where "according to" is Greek *kata*, literally meaning "according to" and not implying authorship. The majority view dates the gospels to within the following time frames: Mark: c. 68–73; Matthew: c. 70–100; Luke: c. 80–100; and, John: c. 90–110. Matthew and Luke show clear signs of having been written based largely on Mark, the earliest of the four canonical gospels. These three are called the synoptic gospels. Scholars found that if large-format pages were ruled off into three columns, it was possible to print the three texts together, one in each column, collating passages chronologically to facilitate comparison. John does not fit this synoptic scheme. In some cases, the events are not even in the same order. John is unusual also with regard to its beginning verses, referring to the "word" as God (*logos*, in Greek). This follows a Hellenistic philosophical formulation, and argues for an author well versed in Greek language, literature and philosophy. Some scholars do not accept that the Johannine epistles were written by the same author as the Gospel according to John, although similarities support the view of others that they were. For what it is worth, many now think that the Gospel of Thomas, discovered in a Coptic text, is actually the earliest gospel to have survived. Its focus was the sayings of Jesus, and may have been a source document for Mark.

The odd man out is the Book of Revelations, which is so different in language and style that most agree that it was written by a different author, and most probably around 95 CE. The early second-century author Justin Martyr was the first to write that the author of Revelations was John the Apostle.[95] However, Eusebius in his *History of the Church* (c. 330) argued that one author wrote the Gospel of John and the First Epistle of John, some other author wrote the second and third epistles of John, and there was no agreement on the identity of the author of Revelations.[96] Sophronius of Jerusalem (560-638) held that some other John, John of Patmos (later sometimes called John the Divine) wrote it. John the Presbyter has also been proposed as the author (by Eusebius of Caesarea and Jerome). The subsequent inclination to ascribe it to the apostle was largely due to the theological hesitation to expand the circle of revelators beyond the twelve apostles (accepting Paul as the replacement for Judas), making this revered body the seal of the era of revelation.

John the Apostle, like his brother James the Apostle, on the other hand, was a fisherman, the son of Zebedee, possibly also a fisherman. He was undoubtedly a native Aramaic speaker, most probably with little or no classical education in Greek. This background does not support the proposal that he authored a gospel reflecting Hellenistic learning, much less the Book of Revelations.

Clearly the *Book of Mormon* is in conflict with modern scholarship with respect to these two scriptures, and even some of the earliest extant NT analysis. The true believer can simply assert that the BOM is right, and the experts are wrong.

Biblical Variant Readings in the *Book of Mormon*

The *Book of Mormon* claims that the Nephites brought with them the Bible as it existed by 600 BCE, already assembled as a single sacred book, and translated into Egyptian on brass plates. The BOM text quoted extensively from these Biblical materials, especially Isaiah from the Brass Plates, and other materials, including the Sermon on the Mount, which Jesus delivered again when he visited the New World after his resurrection, to make the Nephites and Lamanites Christians, at least for two centuries, after which people started falling away from the "truth." The Biblical materials in the *Book of Mormon* are primarily the King James text, which, according to LDS scholars, was used in translating the

---

[95] Justin Martyr, *Dialogue with Trypho*, 81:4.
[96] Eusebius of Caesarea, *The History of the Church*, Book three, point 24.

gold plates because people were used to it. It differs from the King James wording, according to the Mormons, when the original text required different wording to be a correct translation (cf. 1 Nephi 13:24-29). But according to the critics, the variants were devised to make it look as though the inclusions are not just a rote copy of the King James Version, pure and simple. These variants, which are supposed to be the correct, divine translation of the original text, of Isaiah, and other Biblical texts, have been a focus of apologist research. The claim is that some ancient Biblical manuscripts occasionally agree with the *Book of Mormon* variants, and since Smith et al. had no access to these manuscripts, and did not know the languages, they could not have come up with variants that enjoy this ancient manuscript support.

The present study has tried to be exhaustive, although that is always an unattainable ideal. The Biblical passages in the *Book of Mormon* that were gleaned for examination are very close to exhaustive, and certainly include all passages of any significant length.

The insertion of Biblical passages was tricky business. This was supposed to be a divine translation, and so these passages would be expected to be perfect translations of the original text, including much of Isaiah, and the words of Jesus on the Mount. Yet the authors dared not depart too far from the accepted text that their prospective audience knew and cherished. They opted to insert primarily the following (with both Biblical and the BOM references, the latter in parentheses):

Longer passages:

Isaiah 2-14 (in 2 Nephi 12-24)
Isaiah 50-52:2 (in 2 Nephi 7 & 8)
Isaiah 54 (in 3 Nephi 22)
Matthew 5:3—7:27 (in 3 Nephi 12:3—14:27)

Isaiah 48-49 (in 1 Nephi 20-21)
Isaiah 53 (in Mosiah 14)
Malachi 3 & 4 (3 Nephi 24 &25)

Other passages:

Exodus 20:2-4 (Mosiah 12:34-36)
Exodus 20:4-17 (Mosiah 13:12-24)
Isaiah 29:3-5 (2 Nephi 26: 14-19)
Isaiah 29:6-18 (2 Nephi 27:2-6, 25-29)
Isaiah 29:13-23 (2 Nephi 27:25-35)
Isaiah 52:7-10 (Mosiah 12:21-24)

Isaiah 52:11-15 (3 Nephi 20: 41-45)
Micah 4:12-13 (3 Nephi 20:18-19)
Micah 5:8-14, 15 (3 Nephi 21:12-18, 21)
Matthew 3:2 (Helaman 5:32)
Matthew 3:10 (Alma 5:52)

There are other Biblical verses interwoven into the text here and there. These passages are often reworded and blended into the text to the point that they can be thought of as paraphrases. It is not possible to determine what might be a variant of the KJV text and what might be simply due to the BOM composition into which the paraphrase is inserted.

The Distribution of the Variants

The process of identifying the *Book of Mormon* variant readings in the longest Biblical inclusions revealed that they vary in importance. Furthermore, they did not occur randomly. The BOM translation is supposed to have come from God. Therefore, the claim that the Biblical passages were written in "reformed Egyptian" on the gold plates is irrelevant: the translation is of divine origin and would be a revelation of the best English wording for the original text. For Isaiah, that would be his Hebrew composition. A *Book of Mormon* variant that simply changes the spelling of an English word does not imply any difference between the King James wording and Isaiah's original text. A variant that adds a phrase of several or many words does imply that the underlying Hebrew text had this phrase, which is missing in the King James text. These are extreme cases; other variants may or may not imply a discrepancy between the original text and the King James.

To study their distribution, I first divided the variants into the following categories:

I (first order): variants that presuppose at least some sort of difference in the source document (i.e., the wording of the original text required this change).
Ia: first order variants consisting of at least three words.
III (third order): variants that are totally English-language based, and do not raise the presumption of a difference in the underlying text, mostly very minor changes.
II (second order): those that cannot be readily assigned to either order one or three.

The four largest texts listed above were selected for analysis since they are long enough to develop a distribution pattern that can be meaningfully analyzed. The numerical results are found in Table 7 below. I then graphed out the variants according to the categories, as found in Figure 1, below.

Table 7. Distribution of *Book of Mormon* Variants
Orders: I, Ia, II & III   Quarters: 1, 2, 3, 4
Ia: order I variants that exceed three words in length

Passage	Group	Total	Frequency				Per Cent			
			1	2	3	4	1	2	3	4
Isaiah 2:1 to 14:32	Total	374	136	84	70	84	36.4	22.5	18.7	22.5
	III	183	54	44	42	43	29.5	24.0	23.0	23.5
	II	124	45	33	20	26	36.3	26.6	16.1	21.0
	I+II	191	82	40	28	41	42.9	20.9	14.7	21.5
	I	67	37	7	8	15	55.2	10.4	11.9	22.4
	Ia	18	12	0	1	5	66.7	0.0	5.6	27.8
Isaiah 48:1 to 49:26	Total	141	48	40	29	28	34.0	28.4	20.6	19.9
	III	64	18	18	13	15	28.1	28.1	20.3	23.4
	II	38	14	11	6	7	36.8	28.9	15.8	18.4
	I+II	77	30	22	16	9	39.0	28.6	20.8	11.7
	I	39	16	11	10	2	41.0	28.2	25.6	5.1
	Ia	20	9	4	7	0	45.0	20.0	35.0	0.0
Isaiah 50:1 to 52:2	Total	113	44	18	29	22	38.9	15.9	25.7	19.5
	III	55	22	11	16	6	40.0	20.0	29.1	10.9
	II	31	9	4	7	11	29.0	12.9	22.6	35.5
	I + II	58	22	7	13	16	37.9	12.1	22.4	27.6
	I	27	13	3	6	5	48.1	11.1	22.2	18.5
	Ia	11	8	1	2	0	72.7	9.1	18.2	0.0
Matthew 5:3 to 7:27	Total	176	89.	48	23	16	50.6	27.3	13.1	9.1
	III	74	29	23	13	9	39.2	31.1	17.6	12.2
	II	36	20	8	1	7	55.6	22.2	2.8	19.4
	I + II	102	60	25	10	7	58.8	24.5	9.8	6.9
	I	66	40	17	9	0	60.6	25.8	13.6	0.0
	Ia	37	21	11	5	0	56.8	29.7	13.5	0.0

The most obvious observation is that it is always the first quarter of a passage that has the most variants. The probability of this happening, if the distribution should be expected to be random, is a very simple calculation, expressed mathematically as .25 x .25 x .25 x .25 = .00390625, or only four chances in a thousand.[97] Note that this distribution feature becomes more acute with the more serious variants and that in the case of the Sermon on the Mount the variants in the first quarter outnumber those in the last three quarters combined.

---

[97] Based on A. Chris Eccel, *An Analysis of the Distribution of the BOM Variants* (Chicago: unpublished paper, 1972).

Figure 1. Distribution of *Book of Mormon* Variants[98]
(Percent in Each Quarter)

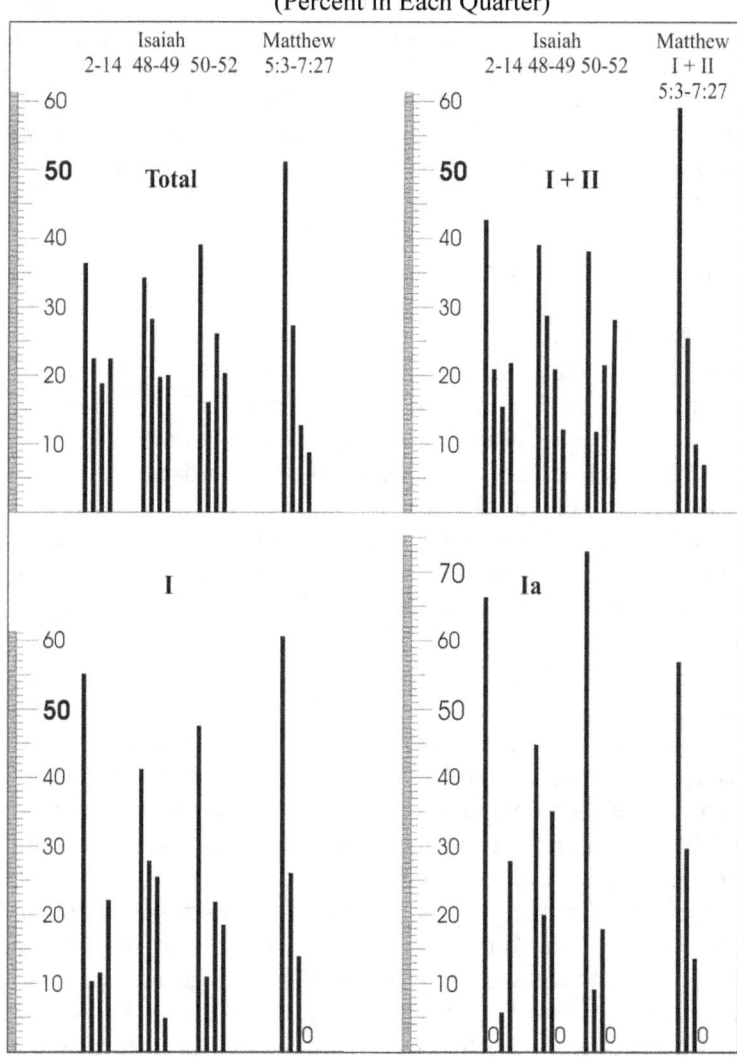

The explanation for this distribution is equally obvious. Changes were made for the purpose of calming suspicions regarding the use of the King James Version. Making these changes was both tedious and time-

---

[98] Eccel, *An Analysis of the Distribution of the BOM Variants.*

consuming. Once it was thought that the reader had accepted the passage as normal, it was no longer necessary to make as many changes. The process seems to be governed either by a time-efficiency principle, a laziness principle or both. In either case, this pattern is not consistent with the claim that the variants occur because the Bible had been changed (cf. 1 Nephi 13:24-29), and that the *Book of Mormon* is correcting the King James in accordance with the original text divinely revealed in the process of translating the gold plates.

And upon all the ships of the sea

Having a BA in Classics (Greek and Latin) and an MA in the Semitic languages, I found the study of *Book of Mormon* variants to be especially fascinating, although the research was long and tedious. I not only used the standard critical editions for the Bible (Rudolf Kittel's *Biblia Hebraica*, Alfred Rahlfs' Greek *Septuaginta*, Eberhard Nestle's *Novum Testamentum Graece*, and Alberto Colunga & Laurentio Turrado's *Biblia Sacra iuxta Vulgatam Clementinam*), but also the principal editions of the Old and New Testaments in Aramaic, Coptic, Ethiopic, pre-Vulgate (Italic) Latin and Arabic.[99] Most of these editions are actually rendered unnecessary by the use of the critical editions.

We do not have Isaiah's original manuscript, or a copy of it. What actually exists is a number of ancient Isaiah manuscripts in Hebrew, and these have differences among them, variant readings. An editor, such as Kittel, selects the manuscript that he considers to be the most reliable as his base text. He then compares it with every other source, not only the other Hebrew manuscripts, but Aramaic, Greek, Latin, Coptic and Ethiopic. At times he will decide that a reading in another Hebrew manuscript is more probable than the reading in his base edition, and will make the substitution. When he does, he lists what his base edition originally said as a footnote, as a variant. When he decides in favor of his base edition, the variant from the other manuscript is listed as a footnote as well. In the end, he produces his edition, called a recension, that is thought to be an improvement over the base manuscript, but in the footnotes he lists all other readings from all the manuscripts used that could reasonably be important. In this manner, he produces a resource that provides the user all significant evidence from all ancient

---

[99] These are found in Bibliography 1.

manuscripts. So no one is required to accept Kittel's decisions. Scholars can examine the other possibilities listed in the footnotes, called the critical apparatus.

Now, let us consider the Mormon apologists' *pièce de résistance*:[100]

Isaiah 2:16	2 Nephi 12:16	Greek Septuagint
And upon all the ships of Tarshish	and upon all the ships of Tarshish And upon all the ships of the sea	And upon all the ships of the sea
and upon all pleasant pictures	and upon all pleasant pictures	And upon every sight of ships of beauty

Defenders of the *Book of Mormon* have been delighted to find that the Greek Septuagint has a phrase that the *Book of Mormon* added: "And upon all the ships of the sea." Joseph Smith, a farmer's son, knew no Greek, and did not have access to the Greek text. This can only be explained, they say, by the fact that the *Book of Mormon* text is a divine translation of Isaiah's original, which must have had this phrase.

For our analysis, first, note the Biblical context is using a style called *parallelismus membrorum* (parallel members). The larger passage is in Isaiah 2:12-17:

12	For the day of the Lord of hosts shall be upon	
	every one that is proud and lofty	and upon every one that is lifted up and he shall be made low:
13	And upon all the cedars of Lebanon that are high and lifted up	and upon all the oaks of Bāshan
14	And upon all the high mountains	and upon all the hills that are lifted up
15	And upon every high tower	and upon every fenced wall
16	And upon all the ships of Tarshish	and upon all pleasant pictures
17	And the loftiness of man shall be bowed down	and the haughtiness of men shall be made low
	and the Lord alone shall be exalted in that day.	

The parallelism is partly obscured by the fact that a single word or two words in Hebrew can be best translated by a clause in English. Allowing

---

[100] Sidney B. Sperry, *Our* Book of Mormon (Salt Lake City: Bookcraft, 1950), 172-73. John Tvedtnes, "Isaiah Variants in the *Book of Mormon*" (1984; transcript accessed on 12/04/2015, at http//:www.publications.mi.byu.edu/people/john-a-tvedtnes/).

for that, the parallelism is in the paired items: *ones proud and lofty* parallel with *ones lifted up*; *cedars of Lebanon* parallel with *oaks of Bāshan*; *high mountains* parallel with *lifted up hills*; *high tower* parallel with *fenced wall*; *ships of Tarshish* parallel with *pleasant pictures*; and *loftiness of man* parallel with *haughtiness of men*. The parallelism of verse 16 is also obscured by a KJ mistranslation. Instead of "pleasant pictures," the translation should be "ships of delight (or pleasant ships)." See Table 9.

The addition of a member in the *Book of Mormon* version of verse 16, increasing the members from two to three, violates this parallelism. This alone makes it improbable.

Furthermore, while the *Book of Mormon* adds the phrase, "and upon all the ships of the sea," the Greek does not; rather, it translates Tarshish as meaning "of the sea." So the Greek does not provide support.

The Alexandrian translator, a native speaker of Greek, Hebrew being already a dead language, knew that Tarshish was a foreign word. He could treat it as a proper name, possibly an unknown toponym as others had done, or he could try to figure out what language it came from, and thereby its meaning. To understand his situation, we must bear in mind these characteristics of Hebrew writing in his day:

1. For the most part, only the consonants were written, although three characters came to do double duty (*matres lectionis*). Initially, *aleph* (א, transliterated as ') was used for the glottal stop (like the pronunciation of *t* in bottle [bo'l] in cockney English), but came also to indicate a long *ā* vowel; *waw* (ו, transliterated as *w*) was used to indicate *w* but came also to indicate a long *ū* vowel; and *yōd* (י, transliterated as *y*) was used to indicate *y* but came to also indicate a long *ī* vowel (pronounced like *e* as in 'delete') or a long *ē* vowel (pronounced like *a* as in 'snake').
2. Double consonants were not indicated, so *s* could be one *s* or two.
3. The Hebrew alphabet, borrowed from Aramaic, did not have characters for all the Hebrew sounds in use at the time. One example is *t* (ת), which could represent either *t* or *th* (as in thin).
4. Hebrew has an "extra" sibilant. Sibilants are consonants with a bit of a whistling sound (sibilant being Latin for hissing or whistling). These are:

5. The Bible Versus the *Book of Mormon*

ש   *sh* (later written with a dot over the right-hand "prong")
ס   *s*
ז   *z*
ש   a sound that is today unknown, and which came to be pronounced like *s* as a matter of convenience (later written with a dot over the left-hand "prong")

5. Ever since the conquest of Alexander the Great, or even earlier, Greek words had been entering into Hebrew, and when they did, there was often a bit of distortion, much like foreign words adopted by English. One possible source of distortion was the common sound shift, *l/r*. This is because the *r* was pronounced by the end of the tongue, in roughly the same position as *l*. This correspondence is also epigraphically possible since a badly made Hebrew *r* can look like a Hebrew *l*.

The Hebrew word Tarshish is תרשיש. It is written right to left. Changing the order to Greek order (the same as English order), and applying the possibilities listed above, we have:

Hebrew letters:	ת	vowel	ר	vowel	ש	י	ש
Possible sounds:	*t/th*		*r/l*		*s/sh*	*ī/ē*	*s/sh*

The Greek speaking Jewish translator would know that others had simply transliterated Tarshish as Θαρσις (Tharsis, an unknown place name). He however, spotted a Greek word, which he settled on as the best rendition:

Hebrew letters:	ת		ר		ש	י	ש
Greek letters:	Θ	α	λ	α	σ	η	σ/ς
English letters:	*th*	*a*	*l*	*a*	*s*	*ē*	*s*

So, the word is Θαλασσης (*thalassēs*). Θαλασσα (*thalassa*) means sea, and the –ης ending is genitive, like our apostrophe *s*. Just as "Bob's book" means "the book of Bob," so *thalassa* with the ending –*ēs* means "of the sea." For our Hellenistic translator, the presence of what can pass for a Greek genitive ending may have promoted his translation from "highly probable" to "quite certain." A ship "of the sea" may have been a vessel for the open sea, bringing treasures from afar.

By translating Tarshish as "of the sea" (rather than a totally unknown place name) he got a meaningful phrase, "all the ships of the sea." He did not add this phrase; he just translated "Tarshish," at least to his satisfaction. His version is totally faithful to the Hebrew original, which was transliterated into English letters by the King James translation. The icing on the cake is the fact that it is a nice parallel to "all pleasant ships," the correct translation instead of "all pleasant pictures." The *Book of Mormon* authors, by contrast, added a whole new element, violating the parallelism in the context, and finding no support at all, in any ancient manuscript, neither in the Greek as an additional member, nor in language versions translated from the Greek. In the BOM, "all the ships of the sea" is nothing more than a common English phrase suggested to the BOM authors by the context.

Examples of Variant Analysis

Before proceeding further, a word about Hebrew. The Semitic languages are what I call "Me Tarzan, you Jane" languages. That is to say, Hebrew does not use the verb "to be" unless it is needed. So "He is David" is "He David", (*Hū Dawīd*, where the *w* is pronounced *v* in later Hebrew). The King James translators were determined to be as literal as possible, and when they had to add a word to make good English, such as the verb *is* in this example, they wrote it in italics. It is important to note that *Book of Mormon* variants often occur where one finds italicized words or phrases. It is clear that the authors thought that italics were a sign that there is something a bit odd here, so it is a good place to throw in a variant. This phenomenon will be evidenced here and there throughout the remainder of this presentation, and the portion of the study found in Appendix 1.

The original language of the Old Testament books is Hebrew (except, primarily, for the stories of Daniel, and part of Ezra, which were originally in Aramaic). The original language of the New Testament is Greek. With respect to the biblical passages in the *Book of Mormon*, all other language sources are translations. The Greek Septuagint is translated from the Hebrew, as is the Aramaic. But the Ethiopic, Coptic and Arabic texts are mostly translations of the Septuagint, and so are translations of translations. Therefore, these are not direct evidence for the Hebrew. Scholars use them to evaluate variant readings in the Septuagint. Unless one is faced with two or more variant readings for the same word or phrase in Hebrew for the Old Testament, or in Greek for the New Testament, the Hebrew text trumps all translations of the OT, and the Greek text trumps all translations of the NT. Even so, a perusal of Bibliography 1 will show that every language tradition has been extensively examined.

To start off, an interesting variant is Exodus 20:11: "For in six days the Lord made heaven and earth, the sea, and all that in them *is*, and rested the seventh day:" Incredibly, the *Book of Mormon* omits "and rested the seventh day." All versions have this clause, but there is a note in one critical apparatus indicating that only one Arabic manuscript omitted it.[101] So, is there a manuscript that supports this huge omission? Indeed, there is. But effectively, there is absolutely no support for it.

Isaiah 53:9 has a variant: violence (KJ)/evil (BOM). The Hebrew uses a noun that means violent treatment, whereas the Greek uses the noun *anomia*, which essentially refers to unlawful behavior, transgression. The *Book of Mormon* receives no support here.

Matthew 5:36 has: white or black (KJ)/black or white (BOM). The Greek original agrees with the KJ, while the Syriac translation of the Greek agrees with the BOM. Greek trumps Syriac; furthermore, this is just a simple change in order, with no change in meaning.

Isaiah 10:23 has the phrase "in the midst of all the land" where the *Book of Mormon* omits "midst of." The meaning is the same. The omission occurs also in Greek, Syriac, Latin and Arabic manuscripts. This is an example of a change that better fits a language into which the text is being translated. Hebrew rules.

In Isaiah 9:3 "Thou hast multiplied the nation *and* not increased the joy," "not" was deleted (2 Nephi 19:3). In a number of Hebrew manuscripts, "the nation and not" is absent, producing "Thou hast multiplied; Thou hast increased the joy." In a sense, one can say that "not" was deleted, but the change is more than that. In Isaiah 29:17 "*Is* it not yet a very little while, and Lebanon shall be turned into a fruitful field," "not" is also deleted, a change that finds some non-Hebrew manuscript agreement, but the change has only slight difference in meaning, and Isaiah 29 is not quoted word-for-word, but has been rewritten into part of a preachment. These verses are of no significance.

In Isaiah 2:21, "glory of his majesty" is changed to "majesty of his glory" with agreement in the Arabic text of the *Biblia Sacra Polyglotta Complectentia* (London, 1657), for what it is worth.

---

[101] Robertus Holmes, ed., *Vetus Testamentum Graecum cum Variis Lectionibus*, (Oxford: Clarendon Press, 1798), vol. 1.

An interesting rewording, with no meaning change, occurs in Isaiah 2:20 and 2 Nephi 12:20:

In that day a man shall cast his idols of silver, and his idols of gold, which they made *each one* for himself to worship... (KJV Isaiah)

In that day a man shall cast his idols of silver, and his idols of gold, which he hath made for himself to worship,.. (2 Nephi)

In Hebrew, the pronoun is part of the verb (although separate pronouns also exist), and in a couple of Hebrew manuscripts '*āsū* (they made) is changed to '*āsā* (he made), providing agreement for the 2 Nephi version. The BOM change was a result of the deletion of the italicized words *each one* thereby requiring "he hath made" to make the verb agree with "for himself."

A similar case is Isaiah 4:3 where "*that he that is* left in Zion, and *he that* remaineth in Jerusalem" is changed to read "they that are left in Zion and remain in Jerusalem" (2 Nephi 14:3). There is no meaning change, but even so, a couple of Coptic manuscripts translate with wording that involves "they that are" similar to the 2 Nephi version. Again, Hebrew and Greek trump Coptic, and the italics prompted the *Book of Mormon* variant.

A less than straightforward variant is found respecting Isaiah 50:2, which reads, "their fish stinketh, because *there is* no water, and dieth for thirst." The BOM reads "I make...their fish to stink because the waters are dried up, and they die of thirst." The Great Isaiah Scroll reads, "their fish dry up for lack of water and die of thirst." The Septuagint has the same. For Tvedtnes, the interesting point is that the latter uses the verb "to dry up" as does the BOM. But there is a critical difference. In the BOM, the waters dry up, but in the Scroll and Septuagint, the fish dry up. The confusion seems to derive from the similarity in the two verbs: *ybš*, to dry up, and *b'š*, to stink. In any case, the BOM reading does not occur in any manuscript.

A word switch occurs in Isaiah 3:1 ("whole stay of bread") and 2 Nephi 13:1 ("whole staff of bread"). There is no manuscript support for this. The change may have been prompted by the English idea that bread is the staff of life.

A revealing case is the variant in Isaiah 5:30, where "if *one* look" is changed to "if they look." In this case, after the removal of the italicized word, the authors mistakenly thought that 'look' is plural, but in reality it is a subjunctive singular. This grammatical misunderstanding prompted the addition of a plural pronoun for the verb. No meaning change is involved.

One cannot omit Isaiah 50:2 (2 Nephi 7:2):

Wherefore, when I came, *was there* no man? when I called, *was there* none to answer? (Isaiah)

Wherefore, when I came there was no man; when I called, yea, *there was* none to answer. (2 Nephi)

This change again turns on King James italicization. But in this case, interrogative is changed to assertion. This change plays on the double meaning of the English word 'wherefore.' The Hebrew is unequivocally interrogative (*maddūa'*), and most of the Septuagint manuscripts as well. But a couple change *ti hoti* to *dioti*, an obvious scribal error that produces the change above (since *h* had ceased to be pronounced in Greek). But the Latin Vulgate, following the Septuagint variant, introduces the verse with *quia*, because, and so agrees with the BOM variant. Here, meaning is involved, but Hebrew trumps.

A variant with some support involves Isaiah 48:14, where the BOM adds 'unto them.' This prepositional phrase is found in the Septuagint and translations based on it (the Latin Vulgate, Targum Jonathan, Arabic mss, the Syriac Hexapla and Coptic). It is not found in any Hebrew ms, which trumps all else, and has little meaning change.

Another interesting case is Matthew 5:22: "whosoever is angry with his brother without a cause shall be in danger of the judgment." 3 Nephi 12:22 says: "whosoever is angry with his brother shall be in danger of his judgment." The phrase "without a cause" is in some Greek manuscripts, but not all; but 'his' in 'his judgment' instead of 'the judgment' has no support.

The *Book of Mormon* also has variants with itself. Isaiah 52:1, as found in 2 Nephi 8:24, begins "Awake, awake, put on thy strength, O Zion; put on thy beautiful garments, O Jerusalem, the holy city..." while in Moroni 10:31 we read, "And awake, and arise from the dust, O Jerusalem; yea, and put on thy beautiful garments, O daughter of Zion;.." This complex rewording enjoys no agreement.

Some *Book of Mormon* passages are so reworked that they are difficult to evaluate. For example, 1 Nephi 10:8 ("he is mightier than I, whose shoe's latchet I am not worthy to unloose") is a composite of Mark 1:7, Matthew 3:11 and Luke 3:16.

Testing, Testing: The Longer Variants

When the *Book of Mormon* variants reach a certain length, and greater significance, there is no longer room for tortuous interpretation. These variants, some additions and others deletions, are as follows.

Table 8. The Longer *Book of Mormon* Variants

These are coded: additions (A) and omissions (O).
Isaiah 2:5 (2 Nephi 12:5): yea, come, for ye have all gone astray, every one to his wicked ways (A)
Isaiah 2:11 (2 Nephi 12:11): And it shall come to pass that (A)
Isaiah 2:14 (2 Nephi 12:14): and upon all the nations (A)
Isaiah 2:14 (2 Nephi 12:14): and upon every people (A)
Isaiah 5:8 (2 Nephi 15:8): *that* lay field to field (O)
Isaiah 9:4 (2 Nephi 19:4): as in the day of Midian (O)
Isaiah 13:8 (2 Nephi 23:8): they shall be in pain as a woman that travaileth (O)
Isaiah 13:22 (2 Nephi 23:22): For I will destroy her speedily; yea, for I will be merciful unto my people, but the wicked shall perish. (A)
Isaiah 14:2 (2 Nephi 24:2): yea, from far unto the ends of the earth; and they shall return to their lands of promise. (A)
Isaiah 14:4 (2 Nephi 24:4): And it shall come to pass in that day (A)
Isaiah 14:11 (2 Nephi 24:4): is not heard (A)
Isaiah 29:6 (2 Nephi 27:2): And when that day shall come (A)
Isaiah 29:7 (2 Nephi 27:3): the multitude of (O)
Isaiah 29:4 (2 Nephi 26:15): low in the dust (A)
Isaiah 29:4 (2 Nephi 26:15): for the Lord God will give unto him power, that he may whisper concerning them, even as it were (A)
Isaiah 29:7 (2 Nephi 27:3): even all that fight against her and her munition (O)
Isaiah 29:9 (2 Nephi 27:4): all ye that doeth iniquity (A)
Isaiah 29:10 (2 Nephi 27:5): because of your iniquity (A)
Isaiah 29:16 (2 Nephi 27:27): But behold, I will show unto them, saith the Lord of Hosts, that I know all their works (A)
Isaiah 29:17 (2 Nephi 27:28): But behold, saith the Lord of Hosts: I will show unto the children of men that (A)
Isaiah 29:20 (2 N 27:31): assuredly as the Lord liveth they shall see that (A)
Isaiah 48:1 (1 Nephi 20:1): or out of the waters of baptism (A)
Isaiah 48:2 (1 Nephi 20:2): who is the Lord of Hosts (A)
Isaiah 48:3 (1 Nephi 20:3): and they came to pass (A)

5. The Bible Versus the *Book of Mormon* 113

(Table 8 continued)

Isaiah 48:5 (1 Nephi 20:5): and I showed them for fear (A)
Isaiah 48:7 (1 Nephi 20:7): they were declared unto thee (A)
Isaiah 48:10 (I Nephi 20:10): but not with silver (O)
Isaiah 48:11 (1 Nephi 20:11): I will not suffer (A)
Isaiah 48:14 (1 Nephi 20:14): yea, and he will fulfill his word which he hath declared by them (A)
Isaiah 48:22 (1 Nephi 20:22): And notwithstanding he hath done all this, and greater also (A)
Isaiah 49:1 (1 Nephi 21:1): And again: Hearken, O ye house of Israel, all ye that are broken off and are driven out, because of the wickedness of the pastors of my people; yea, all ye that are broken off, that are scattered abroad, who are of my people, O house of Israel (A)
Isaiah 49:7 (1 Nephi 21:7): *and* the Holy One of Israel, and he shall chose thee (O)
Isaiah 49:8 (1 Nephi 21:8): O isles of the sea (A)
Isaiah 49:8 (1 Nephi 21:8): my servant (A)
Isaiah 49:12 (1 Nephi 21:12): And then O house of Israel (A)
Isaiah 49:13 (1 Nephi 21:13): for the feet of those who are in the east shall be established (A)
Isaiah 49:13 (1 Nephi 21:13): for they shall be smitten no more (A)
Isaiah 49:14 (1 Nephi 21:14): but he will show that he hath not (A)
Isaiah 50:1 (2 Nephi 7:1): Yea, for thus saith the Lord: Have I put thee away, or have I cast thee off forever? (A)
Isaiah 50:1 (2 Nephi 7:1): Yea, to whom have I sold you? (A)
Isaiah 50:8 (2 Nephi 7:8): and I will smite him with the strength of my mouth (A)
Isaiah 50:10 (2 Nephi 7:10): let him trust in the name of the LORD, and stay upon his God. (O)
Isaiah 51:1 (2 Nephi 8:1): ye that seek the LORD (O)
Isaiah 51:2 (2 Nephi 8:2): and increased him (O)
Isaiah 51:7 (2 Nephi 8:7): I have written (A)
Isaiah 51:9 (2 Nephi 8:9): in the generations of old (O)
Isaiah 51:11 (2 Nephi 8:11): and holiness (A)
Isaiah 51:15 (2 Nephi 8:15): that divided the sea (O)
Isaiah 51:20 (2 Nephi 8:20): save these two (A)
Isaiah 52:6 (3 Nephi 20:39): Verily, verily, I say unto you, that (A)
Isaiah 52:11 (3 Nephi 20:41): And then shall a cry go forth (A)
Isaiah 54:4 (3 Nephi 22:4): and shalt not remember the reproach of thy youth (A)
Isaiah 54:9 (3 Nephi 22:9): nor rebuke thee (O)
Micah 5:8 (3 Nephi 21:12): my people who are (A)

(Table 8 continued)

Micah 5:10 (3 Nephi 21:14): Yea, wo be unto the Gentiles except they repent (A)
Micah 5:15 (3 Nephi 21:21): in anger (O)
Micah 5:15 (3 Nephi 21:21): them; even as upon (A)
Matthew 3:11 (1 Nephi 10:8): that cometh after me (O)
Matthew 5:3 (3 Nephi 12:3): who come unto me (A)
Matthew 5:6 (3 Nephi 12:6); with the Holy Ghost (A)
Matthew 5:12 (3 Nephi 12:12): ye shall have great joy (A)
Matthew 12:13 (3 Nephi 12:13): Verily, verily, I say unto you, I give unto (A)
Matthew 12:14 (3 Nephi 12:14): Verily, verily, I say unto you, I give unto (A)
Matthew 5:18 (3 Nephi 12:18): Till heaven and earth pass away (O)
Matthew 5:19 (3 Nephi 12:19: [total change] And behold, I have given you the law and the commandments of my Father, that ye shall believe in me, and that ye shall repent of your sins, and come unto me with a broken heart and a contrite spirit. Behold, ye have the commandments before you, and the law is fulfilled. (A)
Matthew 5:20 (3 Nephi 12:20: Therefore come unto me and be ye saved. (A)
Matthew 5:20 (3 Nephi 12:20): your righteousness shall exceed *the righteousness* of the scribes and Pharisees (O)
Matthew 5:20 (3 Nephi 12:20): ye shall keep my commandments, which I have commanded you at this time (A)
Matthew 5:21 (3 Nephi 12:21): and it is also written before you, that (A)
Matthew 5:23 (3 Nephi 12:23): bring thy gift (O) shall come unto me, or shall desire to come unto me (A)
Matthew 5:24 (3 Nephi 12:24): Leave there thy gift before the altar (O)
Matthew 5:24 (3 Nephi 12:24): unto thy brother, and (A)
Matthew 5:24 (3 Nephi 12:24): unto me with full purpose of heart, and I will receive you (A)
Matthew 5:25 (3 Nephi 12:25): the adversary deliver to the judge, and the judge deliver thee to the officer, and thou be cast into prison (O)
Matthew 5:26 (3 Nephi 12:25): And while ye are in prison can ye pay even one senine? Verily, verily, I say unto you, Nay. (A)
Matthew 5:27 (3 Nephi 12:27): Ye have heard that (O)
Matthew 5:29 (3 Nephi 12:27): And if thy right eye offend thee, pluck it out, and cast it from thee: for it is profitable for thee that one of the members should perish, and not that thy whole body should be cast into hell. (O)
Matthew 5:29 (3 Nephi 12:27): Behold, I give unto you a commandment, that ye suffer none of these things to enter into your heart. (A)
Matthew 5:30 (3 Nephi 12:30): And if thy right had offend thee, cut it off, and cast it from thee (O)
Matthew 5:30 (3 Nephi 12:30): one of thy members should perish, and not that thy whole body (O)

(Table 8 continued)

Matthew 5:30 (3 Nephi 12:30): ye should deny yourselves of these things, wherein ye will take up your cross, than that ye (A)
Matthew 5:33 (3 Nephi 12:33): ye have heard that (O)
Matthew 5:35 (3 Nephi 12:33): neither by Jerusalem; for it is the city of the great King (O)
Matthew 5:38 (3 Nephi 12:38): Ye have heard that (O)
Matthew 5:43 (3 Nephi 12:43): Ye have heard that (O)
Matthew 5:45 (3 Nephi 12:45): and sendeth rain on the just and on the unjust (O)
Matthew 5:46 (3 Nephi 12:46): For if ye love them which love you, what reward have ye? do not even the publicans the same? (O)
Matthew 5:46 (3 Nephi 12:46): Therefore those things which were of old time, which were under the law, in me are all fulfilled (A)
Matthew 5:47 (3 Nephi 12:47): And if ye salute your brethren only, what do ye more than others? do not even the publicans so? (O)
Matthew 5:47 (3 Nephi 12:47): Old things are done away, and all things have become new. (A)
Matthew 6:1 (3 Nephi 13:1): Verily, verily, I say that I would that ye should do alms unto the poor (A)
Matthew 6:10 (3 Nephi 13:10): Thy kingdom come (O)
Matthew 6:11 (3 Nephi 13:11): Give us this day our daily bread (O)
Matthew 6:25 (3 Nephi 13:25): Remember the words which I have spoken. For behold, he are they whom I have chosen to minister unto this people (A)
Matthew 6:32 (3 Nephi 13:32): (For after all these things do the Gentiles seek) (O)
Mark 1:7 (1 Nephi 10:8): among you whom ye know not; and he is (A)
Acts 3:24 (3 Nephi 20:24): Verily, I say unto you (A)
Acts 3:25 (3 Nephi 20:25): and ye are of the house of Israel (A)
Acts 3:26 (3 Nephi 20:26): and this because ye are the children of the covenant (A)
1 Corinthians 12:5 (Moroni 10:8): but the same Lord (O)
1 Corinthians 12:6 (Moroni 10:8): And there are diversities of operations (O)
1 Corinthians 12:8 (Moroni 10:9): of God, that he may teach (A)
1 Corinthians 12:8 (Moroni 10:10): that he may teach (A)
1 Corinthians 12:9 (Moroni 10:11): exceeding great (A)
1 Corinthians 12:10 (Moroni 10:13): [replacing "prophecy"] that he may prophesy concerning all things (A)
1 Corinthians 12:10 (Moroni 10:16): languages and of divers kinds of (A)
1 Corinthians 13:4 (Moroni 7:45): charity vaunteth not itself (O)
1 Corinthians 13:5 (Moroni 7:45): Doth not behave itself unseemly (O)

Note that the addition to Isaiah 2:5 (2 Nephi 12:5: yea, come, for ye have all gone astray, every one to his wicked ways) was created by inserting wording based on the famous Isaiah verse 53:6, "And we like sheep have gone astray; we have turned every one to his own way; and the LORD hath laid on him the iniquity of us all."

Analyzing Isaiah 13:22, where the BOM adds "For I will destroy her speedily; yea, for I will be merciful unto my people, but the wicked shall perish" (2 Nephi 23:22), Tvedtnes states that the Septuagint adds, "quickly shall it be done, and shall not be delayed" offering some sort of support to the BOM addition. In fact, the Septuagint does not *add* this. It *translates* the KJV clause "and her time is near to come" with "quickly it will come," and the KJV clause "and her days shall not be prolonged" with "and it shall not be delayed." Indeed, a Septuagint variant reading has "and her days shall not be drawn out." The BOM addition finds neither parallel nor support in any version.

Analyzing Isaiah 14:2 where the BOM adds "yea, from far unto the ends of the earth; and they shall return to their lands of promise" (2 Nephi 24:2), Tvedtnes suggests that there is partial support in the Great Isaiah Scroll, which, instead of the KJV phrase "to their place" one finds "to their land and to their place." The BOM variant has "lands of promise," but after "to their place," and after an intervening clause. This is scraping the barrel for lean pickins.

Analyzing Isaiah 48:11 "how should my name be polluted?" where the BOM has "I will not suffer my name to be polluted" (1 Nephi 20:11), Tvedtnes states that there has been a change in the verb, from third person singular to first person singular, with support in the Great Isaiah Scroll, the Septuagint and one Targum. Although this is true of the verb "to pollute," the change in the BOM is in the verb "to suffer" while "to pollute" is an infinitive. No version agrees with the BOM.

An awkward situation exists with respect to the variant involving Isaiah 51:9, where the BOM omits "in the generations of old" (2 Nephi 8:9). Tvedtnes states that some Hebrew mss omit "generations" providing partial support. No Hebrew manuscript omits it according to Kittel's *Biblia Hebraica* or *Biblia Hebraica Stuttgartensia*, or any other source that I have been able to examine. Kennicott does have variant spellings for "generations" (*drt/drwt*, both plural of *dwr*).

These larger, and significantly more substantive variants find no agreement in any ancient manuscript. Sidney B. Sperry and John Tvedtnes were of course aware of these much more substantial variants.

Their rational for themselves to ignore them, as well as others, was that these passages are BOM paraphrases, and not taken from the Isaiah of the Brass Plates. On the contrary, they cannot be explained as being simply scribal glosses, explanatory insertions, since the *Book of Mormon* version is not supposed to be a translation of a text produced by a scribal tradition, but Isaiah's text translated by the power of God. As we have seen in the case of the four long Isaiah inclusions, it is clearly stated that Nephi is simply reading from the Brass Plates. All of the inclusions are commented upon separately, following the reading. The claim that these longer variants are Nephi's glosses is nothing more than a tacit admission that LDS apologetics can do nothing with them. Furthermore, the gloss argument cannot apply to the omissions.

BOM Isaiah and the King James Mistranslations

The King James translation was begun in 1604 and completed in 1611. Several teams (companies) produced it. The First Oxford Company translated from Isaiah to Malachi. They were John Harding (Professor of Hebrew at Oxford; died in 1610), John Rainolds (Reynolds; 1549-1607; a Greek scholar, educator and Puritan protagonist), Thomas Holland (1539-1612; Calvinist scholar and theologian), Richard Kilby (1560-1620; Regius Professor of Hebrew, responsible for translating the latter part of the Old Testament), Miles Smith (1554-1624; Calvinist scholar, accomplished in the Biblical languages), Richard Brett (1567-1637; clergyman and student of Latin, Greek, Aramaic, Arabic, Hebrew and Ge'ez), Daniel Fairchough (1582-1645; a chaplain and theological disputant, especially in debates against the Jesuits) and William Thorne (1569?-1630; a chaplain and orientalist who had been Regius Professor of Hebrew at Oxford). The translation of the Old Testament was based primarily on the Masoretic text of *The Second Rabbinic Bible*, edited by Jacob Ben Chayyim and printed by Daniel Bloomberg in 1525, but for some passages not present in this edition, recourse was had to *First Rabbinic Bible* edited by Felix Praetensis in 1517-18.

The lay believer often assumes that the KJV translation is so good that one can argue from it, word for word, as though it were the Hebrew original. In fact, there are many problems in the translation. The following table presents some of the mistranslations in the book of Isaiah, and compares them with the Jewish Aramaic Targum translation and the Septuagint Greek translation. One must bear in mind that the

Hebrew is the original and trumps all else. The translations are important only when they can shed light on Hebrew words or phrases that are still poorly understood, especially the *hapax legomena*. At times, both the Aramaic and Greek indulge in a bit of translator's license, and even some exegesis (theological interpretation). The Aramaic in particular seems to be concerned to say what the reader should understand Isaiah to have meant, rather than word for word what he actually wrote. The KJ translators used Masoretic Hebrew manuscripts, and also consulted the Greek and Aramaic when found useful.

The Masoretes were a famous family working in Palestine (Tiberias and Jerusalem) and Iraq (Babylon) that was dedicated to preserving the scriptural tradition (*masorah* means "handing down, transmission, tradition," in Aramaic). Their text did not change the consonantal text, but added marks, a form of diacritics, above or below the consonants to indicate vowels (vocalization) and other marks for liturgical intonation. The timeline is approximately the Great Isaiah Scroll (1QIsaa, carbon-14 dated several times with the following results: 335-324 BCE and 202-107 BCE), the Greek Septuagint (possibly as early as late 2nd century BCE), the Aramaic Targum Jonathan (Yonatan, early 1st century CE) and the Masoretic text of the prophets (c. 900 AD). The antiquity of the Great Isaiah scroll is hugely important, as this text confirms the accuracy of the Masoretic text, and shows the great care the rabbis have exercised in passing Isaiah's text down to us. Although it is the best preserved of the Dead Sea Scrolls, it does have some small damaged parts, resulting in occasional lacunae in the text.

The *Book of Mormon* Isaiah inclusions are held to be a divine translation, restoring lost or poorly transmitted scriptures.

> 26 And after they [the scriptures] go forth by the hand of the twelve apostles of the Lamb, from the Jews unto the Gentiles, thou seest the formation of a great and abominable church…they have taken away from the gospel of the Lamb many parts which are plain and most precious; and also many covenants of the Lord have they taken away. (1 Nephi 13:26)

The BOM text is claimed to differ from the King James Version only when such differences were needed to correct errors in the KJV. The BOM emendations are quite numerous. Therefore, the obvious question is: when the King James translation is wrong, or poor, do the BOM "corrections" correct or improve upon it?

The following table reports some of the KJV mistranslations. There are many more in Appendix 2.

Table 9. Mistranslation in the King James Version of Isaiah

HM:	the Hebrew Masoretic text
Q:	the Great Isaiah Scroll found at Qumron
	=Q indicates orthographic differences to HM
T:	the Aramaic Targum Yunatan (Jonathan; Sperber edition)
S:	the Greek Septuagint (edited by Rahlfs)
Editions and Dictionaries are listed in the bibliographies.	
Transliteration: in keeping with the early date of Isaiah, b, g, d, k, p & t are not aspirated after vowels.	

Texts at Issue with Chapter & Verse	Translation & Comments
2:16: pictures (in: "pleasant pictures")	
HM: śəkîyôt (=Q)	HM: ships (so in prominent lexica; for the KJ version, one must posit a root based on Aramaic)
T: kol də-šāran bə-bīrānyāt šiprā	T: on all those dwelling in beautiful palaces
S: πᾶσαν θέαν πλοίων κάλλους	S: every appearance of beautiful ships
3:2: the prudent (one)	
HM: qōsēm (=Q)	HM: the verb means to tell the future, practice divination, and this active participle means a soothsayer or a diviner
T: mištə'ēʸl	T: diviner
S: στοχαστὴν	S: diviner
3:18: bravery	
HM: tip'eret (=Q)	HM: the root meaning is glorification, and this word means beauty, glory, ornament
T: tūšbəḥāt	T: praise, glory
S: δόξαν	S: glory
4:1: to take away	
HM: 'esōp (=Q)	HM: take away! (the form is imperative not the infinitive: ke-'esōp/le-'esōp)
T: kənōš	T: sweep away! (imperative)
S: ἄφελε	S: take away! (imperative)
4:5: every dwelling place of mount Zion	
HM: kol məkôn har-ṣîyôn (=Q)	HM: məkôn means "place": "every place of ..."
T: kōl miqdaš ṭūrā də-ṣiyōn	T: every sanctuary of Mount Zion
S: πᾶς τόπος τοῦ ὄρους Ζιων	S: every place of Mount Zion

5:15: the mean man shall be brought down, and the mighty man shall be humbled HM: *way-yiššaḥ ʾādām way-yišpal ʾîš* (=Q, except Q lacks *way-*)	HM: both *ʾādam* & *ʾîš* mean "man" or "a man" so that one has "a man shall be bowed low, and another shall be abased"; there is no word in the text to be translated "mean" or "mighty" (words introduced by the KJ translators
T: *yimʾak ʾᵃnāšā wə-yiḥlaš təqōp gūbrīn* S: καὶ ταπεινωθήσεται ἄνθρωπος καὶ ἀτιμασθήσεται ἀνήρ	T: man shall be debased and the might of men shall grow weak S: man shall be brought low and man shall be dishonored
5:25: their carcases were torn in the midst of the streets HM: *wat-təhî niblātām kas-sûḥâ bə-qereb ḥûṣôt* (Q reads: *w-thyh*; no meaning difference)	HM: *sûḥâ* is a noun probably meaning rubbish, sweepings, or possibly faeces; so that the verse should be "their carcases are like rubbish in the midst of the streets [for *sûḥâ*, note its usage in Psalms 80:16 (80:17 in Kittel] & cf. Arabic *suwāḥ*, mire)
T: *wa-hwaʾā nəbīlathōn məšuggərā kə-siḥūtā bə-gō šūqayā* S: ἐγενήθη τὰ θνησιμαῖα αὐτῶν ὡς κοπρία ἐν μέσῳ ὁδοῦ	T: "their corpses were cast out like offal in the midst of the streets" S: "their corpses were like dung in the midst of the street"
5:30: in the heavens thereof HM: *ba-ᶜarîpeʸhā* (=Q)	HM: "by its [the land's] clouds" unless emended: *ᶜarîpīyā* (in cloud); there is nothing that can mean "heavens"
T: *min qədām bištā* S: ἐν τῇ ἀπορίᾳ αὐτῶν	T: "from before the shame [or evil]" S: "in their distress (perplexity)"
6:13: shall be eaten HM: *wə-hāyətâ lə-bāᶜēr* (Q: *w-hyyth l-bʿr*; no meaning difference)	HM: *bāᶜēr* means "to kindle" and thus ([the tenth that returns] "shall be to kindle") and like the mighty trees shall sow the holy seed (certainly, this tenth will not be eaten!)
T: *w-îhōn lə-ṣārābā* S: ἔσται εἰς προνομὴν	T: "it will be for burning" (the remnant) S: "it wll be for plunder"

5. The Bible Versus the *Book of Mormon*   121

9:5: for every battle of the warrior is with confused noise HM: *kî kol sə'ôn sō'ēn bə-ra'aš* (=Q)	HM: "for every shoe (boot) of the wearer (marcher) is with noise (tumult, din)"; *sə'ôn* occurs only here in the whole OT but is common in Aramaic (Syriac: *sə'ūnā*, where the verbal root means "to wear a shoe") and Jewish Babylonian Aramaic (*sēʸnā*); while *ra'aš* means a din or noise (not necessarily "confused")
T: *kol miʸsabbəhōn we-mittanhōn bi-ršaʿ* S: ὅτι πᾶσαν στολὴν ἐπισυνηγμένην δόλῳ	T: "all their taking and giving is with wickedness" (v. Jastrow, p. 777) S: "for every garment gathered by treachery"
10:4: without me HM: *biltî* (=Q)	HM: "except"; this is a negative or privative particle, often meaning "not" and "lest"; the *-î* ending is part of the negative particle, and not the first person suffix (as the KJ mistakenly thinks); note that in 48:9 it is rendered "that ... not"
T: *bar min* S: τοῦ μή	T: "except for" S: "to not (lest)..." this is part of and completes the previous sentence
10:18: a standardbearer fainteth HM: *məsôs nōsēs* (=Q)	HM: "an invalid pines away (despairs)." *nōsēs*, a *hapax legomenon*, was interpreted by the KJ based on *nēs* (flag) and *hitnôsēs* (to rally about the flag). Taking *nōsēs* to mean "standardbearer" is pure KJ guesswork, over against T, S & the lexica. The root *nss* (*nōsēs* is the active participle) is found in post-Biblical Hebrew & Jewish Aramaic (*nəsîs*, grieved), Syriac (*nassîs*, frail, sick) and Akkadian *nasāsu* (to lament, bewail). T takes *nōsēs* from *nws*, "to flee." *məsôs* is a better attested root, meaning "to melt, disolve," and hence "to pine away, despair, become faint."
T: *təbīr wə-ʿārīq* S: ὁ φεύγων ὡς ὁ φεύγων ἀπὸ φλογὸςκαιομένης	T: "a lame [broken] person and a fugitive"; as if putting "and" between *məsôs* and *nōsēs*, (T & S derive from Hebrew *nās* (nws), to flee S: "the fugitive like one fleeing from burning flame"

10:26: slaughter	
HM: *makkat* (=Q)	HM: "blow (or defeat)"; the root means to strike; slaughter is a totally different root
T: *maḫḫat*	T: "smiting (blow)"
S: πληγήν	S: "blow"
10:28: carriages	
HM: *kēlā^{y}w* (=Q)	HM: "his weapons (vessels? baggage?)"; the word primarily means "vessels", bowls, used often of the vessels of the temple, altar, sanctuary or tabernacle, but can mean vessels (ships), equipment, instruments (musical) and weapons
T: *yəmannē^y rabbānē^y mašrəyātē^{y}h*	T: "he appoints the heads of his camps, troops"
S: σκεύη	S: "equipment"
11:1: a Branch shall grow out of his roots	
HM: *nēṣer miš-šorāšā^{y}w yipre* (=Q)	HM: "a shoot from his roots shall bear fruit (be fruitful)"; *yipre* comes from the common word for fruit, *pərî*; while the phrase "shall grow" would come from "*yipraḥ*" and the two can be easily confused in orthography (but note: Q also has *yipre*)
T: *məšīḥā mib-bnē^y bənōhī yitrabbē*	T: "the Messaiah shall be reared from the sons of his sons"
S: ἄνθος ἐκ τῆς ῥίζης ἀναβήσεται	S: "a flower shall come up from the root"
11:8: cockatrice	
HM: *ṣipʿônî* (=Q)	HM: "a poisonous snake"; not specifically identified, while the cockatrice is a mythological serpent or dragon born of a cock's egg with a power to kill with its look (the lore is rich re its physical characteristics, and supernatural powers)
T: *ḥiwē^y ḥurmān*	T: "poisonous snake" (for *ḥurmān* [poisonous] v. Dalman, p. 161)
S: ἀσπίδων	S: "asps"
13:12: golden wedge of Ophir	
HM: *ketem ʾôpîr* (=Q)	HM: "gold of Ophir"; no word for wedge here
T: *məsannənā də-ʾōpīr*	T: "refined [gold] of Ophir"
S: ὁ λίθος ὁ ἐκ Σουφιρ	S: "the stone from Souphir
13:14: roe	
HM: *ṣəbī* (=Q)	HM: "gazelle"
T: *ṭəbē^y*	T: "gazelle"; possibly also deer
S: δορκάδιον	S: "fawn" of the gazelle in the Middle East, & deer in Europe

5. The Bible Versus the *Book of Mormon*

13:21: owls HM: *bənôt yaʿănâ* (=Q) T: *bənāt naʿāmyāʸn* S: σειρῆνεσ	HM: "ostriches"; an unclean animal T: "ostriches" S: "sirens" or rather, demon ghosts of the desert
13:2a: high mountain HM: *har nišpe* (=Q) T: *ʿal karkā yātēʸb šēlēʸwā zəqūpū ʾātā* S: ὄρους πεδινοῦ	HM: "wind-swept (bare) mountain"; other words from this root mean to clean off, polish off, while a form in later Hebrew means to make smooth, and roots from cognate languages have similar meaning, and never mean "high" (cf. Jewish Aramaic, Samaritan Aramaic, Syriac, Mandaic & Arabic) T: "on the fortified place standing at ease, set up the sign" S: "a mountain of a plain"
13:22: the wild beasts of the islands shall cry in their desolate houses HM: *wə-ʿānâ ʾīyîm bə-ʾalmənôtāʸw* (=Q) T: *w-inaṣṣəpūn ḥātōlīn bə-bīrānyāthōn* S: ὀνοκένταυροι ἐκεῖ κατοικήσουσιν	HM: ""the jackals shall dwell among their widows"; or "the islands shall sing a dirge among their widows; " *ʿānâ* has other meanings (to answer, to be afflicted, to be occupied, preoccupied, to dwell; the KJ version is unjustified T: "and cats are crying in their palaces" S: "donkey-centaurs dwell there"
14:4: golden city HM: *madhēbâ* (Q reads: *marhēbâ*) T: *sāp təqōp hayyābā* S: ἐπισπουδαστής	HM: mss. differ, some having *madhēbâ* and Q has *marhēbâ*; *madhēba* does not mean "golden" in Hebrew (much less golden city), the word for gold being *zāhāb*, and no "m" preformative from this root exists to read "golden"; while *marhēbâ* comes from a root meaning "to assault, storm, act insolently"; so that we can read with Q: "the insolence (insolent one) has ceased" T: "the strength of the guilty has ceased" S: "compeller"; of labor gang drivers
14:22: son, and nephew HM: *nîn wā-neker* (=Q) T: *bar wə-bar bar* S: κατάλειμμα καὶ σπέρμα	HM: "offspring and progeny" T: "son and son's son" S: "offspring and seed (progeny)"

14:23: bittern	
HM: *qippōd* (=Q)	HM: "hedgehog" (earlier **qinpod* = Arabic *qunfud*, hedgehog)
T: *qūppədīn*	T: "hedgehogs" (Dalman, Levy)
S: ἐχίνους	S: "hedgehogs"
48:3: from the beginning (also 48:7)	
HM: *mē ʾāz* (=Q)	HM: "from then, in advance"; note *me-ʾāz* is rendered "from that time" in 48:8
T: *mib-bə-kēʸn*	T: "from there on"; with the sense of prior time (v. Dalman, p. 201)
S: ἔτι	S: "already"
51:6: abolished	
HM: *tēḥāt* (=Q)	HM: "to be broken"; this is the passive of a common verb meaning "to break"
T: *u-zkūtī lā titʿakkab*	T: "and my judgment (the judgment in my favor) will not be delayed [var.: broken]"
S: δικαιοσύνη μου οὐ μὴ ἐκλίπῃ	S: "fail"
51:9: Art thou not it	
HM: *hᵃlô ʾat hî* (=Q)	HM: "Art thou not she"; *ʾat* ("thou"), *hî* ("she") and the verb are feminine (also in 51:10; all referring to Jerusalem)
T: pronouns not used	T: the circumlocution does however have a feminine verb: *šēʸṣītī*
S: οὐ σὺ εἶ	S: "Is [it] not thou"; Greek does not indicate gender in verbs or these pronouns
51:15: divided	
HM: *rōgaʿ* (=Q)	HM: "stirred up"; a number of passages involving the sea and requiring a meaning such as this have brought some lexicographers to separate the verb in these instances from the more common root having to do with calm and quiet
T: *nāzēʸp*	T: "rebuke"
S: ταράσσων	S: "one who stirs up (troubles)"
51:20: wild bull	
HM: *tôʾ* (Q: *tô*)	HM: "antelope"; possibly the oryx, or the ibex (a species of wild goat)
T: *mizrəqēʸ*	T: "vessels" (to sprinkle blood on the altar; followed by "of the snare, net", which means?)
S: σευτλίον ἡμίεφθρον	S: "beet"; both words together "half-boiled beet"

The concerned reader may wish to check them against the published literal translations of the Hebrew Masoretic text, Aramaic Targum

Jonathan and Greek Septuagint. (v. p. 124) Linguists will find numerous lexical resources in Bibliography 2. Bibliography 1 has an extensive annotated list of published texts. Even though the Greek and Aramaic texts are interesting in their own right, since the original was in Hebrew, the bottom line is: Hebrew rules.[102]

In spite of the fact that the rational for the changes made in the KJ Isaiah text was to correct it, the BOM text retains all of the KJ mistranslations verbatim, except three, where its version is equally incorrect. In Isaiah 51:9, the KJV says "Art thou not it," while the BOM says "Art thou not he," and the Hebrew says "Art thou not she." In Isaiah 51:15, the KJV says "that divided the sea," while the Hebrew says "that stirs up the sea" and the BOM omits the clause. In Isaiah 51:17 the KJV says "wrung *them* out," while the BOM says "wrung out," and the Hebrew says "drained [it]." Apart from the fact that "wrung out" is the mistranslation, the BOM does tangentially delete "them," not present in the Hebrew text, while the KJV has it in italics, which the BOM frequently deletes.

Isaiah 8:3 is a special case. Most Hebrew names have meaning, and they are not usually translated. But the carnal intercourse of Isaiah and the prophetess was to produce an oracle. Yahweh himself speaks, telling Isaiah to name the boy "Hurry, take booty; hasten, take plunder." This is the text of the divine oracle itself, and the whole purpose of the story. It was a revelation that the enemies of Israel were soon to be defeated, and is usually taken to refer to the expected Messiah, the long-awaited new David. Yahweh only rarely speaks to his prophet, and when he does, his oracle, and especially this name, must be translated. Note that it was translated in both the Aramaic Targum Jonathan and the Greek Septuagint.

The passages in the above table are part of a larger study of KJV translation deficiencies in the relevant Isaiah passages. The total included in this study is 108. Table 9 has 30. The remaining 78 can be found in

---

[102] Jay P. Green, editor & translator, *The Interlinear Bible, Hebrew-Greek-English* (Peabody, MA: Hendrickson Publishers, 1986). Lancelot Brenton, *The Septuagint with Apocrypha: Greek and English* (Peabody, MA: Hendrickson Publishers, 2016). J. F. Stenning, *The Targum of Isaiah* [Targum Jonathan], Edited with a translation (Oxford: at the Clarendon Press, 1953 [1949]). The Comprehensive Aramaic Lexicon Project of the Hebrew Union College, which has an interactive text of Targum Jonathan, and is available online (http//:www.cal.cn.huc.edu).

Appendix 2. By far the majority are clear mistranslations, but there are some included that are most probably mistranslations, and a few that are simply very weak. This study has arrived at the following observations:

1. The King James translation is seriously defective.
2. These tables contain numerous opportunities for correction or improvement by a totally or nearly perfect, divine translation of Isaiah.
3. In 105 of 108 cases, the version of Isaiah in the *Book of Mormon* retains the KJV wording *verbatim*. The BOM version introduced some change in only three cases (above), which neither correct a KJV mistranslation, nor improve upon an improbable translation..
4. The BOM Isaiah text has numerous variant readings. These do not find support in the ancient manuscripts. Above all, as many as they are, they do not correct KJ mistranslations or dubious translations. Not even once.

The division of the Isaiah text into chapters evolved over time. We do not know what this division might have been prior to the Great Isaiah Scroll (Q). The beginning and end points of the three long Book of Isaiah inclusions correspond with the chapter divisions in the King James. These divisions were determined by content, so it is not surprising to find that the divisions in Q largely correspond with those in the KJV, but not altogether. The KJV break between 51:23 and 52:1 does not exist in Q. Having all chapter breaks in agreement with KJV breaks is consistent with a nineteenth century origin for the BOM.

New Testament Intrusions

Old Testament material in the Nephite record is explained by the Brass Plates of Laban, presumably essentially most of the Bible through 1 Kings, along with Isaiah. Passages dating after 600 BCE are said to have been given to the Nephites by revelation. Remarkably, these even include New Testament material that appears hundreds of years before Christ, by *Book of Mormon* chronology. Phrases familiar to New England Christians occur throughout. The following table gives some of the passages.

Table 10. Some Pre-Christian NT Passages in the *Book of Mormon*[103]

ye must pray always, and not faint (2 Nephi 32:9)	men ought always to pray, and not to faint (Luke 18:1)
they shall depart "into everlasting fire prepared for the devil and his angels." (Mosiah 26:27)	Depart from me, ye cursed, into everlasting fire, prepared for the devil and his angels (Matthew 25:41)
And then shall the righteous shine forth in the kingdom of God. (Alma 40:25)	Then shall the righteous shine forth as the sun in the Kingdom of their Father. (Matthew 13:43
ye should be steadfast and immovable, always abounding in good works (Mosiah 5:15)	be ye stedfast, unmoveable, always abounding in the good work of the Lord (1 Corinthians 15:58)
when my mortal shall put on immortality (Enos 1:27)	this mortal must put on immortality (1 Corinthians 15:53)
in the nurture and admonition of the Lord (Enos 1:1)	in the nurture and admonition of the Lord (Ephesians 6:4)
he that fighteth against Zion, both Jew and Gentile, both bond and free, both male and female, shall perish (2 Nephi 10:16)	There is neither Jew nor Greek, there is neither bond nor free, there is neither male nor female (Galatians 3:28)
the Spirit is the same yesterday, today and forever (2 Nephi 2:4)	Jesus Christ the same yesterday, and to day, and for ever (Hebrews 13:8)
the righteous...who have endured the crosses of the world, and despised the shame of it (2 Nephi 9:18)	Jesus...endured the cross, despising the shame (Hebrews 12: 2)

New Testament influence can be found in other ways. For example, when Jesus comes to the Nephites, he chooses twelve disciples. One of them is Timothy, a good New Testament name, which, however, happens to be a Greek name. It was only after the conquests of Alexander and the spread of Hellenism in the Middle East that Greek names occurred among the Jews, as can be readily observed in the Old Testament. Timothy should have had a good Nephite or Hebrew name.

This tendency may be greater in utterances experienced as the gift of the tongues, since it is spontaneous. These passages were worked over in private, with pen and ink, and display many types of variants. Still, the basic phenomenon is the same: some changes are clearly suggested by similarity between the KJ word and the BOM word. The *Book of Mormon* throughout reflects the linguistic and religious environment of its authors.

---

[103] H. Michael Marquardt, *The Rise of Mormonism: 1816-1844: Second Edition, Revised and Enlarged*, (Maitland, FL: Xulon Press, 2013), 104-05.

New Testament themes are also used. The story of Salome, with the dance of the seven veils, and the head of John the Baptist on a platter, is given new life in the Jaredite Book of Ether. The daughter of the king's son in exile, who is "exceeding fair," says "And now, therefore, let my father send for Akish, the son of Kimnor; and behold, I am fair and I will dance before him, and I will please him, that he will desire me to wife; wherefore if he shall desire of thee that ye shall give unto him me to wife, then shall ye say: I will give her if ye will bring unto me the head of my father, the king." (Ether 8:10)

Observations.

1) Several aspects of the BOM narrative conflict with the Bible, such as the existence of a Bible at 600 BCE, especially in Egyptian; the departure of Lehi in the first year of Zedekiah, after the sack of Jerusalem; and including on the Brass Plates parts of Isaiah not done by Isaiah, but dating much after Lehi's departure.
2) The BOM variant readings fail to correct even one mistranslation in the KJV.
3) The preparation of the KJV inclusions in the BOM text required considerable effort, as well as the commentary on them, and the paraphrases worked into the Nephite narrative. This was not something that was done by casual composition, nor extemporaneous dictation.

Chapter 6

Nephite-Lamanite Intangible Culture: Religion

The Religion of the Nephites

Although the *Book of Mormon* is often characterized as being a historical narrative covering a thousand years of Israelites in the New World, it is actually a collection of sermons, commentary and religious disputation, within a relatively thin historical narrative that is often presented in homiletic style. Some of these can qualify as informal, somewhat folksy theological dissertations. They call the reader to repentance and a spiritual life, establish the justification for a latter-day restoration of true Christianity along with a latter-day prophet and a new bible, and delineate its largely Pauline theology.

Repent, and Hold to the Iron Rod of the Word of God

Already in the first pages of the text a major rift develops between the protagonist, Lehi's younger son, Nephi, and the antagonists, his two older sons, Laman and Lemuel. Nephi was chosen from the beginning, before his conception, and is to be the founder of the true Christian gospel in the Promised Land early in the seventh century BCE. As he asserts his spiritual and temporal leadership in the family, his two older brothers are affronted, feel threatened, and revolt. This scenario gives father Lehi and Nephi opportunities for speeches calling them to repentance, to hold to the word of God, to seek the spiritual life in preference to the material, and to withstand the mockery of the great many who despise the truth under the influence of Satan. They serve also as Nephi's foil to rebut objections to BOM claims of a Hebrew party settling in the New World.

It is interesting to note that in addition to condemning materialist pursuit of the riches of this world, BOM morality roundly condemns whoredoms, adultery, concubines and plural wives. (Jacob 1:15, 2:24-27, Mosiah 11:2, Ether 10:5)

This preachment aims to put the *Book of Mormon* on a higher spiritual plain, and disarm the reader's natural skepticism, by challenging his own religiosity and morality, and calling him too to repentance.

The Whore of All the Earth

Although John (of Patmos?), in the writing the *Book of Revelations*, directed his bitterness and the indignation of God against Rome, Christian writing after the fall of that empire had already extended it to apply to religious movements that were deemed to be antichrist. The *Book of Mormon*, applying it to absolutely all religions in the 1820's, pulls no punches (1 Nephi 13):

> 5. And the angel said unto me: Behold the formation of a church which is most abominable above all other churches, which slayeth the saints of God, yea, and tortureth them and bindeth them down, and yoketh them with a yoke of iron, and bringeth them down into captivity.
> 6. And it came to pass that I beheld this great and abominable church; and I saw the devil that he was the founder of it.
> 7. And I also saw gold, and silver, and silks, and scarlets, and fine-twined linen, and all manner of precious clothing; and I saw many harlots.
> 8. And the angel spake unto me, saying: Behold the gold, and the silver, and the silks, and the scarlets, and the fine-twined linen, and the precious clothing, and the harlots, are the desires of this great and abominable church.
> 9. And also for the praise of the world do they destroy the saints of God, and bring them down into captivity.

This sounds calculated to please Protestant anti-papist fervor, but its terrible judgment is extended to all churches:

> And he said unto me: Behold there are save two churches only; the one is the church of the Lamb of God, and the other is the church of the devil. (1 Nephi 14:10)

Needless to say, the LDS Church is not a likely candidate to sit at any ecumenical conference table. In opposition to the church(es) of the devil, its mission is to build the kingdom of Christ, and call all mankind to its true restored church, destined to become Christ's world government after his victory over Satan, when he comes again to reign on earth.

One God, the Same Yesterday, Today and Forever

As Smith and his partners proceeded to announce the visitation of God the Father, God the Son, the Angel Moroni, and the mission to miraculously translate a new scripture engraved on gold plates, they encountered considerable skepticism, rising to the level of persecution, and condemnation as heretics on theological grounds. The *Book of Mormon* counters (Mormon 9):

> 9. For do we not read that God is the same yesterday, today, and forever, and in him there is no variableness neither shadow of changing?
> 10. And now if ye have imagined up unto yourselves a god who doth vary, and in whom there is shadow of changing, then have ye imagined up unto yourselves a god who is not God of miracles.
> 20. And the reason why he ceaseth to do miracles among the children of men is because that they dwindle in unbelief, and depart from the right way, and know not the God in whom they should trust.

This unchanging god is forever a god of miracles, a god of revelation, who sends angels to his elect, and a god of one true church. All of these are hallmarks of the Mormon movement. As a result, one true gospel fits all, in every time and every clime. In Mormonism, there is little awareness of historical evidence of religious evolution, from the religion of Israel to Judaism and Christianity. To the extent that it impinges upon the minds of some, assertions are marshaled to refute it, or it is simply ignored.

The Stick of Judah and the Stick of Joseph

The argument in support of the idea that the God of Israel had brought part of the tribe of Joseph to the New World and produced a new bible makes use of a naive misinterpretation of several Biblical passages, taken out of context, probably as a result of total ignorance of Biblical history. Few events are more central or more seminal in the OT narrative than the unification of Israel under Saul and David, who used his considerable military assets to bring the tribes under one yoke, as well as many of the neighboring peoples. Like all expansions, the initial take in booty and slaves was considerable. His successor, Solomon, was a major builder. Since the Hebrew tribes had neither experience nor expertise in such things, he contracted with the Canaanite king Hiram of Tyre to build first his own palace, then the temple and later his fleet. Having exhausted the initial booty resources, and overstrained the imposed tribute obligations, he resorted to heavy taxation of his own people. After his death, the tribes in desperation inquired regarding taxation, and Rehoboam, the successor in Jerusalem, made his famous reply (1 Kings 12:11): "And now whereas my father did lade you with a heavy yoke, I will add to your yoke: my father hath chastised you with whips, but I will chastise you with scorpions." This reply fed an already sharp division between Judea and the tribes of the north, led by the tribes of Ephraim and Manasseh (the two sons of Joseph). Rehoboam emerges as the king of the Kingdom of Judah, with Jerusalem as its capital, and Jeroboam becomes the king of the Kingdom of Israel in the north (composed of ten of the twelve tribes), with its capital in Shechem. This division was a continual irritant to the prophets of Judah, who looked forward to a new David, a Messiah (anointed one, i.e. king) to reunite the twelve tribes. The Kingdom of Israel fell to the Assyrians over about a twenty-year period beginning in 740 BCE, and many were dispersed and/or carried off into captivity, leading to the dissolution of the tribes and the legend of the ten lost tribes. Around 597 BCE Babylon sacked Jerusalem, carrying many off into captivity in Babylon, and c. nine years later destroyed the temple and walls. Meanwhile many Hebrews, like their Canaanite cousins (called Phoenicians by the Greeks) traveled abroad to seek their fortunes elsewhere, as far as India and Persia in the East, and around the Mediterranean, and especially Egypt, at Elephantine Island in the far south, and Alexandria.

The book of Isaiah began as a collection of some prophetic writings by the prophet himself, gathered together and edited by his followers, and received further editing and considerable augmentation over the next hundred years. In the resulting text, and in the books of Jeremiah and Ezekiel, there are occasional prophecies regarding the hoped-for gathering from captivity and dispersion, even from the isles of the sea (the Mediterranean; cf. Esther 10:1). Ezekiel claimed a revelation that indicated that this reunification would be soon (Ezekiel 37):

> 16. Moreover, thou son of man, take thee one stick, and write upon it, For Judah, and for the children of Israel his companions: then take another stick, and write upon it, For Joseph, the stick of Ephraim, and for all the house of Israel his companions:

17. And join them one to another into one stick; and they shall become one in thine hand.
18. And when the children of thy people shall speak unto thee, saying, Wilt thou not shew us what thou meanest by these?
19. Say unto them, Thus saith the Lord GOD; Behold, I will take the stick of Joseph, which is in the hand of Ephraim, and the tribes of Israel his fellows, and will put them with him, even with the stick of Judah, and make them one stick, and they shall be one in mine hand.
20. And the sticks whereon thou writest shall be in thine hand before their eyes.
21. And say unto them, Thus saith the Lord GOD; Behold, I will take the children of Israel from among the heathen, whither they be gone, and will gather them on every side, and bring them into their own land:
22. And I will make them one nation in the land upon the mountains of Israel; and one king shall be king to them all: and they shall be no more two nations, neither shall they be divided into two kingdoms any more at all:

So God will take the children of Israel (the kingdom of the north, scattered among the heathen) and gather them together. Then they shall no longer be two nations (the kingdom of Israel and the kingdom of Judah). This all goes back to the division wrought by the dispute between Solomon's sons, Jeroboam and Rehoboam.

LDS scholars interpret the stick of Judah as being the Bible, and the stick of Joseph as being the new bible from the gold plates. LDS exegesis has claimed that the sticks are scroll sticks, each scroll being a book of scripture, which will be united as the twin scriptures of the restored church. The phrase the "isles of the sea" in Isaiah 24:15 is claimed to refer to the Israelites in the New World, those continents being interpreted as "isles." (2 Nephi 8:10 & 29:7) The *Book of Mormon*, it is claimed, is further referred to in Isaiah 29:4, "And thou shalt be brought down, and shalt speak out of the ground, and thy speech shall be low out of the dust, and thy voice shall be, as of one that hath a familiar spirit, out of the ground, and thy speech shall whisper out of the dust." This is said to apply because the gold plates were dug up "out of the ground," speaking, as it were, "low out of the dust." (See also 1 Nephi 22 & 2 Nephi 6:5-18) Actually, "hath a familiar spirit, out of the ground" refers to necromancy calling for a message from a deceased person in Sheol, the great pit underground, as was the case when Saul sought wisdom from the deceased Samuel, with the aid of the Witch of Endor (I Samuel 28:3-25).

Note that possibly half of the people who became Nephites were descended from Mulek, said to be a son of Zedekiah, and apparently other Judeans who came with him to the New World and founded Zarahemla. It is not clear to what extent the Nephites were descended from Joseph in any case.

Millennialism and Pauline Theology

Having thus laid the foundation for the argument that the Biblical prophets knew that a branch of Israel would be found in the isles of the sea and that their history and preachments would become a second book of sacred scripture, the BOM authors proceeded to delineate Nephite theology.

Hippolytus of Rome likened history to the days of creation plus the Sabbath, and argued that six millennia must precede the millennium of Christ's rule on earth. Some have suggested an apostasy-restoration cycle, although not sticking literally to a 1,000-year period for each cycle. Mormonism has generally accepted a version of this view. For what concerns us here, it is important to note that the *Book of Mormon* holds that each of the main prophets, including Adam, Abraham and Moses, was a Christian and had the full gospel. God's true church has been the same over the millennia, with the exception of the major change occasioned by Jesus' accomplishment of his mission upon the cross. In later LDS theological development, this led some to adopt some version of dispensationalism.[104] It is no accident that general Mormon is killed in 400 CE, exactly one thousand years ALJ.

BOM theology condemns all churches but one as being collectively the church of the devil. It holds that when the Lamanites rejected the truth, they became a dark, loathsome, indolent and savage people. The Jews were not overlooked. They are systematically treated as being Christ-killers, a stiff-necked people that also killed the prophets of God. 2 Nephi 10:3 declares.

> Wherefore, as I said unto you, it must needs be expedient that Christ—for in the last night the angel spake unto me that this should be his name—should come among the Jews, among those who are the more wicked part

---

[104] See William C. Watson, *Dispensationalism before Darby. Seventeenth-Century and Eighteenth-Century English Apocalypticism* (Silverton, OR: Lampion Press, 2015).

of the world; and they shall crucify him—for thus it behooveth our God, and there is none other nation on earth that would crucify their God.

In Alma, notwithstanding some differences, one cannot help but feel that the Jews are caricatured in the form of the Zoramites. They worship in synagogues rather than churches, and deny the Christ. They believe that they were separated from others by God, and are His chosen children:

> Holy God, we believe that thou hast separated us from our brethren; and we do not believe in the tradition of our brethren, which was handed down to them by the childishness of their fathers; but we believe that thou hast elected us to be thy holy children; and also thou hast made it known unto us that there shall be no Christ. (31:16)

Christian anti-Semitism is well represented in the BOM text.

Thus, all the while being Christians, and even baptized into the faith, the believers in the New World were commanded to obey the Law of Moses and keep all of its performances, from the seventh-century BCE to the visit of Christ after his resurrection. Although left somewhat vague, it appears that the law was given to the Israelites to keep them sufficiently in line that their society would be suitable for Christ's mission. Its performances, however, cannot save.

It has often been said that Paul, a Greek speaker and citizen of Rome, with aspirations to be the apostle to the gentiles, was not personally fond of the Law of Moses, and knew well that it would be a hard sell in the centers of empire. It had to end. His formula, which carried the day and marked the transition of the movement started by Jesus from a Jewish sect to a new universal religion, was that it had been given to Israel to prepare them for Christ's coming, and that when he performed the infinite (and last) sacrifice, of himself on the cross, the law was fulfilled. It became no longer valid. This is also the view of the Nephite preachers. It was taught and well understood by them, from 7th-century BCE Nephi on down to the visit of Jesus.

Even while continuing adherence to the performances and strictures of the law, the faithful in BCE pre-Columbian America were eventually organized into churches, were baptized and took upon themselves the name of Jesus Christ, i.e. they were called Christians (2 Nephi 31:5-17, Mosiah 18:13-18, Alma 19:35 & Helaman 3:24-26). They were taught the doctrine of repentance and redemption from their sins by the power of the sacrifice of Jesus on the cross. They even were urged to cross themselves (Alma 39:9).

The BOM narrative contains many passages describing miracles, curses, a person raised from the dead, and prophets delivered from prison, with the walls tumbling down while they emerged unscathed. These accounts are written in the same tone as some of the stories of Daniel.

Although there is some language regarding Jesus and God that might presage Joseph Smith's later polytheism, it is not more clear than similar language in the New Testament, and if Smith had never adopted a doctrine of plural gods, it is unlikely that this language would be interpreted in that way. Apart from this issue, there is a clear anthropomorphic view of deity. The Lord says to the brother of Jared, "Behold, this body, which ye now behold, is the body of my spirit; and man have I created after the body of my spirit; and even as I appear unto thee to be in the spirit will I appear unto my people in the flesh." (Ether 3:16)

The theonym "Jehovah" is found only twice, in an Isaiah inclusion (2 Nephi 22:2) and Mosiah 10:34. In the full form, it occurs only seven times in the Old Testament. Note however that various shortened forms (hypocorisms) of the name are of frequent occurrence in the OT.

Apart from the arguments supporting the basic claims of Smith's election as a prophet, the miraculous translation of the gold plates, and the visitation of the angel Moroni, Jesus and God the Father, the reader finds much material that has the ring of religious propriety, resembling doctrines heard from the pulpits of other churches. This is accompanied with an exhortation to prayer, with the promise that if you repent, and seek with an open mind and contrite spirit, then a testimony of the truth of the *Book of Mormon* will be planted, grow, mature and be confirmed in your heart. We also find discourses on more sophisticated theological issues, such as the law being a type or foreshadowing of Jesus and his crucifixion, arguments against infant baptism and the complexities of the first and second resurrection.

There are also contrasts. The New Testament has the Beatitudes, but Nephi has his "Wo attitudes" (ten statements of "wo unto..." in 1 Nephi 9:27-38). And while the NT Jesus invites, in 3 Nephi he constantly commands. The extent that this is so can be seen in Table 23 *infra*.

The Religion of the Lamanites

Although at times many of the Lamanites accept Christianity and are even described as being more righteous than the Nephites, on the whole this is not the case, and the BOM narrative states clearly that it uses the term Lamanites to refer to those who reject the teachings of God. We find a New England 19th-century stereotype of the Indians, as being dark and loathsome, indolent, savage and bloodthirsty.

The Great Spirit. It is not easy to know exactly what North American pre-Columbian beliefs were about deity prior to European missionary contact. The information is oral, and usually rather late, even, at times, related by European colonists. Yet some concept of a Great Spirit seems to have existed among many. Some names for the Great Spirit, or its equivalent follow: 1) Sioux: *"Wakan Tanka,"* Great Mystery that organizes the spirits or deities, as every object was spirit, or "*wakan;*" 2) the Shoshone: "*Tam Apo,*" Our Father (although the religion involved various legendary spirits and ghost spirits); 3) Chickasaw: "*Ababinili,*" spirit of fire and manifest in fire and the sun, the giver of life, light, and warmth; 4) Many Algonquian speaking tribes of the Great Plains, such as the Ojibwe: "*Gitchi Manitou,*" Great Spirit (translated as "God" in missionary translations of scripture), along with other spirits pictured above doorways; 5) Blackfoot: "*Apistotoke,*" Our Creator, a formless spirit (translated as "God" in Christian scriptures); Arapaho: "*Chebbeniathan,*" Spider-above, the creator god; 6) Abenaki: "*Gici Niwaskw,*" Great Spirit; 7) Huron: "*Ha-Wen-Neyu,*" the creator god, rendered Great Spirit in English, but meaning "Great Voice" or "Great Ruler;" 8) Cheyenne: "*Maheo,*" Great One, creator, but figured in a pantheon including *"Wihio"* (spider trickster), *"Nonoma"* (spirit of thunder), *"Mehne"* & *"Axxea"* (water monsters) and other legendary beings; 9) Seminole: *"Hisagita Misa"* (Creek: *"Hisagita-imisi"*), Breath-maker, associated with the Milky Way. There are others. What they all have in common is that one being is central, although others may exist, and that the religions are shamanistic. It was convenient to tell inquiring Whites simply that they believed in the Great Spirit.

In New England, English-speakers would mostly have heard of the Great Spirit, including the BOM authors. It is not surprising then to discover that the general religion of the Lamanites, to the extent that the BOM treats it, was based on the existence of the Great Spirit. In Alma 18:2, the Lamanite king Lamoni says, "Behold, is not this the Great

Spirit who doth send such great punishments upon this people, because of their murders?" Referring to his belief, "Ammon said: This is God. And Ammon said unto him again: Believest thou that this Great Spirit, who is God, created all things which are in heaven and in the earth?" (Alma 18:28) The king replies in the affirmative.

In view of the fact that Nephite civilization is placed in an area almost perfectly contiguous with or adjacent to Mayan and Olmec culture, we might expect there to be some mention of the false gods, similar to the OT mention of Baal, Baal-Zebub, Bel, Moloch, Ashtoreth, Amon, Chemosh, Dagon, Tammuz and various other regional deities in competition with Jehovah (Yahweh). Surprisingly, or perhaps not so surprisingly, we find no mention of any other deity in the entire BOM text (although there are occasional condemnations of idolatry). Historically, throughout this region, there were impressive representations of numerous deities, and elaborate rituals, in scores of cities and villages, even throughout the two Nephite Christian centuries.

God vs. Belief, and Unbelief. Just as we find the Great Spirit drawn from the New England perception of Native American religion, we find that the BOM authors are primarily concerned with atheism, a concept that was developed among the pre-Socratic philosophers, and scarcely evidenced in the Bible (Psalms 10:4; 14:1; 53:1). Reasoned disputations are totally absent. It was, however, a prevalent concern in 18th and 19th-century New England, in the context of the perceived conflict between science and religion. Ammoron writes in reply to an epistle received from Moroni, "And as concerning that God whom ye say we have rejected, behold, we know not such a being; neither do ye; but if it so be that there is such a thing, we know not but that he hath made us as well as you." (Alma 54:21) There are a number of debates over the existence of God:

> Behold, will ye believe in the day of your visitation— behold, when the Lord shall come, yea, even that great day when the earth shall be rolled together as a scroll, and the elements shall melt with fervent heat, yea, in that great day when ye shall be brought to stand before the Lamb of God— then will ye say that there is no God? (Mormon 9:2)
>
> And Amulek said unto him: Yea, if it be according to the Spirit of the Lord, which is in me; for I shall say nothing which is contrary to the Spirit of the Lord. And Zeezrom said unto him: Behold, here are six onties of

silver, and all these will I give thee if thou wilt deny the existence of a Supreme Being. (Alma 11:22)

And now Korihor said unto Alma: If thou wilt show me a sign, that I may be convinced that there is a God, yea, show unto me that he hath power, and then will I be convinced of the truth of thy words.

But Alma said unto him: Thou hast had signs enough; will ye tempt your God? Will ye say, Show unto me a sign, when ye have the testimony of all these thy brethren, and also all the holy prophets? The scriptures are laid before thee, yea, and all things denote there is a God; yea, even the earth, and all things that are upon the face of it, yea, and its motion, yea, and also all the planets which move in their regular form do witness that there is a Supreme Creator. (Alma 30:43-44)

Alma's argument here is anachronistic. Verses in the Bible used in Christian theology to adduce the wonders of nature as evidence of the existence of God were composed by the Biblical authors to praise God, rather than as part of a reasoned argument against atheism (i.e. the *vestigiae dei* argument). Alma uses the marvels of nature in his disputation just as they have been used in Euro-Christian theology.

Apart from the Great Spirit, and atheism among at least some, the other gulf between the Lamanites and the Nephites is the traditions of their fathers, for the former had preserved a memory of the conflict between Nephi and Laman, and believed that Nephi used religion to cheat his eldest brother out of the rule that was rightly his, and had made off with group property, the Brass Plates, the sword and breastplate of Laban and Liahona. Ultimately, the bottom line is that all of Lamanite and Nephite religion derives from the religious culture of nineteenth-century New England. This includes the condemnation of idolatry, found in the Bible and sermons. There is no trace of the religions of the territory that they should have been in competition against for the hearts and minds of the indigenous populations such as the Mayas and Olmecs.

The Case of the Missing Nephite Christians

The Christian issue in the *Book of Mormon* is based on the assertion that the Nephites were Christians, or at least those who remained faithful to the teachings of Nephi and his prophetic successors. Even more fundamental, a full knowledge of God's plan and its theology was already revealed to Adam. The word "baptism" is found early in the

BOM text (1 Nephi 20:1) where it is inserted into the mouth of Isaiah (48:1). Nephi taught basic Pauline theology regarding the coming Savior, and the atonement: "And it came to pass that I, Nephi, did consecrate Jacob and Joseph, that they should be priests and teachers over the land of my people." (2 Nephi 5:26) The name of the Savior, Christ, was revealed to him (2 Nephi 10:3). He states, "...there is none other name given under heaven save it be this Jesus Christ" (2 Nephi 25:20) by which man can be saved; "And we talk of Christ, we rejoice in Christ, we preach of Christ, we prophesy of Christ..." (2 Nephi 25:26) In Mosiah 3:8 (2nd century BCE) we read "And he shall be called Jesus Christ, the Son of God, the Father of heaven and earth, the Creator of all things from the beginning; and his mother shall be called Mary." (See also Alma 7:10) This is the "Old Testament" as many Christians have always thought it should have been written.

The doctrine of Christ and redemption was accompanied by baptism: "And now, if the Lamb of God, he being holy, should have need to be baptized by water, to fulfil (sic) all righteousness, O then, how much more need have we, being unholy, to be baptized, yea, even by water!" (2 Nephi 31:5). Following that, "... then shall ye receive the Holy Ghost; yea, then cometh the baptism of fire and of the Holy Ghost; and then can ye speak with the tongue of angels." (2 Nephi 31:13; 5th century BCE)

Although already in Nephi's time (the first few decades in the New World) a church with ordained clergy existed, the word "church" first occurs in Mosiah 18:17: "And they were called the church of God, or the church of Christ, from that time forward. And it came to pass that whosoever was baptized by the power and authority of God was added to his church." King Benjamin announces that he would give the faithful a new name (Mosiah 1:11), "the children of Christ." (Mosiah 5:7; cf. 5:8-11) The actual name "Christian" first occurs in Alma 46:13-16. In the BOM narrative, the places of worship are variably called churches and synagogues, although Nephi built a temple, and various cities had a temple. The term "holy order of God" is introduced to refer to the divine authority to officiate in the church. Alma stepped down from the judgment seat and "confined himself wholly to the high priesthood of the holy order of God, to the testimony of the word, according to the spirit of revelation and prophecy." (Alma 4:20) After addressing the church established in Zarahemla, Alma "ordained priests and elders, by laying on his hands according to the order of God, to preside and watch over the church." (Alma 6:1; See Alma 4:7 and Alma 13) By the fifteenth year of the reign of judges, "the church had been established throughout all the land..." (Alma 16:21) After some falling away, "Therefore, Helaman (son of Alma) and his brethren went forth to establish the church again in all the land, yea, in every city throughout all the land which was possessed by the people of Nephi. And it came to pass that they did appoint priests and teachers throughout all the land, over all the churches." (Alma 45:22; cf. 62:46)

The wavering between belief and unbelief continued, until the wickedness became sufficient that, at the time of the crucifixion of Christ, divine judgment befell the people in the form of the Crucifixion Cataclysm, when many cities were entirely destroyed. Those who were spared were apt to accept Christ when he appeared to them after his resurrection. A new era is ushered in, with Christ preaching his gospel and choosing twelve disciples:

> And it came to pass that on the morrow, when the multitude was gathered together, behold, Nephi and his brother whom he had raised from the dead, whose name was Timothy, and also his son, whose name was Jonas, and also Mathoni, and Mathonihah, his brother, and Kumen, and Kumenonhi, and Jeremiah, and Shemnon, and Jonas, and Zedekiah, and Isaiah—now these were the names of the disciples whom Jesus had chosen—and it came to pass that they went forth and stood in the midst of the multitude. (3 Nephi 19:4)

These names are unlikely. Timothy is a well-known Greek name found in the New Testament. In Greek, it means God-fearing. Nephi's brother should not have a Greek name. The BOM authors did not know Greek, and fell into a linguistic trap. Furthermore, unlike the other names of the BOM, there is a concentration of names of the most famous OT figures: Jonas (twice), Jeremiah, Zedekiah and Isaiah. Jonas is especially interesting. It is the New Testament rendering of Jonah in Greek, the *s* being a Greek ending. This too should not appear in a New World disciple list. The governor over the land at the time of the birth of Jesus was Lachoneus (cf. Laconia, region of Sparta [& laconic]; note too Archeantus). Names were chosen for a New Testament atmosphere.

As noted above, there were earlier periods when the whole land became Christian, although this referred to the Nephite lands. Following the mission of the Twelve to preach to all the surviving people, we are told that the whole land was Christian for about two centuries. This time around, the account refers to truly all the land, presumably North and South America, depicting a Christian era, followed by a post-Christian era, characterized by heresy and apostasy (4 Nephi 1):

> 1. And it came to pass that the thirty and fourth year passed away, and also the thirty and fifth [after the birth of Jesus], and behold the disciples of Jesus had formed a church of Christ in all the lands round about. And as many as did come unto them, and did truly repent of their sins, were baptized in the name of Jesus; and they did also receive the Holy Ghost.
> 2. And it came to pass in the thirty and sixth year, the people were all converted unto the Lord, upon all the face of the land, both Nephites and Lamanites, and there were no contentions and disputations among them, and every man did deal justly one with another.
> 7. And the Lord did prosper them exceedingly in the land; yea, insomuch that they did build cities again where there had been cities burned.
> 22. And it came to pass that two hundred years had passed away; and the second generation had all passed away save it were a few.
> 23. And now I, Mormon, would that ye should know that the people had multiplied, insomuch that they were spread upon all the face of the land, and that they had become exceedingly rich, because of their prosperity in Christ.
> 24. And now, in this two hundred and first year there began to be among them those who were lifted up in pride, such as the wearing of costly apparel, and all manner of fine pearls, and of the fine things of the world.
> 26. And they began to be divided into classes; and they began to build up churches unto themselves to get gain, and began to deny the true church of Christ.
> 27. And it came to pass that when two hundred and ten years had passed away there were many churches in the land; yea, there were many churches which professed to know the Christ, and yet they did deny the more parts of his gospel, insomuch that they did receive all manner of wickedness, and did administer that which was sacred unto him to whom it had been forbidden because of unworthiness.
> 29. And again, there was another church which denied the Christ; and they did persecute the true church of Christ, because of their humility and their belief in Christ; and they did despise them because of the many miracles which were wrought among them.
> 36. And it came to pass that in this year there arose a people who were called the Nephites, and they were true believers in Christ; and among them there were those who were called by the Lamanites—Jacobites, and Josephites, and Zoramites;
> 38. And it came to pass that they who rejected the gospel were called Lamanites, and Lemuelites, and Ishmaelites; and they did not dwindle in

> unbelief, but they did wilfully (sic) rebel against the gospel of Christ; and they did teach their children that they should not believe, even as their fathers, from the beginning, did dwindle.
> 40-41. And it came to pass that two hundred and forty and four years had passed away...And they did still continue to build up churches unto themselves, and adorn them with all manner of precious things. And thus did two hundred and fifty years pass away, and also two hundred and sixty years.

The whole land became converted to Christianity, and remained occupied by true Christians for almost the first two centuries, at which point false churches emerged, and eventually one that denied Christ altogether. The BOM authors replicated their own view of what they considered to have been the great apostasy in the early history of Christianity in the Old World, leading to their situation in New England. There is no mention of competition with pagan religions, and the known deities of the New World, nor their worship upon pyramids, or in the caves of cenotes.

This period of the BOM account covers the last two centuries of the late preclassic period of Mayan history. The Mayans and related peoples of Central America are the most relevant pre-Columbian civilizations, due to the specific geographical details in the BOM narrative, tied to the narrow neck of land, which can only be the Isthmus of Panama.

It might be expected that at some point specifically Christian remains would be found, churches perhaps, Christian documents, and burials. It is not clear that we would expect cross icons, but it seems that the cross did have some significance in the *Book of Mormon*:

> Now my son, I would that ye should repent and forsake your sins, and go no more after the lusts of your eyes, but cross yourself in all these things; for except ye do this ye can in nowise inherit the kingdom of God. Oh, remember, and take it upon you, and cross yourself in these things. (Alma 39:9)

Jesus says to the Nephites: "For it is better that ye should deny yourselves of these things, wherein ye will take up your cross, than that ye should be cast into hell." (3 Nephi 12:30) The problem is that the cross is one of the common symbols in various civilizations. Its significance depends on the context, and associated inscriptions, especially when found in distinctly non-Christian settings. An explicitly Christian complex should be expected, but none has been found.

From the evidentiary point of view, by far the most important thing is the prevalence of uninterrupted pagan (Mayan, Olmec, Nazca, Moche, etc.) civilization. It is now recognized that the essential traits of the classic period (c. 250-800 CE) had already developed in the late preclassic period, including writing, the Mayan calendar, monumental architecture including massive pyramids, statuary and murals, replete with typical Mayan religious iconography.[105]

It is clear that two centuries or more of exclusively Christian civilization just simply did not exist, in this time period, conservatively covering modern Ecuador to northern Mexico. The BOM narrative further describes Christian centers all the way from Nephi to the coming of Christ, indicating that Christian sites should be found even in pre-Christian centuries.

Table 2 reviews relevant archaeological sites and relevant finds. The ⸸ sign indicates only a few of the sites with finds related to Mayan-Olmec polytheism in what should be an exclusively Christian BOM era. An examination of the dig reports would uncover many more.

Nephite-Lamanite Curses

The most remarkable curse in the *Book of Mormon* is that put by God on the Lamanites, making them dark and loathsome. Beyond that, it is amply clear throughout the BOM narrative that God curses the land due to the sins of the inhabitants. These curses are not treated as being false teachings or superstitions. In the *Book of Mormon*, curses are real.

---

[105] See, for example, Michael Love & Jonathan Kaplan, eds., *The Southern Maya in the Late Preclassic: The Rise and Fall of Early Mesoamerican Civilization* (Boulder, CO: University Press of Colorado, 2011).

Chapter 7

Nephite-Lamanite Intangible Culture: Language

A major task faced by the BOM authors was the creation of a name list for all the personal and geographic names in their narrative. Research into a somewhat similar phenomenon has been done on speaking in tongues. In 1972, a linguist, William J. Samarin, published his now classic study using extensive recordings made in religious meetings in Italy, the Netherlands, Jamaica, Canada and the USA. He included Puerto Ricans of the Bronx, the snake handlers of the Appalachians and others. One of his main findings was that those presumably speaking in tongues never used sounds alien to their own language. Their discourse was made up of syllables, combined in various ways, with language-like intonation and rhythm, but lacking internal organization.[106] In another study, Felicitas Goodman found similar results.[107]

The generation of names for the Nephite narrative shares some of these traits. But it differs in that the names need not be all made up. The repertoire can include names from the Bible. On the other hand, since many names need not have any referent outside the fertile minds of the authors, their analysis is fraught with hazards.

The Brass Plates of Laban: Establishing the Language Base

For our analysis, the Brass Plates of Laban raise the question: To what extent does one expect to find Hebrew in the *Book of Mormon*, and to what extent Egyptian? Nephi states that his father had lived all his days in Jerusalem, while at the same time referring to Egyptian as the language of his (Nephi's) father. It is hard to imagine that these two statements are not at odds. He claimed to be descended from Joseph. This implies that he would have hailed from the tribe of Joseph. When the tribe of Levi was made into a priestly cast and scattered among the other tribes, their territory was reallocated, along with that of Joseph,

---

[106] William J. Samarin, *Tongues of Men and Angels: the Religious Language of Pentecostalism* (New York: Macmillan, 1972).
[107] Felicitas D. Goodman, *Speaking in Tongues: a Cross-cultural Study of Glossolalia* (Chicago: University of Chicago Press, 1972).

making tribes of each of Joseph's sons, Manasseh and Ephraim. These tribes were located in the north, in what had become the northern kingdom, after the conflict between Solomon's sons, Jeroboam and Rehoboam, which had divided the tribes into two Kingdoms, Judah in the south, and Israel in the North. When Nephi says that he went to the land of his inheritance to get the silver, gold and other precious things (left there by his father) to buy the Brass Plates, he must have gone to the north, to the land of Israel. Lehi was of the tribe of Manasseh (Alma 10:3), perhaps from the capital city Shechem. It would appear that one or some of Lehi's forebears had moved from this land of their inheritance to Jerusalem, possibly during the time of the Assyrian conquest of the Kingdom of Israel in the north, but certainly before his birth. Nephi and his siblings too must have been reared in Jerusalem, with their father. Surely their first language must have been Hebrew.

Even so, Nephi made plates with his own hands (1 Nephi 1:17) and wrote his history in Egyptian. (1 Nephi 1:2) This must have been the Egyptian of the period of the plates, Late Egyptian or Demotic, rather than reformed Egyptian. Nephi states (1 Nephi1 3:19 "And behold, it is wisdom in God that we should obtain these records, that we may preserve unto our children the language of our fathers." That Egyptian was an acquired language even for Lehi is clear.

> For it were not possible that our father, Lehi, could have remembered all these things, to have taught them to his children, except it were for the help of these plates; for he having been taught in the language of the Egyptians therefore he could read these engravings, and teach them to his children, that thereby they could teach them to their children, and so fulfilling the commandments of God, even down to this present time. (Mosiah 1:4)

So he spoke Hebrew, but was taught Egyptian. Even though the first language of the people must have been Hebrew, and in spite of the sacred stamp of the Hebrew language, and its symbolic value for ethnic and religious pride, inexplicably he chose to write in Egyptian. (1 Nephi 1:2) When Alma passed the records to his son Helaman, he said (Alma 37):

> 2. And I also command you that ye keep a record of this people, according as I have done, upon the plates of Nephi, and keep all these things sacred which I have kept, even as I have kept them...

7. Nephite-Lamanite Intangible Culture: Language   147

3. And these plates of brass, which contain these engravings, which have the records of the holy scriptures upon them, which have the genealogy of our forefathers, even from the beginning

Each member in this line of succession taught the Egyptian language to his sons, to pass on the ability to read and continue the record. The fact that this instruction was necessary shows that Egyptian was not their spoken language, but rather a scriptural, literary, liturgical but otherwise dead language. The *Book of Mormon* claim is, therefore, that an elite among the people were bilingual, speaking Hebrew, but using Egyptian largely as a scriptural and possibly liturgical language, a bit like Latin in Italy, confined to the Vatican.

This is reflected in the statement of Mormon, when speaking of his production of the text on the gold plates, saying that he wrote in reformed Egyptian which had been "handed down and altered by us, according to our manner of speech," due to a shortage of gold, apparently implying Egyptian was a more compact language. Notably he added, "if we could have written in Hebrew, behold, ye would have had no imperfection in our record." This indicates that he was able to write in Hebrew better than in Egyptian. Clearly, the first language of the Nephites was Hebrew, although among them there was an elite who handed down a knowledge of the Egyptian needed to read the Brass Plates, i.e. Late Egyptian or Demotic.

The assertion that both Egyptian and Hebrew had been altered over the course of a millennium in the New World is not unusual. Language always changes. Even so, the Semitic languages display remarkable resistance to change, largely due to their triconsonantal structure and the forms used to generate vocabulary. Even Coptic resembles ancient Egyptian to such an extent that Champollion, who knew Coptic, was able to use it to decipher the Rosetta Stone text, once he had identified enough of the phonological characters. Two of the principal factors that promote language change are the adoption of a language by a substrate population that speaks some other language, and influences from neighboring languages, especially languages with considerable cultural dominance. Egyptian and Hebrew among the Nephites would have suffered neither of these influences, since the land is claimed to have been devoid of human beings prior to Lehi's arrival. Especially Egyptian should have remained largely intact, existing in splendid isolation, and used mostly as a written scriptural language. For example, the transformation from classical Latin to church Latin did not produce a major change in the language, and almost no change in script.

Even the nature of change that had befallen Egyptian among the Nephites seems to have affected mostly the system of writing. In Mormon 9:32, Moroni says, "we have written this record according to our knowledge, in the characters which are called among us the reformed Egyptian..." Even so, there would also have been some change in the language itself, similar to the shift from classical to church Latin.

Many other records existed. In Helaman 3:15 we read "But behold, there are many books and many records of every kind, and they have been kept chiefly by the Nephites." By the time of Mosiah, there is a Lamanite language and Nephite languages (Mosiah 9:1: "all the language of the Nephites"). The latter may have included the late Egyptian of the Brass Plates, and already a modified Egyptian in their record-keeping, as well as some regional dialects of Hebrew. Apparently early (classical) Nephite was preferred, the "language of Nephi." Steps are taken to make Nephite the linguistic coin of the realm (Mosiah 24):

> 4. he appointed teachers of the brethren of Amulon, in every land which was possessed by his people: and thus the language of Nephi began to be taught among all the people of the Lamanites.
> 6. they taught them that they should keep their record, and that they might write one to another.

Perhaps what are termed languages are more properly dialects, since Alma says "I attempt to address you in my language." (Alma 7:1)

At this point, the Lamanites "began to increase in riches, and began to trade one with another, and wax great, and began to be a cunning and a wise people, as to the wisdom of the world" (Mosiah 24:7). This trade would require written documents.

Communications by sending epistles was very common (Moroni 8:1; Alma 54:14-15; 56:1; 57:1-3; 59:3-4; 60:1; 60:25; 61:1 & 9; 61:19; 3 Nephi 3:1; 3:10; Mormon 3:4; 6:2; Ether 15:4-5; 15:18; and Moroni 8:6). Messages were often sent, and though some may have been delivered orally, others may have been written (Alma 15:4; 43:24; 47:12; & 47:33). Decrees were issued (Alma 23:2). Proclamations were "published throughout all the land" (Alma 22:27; 23:1; 30:57; 47:1; 61:6; Helaman 9:9; 3 Nephi 3:22 Mosiah 2:1; 7:17; & 27:2). The scriptures were sent out to teach the people: "Now behold, all those engravings which were in the possession of Helaman were written and sent forth among the children of men throughout all the land, save it were those parts which had been commanded by Alma should not go forth." (Alma 63:12) A case of book burning (burning of the scriptures) shows that a burnable material was used for copies of sacred writings: "they also brought forth their records which contained the Holy Scriptures, and cast them into the fire also, that they might be burned and destroyed by fire." (Alma 14:8)

The Nephite/Lamanite civilization is described as being very advanced, with numerous cities, many of them fortified, kingship, coinage, advanced metallurgy, wheeled vehicles, large armies and a written tradition in two languages. Writing must have been essential to keep inventories, write contracts and conduct business. Indeed, in parts of the ancient Middle East, these mundane applications were the earliest and most common use of writing. Since the account of the Nephites and Lamanites spans a period of over 1,000 years, certainly they would have left written material, in both languages, monumental inscriptions, commemorative inscriptions, signet rings, seal stamps and bullae, texts on jars used for votive offerings, royal and business correspondence, documents (contracts, inventories, marriage and divorce writs, and scriptures), tomb inscriptions and inscribed bone boxes. Some principal cities would have had a royal archive. Apparently, metal plates were a common medium for records in the *Book of Mormon*.

Even if the Hebrew writing system was altered, the alphabet has only twenty-two characters. Its form at the end of the seventh century BCE is known to scholars from inscriptions. If a text in altered Hebrew were to be found, a specialist would readily identify the alphabet, and basic translation would be possible in probably no more than a year. Subtle shifts in the meaning of some words, and neologisms, would provide grist for the scholars' publication mills for many years. It is even now so with Biblical Hebrew and the corpus of Hebrew inscriptions. Joseph Smith's transcription of characters from the gold plates would readily identify texts written in reformed Egyptian, but its decipherment would be more complex and take longer. Certainly the character set would be larger, and logograms would exist alongside phonological characters. Even so, there is no reason to assume that this challenge would be greater than that faced by Champollion. Above all, minimally, archaeologists should be digging up textual material that is unidentified, not Mayan, or part of the Zapotec/Oaxacan/Aztec systems. In spite of massive archaeological exploration and excavation in the New World, no unidentified writing has been found that could be a candidate for a Nephite or Lamanite text.

Some Conclusions

1. The claim is extremely unlikely that the Hebrew scriptures had been collected as a sort of Bible, and translated into Egyptian, by the end of the seventh century BCE.
2. The *Book of Mormon* shows that Hebrew was the first language of the Nephites, and Egyptian was a written scriptural language.
3. The *Book of Mormon* states that there were many records of every kind, and correspondence.
4. If the Nephite/Lamanite civilization existed in the Americas without a substrate population and language, or neighbors using other languages, then their Hebrew and Egyptian would have existed in ideal circumstances to resist change.
5. Such a large and advanced civilization, existing for over 1,000 years in the Americas should have left written artifacts that can be deciphered, or at the very least, there should be unidentified texts that are candidates for ancient Nephite texts. No Nephite or Lamanite written material has ever been found, or any unidentified text that could be a candidate for it.

Approaches to the Study of BOM Language Issues

Distribution of BOM Personal Names

The fact that BOM names consist of some taken from the Bible, and others that are decidedly non-Biblical, provides us with our first approach, without even dealing with the analysis of any individual non-Biblical name. As we shall see later, the first part of the *Book of Mormon* was initially written with considerable detail, and the rewrite of that important section omitted much of the detail. Thus the events that took place in the portion that dealt with the Middle East are written in a social, cultural and political vacuum, thereby reducing the chance of errors that could be checked. The authors were much more comfortable giving their imaginations greater rein once they had gotten their little band established in the New World, an more so after King Benjamin. The history and cultures there, so long ago, could never be known well enough to prove them wrong, or so they thought. This is reflected in the roster of personal names that populated their narrative.

The band of Israelites arriving from Jerusalem obviously had to have Hebrew names. This was best done by drawing heavily from the Bible. As soon as the founding generation had died, they switched to made-up names, to give an exotic expression to a world that is uncharted and unknowable, apart from what one learns in their new bible. Even so, they felt that using such names exclusively for the disciples of Jesus would be just too strange for devout readers. To give a sacred cachet to the story of Jesus in the New World, they used some of the most illustrious names in the Bible associated with their period: Isaiah, Jeremiah, Jonas, Timothy and Zedekiah. These are joined by the name of their founding hero and prophet, Nephi. The two Christian centuries were followed by apostasy, a reemergence of the Nephite/Lamanite division, and the annihilation of the Nephites. This period is once again dominated by made-up names.

Table 11. Distribution of Nephite/Lamanite Names

	Biblical Names Are in Bold Type.		
Israel	Enos to the Birth of Christ	The Christian Centuries (34-231 CE)	Apostasy & Annihilation (231-421)
Lehi, Laman, **Lemuel**, Nephi, **Jacob**, **Sam**, **Joseph**, **Sariah**, **Ishmael**, Zoram **Laban**	Enos, **Shem**, Jarom, Omni, Amaron, Chemish, Abinadom, **Amaleki**, Mosiah, **Benjamin**, Mosiah, Mormon, **Aaron**, Abinadi, Amulon, Helorum, Helamon, Himni, **Antipus**, Ammon, Helam, Helem, **Hem**, Limhi, **Amaleki**, Ammon, **Noah**, Zeniff, Laman, Laman, Alma, Alma, Aminadi, Amulon, Helaman, Mulek, Omner, **Gideon**, Amlici, Ammonihah, Zeram, Amnor, Manti, Limher, Antinephilehi, Isabel, Nephihah, Amulek, Giddonah, Ishmael, Zeezrom, Seantum, Zoram, Zoram, Lehi, Aha, Zoram, Antionah, **Lehi**, Lamoni, Abish, Muloki, Antiomno, **Ammah**, Korihor, Helaman, Nephi, Shiblon, Corianton, Gazelem, Zerahemnah, Moroni, Nehor, Amalickiah, Laman, Lehonti, Teancum, **Lehi**, Pahoran, Ammoron, **Jacob**, Paanchi, Pacumeni, Pahoran, Gid, Morianton, Cumeni, Teomner, Pachus,	**Jesus Christ**, Nephi, **Timothy**, **Jonas**, Mathoni, Mathonihah, Kumen, Kumenonhi, **Jeremiah**, Shemnon, **Jonas**, **Zedekiah**, **Isaiah**, Nephi, **Amos**, **Amos**	Ammaron, **Aaron**, Mormon, Mormon, Moroni, Gidgiddonah, Lamah, Limhah, Joneam, Camenihah, Moronihah, Antionum, Amoron, Shiblom, **Gilgal**, **Shem**, Josh, Archeantus, Luram, Emron, Zenephi

(Table 11 continued)

	Moronihah, Hagoth, Coriantumr, Tubaloth, Gadianton, Kishkumen, Cezoram, **Aminadab**, Nephi, **Lehi**, **Samuel**, Lachoneus, Lachoneus, Giddianhi, Gidgiddoni, Zemnariha, **Jacob**			
11 8 Biblical (70%)	106 17 Biblical (15%)		16 9 Biblical (56%)	21 3 Biblical (17%)

Note: A few Biblical entries are not identical with Biblical names, but very close (e.g. Sariah; cf. Sarah, Sarai, Saraiah). Excluding them would not change the results. Sources: Alvin Knisley, *Book of Mormon Dictionary*, and "An Alphabetical Table of the Proper Names in the Old and New Testaments", in *The Holy Bible* (Philadelphia: M. Carey & Son, 1821).

Book of Mormon Phonology

The distribution of words by the first letter in the Nephite narrative is equally interesting. We cannot analyze Jaredite phonology in any meaningful way, since, according to that narrative, their language escaped the Tower of Babel confusion of languages, and so we are left to assume that they spoke the language of Noah, which theological creativity can assume to have existed, and to have been the language of Adam, or some approximation to it. The linguistic heritage of Nephite/Lamanite inhabitants is said clearly to have been Hebrew, as a spoken language, and Egyptian as a scriptural/liturgical language. BOM names should reflect their phonology.

Using Knisley's *Dictionary of All Proper Names in the Book of Mormon*, we can make the following observations regarding non-Biblical personal names in the Nephite narrative:

1. There are no personal names beginning with *b* or *d*, although these are common in both Hebrew and Egyptian.
2. The exception to this is "deseret" which the BOM defines as "honey bee" while there is no phonologically similar word in Middle Eastern languages with this meaning.
3. The letter *c* is used as in English, for both *s* (Cezoram) and *k* (Corianton).

4. The sound *ch* is found pronounced as in "choice" (Chemish) although there is no such sound in Hebrew; while the closest in Egyptian is pronounced differently (more like *ts*).

5. The letter *j* pronounced as in "justice" does not exist in Hebrew. The letter usually written as *j* is *y* in Hebrew. So Jerusalem in Hebrew is *Yerushalayim* (*yərūšālayim*) and Joseph is *Yoseph* (*yōsēp*). When words from Latin passed into French, this sound shifted to the French *j* and so Latin *"Justitia"* (*iustitia*) became *justice* in French, and was so borrowed into English. Many Biblical names that should be pronounced with initial *y* came into English with initial *j*. Some north-European languages have retained the original *y* pronunciation for *j*.

6. This said, many Hebrew words beginning with *y* came into English with initial *i*, such as Israel and Ishmael. In Hebrew, these are *Yiśrā'ēl* and *Yišmā''ēl* respectively. These are often names that are actually third person singular imperfect verbs ("May he [El, God] strive" and "May he [El, God] hear", respectively). These names are common in Hebrew. But in the BOM, there are no names beginning with *y* at all, and none beginning with *i* that were not taken from the Bible.

7. The absence of initial *f* and *ph* personal names is consistent with Hebrew, since it has no letter *f*. Even in late Hebrew this is true in the initial position. In Egyptian initial *f* is used in names.

8. The sound *w* existed in Egyptian, and in early Hebrew (although in late Hebrew it shifted to *v*). No BOM personal name begins with either sound.

Given the number of personal names in the Nephite narrative, it is obvious that there are inexplicable gaps in its phonological lineup, which is consistent with the artificial nature of BOM name creation.

BOM Name Generation

We will never know as much as we would like to know about the generation of the names found in the *Book of Mormon*. It is not possible to learn of all of the source elements that were used in this process, and, above all, one cannot get into the minds of the BOM authors. This said, once again, it is hoped that a real-world comparison might throw some light on the subject. Since it is the Bible that the authors took as their model, at least to a significant extent, one beginning point is to examine its names, and in particular, the degree of multiple occurrence of the same name, but borne by different individuals. The following list has been culled from a dictionary of Biblical names.[108] It is a collection of names that are not borne by more than one person in the Old Testament (and almost always in the New Testament as well), and are sufficiently prominent as OT heroes or eponymous ancestors that one might think that they would have been among the first choices of parents seeking a name for their child.

Table 12. 118 Personal Names Borne by Only 1 Individual in the Old Testament

Abel (also in five compounds), Abigail, Abinadab, Abram/Abraham, Absalom, Adam, Ahab, Ahaz, Ahaziah, Ahijah, Asher, Baruch, Benjamin, Dan, Daniel, David, Deborah, Delilah, Dinah, Elijah/Elias, Elkanah, Ephraim, Er, Esau, Esther, Eve, Ezekiel, Ezra, Gad, Gideon, Gog, Goliath, Habakkuk, Hagar, Haggai, Ham, Hannah, Hosea, Jacob, Japhet, Jeconiah, Jehoash, Jehoiachin, Jeconiah, Jehoiakim/Eliakim, Jephthah, Jeroboam, Jerusha, Jesse, Jethro, Jezebel, Jonah, Joram/Jehoram, Josiah, Isaac, Isaiah, Israel, Issachar, Ithamar, Jubal, Judah, Judith, Kish, Laban, Lamech, Leah, Lemuel, Levi, Lot, Magog, Malachi, Manoah, Medan, Melchisedek, Menahem, Merab, Methuselah, Michal, Miriam, Moab, Mordecai, Moses, Na'am, Na'ashon/Nashon, Nahum, Naomi, Naphtali, Nehemiah, Ner, Nimrod, Noah, Nun, Onan, Ozem, Rachel, Rahab, Rebekah/Rebeccah, Remaliah, Rephael, Reuben, Ruth, Salmon, Samson, Samuel, Sarah/Sarai, Saraiah, Saul, Seth, Shem/Sem, Simeon, Solomon, Terah, Tubal, Uriel, Zebulun, Zeruiah, Zillah, Zilpah, Zipporah

It is surprising that so many prominent names do not recur in the OT books, especially given the large number of names and the near notoriety of some books for their "begats" and genealogical references. This is in spite of the fact that our reference, "The Scripture Dictionary," contains over 3,000 entries.

Our source for BOM names is the work of Knisley,[109] which contains only 506 entries. Both contain entries for locations, and some important words, in addition to personal names. "The Scripture Dictionary" contains some entries that derive from outside the Biblical lands (foreign place names, deities, etc.), while Knisley's work contains

---

[108] "An Alphabetical Table of the Proper Names in the Old and New Testaments," in *The Holy Bible Containing the Old and New Testaments, together with the Apocrypha* (Philadelphia: M. Carey & Son, 1824), 1067-73.

[109] Knisley, *Dictionary of all Proper Names in the* Book of Mormon.

names from Biblical inclusions. All in all, they are comparable name lists.

First we note significant BOM name underpopulation. Although the BOM covers over 1,000 years of history, its name list is under 20% of the number in the OT.

Second, a large proportion of the BOM names are applied to two or more individuals. Unlike the OT, prominent names are especially given to this trend.

Table 13. BOM Name Recurrence

The number of persons bearing the name is in parentheses
Exact Personal Names:
Aaron (3), Alma (2), Amaleki (2), Ammon (2), Amos (2), Cohor (3), Com (2), Coriantum (2), Coriantumr (3), Corihor (2), Helaman (3), Heth (2), Ishmael (2), Jacob (3), Jared (2), Jonas (2), Lachoneus (2), Laman (4), Lamoni (2), Lehi (4), Lib (2), Mormon (3), Moroni (2), Moronihah (2), Mosiah (2), Nephi (4), Noah (2), Pahoran (2), Shez (2), Shiblom/n (3), Zoram
Similar Personal Names:
Abinadi/Abinadom/Aminadab, Aminadi, Aha/Ahah, Amaleki/Amalickiah/Amlici, Amaron/Ammaron/Ammoron/Amoron/Moron/Moroni/Moronihah, Ammon/Ammonihah, Amos/Amoz Amulek/Amulon, Anti-Christ/Anti-Nephi-Lehi, Antiomno/Antionah/Antionum/Antum, Antipas/Antipus, Cezoram/Seezoram/Zeezrom, Com/Comnor, Corianton/Coriantor/Coriantum/Coriantumr, Corihor/Korihor, Cumen/Kumen/Kumenonhi/Kish/Kishkumen/Pacumeni, Emer/Emron, Esrom/Ezrom, Ethem/Ether, Gadiandi/Gadianton/Gadiaomnah, Gideon/Giddianhi/Giddonah/Gidgiddonah/Gidgiddoni, Gilgah/Gilgal, Helam/Helaman/Helem/Helorum, Jashon/Jershon, Jonas/Joneam, Kib/Kim/Kimnor, Lamah/Laman/Lamoni, Limah/Limher/Limhi/Limnah, Morianton/Moriantum, Mulek/Amulek/Mulok/Muloki, Nephi/Nephihah, Nimrah/Nimrod, Omer/Omner/Omni/Teomner, Riplah/Kish/Riplakish/Ripliancum, Seantum/Teancum, Shemlon/Shemnon/Shiblon/Shiblom/Shiblum, Zonock/Zenos, Zeram/Zerin, Zarahemla/Zerahemnah
City Names (Often from Personal Names)
Nephi, Zarahemla, Helam, Lehi-Nephi, Shemlon, Shilom, Aaron, Ammonihah, Bountiful, Gideon, Jerusalem (Lamanite), Lemuel, Shimnilom, Zarahemla, Antiparah, Judeah, Lehi, Moroni, Mulek, Nephihah, Onmer, Zeezrom, Gid, Gad, Gadiandi, Gadiomnah, Gilgal, Gimgimno, Jacob, Josh, Kishkumen, Laman, Moronihah, Onihah, Angola, Desolation, Jashon, Jordan, Shem, Teancum

The first group in this table reflects the need for efficiency, since duplication is the easiest way to generate names. The second group is name generation by free association. A slight modification or recombination of elements already used can readily produce additional names.

Syllable Generation

The production of speech-like utterances in the practice of speaking in tongues differs from the BOM generation of names, in that the former is an extemporaneous phenomenon. The BOM authors still did need to develop a number of syllables that they could recombine, but could do so in a more studied and deliberate manner. An example is the ending *antum* and its permutations. These include: Antum, Irreantum, Coriantum (twice), Coriantumr (thrice), Corianton, Coriantor, Gadianton, Gadianti, Morianton, Ripliancum, Seantum and Teancum. Although we cannot be certain as to the source of this element, we may not have to look further than to the first settlement of Indian converts to Christianity in New England, Nonantum, founded by John Elliot, the Apostle to the Indians, whose work was used as an example and goal in the Second Great Awakening, which exercised the minds and aspirations of so many in the first three decades of the nineteenth century.

Some other examples of syllable components are worth mentioning:

Table 14. Names Ending in *hor*

Cohor (1)	the first rebel in the Jaredite narrative
Cohor (2)	a rebel who killed his own father to gain power
Cohor (3)	one of a group who refused repentance
Corihor (1)	rebelled against his father, raised an army in Land of Nehor, imprisoned his father
Corihor (2)	mentioned with other impenitents
Korihor	an anti-Christ who opposed Alma
Nehor	a false teacher who murdered Gideon
Nehors	Order of the Nehors, a false religious system
Nehor	the refuge, land and apparently city of Corihor

Free association also appears manifest in the *-hor* (whore) names. All such occurrences are names of bad men, impenitents, patricides, and an anti-Christ. In this context, we remember that Nephite theology holds that there is only one true church, and all others are collectively the work of Satan, and are the *Whore of All the Earth*, a key BOM *cri de guerre*.

Table 15. Evil vs. Good: Gad and Gid Names

Gad Names	
Gad	a wicked city that was burned as divine punishment
Gadiandi	a wicked city that was sunk in the earth as divine punishment
Gadianton	the founder of the Gadianton Robbers, based on oaths & secrets inspired by Satan
Gadiomna	a wicked city that was sunk in the earth as divine punishment

(Table 15 continued)

Gid Names	
Gid	a victorious Nephite military officer
Gid	Nephite city, captured by Lamanite Amalickiah, but retaken by Nephite Moroni
Giddianhi	a leader of the Gadianton Robbers
Giddonah	presiding High Priest over the Nephite church
Gideon	Nephite military leader & teacher, who delivered Limhi's people of from bondage
Gideon	Nephite city, threatened by woe by Samuel; not listed among the cites destroyed
Gidgiddonah	a Nephite commander slain in the battle of Cumorah
Gidgiddoni	Commander in Chief of all Nephite armies in the Gadianton-Nephite war

All Gad names are of bad men or cities, while nearly all Gid names are good, including four Nephite heroes and one High Priest. The exception is Giddianhi. In this case, we may have a deliberate dissimulating alteration of the name Gadianton. The association of Gad with evil may have come simply from its rhyming with "bad," or from the fact that the tribe of Gad had joined the rebellion of the Israelite tribes of the north against the Davidic kingdom, and the prophets of Judah, including Isaiah and Jeremiah. Or it may have been drawn from the city name Baal-gad, the northernmost city smitten by Joshua (Joshua 11:17). On a more popular level, it may have derived this connotation from the expression "Egad!"/"Ye Gad!" (By God!), a euphemism for taking the name of God in vain. Even worse was the original more heathen expression, "Egads!"/"Ye Gads". In the still puritanical New England, especially in religious circles, such profanity was not taken lightly. Compare the vowel contrast between God and Gad.

Another element used in name generation is the prefix *-anti*, as in: Anianti, Anti-Nephi-Lehi, Antiomno, Antionah, Antionum, Antiparah, Antipas, Antipus and Archeantus.

Where Are the Expected Hebrew Elements?

There are recurrent elements in language. We would expect personal and location names given by a people speaking Hebrew to have at least some such elements from Hebrew.

These pairs are inseparable. *Aḥijah (Aḥiya)* is "Brother of Yahweh (Jehovah). His name would never be just *Aḥi* (brother), nor could you call him Jehovah. Brother of Jehovah would have had the sense of Godly, as well as one favored by Jehovah. Aḥimelek, brother of the King (God) has similar connotations. Abiel is (my) Father is God, where

Table 16. Name Elements in Biblical Hebrew

adon-	'dn אדנ	lord, as in Adonijah (Adoniya), Adonizedek	None
ab-/abi-	'b/'by אבי/אב	father of	Abinadi, Abinadom—compare both with Biblical Abinadab
aḫi-	'ḫi אחי	brother of, as in Aḫijah (Aḫiya), brother of Jehovah	None (Note that the sound *j* does not exist in Hebrew; but *y* became *j* in French, & English got it through French.)
ben-/beni-	bn/bny בני/בנ	son of, as in Benaiah Son of Yahweh (Jehovah), Bǝnēbǝraq, Sons (clan) of Bǝraq	None, except Biblical Benjamin
bat-/bit-	bn+t ת+בנ	daughter of (the n combines with the t, a feminine ending	None
yo-/-yah-/yahu	y+hwy הוי+י	Short versions of Yahweh (Jehovah), extremely common	Mosiah is possible, pronounced Mosyah, but it is hard to make it have meaning in Hebrew; Elijah (Eliyah) is Biblical
el-/-el	'l אל	God (El)-as in Samuel and Elhanan	Only Elijah (Eliyah), which is Biblical
ebed-/abd-	'bd עבד	servant of	None
ezer-ezr-azar-	'zr עזר	help, as in Azarel, Ezra, Azar, Azariah (Azar-ya)	None
uzz-azaz-aziz-	'zz עזז	strength, refuge, as in Uzziah (Uzzi-ya/Uzzi-yahu)	Uzziah (Biblical)
malk-/melk-/milk-	mlk מלכ	king, usually as in "my king is (God)": cf. Malkiyah, Malkiel	Melek (Biblical), Malachi (Biblical) Mulek, Muloki—not Hebrew names with God
mika-	my-k-'l מיכאל	Mikah is short for Michael; mi-who (is)+ka-like+el (God): Who is like God	None
Place Names			
bet-	byt בית	house of, clan of-, as in Bethlehem	Bethabara (Biblical)
en-	'yn עינ	spring of, as in Engedi, Endor	Enosh, but making this work in Hebrew requires gymnastics
migdal	gdl גדל	tower of, as in Migdal-El, Migdal-Gad	None
qirya-qiryat-	qry קרי	town of, as in Qiryatsefer (book city)	None

(Table 16 continued)

| rama-/ram- | rwm
רום | an elevated town, hence defensible, as in Ramah | Ramath (cf. Biblical Ramoth-Gilead); Ramah (Biblical); Rameumpton (needs to be broken up for interpretation) |

the close relationship of father has a function similar to *Aḥi*. When I had a beard in Egypt, some Arabs called me *Ibn liḥya*, son of a beard, i.e., bearded one. *'Obadiah ('Obadya)* is Servant of Jehovah. In some cases, there may have been hypocorism (short forms, or nicknames). How this might have been done can be seen in Arabic, were *'Abdallah* (servant of God) can be shortened to 'Abduh, His (God's) Servant. The second element is removed only by adding *-uh*, the suffixed possessive pronoun.

The same is true of place names. Engedi, "Gedi Spring," is never just Spring, nor just Gedi. Just as my hometown, Green River is never just Green, nor just River. Bethlehem was never just *bēt*, nor just *leḥem*. Both *bēt* (house, place of, clan of) names and *'ēn* (spring) names are common in Hebrew.

It is inconceivable that a Hebrew people, speaking Hebrew at least as their first language, would not have a good share of these elements, which are not just standard in Hebrew, but in the Semitic languages generally. The *Book of Mormon* names are mostly made up, and the common types of names expected in Hebrew are virtually nonexistent. But given the lack of relevant background of the prospective readership, this defect was not an obstacle to successful proselytism.

Investigation into Specific Names

The easiest names to analyze are those that should not be in the *Book of Mormon*, such as Timothy, Jonas, Lachoneus and Archeantus (all analyzed above).

Lehi, Nephi, Nephites and Lamanites

Although there are many made-up personal and place names in the *Book of Mormon*, one cannot resist speculating about certain key names. Among these are the prophet/patriarch who was commanded to leave Jerusalem, Lehi, and his able, devoted and devout son, Nephi. We can add to these the names of the two main groups, the Nephite protagonists and Lamanite antagonists.

Rick Grunder has referred us to *Walker's Critical Pronouncing Dictionary* published in Boston in 1823,[110] which lists La′ban, Lah′man, Le′hi, and Lem′u-el in close proximity to each other on page 361, and Ne′phi on page 363. This leaves the issue of name selection. Note that Nephi is found in the Catholic Douay-Reims Bible, where it is a toponym in 2 Machabees 1:36.

Lehi appears to be easy, since it is the name of the place where Samson slew a thousand Philistines with a new jawbone of an ass. Given the emphasis on slaughter in the *Book of Mormon*, it is easy to think that this passage would have appealed to Joseph Smith. The name could have been further recommended by the phonology and meaning of Le High, the Le High River, Valley and Pass. In 1822, Le High was made a county of Pennsylvania. Was not Lehi a "high" leader in the eyes of the Lord? To the extent that young Smith identified with Nephi, he may have associated Lehi with his own father, whom he made the new church's first Patriarch, a position comparable to Lehi.

The BOM project was conceived, framed and carried out during part of the Second Great Revival, with one of its emphases being the conversion of the Indians. During this period, Indians who converted to Christianity and were taking their first steps in their new faith were called neophytes. This is an old theological term, meaning a new growth, a term not only applied to converts, but to those entering into a religious calling, such as a person in training to become a monk. Although used for Indian converts commonly in the Catholic missions in the Southwest, the first Methodist mission to western Canada (Alberta) used the term for Indian converts (re Rev. Robert Rundle, 1840).[111] In Smith's fertile imagination, "neophytes" as a term for the Christianized Indians could have readily become "Nephites" for the BOM Christians.

This could have been reinforced by Smith Jr.'s own experience, when he entered into training to be a Methodist exhorter. Like the believer in training to join a monastic order, the exhorter trainee was also a neophyte. In an 1885 source we find a reference to a Methodist

---

[110] John Walker, *Walker's Critical Pronouncing Dictionary, and Expositor of the English Language* [including Scripture Proper Names] (Boston: Lincoln & Edmands, Samuel T. Armstrong, and Charles Ewer, 1823).

[111] John Blue, *Alberta, Past and Present, Historical and Biographical*, Vol 1, Chapter XIV, "Church History in Alberta" (Chicago: Pioneer Historical Publishing Co., 1924).

"neophyte ministry,"[112] which probably was not a neologism at that time. All of this gelled: Christianized Indians were neophytes, Christian Pre-Columbians are Nephites, the Nephites descend from Nephi, akin to Joseph Smith's own Methodist moniker, neophyte.

The neophyte exhorters were in the first stage of possibly becoming a minister, and so were already set apart from the lay members of the church, the laymen. Similarly, Nephi found himself at odds with his older brother, Laman.

As reasonable as this can be made to sound, we must remember that we cannot really put ourselves into the minds of the BOM authors.

Gadianton, and the Gadianton Robbers

Since the Gadianton cabal is a chief antagonist to the Nephites, it is not surprising that there has been some interest in the origin of the name. The simplest hypothesis is that it is simply the result of combining elements already introduced into the BOM narrative (Gadi-anton): Gad, Gadiandi, Gadiomnah, Antianti, Antiomno and Antionum. Need one search further? Gad, as we have seen, is a name element associated with great evil. Conceivably the name Gadianton is composed of two syllabic elements.

Another intriguing possibility has been brought to my attention by Dale Broadhurst. Perhaps it comes from the Gades Pirates. Here we have more than just phonology. There is also a meaning component: robbers and pirates. In addition, fledgling America was somewhat seized with the recent-history event of President Jefferson's war against the Pirates of Barbary (of the Berbers). Both the Gades Pirates and the Pirates of Barbary preyed upon ships in the western Mediterranean. One difference is that the former operated out of the Iberian seaport on the north coast, Gades, while the latter operated out of North Africa, on the southern coast. The problem with this is that Gades is a name found in ancient Greek and Roman sources. By the early 19th century, Gades had long since been known by the Spanish name Cadiz. Perhaps some newspaper article regarding Jefferson's campaign had made reference to the Gades pirates? Lacking the discovery of such an article that the BOM authors

---

[112] Bishop H. M. Turner, *The Genius and Theory of Methodist Polity, or the Machinery of Methodism* (Philadelphia: Publication Department, A. M. E. Church, 1885), v.

cold have read, it is not clear that they would have had access to base Gadianton on the Gades Pirates.

Barring the emergence of additional information, the truth may be that we may never know the genesis of this key BOM name.

The Generation of Aliases

Joseph Smith apparently came to delight in name generation, to the point that he devised various aliases for himself and some of his associates. One, Gazelem, is found in the *Book of Mormon* (Alma 37:23) in connection with a "stone, which shall shine forth in darkness unto light, that I may discover unto my people who serve me, that I may discover unto them the works of their brethren…" This name is used for Joseph Smith in D&C 78:9, where he is called Gazelem, or Enoch. Twenty-four aliases were used in five sections of the 1835 D&C, 78, 82, 92, 96 and 103. These aliases were not original to the original language of the revelations, which used only the real names. Their substitution seems to have been in order to instruct members how to refer to people and places in any situation that could involve persecutors or creditors. It is no accident that all of these refer to the United Firm (United Order) that Smith had established in Kirtland, which was having difficulties with its creditors, and eventually defaulted. In addition, aliases were also used in two sections of the 1844 edition of the D&C, 104 and 105.[113]

Table 17. Names & Aliases after *Book of Mormon* Publication

Name	Meaning with Section References to the 1835, 1864 and Current D&C
Gazelem (seer stone gazer, foretold in the BOM, & used later by Joseph Smith Jr.) Ahashdah (Newel K. Whitney; 1835, 75; D&C 78) Enoch (Joseph Smith, Jr.; 1835, 75; D&C 78) Pelagoram (Sidney Rigdon; 1835, 75; D&C 78) Alam (Edward Partridge; 1835, 86; D&C 82) Mahalaleel (Sidney Gilbert; 1935, 86; D&C 82)	

---

[113] Orson Pratt, "Explanation of Substituted Names in the Covenants," *Millennial Star,* 16 (March 18, 1854): 171–73; & Steven C. Harper, "Selected Teachings on Why Code Names Were Used in the D&C," published online on http//:www.scottwoodward.org (accessed 21/01/2017).

(Table 17 continued)

Horah, (John Whitmer; 1835, 86; D&C 82)
Olihah (Oliver Cowdery; 1835, 86; D&C 82)
Shalemanasseh (William W. Phelps; 1835, 86; D&C 82)
Mahemson (? Jesse Gause, or Martin Harris? 1835, 86; D&C 82)
Shederlaomach (Frederick G. Williams; 1835, 93; D&C 92)
Zombre (John Johnson; 1835, 96; D&C 96)
Seth (Joseph Smith; 1835, 96; D&C 96)
Tahhanes (Tan<n>ery; 1835, 98; D&C 104)
Shinehah (revealed name for Kirtland, Ohio; 1835, 86; D&C 82)
lane-shine-house (printing office; 1835, 86; D&C 82)
Shinelah (print: "to shinelah my words;" 1835, 86; D&C 82)
Shine-lane (printing; 1835, 86; D&C 82)
Ozondah (revealed name for the LDS store in Kirtland, Ohio; 1835, 86; D&C 82)
Mahemson (Martin Harris; 1835, 86; D&C 82)
shule (Ashery, converts wood to lye, potash and pearl ash; 1835, 86; D&C 82)
Talents (dollars; 1835, 86; D&C 82)
Cainhannoch (New York; 1835, 86; D&C 82)
Baurak ale (Joseph Smith ; 1864, 102; D&C 103)
Baneemy (Sidney Rigdon according to Orson Pratt, but currently "my elders;" 1864, 102; D&C 103)
Ahman (Possibly: the LDS deity, the Son & Redeemer [Jesus], presumably from the pure Adamic language)
Adam-ondi-Ahman (Generally held to be the place of Adam and Ahman, i.e. Eden)
Master Mahan, (Cain "master of the great secret, that I may murder and get gain", who "gloried in his wickedness" [also Lamech)]
Nauvoo (name chosen for the LDS capital in Illinois)

Names with Middle Eastern Referents

Since they assumed that the knowledge of Egyptian would never be known, and some other languages of the Middle East were at least not known by their prospective audience, it would be safe to be more adventurous in the realm of linguistics. Not so. Efforts, in the *Book of Mormon* and *The Book of Abraham*, to show off a knowledge of these languages backfired royally.

Not one of these made-up words corresponds phonologically to a word in any Semitic language.[114]

---

[114] See A. Chris Eccel, *Sembase, a Database for the Semitic Languages* (http//:www.sembase.org), prepared for a comparative dictionary of the Semitic languages; work in progress).

Table 18. Names with "Interpreted" Semitic or Egyptian Content

Word	Translation	Is it found in Middle Eastern Languages?
Mormon	more good (source: a statement attributed to Joseph Smith)	Neither component (mor & mon) means 'more' or 'good' in any Middle Eastern language. (As a powerful military man, 'more man' makes more sense, but who knows the authors' thinking?)
Liahona	compass (to guide Lehi in the wilderness east of Canaan/Negev)	There was no compass, much less a word for one; no word with appropriate meaning can be found in any Middle Eastern language
Irreantum	many waters	no
Ripliancum	large, to exceed all	no
Rameumpton	the holy stand	no
Deseret	honey bee	no
Ziff	an unknown metal	no
Elkenah	an Egyptian god	no
Libnah	an Egyptian god	no
Mahmackrah	an Egyptian god	no
Korash	an Egyptian god	no
Rahleenos	hieroglyphics	no
Kolob	the first creation, nearest to the residence of God, first government, a measurement of time	no
Enish-go-on-dosh	one of the governing planets, the sun	no
Kae-e-vanrash	the grand Key, the governing power, governing 15 other fixed planets or stars	nothing in Egyptian to answer to this range of meanings (nor in astronomy)
Floese	the Moon, the Earth and the Sun in their annual revolutions	no
Kli-flos-is-es or Hah-ko-kau-beam	the star represented by the numbers 22 & 23	no for the Egyptian (#'s 22 & 23 in Facsimile 2 are not stars); as for the Hebrew, the second is Smith's rendition of hak-kōkābīm (stars); Smith was studying Hebrew, but was not faring well.

However, note rabbanah (powerful, great king) is not actually a made-up name (cf. NT rabbi and rabboni).

Ziff is a BOM word that has interesting phonological problems. First, even though Early (3rd-millennium) Egyptian shows evidence of the sound *z*, as a legacy from an Afro-Asiatic past, it was mostly merged with *s*, to the extent that Egyptian dictionaries do not list words under the letter *z*. This sound was lost in Middle Egyptian, and absent in Late Egyptian, that of the 1st-millennium BCE, or the time of the destruction of Jerusalem. Second, the letter *f* does not exist in Hebrew. To be sure, the letter *p* shifts to *f* after a vowel in Post-Biblical Hebrew, a phenomenon that developed under Aramaic influence, i.e. during and after the captivity in Babylon, or, more probably later, after Hebrew ceased to be a spoken language. Under the influence of the Aramaic speaking rabbis of Babylon centuries after Christ, this pronunciation was preferred even for reciting Old Testament passages, probably initially for recitation in the synagogues, but made "official" for the OT in the Masoretic text. Even so, a double *p* never shifted to *f*, so there has never been a double *f* in Hebrew. Finally, even allowing for all reasonable phonological alternatives (*zff, zwf, zyf, sff, swf* & *syf* for Egyptian, *zpp* for Hebrew, *zff* for Arabic, and *zpp* for Aramaic and Akkadian), there is no word even roughly corresponding to *ziff*, with the meaning "metal" or any specific metal. Nor is there any pre-Columbian metal that did not have a common English name in the 1820's, thereby requiring the use of a Nephite word. Ziff is phonologically improbable, is unattested in any Middle Eastern language, and lacks a real-world referent.

The *Book of Mormon* also falls into linguistic pitfalls in some of its expressions. A good example is the use of the phrase "straight and narrow" Compare Matthew with 2 Nephi:

> Enter ye in at the strait gate: ... Because strait is the gate, and narrow is the way, which leadeth unto life... (Matthew 7:13-14)

> ..enter into the narrow gate, and walk in the straight path which leads to life... (2 Nephi 33:9)

The verse is paraphrased in various other locations:

> And again, it showeth unto the children of men the straightness of the path, and the narrowness of the gate, by which they should enter... (2 Nephi 31:9)

> straight is the gate, and narrow is the way (3 Nephi 14:14)

Behold, the way for man is narrow, but it lieth in a straight course... (2 Nephi 9:41)

Popular preachers confused *strait* with *straight*, which seems to be a confusion arising from the English language, the two words being homophones, and a confusion between "straight" in Matthew 3:3 ("make his paths straight") and Matthew 7:13-14, above. The wording of 2 Nephi 9:11 shows that this is not just a spelling problem. Actually, the phrase in the New Testament uses a common Semitic form of emphasis through repetition, by using two words with the same meaning: "strait and narrow" means "truly narrow."

The BOM has a tendency to produce words suggested by a word in English. Here are some examples:

my hand hath found the kingdoms of the idols (KJ Isaiah 10:10)
my hand hath founded the kingdoms of the idols (2 Nephi 20:10)

everyone that is found shall be thrust through (Isaiah 13:15)
everyone that is proud shall be thrust through (2 Nephi 23:15)

the raiment of those who are slain (Isaiah 14:19)
 the remnant of those who are slain (2 Nephi 24)

I will break the Assyrians in my land (Isaiah 14:25)
I will bring the Assyrians in my land (2 Nephi 24:25)

As we have seen, producing language-like made-up words from words in one's own language has also been found to be a common phenomenon in the speech of persons claiming to be speaking in tongues.

One Nephite name appears to be a modification of a famous Hebrew OT name: Cumorah from Gomorrah? Cumorah is today almost a Mormon pilgrimage site, the Hill Cumorah being where Moroni buried the plates and then revealed them to Joseph Smith. But in the *Book of Mormon*, it is the place where the Jaredites totally annihilated each other to extinction (Jaredite Ramah being Nephite Cumorah). Under the name Cumorah, it is the place of the last battle where the Lamanites totally annihilated the Nephites. In both cases, it is the place where a people are visited by God with total extinction due to their sins, not unlike Gomorrah. This association could well have been the basis for producing the name Cumorah. Note as well Hermounts, apparently a modification of Mount Hermon.

Another interesting possibility occurs in a passage of the *Book of Moses* (5:31 & 49), which was undertaken only months after the BOM: "And Cain said: Truly I am Mahan, the master of this great secret, that I may murder and get gain Wherefore Cain was called Master Mahan, and he gloried in his wickedness." In the 1820's, there was a campaign against the Freemasons. Given this context, it is impossible to ignore the possibility that Master Mahan is adapted from Master Mason.

Vernal Holley has made a gallant effort to find names in the New York region that could have been the source or inspiration for some *Book of Mormon* names[115] I have added the comments below.

Table 19. BOM Place Names and Locations in the Wider New York Area

Name in the BOM	NY Region Place Name	Comment
Ogath	St. Agathe des Monts, Quebec	No. Founded 1849
Alma, Valley of	Alma, NY	No. Founded 1854
	Alma, WV	? When was it founded?
Antum	Antrim (Hamlet in Ramapo, NY?)	? Difficult phonology
Anti-Anti	Antioch, IL	No. Named in 1843
Boaz	Boaz	No. Named in 1878
Comnor	Conner	Where?
Ephraim, Hill	St. Ephrem de Beauce, Quebec	No. Founded 1866
Helam	Hellam, PA	Possible
Hill Onidah	Oneida County, Oneida Castle, Oneida Indian Nation	Possible.
Jacobugath	Jacobsburg	Difficult phonology
Jordan	Jordan, NY	No. Settlement began in 1825 incorporated in 1835. Why not Biblical Jordan?
Lehi	Lehigh (river, valley, pass, etc.)	Possible
Manti	Mantu? (Mantua, OH?)	Possible
Moroni	Monroe, NY	Difficult phonology
Morianton	Moraviantown	Difficult phonology
Moron	Morin, Ontario	No. Founded 1855
Noah, Land of	Noah Lakes (Noah Lake, MI?)	Why not Biblical Noah?
Omner	Omer, MI	No. Founded 1866
Shilom	Shiloh, NJ	Difficult phonology
Sidom	Sodom, NY	Possible but date unknown
Land of Minon	Minonian Indians	Possible

---

[115] Vernon Holley, Book of Mormon *Authorship*.

(Table 19 continued)

Waters of Ripliancum	On the banks of Lake Superior: Ripple Bay, Ripple Creek, Ripple Reef, Ripple Lake	Possible, as well as a name suggested by *ripple*.
Hill Ramah	Rama Indian Reservation & Rama Township, Ontario, Canada	Rama Township, Ontario is possible, but the Chippewa moved there in 1836. Why not Biblical Ramah?
Angola (fortified city)	Angola, New York (Or Angola, Indiana?)	No. Evans Station was renamed Angola in 1855 due to Quakers who were giving aid to Angola, Africa. Angola, Indiana, dates to even later. Perhaps, Angola Plantation (infamous for enslaving Indians)?
Teancum (city)	Tecumseh (Tenecum), Canada	Possible.
King Gideon	Chief Tadeuskund, baptized in 1750 and christened "Gideon"	Possible, but note Biblical Gideon (place & angel).
Kishkumen (city)	Delaware Indian village Kishkiminetas, near Pittsburgh	Possible. It is about 30 miles northeast of Pittsburgh. Or BOM Kish + Kumen?

Holley's list was made to support the Spalding or Spalding-Rigdon theory of BOM authorship. They are said to be names that these men would have been familiar with. Many turn out to be names that the Smiths and Cowdery might have been familiar with. Another is Irreantum, the name given to the point in Arabia, on the coast of the Indian Ocean, where Lehi and his band constructed a boat and set sail. The narrative says it means "many waters." The BOM authors were quite familiar with both Erie the lake and the canal. The name would simply be Erie with the syllabic element -antum (treated above), or the lakes Erie-Ont(ario)> Irreantum. One drawback is that many of these names are small, little known and remote locations. It is unclear that the BOM authors would have known them. At the time, such places did not figure on the maps of the day. Moreover, for the BOM authors, the important thing was probably to have names with a good ring to them. They may even have tended to avoid local names.

The generation of names shows considerable thought. They could not have been produced in casual composition or extemporaneous dictation.

Chapter 8

The Post-Biblical Euro-Christian Text

When Christianity became rooted in Europe, a process began of developing a new culture, to replace the pre-Christian cultures. This process occurred in widely different European regions, and drew upon pre-Christian elements (Greek philosophy) and the creativity of numerous theologians, church clerics, poets and hymnists. In England, and its New World offshoot, many common cultural elements merged with Biblical elements, to the extent that it was not easy to avoid confusing the two. This was clearly true in the case of the BOM authors, and as a result the BOM text includes Euro-Christian elements that are incompatible with the premise that it was written by pre-Columbian authors, or even pre-Columbian Christian authors.

Post-Biblical Euro-Christian phrases in the BOM text pose a significantly different issue as compared to the Biblical phrases. They cannot be said to be identical elements of divine revelation received by prophets on both sides of the world. In some cases, they are clearly a product of later Christian thought, and in the most serious cases, they are instances of incorrect Biblical interpretation, or even pseudoscientific apologetics.

The assertion that the BOM text quotes Shakespeare helps bring the current study into better focus. The phrase is from lines 79 and 80 in Hamlet, Act 3, Scene 1:

> The undiscovered country from whose bourn
> No traveller returns.

The BOM verse states (2 Nephi 1:14):

> the cold and silent grave, from whence no traveler can return

A tough-minded assessment must not only ask whether these few words, in substantially different contexts, are sufficient to warrant the assertion, but also must face the serious question of transmission. Can we really assume that any of the BOM authors had such familiarity with Hamlet that this phrase would have come to mind? Alternatively, was it part of the common parlance of clerics in rural New England, to the point that they might have heard and acquired it, perhaps not even knowing where it came from? Perhaps. Perhaps not. This example illustrates the problems of asserting the existence of post-Biblical Euro-Christian phrases and/or concepts in the BOM text.

In some cases, the inclusion is a Euro-Christian notion that is an unsustainable interpretation of a Biblical passage. In other cases, it is scientifically wrong. But in most cases, it is a phrase coined in English Euro-Christian devotional or theological literature.

Unsustainable Biblical Interpretation: Satan

Lucifer

> 2 Nephi 2
> 17. And I, Lehi, according to the things which I have read, must needs suppose that an angel of God, according to that which is written, had fallen from heaven; wherefore, he became a devil, having sought that which was evil before God.
> 18. And because he had fallen from heaven, and had become miserable forever, he sought also the misery of all mankind. Wherefore, he said unto Eve, yea, even that old serpent, who is the devil, who is the father of all lies, wherefore he said: Partake of the forbidden fruit, and ye shall not die, but ye shall be as God, knowing good and evil.
>
> 2 Nephi 24:12 (quoting Isaiah 14:12)
> How art thou fallen from heaven, O Lucifer, son of the morning! how art thou cut down to the ground, which didst weaken the nations!

The issue here is not the story itself. The doctrine of a war in heaven is found in the New Testament:

> And there was war in heaven: Michael and his angels fought against the dragon; and the dragon fought and his angels... And the great dragon was cast out, that old serpent, called the Devil, and Satan, which deceiveth the whole world: he was cast out into the earth, and his angels were cast out with him (Revelation 12:7-9; See also Luke 10:18; 2 Corinthians 11:14; & Jude 1:6).

The issue is the interpretation of Isaiah 14:12, as being Old Testament support for this story. The BOM text makes this identification by using the proper name Lucifer. Actually, this passage does not refer to Satan, but is part of a proverb (similitude, tantamount to a curse) that Isaiah was commanded by God to declare against the king of Babylon. The complete curse follows (Isaiah 14, AKJV), with the Lord saying:

> 4. That thou shalt take up this proverb against the king of Babylon, and say, How hath the oppressor ceased! the golden city ceased!
> 5. The LORD hath broken the staff of the wicked, and the sceptre of the rulers.
> 6. He who smote the people in wrath with a continual stroke, he that ruled the nations in anger, is persecuted, and none hindereth.
> 7. The whole earth is at rest, and is quiet: they break forth into singing.
> 8. Yea, the fir trees rejoice at thee, and the cedars of Lebanon, saying, Since thou art laid down, no feller [one who fells trees] is come up against us.
> 9. Hell from beneath is moved for thee to meet thee at thy coming: it stirreth up the dead for thee, even all the chief ones of the earth; it hath raised up from their thrones all the kings of the nations.
> 10. All they shall speak and say unto thee, Art thou also become weak as we? art thou become like unto us?
> 11. Thy pomp is brought down to the grave, and the noise of thy viols: the worm is spread under thee, and the worms cover thee.
> 12. How art thou fallen from heaven, O Lucifer, son of the morning! how art thou cut down to the ground, which didst weaken the nations!
> 13 For thou hast said in thine heart, I will ascend into heaven, I will exalt my throne above the stars of God: I will sit also upon the mount of the congregation, in the sides of the north:
> 14. I will ascend above the heights of the clouds; I will be like the most High.
> 15. Yet thou shalt be brought down to hell, to the sides of the pit.
> 16. They that see thee shall narrowly look upon thee, and consider thee, saying, Is this the man that made the earth to tremble, that did shake kingdoms;
> 17. That made the world as a wilderness, and destroyed the cities thereof; that opened not the house of his prisoners?
> 18. All the kings of the nations, even all of them, lie in glory, every one in his own house.
> 19. But thou art cast out of thy grave like an abominable branch, and as the raiment of those that are slain, thrust through with a sword, that go down to the stones of the pit; as a carcase trodden under feet.
> 20. Thou shalt not be joined with them in burial, because thou hast destroyed thy land, and slain thy people: the seed of evildoers shall never be renowned.

21. Prepare slaughter for his children for the iniquity of their fathers; that they do not rise, nor possess the land, nor fill the face of the world with cities.
22. For I will rise up against them, saith the LORD of hosts, and cut off from Babylon the name, and remnant, and son, and nephew, saith the LORD.
23. I will also make it a possession for the bittern, and pools of water: and I will sweep it with the besom of destruction, saith the LORD of hosts.

This proper name, Lucifer, occurs in the King James Version only once; nowhere else is it used to refer to the Great Serpent. It renders the Hebrew word הֵילֵל (*hēlēl*) in Isaiah 14:12. This word also occurs only once in the Hebrew Bible, and means "shining one, morning star." The Latin Vulgate translated הֵילֵל as *lucifer*, meaning "the morning star, the planet Venus," or, as an adjective, "light-bringing." The Septuagint renders הֵילֵל in Greek as ἑωσφόρος (*heōsphoros*; literally "bringer of dawn"), a name for the morning star.

In this passage Isaiah applies to a king of Babylon the image of the morning star fallen from the sky, an image believed by some scholars to have been borrowed from a legend in Canaanite mythology.

Later Christian tradition came to use the Latin word for "morning star," lucifer, as a proper name ("Lucifer") for Satan as he was before his fall. As a result, Lucifer has become a byword for Satan in much of Euro-Christianity, and in popular literature, as in Dante Alighieri's *Inferno* and John Milton's *Paradise Lost*. However, unlike in English, the Latin word never came to be used almost exclusively in this way, and was applied to others also, including Christ. It is incongruous for a divine translation of Isaiah to use this proper name. It should rather have been "O morning star!"

The morning star is Venus, which was a pagan deity in the Roman pantheon. This may have influenced the evolution of the Roman church's interpretation of Isaiah, and of the Euro-Christian name.

Father of Lies

2 Nephi 2:18. that old serpent, who is the devil, who is the father of all lies (See also 2 Nephi 9:9).

This phrase seems to have derived from John 8: 44,

> Ye are of your father the devil, and the lusts of your father ye will do. He was a murderer from the beginning, and abode not in the truth, because there is no truth in him. When he speaketh a lie, he speaketh of his own: for he is a liar, and the father of it.

The Greek (καὶ ὁ πατὴρ αὐτοῦ.) can say, literally, "the father of it" or "the father of him" or "its/his father." Some modern translations take the interpretive liberty to render the last clauses: "for he is a liar and the father of lies." Many Christian websites ask about this phrase, "father of all lies," so it appears to have become a common Christian phrase, not found in the Bible. "Father of Lies" is the title of a "topic page" of "gospel.com." Similarly, "openbible.info" has a page titled "100 Bible Verses about Father Of All Lies."

Author of All Sin

> Helaman 6:30. And behold, it is he [Satan] who is the author of all sin

The designation "author" is used in the KJ Bible in reference to God ("God is not the author of confusion," 1 Corinthians 14:33) and Jesus ("he became the author of eternal salvation," Hebrews 5:9). By contrast, in English Euro-Christianity, Satan has been called the "author of sin." Ironically, originally it was applied to God. This assertion first appeared in the affirmative by the Gnostic Florinus (c. 180), which was immediately attacked by Ireneaus (130-200), who published a discourse entitled: "God, not the Author of Sin." Florinus' doctrine reappeared in another form later in Manichaeism, of which Augustine was initially a member for nearly a decade before converting to Catholicism. A similar rejection of the charge is found in the work of the American theologian Jonathan Edwards. The assertion that Satan is the author of all sin is found in English Euro-Christianity, but has rarely been stated as boldly and unequivocally as in the BOM passage, since sin is normally treated as being a complex problem involving three actors, God, Satan and man. We find in a sermon of John Wesley ("The End of Christ's Coming"), "'For the devil,' saith the Apostle, 'sinneth from the beginning;' that is, was the first sinner in the universe, the author of sin..." The phrase is exampled in a sermon of Martin G. Collins, "Atonement and this World's Future." (bibletools.org)

Son of Righteousness

3 Nephi 25:2. But unto you that fear my name, shall the Son of Righteousness arise with healing in his wings.

This is the BOM version of Malachi 4:2, where the text reads "shall the Sun of righteousness arise with healing in his wings." This phrase is possibly inspired by the ancient Egyptian image of the winged sun. In Hebrew, sun is *shemesh*, while son is *ben*. The phonological basis for this sun/son confusion is found only in English. In the BOM text, the passage is spoken by none other than Jesus Christ to the Nephites.

It occurs prominently in "Hark! The Harold Angels Sing" by Charles Wesley (1707-1788). In many printings, the word "Sun" is changed to "Son," deliberately or inadvertently. Examples include the versions of the St. Patrick Catholic School Christmas Program Songs (found online); as well as that of Oakton Community College; of Our Lady of Sorrows Church; of Tripod.com; of Mars Hill Music; of the Christmas Songbook of MP3 CDburner.com; of Holly Jolly Christmas; of the Christmas Day Service of the Victoria Point Baptist Church; of the Christmas Song Book of Hillbillyhousewife.com; of Christmaspianosongs.com; in the "Song of Angels" medley, Damaris Carbaugh; of Tab Chords and Lyrics (learn-classic-rock-songs.com); of the Melodic Memories Sing-along Christmas; of a commentated analysis delivered by Rev. Will Nelken, at Trinity Community Church, San Rafael, CA (12/09/07); of the Christmastide of Mona Shores Public Schools; and many others.

The line occurs in other songs, such as in "But for You Who Fear My Name," posted online by Hope College, Campus Ministry; in "Son of Righteousness," Sam Reeves/Robert Robinson; and in "Son of Man, Son of Righteousness" by Tye Tribbett. Given the variation found in printed versions, it is clear that members of congregations, while hearing or singing the hymn, or both, would tend to understand "Son of Righteousness."

Red Sea (dubious identification, in a dubious Biblical account)

The Red Sea is mentioned in the BOM narrative in two contexts, the geography of Nephi's travel in Arabia (1 Nephi 2:5; 1 Nephi 2:8; 1 Nephi 16:14), and the story of Moses leading the Israelites out of Egypt:

8. The Post-Biblical Euro-Christian Text

> 1 Nephi 4:2. Therefore let us go up; let us be strong like unto Moses; for he truly spake unto the waters of the Red Sea and they divided hither and thither, and our fathers came through, out of captivity, on dry ground, and the armies of Pharaoh did follow and were drowned in the waters of the Red Sea. (See also 1 Nephi 17:26-27; 2 Nephi 19:1; Mosiah 7:19; Alma 36:28 & Helaman 8:11)

Red Sea is a direct translation of the Greek *Erythra Thalassa* (Ερυθρὰ Θάλασσα) and Latin *Mare Rubrum*. The OT has ים סוּף (the Sea of Reeds). The BOM usage can be simply an affirmation that its identification with the Red Sea is correct, or, if it is not, then it is a post-Biblical identification that was incorporated into the BOM.

Convincing of the Jews

> 2 Nephi 26:12. And as I spake concerning the convincing of the Jews, that Jesus is the very Christ, it must needs be that the Gentiles be convinced also that Jesus is the Christ, the Eternal God (see also 2 Nephi 25:18).

This phrase originally meant to refute the claims of the Jews, or to condemn them and their rejection of Christ. In English, the meaning of "to convince" changed. The obsolete meaning is "to refute or prove wrong," but eventually this gave way to the current meaning, "to show to the satisfaction of someone else that one's own claims are true." The BOM usage is based on an understanding of the Bible based on this later meaning, while the King James translators were intending the now obsolete meaning. It is this meaning that we find in the original languages:

> Greek: (ἐλέγχει [*elengchei*]): to expose wrongdoing, charge, show fault, prove wrongdoing, convict
> (διακατηλεγχετο; to confute)

> Hebrew: (מוֹכִיחַ; argue, dispute)

> Job 32:12
> there was none of you that convinced Job, or that answered his words (מוֹכִחַ; dispute, refute)
> John 8:45-46
> 45. And because I tell you the truth, ye believe me not.

46. Which of you convinceth me of sin? And if I say the truth, why do ye not believe me? ([ἐλέγχει; accuses, charges with, convicts)

Acts 18

28. For he mightily convinced the Jews, and that publickly, shewing by the scriptures that Jesus was Christ. (διακατηλεγχετο; to confute)

1 Corinthians 14:24-25

24. But if all prophesy, and there come in one that believeth not, or one unlearned, he is convinced of all, he is judged of all:

25. And thus are the secrets of his heart made manifest; and so falling down on his face he will worship God, and report that God is in you of a truth. (ἐλέγχεται; he is convicted)

Titus 1:9

Holding fast the faithful word as he hath been taught, that he may be able by sound doctrine both to exhort and to convince the gainsayers. (ἐλέγχειν; to convict, charge)

James 2:9

But if ye have respect to persons, ye commit sin, and are convinced of the law as transgressors. (ἐλέγχομενοι; convicted [by the law])

Jude 1:15

15 To execute judgment upon all, and to convince all that are ungodly among them of all their ungodly deeds which they have ungodly committed, and of all their hard speeches which ungodly sinners have spoken against him. (ἐξελέγχαι; to convict)

Freemasonry

It is not surprising to find influences from Freemasonry in the *Book of Mormon*. In 1827 Hyrum Smith received Masonic degrees in Palmyra's Mount Moriah Lodge #112. Joseph Smith became a Freemason after the publication of his new Bible, a Masonic lodge was organized in Nauvoo, and the rituals of the LDS temple were strongly influenced by Masonic rites. In a draft of Lucy Smith's biography, regarding the early 1820's, she mentioned "trying to win the faculty of Abrac..."[116] Abrac "derives from Abracadabra and Abraxas." Masons claimed to know the way of obtaining the faculty of Abrac.[117] An encyclopedia of Freemasonry states, "In the so-called Leland Manuscript [sometimes called the Locke Manuscript], it is said that Freemasons 'conceal the way of wynninge the

---

[116] Lucy Mack Smith, in Lavina Fielding Anderson, ed., *Lucy's Book, A Critical Edition of Lucy Mack Smith's Family Memoir* (Salt Lake City: Signature Books, 2001), 323.

[117] Marquardt, *Rise of Mormonism*, 67 n. 22.

facultye of Abrac.' That is, that they conceal the method of acquiring the powers bestowed by a knowledge of the magical talisman that is called Abracadabra (see Abracadabra and Leland Manuscript).[118]

Secret Combinations

> 2 Nephi 9:9. secret combinations of murder and all manner of secret works of darkness. (See also: 2 Nephi 26:22; Alma 37:30-31)

The *Book of Mormon* has numerous passages that warn against "secret combinations," with their oaths and secret signs. It seems that this phrase is used in lieu of "secret societies." The historical context is the Freemasonry controversies that were raging, exacerbated by the anti-Freemason accusations made by Captain William Morgan, stirred up by his persecution, kidnapping and mysterious disappearance, and present in the Presbyterianism of the Second Great Revival in New York, due to the disaffection of revivalist Rev. Charles Finney and others.

The Wayne Sentinel (March 23, 1827) quotes the *Rochester Daily Advertiser*:

> The Freemason, too—not only those who took off Morgan, but every one who bears the masonic name—are proscribed, as unworthy of 'any office in town, county, state, or United States!' and the institution of masonry, . . . is held up as DANGEROUS and detrimental to the interests of the country!"

Regarding the 1827 elections, *The Wayne Sentinel* printed the following (November 16, 1827):

> The election in this county (says the Ontario Messenger) has resulted in the choice of the entire ANTI-MASONIC ticket.

Ironically, the BOM authors were not consistent in their attitude towards Freemasonry, reflected in their use of the following phrases, and the

---

[118] Albert C. Mackey, *Encyclopaedia of Freemasonry and Its Kindred Sciences* (http://www.phoenixmasonry.org/mackeys_encyclopedia/f.htm, accessed 29/03.2017).

subsequent adoption of Masonic rites and symbols in the Mormon temples.

One Eternal Round

> 1 Nephi 10:19. the course of the Lord is one eternal round (See also Alma 7:20; 37:12)

The circle had long been a symbol for eternity, although not in the Bible. This is because the line that circumscribes it has neither beginning nor end. However, referring to it as an eternal round is distinctly Masonic. It has been found as early as 1731, in "The Generous Freemason" (well before Mozart's *Magic Flute*) by William Rufus Chetwood, the first Freemason to write the libretto of an opera. It contains the passage:

> Let Love and Friendship then our cares confound,
> And halcyon days be one eternal round.[119]

Tabernacle of Clay

> Moroni 9:6. we have a labor to perform whilst in this tabernacle of clay

Biblically, this phrase is related to 2 Corinthians 5:1 "For we know that if our earthly house of this tabernacle were dissolved, we have a building of God, an house not made with hands, eternal in the heavens."

The BOM phrase is found in a Freemason funeral ceremony text:

> *Master*: This evergreen is an emblem of our faith in the immortality of the soul. By it, we are reminded of our high and glorious destiny beyond the 'world of shadows' and that there dwells within our tabernacle of clay, an

---

[119] W R Chetwood, *The generous Free-Mason, or, The constant lady: with the humours of Squire Noodle, and his man Doodle: a tragi-comi-farcical ballad opera in three acts: with the musick prefix'd to each song* (London: J. Roberts, 1731). Richard Northcott, "The Generous Freemason, A short History of the First Masonic Opera," published on the website of the Grand Lodge of British Columbia and Yukon (http://www.freemasonry.bcy.ca/fiction/generous_free mason/generous.html, accessed March 2016).

imperishable, immortal spirit, over which the grave has no dominion, and death not power.[120]

Since the phrase is found in other Euro-Christian sources, it cannot be said to be exclusively a Freemason expression. More recently, we find in a poem, "Tabernacle of Clay," on the web under the name of LateefahFreeWOMAN (2014), the line: "In this temple, this tabernacle of clay."

All-searching Eye

>Mosiah 27:31. the glance of his all-searching eye

>Jacob 2:10. the glance of the piercing eye of the Almighty God

This post-Biblical phrase has been thought to have its source in the eye iconography of ancient Egypt, and Freemasonry. The all-seeing eye of God (or Eye of Providence) is often represented as an eye surrounded by rays of light, usually within a triangle. Today, the Eye of Providence is usually associated with Freemasonry, although many associate it primarily with the reverse of the Great Seal of the United States, which appears on the one-dollar bill.

It is found in the hymn "Almighty God, thy piercing eye," written by Isaac Watts (1715), which has been published in 78 hymnals:

>Almighty God, thy piercing eye
>Strikes through the shades of night,
>And our most secret actions lie
>All open to thy sight.

It is also found in a work of a Canon of Westminster Abbey, Christopher Wordsworth (born, 1807; *Holy Year; or, Hymns for Sundays, Holidays, and other Occasions*):

>God, in Whose all-searching eye
>Thy servants stand, to ratify
>The vow baptismal, by them made

---

[120] Most Worshipful Grand Lodge of Ancient Freemasons of South Carolina, "Funeral Service" (Abbeville, SC: Hugh Wilson, Printer, 1899).

Influences from Hymns

Popular hymns of the day not only influenced those who heard them, but provided expressions in use in common parlance. In many cases, worshippers tended to confuse these expressions with those in the Bible itself. As a result, a writer intending to use Biblical expressions might include post-Biblical expressions by mistake. Or one might draw freely and knowingly from both sources, all the while aware that the reader would not be able to distinguish them. These phrases enabled the creation of a text that would have a familiar sound.

Redeeming Love (Sing..., or Song of...)

> Alma 5:9. they did sing redeeming love
>
> Alma 5:26. if ye have felt to sing the song of redeeming love
> (Also Alma 26:13)

This English post-Biblical Euro-Christian phrase is found in a number of hymns, most notably "Redeeming Love," often published as "Now begins the heavenly theme," erroneously attributed to John Langford, who, in 1765, began to preach in a chapel in London, and in 1776, published a collection of *Hymns & Spiritual Songs*. This hymn has been published in 326 hymnals. However, the earliest form in which it is found differs widely from that followed in modern hymnals. In 1763 it appeared in the Appendix to M. Madan's *Psalms and Hymns*, as No. clxxii, thus:—

> "Redeeming Love"
> Now begin the Heav'nly Theme,
> Sing aloud in Jesu's Name,
> Ye, who Jesu's Kindness prove
> Triumph in Redeeming Love.

This is followed by seven additional stanzas, each ending with a "Redeeming Love" phrase.[121] The phrase occurs twice in the sermons of

---

[121] John Julian (ed.), *A Dictionary of Hymnology : Setting Forth the Origin and History of Christian Hymns of All Ages and Nations* (London: John Murray, 1907).

John Wesley, such as "You cannot taste his redeeming love," in sermon #29, "Upon Our Lord's Sermon on the Mount, Discourse Nine." It is found four times in the sermons of George Whitefield, and once in *The Works of Jonathan Edwards*, Chapter XI.

Glad Tidings of Great Joy/Glad Tidings of Salvation

> Mosiah 3:3. for behold, I am come to declare unto you the glad tidings of great joy (See also Alma 13:22)

> Alma 39:15 he cometh to declare glad tidings of salvation

This is an English variation of "I bring you good tidings of great joy" in Luke 2:10. It is not known when the popular variation developed, with "glad" instead of "good," but already we have it in a hymn by Leonard Marshall (1809--1890), as the first line: "Glad tidings of great joy I bring." "Glad tidings of salvation" is likewise extra-Biblical. It developed in English Euro-Christianity, and is evidenced in a text of John Wesley (*Journal*, June 11, 1739.), "I look upon all the world as my parish: thus far I mean, that, in whatever part of it I am, I judge it meet, right, and my bounden duty to declare unto all that are willing to hear the glad tidings of salvation." This phrase is the title and first line of a hymn by Donald S. Lundin, and is the title of a hymn by Robert O. Smith.

Condescension of God

> 1 Nephi 11:16. Knowest thou the condescension of God?

> 2 Nephi 4:26. O then, if I have seen so great things, if the Lord in his condescension unto the children of men

This post-Biblical Euro-Christian phrase is a standard Christian theological term. We find it prominently in a Hymn by the famous and prolific hymnist Isaac Watts (1674-1748), "God's Condescension to Human Affairs."[122] Considered the "Father of English Hymnody," he is credited with some 750 hymns. Many of his hymns remain in use today and have been translated into numerous languages.

---

[122] Isaac Watts, *Hymns and spiritual songs, in three books* (Coventry: M Luckman, 1793).

> 2. He that can shake the worlds he made,
> Or with his word, or with his rod,
> His goodness how amazing great!
> And what a condescending God!

The phrase is common in English-language sermons. Note "The Condescension of Christ, A Sermon (No. 151), Delivered on Sabbath Morning, September 13, 1857, by the REV. C. H. Spurgeon at the Music Hall, Royal Surrey Gardens."

Rejoice My Heart

> 2 Nephi 4:28. Awake, my soul! No longer droop in sin. Rejoice, O my heart, and give place no more for the enemy of my soul.

"Rejoice my heart" is a phrase found in 18th-19th century Christian devotion. See for example "Rejoice my heart, be glad and sing" by Paul Gerhardt (1607-1676, Lutheran), which was translated into English and became cross-denominational:

> Rejoice, my heart, by glad and sing,
> A cheerful trust maintain;

Note too that hymn 388 in the *Complete Collected Hymns of John Wesley* has the line "Come, Lord! the drooping sinner cheer…"

Judgment Bar

> 2 Nephi 33:15. For what I seal on earth, shall be brought against you at the judgment bar; for thus hath the Lord commanded me, and I must obey. Amen.

> 2 Nephi 33:11. I shall stand face to face before his bar
> Alma 5:22. the bar of God (See also 11:44 & Moroni 10:27)

This English phrase is not Biblical; compare with "barrister" and "bar-at-law." "Bar" is defined as the whole body of lawyers, the legal profession (1550's), a sense that derives ultimately from the railing that separated benchers from the hall in the Inns of Court. It is found in a hymn, "God's Judgment bar! Justice complete" (music composed in the late 19th

century, for words by Emily Leader). "How wilt thou stand at the judgment bar?" is found as a refrain of a hymn written and composed in 1917 by Harry D. Loes. The early adaptation of the term to religious discourse is documented in a sermon of John Wesley, "…wherein to Stand at the bar of God in the day of judgment."

God of Nature

> 1 Nephi 19:12. "The God of nature suffers"

This phrase is not Biblical, and developed in Euro-Christianity. Note, in particular, a poem/hymn by James Montgomery (1771-1854, son of John Montgomery, a Moravian minister). He wrote many poems, some of which were made into hymns, such as the stanza:

> The God of nature and of grace
> In all His works appears;
> His goodness through the earth we trace,
> His grandeur in the spheres.

Compare with the hymn of Jeremiah Eames Rankin (Pseudonym: R. E. Jeremy), born at Thornton, New Haven, Jan. 2, 1828: "O God of nature, come and grace our harvest;" as well as a sermon by Charles Kingsley, "The God of Nature (Preached During a Wet Harvest)". "Nature" is not an OT concept, and was developed in Greek literature, where *physis* (nature) and *nomos* (convention, law) were in opposition. From Greek thought, it went into the epistles of Paul, but not regarding the deity.

The Veil of Unbelief

> Ether 4:15. Behold, when ye shall rend that veil of unbelief (See also Alma 19:6)

This is a common extra-Biblical English Euro-Christian phrase, found as early as in a hymn by John Wesley (1703-1791):

> 4. The veil of unbelief remove,
> And by thy manifested love,
> And by thy sprinkled blood,
> Destroy the love of sin in me

The phrase occurs as a theme in Christian sermons and devotional articles.

Valley of Sorrow

> 2 Nephi 4:26. O then, if I have seen so great things, if the Lord in his condescension unto the children of men hath visited men in so much mercy, why should my heart weep and my soul linger in the valley of sorrow

Compare with "Vale of tears," Psalm 84:6.

This phrase does not occur in the Bible. We do find it in "Resurrection of Christ" by M.H. Ware, Jr. (1794-1843):

> But Jesus hath cleared the dark valley of sorrow,
> And bade us, immortal, to heaven ascend

In the hymn "I have been through the valley of sorrow and weeping" of Clement Cotterill Scholefield (1839-1904) we have:

> I have been through the valley of weeping,
> The valley of sorrow and pain

Note too "Rays Of Light In The Valley Of Sorrow" by Henry Wheeler.

Blood from Every Pore

> Mosiah 3:7. blood cometh from every pore, so great shall be his anguish

As part of the cult of Christ's Blood, this is a post-Biblical Euro-Christian interpretation of Luke 22:44:

> his sweat was *as it were* great drops of blood falling down to the ground [Emphasis added]

This description is found only in Luke, and even he qualifies it with "as it were." Contrast it with the couplet in the hymn "O Love Incomprehensible" by Anne Steele (1717 –1778), an English Baptist hymn writer:

> 16. What pain, what soul-oppressing pain, The great Redeemer bore;
> While bloody sweat, like drops of rain, Distilled from every pore!

In "Agony in the Garden" one sings, "His sweat like drops of blood ran down; In agony he prayed," attributed to (Thomas?) Haweis (1734-1820).[123] Reverend Spurgeon (1834-1892), in an oft-quoted sermon, exclaims, "every pore is open, and it sweats!" In "Feast of the Sacred Heart," a devotional by Fr. Francis Xavier Weninger, 1877, we find: "His precious blood burst forth from every pore.".

Atoning Blood of Christ

> Mosiah 4:2. O have mercy, and apply the atoning blood of Christ

This is also relevant to the Euro-Christian cult of Christ's blood. The Biblical inspiration, apart from the Last Supper of Christ, derives from Hebrews 9:13-14 (and cf. Revelations 1:5):

> 13. For if the blood of bulls and of goats, and the ashes of an heifer sprinkling the unclean, sanctifieth to the purifying of the flesh:
> 14. How much more shall the blood of Christ, who through the eternal Spirit offered himself without spot to God, purge your conscience from dead works to serve the living God?

The phrase "atoning blood" is found in hymns of Isaac Watt:

Hymn 1:97, "Christ our wisdom, righteousness, &c."

> Our guilty souls are drown'd in tears
> Till his atoning blood appears

---

[123] Found in J.G. (John Greenleaf) Adams and E.H. (Edwin Hubbell) Chapin (compilers), *Hymns for Christian devotion; especially adapted to the Universalist denomination* (Boston: B. Bradley & Co., 1853).

The phrase also occurs in hymns 1:98 and 2:36. It occurs at least five times in the sermons of John Wesley, and in ten of his hymns.

As for the phrase using the verb "to apply," I have found it online for a Church of Christ congregation in Texas (not related to Mormonism), but I have not found it yet in a source prior to 1828.

Gulf of Death

> Alma 26:20 Behold, he did not exercise his justice upon us, but in his great mercy hath brought us over that everlasting gulf of death and misery

This is a phrase and characterization that developed in English Euro-Christianity. An example is found in the works of Felicia Hemans (1793-1835). In "Communings with Thought" she wrote:

> Go, visit cell and shrine!
> Where woman hath endured!—through wrong, through scorn,
> Uncheer'd by fame, yet silently upborne
> By promptings more divine!
>
> Go, shoot the gulf of death!

In John Wesley's hymn #288, similar wording occurs:

> Thy love shall burst the shades of death,
> An bear me from the gulf beneath
> To everlasting day.

In "Encouragements to Walk with God" in the *Sermons of George Whitefield*, we read, "Death may seize thee, judgment find thee, and then the great gulf will be fixed between thee and endless glory forever and ever."

Bounty of His Love

> Alma 26:15 "they are encircled about with the matchless bounty of his love"

This is an English Euro-Christian phrase, found as early as a hymn published in 1756 by Thomas Cradock, and containing the lines:

All by the bounty of his love are fed;
O'er heav'ns above, o'er earth beneath, he reigns

Word of Truth and Righteousness

Alma 38:9. Behold, he is the word of truth and righteousness.

This extra-Biblical phrase is found among various denominations, such as in "A Hymn" by James M. Whitfield (1822–1871):

And grant that many souls may hear
The words of truth and righteousness

It is found in a newspaper, *The Gospel Trumpet*, of 1899 (o4/06), and in a meditation by Don Swagger (online) we find: "Do you trust in God's grace and mercy and do you submit to his life-giving word of truth and righteousness (moral goodness)?"

Mankind Fallen

Alma 42:14. And thus we see that all mankind were fallen (See also 1 Nephi 10:6; Alma 12:22

Phrases characterizing mankind as "fallen" is post-Biblical. One finds it in the English language as early as John Wesley, in "God's Love to Fallen Man." It is also found in a hymn by Isaac Watts (1674–1748), beginning:

1 Ah, how shall fallen man
Be just before his God!

Redemption of the World

Mormon 7:7. he hath brought to pass the redemption of the world

This post-Biblical phrase is found as early as St. John of Damascus (hymn writer, c. 760),

> We bless you for our creation, preservation,
> and all the blessings of this life;
> but above all for your immeasurable love
> in the redemption of the world by our Lord Jesus Christ

It comes into English usage at least as early as "A Rationale upon the Book of Common Prayer" by Anthony Sparrow, D.D. (London, 1672): "For the Te Deum, Benedictus, Magnificat, and Nunc Dimittis being the most expressive Jubilations and rejoycings for the redemption of the world, may be said more often than the rest." The phrase became common in English. We find it in *"The Worship of the Church (28; v. 632); A Witness for the Redemption of the World, a Sermon"* by F. D. Maurice (1805-1872). It is also in "Plenteous Redemption," (Sermon No. 351, delivered by Rev. C. H. Spurgeon: "and in that day he purchased the redemption of the world from its curse."

Eye of Faith

> Alma 5:15. Do you look forward with an eye of faith...? (Alma 32:40; Ether 12:19)

This is a common English Euro-Christian phrase, as in the hymn "The Eye of Faith" by J. J. Maxfield (19th –century, dates unknown). Another hymn is "Through the Eyes of Faith" by Stephen Hurd. We find it in sermon 4, "Of Contentment" by Isaac Barrow (1630-1677):

> Will it not much please us with an eye of faith to behold our Redeemer sitting in glorious exaltation at GOD's right hand...?

It is a sermon genre (used by Arthur Pink, John Rhodes, Jose Cabajar, Tenette Abanilla, Glenn Schoonover, Stan Coffey, Robert D. Luginbill, Tom Stewart, David Larsen and others).

The Life and Light of the World

Making Jesus not only the light, but also the life of the world, is extra-Biblical. Since this phrase occurs among various denominations, it is not unique to the *Book of Mormon*, even though early nineteenth-century occurrences have not been found. It appears to be a combination of two titles, as indicated in the hymn of Isaac Watts, "The Names and Titles of Christ."

> What winning titles he assumes!
> Light of the World, and Life of Men

The hymn "All Things Are of God"[124] states:

> Thou art, O God, the life and light of all this wondrous world

Clasped in the Arms of Jesus

> Mormon 5:11. ...they might have been clasped in the arms of Jesus.

This phrase is similar to several hymns, including a hymn of Charles Wesley written after his daughter Sarah died, with the line, "clasped in the arms of His love."[125] In the *Free Methodist Hymnal*,[126] "The Savior's melting mercies yearn to clasp thee to his breast." We also find "He leadeth me, for I can feel the clasping of that pierced hand so." (Helen S. Arnold, Charles H. Gabriel, "He Leadeth Me") We note that another hymn reflecting the same idea was written in 1868 by Fanny Crosby: "Safe in the Arms of Jesus."

Theological Euro-Christian Phrases

Typifying of Him (a Shadow, or Similitude)

Early Christianity was essentially an offshoot of the Judaism of Jesus' day. One accusation that the first believers had to face was that Jesus just is not in the pre-Christian scriptures, and certainly not the essential claims regarding the mission of their Christ. There was no way that they

---

[124] So titled in *Hymns for Christian Devotion Especially Adapted to the Universalist Denomination*, 1846, with attribution to "61. Moore" [dates?]; but alternatively, "God's Presence in Nature", the title in Samuel Johnson & Samuel Longfellow, *Book of Hymns for Public and Private Devotion*, 10th ed. (Boston: Ticknor & Fields, 1857/1846).

[125] Sir Thomas Moore, *The English Hymnal*, no. 298.

[126] *Free Methodist Hymnal* (Chicago: Free Methodist Publishing House, 1910).

could challenge the sacred texts, and certainly they would never have thought to argue that important parts had been deleted. Rather, they argued that certain verses, and the sacred law itself, were typifications or foreshadowings of Jesus, the crucifixion and redemption. The Israelites, they held, were not ready for the literal truth. Instead, the law was given as a schoolmistress for Israel, to prepare Israelites for the Advent of the Messiah. Paul taught that the law had been fulfilled in the crucifixion, the passion (suffering) of Christ.

> 2 Nephi 11:4. for this end hath the law of Moses been given; and all things which have been given of God from the beginning of the world, unto man, are the typifying of him

> Alma 33:19. Behold, he [Christ] was spoken of by Moses; yea, and behold a type was raised up in the wilderness, that whosoever would look upon it might live (See also: Alma 13:16; 25:15; 37:43-45)

> Mosiah 3:15. And many signs, and wonders, and types, and shadows showed he unto them, concerning his coming

> Jacob 4:5 offering up his son Isaac, which is a similitude of God and his Only Begotten Son. (See also Helaman 8:14)

The inspiration for this is in the commentaries on the Epistle of Paul to the Hebrews, 11:17-19:

> 17 By faith Abraham, when he was tried, offered up Isaac: and he that had received the promises offered up his only begotten son,
> 18 Of whom it was said, That in Isaac shall thy seed be called:
> 19 Accounting that God was able to raise him up, even from the dead; from whence also he received him in a figure.

In his *Interpretation of Hebrews 11*, Theodoret, Bishop of Cry (Cyrrhus; 393-466 AD), wrote (commenting on Hebrews 11:19):

> Figuratively speaking, he did receive him back, that is, by way of a symbol and type of the resurrection. Put to death by his father's zeal, he came back to life at the word of the one who prevented the slaughter. In him the type of the saving passion was also prefigured. Hence the Lord also said to the Jews, "Your father Abraham rejoiced at the prospect of seeing my day; he saw it and was glad."

8. The Post-Biblical Euro-Christian Text 191

This rationale is present in English Euro-Christianity, at least as early as John Wesley ("The End of Christ's Coming", Sermon 62;), who wrote:

> 3. May we not reasonably believe it was by similar appearances that He was manifested in succeeding ages to Enoch, while he "Walked with God;" to Noah, before and after the deluge; to Abraham, Isaac, and Jacob, on various occasions; and, to mention no more, to Moses? This seems to be the natural meaning of the word: "My servant Moses is faithful in all my house. – With him will I speak mouth to mouth, even apparently, and not in dark speeches; and the similitude of Jehovah shall he behold;" namely, the Son of God.
> 4. But all these were only types of his grand manifestation.

His commentary on the Bible has at least 170 instances of asserting that an OT personage or event was a "type" of Christ, or of the Savior.

Closer to home we have the work of Jonathan Edwards, "Types of the Messiah." Of OT sacrifices, he wrote:

> Gideon was not only the captain of the host of Israel, but was immediately appointed of God to be a priest to build the altar of God, and to offer sacrifice to God, to make atonement for that iniquity of Israel that had brought them sore judgment upon them, that he came to deliver them from. Jdg. 6:20-28. And he offered a sacrifice acceptable unto God, and of which God gave special testimony of his acceptance, by consuming his sacrifice by fire immediately enkindled from heaven. Verse 21. And his sacrifice procured reconciliation and peace for Israel, Jdg. 6:24. These things are exactly agreeable to the prophecies of the Messiah.

And in his "Dissertation Concerning the End for Which God Made the World," Edwards wrote:

> those two great temporal salvations of God's people, the redemption from Egypt, and that from Babylon, often represented as figures and similitudes of the redemption of Christ

The word similitude does occur in the Bible, but to indicate the form of God, or a graven image, or allegories made by Jesus. It does not occur to indicate that an OT event or precept was a similitude of Christ.

As for "shadow" we read in Hebrews 10:1:

> For the law having a shadow of good things to come, and not the very image of the things, can never with those sacrifices which they offered year by year continually make the comers thereunto perfect.

The verse says that the law "has" a shadow, not that it "is" a shadow. It asserts that this shadow is impotent, unable to "make the comers thereunto perfect." This did not prevent later interpretation to mean that the law was a shadow of Christ and redemption, a sort of revelation of them. The use of the word "shadow" in English Euro-Christianity is illustrated in John Wesley's Commentary on the Bible, Notes on Joel," 3:18:

> Of the flowing waters in this verse, he wrote, "This no doubt is a shadow of the purifying blood of Christ, and his sanctifying spirit and word."

Of the words "type," "similitude" and "shadow," only the last was used in the Bible with a meaning that can be easily confused with the meaning it acquired in English Euro-Christianity, the meaning that found its way into the BOM narrative.

Plan of Salvation or Plan of Redemption

> Jarom 1:2. For have not they revealed the plan of salvation? (See also: Alma 24:14; 34:9; 42:5)

> Alma 12:30. ...the plan of redemption, which had been prepared from the foundation of the world (See also Alma 12:25; 18:39; 22:13; 29:2; 34:16; 39:18; 42:13)

Although Christians have always perceived that the Bible teaches God's provisions for salvation, the phrases "plan of salvation" and "plan of redemption" are not Biblical. At least in English Euro-Christianity, the phrases have become common to Catholics and various Protestant denominations. A sermon on the topic was delivered by John Wesley, "The Way of Salvation," in which he states, "Here I design to take a brief view of the gospel plan of salvation, and exhibit it especially in contrast with the original plan on which it was proposed to save mankind."

Ends of the Law

> 2 Nephi 2:10. Wherefore, the ends of the law which the Holy One hath given, unto the inflicting of the punishment which is affixed, which punishment that is affixed is in opposition to that of the happiness which is affixed, to answer the ends of the atonement.

This post-Biblical Euro-Christian phrase is common in English, both in theology and in legal studies. We have an example in the sermon "The Law Established Through Faith, Discourse 1" by John Wesley:

> Their grand plea is this: That preaching the gospel, that is, according to their judgment, the speaking of nothing but the sufferings and merits of Christ, answers all the ends of the law. But this we utterly deny.

Forbidden Fruit

> 2 Nephi 2:15. there was an opposition; even the forbidden fruit in opposition to the tree of life

All Judeo-Christians have heard that there was a fruit forbidden to Adam and Eve in the Bible. But this phrase "forbidden fruit," although a common Christian phrase, is not in the Bible. Surprisingly, the word "forbidden" is found only three times. Its incidence in English Euro-Christianity is exampled in the sermon "On the Fall of Man" by John Wesley:

> And if this was the case, there is no absurdity in the assertion of a great man, "That Adam sinned in his heart before he sinned outwardly; before he ate of the forbidden fruit;" namely, by inward idolatry, by loving the creature more than the Creator.

In the Sermons of George Whitefield, this phrase occurs nineteen times, and twenty times in *The Works of Jonathan Edwards*. Although I have not found it in hymns, it is common in modern music and film.

Eternal Head

> Helaman 13:38. that righteousness which is in our great and Eternal Head

This non-Biblical phrase may have been introduced by James (Jacob) Arminius (1560-1609) who wrote: "that Christ may be the eternal head of the predestinate." His work and theology became especially dominant in the United States, through John Wesley and Methodism.

Eat, Drink and Be Merry, for Tomorrow We Die

> 2 Nephi 28:7. Yea, and there shall be many which shall say: Eat, drink, and be merry, for tomorrow we die; and it shall be well with us

> 1 Corinthians 15:32. let us eat and drink; for to morrow we die

> Ecclesiastes 8: 15. Then I commended mirth, because a man hath no better thing under the sun than to eat, and to drink, and to be merry: for that shall abide with him of his labour the days of his life

> Isaiah 22:13. let us eat and drink; for to morrow we shall die

This common English phrase is based on a composite of these Biblical passages (eat, drink, be merry), but inserted into the BOM text with the exact wording of the later Euro-Christian phrase.

Upon the Wings of His Spirit

> 2 Nephi 4:25. And upon the wings of his Spirit hath my body been carried away upon exceedingly high mountains

This phrase occurs in devotional material of various denominations. For example,

> As the wind of the eternal purpose blows along from generation to generation, the sound of God's voice is being borne upon the wings of His Spirit to certain men and women of His own choosing.[127]

In the Presbycan (Presbyterian) Daily Devotional we find:

> Let us cast aside false guilt and discouragement when we feel that we haven't measured up, and let us rise on the wings of His Spirit to

---

[127] Stephen T. Kia, "Christ, the Synthesis of Independent Fellowship" (online at http//:www.2liveischrist.net/articles/synthesis.htm, accessed March 2016).

praise and glorify His name with bright and cheerful hearts full of the sunshine and beauty of the Son's transformation.

Clearly this is an English Euro-Christian phrase, not limited to the BOM.

Join the Choirs Above in Singing the Praises of a Just God

> Mosiah 2:28. that I might go down in peace, and my immortal spirit may join the choirs above in singing the praises of a just God (cf. 1 Nephi 1:8; Mormon 7:7)

> Psalms 148:1 Praise ye the LORD. Praise ye the LORD from the heavens: praise him in the heights. 2. Praise ye him, all his angels: praise ye him, all his hosts. 3. Praise ye him, sun and moon: praise him, all ye stars of light. 4. Praise him, ye heavens of heavens, and ye waters that be above the heavens.

> Luke 2:13. And suddenly there was with the angel a multitude of the heavenly host praising God, and saying, 14. Glory to God in the highest, and on earth peace, good will toward men.

In the Bible, an angel (less commonly angels) is sent for specific purposes: to deliver a message, to protect, to destroy, to reap men for judgment, to gather the elect, etc. In Psalms 148, they are commanded to praise God, but apparently figuratively, since they are included with inanimate objects, such as stars and waters. This is reflected in the Hebrew word for angel, *mal'akh*, envoy, from a Semitic root "to send." In the New Testament, the word *angelos*, envoy, is a translation of the Semitic.

"Choir" does not occur in the Bible, and there is no mention of a group of angels singing, a "choir" (from Greek χορός [*choros*], a group of dancers or singers). At some point in the development of Euro-Christianity, the image of a "choir" of angels developed. Eventually, the angels were divided into various orders called choirs (9 choirs [orders] according to some, each with its own function. No choir has singing, or singing praises, as its function. Even so, in popular religion, this gave rise to the image of angels floating on clouds playing the harp. Whatever the meaning in this passage in Mosiah, this phrase obviously comes from post-Biblical Euro-Christianity. The phrase is found in a hymn of Charles Wesley:

> 2. Thy will by me on earth be done, As by the choirs above,
> Who always see thee on thy throne, And glory in thy love.

Contrast this with the Spurgeon sermon "Royal Homage" (no. 1102, 1873), "Nor can we expect that untrained voices should be admitted into the choirs above."

Chains of Hell

> Alma 26:14. has loosed our brethren from the chains of hell.

> 2 Peter 2:4. For if God spared not the angels that sinned, but cast them down to hell, and delivered them into chains of darkness

A common extra-Biblical English Euro-Christian phrase, found in *A Gospel Glass*, Part IV, Chapter 21: "Their Pride" by John Wesley:

> Knock off the chains of hell from your children while you may. Lay not out all your time how they may be rich

It is found in later devotional material, such as a sermon of Dieter Reinstorf, Cape Town, "Sermon for the Sunday Cantate." We find the phrase in an 1827 sermon of Rev. John Chambers, Presbyterian Church:

> for it will entail upon your souls the everlasting chains of hell, where there will be nought but weeping, wailing, and gnashing of teeth.

We also find the passage "let monarchs now in the chains of hell bear witness to their own utter confusion" in the sermon delivered in 1854 by C. H. Spurgeon. The image found its way into literature, such as the chains of Jacob Marley in Dickens, *A Christmas Carol*, first published in 1843.

The Damned Soul

> Alma 36:16. for three days and for three nights was I racked, even with the pains of a damned soul

This is a post-Biblical English Euro-Christian phrase, made popular if not introduced by none other than John Bunyan (author of *The Pilgrim's*

Progress) in *A Few Sights From Hell, or the Groans of The Damned Soul or An exposition of those words in the Sixteenth of Luke* (1658). Closer to home, it is found in "Surprised by God's Judgment" by Jonathan Edwards (1703-1758):

> Even those proud and sturdy spirits, the devils, tremble at the thoughts of that greater torment which they are to suffer at the Day of Judgment. So will the poor damned souls of men.

It is possible that the phrase developed in early Christianity.

Cup of Wrath

> Mosiah 3:26: Therefore, they have drunk out of the cup of the wrath of God

> Revelation 14:10: he also will drink of the wine of the wrath of God, which is mixed in full strength in the cup of His anger; and he will be tormented with fire and brimstone in the presence of the holy angels and in the presence of the Lamb.

This has long been a common Christian phrase, although not found in the Bible in this form. It is found in "The Life of Christ, the Pith and Kernel of All Religion," by R. Cudworth, B.D., preached before the Honorable House of Commons, 1647: "will prepare flaming ingredients for the cup of wrath, and fill it up to the very brim." It is found in Hymn 1:56 of Isaac Watts, "The Song of Moses and the Lamb; or Babylon Falling":

> The cup of wrath is ready mix'd
> And she must drink the dregs

Note too, its usage in a hymn penned by Witness Lee, "Thou didst drink the cup of wrath." In a sermon, "Jesus Sweats Blood," preached by Pastor Mark Driscoll out of Luke 22:39–46, we read:

> What is the cup he [Jesus] is so grieved about? It is the cup of the wrath of God. It refers to the cup Jesus had to drink, as every drop was a sin of the people for whom he drank it.

Sword of Justice

> Helaman 13:5: the sword of justice hangeth over this people (See also 3 Nephi 20:20; 29:4 & Alma 60:29)
> 3 Nephi 2:19: the sword of destruction did hang over them

This non-Biblical expression drives from other Biblical material about God's judgment and the common expression of the sword of Damocles, hanging over the head of his guests. Perhaps it was popularized among preachers by Thomas Watson (c. 1620-1686), who still has many works in print, including *The Ten Commandments*, "The Wrath of God":

> but the sword of God's justice hangs over a sinner, and when the slender thread of life is cut asunder it falls upon him.

It is found in a sermon of Rev. C. H. Spurgeon, "Mercy, Omnipotence, and Justice" (June 21, 1857):

> God's sword of justice is in its scabbard: not rusted in it–it can be easily withdrawn–but held there by that hand that presses it back into its sheath, crying, "Sleep, O sword, sleep; for I will have mercy upon sinners."

The "sword of Divine Justice" occurs in John Wesley's commentary on Ezekiel 32:32. In the hymn of Isaac Watts, "Christ's dying love; or Our Pardon bought at a dear price," we find:

> When Justice by our sins provok'd
> Drew forth its dreadful sword,

Reap the East Wind

> Mosiah 7:31: they shall reap the east wind, which bringeth immediate destruction.

> Mosiah 7:30: they shall reap the chaff thereof in the whirlwind.

> Hosea 8:7: For they have sown the wind, and they shall reap the whirlwind.

Ezekiel 17:10: shall it not utterly wither, when the east wind toucheth it?

This phrase is not Biblical, but is a blend of "reap the whirlwind" and "the east wind" (the latter being found in the OT as a wind of destruction). Since Hosea was not on the Brass Plates, there is no OT basis for the blend in the BOM. Early occurrences in English Euro-Christian usage have not been found, but note the novels *Reap the East Wind* (*Dread Empire* series) by Glen Cook and *Reap the East Wind* by Anne Smart-Pearce. This blend is so natural that it could be done by anyone with a knowledge of the two Biblical expressions.

Isabel in Siron

Alma 39:3: thou didst... go over into the land of Siron, among the borders of the Lamanites, after the harlot Isabel.

The sirens were legendary alluring women appearing to sailors at sea who (mis)led them onto rocky shoals and to a watery grave. In English, a siren became a woman of low morality who uses her charms to seduce a man into danger or sin. Isabel seems suggested by the name Jezebel (Hebrew אִיזֶבֶל, Izabel), a Canaanite princess who married Ahab, king of the northern kingdom Israel, and caused him to worship Baal and Asherah. (See 1 Kings 16, 18 & 21) The co-occurrence of the possible Isabel/Jezebel association, and the possible Siron/Siren association, seems like more than a coincidence.

Cross Yourself

Alma 39:9: Oh, remember, and take it upon you, and cross yourself in these things

The sign of the cross, or blessing oneself or crossing oneself, is post-Biblical, but became a ritual act done by members of many branches of Christianity. The use of the cross as a symbol of Christianity was rare in early Christianity, but apparently established by 200 CE. Signing the cross on one's forehead was common by the time Tertulian wrote "We Christians wear out our foreheads with the sign of the cross." The LDS Church rejects the use of the cross, regarding it to be a symbol of torture unworthy of their faith in Jesus.

A Bitter Cup

> Alma 40:26. ...they drink the dregs of a bitter cup

"A bitter cup" is not a Biblical expression, but became common in English Euro-Christian culture. We find it in a popular eighteenth-century hymn, "Jesus drinks the bitter cup" by Charles Wesley (1707-1788). In the sermon "On Eternity" by John Wesley we read:

> I know not if it would not seem as a thousand years. But (astonishing thought!) after thousands of thousands, he [the damned] has but just tasted of his bitter cup! After millions, it will be no nearer the end than it was the moment it began!

The *Book of Hymns for Public and Private Devotion* has a hymn by Jane Roscoe, "The Bitter Cup." The same collection has two other hymns containing this phrase. In the hymn "Agony in the Garden" (referenced above), we find "Father, remove this bitter cup."

Kingdom of the Devil

> 1 Nephi 22:23: all those who belong to the kingdom of the devil (See also v. 22 & 2 Nephi 28:19; Alma 5:25; 41:4)

This is a common post-Biblical English Euro-Christian expression, most usually referring to this world, before the coming of the kingdom of Christ. For a reference in the work of Martin Luther, see *Devotional Writings I*.[128] In "The Happy Ascetic," a sermon of Anthony Horneck (1641-1697), we find:

> how men, under a show of strictness, would prohibit what GOD had, like an indulgent Father, permitted to his creatures; under pretence (sic) of doing more than GOD has commanded, would set up the kingdom of the Devil.

We find it in John Wesley's notes on Genesis 3:

---

[128] Jaroslav Jan Pelikan, Hilton C. Oswald and Helmut T. Lehmann, eds., *Devotional Writings I* (Philadelphia: Fortress Press, 1999), 38-39.

> A perpetual quarrel is here commenced between the kingdom of God, and the kingdom of the devil among men; war proclaimed between the seed of the woman, and the seed of the serpent, Rev 12:7.

State of Nature

> Alma 41:11. And now, my son, all men that are in a state of nature.

A non-Biblical Euro-Christian concept, it was developed as early as Thomas Aquinas, for the concept of natural law in political philosophy. Alternatively, it has been used to refer to man's natural sinfulness. In the sermon by John Wesley, "Awake, Thou That Sleepest," we read:

> The state of nature is a state of utter darkness; a state wherein "darkness covers the earth, and gross darkness the people."

Nature of God

> Alma 41:11. they have gone contrary to the nature of God

This is a post-Biblical Euro-Christian concept/phrase that became common in Christian devotional material and speculative theology. We find it in Disputation #15 of James (Jacob) Arminius, "On the Nature of God". In his sermon (# 15) on the "Nature of God," John Wesley wrote:

> Now God saw that all this, the whole thereof, was evil; -- contrary to moral rectitude; contrary to the nature of God, which necessarily includes all good.

Days of Probation

> 1 Nephi 15:32. the works which were done by the temporal body in their days of probation

> Mormon 9:28. Be wise in the days of your probation (See also: 1 Nephi 10:21; 2 Nephi 2:30; 2 Nephi 33:9; Alma 12:24; Alma 42:4, 10, 13; and Helaman 13:38)

This is an English Euro-Christian concept and expression, not found in the Bible. In the commentary on the Bible of Daniel Whedon (1808-1885), we find:

Acts 3:22-26. Peter now contemplates those prophecies—which are being fulfilled during the Saviour's residence in heaven, namely, during these days of probation under the Christian dispensation—of a predicted, and once present, but now absent Christ.

Example of the Son

2 Nephi 31:16: in following the example of the Son of the living God.

The path to perfection of the soul developed to a high point in Euro-Christianity. Although implied in 1 Corinthians 13:1, this phrase is not in the KJV (although it has been used in more loosely translated modern versions). The classical Catholic work to assist the believer is *Imitatio Christi*. In English-language Protestant worship, following the example of Jesus has long been a theme for sermons, usually adding words to focus on a particular behavior, such as example of Jesus in charity, in praying, etc. Methodism also stresses the example of Jesus in its path to perfecting the soul. In an introduction to John Wesley's sermons, we find: "Wesleyans to this present day still believe that holiness of heart and life is essential to the Christian sojourn. Love perfected in the individual, mirrored after the example of Jesus, will always be a mainstay of a Wesleyan understanding."[129]

Strangers to God

Alma 26:9. they would also have been strangers to God

This phrase is an extra-Biblical English Euro-Christian phrase, found in devotional material and hymns, such as "The Strangers to God," by Charles Austin Miles (1868-1946). In John Wesley's Commentary on the Bible, his note for Genesis 6:4 states: "The sons of God—those who were called by the name of the Lord, and called upon that name, married the daughters of men—those that were profane, strangers to God." In the same spirit, we find it in sermon #104 "On Attending the Church Service" by John Wesley: "Can we imagine that they who are themselves strangers to the grace of God will manifest that grace to others? ...Were

---

[129] Ryan N. Danker, "The Sermons of John Wesley [1872 Edition] - An Introduction," in *The Sermons of John Wesley* - 1872 Edition (Thomas Jackson, editor; online version at Wesley.nnu.edu, accessed 03/05/2017).

not the priests, and public teachers, equally strangers to God, from this time to that of the Babylonish captivity?" Note as well its usage in later sermons: "I once was a stranger to God and his grace" by Adrian V. Miller; and "Stop Being a Stranger to God," preached in the Bethany Bible Church.

Wanderers in a Strange Land

> Alma 13:23 because of our being wanderers in a strange land
>
> Acts 7:6 That his seed should sojourn in a strange land

In the Bible, this phrase refers to alien residents in a city or land, not wanderers. But the wording with 'wandering' has become common, to the extent that it occurs in some so-called modern-English translations. The earliest occurrence I have found is dated 1832:

> Friends, my attachment to my native land was strong—that cord is now broken; and we must go forth as wanderers in a strange land. ("George W. Harkins [Chief of the Choctaw Tribe] to the American People, February 25, 1832," posted on ushistory.org, accessed 09/18/2016)

Give thanks to his holy name

> Alma 26:8. let us give thanks to his holy name (see also 2 Nephi 9:52)

This verse poses an interesting problem. The closest in the Bible is Psalms 30:4, "give thanks at the remembrance of his holiness" (KJV). Strangely, various modern translations render it "give thanks to his holy name" (Jewish Publication Society *Tanakh* of 1917, English Standard Version, New American Standard Bible, NET Bible, English Revised Version). However, the Hebrew text is clear: *və-hōdū lə-zēker kodšō*, "praise (or give thanks to) the remembrance (or at the mention) of his holiness." The word for name, *šem*, is not even present. Other modern translations remain faithful to the Hebrew text. Since it is found in Christian sermons as well as translations of Isaiah, this too qualifies as a Euro-Christian phrase.

Weeping, wailing and gnashing of teeth

>Alma 40:13. weeping and wailing and gnashing of teeth

>Matthew 8:12, 22:13, 24:51, 25:30 & Luke 13:28. weeping and gnashing

>Matthew 13:42 & 13:50. wailing and gnashing

The BOM combines all three (weeping, wailing, gnashing), as does George Whitefield in sermon number 40 and John Wesley in sermons 73 and 119. Note the 1827 sermon of Rev. John Chambers, Presbyterian Church:

>for it will entail upon your souls the everlasting chains of hell, where there will be nought but weeping, wailing, and gnashing of teeth.

Enlightened (Lamanites, i.e. Savages)

>Helaman 15:10. And now, because of their steadfastness when they do believe in that thing which they do believe, for because of their firmness when they are once enlightened, behold, the Lord shall bless them and prolong their days, notwithstanding their iniquity

Enlightening people, and especially the "savages," is not Biblical. The term emerged to describe the transformation from an earlier benighted state to the scientific age, the age of enlightenment. It developed in the missionary work, as an English equivalent of "*la nation civilisatrice*" (France). Urging the colonization of Virginia, Samuel Purchas (1577?-1626) wrote: "God in wisdom having enriched the Savage Countries, that these riches might be attractives for Christian suters, which there may sowe spirituals and reape temporals."[130] It is evidenced in a journal entry of Rev. Cyrus Brington on his 1820 mission:

>The Missionary Boat has arrived from Marietta on her way to the Choctaw Nation. The plan of enlightening the Savages is certainly philanthropic, to say nothing of the importance of giving them the gospel. They are an injured people; have been driven from their rightful possessions by the

---

[130] Samuel Purchas, *Hakluytus Posthumus, or, Purchas his Pilgrimes (a Discourse on Virginia)* (Glasgow: James MacLehose & Sons, 1905), XIX, 232-233).

whites; have became (sic) as it were a remnant that will soon be extinguished unless arrested in their downward career; the plan of Missions and schools has been devised for that purpose.

Similarly, as we have seen, Thorowgood held that "If we meane the Indians shall be Gospellized, they must first be civilized..."

Addressing Modern Issues

The advent of the scientific age and a more liberal culture had its own effect. The BOM authors wanted to show that God knows science. They also felt a need to address what some thought was a scourge of atheism.

No God and No Hell

The *Book of Mormon* has numerous passages attacking atheism. These BOM passages reflect a preoccupation of later Euro-Christian writers and preachers.

> 2 Nephi 2:13. And if ye shall say there is no law, ye shall also say there is no sin. If ye shall say there is no sin, ye shall also say there is no righteousness. And if there be no righteousness there be no happiness. And if there be no righteousness nor happiness there be no punishment nor misery. And if these things are not there is no God. And if there is no God we are not, neither the earth; for there could have been no creation of things, neither to act nor to be acted upon; wherefore, all things must have vanished away.

> 2 Nephi 28:22. ...there is no hell; and he saith unto them: I am no devil, for there is none.

Disputation regarding the deity in the Bible was mostly a contest between the deity of Israel and its competition among the divinities of Israel's neighbors. The word "atheism" does not occur in the Bible. A reference to the lack of belief in God is extremely rare. When it occurs at all, it is in the form of a condemnation of evildoers (Psalms 10:4; 14:1; 53:1).

Our interest here is not just the concept of atheism, but disputation over the issue and the classical arguments against it. It developed as a philosophical concept, in the West in pre-Socratic Greek philosophy. By the eighteenth century, in the face of the emergence of modern science, atheism had become a matter of concern for Christian preachers. In the sermons of John Wesley, "atheist" occurs sixteen times. In "Without God in the World" he maintains "I do not mean that they are Atheists, in the common sense of the word. I do not believe that these are so numerous as many have imagined...who seriously disbelieved the being of God...nay, I have found only two of these (to the best of my judgment) in the British Islands." Even though the majority of Americans believe at least in a "higher being," it is clear that the concern among preachers remains considerable.

What we might translate as "hell" in the OT is *šə'ōl*, sometimes rendered as the "pit" (i.e. the grave). It comes from a common Semitic root meaning "to ask" and possibly derives from necromancy. The witch of Endor brings Samuel up from *šə'ōl*. The curse uttered against the king of Babylon (Isaiah 14) says, "All they shall speak and say unto thee, Art thou also become weak as we?" This has been taken to imply that the original Hebrew view of Hell was the great leveler, much like Hades among the Greeks, where both the exalted and the lowly are weak shades (ghostly beings). Closer to home, Joseph Smith Sr. was at one point a member of the Universalists, who held that all mankind will be saved. Regarding disbelief in the existence of hell, not evidenced in the Bible, in a sermon of George Whitefield, "The Lord Our Righteousness," when the Earl of Rochester remains unconvinced of the "invisible realities of another world," he is told "Well, my lord, if there be no hell, I am safe. But if there should be such a thing as hell, what will become of you?" Hell has often been used as a sort of theological terrorism.

Your Nothingness, & Unworthy Creatures

> Mosiah 4:5. For behold, if the knowledge of the goodness of God at this time has awakened you to a sense of your nothingness. (See Mosiah 4:11. "your own nothingness, and his goodness and long-suffering towards you, unworthy creatures.")

Reducing man to nothingness, or abject unworthy creatures, is not Biblical. Likewise, it has now gone out of fashion. But it was emphasized in certain Euro-Christian doctrines. This negative view of humanity is especially famous in the theology of some New England Puritanism. In BOM sermonology, it is most extreme in Mosiah

This self-denying view of the worth of man developed in Euro-Christianity. An explanation of the Greek Orthodox way of life states: Saint Theophan says that the ancient Church Fathers tell us, "The feeling of one's nothingness and dedication to God unfolds best under constant sorrows and especially through extreme, providential crosses..." A Roman Catholic comments on the view of St. Therese of Lisieux: "When asked what she meant by 'remaining a little child before God', Therese responded: 'It is to recognize our nothingness, to expect everything from God.'" The views of New Englander Jonathan Edwards are well known. He wrote: "whereby there has been wanting a sense of the awful and holy majesty of God as present with them, and their nothingness and vileness before him."[131] A hymn by Greg Metcalf has a line "Your blessings are to us as creatures unworthy."

The Earth

> Helaman 14:21. the rocks which are upon the face of this earth, which are both above the earth and beneath, which ye know at this time are solid, or the more part of it is one solid mass, shall be broken up

The BOM authors inserted comments to show that scripture is not unaware of scientific truth. In Helaman 12:15 we find a description of a solar-centric system. Even so, they explain God's stopping the sun in its path by asserting that actually, it is the earth that stops its rotation. In 14:21, they address the structure of the earth, and reveal a view of the earth that is unaware of the earth's complex structure, with a solid crust, a mantle that is largely ductile, and a core that behaves like a liquid. At the time, a lively debate was ongoing between the emerging science of the origin, history and structure of the earth, and various scripture-based arguments to counter what was perceived to be a challenge to the validity of scripture. The BOM authors thought that they had a sufficient understanding of the issues that they could include a scientifically valid statement to show that BOM prophets had a sound understanding of the truth on this topic.

---

[131] Jonathan Edwards, *Some Thoughts Concerning the Present Revival of Religion in New England*, Part IV. Sect. III, 2. *The Works of Jonathan Edwards*, Peabody, MA: Hendriksen Publishers, 1993).

God and Country

> Alma 56:11. died in the cause of their country and of their God (See also Alma 58:8; 59:13; 60:29, 36; 61:6, 21; 62:1-2; 62:4, 9; 62:37; Helaman 6:23-24; & 3 Nephi 3:2)

Prior to the era of the nation state, one did not think in terms of "our country," but rather, our city, people, tribe, or land (of Judea, etc.). Country, as an abstract political or nationalist idea, did not exist. "Country" and "God and country" fit perfectly into nineteenth-century American discourse. For the emergence of the idea of the nation state, see the classic *Idea of Nationalism* by Hans Kohn.[132]

The assessment of these passages involves keeping the following in mind:

> 1) As Christianity spread throughout Europe, it tended to merge to some extent with local cultures. A notable example is the major role that pre-Christian Greek philosophy played in the development of Euro-Christian theology. Indeed theology, in its most rigorous sense, is an adaptation of Greek, especially Aristotelian learning to the Middle Eastern religious heritage. On a more devotional level, many Christian leaders produced a legacy of sermons, poetry and hymns that had a profound effect on English-language discourse by the nineteenth century.
> 1) It is not easy to retrieve the religious discourse of the early nineteenth century. There is a huge amount of material that no longer exists, and what does exist is not easily searched. Nor has it been possible to resurrect a random sample of Upstate New York inhabitants of the 1820's. These examples only scratch the surface of what must still be extant, waiting to be discovered.
> 2) One's analysis should not hinge on any particular example. Taken altogether, one can readily see that the BOM text is replete with English Euro-Christian phrases and concepts.

---

[132] Hans Kohn, *The Idea of Nationalism, a Study in its Origins and Background* (New York: Macmillan, 1944).

8. The Post-Biblical Euro-Christian Text   209

3) There is no intention here to imply that any BOM author consulted the sermons of John Wesley, or any other source cited above. Even Wesley most probably did not invent the phrases in his sermons, but drew from language that had already become the common coin of the Christian realm in England. English is a language of idioms and expressions. For the religiously inclined, growing up Christian meant acquiring fluency in this heritage.

What is not clear is whether the BOM authors wrote in this manner totally unaware that certain phrases are post-Biblical and therefore inappropriate, being the creations of later times and religious culture; or if they deliberately used these phrases to make their text more familiar and easily accepted; or, perhaps more probably, as a combination of the two. However this may be, although we are accustomed to material such as this being used to assess the *Book of Mormon*, this material can be studied the other way around, using the BOM text as documentation for the analysis of the religious culture of Upstate New York in the 1820's.

Chapter 9

Restoring and Supplementing Biblical Texts

Even before the *Book of Mormon* was completed, Joseph Smith's calling to restore lost scripture was envisaged as extending beyond it.

The Book of Abraham

Reformed Egyptian Exists

Egyptian writing has had a very long and continuous history of change. Characters have been found on Gerzean pottery resembling hieroglyphs, dating to c. 4,000 BCE. Günter Dreyer found about 300 clay labels in tomb U-j bearing protohieroglyphs dated to the 33rd century BCE. The first full sentence discovered so far is from the tomb of Seth-Peribsen of the 28th century BCE, at Umm el-Qa'ab. By the 25th century BCE an extensive sign list had developed (note the pyramid text at the pyramid of Unas). These included logograms, i.e. signs representing a complete word, independent of phonological content. Other signs were phonological, including signs for one consonant, for two consonants, and even for three. For the most part, vowels were not indicated (unlike ancient Sumerian and Akkadian).

But also very early, those who needed to write in their daily activities, primarily merchants and administrators, needed something less time-consuming than having to draw a picture of a particular species of bird, just to represent the letter *m* (for example). The same logogram was used, but simplified, requiring fewer strokes. This process resulted in hieratic. It is mostly possible to recognize the original hieroglyph in the hieratic character. Much later, a further simplification occurred, demotic. This was now so different that it is generally not possible to see the hieroglyph in the character, but the connection with the hieratic antecedent is clearer. Finally, the latest form of Egyptian, before it went extinct, is Coptic (*copt* related to *-gypt* in Egypt). To write this, the Greek alphabet was used, supplemented by Egyptian-origin characters for sounds not in Greek. Now, finally, the language was rewritten to reflect much of the linguistic change that had happened in the spoken language over two millennia. But Coptic remains, at base, still Egyptian. For example, the word for god is *n-tch-r* (vowels not written) in hieroglyphic, but *noute* in Coptic (dialects varying slightly). The freestanding pronouns are as follows:

Table 20. Middle Egyptian and Coptic Pronouns Compared

Person	Singular		Person	Plural	
	Egyptian	Coptic		Egyptian	Coptic
1. c. (I)	ínk	anok	1. c. (we)	ínn	anon
2. m. (you)	nt.k	ntok	2. c. (you)	nt.tn	ntôten
2. f. (you)	ntt	nto			
3. m. (he)	nt.f	ntof	3. c. (they)	nt.sn	ntôou
3. f. (she)	nt.s	ntos			

Champollion had studied Coptic, and when he succeeded in deciphering some of the Egyptian characters on the Rosetta Stone, he suddenly had a breakthrough realization: "Hey, I already know this language, sort of. It is the antecedent of Coptic." Coptic had never gone extinct, and is still used as the liturgical language for Coptic Christian services in Egypt today. It was a great aid in deciphering earlier stages of Egyptian.

But note, some sort of "reformed" Egyptian as a code has never been found, where one character can represent a sentence, a paragraph or even a high mystery of the initiate.

Joseph Smith's Notion/Rational for Reformed Egyptian

The mention in the *Book of Mormon* that the Brass Plates of Laban were written in Egyptian is remarkable, being the record of Lehi's Hebrew fathers (the Old Testament up to his departure). It is not impossible, of course, that that family had returned to Egypt, possibly to carry on commerce, and had become bilingual. Even if they were bilingual, certainly Hebrew would have been their choice, the sacred language. A more remarkable mention of this language is found in connection with the gold plates, in Mormon 9:32-34:

> 32. And now, behold, we have written this record according to our knowledge, in the characters which are called among us the reformed Egyptian, being handed down and altered by us, according to our manner of speech.
> 33. And if our plates had been sufficiently large we should have written in Hebrew; but the Hebrew hath been altered by us also; and if we could have

written in Hebrew, behold, ye would have had no imperfection in our record.
34. But the Lord knoweth the things which we have written, and also that none other people knoweth our language; therefore he hath prepared means for the interpretation thereof.

We find here some interesting points. First, apparently their first language was Hebrew, although it too had undergone change. They could write in it more perfectly. Second, the use of reformed Egyptian was dictated by a shortage of gold, indicating a belief that writing in reformed Egyptian is more compact than in reformed Hebrew. That this most probably is not the case, or not to any great degree, can be seen in Figure 2, *infra*. Even with this description we are not able to know what "reformed" means, since it states that the characters had been reformed. Were only the characters reformed, or the vocabulary, morphology and syntax as well? The same holds true regarding the reference to Hebrew. In what sense and to what degree was it altered?

The text seems to also make clear the real reason for the Brass Plates to be in Egyptian, and the gold plates in reformed Egyptian. It is said in the statement, "none other people knoweth our language." The introduction of the Brass Plates in Egyptian is intended as an explanation for their ability to write the gold plates in Egyptian, albeit reformed Egyptian. And the gold plates are in Egyptian in order for Joseph Smith to have plates in a language that he believed, at that time, to be unknown. Indeed, in the statements of his contemporaries, both believers and detractors, I have never seen a mention of Champollion. The authors of the *Book of Mormon* could not be called to task in regard to the language of the plates.

Before the discovery of the Rosetta Stone, and the subsequent decipherment of ancient Egyptian, a common view was that in Egyptian writing, a single character could represent a whole sentence, or more. Thus even small texts were being "translated" into long documents. The most famous and influential of these was the work of Athanasius Kircher (c. 1601-1680). He, for example, translated two characters, d̲d̲ Ws̲r̲ ("Osiris says") to mean: "The treachery of Typhon ends at the throne of Isis; the moisture of nature is guarded by the vigilance of Anubis."[133]

---

[133] Examples of his translations may be found in his *Sphinx mystagoga: sive Diatribe hieroglyphica, qua Mumiae, ex Memphiticis Pyramidum Adytis Erutae...* (1676 edition).

Figure 2. Does Egyptian Have a More Compact Script?

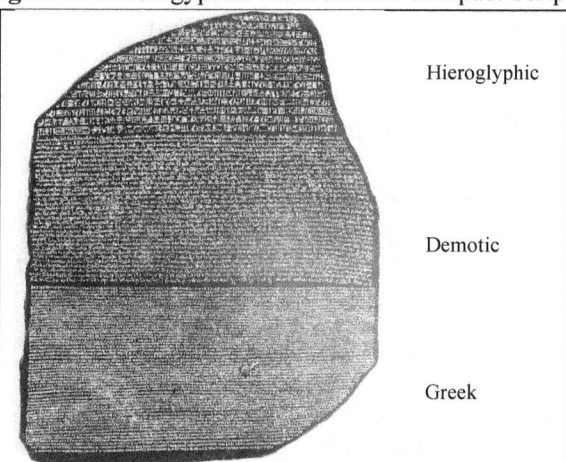

Hieroglyphic

Demotic

Greek

It is difficult to compare languages for compactness. A good basis for our interest is the Rosetta Stone. We do not have the whole hieroglyphic section, but can see that the Demotic and Greek texts occupy about the same space. To evaluate this observation, it is necessary to know that the Greek text is written in smaller characters (and in Greek, this is possible), and that the Greek writes the vowels, while the Demotic writes only the consonants. On balance, it is not clear that Demotic is more compact than Greek. Like Demotic, Hebrew does not write vowels. Like Greek, Hebrew characters are capable of being written small.

The famous Egyptologist, Sir E. A. Budge wrote of him:[134]

> Many writers pretended to have found the key to the hieroglyphics, and many more professed, with a shameless impudence, which is hard to understand in these days, to translate the contents of the texts into a modern tongue. Foremost among such pretenders must be mentioned Athanasius Kircher, who, in the 17th century, declared that he had found the key to the hieroglyphic inscriptions; the translations which he prints in his *Oedipus Aegyptiacus* are utter nonsense, but as they were put forth in a learned tongue many people at the time believed they were correct.

---

[134] E. A. Wallis Budge, *Egyptian Language: Easy Lessons in Egyptian Hieroglyphics* (Mineola, NY: Dover, 1983 [1910]),15.

On several occasions Joseph Smith said that he was working on a translation of the Egyptian alphabet, and grammar. The text of this work has been preserved in the Church historian's office and has been published. He also did a work that I call the translation document, which lists characters from this papyrus in a column, and opposite each, a phrase or sentence found in *The Book of Abraham*.

The concept reigning in America of the Egyptian language seems to have been untouched by Champollion's work, and so it is not surprising to find, in Joseph Smith's *Egyptian Alphabet and Grammar* a similar pre-19th century approach, reproduced in part below.

Table 21. Examples from Smith's Egyptian Alphabet and Grammar

Character	Smith's Rules
1.	This is called Za Ki-oan hiash, or chaslidon hiash. This character is in the fifth degree, independent and arbitrary. It may be present in the fifth degree while it stands independent and arbitrary. That is, without a straight mark inserted above or below it.
2.	By inserting a straight mark over it thus, (2) it increases its significance five degrees;
3.	by inserting two straight lines thus, (3) its signification is increased five more.
4.	By inserting three straight lines thus, (4) its signification is again increased five more degrees than the last.
5.	By counting the number of straight lines, or considering them as qualifying adjectives, we have the degrees of comparison. There are five connecting parts of speech in the above character, called Za Ki-on hish. These five connecting parts of speech [are] for verbs, participles, prepositions, conjunctions, and adverbs. In translating this character, the subject must be continued until there are as many of these connecting parts of speech used as there are connections, or connecting points, found in the character. But whenever the character is found with one horizontal line, as at (2), the subject must be continued until five times the number of connecting parts of speech are used, or the full sense of the writer is not conveyed. When two horizontal lines occur, the number of connecting parts of speech are continued five times further—or five degrees. And when three horizontal lines occur, the number of connecting parts of speech are continued five times further. The character alone has 5 parts of speech increased by one straight line thus: 5 x 5 is 25; by two horizontal lines thus: 25 x 5 = 125; and by three horizontal lines thus: 125 x 5 = 625. When this character has a horizontal line under it reduces it to the fourth degree, consequently it has but four connecting parts of speech.

(Table 21 continued)

| 6. | *f* | When it has two horizontal lines, it is reduced into the third degree and has but three connecting parts of speech, |
| 7. | *f* | And when it has three horizontal lines it is reduced into the second degree and has but two connecting parts of speech. |

Nothing here addresses the problem of identifying the phonological or semantic content of the characters on the papyrus. What do they mean?

Among comparative linguists, there are those who specialize in language universals. Enough universals have been found to seriously suggest that the human brain has evolved to be "hard-wired" for language. In any case, all languages (even the so-called ergative languages) have subjects, verbs and objects. Writing systems all have a way to unambiguously represent each of these, whether through logograms (Chinese), phonological signs (English) or a combination of logograms and phonological signs (Egyptian and Akkadian). It is inconceivable that a system such as that attempted by Smith could work. Still wedded to the approach destroyed by Champollion, he is trying to answer the question, "OK, so how can one know how much meaning a single sign can represent." For Smith, it can be huge. It is hard to understand how he planned to use such a method, since the Egyptian characters in the papyrus don't have these lines above and below. The Egyptians, on one line, could place one character above another. What Smith may have thought was a line is possibly the letter *n* (a horizontal zigzag line like saw teeth). In a late text, this can look like a horizontal line.

What Should Be Found, and Actually Has Been Found

The written materials, in books (metallic plates, vellum, etc.) or stone inscriptions, of the Nephite/Lamanite civilization, can be expected, first of all, to look like the writing that Smith claimed to have transcribed from his gold plates, at least that written in the late period. He made this transcription, or so he claimed, of the alphabet he found there, for his first scribe, Martin Harris, to take to some "learned men." (See Figure 3, *supra*) This was in the RLDS church archives, and when I was sent off as a Mormon missionary, I was armed with a plastic-laminated copy of it to show to my contacts. It may be our best clue of what archaeologists should dig up, but Anthon's two descriptions stated the characters were arranged in columns, raising issues regarding this copy. It may be a second version, after Harris' visit to Anthon.

On the other hand, the Brass Plates of Laban were written in Egyptian, presumably late hieratic or possibly demotic at 600 BCE, and any written material at an early date would, presumably, be closer to it.

Figure 3. Copy Made from the Anthon Transcript

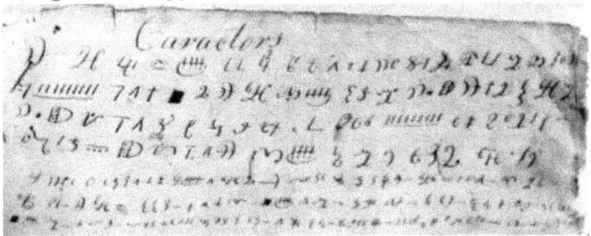

What we have actually found is totally different. Mesoamerican writing scripts include Olmec, Zapotec, Isthmian, and Mayan. The Aztecs did begin to adopt writing as well, under Zapotec influence, but it was not as developed. The Incas did not write, nor any other group that we have studied.

For a long time the Mayan glyphs were thought to be highly ornamental and only suggestive of meaning, perhaps a bit like what was assumed about Egyptian before the Rosetta Stone. An amazing documentary, *Breaking the Mayan Code*, shows blow by blow how Mayan was deciphered. One can also consult the book, *Breaking the Mayan Code*, by Michael Coe. The bottom line is that, like Egyptian, there is a mixture of logograms and phonological characters. But unlike Egyptian, Mayan phonological signs are syllabic (like Sumerian, Akkadian, and ancient Ethiopic). That is to say, there is a character for *bi*, another for *bo*, another for *ba*, another for *bu*, and so on, for all the consonants. Here again, one cannot get a sentence or a whole paragraph out of a single character. One of the great breakthroughs was the realization that Mayan, and indeed Aztec, are still spoken languages in Mexico. As a student at Harvard, I met a native Aztec speaker. At some point in the decipherment process, it was realized that spoken Mayan had not changed hugely from the Mayan of the stelae and the few books that survived the book-burning priest, Diego de Landa. Grammar books and a dictionary had already been written for a modern Mayan language, a great help. Certainly there are issues remaining to be solved, including words yet to be figured out. But this is always the case in ancient languages. Even in Biblical Hebrew, there are a great number of *hapax legomena*, words that occur only once in the whole Old Testament. The exact meaning of many of these remains debated today.

Mayan is a very distinctive language, and is absolutely in no way related to Hebrew, or any other Semitic language, or to Egyptian, or any other Hamito-Semitic language. The conclusion: the assertions of the *Book of Mormon* require that we find some sort of Hebrew or Egyptian, and if ever it were found, it would not be hard to recognize it.

Abraham Found?

An American in Philadelphia, Michael Chandler, came into possession of eleven mummies around 1833. Apparently he collected them from customs in New York, possibly under contract with representatives of the estate of the late Antonio Lebolo of Castellamonte, a rich Italian merchant, who had acted as superintendent of the archaeological digs in Egypt for Bernardino Drovetti. In this capacity, he had acquired eleven mummies. The identification of Lebolo's mummies with those Chandler took possession of is not completely proven, but a good case has been made for it by H. Donl Peterson and H. Michael Marquardt.[135] Chandler was touring to exhibit them for profit, but was occasionally selling a mummy, and was to pay a share of the profits to Lebolo's estate. Unwrapping them, Chandler found some Egyptian papyri. Probably while on tour with his mummy exhibit he heard of Joseph Smith, who claimed to have translated a gold bible from Egyptian, but his angel had taken the plates back. Certainly he would have liked to have something of this nature, to show his followers and prospective converts.

One can imagine the buzz in the Mormon community when, in June of 1835, Chandler arrived with his mummies and papyri in the Mormon center at that time, Kirtland, Ohio. Joseph Smith purchased four mummies and a collection of papyri. Reportedly he was only interested in the papyri, but Chandler insisted on a package deal. When later he had had an opportunity to study the papyri a bit, he announced that one of them was *The Book of Abraham*. For his followers, the mission of their

---

[135] H. Donl Peterson, *The Story of The Book of Abraham, Mummies, Manuscripts and Mormonism* (Salt Lake City: Deseret Book Company, 1995). H. Michael Marquardt, "Joseph Smith's Egyptian Papers: A History," in Robert K. Ritner, *The Joseph Smith Egyptian Papyri, A Complete Edition* (Salt Lake City: Signature Books, 2013), 11-68.

prophet to bring forth lost scriptures was ongoing, but this time, even better, as the Egyptian documents were there for all to see.

Smith said that the project of translation required preliminary work. He wrote, "The remainder of this month (July, 1835) I was continually engaged in translating an alphabet to '*The Book of Abraham*,' and arranging a grammar of the Egyptian language as practiced by the ancients."[136] After some tumultuous years, and when the Mormons had moved to Nauvoo, Illinois, he published what he called *The Book of Abraham*, claimed to be a translation from one of the papyri, in March of 1842. Eventually, the LDS Church accepted this work as divine scripture. It has been a source of some uniquely Mormon theology, making it indispensable. In the turmoil accompanying and following the murder of Joseph Smith, the mummies and papyri disappeared. Many were certain, and perhaps wished to believe, that they had found their way to a museum in Chicago that was destroyed in the Chicago fire.

In 1967, the founder of the Middle East Center at the University of Utah, Dr. Aziz Suryal Atiya, a renowned expert on the Crusades and on the history of the Coptic Christians in Egypt, he himself being a Copt, was searching the storage area at the Metropolitan Museum of Art for Coptic materials, where he found the Joseph Smith papyri, with a bill of sale signed by Joseph Smith's first wife, Emma. This included some, but clearly not all, of the papyri (at least, a hypocephalus, or solar disk, published in the *Pearl of Great Price*, has not been recovered). On 27 November 1967, the Museum presented them to the LDS Church. Later they were locked up in the university's vaults, and many feared that they would become inaccessible. Rumor had it at the time that the staff of *Dialogue, a Journal of Mormon Thought*, put pressure on the Church to make them available. Apparently fearing nothing, the Church published them in very beautiful images in *The Improvement Era*, its official organ. Subsequently, Egyptologists translated them. The papyrus that had been identified conclusively as being the one that Smith said he translated into *The Book of Abraham* turned out to be an ancient Egyptian funerary text called the *Sensen* (breathing) document, or Breathing Permit of Hor, for the reanimation of the mummy. This, of course, created a great stir, and some intellectual exodus from the Church. How could the LDS establishment respond to this challenge?

---

[136] Joseph Smith, *History of the Church of Jesus Christ of Latter-day Saints* (Salt Lake City: Deseret News, 1902), 2:238.

Facsimile No. 1. The Lion Couch Scene

The identification of the *Sensen* papyrus with the papyrus that Joseph Smith claimed to have translated into *The Book of Abraham* has been made decisively by *"Facsimile No. 1,"* a detailed reproduction in the BOA of a distinctive vignette found in the papyrus.

Figure 4. Facsimile No. 1 (*The Book of Abraham*)

EXPLANATION OF THE ABOVE CUT

Fig. 1. The Angel of the Lord. 2. Abraham fastened upon an altar. 3. The idolatrous priest of Elkenah attempting to offer up Abraham as a sacrifice. 4. The altar for sacrifice by the idolatrous priest, standing before the gods of Elkenah, Libnah, Mahmackrah, Korash, and Pharaoh. 5. The idolatrous god of Elkenah. 6. The idolatrous god of Libnah. 7. The idolatrous god of Mahmackrah. 8. The idolatrous god of Korash. 9. The idolatrous god of Pharaoh. 10. Abraham in Egypt. 11. Designed to represent the pillars of heaven, as understood by the Egyptians. 12. Raukeeyang, signifying expanse, or the firmament over our heads; but in this case, in relation to this subject, the Egyptians meant it to signify Shaumau, to be high, or the heavens, answering to the Hebrew word, Shaumahyeem.

Source: *The Book of Abraham* (Times & Seasons, 1842. "Explanation" is reformatted).

This "vignette of the corpse in the process of reanimation is common in Books of Breathings..."[137] with the deceased lying on the lion couch, the jackal-headed mummification god Anubis standing behind, and the *ba* spirit of the deceased in the form of a bird with a human head. Beneath the couch are the four standard canopic jars, holding the key organs of the deceased that were extracted during mummification. Each jar is identified by its head (lid). To communicate reanimation, the ancient artist depicts the posture of the deceased with arms uplifted and legs apart, with one leg uplifted.[138]

Figure 5. Egyptologist Bell's Proposed Reconstruction

Source: Lanny Bell.

In an early criticism of *The Book of Abraham*, it was claimed that Facsimile No. 1 had been modified, that the head of the figure behind the lion couch must originally have been Anubis, the mummification god, with the head of a jackal. Now that the original papyrus has resurfaced and has been studied, it turns out that a large area is missing, including the head of Anubis, the hand of Anubis' outstretched arm including what he is grasping, the arms of the deceased, and part of the head of the *ba*

---

[137] Ritner, *The Joseph Smith Egyptian Papyri*, 115.
[138] The reconstruction of Figure 5 is from Lanny Bell, "The Ancient Egyptian 'Books of Breathings,' the Mormon 'Book of Abraham,' and the Development of Egyptology in America," in Stephen E. Thompson & Peter Der Manuelian, eds., *Egypt and Beyond, Essays Presented to Leonard H. Lesko upon his Retirement* (Providence, RI: Brown University, 2008), 30.

spirit. In the gap, in pencil, the head of Anubis is drawn as a human head. His outstretched hand holding a sacrificial knife, the two arms of the deceased and the head of the ba spirit were drawn in to befit *The Book of Abraham* story. This was drawn on the paper upon which the papyrus had been mounted.

Figure 6. The Papyrus used for a part of *The Book of Abraham*

Figure 7. Smith's Modified Papyrus for Facsimile No. 1

Note the top damaged area above the image has a shallow swoop on the left and a deeper swoop on the right. The same is true of the text panel to the left. Comparing the deep swoops, we find the latter is very frayed, but the one above the lion couch has clean edges. It seems a pen knife was used to remove unwanted material, to create space for the pencil drawing. This is further evidence of deliberate modification.

A number of leading Egyptologists have worked on these papyri. The first to do so was John A. Wilson, Andrew MacLeish Distinguished Service Professor of Egyptology at the Oriental Institute of the University of Chicago,[139] and Richard A. Parker, Wilbour Professor of Egyptology and Department Chairman at Brown University. They were followed by Klaus Baer, Associate Professor at Chicago's Oriental Institute,[140] and more recently, Robert K. Ritner, Professor of Egyptology also at the Oriental Institute, who has published a complete definitive edition.[141]

Some have claimed that although it is the right papyrus, Joseph Smith mistakenly thought he was translating it, while at the time he was actually receiving the text of *The Book of Abraham* by revelation. He was killed before he could realize or correct his error. This argument is also impossible, because in *The Book of Abraham*, Abraham himself makes a first-person reference to Facsimile No. 1:

> 12. And it came to pass that the priests laid violence upon me, that they might slay me also, as they did those virgins upon the altar; and that you may have a knowledge of this altar, I will refer you to the representation at the commencement of this record.
> 13. It was made after the form of a bedstead, such as was had among the Chaldeans, and it stood before the gods of Elkenah, Libnah, Mahmackrah, Korash, and also a god like unto that of Pharaoh, king of Egypt.

Figure 8 shows the text found to the left of the lion couch scene. Parts of the Abraham translation document and hypocephalus (v. *infra*) draw from the first four of these lines. These are shown more clearly in Figure 9, where the lines have been numbered to facilitate discussion .

---

[139] *Dialogue, a Journal of Mormon Thought*, Vol. III, No. 2, 67-85.
[140] *Dialogue, a Journal of Mormon Thought*, Vol. III, No. 3, 109-134.
[141] Ritner, *The Joseph Smith Egyptian Papyri*.

9. Restoring and Supplementing Biblical Texts 223

Figure 8. The Passage to the Left of the Lion Couch Scene

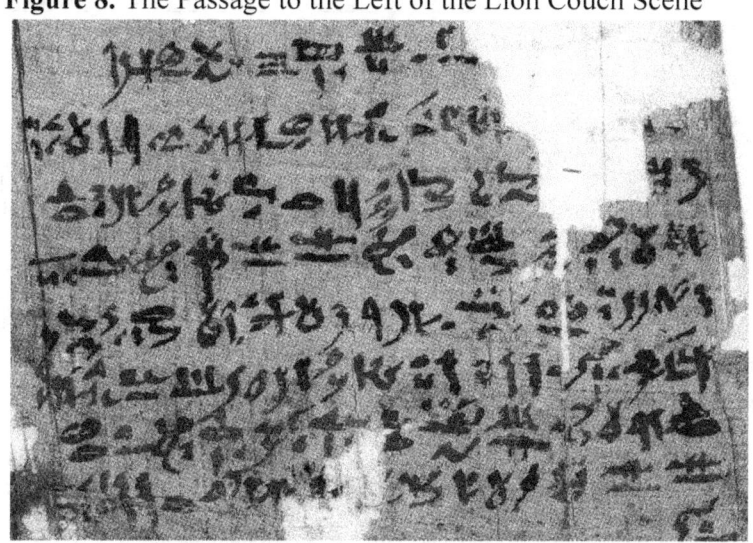

Figure 9. The Texts Used to Produce Abraham and the Hypocephalus

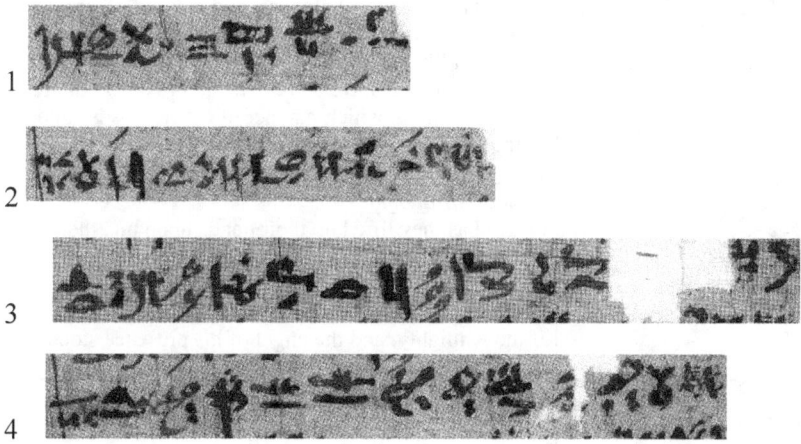

Table 22 is based on a Joseph Smith translation document. In the column on the left, it lists characters from Figure 9. There we see the photographed character on the left, Smith's transcription to its right, the egyptologist's translation of the character below these, and Smith's translation opposite each character in the column on the right.

Table 22. Smith's BOA Translation of Characters from the Abraham Papyrus

Egyptologist Translation (photo from the papyrus, with Smith's transcription, & the egyptologist's translation.)	Smith's Attempted Translation of the Character.
Egyptologist: The, this (Figure 9, line 1)	*Book of Abraham* text 11. Now, this priest had offered upon this altar three virgins at one time, who were the daughters of Onitah, one of the royal descent directly from the loins of Ham. These virgins were offered up because of their virtue; they would not bow down to worship gods of wood or of stone, therefore they were killed upon this altar,
Egyptologist: pool, lake (Figure 9, line 1)	*Book of Abraham* text: and it was done after the manner of the Egyptians. 12. And it came to pass that the priests laid violence upon me, that they might slay me also, as they did those virgins upon this altar; and that you may have a knowledge of this altar, I will refer you to the representation at the commencement of this record.
Egyptologist: Water determinative (for clarification, not for translation) (Figure 9, line 1)	*Book of Abraham* text: 13. It was made after the form of a bedstead, such as was had among the Chaldeans, and it stood before the gods of Elkenah, Libnah, Mahmackrah, Korash, and also a god like unto that of Pharaoh, king of Egypt. 14. That you may have an understanding of the figures at the beginning, which manner of the figures is called by the Chaldeans Rahleenos, which signifies hieroglyphics.
Egyptologist: great (Figure 9, line 1)	*Book of Abraham* text: 15. And as they lifted up their hands upon me, that they might offer me up and take away my life, behold, I lifted up my voice unto my God, and the Lord hearkened and heard, and he filled me with the vision of the Almighty, and the angel of his presence stood by me, and immediately unloosed my bands;
Egyptologist: Khonsu (the moon god of Thebes) (Figure 9, line 1)	*Book of Abraham* text: 16. And his voice was unto me: Abraham, Abraham, behold, my name is Jehovah, and I have heard thee, and have come down to deliver thee, and to take thee away from thy father's house, and from all thy kinsfolk, into a strange land which thou knowest not of; 17. And this because they have turned their hearts away from me, to worship the god of Elkenah, and the god of Libnah, and the god of Mahmackrah, and

9. Restoring and Supplementing Biblical Texts   225

(Table 22 continued)

	the god of Korash, and the god of Pharaoh, king of Egypt; therefore I have come down to destroy him who hath lifted up his hand against thee, Abraham, my son, to take away thy life. 18. Behold, I will lead thee by my hand, and I will take thee, to put upon thee my name, even the Priesthood of the father, and my power shall be over thee. 19. As it was with Noah so shall it be with thee; but through thy ministry my name shall be known in the earth forever, for I am thy God.
Egyptologist: Born of (Figure 9, line 2)	*Book of Abraham* text: 29. Now, after the priest of Elkenah was smitten that he died, there came a fulfillment (sic) of those things which were said unto me concerning the land of Chaldea, that there should be a famine in the land. 30. Accordingly a famine prevailed throughout all the land of Chaldea, and my father was sorely tormented because of the famine, and he repented of the evil which he had determined against me, to take away my life. 31. But the records of the father, even the patriarchs, concerning the right of Priesthood, the Lord my God preserved in mine own hands; therefore a knowledge of the beginning of the creation, and also of the planets, and of the stars, as they were made known unto the fathers, have I kept even unto this day,
Egyptologist: Tai (first part of a name) (Figure 9, line 2)	*Book of Abraham* text: And I shall endeavor to write some of these things upon this record, for the benefit of my posterity that shall come after me.
Egyptologist: Khibit, (2nd half of the name) (Fig. 9, line 2)	*Book of Abraham* text: 1. Now the Lord God caused the famine to wax sore in the land of Ur, insomuch that Haran, my brother, died; but Terah, my father, yet lived in the land of Ur, of the Chaldees. 2. And it came to pass that, Abraham, took Sarai to wife and Nehor, my brother, took Milcah to wife.
Egyptologist: determinative for a woman's name (not to be translated) (Figure 9, line 2)	*Book of Abraham* text: Who was the daughter of Haran.

(Table 22 continued)

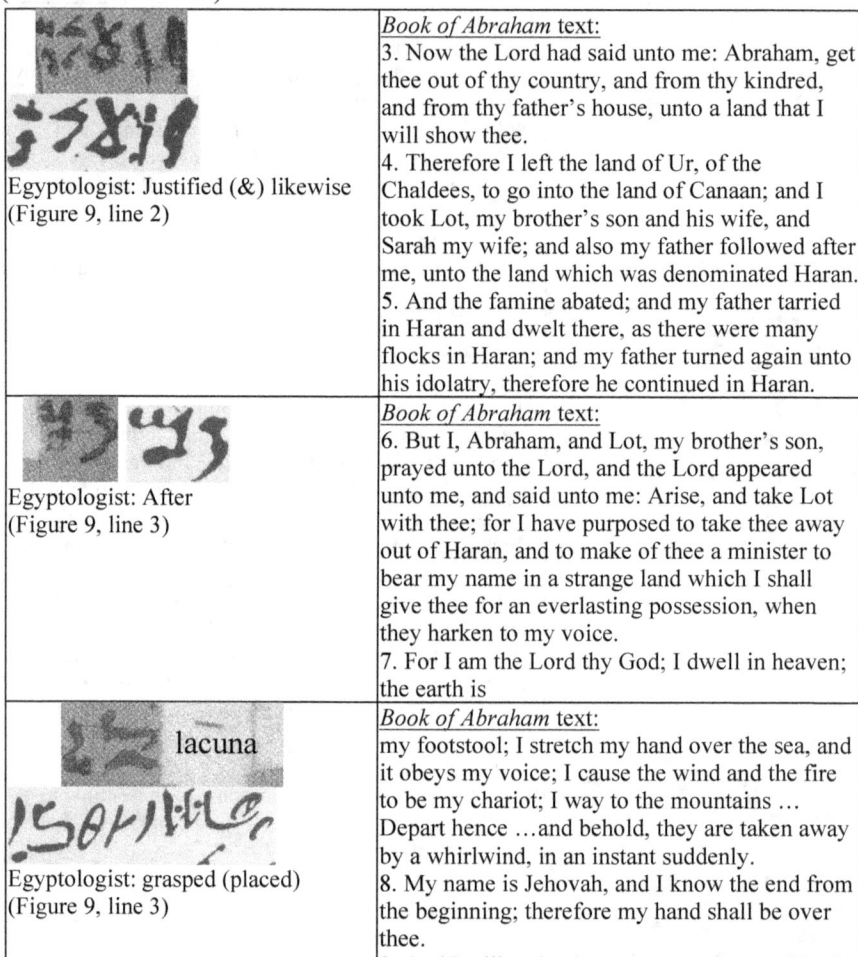

	Book of Abraham text:
Egyptologist: Justified (&) likewise (Figure 9, line 2)	3. Now the Lord had said unto me: Abraham, get thee out of thy country, and from thy kindred, and from thy father's house, unto a land that I will show thee. 4. Therefore I left the land of Ur, of the Chaldees, to go into the land of Canaan; and I took Lot, my brother's son and his wife, and Sarah my wife; and also my father followed after me, unto the land which was denominated Haran. 5. And the famine abated; and my father tarried in Haran and dwelt there, as there were many flocks in Haran; and my father turned again unto his idolatry, therefore he continued in Haran.
Egyptologist: After (Figure 9, line 3)	Book of Abraham text: 6. But I, Abraham, and Lot, my brother's son, prayed unto the Lord, and the Lord appeared unto me, and said unto me: Arise, and take Lot with thee; for I have purposed to take thee away out of Haran, and to make of thee a minister to bear my name in a strange land which I shall give thee for an everlasting possession, when they harken to my voice. 7. For I am the Lord thy God; I dwell in heaven; the earth is
Egyptologist: grasped (placed) (Figure 9, line 3)	Book of Abraham text: my footstool; I stretch my hand over the sea, and it obeys my voice; I cause the wind and the fire to be my chariot; I way to the mountains … Depart hence …and behold, they are taken away by a whirlwind, in an instant suddenly. 8. My name is Jehovah, and I know the end from the beginning; therefore my hand shall be over thee. 9. And I will make thee a great nation, and I will bless thee above measure, and make thy name great among all nations,

There exists a collection of translation material.[142] Much of it is unclear. Ritner has selected the passages where Smith's Egyptian character is clear enough to be recognized in the papyrus text in Figure 9. His translation of the characters in the column on the left, put together as

---

[142] H. Michael Marquardt, *The Joseph Smith Egyptian Papers* (Cullman, AL: Printing Service, 1981).

they originally were to form a continuous text, albeit out of context, reads: "the great lake of Khonsu, and likewise born of Taikhibit, the justified, after his two arms have been [placed/grasped] at his heart,.."[143]

To emphasize how wrong Smith's translation is, note the character on row three that was transcribed to look like a backwards E (Ǝ, but should be three horizontal lines). This is a determinative. Far from writing in a way that allowed a single sign to be interpreted as having lengthy meaning, the ancient scribes were concerned to reduce ambiguity. They developed a set of semantic category signs to help clarify the word associated with it, by indicating what semantic category it belonged to. An example is the word for sun, written with a circle and a tiny circle inside it, a logogram, representing the sun. It could also be written phonologically, with the two consonants—*r'*—(no vowel indicated, but English writes it *re*, *ra* or *ra'*). When it meant simply the sun itself, the object we see in the sky, it could be accompanied by the circle sign. But if it meant the sun god Re, it could be accompanied by a deity determinative, a picture of a seated god. The determinative only clarified the word it accompanies, without adding meaning, and is neither pronounced nor translated. Here, the scribe is simply indicating that the word "lake" is in the water category, and should not be mistaken for any homonym. A rough example in English is our use of quotation marks, signs to eliminate ambiguity, distinguishing what is quoted from the rest of the text. Quotation marks are not translated into sentences, or verses. To render quotation marks separately, and make them into two verses of *The Book of Abraham*, would be as silly as doing just that with the Egyptian water determinative. Smith also translated the determinative for a woman's name. A name sign is useful. I was born in Green River, located on the Green River. In Egyptian, the first might have a city determinative just so no one would mistakenly think that I was born in a river.

Apparently Smith continued to think that no one would ever be able to read Egyptian, or come to know the many gods of the Egyptians, and their names. The sacrifice of virgins on an altar is not Egyptian practice. The four gods mentioned are the four canopic jars for the deceased's key organs, typical of a funerary papyrus illustration. By the time of this papyrus, they also represented the four points of the compass: Hapi (the baboon-headed god—north; jar for the lungs), Duamutef (jackal-headed

---

[143] Ritner, *The Joseph Smith Egyptian Papyri*, 127.

god—east; jar for the stomach), Imseti (human-headed god—south; jar for the liver), and Qebehsenuef (falcon-headed god—west; jar for the intestines). Once again, Smith's score is zero.

The Egyptians Never Occupied Ur of Chaldea

Between the 10th and 11th centuries BCE, tribes of West Semitic origin migrated into southern Iraq. These are identified as the Suteans and Arameans, followed perhaps a century later by a tribe called the Kaldu, usually referred to as the Chaldeans or Chaldees. After the Chaldeans had become masters of Babylon (9th century BCE), the term Chaldea became synonymous with Babylonia. The Assyrian empire prevented them from expanding into northern Iraq, and in 689 BCE the Assyrians cemented their control by completely razing the city. To put this in historical perspective, David ruled Israel in the 10th century, long after the time ascribed by the Bible to its great patriarch, Abraham.

Ur, located in the deep south of Mesopotamia (Iraq, ten miles from the modern city of Nasiriyah), became a significant settlement in the 4th millennium BCE, and the capital of an empire in the 21st century BCE. It fell into serious decline in the 1st millennium BCE.

Due to its considerable distance from the Fertile Crescent, it has been felt by some biblical scholars that the city referred to in the OT in connection with Abraham must have been some other city. This has led to a search for place names sounding like Ur. The only plausible identification is Urha, in present-day southern Turkey. Since the Chaldeans were clearly far too late to be associated with Abraham, even some LDS scholars have joined the quest for an alternate Ur.

Although Canaanites had established a realm in the eastern Egyptian delta in the 18th century BCE, the principal contact that ancient Egypt had with the Semites was the invasion of the Hyksos, who invaded the delta in c. 1650 BCE, and ruled there until expelled by the campaigns of Seqenenre Tao, Kamose and Ahmose, around a century later. The Egyptians used a term for peoples east and northeast of the delta that Egyptologists have usually translated as "Asiatics," which includes the Semites and peoples of Anatolia and Persia. Apart from the initiatives of Senusret I in the land of Canaan, the beginning of Egyptian extension into Canaan and Syria was the military campaigns of Thutmose I. After quelling a Nubian revolt, he led a military campaign across Canaan and to the northern reaches of Syria. After crossing the Euphrates, he set up a stele to commemorate his presence (although this has never been found), and returned to Egypt. As long as his military force was present in Syria, cities there conveniently capitulated and paid tribute, but as soon as he returned home they stopped their payments and began preparations to repel a possible recurrence of this invasion. His son and successor, Thutmose II, only made raids into Nubia to the south and to a limited extent north into Syria,. The most penetrating of the Egyptian campaigns was conducted by Thutmose III, after acceding to the throne in the wake of the regnant queen Pharaoh (usurper) Hatshepsut. Of most importance is the fact that he kept a personal record (day-book) of his exploits.

We cannot expect that the Pharaoh's own account would be an understatement of his campaign. In it we learn that he traveled across the full extent of modern Syria, and, in his eighth campaign, as far north as Carchemish, on the west bank of the Euphrates, in what is now southern Turkey (mid-15th century, BCE). The only real kingdom opposing him was Mittani, in what is now eastern Turkey. Its king had not expected that the Egyptian campaign would be anything more than brief incursions, and certainly not that Thutmose III would cross the river. When they arrived on the east bank of the Euphrates, the Mittani king was not prepared for war, and withdrew most of his forces. The Pharaoh erected a stele, destroyed some Mittani towns, and withdrew. He did not go as far as Orhay (Syriac; Urha, Urfa, Edessa and Turkish Şanlıurfa). His time on the east side of the Euphrates was limited, and purely military.[144]

Donald B. Redford, the preeminent authority on the campaigns of Thutmose III, wrote:

> While Thutmose lived, the administration of the Levant (if we can even use this formal term) was rudimentary in the extreme. The Egyptian army marched forth at such regular intervals that "resident governors" were unnecessary, and specific tasks in the north were assigned on an ad hoc basis to civil administrators. Only later in the reign (year 47) is mention made of permanent troops in the Akkar plain (Ullaza [north of Biblos, now north Lebanon]), and they have been stationed there for three purposes: to

---

[144] George Steindorff & Keith C. Seele, *When Egypt Ruled the East* (Chicago: The University of Chicago Press, 1957), 58-59; and Donald B. Redford, *The Wars in Syria and Palestine of Thutmose III* (Leiden: Brill, 2003), 220-228.

guard the stores in the "harbors," to supervise the cutting and transport of timber and to keep Eluetheros valley under surveillance.[145]

Map 6. The 8th Campaign of Thutmose III

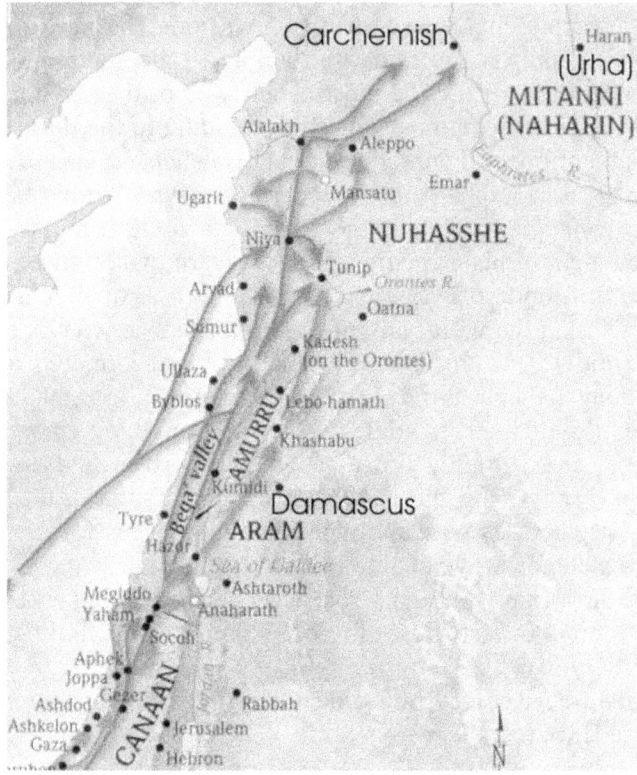

The Mittani became more prepared for Egyptian incursions into their territory, and a new power moved south into north Syria, the Hittites. This formidable kingdom effectively kept the Egyptians out of lands north of Kadesh, famous as the site of the great battle where the Hittite Muwatalli II and Ramses the Great fought to a stalemate, ending with the Hittites remaining in control of this city.

The bottom line is that the Egyptians never had a presence in southern Turkey, certainly not anywhere near Urha, nor even in Syria, that would involve a religious establishment overseen by the priest of Pharaoh. The account in *The Book of Abraham* is historically impossible.

---

[145] Redford, *Wars in Syria and Palestine of Thutmose III*, 256-7.

The Egyptians were not in Ur, and the Chaldeans were in southern Iraq, and even there only from about the time of King David. No other city has been found that could be a plausible Ur to meet the needs of *The Book of Abraham*.

Human Sacrifice and the Egyptians

Human sacrifice in its most normal form is the ritual killing of an individual to propitiate a god or the gods. It can be a relatively routine practice, such as among the Aztecs, or a special-circumstance practice, such as when a people face conquest by an enemy, or prior to launching a military campaign (cf. Euripides' tragedy *Iphigenia at Aulis*), or to seek divine help in a time of plague or famine. This form of human sacrifice is not evidenced in Egypt. This is notable, in that Egypt has been documented by many thousands of structures, statues, stelae, inscriptions, bas relief scenes and documents. All of this has a strong focus on religious matters, and some sort of evidence of human sacrifice should have been discovered, if the institution existed.

Another form of human sacrifice is retainer sacrifice. During the first dynasty (c. 3080-c. 2886 BCE) pharaonic burials contained burials of retainers of the pharaoh as well as his own burial. Since these tombs were covered over by a continuous roof, it is believed that the retainers must have been killed to be buried with their master, to serve him in the afterlife. This was discontinued in the second dynasty, apparently because the retainers no longer believed that their demise was needed for the Pharaoh's well-being, and that they could serve him better alive to maintain his cult. Also, the *ushabtis*, figurines buried with the deceased to come alive and serve their master after resurrection, were viewed to be just as good, and could be much more numerous.

Those who desperately attempt to have human sacrifice in Egypt make reference to representations of executed prisoners of war. There are usually two groups depicted, those who will be prisoners and probably slaves, and those who have been killed. An iconographic device is used to distinguish the two groups. The captives are bound by a cord, while the executed are beheaded. There is never a reference to the latter to indicate that they have been killed to propitiate a deity. Rather, the message is to emphasize the power of the pharaoh, and the fate of those who dare to fight him.

Summary

1. The so-called Abraham papyrus is the Book of Breathing (Breathing Permit) of the Book of the Dead.
2. This papyrus was seriously and deliberately modified to make it fit the story in *The Book of Abraham*.
3. Because in Smith's text, Abraham himself refers to Facsimile 1, speaking in the first person, it is not possible to divorce this papyrus from *The Book of Abraham*.
4. There is no evidence that Egypt practiced any sort of human sacrifice, in the millennium to which Abraham is ascribed.
5. Scholars attempting to find a location that could be the Biblical Ur of Chaldea have only found Urha in modern-day Turkey. This toponym is phonologically improbable, and in any case, even the great conqueror Thutmose III did not get that far in the most far-reaching Egyptian incursion. Indeed, Egypt did not have any real administrative presence north of Palestine.

Facsimile No. 2. The Hypocephalus

The hypocephalus in Figure 10 has been found in the *Book of Abraham* every since its first edition, where it is labeled Facsimile No. 2. Joseph Smith attributed it to Abraham. This too was seriously modified.

For example, the original text around the circumference is in cursive hieroglyphs, whereas the text copied in is in hieratic script. This is like suddenly shifting a text, say on the front of a Washington government building, from block printing to handwriting. Furthermore, the meaning of the hieratic text does not fit that of the cursive hieroglyphic text. It is interesting that this hieratic text was copied in upside-down, [146] apparently on purpose.

That it was no accident can be seen by examining the text on the horizontal lines 12-15. Not only is it also upside down, but note that the numbers are also upside down in the 1842 *Times and Seasons* first printing (Figure 10). This happened because the scribe was holding the hypocephalus upside down when copying the text. It was easy to get the

---

[146] Ritner, *The Joseph Smith Egyptian Papyri*, 263-66.

9. Restoring and Supplementing Biblical Texts   233

Figure 10. BOA Facsimile No. 2: Smith's Hypocephalus Fabrication

Source: The *Book of Abraham*, first printing in *The Times and Seasons*.

Figure 11. BOA Facsimile No. 2: Scribe's Copy Showing the Missing Sections

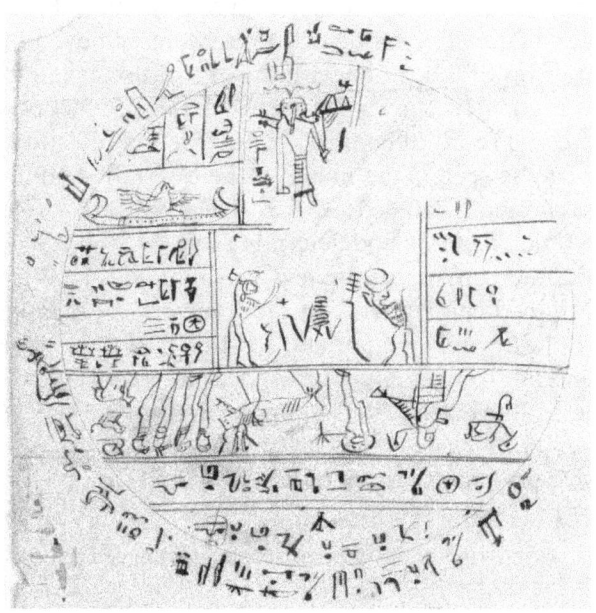

source text (Figures 7-9) right side up since it was from the section of the papyrus to the left of the lion couch scene, an image clearly indicating the correct orientation. The scribe deliberately rotated the papyrus 180° before copying. He copied upside down to obscure the source of his borrowed texts, a clear sign of deliberate albeit clever deception. Presumably, Smith expected that the printer would not print the numbers upside down, just as their orientation was corrected in subsequent editions.

Figure 12 shows another source papyrus used to obtain authentic material to occupy part of the missing section. The boat scene at the bottom right was copied into the upper right-hand part of the empty space of what was originally a damaged hypocephalus. There was no rational for doing this, other than to produce an impressive and "complete" graphic to accompany his *Book of Abraham*. It is not part of the Abraham story. Smith seemingly hoped to use it to demonstrate his Egyptian language credentials, much as he had attempted to do with his "Egyptian Alphabet and Grammar." The text to the left of the lion couch scene (Figure 6) was used to fill in some of the remaining damaged part, labeled 12 through 15 (upside down in Figure 10). Note that on these lines the scribes had made an effort to copy some indistinct text still remaining on the hypocephalus, leaving the far right of each line empty. This can be seen in the scribe's copy (Figure 11), but in Figure 13, I have left these lines blank. The fabricated lines were achieved by combining the indistinct effort of the scribe with the bits of text taken from the lines of Figure 9. Figure 13 shows the steps in the production of the final graphic. There, the result of combining the existing indistinct text and the inserted text can be seen in the image at the top right, and in the last four lines at the bottom, labeled 12-15. Clearly, this project required considerable time, planning and determination.

This said, the copying of the text was not well done from the point of view of a trained epigrapher. Nor did it have to be. No one could read it anyway. It was only important to fill the gaps with characters sufficiently similar to their source to appear to match the rest to give the appearance of authenticity. Some imprecision in the process would go unnoticed.

The discovery and translation of these papyri are important because this shows that the *Book of Abraham* was a 19th-century composition. But how it was done is equally important, since it shows conscious

9. Restoring and Supplementing Biblical Texts   235

deception. Logically, it is not possible to conclude that Smith sincerely thought he was translating.

Figure 12. Papyrus JS IV: Smith's Source for the Boat Insert

Figure 13. How to Customize a Hypocephalus

	 before 	after
3	Taken from 	JS fragment IV
rim	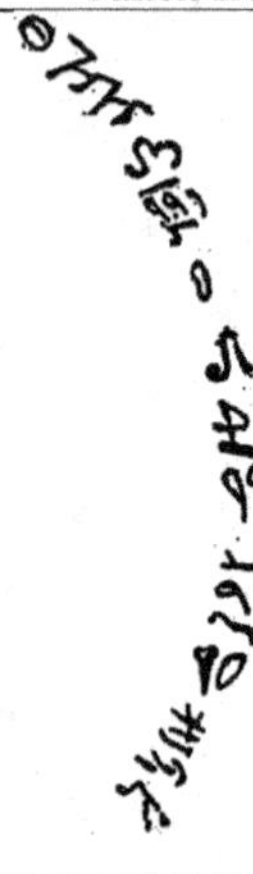	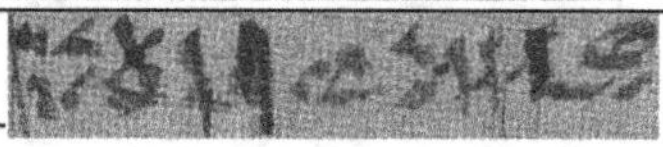 (from line 2 of Figure 9) 
		(from line 3 of Figure 9)
		These texts, are inserted upside down (from the panel to the left of the lion couch scene, Figures 6, 8, & 9). 
		(from line 4 of Figure 9)
	The texts below were inserted upside-down and backwards.	

9. Restoring and Supplementing Biblical Texts 237

(Figure 13 continued)

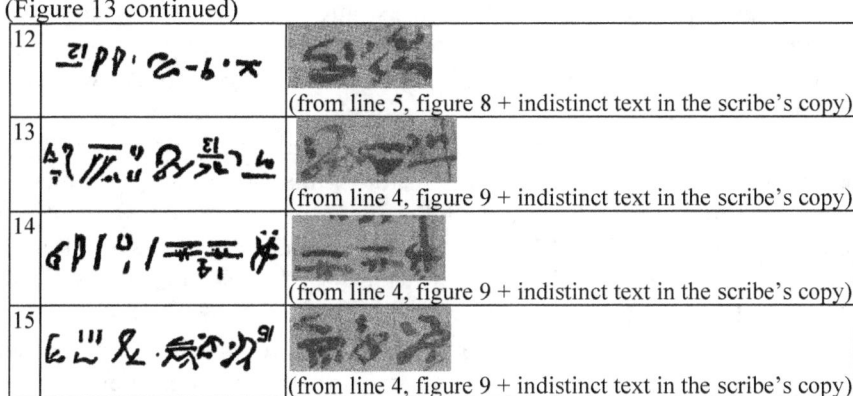

Facsimile No. 3

Figure 14. Book of Abraham facsimile No. 3

EXPLANATION OF THE ABOVE CUT
1. Abraham sitting upon Pharaoh's throne, by the politeness of the king, with a crown upon his head, representing the Priesthood as emblematic of the grand Presidency in Heaven; with the scepter of justice and judgment in his hand.
2. King Pharaoh, whose name is given in the characters above his head
3. Signifies Abraham in Egypt—referring to Abraham, as given in the ninth number of the Times and Seasons. (Also as given in the first facsimile of this book.)
4. Prince of Pharaoh, King of Egypt, as written above the hand.
5. Shulem one of the kin's principal waiters, as represented by the characters above his hand.
6. Olimlah, a slave belonging to the prince.
Abraham is reasoning upon the principles of Astronomy, in the king's court.

Source: The *Book of Abraham* (including the "Explanation").

Joseph Smith attributed a third illustration to Abraham (Figure 14). Unfortunately, the original was not among the recovered papyri. His "Explanation of the Above Cut," again, has nothing to do with the vignette.

The Book of Abraham is never studied totally on its own merits or demerits. The few believers who study this issue are completely committed to their faith. Some of the others are in fact just what the believers call them: anti-Mormons. Even secular scholars who attempt objective research are influenced by what they know about the *Book of Mormon*. It is hard for a secular scholar to move from the previous chapters of this work to the current one without having in mind the fact that *The Book of Abraham* was brought forth by the same person who must be considered a principal author of the *Book of Mormon*.

The Book of Ether

Although the *Book of Ether* was published in the the *Book of Mormon*, it is a separate history, included, almost as an afterthought, just in case there should turn out to be Pre-Columbian ruins dating prior to the Nephites. It also helps explain how it is that Lehi et al. found animals that should have been killed in Noah's flood. This record of the Jaredites is sufficiently interesting to warrant inclusion here. The basic points are as follows:

1. A prophet Jared sought an exception from the Lord from divine wrath at the Tower of Babel, so his group would not suffer the confusion of tongues.
2. The Lord obliged him, and, guided Jared's group through a wilderness to the sea for the voyage to the New World, kept empty, just for them for an inheritance.
3. The Lord instructed them so they could build eight barges, totally sealed "like a dish" with only a small pluggable hole in the top, so when plunged to the depth of the sea they would not drown. Water pressure is not taken into consideration; these submarines are made of wood.
4. The brother of Jared "did molten out of the rock sixteen small stones" and the Lord touched each to emit light, providing light in the vessels when submerged.
5. They gathered "flocks of every kind; and also of the seed of the earth of every kind," the "fowls of the air," "a vessel in which they did carry

with them the fish of the waters" and honey bees. Thus each barge was a scaled-down Noah's ark. (Ether 1:41 & 2:1-3) Apparently the authors wrote on the assumption that most or all animal life might not have existed on isolated distant lands after Noah's flood.

7. The Lord gave him two special stones, interpreters (seer stones).

8. They included food for themselves and all of these animals, sufficient for their voyage of 344 days at sea.

9. They arrived in the New World and quickly populated much of the same area where the Nephites and Lamanites would later be (but only as far south as the "narrow neck of land"). Imitating the book of Genesis, the Book of Ether is full of "begats." One individual has 31 children.

10. Shortly after their arrival, a leader named Shule smelted ore from a mountain, and made steel swords (not bronze, or just iron, but steel), before the Iron Age elsewhere.

11. They filled the land with many cities.

12. At the end, shortly before the arrival of Lehi, their internecine wars totally exterminated every last soul. In one sequence of battles, about two million warriors were killed on just one side. Then, during a truce of four years, each side rounded up every last soul of the Americas to what is now upstate New York, near the Hill Cumorah, for the last major confrontation: on each side, "they were all gathered together, every one to the army which he would, with their wives and their children—both men, women and children being armed with weapons of war, having shields, and breastplates, and head-plates, and being clothed after the manner of war..." Eventually all were dead, except the two enemy commanders: Coriantumr and Shiz. The former killed the latter. Then Coriantumr wandered until eventually he arrived in Zarahemla, where he spent the last months of his life. In this manner, the *Book of Mormon* authors manage to provide for the possibility of pre-Nephite ruins, while retaining a central theme of the gold plates, to wit, that Lehi was guided to an empty land for his people's exclusive inheritance.

The Book of Moses

Even though the *Book of Mormon* is the founding scripture of the Mormon community, it contains little of what would become their distinctive theology. In June of 1830, shortly after the publication of the *Book of Mormon* and the founding of the new church, Joseph Smith turned his attention to more theological matters. From June of 1830 through February of 1831, he and colleagues produced for his followers another book of scripture, in keeping with his role as having been called by God to restore important and precious truths in lost scripture. The work went through a redaction process:

> Examination of the original manuscripts of the JST shows that soon after the initial writing, Joseph further modified and revised these early chapters in a number of ways. This included a complete rewriting of the early chapters of Genesis, which was then followed in the editorial process by a number of interlinear inserts and deletions. In some instances, additional material was written on small pieces of paper and pinned to the manuscript at places needing still further correction.
>
> Thus, there were two drafts of the manuscript for the first twenty-four chapters of Genesis, with the second copy being more complete and presenting a more extensive text than the first draft...
>
> The portions of the JST that were published in the *Evening and Morning Star* and later incorporated into the Book of Moses are as follows:
>
> August 1832—Moses 7:1-69; March 1833—Moses 6:43-68; April 1833—Moses 5:1-16; Moses 6:52, 58-61; Moses 7:5-11; Moses 8:13-30.[147]

This redaction process, to produce not just one but two drafts, is a good indication how the drafts were done to produce the BOM ms O (the partially extant original manuscript of the entire work). There were mss[i] (initial drafts) and an mss[c] (completed drafts). Work on the BOM drafts was also done with the assistance of scribes. For the *Book of Moses*, these were (with the portion he wrote): Oliver Cowdery (1:1-5:43), John Whitmer (5:43-6:18), Emma Smith (6:19-52), John Whitmer (6:52-7:1) and Sidney Rigdon (7:2-8:30). This list does not track specifically with the production of two versions. We are left to wonder who did what of each version? It is also not clear how the scribal work interfaced with the edits and insertion of additional material.

The mss were in the possession of the Reorganized Church of Jesus Christ of Latter Day Saints, and the material published above, and a partial copy in the possession of the LDS Church served as the basis for an inadequate version published in the 1851 edition of the *Pearl of Great*

---

[147] Robert J. Matthews, "How We Got the Book of Moses," *Ensign*, January 1986.

Price. Orson Pratt prepared the current version for the 1878 edition. It was officially canonized in 1880.

This text is often called a revision of Genesis. Although similar to parts of Genesis, it is a major understatement to call it a simple revision. Although it more or less revises Genesis in some chapters, it contains major totally extraneous expansions. In Moses 1, God is speaking to Moses regarding a mission for him, partially to show the close relationship between the deity and his prophet. Even in the chapters shadowing the Genesis text, there are theologically major insertions, such as all things having been created spiritually in heaven before their material creation on the face of earth (3:5, 7); freewill (3:17); trees, beasts of the field and fowls of the air having souls (3:9, 19); God working with his Beloved Son from the beginning (4:1-4, 28, 5:6-15, 5:57-59; animal sacrifice as a similitude of the sacrifice of the Son of God (5:7); evil arising even in Adam's day in the form of secret combinations (5:51, 6:15); the institution of priesthood (6:7, 8:19); Cainan called the promised land (6:17); the atonement of the Son of God for original guilt (6:53) and the baptism of Adam and his receiving the gift of the Holy Ghost (6:65). The passages Joseph Smith chose for publication are an almost total miss with respect to these passages. Those published in his lifetime dealt exclusively with the stories of Enoch and Noah, comprising material not found in Genesis. It may be that he was hesitant to publish at that time yet more direct modifications of the KJV that his followers had grown up with. Perhaps too the passages he did not publish were those he wished to modify further.

One important point of its difference from Genesis is that the creation story purports to be the words of God himself, not the inspired writing of Moses or of some other ancient author or redactor. The creation in six days, the seventh day of rest, the creation of Adam from the dust, and of Eve from his rib, are all literally the word of the Lord, a point that is specifically emphasized in Moses 4:32. This does not mean that all or even most Mormons have been unable to reason their way around the details, to embrace the modern geological and biological sciences, but for some this text rendered the process more complicated, if not more difficult, and certainly more sensitive.

The Enoch story in the Book of Moses is not in itself notable, although it has been expanded beyond the original in Genesis. There, we find two Enochs. The first is a son of Cain, in Genesis 4:17: "and [the wife of Cain] bare Enoch: and he [Cain] built a city, and called the name of the city, after the name of his son, Enoch." This Enoch sired Irad. The second Enoch is in the line of Adam in Genesis 5:18, 21-24 (cf. Moses 6:21). The main Enoch story in KJV Genesis follows:

> 21. And Enoch lived sixty and five years, and begat Methuselah:
> 22. And Enoch walked with God after he begat Methuselah three hundred years, and begat sons and daughters:
> 23. And all the days of Enoch were three hundred sixty and five years:
> 24. And Enoch walked with God: and he was not; for God took him.

The statement "and he was not; for God took him" has been interpreted to mean that he was not made to suffer death. We find in Hebrews 11:5, "By faith Enoch was translated [i.e. "carried across] that he should not see death; and was not found, because God had translated him: for before his translation he had this testimony, that he pleased God."

The Book of Moses elaborates on this passage, detailing the calling God gave to Enoch and the message of his testimony. Enoch teaches the word and name of Jesus Christ, baptism and the gift of the Holy Ghost. This Enoch also builds a city, which is named Zion. Enoch saw the seed of Adam "save it was the seed of Cain, for the seed of Cain were black, and had not place among them."

This Enoch story is not remarkable in itself, apart from the fact that it has become a focus of LDS apologetics, beginning with a work of Hugh Winder Nibley, to be treated below.

The Doctrine and Covenants

Even before completing the *Book of Mormon*, Joseph Smith had discovered that he could simply receive a revelation from God, without the aid of gold plates, or even a seer stone. Over the course of his career he gave to his church a large number of revelatory texts. These included instructions to the prophet himself, the will of God regarding the role of the cofounders of the church and other later principal persons, and details regarding the organization of the Church and the affairs of the community. But they also contain elements of an inchoate theology.

Revelations received and published were not final. Many of them have a history of revision, even from printing to printing. The early revelations exist in a few original copies, but mostly in copies and early publications. In 1831 a series of conferences were held in Hiram, Ohio, and on 1 November it was decided that 10,000 copies should be printed of what was to be called the *Book of Commandments*. Cowdery and John Whitmer arrived in Independence, Missouri, on 5 January 1832, where William W. Phelps was to establish his press and printing company. Although Smith Jr., Harris, Cowdery, Whitmer, Rigdon and Phelps were made stewards over the revelations and commandments, it appears that the person actually in effective charge of the project was Cowdery. On 30 April, in a meeting of the council of the Literary Firm, the project was scaled down to an initial printing of 3,000 copies. Apparently as a stop gap, between June 1832 and July 1833, the earliest to appear were published in the *Evening and Morning Star*. Meanwhile, work was progressing on the publication of the *Book of Commandments*. But, on 20 July, citizens of Independence demolished the printing office throwing the press from the upper story window and scattering the type. Sheets of what had been done up to then on the *Book of Commandments* were gathered up, from which it was possible to assemble around 100 copies comprising 160 pages of the unfinished work. Between January and June 1835 the *Evening and Morning Star* again published revelations and commandments. After extensive research, Michael Marquardt found that "if any original manuscripts (previous to 1835) were used, their exact wording was not adhered to… [the Star] altered texts, deleted previously published material and inserted editorial comments by Cowdery."[148] Cowdery wrote, "On the revelations we merely say, that we were not a little surprised to find the previous print so different from the original."[149] As an explanation, RLDS Church historian Richard P. Howard wrote:

> It may be that Cowdery's surprise at the remarkable differences between the "original" and that which he had previously published arose from the fact that in late 1834 or early 1835, as he was beginning to republish the revelations, he was working from a *different* "original"—different, that is, from the one he and John Whitmer had copied from in 1831 in preparing the *Book of Commandments* manuscript for the Independence printer.[150]

---

[148] Michael Marquardt, *The Joseph Smith Revelations, Text and Commentary* (Salt Lake City: Signature Books, 1999), 10-11. This entire discussion depends on Marquardt, *ibid*, 3-19.

[149] Oliver Cowdery in the *Evening and Morning Star* (Kirtland reprint) 1 (June 1832), 16; reprinted Jan. 1835; see Marquardt, *ibid*, 11.

[150] Richard P. Howard, *Restoration Scriptures* (Independence, MO: Herald House, 1969), 202; Marquardt, *Joseph Smith Revelations*, 11.

These changes do not include those done in the process of arriving at the text of the earlier "original" drafts. This skeletal review indicates the degree to which the revelations were subject to editing and modification. The revisions of those involved can be found in Marquardt's work.[151]

Other doctrines, now popularly associated with the Mormon community, were given in the *Doctrine and Covenants*. These include the text that counsels against tobacco, wine or strong drink, and hot drinks, given as a word of wisdom, and not a commandment, but the will of God (Section 89). It also includes the institution of polygamy, or plural wives, and a justification for concubinage at least for some (D&C 132). Another doctrine of interest came in Section 19, addressing relations with non-Mormons:

> 21. And I command you that you preach naught but repentance, and show not these things unto the world until it is wisdom in me.
> 22. For they cannot bear meat now, but milk they must receive; wherefore, they must not know these things, lest they perish.

In the BOM Book of Alma (12:9) we find the earliest articulation of this policy:

> And now Alma began to expound these things unto him, saying, It is given unto many to know the mysteries of God; nevertheless they are laid under a strict command, that they shall not impart only according to the portion of his word, which he doth grant unto the children of men, according to the heed and diligence which they give unto him.

This is essentially a doctrine of collective dissimulation when replying to prying questions about doctrines or practices outsiders might consider disturbing and/or unorthodox. It does not encourage telling untruths, but simply says that it is not always wise to tell the whole truth.

Joseph Smith's Translation (Revision) of the Bible.

The LDS believe in the Bible only as far as it is translated correctly, unlike their other scriptures, which are seen to be fully correct. Joseph Smith began this revision shortly after the Church was organized, and at

---

[151] Marquardt, *Joseph Smith Revelations*.

least some preparations were envisaged for publication as early as 1833. Some work continued until his death. Although over three thousand verses of the KJV were modified in some way, proportionately Genesis received the most modification. The original manuscripts are in the possession of the Community of Christ, which has done the most scholarly work on them. The LDS Church has stood a bit aloof, but does consider some parts of this work to be doctrinally significant.

The Book of Abraham purports to be the writing of the patriarch by his own hand. At least chapters two through four of the Book of Moses clearly claim to be the word of God himself spoken to Moses. Likewise the D&C is mostly the word of the Lord spoken in the first person to Joseph Smith. When we see how they were produced, edited and partially rewritten as needed, we gain an understanding regarding their purely human character. But beyond this, we are given considerable insight into the process of producing the initial drafts of the principal books of the *Book of Mormon*, and of their Smith-Cowdery collaborative redaction prior to being copied to produce ms 𝒪.

Chapter 10

Lehi: A History to Convert the Lamanites

A now lost text produced as restored scripture is the work drafted by Joseph Smith, assisted by Martin Harris, in the first half of 1828. It came to be known as the Book of Lehi.[152] In the summer of that year, a person (or persons) unfriendly to Smith's claims stole the only copy of this work, according to the official account. This has also come to be called the purloined 116 pages. Following this loss came Smith's first recorded revelation dated July 1828[153] giving us his view at that pivotal moment of the purpose of the plates.

"For This Very Purpose Purpose Are the Plates Preserved"

> as the knowledge of a Savior has come into the world, even so shall the knowledge of my people [Nephites, Jacobites, Josephites and Zoramites] come to the knowledge of the Lamanites... and for this very purpose are these plates preserved, which contain these records, that the promises of the Lord might be fulfilled, which he made to his people; and that the Lamanites might come to the knowledge of their fathers, and that they might know the promises of the Lord, and that they may believe the gospel and rely upon the merits of Jesus Christ, and be glorified through faith in his name (BC 2)

Here we find only one set of plates. There is no mention of a new bible, nor of the Jew or the Gentile. At this point, "the knowledge of a Savior has come into the world." The purpose at this early date did not go further than to bring the Native Americans to an awareness of their Israelite origin and to accept Christ. Some seven months later, Smith delivered a revelation said to be for his father on the occasion of the latter's February visit, announcing that "a marvelous work is about to come forth among the children of men..." (BC 3; D&C 4:1) To more fully appreciate the transition from the history to the new bible, one must have a fuller understanding of the contents of the Book of Lehi.

---

[152] Joseph Smith, "Preface" to the 1830 edition of the *Book of Mormon*.
[153] Marquardt, *The Joseph Smith Revelations*, 24.

The Book of Lehi: The More Particular Record

If indeed divine assistance had caused words to appear to Smith in his scryer's hat and he just read them off for Harris to copy down, then surely he could produce a second and virtually identical copy of the purloined 116 pages. To duck this challenge, it was decided to replace Lehi with the Book of Nephi, in circumstances that we will examine in the next chapter. Both books were said to be on the gold plates, covering the same period of the BOM narrative, although the first of these was said to have been originally engraved on plates called the large plates of Nephi, replete with historical detail. In 1 Nephi 19:2 we read:

> And I knew not at the time when I made them that I should be commanded of the Lord to make these plates; wherefore, the record of my father, and the genealogy of his fathers, and the more part of all our proceedings in the wilderness are engraven upon those first plates of which I have spoken

The phrase "these plates" refers to the small plates of Nephi. The phrase "those first plates" refers to the large plates of Nephi, which began with the Book of Lehi. For the period in the New World, they also contained "an account of the reign of the kings, and the wars and contentions of my people." (1 Nephi 9:4) The details were "more particularly made mention upon the first [large] plates." (1 Nephi 19:2) Of the small plates of Nephi, he wrote, "I do not write anything upon [these] plates save it be that I think it be sacred." (1 Nephi 19:6) Although the 116-page text is not extant as far as anyone knows, the *Book of Mormon* itself gives us enough information to reconstruct Lehi in general. This chapter will investigate the degree to which the Nephi replacement text struck a radically different course rather than simply replacing Lehi. As Smith moved from the Book of Lehi to the Book of Nephi, his history, designed to gather the Pre-Columbian Israelite Americans to Jesus, became a new bible for a far grander mission, to restore Christ's true church for all mankind in preparation for the Second Coming.

The Devils in the Details: The First Centuries in the New World

The first of these devils was the persistent fear that once the book was published the purloined 116 pages would resurface and be compared with the text composed to replace them, with disconfirmatory results. The sort of detail Smith would have included even after their arrival in the New World, according to his mother, is illustrated by the ability of his imagination to invent Indian manners and customs well before he claimed to have the gold plates.[154] If he had decided to merely attempt a reworded version, the events and actors involved in the Book of Lehi would have proven to be a major challenge to Smith's memory, and numerous opportunities to contradict his original work. The solution to this problem did not require a degree in physics, and probably was rather quickly devised. The new text would eschew detail. As a result, there is a dearth of detail from Nephi to Amaleki (in the book of Omni). Beginning with Mosiah, we suddenly encounter numerous events, and the number of personal names rapidly increases, as do the toponyms, including cities and natural features of the BOM setting. This said, it is clear that there should have been no bar on introducing new events that clearly were not in the Book of Lehi. A good illustration of this is found in the gospels, with which the BOM authors were quite familiar. The so-called Slaughter of the Innocents, when Herod the Great is supposed to have ordered the death of all young male children in the vicinity of Bethlehem, is reported only in Matthew, as well as the flight of the Holy Family with Baby Jesus to take refuge in Egypt. This is a very major event. Yet somehow it escaped the notice of Mark, Luke and John. Similarly, some additional events that had not been reported in the purloined pages would not look out of place in the replacement text.

The Devils in the Details: "Our Proceedings in the Wilderness"

The next devil is the very real fear that at least with regard to events and associated detail in Judea and Arabia one might make serious errors. For almost two millennia scholars had studied the Biblical lands and Arabia, including Moab, Edom, Midian, Arabia, Saba (Sheba) and the rest of Arabia Felix (Yemen). Any effort to produce Semitic personal and place names along the way would have been a minefield. But there were so many opportunities to do so. Lehi's group would have had to go across Arabia to the Indian Ocean from oasis to oasis, always finding people there who had limited provisions for their own families, and jealously guarded water sources and family and tribal cisterns. Either they would have had to make a living themselves, or carry with them considerable

---

[154] Lucy Smith, in Anderson, *Lucy's Book*, 345. This would be c. 1824 prior to claiming to have the gold plates.

10. Lehi: A History to Convert the Lamanites

valuable trade goods, enough for eight years, under threat of nomadic robber-band attacks. Any effort to recount the adventures of this group in the wilderness would encounter many a pitfall. It may be that Joseph Jr. was at least initially naïve respecting the degree to which these areas were known even in his day, but once the project became a Smith family project assisted by Cowdery, this great storyteller must have been made to understand that it would be better for these eight years before getting onboard their ship to take place mostly in a vacuum.

Even so, occasionally some details were included, usually with predictable results. An example is found in Lehi's first two months in the wilderness. After traveling in the wilderness, and descending to the shore of the Red Sea, he camped in a valley near the mouth of a river that emptied into the Red Sea. He travelled three days in the wilderness. (Is this overall from Jerusalem to this camp site, or from his first arrival at the Red Sea to this site?) The account follows1 (Nephi 2:5-9):

> 4. And it came to pass that he departed into the wilderness...
> 5. And he came down by the borders *near the shore of the Red Sea*; and he traveled in the wilderness in the borders which are nearer the Red Sea; and he did travel in the wilderness with his family, which consisted of my mother, Sariah, and my elder brothers, who were Laman, Lemuel, and Sam. (emphasis added)
> 6. And it came to pass that when he had traveled three days in the wilderness, he pitched his tent in a valley by the side of a river of water.
> 7. And it came to pass that he built an altar of stones, and made an offering unto the Lord, and gave thanks unto the Lord our God.
> 8. And it came to pass that he called the name of the river, Laman, and it emptied into the Red Sea; and the valley was in the borders near the mouth thereof.
> 9. And when my father saw that the waters of the river emptied into the fountain of the Red Sea, he spake unto Laman, saying: O that thou mightest be like unto this river, continually running into the fountain of all righteousness!

The Arabian peninsula essentially approximates a wedge that begins at sea level at the Persian Gulf and rises to the Hijaz escarpment overlooking the Red Sea from heights ranging from 3000 feet to over a mile. As the west side of the peninsula was lifted up to form the wedge it exposed the bottom of the Red Sea all along its Arabian shore, forming an arid and highly saline coastal plain, the Tihama.

Map 7. Jerusalem to the Red Sea

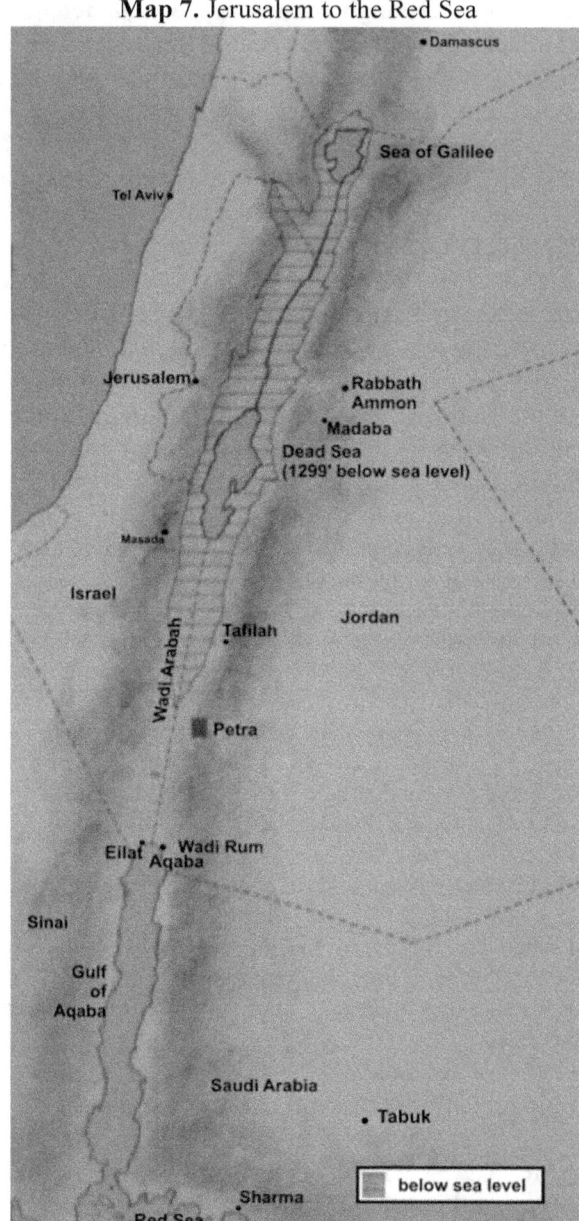

Source: Based on Iain Browning, *Petra*, 12.

10. Lehi: A History to Convert the Lamanites

Map 8. Arabian Trade Routes

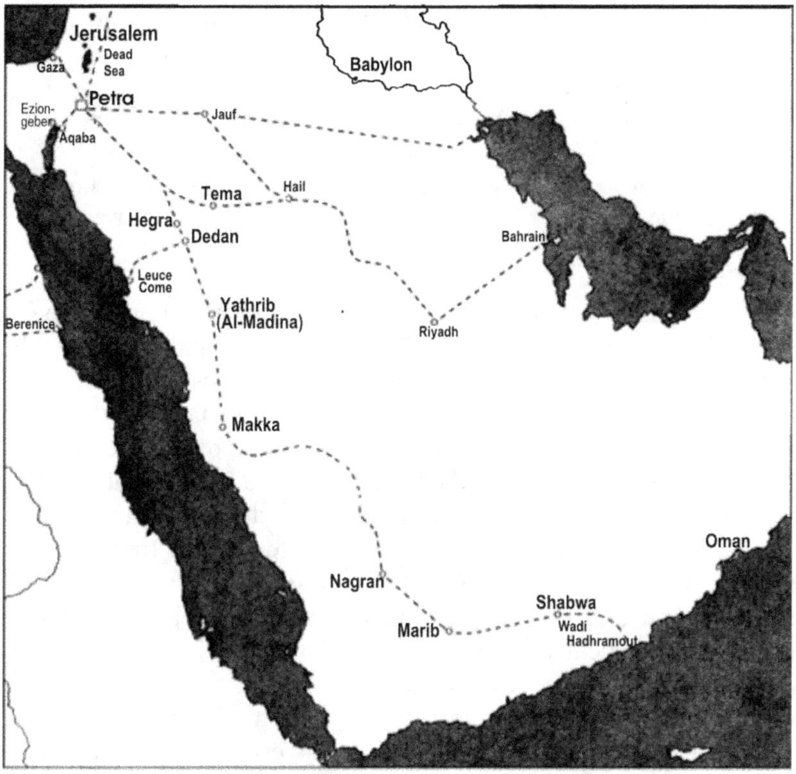

Source: Iain Browning, *Pera*, 14 (slightly edited)

The absolutely shortest route to a point "near the shore of the Red Sea" is to follow the modern Israeli road to the ancient Israelite port of Eilat on the Gulf of Aqaba. This road passes along the west side of the Dead Sea to Ayn Gedi, then Masada and on down to Eilat. It has a very long stretch in the worst of Wadi Arabah, which as badlands go, is at the top of a scale from one to ten. At Aqaba it is not possible to follow the east coast of the gulf due to mountain cliffs that plunge directly into the sea. A winding road follows mountain passes over to Sharma. The total distance is 346 miles according to Google Maps. Since this is a nearly straight route most of the way, there is little room for camels to take shortcuts. We have solid evidence regarding the distance a caravan travels in a day. Along various trade routes, premodern governments built inns (caravanserai) where the caravans could sleep overnight, eat and take care of their camels. These are routinely spaced twenty to thirty miles apart. Averaging thirty miles a day, to get to the Red Sea would require about twelve days. From this point they traveled three more days to Lehi's campsite in the Valley of Lemuel.

The route followed raises concerns. In 1 Nephi 16:14, we find:

> we did go forth again in the wilderness, following the same direction, keeping in the most fertile parts of the wilderness, which was in the borders near the Red Sea.

This is the Tihama. It is saline, dry and about as inhospitable as can be to plants other than halophytes, very similar to the wasteland bordering the Great Salt Lake. The "borders near the Red Sea" is absolutely not "the most fertile parts." It is eschewed by the caravans in favor of the very tractable and cooler highland plateau on the east side of the escarpment. (Map 8) The distance from Sharma to Jizan, near the border with modern Yemen, is 1000 miles (Google Maps). I have only driven this route once, just to see it. The normal trade route from Jerusalem to the Indian Ocean crossed Wadi Arabah (part of the Great Rift, 1300 feet below sea level at the Dead Sea) over and up to either Madaba or to Petra at Wadi Musa. The caravan route basically followed the possible, avoiding rugged steep hills while heading for the next oasis, in an unforgiving mountain and desert region. From Petra it made its way south to Hegra (Al-Hijr, or Mada'in Salih). Even on the land bordering this escarpment, settlements exist only in scattered oases, such as Tabuk, Al-'Ula, Yathrib (Al-Madina), Makka, At-Ta'if, Al-Baha, Abha and Najran (Nagran in Yemeni Arabic).[155] There it turned southeast to avoid the forbidding mountains of Yemen, where the capital, San'a, perches at 7000 feet. From Najran it made its way to Ma'rib in ancient Saba (seat of the legendary Queen of Sheba). At Shabwa it entered Wadi Hadhramout and descended to the Indian Ocean. (Map 8) Proceeding south-east along the Hijaz escarpment, the route either continued on south into what is now

---

[155] Apart from considerable literature on the ecology of the area, this passage is buttressed also by the author's personal experience, having lived three years in Jeddah, during which I was the President of the Natural History Society of Western Arabia, and three in San'a, Yemen. I have travelled numerous times along the routes from Tabuk to Najran, and within Yemen, to Hadhramawt and on to Masqat, Oman.

Yemen, or to Najran, and then on to the Hadhramawt and to the Indian Ocean.

Some problems arise. First, from Lehi's campsite at the Valley of Lemuel, Nephi and his brothers had to travel back to Jerusalem twice, once for the Brass Plates of Laban and once for Ishmael and his family, two round trips requiring fifteen days each way, or a total of sixty days of hard travel. All of this could be classified with the Labors of Heracles.

The second is the river Laman. From Petra to Najran, the caravan route stays on the highland plateau overlooking the Dead Sea and the Gulf of Aqaba. I have driven from Amman to Aqaba several times, and always been amazed as the road plunges from the escarpment heights to Aqaba. No river exists in any of this area. Even in wetter times, if one existed in Lehi's time, the formation of a constant river befitting this passage requires a substantial drainage area sloping westward to feed the river. But the plateau slope is from the escarpment eastward, away from Aqaba and the Red Sea. The drop to the west is precipitous and made up of numerous gorges, hardly a terrain conducive to the formation of such a river. Furthermore, the BOM narrative specifies that Lehi camped near the mouth of the river, pouring into the Red Sea. What seasonal flows and flash floods exist in the winter disappear into the sand before reaching the sea. At present, no river exists that could qualify, and the terrain militates against such a river in Lehi's time.

The historical hydrology of the Arabian Peninsula is not fully known. Certainly in some very remote times it was more verdant. In the historical period, ancient sources make it clear that camels had replaced donkeys and mules on the caravan routes by sometime in or before the second millennium BCE. We also know that the verdant climate in the Sahara dried up one or several thousand years before the predynastic period of ancient Egyptian history, drying up the Nile swamp and forcing population migration, partly into the Nile valley, resulting in what became the Egyptian people. In Arabia there have long been dry gulches (wadi, sayl) that flowed intermittently in the rainy season, often producing raging flash floods. The famous pre-Islamic poet, 'Umru' al-Qays, commemorated this in an encomium to his horse (a *munjarid*):

> *Mikarrin mifarrin muqbilin mudbirin ma'an*
> *Ka-julmūdi ṣaḥrin ḥaṭṭahu s-saylu min 'āli*

> Turning, bolting back, charging forth, dashing back, all at once,
> Like a stone bolder that the torrent drives down from above.

The period of a wetter Arabia appears to have been up to as late as around 8,000 years ago, an approximate date given to a prehistoric lake in the Great Nufud Desert.[156] A map of prehistoric rivers in Arabia shows the closest one descending down the escarpment and emptying into the Red Sea at about 360 miles southeast of Sharma, well beyond Lehi's three-day journey in the wilderness. On this map ancient rivers forming east of the escarpment further north flowed inland. The Paleodesert Project of the Max Planck Institute, directed by Michael Petraglia (Oxford), is doing extensive archaeological hydrology research of the Arabian Desert, and some surrounding areas, covering a period from the first arrival of humans nearly to the present time. Hopefully we will know more about when and where real rivers flowed in Arabia.[157]

Apart from warring tribes, one had to face desperate armed robbers. Adult male misfits were cast out (cut off) from their tribe. Like lion brothers striving to survive, they banded together. Traveling in Yemen with a caravan, the fearless explorer Ulrich Jasper Seetzen was killed by an armed band that preyed on richly laden caravans.[158] In the area of Makka, a tribe was specialized in attacking caravans, even those taking Muslim pilgrims to Makka. They had to pay *khuwa* (a weirdly named "brotherhood tax") for safe passage. Even pilgrims! Perhaps we should think of it as a sort of customs duty. It is unclear how the party made a living other than hunting. Lehi left his silver, gold and precious things behind (1 Nephi 2:4). How would they have paid for passage rights, grain, water and fodder or pasturage. As for hunting, the problem of Nephi's steel bow was addressed in Chapter 2. The party's equipment, clothing and beasts of burden would have been attractive goods for desperate robber bands.

The difficulties of making this eight-year trip is further illustrated by the Roman campaign along virtually the same route, a few decades

---

[156] Jonathan Gornall, "When Arabia Was Green: Lush Grasslands Helped Early Man Make Leap Out of Africa," *The National* [UAE], 14 May 2015 (http://www.thenational.ae/uae/heritage/when-arabia-was-green-lush-grasslands-helped-early-man-make-leap-out-of-africa, accessed 08/01/2017).

[157] Andrew Lawler, "In Search of Green Arabia." Accessed online, 08/01/2017 & sourced to http://www.andrewlawler.com/in-search-of-green-arabia/, the map was adapted from H.S. Edgell, *Arabian Deserts, Nature, Origin and Evolution* (New York: Springer Pub., 2006). Michael Petraglia, www.paleodeserts.com.

[158] Introduction to *Ulrich Jasper Seetzen's Reisen*, published posthumously by family and friends (Berlin: Verlag bei G. Reimer, 1855).

BCE, led by Aelius Gallus by order of Augustus Caesar. Disease significantly reduced his troops, and he encountered armed Arabian resistance. After taking Ma'rib in Arabia Felix (Yemen), and making his way back to the Red Sea, he had lost most of his military. He decided not to attempt a return by the same route, harassed by hostile Arabian warriors, but crossed just north of Bab al-Mandab (The Gate of Wailing) to Abyssinia (now Ethiopia) and marched back to Alexandria, tail between his legs.[159]

Moreover, eight years is excessive. The armed Arab caravans that made the trip successfully traveled from the Indian Ocean to Petra in less than a year. This is a perfect setting for Joseph Smith to fill an eight-year journey from Jerusalem to the Indian Ocean with interesting encounters and adventures. And yet, in Nephi, there is no single mention of any other people, any attempts to announce the gospel of Christ, any conflicts, or any dealings to reprovision themselves with food, water and fodder. This total vacuum is in contrast with the greater detail of the original version, mentioned in the *Book of Mormon*. Even after the BOM narrative gets the Lehi party to the New World, the need to avoid detail continues all the way up to the Book of Mosiah. This is the period that the purloined 116 pages covered, showing that the threat that they posed was equally responsible for a dearth of detail, even in the land of promise. By having Mosiah relocate the Nephites to lands north of the Isthmus of Panama, the BOM authors provided themselves with a virgin territory where they could develop a geography replete with many place names, without fear of contradicting toponym detail in the lost pages.

A Bible! We have got a Bible!

Initially, the Smith-Harris partnership appears to have been limited to produce a history of the Indians as Israelites in pre-Columbian America, for profit. Smith himself admitted, in his 1832 history, that he had sinned in that he "sought the Plates to obtain riches."[160] It eventually focused on bringing the Native Americans to Jesus. Later the expanded BOM team undertook to produce an Israelite New World bible to restore the "true" gospel and church.

---

[159] Strabo, xvi 4:21-25.
[160] Joseph Smith, 1832 history, in Dean C. Jessee, ed., *Papers of Joseph Smith* (Salt Lake City: Deseret Book Company, 1989), I:8.

Here we can make some initial observations. First, Mormon was attracted to the sermons and teachings of the gospel in the small plates of Nephi as opposed to the large plates, the Book of Lehi, which was mostly devoid of these (Words of Mormon vss 3-4). Second, the competing claims of Martin Harris and Professor Charles Anthon mentioned only plates bearing curious characters, not a new bible.[161] Third, prior to starting even the Lehi text, Joseph Smith undertook to train as a Methodist exhorter while still in Palmyra, where he was observed exhorting in Methodist camp meetings.[162] He attended a Methodist class after his arrival in Harmony, Pennsylvania, although how long is disputed.[163] It is quite possible that Smith sought training as a Methodist exhorter to acquire the background needed to produce a history of Israelites in America based on the Old Testament, without the audacity of trying to create a new bible per se. The decision to do so required appropriate content in the text to replace Lehi.

The Ministry Material

The Nephi replacement text (the Book of Nephi) focused on "the ministry and the prophecies" (1 Nephi 19:3), the prophecies of the coming of Christ (Words of Mormon vs 4), and other prophesyings and revelation (ibid, 1:6). These materials include chastisements & exhortations (often to Laman and Lemuel), the patriarchal blessings of Lehi to his sons, gospel-related teachings and Isaiah inclusions with commentary. These materials were absent from the Book of Lehi, which contained "the record of my father, and the genealogy of his fathers, and the more part of all our proceedings in the wilderness" (1 Nephi 19:2), and "a greater account of the wars and contentions and destructions of my people." (1 Nephi 19:4) This was probably seen to detract from the desired image of the work as a new bible. Mormon was also pleased by the small plates of Nephi because of "the prophecies of the coming of

---

[161] Charles Anthon, letter to E. D. Howe dated 17 February 1834, in Vogel, *Early Mormon Documents* (Salt Lake City: Signature Books, 2002), IV:377-81. Joseph Smith, Joseph Smith's History of 1838-39, in Jessee, *Papers of Joseph Smith*, I:285.

[162] O[rsamus] Turner, *History of the Pioneer Settlement of Phelps and Gorham's Purchase* (Rochester, NY: William Alling, 1851), 214, 400; quoted here from Marquardt, *Rise of Mormonism*, 30

[163] Marquardt, *Rise of Mormonism*, 30-31.

Christ." (Words of Mormon 4) Presumably this too is in contrast with the content of the Book of Lehi, which may have kept closer to the Old Testament with only foreshadowing of Christ, while the Book of Nephi mentions Jesus Christ, baptism and ordination of priests and teachers.

The Isaiah Package

The addition of Isaiah inclusions to the replacement text produced an interrelated chain of changes that constitute a single package.

The Package: the Isaiah Inclusions

The ministry material is bolstered by the lengthy Isaiah inclusions, and the commentary on them: Isaiah 2-14; 48-49; 50-51; 29:3-5; 29:6-24; and 29:13-23; as well as other Biblical passages. Clearly the main purpose of these inclusions was to show that the Old Testament prophets were no strangers to the gospel of Christ, knew of some Israelites going off to distant isles of the sea, the coming forth of the *Book of Mormon*, the New World Israelites' future gathering to Christ and the restoration of the true gospel. Unlike the old approach of the book of Lehi, the Nephi replacement text has a new focus. Up front and center is the *Book of Mormon* arguing the case for the *Book of Mormon*. The text is replete with examples, but a couple will suffice here, such as 1 Nephi 19:21:

> And he surely did show unto the prophets of old all things concerning them; and also he did show unto many concerning us; wherefore, it must needs be that we know concerning them for they are written upon the plates of brass.

Introducing Isaiah 48-49, Nephi says (1 Nephi 19:24):

> Hear ye the words of the prophet, ye who are a remnant of the house of Israel, a branch who have been broken off; hear ye the words of the prophet, which were written unto all the house of Israel, and liken them unto yourselves, that ye may have hope as well as your brethren from whom ye have been broken off; for after this manner has the prophet written. (See also 1 Nephi 19 through 2 Nephi 25 *passim*, and specifically 1 Nephi 19:21-24; 20:21; 22:3-13; 2 Nephi 9:1-7; 11:8; 25:1-4.)

The Isaiah inclusions contain 133 variant readings of the first order, and 326 variants of the first and second orders (Chapter 5). If these inclusions were in the Book of Lehi, Smith would not have been able to replicate them, and would not have put them in Nephi. Since they are in Nephi, they must not have been in Lehi. Combined with the evidence in Words of Mormon, this is strong presumptive evidence that Lehi did not contain the Isaiah inclusions.

The Package: The Brass Plates

Quoting from Isaiah and the Pentateuch required that the Nephites be in possession of those works. Obtaining a copy of these texts to bring with them was not the only way. Since the Apostle Paul is quoted before he was even born, the reader must surmise that these verses were received by revelation. So too, Isaiah could have been received by revelation, just as Joseph Smith later claimed to have received the *Book of Moses*. Or Providence could have provided a scroll in Hebrew. These options were clearly on the table. Alternatively, the Nephi replacement text of their new Bible could take care of this through the acquisition of the Brass Plates, a sort of pre-exilic Bible, compiled long before the concept of a bible even existed (1 Nephi 5:11-13):

> 11. And he beheld that they [the Brass Plates] did contain the five books of Moses, which gave an account of the creation of the world, and also of Adam and Eve, who were our first parents;
> 12. And also a record of the Jews from the beginning, even down to the commencement of the reign of Zedekiah, king of Judah;
> 13. And also the prophecies of the holy prophets, from the beginning, even down to the commencement of the reign of Zedekiah; and also many prophecies which have been spoken by the mouth of Jeremiah.

They also contained the prophecies of Joseph (1 Nephi 4:2) and Lehi's genealogy (1 Nephi 3:3). For the prospective 19th-century reader, this would seem normal. This band of Israelite immigrants would be analogous to the Europeans who left for the New World, Bible in hand.

In Nephi, this brass bible was in the possession of a wealthy military leader named Laban. Nephi is commanded to get it from him, and when the latter resists and confiscates the precious items brought to exchange for them, Nephi is commanded to kill Laban to take the plates. It is not clear that some similar account was absent from Lehi. This is because the Zoramites are mentioned in a list of BOM peoples in Smith's first revelation, dated July of 1828 in the Book of Commandments,. If the date is correct, and this list is retrospective (to Lehi) rather than prospective (to the intended Book of Nephi), then Zoram may have existed in Lehi. The same list, in the same order, exists in Jacob 1:13. The order is irrelevant since it is obvious: Nephi followed by Jacob and Joseph (in order of birth), followed by Zoram (completing the believers), and then Laman, Lemuel and Ishmael (the rebels). In Alma a possibly different group of Zoramites are the enemies of the Nephites. Presumably in 4 Nephi, the Jacobites, Josephites and Zoramites emerge as "true believers" among the Nephites (4 Nephi 1:36) because they had been mentioned as such in the July 1828 revelation. Conspicuously absent from the list is Sam. If there was already a Zoram in Lehi, we might assume that there was also a Laban, and so too a conflict between either Nephi or Lehi and Laban, possibly over Lehi's call to repentance, or the genealogy of Lehi, or Lehi's soon-to-be-abandoned property, or a record of the Jews. If this record was part of the story, its contents may not have been mentioned (or possibly just the Law of Moses). None of the foregoing requires a mention of plates of brass. The option of the brass plates was eventually chosen because they had other more intrinsic utilitarian value, as we shall see.

The Package: Egyptian and the Scriptures

One such intrinsic value lies in the fact that the Nephi replacement text could be crafted to take place in a linguistic vacuum, by making the text of the Brass Plates in Egyptian, a language they thought would never be deciphered. The gold plates must be in an epigraphic vacuum as well; to wit, by making them in "reformed" characters, they hoped to establish a vacuum of script, and made it impossible for anyone to test them by asking Smith Jr. to reproduce known ancient Egyptian characters off the top of his head. By placing the history in pre-Columbian America, a land that no one knew or would ever truly know, or so they thought, they were able to write their history in a historical and cultural vacuum, a sort of *tabula rasa*. By contrast, when producing the Book of Lehi, Joseph Jr. did not feel constrained by an imperative to avoid detail.

There is no document dated to before 1829 that identifies the characters on the plates as Egyptian. Professor Anthon stated that the characters shown to him were a hodgepodge from various Middle East languages. There is nothing clearly Egyptian in appearance on the transcription of characters usually attributed by the Church to Harris' mission of c. February of 1828 (Figure 3). Egyptian first clearly emerges in connection with the Brass Plates in the Book of Nephi. This would mean that the addition of these plates provided the opportunity to supply the precedent for the Nephite records to be also in Egyptian, including the gold plates of the *Book of Mormon*. The plates of Laban thus did double duty, being Israelite scriptures in Egyptian. This language was thought to be undeciphered, and never to be deciphered (Mormon 9:34):

> But the Lord knoweth the things which we have written, and also that none other people knoweth our language; and because that none other people knoweth our language, therefore he hath prepared means for the interpretation thereof.

Moreover, making Nephite elites bilingual in Egyptian and Hebrew allowed the authors free rein in devising the many Nephite and Lamanite personal and place names.

The Package: Metallic Plates Rather Than Scrolls

Herein lies a second intrinsic value of the Brass Plates. The story of Smith's acquisition of the BOM text imposed on the project the need to assert that indeed a bible could be inscribed on gold plates. This was given a precedent by making the bible brought by Lehi to the New World a text inscribed on brass plates. These two intrinsic values of brass plates gave them the edge over simply having Isaiah be received in Hebrew through revelation, or even penned on a scroll.

The Package: King James English

Initially, Smith Jr. and Harris would have had little inclination to write Lehi's history in anything other than the familiar English of their day, much as Spalding had done in his romance. Knowing their own limitation in the English language, they may have steered away from attempting to write in what they could even have considered a stultified English. When drafting the replacement text, to make the acceptance of the Isaiah passages easier it was necessary to keep them in King James English. But if they were inserted into a larger text written in nineteenth century English, the contrast would make the overall work look like a modern composition quoting KJV Biblical passages. The Biblical inclusions settled this language issue. However, since writing in correct

King James English should have lain well within divine capabilities, the work would have to be written in their best approximation to it. Although well versed in the Bible, this BOM A-team made numerous errors, such as confusing 'thou,' 'ye' and 'you,' as well as verbal endings.[164] Fortunately for the project, their prospective readers would not notice occasional errors of this nature. Indeed, there was an additional compensation for their effort. They could hope that the result would have an aura of sacred text, appropriate to a new Bible.

The Life of Lehi

The BOM begins its list of components of the purloined pages with "the record of my father." This would be the life of Lehi. Since it lists it before the record of the travails in the wilderness, this would include the dealings of Lehi with the Judeans prior to his departure. It is abbreviated in the Nephi replacement text (1 Nephi 1):

> 17. ... I make an abridgment of the record of my father, upon plates which I have made with mine own hands; wherefore, after I have abridged the record of my father then will I make an account of mine own life.
> 18. Therefore, I would that ye should know, that after the Lord had shown so many marvelous things unto my father, Lehi, yea, concerning the destruction of Jerusalem, behold he went forth among the people, and began to prophesy and to declare unto them concerning the things which he had both seen and heard.
> 19. And it came to pass that the Jews did mock him because of the things which he testified of them; for he truly testified of their wickedness and their abominations; and he testified that the things which he saw and heard, and also the things which he read in the book, manifested plainly of the coming of the Messiah, and also the redemption of the world.

---

[164] Royal Skousen, *The History of the Text of the* Book of Mormon. *Part One, Grammatical Variation* (Provo, UT: The Foundation for Ancient Research and Mormon Studies, 2016), 455-97; & Royal Skousen, *The History of the Text of the* Book of Mormon. *Part Two, Grammatical Variation* (Provo, UT: The Foundation for Ancient Research and Mormon Studies, 2016), 1144-79.

20. And when the Jews heard these things they were angry with him; yea, even as with the prophets of old, whom they had cast out, and stoned, and slain; and they also sought his life, that they might take it away...

This then is a detail-free outline of the record of Nephi's father, omitting "things which he saw in visions and in dreams; and he also hath written many things which he prophesied and spake unto his children," (v. 16), while only making slight mention of the warnings preached to the Judeans, attempts on his life, and possibly miracles of divine protection. One wonders how all of this would have been fleshed out, and would have been interfaced with the mission of Jeremiah, as he undertook the same divinely imposed task, and was cast into prison. What details of Jerusalem and the religious and political elites would have been included? Here again is a minefield for an unsuspecting neophyte exhorter, who probably thought he knew more than he actually did.

The Genealogy Quagmire

A major deletion from the Book of Lehi in producing the version to replace the purloined 116 pages, is the genealogy of Lehi, said to have been on the Brass Plates of Laban, and then recorded in the book of Lehi (1 Nephi 3:12, 5:14-16, 6:1). The BOM asserts that Lehi was a descendant of Jacob through Joseph. Although there is a lot of genealogy in the Bible, the so-called "begats" are not given for everyone. The focus is on the line of descent from Adam to the patriarchs, from Abraham to Jacob, and then on to David, presumably descended from Judah. Even his genealogy is tricky. The OT text does not provide enough information to trace the genealogy of 7th century BCE nonroyal notables of the northern Kingdom back to Manasseh. It is largely a Judean document, focused on Judean kingship. The New Testament focuses, understandably, on the descent of Jesus from David. Joseph Smith, in attempting to invent such a genealogy, would be rushing in where angels fear to tread. The advice of Paul is clear: "But avoid foolish controversies and genealogies..." (Titus 3:9)

Outlining the Book of Lehi

Based on this description derived from the BOM and Smith's first revelation, it is possible now to get a clear idea of what the lost Book of

Lehi, looked like, albeit minus the details of the text itself. It began with the record of Lehi. This was followed by the genealogy of the fathers of Lehi, his mission to call the Jews to repentance with adventures or misadventures in so doing, his calling to lead his family to the New World, an account of many years in the wilderness replete with details of their travails and adventures and finally a relatively political account of these immigrants once in the New World. It lacked the preaching of the gospel of Jesus, and Lehi's dreams, prophecies, exhortations, calls to repentance and patriarchal blessings, all required for the production of a new bible. Moreover, it lacked the Isaiah package, including the Isaiah inclusions, the commentary on them to show that Isaiah knew that Israelites would go to the New World, and was himself Christian. It did not need the source of Isaiah inclusions, i.e. the Brass Plates, which would be used in Nephi to place the *Book of Mormon* into a linguistic and epigraphic vacuum, and set a precedent for recording sacred scripture in Egyptian on metallic plates.

There is enough meat on this skeleton to conclude firmly that the Nephi replacement text was clearly not just a retelling of the Book of Lehi in different words, and perhaps with a few omissions or additions of story details, all justified as being a different composition. Rather, this new version, cast in King James English, was to be a total remake, a totally new concept of what the first fifth of the *Book of Mormon* ought to be, and therefore the *Book of Mormon* itself, and its mission. The wording of Smith's July 1828 revelation, "a marvelous work...about to come forth among the children of men," was incorporated into 1 Nephi 14:7: "For the time cometh, saith the Lamb of God, that I will work a great and a marvelous work among the children of men."

Chapter 11

The Book of Lehi: Its Genesis and Exodus

According to Willard Chase, Joseph Smith worked for him in 1822 to help with digging a well. About twenty feet down, a stone was found that Smith claimed to be a seer stone. He took possession of it for his use.[165] At that point he would have been about seventeen years old. By 1825 he already had a reputation for this activity. Based on this renown, Josiah Stowell sought him out to assist in locating treasure on his property in the latter half of that year.[166] This is how it all began.

Joseph Smith's 1826 Pretrial Examination

According to Smith's account, he stayed on the Stowell farm and worked for about a month. According to his mother's account, he worked for him "by the month," while the account of Oliver Cowdery reports the period as having been "a few months."[167] Smith admitted that he failed. Josiah Stowell was apparently not unhappy with the situation. The original legal proceeding (20 March 1826), a pretrial examination, was for disorderly conduct, which included pretending to find lost goods.[168] It appears that this proceeding did not lead to an actual trial. After the publication of the *Book of Mormon*, there was a new attempt to try him on the same charge. The constable's bill is dated 4 July 1830.

Smith was apparently acquitted. He was subsequently arraigned on similar charges before another judge and in a different jurisdiction for his activities, but it appears he was acquitted or charges were dismissed. In the case of farmer Stowell, the person who might have standing was not complaining. In another case, apparently the statute of limitations had run out.[169] In any case, he was only doing what so many other seer stone scryers and rodsmen were doing. One assumes that it was even difficult

---

[165] The statement of Willard Chase was printed in Eber D. Howe, *Mormonism Unvailed* (Salt Lake City: Signature Books, 2015), 338. The first edition was in 1834. See also Marquardt, *Rise of Mormonism*, 33-46.
[166] Marquardt, *Rise of Mormonism*, 38.
[167] *Ibid*, 38-39.
[168] *Ibid*, 40-45.
[169] For a detailed discussion, see Marquardt, *Rise of Mormonism*, 140-47.

to find a statute that specifically applied. *Nullum crimen sine lege.* The details of the trials are not important here. The cases indicate the extent to which Joseph Smith Jr. was involved in gold hunting with his seer stone.

New England settlers were sorely aware of the fact that while the English were farming the stubborn stony New England ground, Spanish ships were carrying tons of gold back to their homeland. They can be forgiven for thinking that certainly there must also be gold to be found in their vicinity, and possibly on their own farm. On 1 February 1831, a Palmyra newspaper, *The Reflector*, taking a critical look at Smith's "GOLDEN BIBLE,' can be quoted here as a reflection of the atmosphere in Palmyra in the 1820's:

> It may not be amiss in this place to mention that the MANIA of money-digging soon began rapidly to diffuse itself through many parts of the country; men and women without distinction of age or sex became marvelous wise in the occult sciences, many dreamed, and others saw visions disclosing to them deep in the bowels of the earth, rich and shining treasures and to facilitate those *mighty* mining operations, (money was usually if not always sought after in the night time,) divers devices and implements were invented, and although the *SPIRIT* was always able to retain his precious charge, these discomfited as well as deluded beings, would on a succeeding night return to their toil, not in the least doubting that success would eventually attend their labors.
>
> Mineral rods and balls, (as they were called by the impostor who made use of them,) were supposed to be infallible guides to these sources of wealth—"*PEEP STONES*" or pebbles taken promiscuously from the brook or field, were placed in a hat or other situation excluded from the light, when some WIZARD or WITCH (for these preformances [sic] were not confined to either sex) applied their eyes and nearly starting their balls from their sockets, declared they saw all the wonders of nature, including of course, ample stores of silver and gold.[170]

Edward Augustus Kendall observed in his *Travels Through the Northern Parts of the United States in the Years 1807 and 1808*, "The settlers of Maine, like all the other settlers in New England, indulge an

---

[170] Reprinted in Francis W. Kirkham, *A New Witness for Christ in America, "The Book of Mormon"* (Independence, MO: Press of Zion's Publishing Company, 1951), vol. 2, 69.

unconquerable expectation of finding money buried in the earth," a passion encouraged by the fact that money chests "have been dug for in all parts of the United States; and, as the history further goes, they have not unfrequently been found."[171]

The belief in witchcraft in New England immediately brings to mind the Salem witch trials. A Samuel Smith of Boxford accused Mary Easty of witchcraft at Topsfield, and a John Gould accused Sarah Wilds of witchcraft. Both women were hanged as witches at Salem partly based on these accusations. This Samuel Smith was Joseph Smith's great-grandfather Samuel, and John Gould was Samuel's father-in-law.[172] There are contemporary accounts that state that both Joseph Smith, and his father, Joseph Smith Sr., believed in witchcraft.[173] This belief is recorded in Mormon scripture: *Book of Mormon* (Alma 1:32, 3 Nephi 21:16 & 24:5, Mormon 1:19 & 2:10); and *Doctrine and Covenants* (63:17 & 76:103). A curious claim is that a Smith neighbor observed Smith Sr. enchanting guns at a turkey shoot so that they would miss the turkey.[174]

Early nineteenth-century New England had a large number of rodsmen, practitioners of the art of divining rods, used to find water, gold and hidden information. The *Palmyra Herald and Canal Advertiser* carried an article on 24 July 1822, titled "MONEY DIGGERS," claiming "Much, however depends on the skillful use of the genuine mineral rod," and recounts that one Vermont man "after digging with sufficient unyielding confidence and unabating diligence for ten or twelve years, found a sufficient quantity of money to build him a commodious home for his own convenience, and to fill it with comforts for weary travelers." Another person dug up treasure worth "the enormous sum of fifty thousand dollars!" In the manuscript and first published version of the *Book of Commandments*, the promise given to Oliver Cowdery was stated in these words: "Now this is not all, for you have another gift, which is the gift of working with the rod: behold it has told you things: behold there is no other power save God, that can cause this rod of

---

[171] Edward Augustus Kendall, *Travels Through the Northern Parts of the United States in the Years 1807 and 1808*, 3 vols. (New York: I. Riley: 1809), 3:84, 87-88.

[172] D. Michael Quinn, *Early Mormonism and the Magic World View*, 2nd ed. (Salt Lake City: Signature Books, 1998), 31.

[173] *Ibid*, 291.

[174] *Ibid*, 31.

nature, to work in your hands, for it is the work of God; and there whatsoever you shall ask me [God] to tell you, that you shall know." Quinn notes that "The 1835 *Doctrine and Covenants* substituted the phrase 'the gift of Aaron' in place of 'working with the rod' and 'rod of nature' in the 1833 *Book of Commandments*."[175] Joseph Smith senior, and his sons Joseph and Hyrum, along with a proficient rodsman Alva(h) Beman (Beaman), frequently went on treasure quests. In addition to using the mineral rod, the Smiths and many others used the seer stone, both for gold and for information.[176] There is even a report that Joseph Smith's mother, Lucy Mack Smith used a seer stone.[177] One account reports that the fee Joseph Smith charged E. W. Vanderhoof was 75 cents to use his seer stone to find a lost mare.[178]

The use of the seer stone by Joseph Smith is reflected in the standard title of the President of the LDS Church: Prophet, Seer and Revelator. A seer stone that belonged to Smith is currently in the office of the Church Historian.

An Angel by Any Other Name...

From his first use of a seer stone, Joseph Smith began to believe he had a special blessing. The scryer is able to do what others cannot. He or she is claiming to be assisted by some divine or spiritual source. The whereabouts of a treasure was believed to be revealed, at times, by a dream or vision. As a revelation tells rodsman Oliver Cowdery, "there is no other power save God, that can cause this rod of nature, to work in your hands."

What came to be called the second vision, involving the visit of the angel that revealed the gold plates, also underwent some evolution.[179] Buried treasure was often said to be secured by guardian spirits. "Typically the treasure 'moved off' through the earth when guardian spirits were not securely bound by proper ceremony or were offended when the diggers breached the necessary silence."[180] The belief in

---

[175] Quinn, *Early Mormonism and the Magic World View*, 37.
[176] *Ibid*, 41.
[177] *Ibid*, 42.
[178] *Ibid*, 43.
[179] Marquardt, *Rise of Mormonism*, 47.
[180] Quinn, *Early Mormonism and the Magic World View*, 60.

guardian spirits, and that the location of treasure could be learned by revelation, readily becomes a story that a guardian spirit had hidden his people's history engraved on gold plates, a spirit that revealed the location of this treasure to Joseph Smith.

It is significant to note that it was a messenger or an angel that visited Smith in the earlier accounts, but more specifically the angel Moroni visited him in the later and now official account. It was not possible to call him the angel Moroni before the character had been named, or even created. An interesting evidence of this evolution is the fact that in the 1838 version of the vision Smith gave the name as Nephi. This was edited, writing Moroni above Nephi.

> He called me by name and said unto me that he was a messenger sent from the presence of God to me and that his name was Nephi ⟨Moroni⟩.

Joseph Smith himself dictated this text to a scribe, James Mulholland. Much later, B. H. Roberts made the correction, Nephi to Moroni, at the turn of the century, when he was preparing the *History* for publication. Today, no eighteen-year-old missionary, or lay Sunday school teacher would make such a slip of the tongue. It is possible that Nephi had been a candidate for the messenger, and so was still stuck in Smith's mind, giving rise to the error.[181]

Even though we read in the current D&C 28:5 (section 28 dated August, 1830), "Moroni, whom I have sent unto you to reveal the *Book of Mormon*," this text was not found in the 1830 section 28 of the *Book of Commandments* (precursor to the D&C), and was added into the 1835 D&C text of section 28.[182]

The currently official account of receiving the gold plates is:

> 51. Convenient to the village of Manchester, Ontario county, New York, stands a hill of considerable size, and the most elevated of any in the neighborhood [later called the Hill Cumorah]. On the west side of this hill, not far from the top, under a stone of considerable size, lay the plates, deposited in a stone box. This stone was thick and rounding in the middle

---

[181] Jessee, The *Personal Writings of Joseph Smith* (Salt Lake City: Deseret Book Company, 1984), 203 & 667, note 12.
[182] Marquardt, *The Joseph Smith Revelations*, 72-73.

on the upper side, and thinner towards the edges, so that the middle part of it was visible above the ground, but the edge all around was covered with earth.

52. Having removed the earth, I obtained a lever, which I got fixed under the edge of the stone and with a little exertion raised it up. I looked in, and there indeed did I behold the plates, the Urim and Thummim, and the breastplate, as stated by the messenger. The box in which they lay was formed by laying stones together in some kind of cement. In the bottom of the box were laid two stones crossways of the box, and on these stones lay the plates and the other things with them.

53. I made an attempt to take them out, but was forbidden by the messenger, and was again informed that the time for bringing them forth had not yet arrived, neither would it, until four years from that time; but he told me that I should come to that place precisely in one year from that time, and that he would there meet with me, and that I should continue to do so until the time should come for obtaining the plates.

54. Accordingly, as I had been commanded, I went at the end of each year, and at each time I found the same messenger there, and received instruction and intelligence from him at each of our interviews, respecting what the Lord was going to do, and how and in what manner his kingdom was to be conducted in the last days.

55-58. [an account of events in his family, and of persecution]

59. At length the time arrived for obtaining the plates, the Urim and Thummim, and the breastplates. On the twenty-second day of September, one thousand eight hundred and twenty-seven, having gone as usual at the end of another year to the place where they were deposited, the same heavenly messenger delivered them up to me with this charge: that I should be responsible for them; that if I should let them go carelessly, or through any neglect of mine, I should be cut off; but that if I would use all my endeavors to preserve them, until he, the messenger, should call for them, they should be protected.[183]

Another observation is presently more pertinent, and possibly more important. Since the earlier "messenger" designation does not specifically involve the BOM, i.e. the new bible, it was appropriate for a period when a gold record engraved with curious characters was to be translated as a more secular history. The treasure aspect lay in the expected book sales.

---

[183] *The Pearl of Great Price*, Joseph Smith 2:51-59.

The Ordeal of Getting the Plates

There are other, earlier, accounts.[184] In one account, Joseph Smith Sr. reportedly told a neighbor, Willard Chase, that "On the 22d of September, he [Joe Jr.] must repair to the place where was deposited this manuscript, dressed in black clothes, and riding a black horse with a switch tail, and demand the book in a certain name, and after obtaining it, he must go directly away, and neither lay it down nor look behind him. They accordingly fitted out Joseph with a suit of black clothes and borrowed a black horse."[185] Smith's own earliest account (1832) reads:

> and it was on the 22d day of Sept. AD 1822 [1823] and thus he [the messenger] appeared unto me three times in one night and once on the next day and then I immediately went to the place and found where the plates was (sic) deposited as the angel of the Lord had commanded me and straightway made three attempts to get them and then being exceedingly frightened I supposed it had been a dream of Vision but when I considered I knew that it was not therefore I cried unto the Lord in the agony of my soul why can I not obtain them behold the angel appeared unto me again and said unto me you have not kept the commandments of the Lord which I gave unto you therefore you cannot now obtain them for the time is not yet fulfilled therefore thou was left unto temptation that thou mightest be made acquainted with the power of the advisary [adversary] therefore repent and call on the Lord thou shalt be forgiven and in his own due time thou shalt obtain them for now *I had been tempted of the advisary and sought the Plates to obtain riches* and kept not the commandment that I should have an eye single to the glory of God.[186] (emphasis added)

In this account, Smith himself states that his original desire was to get riches from the plates (or a claimed translation of them).

A curious account of a statement Willard Chase attributed to Joseph Smith Sr. reads:

> but fearing some one might discover where he got it, he laid it down to place back the top stone, as he found it; and turning around, to his surprise there was no book in sight. He again opened the box, and in it saw the

---

[184] Marquardt, *Rise of Mormonism*, 47-48; Joseph Smith's history of 1838, in Jessee, *Personal Writings of Joseph Smith*, 202-208. Lamar Petersen, *Problems in Mormon Text* (Concord, CA: Pacific Publishing Company, no date), 63-69.
[185] Marquardt, *Rise of Mormonism*, 48.
[186] Jessee, *Papers of Joseph Smith*, I:7-8.

book, and attempted to take it out, but was hindered. He saw in the box something like a toad, which soon assumed the appearance of a man, and struck him on the side of his head.[187]

After trying again, and being struck again, he was told:

> come one year from this day, and bring with you your oldest brother, and you shall have them. This spirit, he said, was the spirit of the prophet who wrote the book, who was sent to Joseph Smith, to make known these things to him.[188]

In this account, "the [nameless] prophet who wrote the book" is a strange expression, since that would presumably be Mormon, perhaps also an early candidate for the messenger. Or perhaps here again we have Nephi as the messenger (i.e., author of the Book of Nephi).

Smith was commanded to return in a year with his oldest brother. Since that brother died during the year, Smith returned without him, and showing up without his oldest brother, he was ordered to return again a year later, and bring a man with him. On asking who might be the man, he was answered that he would know him when he saw him. Marquardt[189] reports several other accounts, including accounts by Joseph's mother Lucy, his sister Catherine, his brother William and a joint account by two cousins of Joseph's wife, Emma Hale Smith. Accounts by non-Mormons can be challenged, accounts by close relatives were memories later in life, and the official account is just that. The earliest account, by Smith himself, differs from the official account; but it too is probably already an effort to spin an official account. In any case, Smith's mea culpa that he had wanted to get gain from the plates probably would assuage the concerns of some who had known him in the early days, when he sought gold treasure, or later on, when his more secular claims spoke of gold plates and a forthcoming translation from which he and Harris would make a lot of money. Also, it may be that this long period of attempting to get the plates is nothing more than a period of claiming to have found gold plates prior to coming up with the plan to turn his claim into profit by publishing a translation. Harris' enduring

---

[187] Marquardt, *Rise of Mormonism*, 48.
[188] Marquardt, *idem*.
[189] Marquardt, *ibid*, 51-53.

focus on profit would be a continuation of what had initially been a shared Smith-Harris motivation.

Once he claimed to have obtained the plates in late September of 1827, he soon began to assert that persons who had learned of his gold plates were attempting to steal them. This is possible. Apparently some claimed that there was an agreement with Smith that they should share their findings. After their arrival in Harmony and with great expectations, Joseph signed the "Articles of Agreement" (1/11/1825), also signed by his father and seven others to share their findings.[190] In 1881, David Whitmer stated, 'I had conversations with several young men who said that Joseph Smith had certainly golden plates, and that before he obtained them he had promised to share with them, but had not done so, and they were very much incensed with him.'"[191] Accordingly, Smith began to hide them in various locations, in a hollow log, in an old black oak tree, beneath the family hearth, in his father's cooper shop and in a barrel of beans.

It would appear that after his experience with the 1826 pretrial investigation, Smith sought a better way to profit from seeking the gold that he simply had not been able to find. Th claim that he had found gold plates could not be challenged, since he had been commanded by their guardian, the messenger, to not show them to anyone. His prior reputation, and the 'Articles of Agreement' prompted many to assume that he had indeed found the plates, and was claiming he could not show them to avoid sharing his treasure.

The Weighty Issue of a Gold Record

Since many involved believed that they could heft the plates, it is clear that no one really had any idea how heavy gold is. The table below reviews the options, with different metals. The accounts of hefting the plates need to be evaluated in the light of the weighty facts: if they were gold, they would weigh 135 pounds, calculated with a very generous estimate that the air between the plates could account for one third of the volume. In fact, 10% is more likely. On the other hand, the plates may have been only 80% gold, and 20% copper, an alloy called tumbaga actually used in South America in *Book of Mormon* times. Tumbaga

---

[190] Vogel, Early Mormon Documents, IV:407-13.
[191] Petersen, *Problems in Mormon* Text, p. 65.

plates with these proportions would weigh 120 pounds, again with the same generous allowance for air between them. It seems clear that very few witnesses would be able to heft 120 pounds. The testimonies would read more in the vein of attempts: "I tried to heft them, but could not lift them."

In the table below, the assumption that the volume occupied by the plates could have been 33% air seems more than generous. Smith described the plates as being about one eighth of an inch thick. If flat, there would have been 48 plates (6"X8"). Inscribed on both sides, they could have been somewhat less than flat, although the serious weight of the gold would have served to press the lower plates in the stack relatively flat and tight. Gold is a very soft metal.

Table 23. Weight of the Plates (Various Metals Compared)

Weight of Each Option Adjusted for the Percent Air Solid block is 6"x8"x6" or 288 cubic inches (weight is in pounds.)							
Plate option by substance of the plates	Weight gold per cubic inch	Weight copper per cubic inch	Weight brass[4] per cubic inch	Weight lead per cubic inch	Volume: G gold C copper	Weight per solid block	% air	Total (67% of a solid block)
Gold	.7					201.6	33	135
Copper		.31				89.28	33	59.8
Brass			.2876			84.64	33	55.5
Tumbaga A	.42	.124			G 80% C 20%	179.14	33	120
Tumbaga B	.525	.078			G 75% C 25%	156.67	33	116

1. The weights per cubic inch of gold, copper and brass are multiplied by 288 to get the weight of a solid block. The weight of the plates for each is this times .67 (adjusting for air).
2. The tumbaga A is rated here as being 80% gold & 20% copper. The weight of copper per cubic inch tumbaga is .31x .2=.062, and the weight of gold is .7x.8=.56. So:
[(288x.062)+(288x.56)]x.67= 120 pounds of tumbaga.
3. The tumbaga B is rated here as being 75% gold & 25% copper. The weight of copper per cubic inch tumbaga is .31x .25=.078, and the weight of gold is .7x.75=.525. So:
[(288x.078)+(288x.525)]x.67= 116 pounds of tumbaga. Reducing the weight of Tumbaga is limited by the weight of its copper.
4. The weight of brass varies. Common brass for cold working applications is 65% copper and 35% tin (.246 pounds per cubic inch), and the weight of the two combined is given here:
(.31x.65)+ (.246x.35)=.2876.

In the case of tumbaga, although the ratio was as high as 80% gold, more usually it was only 75%, but could be even lower. It has higher tensile strength and a lower melting point than either metal alone, and can be gilded by applying a mild vegetable acid. This dissolves away the surface copper, leaving a pure gold surface film, and the process can be repeated when wear occurs. However, tumbaga can corrode:

> Non-gilded archaeological metals having a high percentage of copper are known to survive in better condition than gilded tumbaga objects primarily due to galvanic forces and preferential corrosion between gilded layers and the underlying alloy in a burial environment. The less noble copper will eventually corrode, the resulting corrosion products will undermine the gilding, and the thin gilded layer may eventually become detached from the heavily mineralized base alloy.[192]

Alloys must be above fifty *atomic percent* (At.%) gold to be corrosion resistant.[193] Atomic percentage is the percent of the atoms in the alloy that are a particular metal. To the extent that the copper atoms outnumber the gold atoms, they will be more susceptible to oxidation, producing serious deterioration. The following formula calculates the weight percentage when the atomic weights and atomic percentages of two metals in an alloy are known. I am using x for gold and y for copper. This example has 50 At.% (.5) for each metal.

$$\text{Wt. \% x} = \frac{(\text{At. \% x})(\text{At. Wt. x})}{(\text{At. \% x})(\text{At. Wt. x}) + (\text{At. \% y})(\text{At. Wt. y})} \times 100$$

$$= (.5 \times 196.966)/[(.5 \times 196.966)+(.5 \times 63.546)] \times 100 = 75.6\%$$

Therefore, more than 76% gold, by scale weight, is needed for the plates to be relatively corrosion resistant. If the gold is 67% by scale weight, the atomic weight percent falls to 40%. Over a period of 1500 years, serious corrosion would occur. Presumably, corroded plates with the gilding scaling off are no one's image of Smith's gold plates.

---

[192] Scott Fulton and Sylvia Keochakian, "The conservation of tumbaga metals from Panama at the Peabody Museum, Harvard University," *Objects Specialty Group Postprints*, Volume Twelve (2005), 76-90.

[193] Lyndsie Selwyn, "Corrosion Chemistry of Gilded Silver and Copper," in Terry Drayman-Weisser, *Gilded Metals, History, Technology & Conservation* (London: Archetype Publications, 2000), 21-47.

11. The Book of Lehi: Its Genesis and Exodus

So bearing in mind that gold plates would weigh at least 135 pounds, and even tumbaga plates would weigh from 116 to 120 pounds to survive relatively free of corrosion, we read his mother's account of how he got them out of their hiding place in a log in the woods and home:

> Joseph...wrapping them in his linen frock, placed them under his arm and started for home...travelling some distance after he left the road, he came to a large windfall, and as he was jumping over a log, a man sprang up from behind it, and gave him a heavy blow with a gun. Joseph turned around and knocked him down, then ran at the top of his speed. About half a mile further he was attacked again in the same manner as before; he knocked the man down in like manner as the former and ran on again; and before he reached home he was assaulted the third time. In striking the last one he dislocated his thumb...he threw himself down in the corner of the fence in order to recover his breath.[194]

Joseph runs more than a mile with a weight of at least 116 pounds. He carries it under his arm, like a schoolbook. With it, he jumps over a log. And during this whole time, carrying it from place to place, there is no mention that he can hardly even lift it. Moreover, he was still suffering the effects of the removal of a large abscess in a leg. Smith's mother also reportedly said that she had herself handled and hefted the plates.[195]

Martin Harris had spent his life working on his farm, and was no stranger to hefting heavy objects. Reportedly he claimed to have hefted the plates, and said that they weighed forty or fifty pounds.[196] William Smith recounted that when Smith first got the plates home, although he did not see them uncovered, "I handled them and hefted them while wrapped in a tow frock;" and that "Father and my brother Samuel saw them as I did while in the frock. So did Hyrum and others of the family."[197] Lucy Smith wrote that she invited Mrs. Harris over to see them. In an interview to Edward Stevenson, Martin Harris stated that his wife and daughter had hefted the plates and felt them under cover; he

---

[194] Lucy Smith in Anderson, *Lucy's Book*, 385-86.
[195] Sally Parker to John Kepmpton, 26 August 1838, in Vogel, *Early Mormon Documents* (Salt Lake City: Signature Books, 2002), I:218-19.
[196] Martin Harris as quoted in Joel Tiffany, "Mormonism—No. II," Tiffany Monthly (August 1859, in Vogel, *Early Mormon Documents*, II:306.
[197] William B. Smith, "Wm. B. Smith's last Statement," *Zion's Ensign* 5: Jan. 13, 1894, in Marquardt, *Rise of Mormonism*, 72.

said, "My daughter said, they were about as much as she could lift. They were now in the glass-box [a wood box for window panes], and my wife said they were very heavy. They both lifted them."[198]

In summary, whether we consider the many who hefted the book, even Mother Smith, Martin Harris' estimate of their weight, or the adventures of Joseph running through the woods, the bottom line is that the sheer weight of even tumbaga plates cannot be reconciled with any of these stories. And the weight of even these hypothetical tumbaga plates was generously underestimated.

The writing area is also a problem. With the plates numbering around fifty, there could have been 100 pages, if inscribed on both sides. But one half to two thirds of the plates were sealed and not translated. So the available pages would have numbered only 50 at the most, especially if the plates did not lie perfectly flat. There must have been a margin, and a wider gutter to accommodate the binding rings. The *Book of Mormon* in English, published with around 10-point type, takes over 500 pages, plus 100 for Lehi. The plates, as described by Smith, would have had to have the equivalent of twelve pages in English per side, in reformed Egyptian. It is hard to imagine compressing any real script to this extent.

How about Brass Plates?

To cover other possibilities, it is instructive to have some knowledge of metallurgy in the early Americas, as well as in early nineteenth-century New England. Smelting gold, silver and copper began in the Andes, where alloying also emerged. Well before the Common Era, bronze and tumbaga were produced. The Moche culture was especially advanced, and South American trading ships carried on an active trade with Mesoamerica, resulting in local metallurgy among the Mayas at least by the time of their classic period (c. 250-900 CE).

In colonial America, the British tried to prevent the local development of the metal industries. Still, the world's largest identified lead deposit is in Missouri's lead belt, and it was being mined as early as 1720. Frontiersmen needed it to cast balls for their muskets. Prior to 1800, brass was mostly used in the button industry. Buttons were formed from sheet brass, and these craftsmen got their brass rolled in early steel

---

[198]Martin Harris as quoted by Joel Tiffany in "Mormonism—No. II," Tiffany Monthly (August 1859, in Vogel, *Early Mormon Documents*, II:309.

rolling mills. The center of the New England brass industry came to be in Waterbury, Connecticut, the self-dubbed "Brass Town." Aaron Benedict began rolling sheet brass in 1824, and quickly found a market for his product. Joseph Smith came from a cooper family. His grandfather and father had been coopers, he was a cooper's son, and his family had a cooper shop. It is interesting to observe that this shop was one of the first places where he claimed he was hiding the plates.

The weight of brass plates would be at least 55.5 pounds, more than the upper end of Martin Harris' estimate for the weight of the gold plates. The unsealed portion of brass plates could have been easily inscribed with Smith's character set using an awl, or even an ice pick. But does this mean that the Smiths had actually produced this sort of prop for their project? Not necessarily. Everyone who claimed to have hefted or otherwise examined the plates may have been a confederate. But having a brass-plate prop would have been effective, even just for feeling it through a cloth and hefting it. After all, we do not know that all those who might have had this privilege got their experience into print.

Conclusions

1. The weight of the plates, if gold, is completely incompatible with the stories told about their being carried and hefted.
2. Corrosion-resistant tumbaga plates could look like gold, but are still too heavy.
3. It was possible in the mid 1820's for a cooper's son to fabricate a brass-plate prop, although there is no need to assume that this happened.
4. The writing area of the plates as described could not have held the entire *Book of Mormon* text.

The Production of the Book of Lehi

Joseph and Emma moved to Harmony, Susquehanna Co., Pennsylvania, in December of 1827. Initially he got more acquainted with her family, and set up their new living quarters. At some point, he began dictating his "translation" of the Book of Lehi to "scribes," his wife Emma, and her brother, Reuben Hale.[199] Later, Martin Harris took up that duty. In February, 1828, Harris traveled to Harmony, picked up a copy of

---

[199] Marquardt, *Rise of Mormonism*, 75, 80-81.

characters claimed to be from the gold plates, and traveled to Utica, Albany and New York City to show them to learned scholars. After his return to Harmony, he went back to Palmyra in upstate New York and returned with his wife, Lucy Harris, attempting to change her mind about the project. Then he took her back to Palmyra. He returned to Harmony in April to be Joseph's scribe. The period of his scribal duty then was from April 12 to June 14, picking up after Emma and her brother.

According to Lucy Smith, she and Joseph Smith Sr. visited their son to meet Emma's parents and returned in late September or early October 1828, after his visit to them, although Vogel has published evidence for a possible date before 11 September (Table 37).[200] They visited him again in February 1829.[201] So, the Lehi ms was done entirely in Harmony and the first opportunity for Joseph Sr. to see it would have been when Joseph visited them in Manchester in July of 1828.

Martin Harris: A Doubting Thomas? Or a Scout?

Translation was described as being by means of divine power, using the "spectacles" or "interpreter," two names for the Urim and Thummim. But this device and the gold plates had to be kept unseen. The former were mostly hidden away, in the woods or elsewhere to be protected from thieves. Since translation was done in their absence, it was more practical to simply use a seer stone. With his face in his hat, he could not see the plates anyway, and with the text coming by divine power, he did not need the plates nor the spectacles (nor even the seer stone?).

The LDS account states that he translated with the use of a scribe. Even with this orthodox interpretation, the scribe could serve as an interface to improve on Smith's spelling deficiency, although even the scribes would never win any spelling bee. Like those who cannot write well, but who can compose very well by speaking verbally to a computer text processor enabled with speech recognition, Smith may have been a much better storyteller than writer.

His principal collaborator initially was a prosperous farmer, Martin Harris, for whom Joseph had worked from time to time. Although on occasion several other people acted as scribes, for the Book of Lehi, it

---

[200] Lucy Smith in Anderson, *Lucy's Book*, 423. See also, Vogel, *Early Mormon Documents*, III:439. See Table 37.
[201] Joseph Smith, *History of the Church*, 1:28.

was mostly Harris. He was also an absolutely essential member of the team as the financial backer without whom they would not have the funds to publish the book (over 500 pages in the traditional edition). Shortly after Smith claimed to have the plates, Harris provided him with fifty dollars, a substantial sum at that time, to cover translation expenses. Perhaps it was to court this funder that Hyrum Smith escorted him for his first visit to Joseph's home in Harmony.[202]

According to the official account, at some point, Harris began having doubts about the existence of the plates and Smith's calling. To assuage this doubt, Smith copied characters from the plates to produce a reformed Egyptian alphabet, so that Harris could show them to learned men for reassurance. This account is totally suspect. If Harris were having doubts, sending him on such a mission would have been highly risky. Smith was no dummy, and certainly must have known that he could not be sure how learned men would react to what he claimed to be a transcription, and, accordingly, whether this mission would in fact mark the end of Harris' confidence, and financial commitment to the cause. Alternatively, both Smith and Harris may have thought that a transcript from the plates might be useful to market the book. The expedition to the learned may have been to test Smith's characters, but also to fulfill an OT revelation, wherein a book is delivered to a learned man, who declares that he cannot read it, for it is sealed (Isaiah 29:11).

Harris went off to show Smith's transcription of characters to Dr. Samuel L. Mitchill (Mitchell), Vice President of Rutgers Medical College, and, most notably, to the very erudite Professor Charles Anthon (1797-1867) at Columbia University. The Egyptian qualifications of the latter have at times been overstated. Although evidence indicates that a copy of Jean François Champollion's, *Précis du Système Hiéroglyphique des Anciens Égyptiens* eventually was added to Anthon's library, since Harris' trip was made in 1828, and Champollion's *Précis* was not even published in France until 1824, we cannot say that Anthon had even seen it. Even the Library of Congress has only the second edition (1827-28). But Champollion had published two preliminary studies that Anthon may have seen.

As for the results of the trip, we do not have a report from Harris himself. In 1837, he was excommunicated, and still in 1839 he was

---

[202] Lucy Smith, in Anderson, *Lucy's Book*, 402.

speaking out against Smith. This may have made it easier for Smith, in his 1839 history, to ascribed to Harris a report that says, in part:

> Professor Anthony stated that the translation was correct, more so than any he had before seen translated from the Egyptian.
>
> I then showed him those which were not yet translated, and he said that they were Egyptian, Chaldeak, Assyriac and Arabac...He gave me a certificate certifying to the people of Palmyra that they were true characters and that the translation of such of them as had been translated was also correct. I took the Certificate and put it into my pocket, and was just leaving the house, when Mr Anthon called me back and asked me how the young man found out that there were gold plates where he found them. I answered that an Angel of God had revealed it unto him. He then said to me, let me see that certificate, I accordingly took it out of my pocket and gave it him when he took it and tore it to pieces saying that there was no such thing now as ministering of angels, and that if I would bring the plates to him, he would translate them.[203]

About five years earlier, Eber D. Howe had informed Anthon regarding the claim the Mormons were making that he had stated that some translated characters from the gold plates were an accurate translation of Egyptian. Anthon sent the following reply:

> This paper was in fact a singular scrawl. It consisted of all kinds of crooked characters disposed in columns, and had evidently been prepared by some person who had before him at the time a book containing various alphabets. Greek and Hebrew letters, crosses and flourishes, Roman letters inverted or placed sideways, were arranged in perpendicular columns, and the whole ended in a rude delineation of a circle divided into various compartments, decked with various strange marks...and [I] remember well that the paper contained anything else but *'Egyptian Hieroglyphics.'* [204]

Anthon makes his pointed denial regarding Egyptian in response to Howe's specific query regarding the Mormon claim that he had found Smith's translation of Egyptian to be correct. This claim is itself odd in

---

[203] Martin Harris as quoted in Joseph Smith's history, 1838-39, readily found in Jessee, *Papers of Joseph Smith*, I:285; v. Marquardt, *Rise of Mormonism*, 76.
[204] Charles Anthon to Eber D. Howe, in Howe, *Mormonism Unvailed*, 382. See Stanley B. Kimball, "The Anthon Transcript, People, Primary Sources and Problems," *BYU Studies*, vol. 10, no. 3 (1970), 325-352.

that the *Book of Mormon* says that no one could read the reformed Egyptian text, including Anthon. In a second letter, in 1841, Anthon gave nearly the same description of the characters to Thomas Winthrop Coit, but this time with no mention of Egyptian being among the characters.[205] Anthon's description of the paper with the characters cannot be reconciled with Figure 3. He described the characters as being in vertical columns, while those in Figure 3 are in rows. The layout of characters is the feature that one might most reliably remember. Note too that it is difficult to identify most of the characters found in Figure 3 as being modified Greek, Hebrew, Assyrian or Arabic (cursive!) with any degree of confidence. Indeed, Smith's version of Harris' description is more consistent with Anthon's than either is with Figure 3.

Since it is known that there have been several versions of the gold plates transcript,[206] it is probable that all of the above are roughly accurate. Apparently, Smith initially made a character list in columns. This is what Anthon saw. But Harris' mission was very helpful. They had learned that a simple hodgepodge of modified known characters was not acceptable. Smith would have to invent his own. The original attempt, with characters in columns, was replaced by a text similar to Figure 3. Anthon reported that one character was "a rude delineation of a circle divided into various compartments, decked with various strange marks" located at the end of the character list. In fact we find a character that seems to fit this description, but it repeats several times. Apparently, after getting Harris' report, Smith would have proceeded to create a transcript of a text, drawing from his list while avoiding characters too transparently copied from known alphabets, and adding some characters not found in the list. In this transcript, certain characters repeat so as to mimmic real language.

Harris' trip produced results that would become important when developing the strategies for the *Book of Mormon* remake. For it, the best way to avoid these issues was to create a linguistic and epigraphic vacuum, by having the gold plates in reformed Egyptian. Harris observed his partner at work daily, in the absence of the plates and the spectacles. It is certain that at times the translation had to be substantially edited.

---

[205] Charles Anthon to Thomas Winthrop Coit, in Vogel, *Early Mormon Documents*, IV:383.
[206] Michael Hubbard MacKay, Gerrit J. Dirkmaat, and Robin Scott Jenson, "The 'Charactors' Document: New Light on an Early Transcription of the *Book of Mormon* Characters", in *Mormon Historical Studies*, vol. 14, no. 1, 131-52.

During the development of the transcript, he also observed character transmogrification. There is no indication that any of this bothered him.

The possibility that the characters were devised to promote the book becomes more probable when we note that in fact just this tack was taken in a broadside (essentially a poster) of the short-lived *The Prophet* published in 1844 in New York, New York. It reads:

the
STICK OF JOSEPH,
taken from the
HAND OF EPHRAIM

A CORRECT COPY
of the characters taken from the plates the
BOOK OF MORMON!!
Was translated from—the same that was taken to Professor Anthon of New York, by Martin Harris, in the year 1827 in fulfilment of Isaiah 29.11, 12.
(characters)
text
(characters)
text
(characters)
text

The first two lines of characters are virtually the same as the first two lines in Figure 3, but the third differs, especially the second half of it. We do not know what response this broadside got.

By July of 1828, Smith and Harris, working in Harmony, Pennsylvania, had produced at least 116 manuscript pages of what Joseph Smith eventually called the Book of Lehi. They had every right to feel a profound sense of accomplishment.

The Fate of the Purloined Pages

According to the official LDS account, Martin Harris, a prosperous farmer bankrolling Joseph Smith's *Book of Mormon* project, and his principal scribe at the time, was having difficulties with his wife, who was totally opposed to her husband's relationship with Smith. Quite rightly, she viewed family property to be as much hers as his, and feared that the Smiths would succeed in bilking her husband out of everything. In June of 1828, he requested permission to take 116 pages, all or nearly all of the only copy of the work completed up to that time, to his home in upstate New York, to read them to his wife in hopes of getting her support for his expenses and work as Smith's scribe.[207] Incredibly, according to the official story, Smith allowed Harris to take their only copy of their work into what both knew was enemy territory, even though he himself was planning to make a trip to Manchester, and could have taken them himself. In Smith's 1839 history, Harris had promised to show the manuscript only to his wife, his father, his mother and a sister of his wife.[208]

In late June or early July, Joseph went to visit his parents. The exact date is unknown. His wife had delivered a son that died the day of his birth on June 15 (dated by his tombstone), and Joseph was able to leave his wife in the care of her parents. This was a considerable journey at the time, by stagecoach from Harmony, Pennsylvania to Manchester in upstate New York. On the morning of his arrival Harris was invited to breakfast. According to the account of Joseph's mother, Lucy Mack Smith, Harris arrived over four hours late, and when he arrived, he joined the group at the table but did not eat. She wrote:

> [Harris] cried out in a tone of deep anguish, "Oh, I have lost my soul! I have lost my soul!"
>
> Joseph, who had not expressed his fears till now, sprang from the table, exclaiming, "Martin, have you lost that manuscript? Have you broken your oath, and brought down condemnation upon my head, as well as your own?"
>
> "Yes, it is gone," replied Martin, "and I know not where."
>
> "Oh, my God!" said Joseph, clinching his hands. "All is lost! All is lost! What shall I do? I have sinned—it is I who tempted the wrath of God. I should have been satisfied with the first answer which I received from the Lord; for he told me that it was not safe to let the writing go out of my possession." He wept and groaned, and walked the floor continually.[209]

This is just her recollection, and these words are her composition. What seems clear, since I see no reason why she would invent the whole incident, is that the loss of the plates was announced to all present.

---

[207] For a discussion of this episode, see H. Michael Marquardt, *The Rise of Mormonism*, 81-84.
[208] Joseph Smith, "History, 1839," in Jessee, *Papers of Joseph Smith*, I:286.
[209] Lucy Smith, in Anderson, *Lucy's Book*, 417-18.

Allowing for some embellishment of the language these histrionics seem extreme, even realizing that people expressed themselves differently back then, in a time when apparently women really did swoon,. More to the point, they seem to be intended for an audience. If I had been Martin, I would simply have called Joseph aside, terribly embarrassed, and in private I would have said, "Joe, we have a problem."

In the LDS view, this was Satan's plan from the beginning, and God had prepared to foil it. As the *Book of Mormon* story unfolds, we learn that by commandment of God Nephi kept two records covering the same period, as a sort of textual redundancy strategy (1 Nephi 19):

> 1. the Lord commanded me, wherefore I did make plates of ore that I might engraven upon them the record of my people....the record of my father...our journeyings in the wilderness, and the prophecies of my father; and also many of mine own prophecies have I engraven upon them.
> 2. And I knew not at the time when I made them that I should be commanded of the Lord to make these plates; wherefore, the record of my father, and the genealogy of his fathers, and the more part of all our proceedings in the wilderness are engraven upon those first plates of which I have spoken; wherefore, the things which transpired before I made these plates are... more particularly made mention upon the first plates.
> 3. And after I had made these plates by way of commandment, I, Nephi, received a commandment that the ministry and the prophecies, the more plain and precious parts of them, should be written upon these plates; and that the things which were written should be kept for the instruction of my people, who should possess the land, and also for other wise purposes, which purposes are known unto the Lord.
> 4. Wherefore, I, Nephi, did make a record upon the other plates, which gives an account, or which gives a greater account of the wars and contentions and destructions of my people. And this have I done, and commanded my people what they should do after I was gone; and that these plates should be handed down from one generation to another, or from one prophet to another, until further commandments of the Lord.
> 5. this I do that the more sacred things may be kept for the knowledge of my people.

Thus we learn that Nephi had been commanded to make one set of records, often referred to as the Large Plates of Nephi (or the Plates of Lehi) and a second set referred to as the small plates of Nephi. Mormon mentions them again in a brief statement inserted just at the point where the lost pages left off (Words of Mormon):

11. The Book of Lehi: Its Genesis and Exodus 285

3. ... after I had made an abridgment from the plates of Nephi, down to the reign of this king Benjamin, of whom Amaleki spake...I found these plates, which contained this small account of the prophets, from Jacob down to the reign of this king Benjamin, and also many of the words of Nephi.

4. And the things which are upon these plates pleasing me, because of the prophecies of the coming of Christ; and my fathers knowing that many of them have been fulfilled; yea, and I also know that as many things as have been prophesied concerning us down to this day have been fulfilled, and as many as go beyond this day must surely come to pass—

5. Wherefore, I chose these things, to finish my record upon them, which remainder of my record I shall take from the plates of Nephi...

6. But behold, I shall take these plates, which contain these prophesyings and revelations, and put them with the remainder of my record, for they are choice unto me; and I know they will be choice unto my brethren.

7. thus it whispereth me, according to the workings of the Spirit of the Lord...I do not know all things; but the Lord knoweth all things which are to come; wherefore, he worketh in me to do according to his will.

God, in His wisdom, had provided some failsafe redundancy in the form of a second set of plates covering the same period of time, i.e. that of the lost pages, in anticipation that the translation of the Large Plates would be lost. This is made more specific in a revelation to Joseph Smith (D&C, 10:10-13, 30-31, & 38-45; compare with D&C 3 & 5), in which God says:

10. And, behold, Satan hath put it into their hearts to alter the words which you have caused to be written...which have gone out of your hands.

11. ...because they have altered the words, they read contrary from that which you translated and caused to be written;

12. And, on this wise, the devil has sought to lay a cunning plan, that he may destroy this work;

30. Behold, I say unto you, that you shall not translate again those words which have gone forth out of your hands;

31. For, behold, they shall not accomplish their evil designs in lying against those words. For, behold, if you should bring forth the same words they will say that you have lied and that you have pretended to translate, but that you have contradicted yourself.

> 38. I say unto you, that an account of those things that you have written, which have gone out of your hands, is engraven upon the plates of Nephi;
> 39. Yea, and you remember it was said in those writings that a more particular account was given of these things upon the plates of Nephi.
> 40. And now, because the account which is engraven upon the plates of Nephi is more particular concerning the things which, in my wisdom, I would bring to the knowledge of the people in this account—
> 41. Therefore, you shall translate the engravings which are on the plates of Nephi, down even till you come to the reign of king Benjamin, or until you come to that which you have translated, which you have retained;
> 42. And behold, you shall publish it as the record of Nephi
> 45. Behold, there are many things engraven upon the plates of Nephi which do throw greater views upon my gospel

So, it was the translation from the Large Plates of Nephi (the Book of Lehi) that was lost. The account for the same period from the small plates of Nephi was to be translated to replace it. The replacement text was to be a new book, the Book of Nephi. In this manner, those who had the purloined pages would not be able to say that Smith was unable to produce the same divine text a second time. The new text would be a translation of a different set of plates.

This account is a matter of some embarrassment to true believers, who mostly shrug it off as being just one more thing to be ignored, or tolerated, while relying on their prayers and testimony. It is at the same time an important point for the critics of the BOM. For them, the incident exposed Smith's imposture.

Lucy Smith on the Purloined Pages

Apparently, Lucy Smith, Joseph's mother, and Lucy Harris, Martin Harris' wife, were initially on good terms. We do not know if their relationship deteriorated due to anything more than the pecuniary interests involved. As it became clear that Mrs. Harris was not going to convert, and was determined to get her husband to withdraw his essential financial support from the *Book of Mormon* project, a great antipathy developed between the two Lucy's. Mother Smith's account reads as follows:

> The manuscript has never been found, and there is no doubt but Mrs. Harris took it from the drawer, with the view of retaining it, until another translation should be given, then, to alter the original translation, for the

purpose of showing a discrepancy between them, and thus make the whole appear to be a deception.

It seemed as though Martin Harris, for his transgression, suffered temporally as well as spiritually. The same day on which the foregoing circumstance took place, a dense fog spread itself over his fields, and blighted his wheat while in the blow, so that he lost about two-thirds of his crop, whilst those fields which lay only on the opposite side of the road received no injury whatever.[210]

Much later (1884), Lorenzo Saunders claimed, in an interview to E. L. Kelley, that he had heard Lucy Harris say that she had burned the papers [the lost 116 pages].[211] Initially Martin Harris was reported as making a statement that seemed to indicate that she had given them to some other person.[212] At a much later date, as he was ill and approaching his death in 1875, he was reported as saying that he believed that Mrs. Harris had burned the pages.[213]

Joseph Smith on the Purloined Pages

Joseph Smith undoubtedly knew Harris' actions in all of this more than anyone else, and must have grilled him regarding the fate of the pages. He wrote of them in the "Preface" to the first edition of the *Book of Mormon*, "which said account [the 116 pages], some person or persons have stolen and kept from me..." In his 1832 History he reiterated essentially the same assertions made in the *Book of Mormon* and his earliest revelations on the subject. Smith says:

> the Lord said unto me let him [Martin Harris] go with them [the 116 pages] only he shall covenant with me that he will not show them to only but four persons and he covenanted with the Lord that he would do according to the word of the Lord therefore he took them and took his journey unto his

---

[210] Lucy Smith in Anderson, *Lucy's Book*, 422-23.
[211] E. L. Kelley Papers, "Miscellany," RLDS Church Library-Archives (Independence, MO: 1884).
[212] Claim of John A. Clark, made in a letter addressed to "Dear Brethren" dated August 31, 1840, published in *The Episcopal Recorder* (Philadelphia: 12 September, 1840), 98-99. See Vogel, *Early Mormon Documents*, II:269-71.
[213] Statement of William Pilkington, with his affidavit of 1934; v. Vogel, *Early Mormon Documents*, II:354.

friend to Palmira Wayne County and State of New York and he brake the covenant which he made before the Lord and the Lord suffered the writings to fall into the hands of wicked men.[214]

We do not know who this friend might be. In his 1838-39 History, Smith wrote:

> Notwithstanding however the great restrictions which he had been laid under, and the solemnity of the covenant which he had made with me, he did shew them to others and by stratagem they got them away from him, and they never have been recovered nor obtained back again until this day.[215]

Harris was strictly told that he could show the pages only to his brother, Preserved Harris, his wife Lucy, his father, his mother, and his wife's sister, Mrs. Cobb.[216] The preface of the 1837 BOM edition made no mention of the issue. This is understandable, as it is not faith-promoting, for either believers or those who might become believers.

This account points the finger at "others," not Lucy Harris. If she indeed made the statement that she had burned them, the cause could be nothing more than her fear of what certain persons might do if they thought that she still had them. In effect, such a claim may have been nothing more than, "I burned them. They no longer exist. So leave me alone."

Since Lucy Smith also claimed that Harris had shown the pages to others,[217] one of the things we can take away from the two accounts is that a number of people, not all of them friendly, had had the opportunity to learn what the lost pages contained, especially the first part of them, the part that they were most likely to have read.

Baseless Fears, or Lame Explanation?

All LDS accounts are based on the view that "Satan hath put it into their hearts to alter the words which you have caused to be written… because they have altered the words, they read contrary from that which you translated and caused to be written… that by lying they may say they

---

[214] Smith, 1832 History, in Jessee, *Papers of Joseph Smith*, I:10. This was most probably written November of 1832.
[215] Smith, 1838-39 History, in Jessee, *Papers of Joseph Smith*, I:286.
[216] *Idem*.
[217] Lucy Smith, in Anderson, *Lucy's Book*, 421-22.

have caught you in the words which you have pretended to translate." (D&C 10-13) Was this really a possibility, or even conceivable? Clearly one could not erase passages in the lost pages, written in ink, and then write in new wording. A note by Skousen regarding ms 𝒫 is pertinent: "In addition, there are cases where the scribe first tried to erase the text, then lined it out. In fact, this is fairly common in the printer's manuscript."[218] Such an imposture would have required redoing the entire text, with important differences. This would require writing a very long text in the handwriting of Martin Harris, and a few other scribes known to have taken dictation on occasion. Surely this was likewise impossible. In other words, the threat that Smith alleged patently did not exist. He, and indeed the entire Smith family must have known this, and the truth as well, that Joe Jr. could not reproduce the same text, and that there were no gold plates. Serious analysis of this episode has to accommodate the clear fact that the claimed threat was impossible.

Demise of Lehi, Birth of a Bible and Confederates All

The problem that the Smiths faced was detail. If all the material in the Book of Lehi that could not be replicated in a new telling were to be eliminated, what would remain would be "slim pickins," surely not enough to constitute a replacement text. The answer to the problem may not have come immediately, and it may not have come from Joseph Jr. He had worked long and hard on a history of the Indians as Jews in America, and when he arrived back in upstate New York, at his father's home, he was undoubtedly inspired by a keen sense of accomplishment, and pride of authorship. We have no indication that he had any qualms regarding the text he had produced so far. The decision to essentially scrap the original conception of what he had done, and start over to produce a very different sort of work, would not likely have come from him, or at least not from him alone. At first he had to return to Harmony and farm, to support his family. He would have another opportunity to explore options with his father when his parents visited him in Harmony in August/September 1828. If no solution was devised during this visit,

---

[218] Royal Skousen, *The Printer's Manuscript of the* Book of Mormon*: Typographical Facsimile of the Entire Text in Two Parts* (Provo, UT: Foundation for Ancient Research and Mormon Studies, 2001), I:26.

his father, and eventually he plus Oliver Cowdery, could study the problem in Manchester.

When eventually it was decided that the new work should replace the detail with prophecies, preaching and exegesis of Isaiah, out of the ashes of Lehi there arose the phoenix of a new bible, and the birth of a new Christian faith. Book sales would be enhanced by the desire of converts to own a copy of their new bible. And a new church, even one with a lay clergy, might provide the central leadership, the Smiths, with long-term employment and status.

The suggestion that a new bible project began after the loss of the 116 pages encounters an obstacle in the form of articles published in 1840 in the *Episcopal Record*, written by John A. Clark, Pastor of Palmyra's Zion's Episcopal Church. He recounts, apparently from memory, two visits of Martin Harris, who described his activity with Joseph Smith, and mentioned a "gold bible" in the earlier of the two visits, in the autumn of 1827. It is clear that this date cannot be correct since Harris is supposed to have mentioned the characters to be taken to Professor Anthon, which he did not even have until some date in February, 1828[219]. He wrote,

> One thing is here to be noticed, that the statements of the originators of this imposture veried (*sic*), and were modified from time to time according as the plans became more mature. At first it was a gold bible—then gold plates engraved—then metal plates stereotyped or embossed with golden letters. At one time Harris was to be enriched by the solid gold of these plates, and at another they were to be religiously kept to convince the world of the truth of the revelation—and, then these plates could not be seen by any but three witnesses...[220]

It is not clear where this sequence of changes of plan came from. If Harris was at some point supposed to enrich himself from the gold of the plates, this would not follow the assertion that the find was a gold bible. A more probable order would be the idea of enrichment from the plates, and then progression to a plan for a gold bible. Harris may have mentioned the gold bible in his second visit, after the loss of the 116 pages. Since this account was written over a decade after the details mentioned, confusing some details would not be surprising. It was a

---

[219] Vogel, *Early Mormon Documents*, II:261, note 4.
[220] *Ibid*, II:267.

clergyman's effort to discredit Mormonism in an Episcopal publication. In June of 1829 the *Wayne Sentinel* and the *Rochester* (NY) *Gem* printed the earliest known mentions of a gold bible published before 1830.

It is not known how many of the Smiths were involved in the project to produce a translation of the gold plates prior to the loss of the 116 pages. Joseph's brother Hyrum may have had something to do with it, since he accompanied Martin Harris to Harmony prior to his visit to New York to show the characters to professor Anthon. But in the period immediately following the loss of these pages, it would not have been possible for any Smith to be unaware of the problem, nor to be acutely unaware of two things. First, if ever the stolen pages resurfaced to be compared with any replacement text, they would have to be in the same condition as when they were stolen, or with very obvious changes, and therefore no problem. Second, in any case, Joe Jr. was unable to produce a second copy with the same wording, or even all of the same details. At least at this point, every Smith had to have known that he could not do this, and the correlate as well, that there were no gold plates, nor any translation thereof. Since their involvement henceforth would only grow, it would be in the status of confederates all, united in a family project. According to Irene M. Bates, "Much of Lucy's consciousness during this period was that her *family* was to be the instrument in bringing salvation to the whole human family. It was clearly a Smith family enterprise. As Jan Shipps has pointed out, Lucy employs the pronouns *we*, *ours*, and *us* rather than simply referring to Joseph's particular role (*Mormonism*, 107)."[221]

As for Harris, we have noted that he was not at all bothered by Smith's switch from a hodgepodge of known albeit modified Middle East characters arrayed in columns to his mostly invented characters of his own design. He also had worked with Smith cheek by jowl as the text was produced, undoubtedly with at least occasional substantial editing. This supports the view that he was initially fully engaged with his partner in the production of a money-making history of the Indians, justified as being an instrument to bring them to Jesus.

---

[221] Irene M. Bates, "Foreword. Lucy Mack Smith—First Mormon Mother," in Anderson, *Lucy's Book*, 7-8. For her reference, see Jan Shipps, *Mormonism: The Story of a New Religious Tradition* (Urbana: University of Illinois Press, 1985), 107.

The loss of the Book of Lehi had a major effect on the *Book of Mormon* project:

1. The production of the first text could have been a benefit, as a dry run for the not-so-simple task of creating a new bible.
2. Its disappearance provided the opportunity and catalyst to switch over to the more ambitious task of producing a new bible. No longer would the "very purpose" be to convert the Lamanites to the gospel, but for "a marvelous work…about to come forth among the children of men."
3. The loss of the Lehi ms gave the project a breather, to consider what should be the guidelines for the execution of the project.
4. This fresh start could be based on lessons learned, marked by a policy of creating the work in a total vacuum, and placing more emphasis on preaching and pre-Columbian Nephite Christianity.
5. From this point on, no Smith could have had any illusions regarding the nature and objectives of their project.

Chapter 12

BOM Authorship: From Drafts to Ms 𝒪

Over a period of an undetermined number of months in 1829 and early 1830, a manuscript was produced that LDS scholars call manuscript 𝒪, the original manuscript. It appears to have been the first manuscript of the entire *Book of Mormon* as it was published in 1830. Joseph Smith placed it in the cornerstone of Nauvoo House, which was to serve as his boarding house. Some forty years later, the second husband of Emma Smith, Lewis Bidamon, removed it, and found it had been seriously damaged by water and mold. Although it was originally intended to be for the printer, the scribes of Joseph Smith, primarily Oliver Cowdery, produced for the printer a highly faithful copy (apart from the correction of scribal errors and English mistakes), manuscript 𝒫. Royal Skousen of BYU has produced an excellent professional edition of both manuscripts.[222] He has estimated that the surviving parts of ms 𝒪 constitute about twenty-eight percent of the original.

A number of sheets of foolscap paper, often around six, but in one case twenty-eight sheets (96 pages, most of Alma), were folded and sewn together, each group into a "gathering." For most of the extant work, the fold was "widthwise," made by bringing the top of the gathering in portrait orientation to the bottom, and folding across the width. Others were folded "lengthwise," by bringing the left edge of the gathering in portrait orientation over to the right edge (or vice versa), and folding. The text was written in ink on both sides of the sheet. Since each side of the fold was a page, one sheet yielded four pages. The pages were numbered much like the signature of a book. For a six-sheet gathering, there were thus twenty-four pages. The outer side of the gathering had page one (of the first gathering) on the right side of the fold, and page twenty-four on the other side. This work was done prior to writing, to enable the scribe to avoid the gutter.

---

[222] Skousen, Royal, *The Original Manuscript of the* Book of Mormon. *Typographical Facsimile of the Extant Text* (Provo, UT: Foundation for Ancient Research and Mormon Studies, 2001); and Skousen, *The Printer's Manuscript of the* Book of Mormon.

The extant pages of this original of the first unified work were written mostly in the hand of Oliver Cowdery, but with two unidentified scribes doing parts of 1 Nephi. The hand of Joseph Smith occurs, but oddly, for only about three lines in Alma. The extant pages and the scribe for each can be found in Appendix 3, which gives line numbers to allow the reader to have some idea of the degree of preservation. One caveat: since many deteriorated pages have large lacunae, including sometimes the absence of the whole left or right half of a page, for scholarly use one must consult Skousen's edition.

From Drafts to Ms O

The fact that Skousen found only minor occasional corrections of what would today be called typos, and far fewer instances of one word being changed for another, indicates that ms O was written continuously while taking down dictation. There are only occasional instances of insertions of several words or multiple-word substitutions, and no indications of major changes involving whole lines, sentences or paragraphs, whether scratched out or inserted, or of any cut-and-paste editing. After the pages of the gathering were full, the sheets were sewn together along the fold like a book signature. This is exactly what the reverent LDS scholar would expect: a text written down faithfully as Smith dictated it by reading out loud the words he saw, revealed by a divine translator.

Due to the complexity of the BOM narrative (the editing of the Isaiah inclusions and interweaving of Biblical paraphrases into the text, its theological arguments, geographical complexities and consistency, combination of Biblical and made-up names, military campaigns and the coinage system), the secular scholar who operates on the basis of the archaeological verdict must admit that the work could never have been executed by a nineteenth-century author dictating it extemporaneously, or even from notes. Consequently, there is only one conclusion: highly developed drafts had been produced, with the expected interlinear editing, cut-and-paste and page substitution, much like the drafts of the *Book of Moses*. These drafts were individual works by one drafter or more. They served as the basis for the production of ms O. Statements to the contrary from members of the BOM team are expected and may provide additional evidence of their complicity.

Joseph Smith wrote that both Emma and Samuel had served as scribes before the arrival of Oliver Cowdery. The first page of the extant portion of ms O begins at 1 Nephi 2:2 and was written by Cowdery. Neither of the two unknown scribes working on this manuscript was Emma or Samuel. A plausible conclusion from Smith's comment is that they were taking dictation for a prior first draft, probably of Nephi.

The Page Headings: A Nonissue?

Ms O provides additional evidence of preexisting drafts. First, a content summary was placed at the beginning of most principal books. Unfortunately, book beginnings survived only for two traditional BOM books: 2 Nephi and Helaman (Helaman the Younger). It also has a book synopsis for Helaman the Elder (located between Alma 44 and 45) and for a presumptive 3 Nephi B (see below). Furthermore, the first line of each page contained a page content heading. Unfortunately, this part of the pages tended to fall victim to water and mold damage. Some wording of the more important page content headings, and the book content synopses, are provided in Table 24. Those found in the printer's copy (ms P) were most probably also in ms O.

Table 24. Page Content Headings and Book Synopses in Mss O & P

Book Synopsis (P)

    First   Chapter 1 st
The ^ Book of Nephi ^ his reign and ministry. An account
of Lehi, & his wife Sariah, & his Sons, being called, beginning at
the eldest⟨,⟩ Laman, Lemuel, Sam & Nephi —the Lord warns Lehi to dep
art out of the land of Jerusalem because he prophesieth unto the people co
ncerning their iniquity—and they seek to destroy his life—he taketh three days jou
-rney ⟨un⟩ into the wilderness with his family—Nephi taketh his brethren & retur
-ns to the land of Jerusalem after the record of the Jews—the account of their
sufferings—they take the daughters of Ishmael to wife—they take their
families & depart into the wilderness—their sufferings & afflictions in
the wilderness—the course of their travels—the come to the large waters
—Nephis Brethren rebelleth against him he confoundeth them & bu|i|
-ldeth a ship—they call the place Bountiful—they cross the large waters
Into the promised land &C. this is according to the account of Nephi
or in other words I Nephi wrote this record.

(Table 24 continued)

Relatively intact wording from the longer passages of page content headings:

1 Nephi 2:23: "(N)ephi goeth up to Jerusalem to bring the Records of the jews"
1 Nephi 3:18: "The brethren of Nephi Smite him with a Rod"
1 Nephi 4:2: "Nephi slayeth Laban &C"
1 Nephi 4:20: "Nephi obtains the Records"
1 Nephi 4:38: "Lehi searcheth the Records"
1 Nephi 5:14: "Lehi Prophesyeth conserning his seed"
1 Nephi 7:3: "Laman and lemuel rebelleth Against Nephi"
1 Nephi 7:17: "laman and lemuel Repent g[ ] with Nephi"
1 Nephi 8:11: "Lehies dream of the Pressious fruit"
1 Nephi 8: 27: "Lehies p/fears for laman and lemuel and he exorts (th)e(m)"
1 Nephi 9:4: "Lehi Prophesies of the messiah and so forth"
1 Nephi 10:11: "(N)ephi Desireth the Spirit of (P)rophesy"
1 Nephi 11:1: "Nephi caught Away in the Spirit an(d so fo   )"
1 Nephi 11:18: "Nephi beholdeth the Lam of God &{C}"
1 Nephi 11:32: "The Masiah Crusafied &C"

Book Synopsis ($\mathcal{O}$ & $\mathcal{P}$)

2 Nephi:

                ~~I~~
         ~~Chapter V VIII~~
Second   Chapte[r] I

The ^ Book of Nephi ^ An account of the death of Lehi ~~the Lord~~ Nephis Brethren rebelleth against him—the Lord warns Nephi to depart into the wilderness — &C his journeyings in the wilderness—&C

Book Synopsis ($\mathcal{P}$)

The Book of Jacob (‹Chapter I.››
       Chapter I
The Brother of Nephi ^ the words of his preaching unto his Brethren—He confoundeth a man who seeketh to overthrow the doctrine of Christ—A few words concerning the histo -ry of the People of Nephi

Book Synopses (in either $\mathcal{O}$ or $\mathcal{P}$)

No synopsis for Enos, Jarom, Omni, the Words of Mormon or Mosiah.

Book Synopsis ($\mathcal{P}$)

(Table 24 continued)

Alma (Alma the Younger)

                the Book of Alma Chapter 1/st
                          _____the son of Alma
The account of Alma who was the Son of Alma the First and
Chief {g|J-}udge over the people of Nephi & also the high Priest over the
Church. An account of the Reign of the Judges and the wars & contentions
Among the people, And also an account of a war between the Nep
-hites & the Lamanites According to the Record of Alma the first and Chief Judge

Section Synopsis: Alma 17-26 ($\mathcal{P}$)

Alma the Younger (drawing from the account of Ammon)

An ac{c}ount of the Sons of Mosiah, w[h]o reje{c}ted the{i}r rights to the {K}ing
-{d}om for the word of God, & went up {ro} the land of Nephi, to prea{c}h to the
Lamanites. [T]heir sufferings & deliverance{e}, according to the record of Alma.

Relatively intact wording from the longer passages of page content headings:

Alma 23:7: "(AntiNe)phiLehi (R)e(ig)ns in (h)is s(te[ad])"
Alma 25:16: "Alma & his (   )"
Alma 26:24: "Ammo{n}s discours(   )"
Alma 26:35: "(h)is Brethren {of th}e People of AntiNephi[L]ehi"
Alma 27:12: "[th]e Peo{[}le of Anti{N}eph{i}Lehi   )"
Alma 27:24: "(th)e People [o]f Ammon &C."
Alma 28:6: "exertation of Al(ma   )"
Alma 30:2: Korihor who is called (A)n(ti   )"
Alma 30:28 "Korihor before A(lm   )"
Alma 30:53: "[K]orihor is trodden to (D)e(a   )"
Alma 35:1: "([the people of Am]mon) [go to] the land of Melek [&]C"
Alma 35:14: "Amas [C]harge to (   )"
Alma 36:10: "(   ) his Son Helaman &C"
Alma 37:30: "(n)dments to his Son Helaman &C"
Alma 38:8: "(e)nts to his Son Corianto{n}"
Alma 43:47: "the La{m}anites ensercl{e}d"

Book Synopsis ($\mathcal{O}$ & $\mathcal{P}$)

Helaman the Elder (text inserted between Alma 44 & 45)

(Table 24 continued)

> T{he} account{n}t of the {P}eople of Nephi and the{i}r wars & d{e}se{n}sions in the days of Hela{m}an accord{i}ng to the Reckor{d} of H{e}lam{a}n which {he} {k}ept in his days
>
> **Relatively intact wording from the longer passages of page content headings:**
>
> Alma 47:23: "[A]melecki{a}h Caus{e}s the King to (d   )"
> Alma 49:9: "the La{m}anites go to the C(ity   )"
> Alma 50:1 "Moroni drive[s] the (L)ama(nite   )"
> Alma 50:26: "Morionton slain [&]C the Ch(ief   )"
> Alma 51:8: "A[m]eleck{i}ah comes up to a({tta[k]   )"
> Alma 52:17: "Moron{i} {u}ses stratagem to (   )"
> Alma 53:22: "Moroni sends a{n} Epistle"
> Alma 54:24: "Moroni sends Laman to (de   )"
> Alma 55:28: "Helama{n} sends an (E)pistle   )"
>
> **Book Synopsis ($\mathcal{O}$ & $\mathcal{P}$)**
>
> Helaman the Younger
>
>   The Book of Helaman
>   Chapter I
> An account of the Nephites t(h)eir W(a)rs & Conten(TIONS & THEIR DISSENSIONS & ALSO) the Prop(h)es{i}es of many Holy Prophets before the coming (Of CHRIST ACCORDING TO THE REC)k[o]rd of Helaman which was the Son of Helaman & also a(cCORDING TO THE RECKORDS OF HIS SONS) even down to (t)he comeing of Chr{i}st & also many of the Lam(aNITES ARE CONVERTED AN ACCO)unt of their conve[r]sion an account of the r{i}ghteousness o(f tHE LAMANITES & THE WICK)e{d}ne{s}s & abominat{i}ons of the Nephites accord{i}ng to the Reckord of (H)el{a}m(an (& HIS SONS EV)en do{wn} to the come{i}ng of Chr{i}st wh{i}ch is c{a}lled the Book of Helaman &C.
>
> **Relatively intact wording from the longer passages of page content headings:**
>
> Helaman 1:17: "the [Lam]a[n]it[es] take [City [of] [Za]r[a](hem   )"
>
> **Book Synopsis (in either $\mathcal{O}$ or $\mathcal{P}$)**
>
> No synopsis for 3 Nephi (just preceded by his genealogy). However, there is a synopsis between chapters 10 and 11:

(Table 24 continued)

> Jesus Christ shweth himself unto the people of Nephi, as the multitude were gathered together in the land of Bountiful, and did minister unto them; an [and] on this wise did he shew himself unto them.
>
> On this basis, 3 Nephi is divided presumptively into 3 Nephi A and 3 Nephi B.
>
> No synopsis exists for 4 Nephi, Mormon, Ether or Moroni.

LDS scholars are concerned to show that the heading line was left blank when beginning a page, and after finishing it, the heading was written in the blank space. This appears to be because the content of the page should not have been known, even to Joseph Smith, before receiving the translation. Royal Skousen refers to ms 𝒪 page 6, where the heading is in the hand of Cowdery, but the page was done by unknown scribe two down through line 40, and Cowdery took over at line 41, to the end. If the heading line was left blank, then Cowdery, being the last scribe standing, pen in hand, would naturally fill in the heading to finish the page.

At least for some time, scribe three did headings. On pages 7-18 the heading and the text body were both done by scribe three.

Scribe two does not do page content headings. In two cases, two was the last scribe standing, but scribe three did the heading. The text of page four was done mostly by Cowdery, following his work on page three, but on line 49 he inserts a supralinear edit, after which scribe two continues to the end. The heading is done by scribe three. On page 5, scribe two did the text and scribe three did the heading. In other cases, the heading was left blank. Page nineteen was begun by scribe three, who did just three words, and then scribe two took over to the end. Although the area for the heading is intact, no heading was written. On pages 20 and 22, scribe two wrote the page number and the text, but no heading, although the space is intact. On six extant pages, 21 & 25-29, scribe two wrote the text, but put in no heading.

Skousen explains the absence of headings, where clearly a line was left blank (mostly pages where scribe two did the text), as follows: "It appears that unknown scribe 2 did not like to do these headings..."[223] On the other hand, when beginning a page, scribe two always left a space for a heading.

---

[223] Skousen, *Original Manuscript of the* Book of Mormon, 25.

Most of the pages 31-233 have damage in the heading area, but there is evidence that Cowdery had also ceased to put in headings. He did the text for all of these pages. Pages 111-114 (Jacob 6:11 through Enos 1:14) are sufficiently intact to see that Cowdery did not put in their headings. Later he resumed putting in page content headings. The next extant page (after 1 Nephi 2:2-Enos 1:14) is page 225' (Alma 10:31; primes indicate estimated page numbers). From this point on, Cowdery did all of the remaining extant pages, up to 472' (ending with Ether 15:17). All of these pages have headings, and both they and the texts are in the hand of Cowdery. He also did both the heading and text of the first extant page, page 3.

A more important issue than whether the heading line was left blank or not is why the headings were done in the first place. It seems to be a bit of work, and must have had a function. Perhaps they were first done simply to emulate the appearance of the Bible and its headings. Then, both Cowdery and Smith must have realized that the pages of ms *O* would not track with the pages of the printed edition. At this point they were abandoned. But when they accumulated more and more pages, and got into the more complex books, with many city and personal names, articulations of theological positions, and geographical locations, the need became apparent to be able to go back, efficiently, to crosscheck with what had been written 30, 50 or 200 pages earlier. The headings were recommenced to serve as a sort of index to facilitate finding the key locations relevant to this crosschecking process. In addition, they would have enabled the work to resume without confusion or duplication after a hiatus, due to a lunch or coffee break or an unexpected visitor. They were not inserted into the copy made for the printer, and ms *O* was thought to be safe from prying inspection, at first in Smith's possession, and then in the foundation stone.

Actually, the heading issue is not as threatening to the LDS position as one might think. If divine power could translate reformed Egyptian, surely it could supply page headings prior to translating the page. Similarly, BOM critics can be perfectly at ease with the view that the page headings were done after the pages. The nature of the drafts for the Book of Moses is known to us, with supralinear edits and additions, and slips of paper pinned to pages with additional text to be inserted. If Smith was reciting from such a complex draft, it may not have been clear how much draft material would fill a page. Putting in page headings after the fact would accommodate this uncertainty. In any case, Wisdom counsels that we not presume to know more than we do.

Furthermore, this issue is irrelevant to the Mosiah priority issue since that question goes to the order of the production of the drafts. As we shall see in chapters 14-16, there is evidence of multiple authorship. Different drafters may have done Nephi, Alma and possibly even Mosiah simultaneously. Furthermore, ms 𝒪 has page numbers showing that when the drafts were copied into it, the work began with Nephi. Unfortunately, neither Mosiah nor Moroni is found in the extant ms 𝒪 materials.

Book Summaries and the Division of the Book of Nephi Draft

In any case, the introductions present in the body of the text, introducing 2 Nephi, Helaman the Elder (between Alma 44 &45) and Helaman (the Younger), cannot be explained away in this manner. These three book-content introductions were retained in Cowdery's printer's copy. There, we find a similar book content introduction for the Book of Jacob, but none for the very small works, from Enos through the Words of Mormon. It is also lacking at the beginning of Mosiah, which has an unusual beginning, having been at first treated as a continuation of Words of Mormon, to the extent that the title, "the Book of Mosiah," was omitted, and had to be added in as a correction. An introduction is found for 3 Nephi B (between 3 Nephi 10 and 11). Given the extreme care to copy ms 𝒪 exactly, and the presence of two book introductions, it is highly likely that the other introductions in ms 𝒫 were retained from ms 𝒪. Even so, some books lack this introduction, at least in the printer's manuscript. The book-content summaries constitute additional evidence for the use of prior drafts.

When Cowdery arrived in Harmony, the duo's first task was to study and revise any drafts completed so far. The books already in draft would have been improved also by the talents of Joseph Smith, the innate storyteller, trained exhorter and extemporaneous speaker extraordinaire. As a matter of efficiency, Smith would have read the highly edited drafts while Cowdery wrote to produce ms 𝒪. First in Harmony and later in the Whitmer home, Cowdery would have served as a sort of (imperfect) grammar and spell check for Smith, and the two would discuss the next day's work. His typically neat work indicates that Cowdery did not hurry. At any time, they could pause and consult each other. Some idea of the number of drafters will be shown through analyses of the distribution of style.

While we are on this topic, note that there is evidence from the earliest extant manuscript that Nephi was originally intended to be just one book. The manuscripts, and the 1830 first printed edition, have rather large chapters, retained by the later RLDS edition. First Nephi was done in seven long chapters, with headings in the manuscript such as "Chapter 2" or "Chapter VII." Second Nephi begins as follows:

```
              Chapter (V|I) VIII
      second           Chapter I
The   Book of Nephi    An account of the death of Lehi…
```

Skousen's editorial notation, not fully represented here, indicates that Cowdery dropped down to the first line below the end of 1 Nephi (its chapter VII) and wrote Chapter V, apparently intending to write VIII. Then he overwrote V with I. Perhaps at this point he continued with Smith's dictation, and wrote "The Book of Nephi   An account…" It appears that the protocol for formatting 𝒪 had not yet been fully established. Nephi was to be divided into two books. But did that mean that the chapter numbering would begin with chapter one? Smith had spoken "Chapter VIII," but Cowdery initially thought that was wrong. He began VIII, but overwrote the V to change it to Chapter I. Then, not sure, he crossed it out and wrote VIII. After finishing the page, he and Smith discussed it, and decided that 2 Nephi needed to begin with Chapter I. So Cowdery crossed out the first chapter entry, wrote "second" above *the* and *book,* and "Chapter I" above *Nephi* and *An…* Problem solved. He wrote (where V|I means V is overwritten with I and angle brackets indicate a supralinear insertion):

> [first] Chapter V [then] V|I [then] [Chapter] VIII [and finally,
> all the foregoing was crossed out for the following]
> The ⟨second⟩ Book of Nephi ⟨Chapter I⟩ An account of the death…

Clearly in the draft of the work, there was to have been only one Nephi, as indicated in D&C 10:42, where the instruction was given for the record of the small plates of Nephi, all the way down to King Benjamin: "you shall publish it as the record of Nephi." Judging from the practice observed in the outline for the *Book of Moses,* which survives, the decision to start 2 Nephi after 1 Nephi VII was marked by the composition of a book summary, and by pinning it to the draft page where 2 Nephi was to begin. Inadvertently, Smith read the earlier chapter number still found in the draft, which seems to have not been updated, before realizing his error. This ms 𝒪 episode gives us a rare window into an event in the layout of the BOM narrative.

Based on the evidence regarding the original drafts, I will use the following seventeen-book divisions for the analysis of BOM style:

Traditional BOM Books	*Books Based on Chapter Synopses*
1 Nephi	1 Nephi
2 Nephi	2 Nephi
Jacob	Jacob
Enos	Enos
Jarom	Jarom
Omni	Omni
Words of Mormon	Words of Mormon
Mosiah	Mosiah
Alma	Alma the Younger (Alma 1:1-44:24)
	Helaman the Elder (Alma 45:1-60:17)
Helaman	Helaman the Younger
3 Nephi	3 Nephi A (1:1-10:19)
	3 Nephi B (11:1-30:2)
4 Nephi	4 Nephi
Mormon	Mormon
Ether	Ether
Moroni	Moroni

The evidence for these divisions can be found in Table 24 *supra*. In spite of the evidence that Nephi was originally one book, the traditional division (1 Nephi and 2 Nephi) has been retained due to the sharp difference in content. Citation references are always to the traditional books. The importance of the draft divisions will become clear as we get into the study of stylistic distribution among the books.

Careful analysis of MS 𝒪 repays with interesting observations. Of these, the most important by far is the fact that its largely unedited condition requires the conclusion, at least for the secular scholar, that it is the result of dictation from highly developed drafts. The analysis of Mosiah in Chapter 15 will provide additional evidence.

Chapter 13

BOM Authorship: The Spalding-Rigdon Theory

The fundamental argument that led to the Spalding-Rigdon theory is a syllogism. When the *Book of Mormon* was published, those who took the trouble to read it were somewhat impressed. Although judging it to be a hoax, they were nonetheless surprised to find it complex and theologically substantial. This was occurring in an environment of efforts to undermine the credibility of the Smith family, to brand them a people of bad character, semiliterate and uneducated. So the three-point argument emerged. 1) The quality of the book required some sophistication and background; 2) the Smiths and Cowdery lacked these characteristics; 3) so *therefore* someone else must have written it. But who?

Shortly after the *Book of Mormon* was published, a new church was established, then called the Church of Christ. Some felt strongly that they were witnessing a dangerous heresy, a new church, based on a new bible authored by a person claiming to be a latter-day prophet. Without doubt some of these considered it to be the work of Satan to undermine the true Christian faith at a time when they expected the events of the Apocalypse and the Second Coming of Christ. The more activist among them felt that the best offensive against this heresy was to prove that the new bible was false. At that time the means for conclusive archaeological investigation did not exist. The best vehicle to challenge the book was to brand it a plagiarism of a work done around two decades earlier, penned by Solomon Spalding. The accusation of plagiarism was first leveled at Sidney Rigdon, whose work was recast into the BOM narrative by Smith and Cowdery.

The Spalding-Rigdon Theory

One of the principal early arguments to ascribe authorship is based on statements alleging that a one-time minister, Solomon Spalding, wrote a historical romance based on the premise that the Indians descend from a lost tribe of Israel. Although he died in 1816, it is argued that he took his manuscript to a publisher in Pittsburgh. Years later, a Baptist minister, Sidney Rigdon, came to possess it and plagiarized it, in particular adding some religious material, to become at least a precursor draft of the BOM text. Smith and Cowdery published it, having made modifications of their own to adapt it to their needs. Consequently, whether the text published in 1830 was the work mostly of Spalding, or Rigdon or Smith and Cowdery, the new bible is nothing more than a plagiarized version of Spalding's work. Table 25 presents key points in Spalding's life.

Table 25. Solomon Spalding (also Spaulding)

Date	Event
1761	Born in Ashford, Connecticut
1782	Entered Dartmouth College in Hanover, New Hampshire
1785	Graduated with the class of 1785
1787	Ordained a Congregationalist preacher
1795	Married Matilda Sabin (Sabine)
	Opened a store with his brother in Cherry Valley, New York
1799	Moved the store to Richfield, New York
18??	Bought land and lived in Conneaut, Ohio
18??	Wrote "Manuscript Found," the Oberlin ms, or both (1809-1812?)
1812	Moved to Pittsburgh, Pennsylvania
	Reportedly took his manuscript to Patterson & Lambdin
1814	Moved to Amity, Pennsylvania
1816	Died in Amity

In 1812 Spalding moved to Pittsburgh, Pennsylvania, and in 1814 to Amity, Pennsylvania, where he died in 1816. The argument usually made is that the alleged Israelite-origin manuscript had been taken to a publisher in Pittsburgh but was never published. It is also claimed that at a later date Sidney Rigdon, then working as a tanner, periodically visited the publisher and acquired or stole the manuscript. The Spalding-Rigdon argument got its start when individuals who claimed some knowledge of a Spalding manuscript alleged similarity to the *Book of Mormon*.

Hurlbut: Providing the Syllogism's Minor Premise and Conclusion

Originally a Methodist lay minister, Doctor Philastus Hurlbut (1809-1883), "Doctor" being his first name, was converted to the Mormon faith and ordained an elder.[224] He was excommunicated in June of 1833.

---

[224] Dan Vogel, "Preface" in Howe, *Mormonism Unvailed*, i-xxvii, and "Addenda" to the same, & 408-12.

Sidney Rigdon, who had ordained him, wrote that this was due to his "using obscene language to a young lady, a member of the church," a charge that Hurlbut denied. Although there certainly is a difference between anti-Mormons and Mormonism critics, Hurlbut was the epitome of the former. Initially he began simply lecturing against Mormonism, but soon he obtained funds from a group of anti-Mormons to collect statements from individuals in both Palmyra and Harmony expressly to expose Joseph Smith, the entire Smith family and the *Book of Mormon*. These supplied material to support the minor premise that the BOM could never have been written by Smith whose bad character would certainly not qualify him to be a prophet of God. Believing that he had secured the minor premise of the syllogism, he then needed to address the question it posed, to wit, so "who did it?" To this end, he also collected statements regarding the historical romance of Solomon Spalding from Spalding's brother and sister in Conneaut, Ohio, from his widow Matilda Spalding Davidson in Massachusetts, and others who claimed an association with Spalding. With these he claimed he had identified the ultimate source of the precursor to Smith's new bible. Both sets of statements were published in Eber D. Howe's anti-Mormon book *Mormonism Unvailed* (sic) in 1834. Later, Hurlbut had an association with Oberlin College, becoming a member of the board of trustees in 1847.

Table 26. Doctor Philastus Hurlbut

Date	Event
1809	born in Chittenden County, Vermont
late 1820's	became a Methodist class leader, exhorter & lay minister in Jamestown, New York
Late 1832	converted to Mormonism
March, 1833	ordained an elder by Sidney Rigdon; sent on a mission to Pennsylvania
1833	told by a Methodist, Lyman Jackson, in Albion, that the BOM resembled a manuscript of Solomon Spalding
1833	left his mission to interview John and Martha Spalding, Solomon Spalding's brother and sister, in Conneaut
June 3, 1833	while interviewing the Spaldings he was excommunicated
June 21, 1833	reinstated because of his "liberal confession"
1833	excommunicated for attempting to discredit Joseph Smith

13. BOM Authorship: The Spalding-Rigdon Theory 307

(Table 26 continued)

1833	Collected funds from anti-Mormons Orrin Clapp, Nathan Corning, Grandison Newell and others "to obtain affidavits showing the bad character of the Mormon Smith family"
c. 9/1833-?	collected statements, first from the Spaldings, regarding the "Manuscript Found" connection
12/21/1833	on complaint of Joseph Smith, a writ against Hurlbut was issued by John C. Dowen, Justice of the Peace
1/13-15/1834	in preliminary hearings, Hurlbut said he would kill Joseph Smith, which Dowen said he meant he would kill Mormonism
2/1834	Eber D. Howe agrees to publish Hurlbut's collected statements in a book authored by Howe, paying Hurlbut in books
2/9/1834	Hurlbut's letter to Charles Anthon for his statement
4/9/1834	the decision of the Geauga County Court issued deciding that "the said complainant had ground to fear that the said Doctor Ph Hurlbut would wound, beat or kill him, or destroy his property" setting bail at $200, & charging Hurlbut to keep the peace
11/1834	publication of his collected statements in *Mormonism Unvailed*
1846	ordained an elder in the United Brethren Church
1847	member of the Board of Trustees of Otterbein College

Hurlbut's Spalding-Related Statements

Howe's exposé of Mormonism included statements of persons claiming that Solomon Spalding had written a fictional history of persons from the Old World coming to America, which was very similar to the text of the *Book of Mormon*. Even after two decades, some of them claimed to remember that it was titled "Manuscript Found." In 1885, a former Ohio antislavery editor Lewis L. Rice went through antislavery manuscripts in his possession, and happened to find a Spalding manuscript. His search was on the occasion of the visit to his home then in Honolulu of James H. Fairchild, President of Oberlin College. Rice gave his friend some mss, including the Spalding manuscript, to be donated to the Oberlin Library. The document was not titled, but was accompanied by a wrapper on which Rice had written in ink "Solomon Spalding's Writings." Earlier writing in pencil identifies the contents in the wrapper. When computer-analyzed, it clearly reads "Manuscript Story Conneaght Creek". Proponents of the Spalding-Rigdon theory have taken this to correspond to Conneaught River, the site that the manuscript identifies as the location where marooned Romans had deposited twenty-eight sheets of parchment over fifteen hundred years earlier. They have used this wrapper to ascribe the title "Manuscript Story Conneaught (Conneaut) Creek," or simply "Manuscript Story" to this historical romance of Solomon Spalding. Two camps of researchers developed, one claiming that both this designation and "Manuscript Found" apply to the same manuscript, and the other claiming that these are titles identifying two different Spalding compositions, one donated to the Archive of Oberlin College, and the other lost. I will follow the lead of many others, and call the only presently existing one "the Oberlin Manuscript." Spalding would be surprised to know that it was eventually published (in 1885 by the Reorganized Church of Jesus Christ of Latter Day Saints, and twice, in 1886 and 1910, by the Church of Jesus Christ of Latter-day Saints).

About October of 1833, Spalding's widow Matilda Sabin Spalding Davison informed Hurlbut that she knew her husband had produced some manuscripts but that she did not know anything of their contents. She also stated that her husband's papers were stored at a cousin's home in Otsego County, New York. Assuming that this manuscript was about Israelites coming to America, he continued his quest. When he located Spalding's papers, and the manuscript thought to be the one in question, he found very little similarity to the *Book of Mormon*. He described its contents as follows:

> This is a romance purporting to have been translated from the Latin, found on 24 rolls of parchment in a cave, on the banks of Conneaut Creek, but written in modern style, and giving a fabulous account of a ship's being driven upon the American coast, while proceeding from Rome to Britain, a short time previous to the Christian era, this country then being inhabited by the Indians.[225]

This description is more than sufficient to identify the Otsego manuscript as being the Oberlin manuscript. Undaunted by this untoward discovery, and being convinced already that Smith had plagiarized Spalding, he saved his argument by concluding that in fact Spalding must have had two manuscripts regarding old-world visitors to the Americas, the one later found among the mss of Lewis L. Rice in Honolulu, wherein the settlers are Romans, and a lost manuscript wherein a tribe of Israel comes to the Americas and eventually becomes the American Indians. For Hurlbut, Howe and those arguing the Spalding-Rigdon origin of the

---

[225] Howe, *ibid*, 404.

13. BOM Authorship: The Spalding-Rigdon Theory

Book of Mormon, the manuscript hypothesized by Hurlbut is referred to as "Manuscript Found."

Table 27. Hurlbut's Statements Collected in 1833 re Spalding's Manuscript

John Spalding, brother of Solomon, Crawford County, PA	• About 1812, he visited Solomon, who was working on a book titled "Manuscript Found" which he hoped would pay off his debts. • Solomon read "many passages" to his brother John. • It was a historical romance to show that the Indians are the descendants of Jews who had come to America. • The protagonists were Lehi and Nephi, and the group divided into Nephites and Lamanites. • He wrote it in the old style. • He had recently read the BOM.
Martha Spalding, Wife of John, Crawford County, PA	• Visited Solomon a short time before he left Conneaut. • He was writing a historical novel. • In it the Indians are some of the lost tribes of Israel. • The protagonists were Lehi and Nephi. They divided into Lamanites and Nephites. • It was written in the older style. • She had read the BOM, which brought these details fresh to her recollection.
Henry Lake, Conneaut, Ashtabula County, OH	• Partnered with Spalding to build a forge in Conneaut. • For many hours, Spalding read passages from a manuscript he said had been found in Conneaut called "Manuscript Found." • It represented the Indians as being descendants of the lost tribes. • He remembered the tragic account of Laban. • Later he had examined the BOM and said it is the source of the historical part of the BOM.
John N. Miller, Springfield, PA	• He had lodged with Spalding for several months. • Spalding often read to them from "Manuscript Found." • It tells how the Indians came from Jerusalem. • He remembers the protagonists were Nephi, Lehi and Moroni, and that the group landed at the Straits of Darien which he called Zarahemla. • He had recently read the BOM & found it contains religious material he did not see in Manuscript Found.

(Table 27 continued)

Aaron Wright, Conneaut, Ashtabula County, OH	• He became acquainted with Spalding in 1809 or 1810. • On day in Spalding's home, he read to him from a history he was writing. • Apart from the religious material, it was the same as the BOM. It traced a lost tribe of Israel from Jerusalem to America. It had the same names as the *Book of Mormon* with no alteration.
Oliver Smith, Conneaut, Ashtabula County, OH	•Spalding boarded at is home for about six months. •Oliver read and Spalding read to him at least one hundred pages from his manuscript. •It told how Lehi/Nephi brought Israelites to America. •He had read the BOM; it had added religious text.
Nahum Howard, Conneaut, Ashtabula County, OH	•He frequently saw Spalding at his house and his own. •Spalding frequently showed him his writings. •When I later read the BOM, I found it the same as what Spalding wrote, except the religious material. • He said he planned to get it published in Pittsburgh.
Artemas Cunningham, Perry, Geauga County	•Spalding showed him a manuscript that he hoped would raise the money to pay his debt to Artemas. •It was an account of Israelites as the first Americans. • It was found buried in the earth, or in a cave. •He had partially examined the BOM & found it to be the same as Spalding's work, except the religious part. • He remembered the name of Nephi. •He intended to publish it in Pittsburgh.

Source: Eber D. Howe, *Mormonism Unvailed*, 392-402.

Although she did not make a signed statement, Howe ascribes to Solomon Spalding's wife Matilda the following: she remembered Solomon had many manuscripts, of which one was called "Manuscript Found." She could not remember any of its contents, but thought it was the one he took to Patterson & Lambdin in Pittsburgh to be published. She did not know if the manuscript had been taken back home or not.[226]

The statements collected by Hurlbut are usually referred to as affidavits. An affidavit is actually a well-established term, "a written declaration written under oath before a notary public or other authorized officer."[227] Dan Vogel states, "In any case, the affidavits were signed and

---

[226] Howe, *Mormonism Unvailed*, 403.
[227] *The American Heritage Dictionary of the English Language. Fifth edition.* (Boston: Houghton, Mifflin Harcourt Publishing Company, 2011).

many were notarized."²²⁸ He gives no information to indicate which were notarized, but does quote Cornelius R. Stafford, who "remembered that Hurlbut arrived at 'our school house and took statements about the bad character of the Mormon Smith family, and saw them swear before him.'"²²⁹ He balances this with a statement by Benjamin Saunders, who said Hurlbut "came to me but he could not get out of me what he wanted; so [he] went to others."²³⁰ Swearing to Hurlbut does not make the statement an affidavit. It is incorrect and misleading to dignify these statements as affidavits. With respect to the *Spalding-related* statements, without further information re each one, the most we can assume is that they were signed. Possibly one or more was actually notarized, although if this were the case, Howe's text would almost certainly have said so.

Given the circumstances of his exit from Mormonism, and the preliminary judgments against him in the Joseph Smith v. Hurlbut case, it is clear that he was about as anti-Mormon as one can get. Furthermore anti-Mormons were funding him specifically to expose Joseph Smith, the *Book of Mormon* and Mormonism in general. He had to get results. He was a man on a mission, aided by the anti-Mormon atmosphere of the day. Still, he did not invent the Spalding issue. Persons unfriendly to Joseph Smith, the *Book of Mormon* and Mormonism were discussing a Spalding romance before Hurlbut began his mission.

Rumor Dynamics and Memory Reconstruction

The publication of an American bible, and establishment of a new church headed by a latter-day prophet caused no little stir at a time when many were expecting some sort of end-of-times scenario leading up to the Second Coming. In Ohio, the conversion of a well-known and influential clergyman named Sidney Rigdon became a topic of concern. Since he had been a prominent Campbellite figure, Alexander Campbell himself made a trip to Ohio to determine how much damage had been caused to his own movement. On 24 March 1832, both Joseph Smith and Sidney Rigdon were tarred and feathered. Hurlbut's mission was conducted in special circumstances, marked by intense anti-Mormon feelings and rumor dynamics. His informants were not randomly selected, but at least

---

[228] Vogel, "Preface" to Mormonism Unvailed, xvii.
[229] Vogel, *ibid*, xvi.
[230] Vogel, *idem*.

partially self-selected. What percent of the persons he contacted actually came to be numbered among his informants? We cannot know. As he went about, news of his coming probably preceded him. Whatever one's belief might have been regarding life after death, people are also interested in how they are remembered among the living. In normal circumstances, after the passage of three or four generations, our entire existence is summarized by a name on a tombstone, at best. Hurlbut offered the opportunity to have one's name and statement published in a book, and to be numbered among a chosen group who had helped to end a heresy mounted by Satan leading up to the coming of Jesus. This is heady stuff.

Rumor dynamics have been studied for many decades. The classical study is the 1947 *Psychology of Rumor*, by Gordon Allport and Joseph Postman.[231] They identified three processes: *leveling, sharpening*, and *assimilation*. In the first, there is a loss of detail as a result of the process of transmission facilitating the spread of the rumor. Sharpening involves the selection of the key elements to be included in its transmission. The process of assimilation refers to distortion as a result of subconscious motivations and the intrusion of extraneous information. There can be considerable competition or one-upmanship. A stereotypical example is a housewife saying to her neighbor over the clothesline, "Very interesting. But wait till I tell you what *I've* heard she did." Those who had known Spalding were ideally situated to participate. "I've been thinking a lot about this lately, and suddenly I remembered..."

The importance of rumor in this discussion is that it provided an important backdrop for the process of memory reconstruction. Suggesting this process is not an accusation directed at any individual. It is the way memory works for us all. In this context, it means that the process of memory reconstruction was already underway even before Hurlbut came along. To complete their qualifications for participation in the rumor mill, even those who had a claim to having had an association with Spalding should have some knowledge also of the *Book of Mormon* in order to say that they had noticed a similarity. At least they should have read the first ten or twenty pages. This provided the occasion for the more salient details of the BOM narrative to be subconsciously incorporated into and shape their old and faint memories. This is not

---

[231] Gordon Allport and Joseph Postman, *Psychology of Rumor* (New York: Henry Holt and Company, 1947).

simply speculation; a statement collected from John N. Miller refers to the phenomenon: "The names of Nephi, Lehi, Moroni, and in fact all the principal names, are bro't fresh to my recollection, by the Gold Bible."[232] In the *International Encyclopedia of the Social & Behavioral Sciences* we read:

> Cognitive processes are active. When we perceive and encode events in the world, we construct (rather than copy) the outside world as we comprehend the events. If perceiving is a construction, then remembering the original experience involves a reconstruction. Reconstructive memory refers to the idea that remembering the past reflects our attempts to reconstruct the events experienced previously. These efforts are based partly on traces of past events, but also on our general knowledge, our expectations, and our assumptions about what must have happened. As such, recollections may be filled with errors, when our assumptions and inferences, rather than traces of the original events, determine our recollections. Errors—false memories—constitute the prime evidence for reconstructive processes in remembering. Several different sources of error (inferences during encoding, information we receive about an event after its occurrence, our perspective during retrieval) exist. Contrary to popular belief, memory does not work like a video-recorder, faithfully capturing the past to be played back unerringly at a later time. Rather, even when we are accurate, we are reconstructing events from the past when we remember. (H. L. Roediger)[233]

Simply accessing one's memory many years later is one thing. Doing so at the behest and under the influence of an interviewer is another. At this point memory reconstruction is influenced by the questions. This introduces the issue of the leading question. Having myself taught survey methods at the university level, I can assure that one of the most common mistakes of untrained interviewers or questionnaire designers is to ask leading questions. It is not only possible, but even probable that Hurlbut committed this fallacy, with or without conscious intent of coaching the informant. For example, instead of asking "Do you remember any of the names in the manuscript Spalding read from?" he might very well have asked, "Now try hard. Did

---

[232] Howe, *Mormonism Unvailed*, 398.
[233] H.L. Roediger III, "Psychology of Reconstructive Memory," *International Encyclopedia of the Social & Behavioral Sciences* (Amsterdam: Elsevier B.V., 2001), 12844–12849; accessed online, 04/02/2017.

the name 'Nephi' occur, or Lehi? How about 'Laban?'" In this manner, an informant's statement can be influenced, even coached. Usually a long discussion ensues, and then the interviewer draws up a draft statement and asks, "Is this a fair summary of what you have just told me?" We have all seen this in CSI documentaries.

Furthermore, even though John and Martha Spalding knew Solomon very well, it is his widow Matilda who actually lived with him throughout the period that he worked on his romance, and she could not remember anything about the contents.

Spalding died in 1816. He moved from Conneaut to Pittsburgh in 1812. By 1833, the statements listed *supra* would have been made *circa* twenty years later. The now considerable psychological evidence regarding memory, especially over time, informs us that normally it is impossible to access a memory without altering it. The act of trying to remember an old and faint memory is itself a process of memory *creation*. Reading the *Book of Mormon* feeds details into the mind, to supplement memories.

Depriving Informants of Relevant Key Information

A statement by Howe regarding the Otsego (i.e. Oberlin) manuscript reveals the nature of Hurlbut's method in obtaining statements from his informants. He stated as follows:

> This old [Oberlin] M.S. has been shown to several of the foregoing witnesses, who recognize it as Spalding's, he having told them that he had altered his first plan of writing, by going farther back with dates, and writing in the old scripture style, in order that it might appear more ancient. They say that it bears no resemblance to the "Manuscript Found."

This is located on the third page from the end of his book, after Hurlbut's Spalding-related statements summarized above. The title "Manuscript Found" occurs in the statements of Solomon's brother John, Henry Lake and John N. Miller. The claim made regarding "several of the foregoing witnesses" is strange since in their statements there is absolutely no mention of having been shown a second manuscript bearing no resemblance to "Manuscript Found." If Hurlbut had indeed shown the Otsego manuscript to his informants, and gotten the reply indicated by Howe, this would have been the purest gold for his campaign, and he would certainly have included it in the statement of each informant making this denial. The fact that it is absent from the statements shows that he did not share this document with them even though it was in his possession. We have one telling example. After the interviews, he returned to Aaron Wright to get a statement that the Otsego ms was not the one he had described in his original statement, which described Spalding's ms as being the account of a tribe of Israel that became the first settlers in America, with BOM names. Already on record, Wright had no choice. He could only say, in his follow-on statement, that the Otsego ms was not the one mentioned in his statement.[234] The letter is not in Wright's handwriting, but closely resembles Hurlbut's,[235] indicating that the latter may have composed a summary of their conversation that the former agreed to.

Since he was in possession of the Oberlin ms and did not reveal it when obtaining the initial statements, clearly Hurlbut had decided that if he had a cooperating informant merging a faint memory with *Book of Mormon* details, it was not advisable to share with him a document that would only confuse his memory. Howe, or Hurlbut's backers, or both decided rather belatedly that the authors of these statements certainly should have been shown the manuscript Hurlbut had acquired, and should have been asked if it was the one that they remembered. Hurlbut's visit to Wright may well have been at Howe's prompting, to get from him an addition to his original statement to provide a basis for Howe to supplement their original statements with the foregoing quote.

When Names Are a Double-edged Sword

The most damning aspect of the statements is their feature that Howe thought to be one of their strongest points: "most of the names" of the *Book of Mormon* were found in the Spalding manuscript.[236] In fact, we find only Lehi, Nephi, Laban, Nephites, Lamanites, Moroni and Zarahemla in the foregoing statements. Aaron Wright stated, "the names

---

[234] Aaron Wright draft letter dated 31 December 1833 in the New York Public Library. Photos of the letter and a transcription can be fount at "Ashtabula county, Ohio: Spalding Source Part Three" on Dale Broadhurst's Solomon Spalding website (http//:www.solomonspalding. Com, accessed 25/03/2017).
[235] Dale Broadhurst, "Ashtabula county, Ohio: Spalding Source Part Three," on his website (http//:www.solomonspalding. Com, accessed 25/03/2017).
[236] Howe, *Mormonism Unvailed*, 405.

more especially are the same without any alteration."[237] The specificity here, after two decades, is indicative of reconstructive memory. We are asked to believe that the Smiths and Cowdery were so stupid that in plagiarizing Spalding's work, they did not even think to change the names of the most important protagonists. Since the Spalding-origin claim is usually argued in the form of the Spalding-Rigdon origin, we are actually asked to believe that Sidney Rigdon was so so stupid as to retain the most obvious evidence of his plagiarism

The Origin of the Title for a Second & Missing Manuscript

As we have seen, in their original statements, the informants make no mention of two Spalding historical romances. Hurlbut had already become convinced that a Spalding manuscript would look very much like the BOM narrative at least in broad outline. When he acquired the Otsego (i.e. Oberlin) manuscript and found that it dealt with Romans, he must have been greatly disappointed. The idea that there had to have been a second manuscript probably came to him rather quickly. As we have seen, his initial strategy was to fail to reveal the manuscript that he had acquired. Later writers would supplement Hurlbut's second-manuscript claim by giving it a title.

Using the wrapper found with the Oberlin manuscript as their evidence, they called it "Manuscript Story Conneaught (Conneaut) Creek" or with more effect, simply "Manuscript Story." If Hurlbut had seen the wrapper, or Howe, he could have construed it as evidence for a title for this manuscript to differentiate it from the "Manuscript Found" mentioned by the informants. This too would have been the purest gold, and Howe would not have failed to mention it. In fact, the "Manuscript Story" title occurs neither in Hurlbut's statements nor in *Mormonism Unvailed*. This establishes a time frame for the wrapper: sometime after Howe's book and before Rice donated it.

Furthermore, this title appears to read "Conneaght Creek." [238] Connaught is the name of a very large and celebrated region in Ireland. Both the Irish and the English would know about it. It was at one time almost a separate kingdom, under the Duke of Connaught. An equally

---

[237] Howe, *Mormonism Unvailed*, 399.
[238] Dale R. Broadhurst, "The Oberlin Spalding Manuscript, An Overview" solomonspalding.com, accessed 2 February 2017.

celebrated Irish regiment in the English Army was the Connaught Rangers, established in 1793. There is a Connaught Road on Hong Kong Island, and a Connaught Man's Rambles (a jig), as well as a hotel, the Connaught, in London. This said, the creek or river in question has been variously spelled. According to the Geographic Names Information System, Conneaut Creek has been known historically as: Conneaut Creek, Caneaught Creek, Conneaut River, Coneaught Creek, Conneaut River, Conneought Creek, Conyeayout Creek and even Counite Riviere.[239] It does not list Conneaght.

Figure 15. Computer Enhanced Oberlin Ms Wrapper

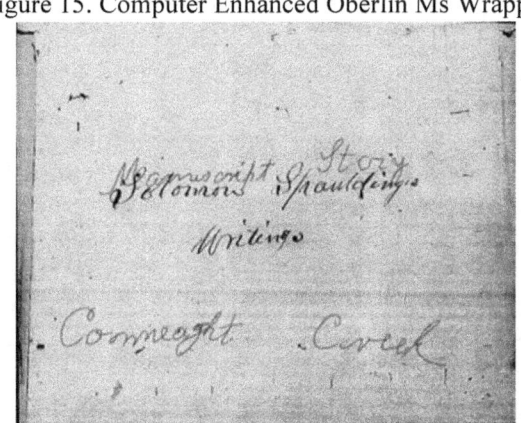

The first line of Spalding's "Introduction" refers to Conneaught River as the place the ancient document was found. Whoever penciled this title on the wrapper would have read at least this line and when writing on the wrapper he erroneously wrote Conneaght Creek instead of Conneaught River, an error that Spalding would never have made. This evidence also indicates that the title attributed to the extant Spalding romance only came into existence decades after 1816. The actual manuscript is untitled.

---

[239] "Conneaut Creek". Geographic Names Information System (https://geonames. usgs.gov/apex/f?p=gnispq:3:::NO::P3_FID:1067126, retrieved 25/03/2017).

The Oberlin Manuscript

Although this document clearly does not support the claim that it was the origin of the *Book of Mormon*, interesting similarities exist:

1. It is the account of an Old World (Roman) discovery of and settlement in the New World.
2. It professes to be a translation of an ancient language.
3. The supposed translator himself found the document he translated.
4. The document was found hidden in the earth.
5. The cavity made to hide the document was lined with stone and covered with a flat stone.
6. The "author" originates from the Old World.
7. He and his group arrive by ship.
8. He anticipates the coming of future Europeans.
9. The "author" hid the document specifically to inform the future Europeans about his people.
10. Some Indians are described as having been a great, relatively enlightened people who later declined.
11. Just as the *Book of Mormon* begins in the first person, this document begins "My name is Fabius…"
12. A storm arises at sea and the people onboard become very frightened. They turn to their god for help, a prophet communes with the divinity, and calm is restored.
13. Those who arrive at the New World are Christians, so there were Christians in the New World prior to Columbus.
14. The history has a "Reign of Judges."
15. They hold their property in common.
16. Some Indians are described as "savages."
17. The color distinction is made between the white Christians and dark Indians.
18. Churches were built.
19. The Indians worship the Great Spirit.
20. The heliocentric solar system is mentioned.
21. New World fauna includes mammoths.
22. The natives produce a sort of iron.[240]

---

[240] Solomon Spaulding [Spalding], *The "Manuscript Found" or "Manuscript Story," of the Late Rev. Solomon Spaulding; from a Verbatim Copy of the*

There is plenty here to feed the memories of any who might have read it, or part of it, or heard Spalding read from it. Some informants stated that they remembered after a hiatus of two decades that "Manuscript Found" was similar or identical to the historical part of the *Book of Mormon*, without the religious material. The similarities here are sufficient to become the manuscript the informants strove to remember. The process of memory leveling eliminated some details, sharpening focused on others, and assimilation merged the memory with details from personal prejudice, anti-Mormon rumor and the *Book of Mormon*, under a bit of coaching from Hurlbut. For Hurlbut, this similarity, unenhanced by reconstructive memory, was not sufficient to make his more specific and extravagant claims, and after his disappointment in Otsego County, he proposed the existence of a second document.

Note too that we have no reason to believe that each informant signed a summary of the discussion with him. Those who could not agree to a statement that Hurlbut could use were never mentioned. He may have deemed their memories inadequate. In the case of the others, he probably wrote a discussion summary that they agreed to. This accounts for the considerable uniformity in their comments.

Sidney Rigdon

The argument that Rigdon contributed to the text of the *Book of Mormon* was made possible primarily by the fact that the image of Joseph Jr. as an uneducated farm boy, with the rest of the family in the shadows, was successful then, and still impresses the minds of some BOM critics even today. Some knowledge of Rigdon's life leaves little doubt that he could not have been involved. Instead he was totally absorbed in Campbellism and the Reformed Baptist movement, in which he was competing for a leading role. Failing to rise to prominence in that movement, he undertook to achieve his aspirations with the Mormons.

Sidney Rigdon's pre-Mormon life was a struggle. In his youth, according to his son John W. Rigdon, "He was never known to play with

---

Original Now in the Care of Pres. James H. Fairchild, of Oberlin College, Ohio, *Including Correspondence Touching the Manuscript, Its Preservation and Transmission until It Came into the Hand of the Publisher* (Lamoni, Iowa: The Reorganized Church of Jesus Christ of Latter Day Saints, 1885); *Manuscript Found: The Complete Original* (Provo, UT: BYU Religious Studies Center, 1997).

the boys; reading books was the greatest pleasure he could get. He studied English Grammar alone and became a very fine grammarian. He

Table 28. Sidney Rigdon

1793	Rigdon was born in St. Claire Township, Allegheny County, PA. He remained on the family farm until his mother sold it in 1818. Rigdon completed basic education (elementary school?).
1817	He was baptized Baptist at Peter's Creek, a tributary of the Monongahela River.
1818	He moved to North Sewickley to apprentice to Baptist minister Rev. Andrew Clark.
1819	He received his license to preach for the Regular Baptists.
1819	He moved to Trumbull, Ohio, and preached there until 1822.
1820	Rigdon moves to Warren (Western Reserve).
01/04/1820	He delivers his first sermon to the small Warren congregation. He supplements this monthly service as a circuit preacher.
12/06/1820	Rigdon and Phebe [Phoebe] Brooks were married.
1820	Rigdon, his cousin Charles Rigdon and his brother-in-law Adamson Bentley were asked to draft the "Corresponding Letter," used for various Baptist associations to keep in touch.
1821	Rigdon's daughter Athalia was born.
07/1821	Rigdon and Bentley meet with Alexander Campbell, noted for his beliefs in dispensationalism, New Testament supremacy over the Old Testament and baptism by immersion. Both joined the Disciples of Christ movement.
1822	Rigdon's daughter Nancy was born.
28/01/1822	Rigdon reported as minister of the First Baptist Church of Pittsburgh and subsequently there.
1823	Rigdon's daughter Elizabeth (or Eliza) was born.
1823	Rigdon worked to advocate Campbell's reforms, and argued against infant damnation (should they die unbaptized) in a debate with Rev. John Winter. The latter formed an opposition group within Rigdon's congregation. Each claims that its group is the First Baptist Church of Pittsburgh. Each, Rigdon and Winter, expels the other. A commission is set up to investigate the heresy charges brought by Winter against Rigdon.
11/10/1823	Rigdon is excluded (cut off, a form of excommunication) from the Baptist denomination, valid only within the Redstone Association of Baptist churches.

(Table 28 continued)

Fall, 1823	Rigdon's group lost its meeting house and informally joined with Walter Scott's Independent Church, holding joint meetings. Even so, at this point, Rigdon had no income.
1824	Rigdon's daughter Phebe Jr. was born.
1824-26	Rigdon first worked as a journeyman tanner, then as a tanner, possibly acquiring part ownership of the tannery. It had dealings with publishers, possibly supplying material for leather book binding. Apparently he took occasional preaching engagements to keep in touch with his chosen clerical occupation.
12/1825	A new tannery opened up in Bainbridge, Geauga County, Ohio, and Rigdon moved there. Reportedly he was called there by a small Baptist congregation. This group embraced a Calvinistic creed, but Rigdon was not required to endorse it. At Bainbridge, he was forced to resort to circuit preaching
1826	A new tannery opened up in Mentor, Ohio, and Rigdon moved to work there. Rigdon appears to have become the minister of this congregation, but served the area as a circuit preacher, which required him to travel about.
c. 11/1826	Rigdon became the new minister, or preaching elder, at Mentor, Ohio.
1826-1830	Rigdon's circuit preaching continued. He preached in the Kirtland area: Bainbridge, Mentor, Kirtland, Warren, etc.
1827	The first eight months of Rigdon's ministry in Mentor are described as being "turbulent."
Early 09/1830	Rigdon's associate, Parley P. Pratt, was baptized into Smith's Church of Christ.
08/11/1830	Sidney and Phebe Rigdon were baptized into the Mormon faith.
30/08/1831	Smith rebuked Rigdon for exalting himself (D&C 63:55).
05/07/1832	Rigdon declared the Keys of the Kingdom have been taken away.
06/07/1832	(Quinn, *Mormon Hierarchy*, 42) Rigdon was disfellowshipped. (Quinn, *Mormon Hierarchy*, 42)
07/07/1832	Smith rebuked him again and took the high priesthood from him.
28/07/1832	Smith re-ordained Rigdon to the high priesthood. (Quinn, *Mormon Hierarchy*, 42)
1844	Joseph Smith was murdered.

(Table 28 continued)

03/08/1845	Rigdon claimed a revelation for him to be the "Guardian of the Church."
08/09/1845	Sidney Rigdon was excommunicated.
1845	He established The Church of Jesus Christ of the Children of Zion.

was very precise in his language."[241] Like many men of the cloth, he may have sought a career in the ministry to escape from the drudge of farm labor. He was ordained a Regular Baptist minister in 1819, preached in Trumbull, Ohio, until 1822, when he reported to be the minister of the First Baptist Church in Pittsburgh, PA. This was the peak of his Baptist career. His upward trajectory ended as a result of a fateful meeting with Alexander Campbell, the prominent leader of a theological reform movement that sought a return to his version of early Christianity, teaching New Testament primacy over the Old Testament, and dispensationalism. Rigdon became a major proponent of Campbellism, in the face of growing opposition from the Regular Baptists. In 1823, he was opposed in his own congregation by Rev. John Winter, who argued more orthodox doctrine. Rigdon was investigated for possible heresy and was cut off from the Redstone Baptist Association to which he belonged. He took those loyal to him to found an independent Baptist congregation, but was unable to raise enough money to pay the rent at his new location, and found himself without a parish, without employment, and without an income. This devastating blow came when he was struggling to support his wife and three daughters Athalia, Nancy and Elizabeth (or Eliza), with a fourth daughter on the way, Phebe. Since his father-in-law was an established tanner, it was possible for him to hire on as a journeyman tanner. At this juncture, he could have been swallowed up in the tannery business.

But Sidney persisted. He made use of his contacts and began networking at a time when that meant personal visits, going to and from on foot in muddy or dusty streets. He sought every opportunity to preach at a church service, or for a funeral. This consumed much of his time when he was not working as a tanner, but it paid off. At the end of 1825, a tannery had opened up in Bainbridge, Geauga County, Ohio, which may be the reason he moved there. But he was also reportedly called to

---

[241] John Wycliffe Rigdon, "The Life and Testimony of Sidney Rigdon," *Dialogue: A Journal of Mormon Thought*, 1:4, 1966, 20.

serve as the preacher for its congregation. Due to its small size, his clerical position could not have supported him and his growing family. In the next year, a tannery opened up in Mentor, Ohio, and he moved there, where he may have served as the preacher of its congregation. This, however, marked a return to his earlier more junior status working as a circuit preacher, traveling about to various congregations in the area. A circuit preacher was a bit like a circuit judge. He did not travel with the speed of the pony express. A distance of thirty miles took a day on horseback or horse-drawn conveyance. The next day he would preach, attending to other pastoral duties, baptisms, marriages, counseling and funerals. The following day would be another travel day. The life was hard, and far from his glory days in Pittsburgh. From 1826 to 1830, he continued his circuit preaching operating out of Mentor, preaching at Mentor, Kirtland, Bainbridge, Warren, etc. Fawn Brodie has given us a list of official acts of Sidney Rigdon as a preacher in Ohio from November 1826 through November 14, 1830, from which she concluded, "It is clear from the following chronology that he was a busy and successful preacher..."[242]

According to Eber D. Howe, in 1823 Rigdon abandoned his preaching and employment to study the Bible for a year. Actually, it was not until 11/10/1823 that his release from his position at the First Baptist Church of Pittsburgh issued. After attempting to form an independent congregation and losing their meeting house due to inability to pay rent, he and his flock informally joined with Walter Scott's Independent Church, holding joint meetings. In May of 1824, Rigdon wrote the Preface to Campbell's report on his debate with Reverend W. L. McCalla, *A Debate on Christian Baptism*, published that summer. Rigdon worked as a journeyman tanner in Pittsburgh from sometime in 1824 up to his move to Bainbridge in December of 1825. There is no place in this period for Howe's claim to be correct.

The author/s of the *Book of Mormon* must have had some serious involvement with the plight of the American Indians, the efforts to convert them to Christianity and the claim that they descended from Israelites. Rigdon's total involvement was with congregations of settlers, and the doctrines of the theological reforms of Campbellism. There is no

---

[242] Fawn Brodie, *No Man Knows My History. The Life of Joseph Smith*. Second edition, revised and enlarged (New York: Alfred A Knopf, 1986 [1945/1971]), 453-55.

indication that he was concerned regarding the Indians, either in his proselyting or his theology. By contrast, Lucy Smith reported that her son Joseph had been fascinated by the Indians as a youth. His brother, Hyrum, attended Dartmouth, a school established to educate and convert the Indians. Ethan Smith, author of *View of the Hebrews* (1823), graduated from Dartmouth in 1790 and was installed pastor at Poultney, Vermont on 21 November 1821 where he preached until December of 1826. The family of William Cowdery Jr. was listed in the Federal Census as living in Poultney as late as 1820, and it was about 1825 that Oliver Cowdery left Vermont. His exposure to the ideas of Ethan Smith is highly probable.

After Sidney Rigdon's encounter with Alexander Campbell in July of 1821, his efforts to promote Campbellism with all his characteristic fervor not only included its rejection of infant baptism, a growing position in his day, but also the belief in the primacy of the New Testament over the Old Testament, and opposition to speculative theology, with his *cri de guerre* "The Bible Alone." As Campbell's father had put it, "Where the Bible speaks, we speak, and where the Bible is silent, we are silent." The latter of these positions is inconsistent with a major effort to produce a new bible, and reminds us of Nephi's anticipated opposition to the *Book of Mormon* saying, "A Bible! We have got a Bible" (2 Nephi 29:3-6). Downgrading the Old Testament is in contrast with the extensive Isaiah inclusions in the BOM, its adoption of the interpretation of some OT texts as prefiguring the coming of Christ and other OT texts to show a knowledge that some Israelites would go to the isles of the sea and produce a new bible. Campbell opposed Mormonism, referring to it as "delusions and religious imposition." After his conversion, Rigdon met his former friend in Kirtland and found him unreceptive to efforts to convert him.[243] It is hard to imagine that in former days a dyed-in-the-wool Campbellite such as Rigdon would be the originator of a new bible inconsistent with the positions for which he was risking his career in the Baptist ministry.

Furthermore, manuscript *O* is full of grammatical errors. Subject and verb often do not agree in number. The past form of the verb is used as a past participle, such as "When I had came..." Its deplorable English rules Rigdon out as an author (as well as God), due to his reputation for

---

[243] Richard S. Van Wagoner, *Sidney Rigdon, A Portrait of Religious Excess* (Salt Lake City: Signature Books, 1994), 96.

good grammar, and experience as a writer. Judging from the published "Manuscript Found," even Spalding's English was much better.

A Multiple-Contingency Hypothesis: Beware the Weakest Link

The Spalding-Rigdon argument is a multiple-contingency hypothesis, dependent on the following contingencies:

1. Did Solomon Spalding write not just one but two historical romances on pre-Columbian migration to America, the Oberlin manuscript featuring a party of Romans, and a second history featuring Israelites? (This might be inferred from the follow-up interviews done by Hurlbut.)
2. Did Spalding take a manuscript to a publisher in Pittsburgh, possibly Patterson &Lambdin, hoping to get it published? (Hurlbut's statements.)
3. If so, was the manuscript taken to Pittsburgh the Israelite one, not the Roman one? (Totally unevidenced.)
4. Although the publisher did not undertake to publish it, did Spalding simply leave it there, rather than reclaiming it for submission elsewhere, or to keep it with his prized manuscripts out of pride of authorship? Did this manuscript languish with the publisher after Spalding's death, even for years? If so, did it stay there until Rigdon showed up in 1822? (Totally unevidenced.)
5. Did Sidney Rigdon gain sufficient access to the publisher's office to rummage through accumulated papers and discover this manuscript? The time window is very narrow, since his release from the Pittsburgh congregation was near the end of 1823, he became a journeyman tanner in 1824, and moved to Bainbridge at the end of 1825. (A late statement suggests a possibility, but his having done so is totally unevidenced. This would be nearly a decade after Spalding might have left it there.)
6. Did Rigdon, who had never shown any interest in the claim that pre-Columbian populations are of Israelite origin, or interest to gospelize them, nevertheless take interest in this manuscript? (Totally unevidenced.)
7. Did Rigdon get possession of the manuscript, either by theft, purchasing it or receiving it for free? (Totally unevidenced.)
8. In spite of his difficult circumstances, dedication to Campbellism and work as a tanner to support his growing family, did Rigdon get the many months free that would be required to plagiarize Spalding's work to

produce what would become the precursor to the *Book of Mormon*? (Totally unevidenced, and seemingly impossible.)

9. Did Rigdon, living in Ohio, have some sort of encounter with either the Smiths or Olive Cowdery, or both? (There is a vague report of contact with some stranger, but actual contact with Smith or Cowdery is totally unevidenced.)

10. Overcoming his own pride of authorship or personal agenda, did Rigdon provide this manuscript to the Smiths, with whom he could only have had the slightest acquaintanceship, but probably none at all? Was Rigdon the sort of man to just give his work away? (Totally unevidenced.)

11. Did Smith decide to plagiarize this work? If so, in the process, were he, Cowdery and even Rigdon not even clever enough to change the names of the principal protagonists? (Totally unevidenced.)

12. Did Rigdon provide a replacement text for the 116 lost pages? (Totally unevidenced. This suggests a scenario where Smith or Cowdery approach Rigdon to say, "Sidney my friend. It seems I have lost the first quarter of my work, and need a replacement text with less history and more religion. Can you help me out?")

13. Would Rigdon keep this secret all his life, even after leaving the LDS Church, and in his lowest and bitterest moments?

One might be tempted to treat this as a simple multiple probability problem. Just for illustration however, let us reduce the first eleven contingencies to only six, each with an independent probability of fifty-fifty (p=.5). Then the probability is $.5^6$ (i.e. .5X.5X.5X.5X.5X.5), which yields .015625, or less than two chances in 100.

In fact, the Spalding-Rigdon hypothesis is more complex. It hangs from a chain of contingencies, and if even just one fails, out of at least the first eleven, the hypothesis falls entirely. To simplify matters, assume there are nine contingencies, and liken this to throwing a single die nine times. In three cases you allow a "success" to be any number but three, or 5 chances out of six, with probability (P) equal to .83 (eighty-three chances out of a hundred). In two cases a "success" is scored with any even number (3 out of 6, or P=.5). In two cases you need to get either a three or a five (2 out of 6, or P=.33). And finally, in two cases either a one or a two or a four or a six is needed, or four chances out of six (P=.67). Just as order is essential in the eleven contingencies above, these must occur in a particular order.

Nine throws, their order and probabilities: .5|.83|.67|.83|.33|.5|.33|.83|.67

This yields only seven chances out of a thousand. Strictly speaking, the probabilities of getting any given face of a die are not mathematically analogous to the assigned probabilities of these nine events. This has been addressed by assigning them probabilities that are much higher than my own personal estimates. Even so, there are two features that are totally valid. First, the combined probability of the nine events is significantly smaller when required to occur in a fixed order. Second, the house rule for the die toss is that on any throw of the die, if the required number fails to come up, one loses the entire game. Thus, on your first role of the die you have a fifty-fifty chance for a success. If you get it, you move on to the next throw. If not, it is game over and you lose your entire stake. You can only win if you get all nine "successes." The same is true of the nine hypothetical historical events. If just one failed to occur, the Spalding-Rigdon conclusion falls. Of course there is no game like this in Vegas. This is because no gambler would play it, even when well oiled with booze.

Sophisticated content analysis has been done in an attempt to provide independent evidence for the conclusion of the Spalding-Rigdon hypothesis. The results are far from proof, and are refuted by other equally good statisticians. For a researcher who feels he has very strong stylistic evidence for his hypothesis, there can be the temptation to feel so sure that the hypothesis is true that it can be used to prove the contingencies. This line of reasoning proceeds as follows. Since Smith plagiarized a Spalding-Rigdon BOM-precursor text (or so this researcher thinks he has shown), therefore "Rigdon must have provided it." Since he did, therefore "Rigdon must have known Smith or Cowdery." Since he did, he must have had a manuscript to provide. Since he did, "Rigdon must have found the time to dedicate himself to produce such a text." Since he did, "he had so much interest in the native American issues that he was motivated to do so." This mode of argument continues all the way down the chain to therefore, "Spalding wrote a history featuring Israelites." In this approach, the unproven hypothesis proves the chain of contingent premises upon which it rests. This is as fallacious as it gets.

Chapter 14

BOM Authorship: One Author or More?

Happily, there are other approaches to investigating authorship. The arguments that Sidney Rigdon or Joseph Smith authored the *Book of Mormon* have prompted an interest among LDS scholars to show that just one person could not have authored the *Book of Mormon*. Ironically, multiple authorship can be consistent with some BOM-critic perspectives as well.

The War of the Statisticians

The work that got the quest off to a quantitative start is that of three BYU scholars, Wayne A. Larsen, Alvin C. Rencher and Tim Layton in 1978.[244] The method they adopted holds that authors have distinct styles that they cannot mask, and that authors can be stylistically identified through their "wordprints," a term taken from CSI "fingerprints." They established a list of noncontextual words, such as *and*, *with*, *the*, etc., and analyzed the rate of usage of these in each sample text. One might think that if this is done for two texts by the same author, the rates would be the same. However, the rates of usage in two texts by the same author will never be identical. So how different can they be, and still be by the same author? Statistical procedures were used in an effort to determine the probability that just one author could produce the observed difference. If the probability is sufficiently low the conclusion is that most probably the texts were authored by different individuals.

This research was challenged by Vernal Holley who did his own wordprint study. His data showed sufficiently small differences between books that, in accordance with his methodology, he was able to conclude in favor of a single-author hypothesis.[245]

---

[244] Wayne A. Larsen, Alvin C. Rencher and Tim Layton, "Who Wrote the *Book of Mormon*? An Analysis of Wordprints," in Noel B. Reynolds, ed., Book of Mormon *Authorship* (Salt Lake City: Bookcraft, 1982).

[245] Vernal Holley, Book of Mormon *Authorship*.

Responding to the challenges to the 1978 BYU study, John Hilton, an adjunct professor in the Department of Statistics at BYU, developed a more refined approach, adapting the analysis of word-pattern ratios developed by Rev. A. Q. Morton in Scotland.[246] This technique uses an analysis of patterns of noncontextual words, rather than just occurrence of those words. One must not be misled by the word "pattern." For example, one pattern is the article *a* as the first word of a sentence, while another is *a* as the next to last word. A third is *a* followed by a space, a word, another space and *and* (as in "a Nephite and..."). Hilton adopted Morton's method, which used sixty-five such patterns.

His study analyzed the occurrences of these patterns in three 5000-word texts from Nephi and three from Alma. These texts were sampled from the longest "didactic" passages in each book. Selection from "didactic" (eg. preachment) material was done to further reduce the effect that differing subject matter might have on the results. Without going into statistical detail, the conclusion reached was that it is statistically improbable that the same person authored the English texts of both Alma and Nephi.[247] A study by Utah State University professors Todd K. Moon, Peg Howland and Jacob H. Gunther analyzed BOM texts from Nephi and Mormon and found evidence consistent with the Hilton study. They refer to these results as distinguishing the underlying actual compositions of these personages.[248] Note that for these researchers, Nephi was written by Nephi in the BOM, and Mormon was written by Mormon, as was Alma.

John C. Fortier criticized the wordprint method, having found the method deficient when attributing three anonymous works to Hobbes.[249]

Another highly competent study, using stylometry, is that of D. I. Holmes, Senior Lecturer in Statistics at Bristol Polytech in the UK. His work has less bias *prima facie* than the work of the BYU scholars, in that

---

[246] A. Q. Morton, *Literary Detection: How to Prove Authorship and Fraud in Literature and Documents* (New York: Charles Scribner's Sons, 1978). For his later work used by Hilton, v. John L. Hilton, "On Verifying Wordprint Studies: Book of Mormon Authorship," Appendix 1, in *BYU Studies* 30, no. 3 (1990).

[247] Hilton, "On Verifying Wordprint Studies."

[248] Todd K. Moon, Peg Howland and Jacob H. Gunther, "Document author classification using Generalized Discriminant Analysis," Proc. Workshop on Text Mining, SIAM, 2006.

[249] John C. Fortier, "Hobbes and a 'Discourse on Laws': The Perils of Wordprint Analysis," in *The Review of Politics*, vol. 59, no. 04, fall 1997, 861-88.

he felt no inhibition deterring him from including non-BOM LDS scriptures for comparison. He used text blocks of approximately 1000 words, of similar subject matter, one from 1 Nephi, one from 2 Nephi, one from 3 Nephi, one from Jacob, one from Lehi (in 2 Nephi), two from Moroni, five from Mormon (found in various books) and two from Alma. He also included three text blocks from Joseph Smith's personal writings, either in his own hand, or that of scribes who stated that they had taken the dictation from Smith. Three independent samples were included from the D&C, three from the BOM Isaiah (KJ) inclusions, and one from *The Book of Abraham*. One only regrets that he did not also include the *Book of Moses*. The study analyzed the occurrence of nouns in the passages (a richness of vocabulary approach), using methods established by others before him. The conclusion was that most of the BOM authors, two of his three D&C samples and his *Book of Abraham* sample clustered together, indicating common authorship. He did not find evidence for separate authorship of individual record engravers (or prophets) in the BOM, although 1 Nephi was somewhat of an outlier. His three Isaiah samples, each from a different large Isaiah BOM inclusion, grouped together but apart from the others, indicating the BOM authors may have imitated King James English, but could not replicate King James style.[250] Like the LDS authors, he failed to give the exact chapter-and-verse references for the samples selected for study.

G. Schaalje, John L. Hilton and John B. Archer took this work to task in a follow-up to Hilton's study.[251] Their work does not attack either the mathematical or theoretical validity of Holmes' approach, but rather claims that his richness of vocabulary methodology inherently lacks the comparative power to adequately differentiate authors. Their list of noncontextual words is: *a, an, and, any, all, of, the, as, but, by, in, it, no, not, that, to, up, upon, with, without* (deleting *you* from Morton's list, and adding *up* without explanation).

A different mode of analysis is that of researchers at the time at Stanford University, Matthew L. Jockers (Dept. of English), Daniela M. Witten (Dept. of Statistics) and Craig S. Criddle (Dept. of Civil and

---

[250] D. I. Holmes, "A Stylometric Analysis of Mormon Scripture and Related Texts," in the *Journal of the Royal Statistical Society. Series A (Statistics in Society)*, vol. 155, no. 1 (1992).

[251] G. Bruce Schaalje, John L. Hilton and John B. Archer, "Comparative Power of Three Author-Attribution Techniques for Differentiating Authors," *Journal of Book of Mormon Studies*, 6/1 (1997).

Environmental Engineering).[252] Their work examines the entire BOM text, with each chapter being a text for comparison with samples from the following authors: Oliver Cowdery, Parley P. Pratt, Sidney Rigdon, Solomon Spalding, Isaiah-Malachi, Henry Wadsworth Longfellow and Joel Barlow. The basic unit of analysis is words, which can be either contextual or noncontextual. They have a complex methodology to select the set of words to be included. The first hurdle to qualify is that a word must have occurred at least once in the works of each author listed above, and once in the entire BOM text. This yielded a set of 521 words. Across their 456 samples, those that did not have at least a mean relative frequency of 0.1% were eliminated, yielding a subset of 114 words. Finally, the following words were eliminated as being too religious: *god*, *ye*, *thy* and *behold*. The effect of this is that any word that is typical of BOM English or subject matter can be excluded simply because it does not occur in just one of the other author's material. Arguably it is just this type of material that one might focus on to consider authorship. Its elimination assures a greater similarity between BOM passages and at least some of the comparison authors, enhancing the possibility of getting results that can be interpreted to be influence from them.

They concluded that their *closed-set* NSC (Nearest Shrunken Centroid) results were consistent with the Spalding-Rigdon theory of authorship. Note however that they did not include Joseph Smith in the study, although they were favorably impressed by the work of David I. Holmes. G. Bruce Schaalje, Matthew Roper and Gregory L. Snow did a sophisticated analysis of this work, showing that an *open-set* NSC method produced dramatically different results compared to the closed-set NSC method of Jockers, et al. They found that less than 9% of texts were attributed by their methodology to Rigdon or Spalding, and these were randomly distributed in the BOM text, presumably refuting the closed-set results supporting the Spalding-Rigdon thesis.[253] They conclude, "The writing styles throughout the book do not credibly match

---

[252] Matthew L. Jockers, Daniela M. Witten and Craig S. Criddle, "Reassessing authorship of the *Book of Mormon* using delta and nearest shrunken centroid classification," *Literary and Linguistic Computing* Advance Access (17 February 2009).

[253] G. Bruce Schaalje, Matthew Roper and Gregory L. Snow, "Extended nearest shrunken centroid classification: A new method for open-set authorship attribution of texts of varying sizes," *Literary and Linguistic Computing*, vol. 26, no. 1, 2011.

Rigdon, Spalding or any of the other candidates, as claimed by Jockers et al. (2008)."[254]

One unsettling observation is obvious: statisticians have not been able to produce the same or even similar results across the board. Real science operates the same on every continent; $E=MC^2$ is universal. Part of the problem may be sampling. This is amplified when the readers of the research reports have not even been given the chapter-verse coordinates of the samples used. The effect of widely different sample sizes for each author examined, as in the Jockers et al. study, may be another problem and needs to be assessed. Unfortunately in these studies, the reader is also put off by inadequate or unclear explanation of the methods used. An example is Hilton's failure to clearly define and example his method of using a wrap-around word group to break apart clusters, a method which affects his counts to produce his data for analysis.[255] In some cases, an important claim is largely asserted, without sufficient research to back it up. An example is the claim that an author cannot alter or disguise his wordprint (or any other patterns). This claim is partially at odds with the work of two researchers at the Department of Computer Science, Drexel University, Michael Brennan and Rachel Greenstadt, showing that persons can engage in obfuscation attacks and imitation attacks sufficiently to defeat at least some authorship recognition techniques.[256] Even Hilton acknowledges that "deliberately writing to an externally imposed pattern which restricts the normal noncontextual word choices of the writer or repetitively using normally contextual words in textually important ways can also change the wordprint patterns."[257] The use of KJ English might function as just such an externally imposed pattern.

The primary validation for Hilton's adaptation of Morton's word pattern method was the use of control texts to test it. Works of eleven authors were used, and tests were done within and between authors. When the method was tweaked sufficiently to differentiate authors, without differentiating works by the same author, it was deemed ready to

---

[254] Schaalje, Roper & Snow, "Extended nearest shrunken centroid classification," 84.
[255] Hilton, "On verifying wordprint studies," 96.
[256] Michael Brennan and Rachel Greenstadt, "Practical attacks against authorship recognition techniques," Association for the Advancement of Artificial Intelligence, 2009.
[257] Hilton, "Verifying wordprint studies," 107, note 4.

apply to BOM tests. Hilton's conclusion that Nephi and Alma were not authored by the same person cannot be dismissed out of hand.

Wordprinting Egyptian?

For those hoping that the results of wordprinting would differentiate between presumed Nephite authors, the selection of words used by Morton and Hilton is problematic. Egyptian grammar, syntax and even some vocabulary are radically different from English. Egyptian lacked the word *and* altogether. "Middle Egyptian had no word for 'and.' Conjunction is normally expressed just by one noun following the other." [258] "Egyptian has no special word for 'and'." [259] Although Egyptian had a definite article, it was usually unexpressed. Originally, there was no indefinite article, although later *w'* (one) was occasionally used: "One man [a man] once told me…"[260] The genitive is expressed, as in Hebrew, using the construct state: "wife the priest" means "the wife of the priest." No word for 'of' is used in this case. *Any* and *all* are also a problem: *nb* (*neb*) means *all*, *any* and *every*, depending on context.[261] These words are particularly a problem for the wordprint method because each occurs in more than one word pattern, magnifying the distortion. The bottom line is that a wordprint analysis of an English translation of an Egyptian document cannot differentiate the authorship of supposed underlying Egyptian texts. If it does show multiple authors, these must be English-language writers in the 1820s.

BOM Segmentation: A Facilitator for Division of Labor

The BOM narrative is highly segmented. It is composed of longer major segments, each with a distinct function, and shorter fast-forward segments, intended to jump to a significantly later date. These segments are ideally suited to collaboration by multiple authors.

---

[258] James P. Allen, *Middle Egyptian. An Introduction to the Language and Culture of the Hieroglyphs* (Cambridge: Cambridge University Press, 2000), 40.
[259] Alan Gardiner, *Egyptian Grammar, Being an Introduction to the Study of Hieroglyphs* (London: Oxford University Press, 1973), 68.
[260] Gardiner, *Egyptian Grammar*, 29, 194.
[261] Gardiner, *Egyptian Grammar*, 47.

The first two segments (originally one) are major: 1 and 2 Nephi. They have perhaps the most important functions, which are to describe and explain the migration of the Lehi band to what will become the land of their inheritance in the New World (1 Nephi), and to use extensive OT material to provide Biblical support for this radical innovation in Israelite history (primarily 2 Nephi). This is done with the large Isaiah inclusions and extensive commentary interwoven with Isaiah and other OT material. Laman and Lemuel, depicted as somewhat irksome naysayers, serve as foils for Lehi's arguments against various objections. Nephi is the earliest work in BOM apologetics.

This is the *Book of Mormon* arguing in defense of the *Book of Mormon*.

The first fast-forward material consists of the books of Enos through Omni, collectively, which occupy only 7 pages, but a huge amount of time, from c. BCE 500 to c. BCE 130.

Words of Mormon has the essential function of explaining the two sets of plates of Nephi, thereby providing the material for the replacement of the lost Book of Lehi, and enabling a total redesign and reorientation of the BOM project.

The Book of Mosiah begins the account found on the large plates of Nephi with its historical and geographic detail. Its original first chapter, relocated to Omni and Words of Mormon in ms $\mathcal{O}$ (v. Chapter 15) tells the story of Mosiah's relocation of the Nephites to the Land of Zarahemla, leaving the Lamanites in occupation of the Land of Nephi, thereby setting the geographical scene for the remainder of the *Book of Mormon*. This gets the narrative out of the territory of the purloined 116 pages, enabling the authors to make use of far more toponyms without fear of contradiction and to develop a *Book of Mormon* geography. This segment loosely links to the Nephi segment by quoting or paraphrasing Isaiah, and contains the BOM version of the Decalogue. The Nephi references to Christianity are followed up by the establishment of the Christian Church of God.

Alma is another core segment. It contains a fuller presentation of BOM Pauline theology, most of the BOM geographical detail and many of the proper names. It builds extensively on the Lamanite-Nephite conflicts, and missionary activity to Christianize the Lamanites. This book alone occupies over 30% of the *Book of Mormon*. By comparison, First and Second Nephi together occupy only 20%. Its size resulted from the joining of Alma the Younger with Helaman the Elder to form a single book.

The Book of Helaman (the Younger) prepares the reader for the coming of Christ, details the hardening of the hearts of many to justify the divine wrath that will result in the Crucifixion Cataclysm, and foretells the signs of the birth and death of Jesus.

The Third Book of Nephi is a central segment, detailing events in the New World leading up to the Crucifixion and the events of the Crucifixion Cataclysm (3 Nephi A). It covers the time of Jesus' ministry among the Nephites and the establishment of the Christian Church (3 Nephi B). Here we find some Church establishment material currently in use in LDS chapels today.

Although Fourth Nephi covers the two-century period of Christianity in all the land, and the apostasy, it is also another fast-forward segment. Being recorded by several people, in only four pages it covers 286 years.

The BOM book titled the Book of Mormon is largely the history of the destruction of the Nephites at the hands of the Lamanites. Its other essential contribution is the account of Mormon engraving the BOM text onto the gold plates. It was originally written to conclude the *Book of Mormon*.

The Book of Moroni is quite short, and was added essentially to supplement the church establishment material in 3 Nephi, drawing from a revelation received by Oliver Cowdery months earlier. With this material, they would be ready to establish their new church immediately following the printing of their new bible.

Incongruously tucked in just before the Book of Moroni is the Book of Ether, which is the history of the pre-Nephite Jaredite civilization. Since its themes are largely the same as the story of the Nephites, its principal *raison d'être* is to cover the possibility that pre-Columbian remains might be discovered dating to a period prior to 600 BCE, and to account for the presence of various animals found by the Nephites in postdiluvian America. The placement of the discovery of the twenty-four gold plates just after the replacement for the purloined pages indicates that the decision to include a record of an earlier civilization was part of the planning for the BOM remake. Ether was originally to have been a separate record apart from the *Book of Mormon*, i.e. following Mormon and without a book of Moroni.

An additional element of segmentation partially reinforces this factor. This is the segmentation of grammatical person. The first person is used in the narration of 1 & 2 Nephi, Jacob, Enos, Jarom, Omni, Words of Mormon, Mormon, Ether and Moroni. Mosiah, Alma, Helaman, 3 Nephi and 4 Nephi use mostly the third person, these being told by Mormon.

With only minor exceptions, the BOM narrative is presented as being the composition of three individuals, Nephi, Mormon and Moroni. The composition of Mormon and Moroni is said to have been in reformed Egyptian, but Nephi, being so early, must have been still in Late Egyptian of the 7th century BCE, the language and script of the Brass Plates.

Chapter 15

BOM Authorship: Interfacing Nephi & Mosiah

Because the Nephi material and Mosiah are largely independent compositions, it was not easy to bridge from one to the other. The first problem was the huge time gap between Jacob and Mosiah, which was largely solved by the insertion of several fast-forward books. The second problem was the somewhat jarring story-line disjuncture. To address this problem, the first chapter of Mosiah was moved partly to Omni and partly to Words of Mormon, thereby beginning the new storyline in the material of the small plates of Nephi (the replacement text). For some scholars, this analysis cannot be divorced from the question, "Which came first?" This has been called the Mosiah priority issue.

The Great Mosiah Mystery

The mystery is in the chapter numbering and the assertion of a missing chapter. Unfortunately, none of Mosiah survived in the extant portions of ms $\mathcal{O}$. But in the printer's manuscript (ms $\mathcal{P}$), usually almost a rote copy of ms $\mathcal{O}$, it initially had neither title nor synopsis. The chapter numbering in the manuscript is as follows:

		8th	
I~~II~~	1	~~IX~~ | I | X	8
II	2	I | X	9
III {~|X}~~~	3	X~~I~~	10
IIII	4	XI~~I~~	11
V ~~{~|{X}}~~~	5	1{3}	12
VI	6	3 14\th	13
VII. —	7		

In ms $\mathcal{O}$ (evidenced in ms $\mathcal{P}$), Mosiah originally began with "Chapter III." There was neither a book title, nor a book synopsis. The title, "book of Mosiah" was added in above the line, and the "Chapter III" was changed to "Chapter I." The next six chapters follow this corrected numbering sequentially, but beginning with chapter eight to the end (chapter thirteen, these being the long chapter divisions seen in the 1830 edition of the BOM) the chapters are all numbered one ahead, and corrected. This erroneous sequence is based on the first chapter originally being II in the draft. This is a reversion to numbering that must have been present in ms *O* and its draft. Omni, Words of Mormon and Mosiah 1-11 (1830 chapter numbers) are all in the hand of Cowdery, so the initial error, and then the return to that error at Chapter 8 were not due to a shift in scribes, and Cowdery is usually very careful in his work. It is improbable that either Cowdery or Smith would suddenly revert to out-of-sequence numbering without a trigger indicating what alternate number to use. Smith was clearly reading from a draft that had been finished to such an extent that it already had numbered chapters. At chapter eight he began to read out the chapter number in the draft. Cowdery did not catch the error and corrected it while proofing his work. The ultimate cause for this numbering error in both mss can only be that the original draft of Mosiah had a first chapter. This chapter was used elsewhere (see below) leaving the book to be titled Mosiah in ms *O* to begin with its second chapter of the draft, but numbered "Chapter III."

When Joseph Jr. and Oliver began work together, and began interfacing the small plates of Nephi with Mosiah, they faced important issues. The first was chronology. Nephi died around 540 BCE. Mosiah begins the lead-up to the coming of Christ, and so begins around 130 BCE. Its timing is fixed by the birth of Jesus. The gap of 400 years is major. Even after Jacob, Enos and Jarom there remained a major gap. The Book of Omni, only one chapter in length, is attributed to Omni, Chemish (his brother), Abinadom and Amaleki. This fast-forward book filled a major chronological gap in only a few pages. The BOM authors were not prepared to come up with enough additional large books to fill this gap.

Second, there was a need to reduce the feeling of disjuncture in the story-line from Nephi to Mosiah. This was addressed by inserting the first chapter of Mosiah into the Nephi material. The assertion that the small plates of Nephi had to be translated, having at least broached Mosiah the elder and his son, King Benjamin (D&C 10:38-45) may be a reference to what had already been done in the drafting stage.

Third, an explanation was needed for how it came to be that there were two sets of plates. This was done in Words of Mormon, but only took eight verses. It was amplified with part of the first chapter of Mosiah.

Some have argued that Mosiah began initially with Chapter II because Chapter I was lost. This makes no sense, since the *raison d'être* for the introduction of the small plates of Nephi was for divine wisdom

15. BOM Authorship: Interfacing Nephi & Mosiah 339

and ability to restore what was lost in the absence of the 116 pages, and certainly the divine plan to foil Satan's scheme would not have failed to restore that first part of Mosiah.

Mosiah Restored

Rather than being lost, the first chapter of the pre-$\mathcal{O}$ draft of Mosiah was divided. The first part was assigned to Amaleki (Omni 12-30), at which point he signs off with "I am about to lie down in my grave; and the plates [small plates of Nephi] are full." The mission-critical part of the Words of Mormon, the explanation of the small plates of Nephi, only took eight verses. This was too small to be a stand-alone document, which would look strange and possibly give rise to suspicion. So it was amplified by adding the second part of the original first chapter of Mosiah. Thus the real role of Words of Mormon was further disguised.

The process of figuring out the continuity problem between Omni and Mosiah went through stages. Incongruously, this small single-chapter book began with the words "The Book of Omni Chapter first" (in ms $\mathcal{P}$). Similarly, Words of Mormon began "The Words of Mormon Chapter 2.d I." The insertion of "Chapter 2.d I" was done as a supralinear edit. This explains why Mosiah originally began with "Chapter III" [i.e. III]. Omni was chapter one, Words of Mormon was chapter two, and the first chapter of Mosiah was three. The decision to make each of the three a separate book reduced Mosiah III to Mosiah I. Before it lost its first chapter, in the draft it was Mosiah II, and the successive chapters numbered III, IV, etc. This gave rise to the chapter numbering problem. Alternation between various numerical formats in chapter numbering (as seen in the above table) is not unusual in ms $\mathcal{O}$.

Here I give my restoration of the beginning of Mosiah. The verses are renumbered, with the verse numbers of Omni and Words of Mormon in parentheses.

[The portion from Omni.]

Chapter I

1 (12). Behold, I [Mormon, proceed from the record of Amaleki, the son of Abinadom, regarding] Mosiah, who was made king over the land of Zarahemla; for behold, he being warned of the Lord that he should flee out

of the land of Nephi, and as many as would hearken unto the voice of the Lord should also depart out of the land with him, into the wilderness—
2 (13). And it came to pass that he did according as the Lord had commanded him. And they departed out of the land into the wilderness, as many as would hearken unto the voice of the Lord; and they were led by many preachings and prophesyings. And they were admonished continually by the word of God; and they were led by the power of his arm, through the wilderness, until they came down into the land which is called the land of Zarahemla.
3 (14). And they discovered a people, who were called the people of Zarahemla. Now, there was great rejoicing among the people of Zarahemla; and also Zarahemla did rejoice exceedingly, because the Lord had sent the people of Mosiah with the plates of brass which contained the record of the Jews.
4 (15). Behold, it came to pass that Mosiah discovered that the people of Zarahemla came out from Jerusalem at the time that Zedekiah, king of Judah, was carried away captive into Babylon.
5 (16). And they journeyed in the wilderness, and were brought by the hand of the Lord across the great waters, into the land where Mosiah discovered them; and they had dwelt there from that time forth.
6 (17). And at the time that Mosiah discovered them, they had become exceedingly numerous. Nevertheless, they had had many wars and serious contentions, and had fallen by the sword from time to time; and their language had become corrupted; and they had brought no records with them; and they denied the being of their Creator; and Mosiah, nor the people of Mosiah, could understand them.
7 (18). But it came to pass that Mosiah caused that they should be taught in his language. And it came to pass that after they were taught in the language of Mosiah, Zarahemla gave a genealogy of his fathers, according to his memory; and they are written, but not in these plates.
8 (19). And it came to pass that the people of Zarahemla, and of Mosiah, did unite together; and Mosiah was appointed to be their king.
9 (20). And it came to pass in the days of Mosiah, there was a large stone brought unto him with engravings on it; and he did interpret the engravings by the gift and power of God.
10 (21). And they gave an account of one Coriantumr, and the slain of his people. And Coriantumr was discovered by the people of Zarahemla; and he dwelt with them for the space of nine moons.
11 (22). It also spake a few words concerning his fathers. And his first parents came out from the tower, at the time the Lord confounded the language of the people; and the severity of the Lord fell upon them according to his judgments, which are just; and their bones lay scattered in the land northward.

12 (23). Behold, [I,] Amaleki, was born in the days of Mosiah; and [I have] lived to see his death; and Benjamin, his son, reigneth in his stead.
13 (24). And behold, [I have seen there arose] in the days of king Benjamin, a serious war and much bloodshed between the Nephites and the Lamanites. But behold, the Nephites did obtain
much advantage over them; yea, insomuch that king Benjamin did drive them out of the land of Zarahemla.
14 (25). And it came to pass that [I Amaleki] began to be old; and, having no seed, and knowing king Benjamin to be a just man before the Lord, wherefore, [I shall he did] deliver up these plates unto him, exhorting all men to come unto God, the Holy One of Israel, and believe in prophesying, and in revelations, and in the ministering of angels, and in the gift of speaking with tongues, and in the gift of interpreting languages, and in all things which are good; for there is nothing which is good save it comes from the Lord; and that which is evil cometh from the devil.
15 (26). And now, my beloved brethren, I would that ye should come unto Christ, who is the Holy One of Israel, and partake of his salvation, and the power of his redemption. Yea, come unto him, and offer your whole souls as an offering unto him, and continue in fasting and praying, and endure to the end; and as the Lord liveth ye will be saved.
16 (27). And now I would speak somewhat concerning a certain number who went up into the wilderness to return to the land of Nephi; for there was a large number who were desirous to possess the land of their inheritance.
17 (28). Wherefore, they went up into the wilderness. And their leader being a strong and mighty man, and a stiffnecked man, wherefore he caused a contention among them; and they were all slain, save fifty, in the wilderness, and they returned again to the land of Zarahemla.
18 (29). And it came to pass that they also took others to a considerable number, and took their journey again into the wilderness.

[Here the portion put into Words of Mormon begins.]

19 (12). And now, concerning this king Benjamin—he had somewhat of contentions among his own people.
20 (13). And it came to pass also that the armies of the Lamanites came down out of the land of Nephi, to battle against his people.
But behold, king Benjamin gathered together his armies, and he did stand against them; and he did fight with the strength of his own arm, with the sword of Laban.
21 (14). And in the strength of the Lord they did contend against their enemies, until they had slain many thousands of the Lamanites. And it

came to pass that they did contend against the Lamanites until they had driven them out of all the lands of their inheritance.
22 (15). And it came to pass that after there had been false Christs,
and their mouths had been shut, and they punished according to their crimes;
23 (16). And after there had been false prophets, and false preachers and teachers among the people, and all these having been punished according to their crimes; and after there having been much contention and many dissensions away unto the Lamanites, behold, it came to pass that king Benjamin, with the assistance of the holy prophets who were among his people—
24 (17). For behold, king Benjamin was a holy man, and he did reign over his people in righteousness; and there were many holy men in the land, and they did speak the word of God with power and with authority; and they did use much sharpness because of the stiffneckedness of the people—
25 (18). Wherefore, with the help of these, king Benjamin, by laboring with all the might of his body and the faculty of his whole soul, and also the prophets, did once more establish peace in the land.

[Chapter II begins here, as it originally appeared in the draft.]

Chapter II
1 (1). And now there was no more contention in all the land of Zarahemla, among all the people who belonged to king Benjamin, so that king Benjamin had continual peace all the remainder of his days.

[Chapter II, first renumbered Chapter III, and then Chapter I, continues.]

The flow of topics and even wording, ending at Omni 29 to resume at Words of Mormon 12, and ending at Words of Mormon 18 to resume at Mosiah 2:1 (renumbered 1:1) indicates the unity of these passages. The original first chapter of Mosiah was placed part in Omni and part in Words of Mormon. The chapter numbers in ms $\mathcal{P}$ underlying the Great Mosiah Mystery are explained by the same error having existed in $\mathcal{O}$, and that is explained by the numbering in the pre-$\mathcal{O}$ Mosiah draft.

This restored chapter consists of 1,336 words. This compares well with the length of chapters in traditional Mosiah in the 1830 edition, which has chapter divisions based on ms $\mathcal{P}$. The lengths of the first five chapters in the 1830 edition are: 4186, 1595, 789, 307 and 2455.

Note too that some books of the BOM narrative begin with the author speaking in the first person. This is true of Nephi through Omni, and Mormon through Moroni. The portion written by Mormon stretches from Words of Mormon through 4 Nephi. This pattern ("I Mormon") had to be deleted from Mosiah Chapter I when it was inserted into Omni, but is followed at the beginning of the explanation of the two sets of plates (Words of Mormon 1:1), and, once again, when Mormon begins his account of Mosiah, "And now I Mormon..." (WOM 1:9) In addition, if the Mosiah draft originally began with a book summary, it had to be sacrificed when Chapter 1 was split between Amaleki and Mormon.

By the way, additional confusion exists regarding King Mosiah and King Benjamin. Ether 4:1 states in the first edition, "for this cause did king Benjamin keep them [the records of the Jaredites]." In later editions, Benjamin was changed to Mosiah.

One of the more important observations is that the initial formatting in ms O of 2 Nephi and Mosiah reveals anomalies that are best explained by errors arising from chapter numbering in drafts that were originally written with no intention at the time to change the original draft chapter numbering. It seems clear that Smith was not only not dictating from notes or outlines, but was dictating from drafts so developed that they were already divided into numbered chapters.

The Issue of Mosiah Priority: D&C 10

When Smith returned to Harmony in late summer of 1828, and eventually got back to work, did he begin with the small plates of Nephi, introduced to replace the now absent Book of Lehi (the infamous 116 pages), or did he begin with Mosiah, the first book following the Book of Lehi? For LDS scholars, this is the issue of the order of translation, and for BOM critics it is the issue of the order of its 19th-century composition, possibly tied to the issue of whether there could have been more than one author. After all, if Smith was primarily plagiarizing the text of another author, then who wrote the replacement text? The Mosiah priority argument is important for some BOM critics who argue that Joseph Smith authored the whole work. For them, it shows that at first Smith did not know what to due after the 116 pages went missing. To not waste time, he just continued where he had left off.

The scriptural base for the view that when he went back to work he began where he left off, with Mosiah, is D&C 10:3. Many read it to mean that the project should recommence beginning with Mosiah.

> Nevertheless, it [the gift to translate] is now restored unto you again; therefore see that you are faithful and continue on unto the finishing of the remainder of the work of translation as you have begun.

Smith was told that he had lost the Urim and Thummim because he had delivered the 116 pages "into the hands of a wicked man" (v. 1), and had lost his gift to translate as well (v. 2). In verse three he was told that these have been restored and he may continue the work. The verb *continue* is intransitive. It is modified by the adverbial prepositional phrase *unto the finishing of the remainder of the work of translation*. This phrase specifies the period of continuation as being to the completion of the whole work of translation, including both sets of plates. The subordinate clause "as you have begun" specifies that the remainder of the whole project must be finished just as Smith had begun it before. He began it with Lehi 1:1, but the revelation goes on to clarify that this second time, instead of redoing Lehi, Smith must do Nephi. So, he must begin again, but with Nephi 1:1. This is as close as one gets to a mention of a specific text location to recommence his project.

In D&C 10 we find an ordered sequence of the two segments of the BOM narrative. Verses 5-29 delineate Satan's plan to destroy the work, wherein evil men challenge Smith to begin again by producing a word-for-word reproduction of the lost pages. In verse 30, addressing this recommencement, God commands Smith, "you shall not translate again those words." In 34, Smith is cautioned against showing his work to the world until he has "accomplished the work of translation." Instead of going back to retranslate the Book of Lehi, in verse 41 He commands, "Therefore you shall translate the engravings which are on the [small] plates of Nephi," up to King Benjamin. Verse 44 assures that after all, the evil men "have only got a part, or an *abridgment* of the account of Nephi" [i.e. of the large plates]. Leaving the replacement text for the first time, verse 46 proceeds further and addresses "all the remainder of this work..." (from Mosiah on). The sequence begins addressing the small plates of Nephi, and continues with the text from Mosiah on.

Extratextual evidence has been adduced for further clarification.:

The Issue of Mosiah Priority: The Gathering Folds

LDS scholars, and some others, believe that when Smith got back to work he dictated for Cowdery to write into ms 𝒪. These have used the gathering folds as evidence for the sequence of the books. All of Alma, and up to 3 Nephi 4:2 are folded *widthwise*. (and also 1 Nephi 14:11 through Enos 1:14) The gathering containing 3 Nephi 19:26 to 27:7 was folded *lengthwise*, as well as the gathering containing the extant part of Ether, 3:9-15:17. From this, some have speculated that lengthwise folding continued to the end of Moroni, and then into the first gathering of 1 Nephi, with 2:2-13:35 extant. If true, this might serve as evidence that the pages composed to replace the purloined 116 pages (the Book of Lehi) were added by Moroni to the end of his record, and then translated (or composed) in that order.

There is evidence that indicates that this was the case. First, the folds are only relevant to the copying of the text into ms 𝒪. It says nothing about when the initial drafts were composed. Second, the ms 𝒪 texts of Mosiah, 4 Nephi, Mormon and Moroni are not even extant. Third, we need to know *why* some gatherings are folded widthwise and others lengthwise. Note that Cowdery was the sole scribe for all extant portions of 2 Nephi and on to 3 Nephi 4:2. These were folded widthwise. But Cowdery, who was very consistent in his procedures, was also the scribe for the gathering with 3 Nephi 19:26-27:7 (extant), and the next gathering with Ether 3:9-15:17 (extant), both exhibiting lengthwise folds. Even though the first gathering of 1 Nephi has lengthwise folds, its second gathering has widthwise folds. Cowdery was the chief scribe for both of these. Why does the same scribe, and a somewhat fussy one at that, change the fold orientation in the middle of a book?

Perhaps the solution to the fold orientation mystery is both mundane and very simple. If the person sent to get paper rolled it tightly in some old newspaper to protect it in his saddle bag, and kept it rolled up in storage, then Cowdery may have folded it lengthwise to make it lie flat. This may have been particularly important when writing with a quill pen. I have myself folded paper towels lengthwise to make them lie flat. Evidence indicates that he preferred widthwise folds, and so he would revert to his preference whenever lengthwise folding was not needed, even in the middle of 1 Nephi.

Paper was probably acquired by the quire, i.e. 24 sheets. This explains why six sheets (24 pages) was a common size for a gathering, with four gatherings per quire. So, was the paper for Ether, 3:9-15:17 (extant) and 1 Nephi 2:2-13:35 (extant) from the same quire, which had possibly been rolled up? This is not the case. The evidence is in the paper type. Robert J. Espinosa, conservator at the Harold B. Lee Library at BYU, identified five different paper types in ms O, and these two gatherings are of different paper types. So 1 Nephi 2:2-13:35 does not follow from the last books of the BOM. Actually, the next four gatherings (1 Nephi 14:11 through Jacob 4:14) are of yet another type, clearly coming from the same quire. The first gathering of ms O used a paper type not found elsewhere in the extant materials, likely left over from another quire and possibly one used in producing drafts, and perhaps already folded.

The Issue of Mosiah Priority: Page Numbers Count

The pages of ms O were numbered. Thus, if the first gathering had six sheets, the pages would have been numbered from 1 through 24. The sheets after Enos lack the page numbers due to damage. Skousen lists the readable page numbers as follows:[262]

Cowdery: 6, 44, & 111-114.
S^2: 20 & 22.
S^3: 5, 7, & 11-18.

These page numbers enable this whole section to be reliably numbered, pages 3 through 114. Skousen expects that the entire work also was numbered, and provides pages with estimated numbers indicated with a prime (315`, 316`, etc.). The scribes had their own preferred location to put the numbers, Cowdery being the most particular. This indicates that the numbers were not written after the fact. Each scribe numbered his pages during the process of writing them. Skousen comments: "In two cases, it is possible to determine that the scribe wrote the page number at the same time he wrote the summarizing heading at the top of the page—namely, page 5 (by scribe 3) and page 6 (by Oliver Cowdery)."[263]

---

[262] Skousen, *Original Manuscript of the* Book of Mormon, 33.
[263] Skousen, *Original Manuscript of the* Book of Mormon, 33

15. BOM Authorship: Interfacing Nephi & Mosiah   347

Whatever one might think regarding the order of the composition of the various book drafts, the page numbers indicate that they were written into ms 𝒪 in Nephi priority order. But, if we were to assume the Mosiah-priority order of composition, and that drafts were first prepared prior to doing ms 𝒪, we would be faced with the scenario of drafts being prepared and fully edited for Mosiah through Moroni, and also at least 1 Nephi, prior to beginning the process of copying them into ms 𝒪. This has serious implications for the BOM production timeline, which we will revisit in Chapter 18.

Another observation militating against the view that the composition of Nephi followed Moroni is the probability that the latter was not even thought of until long after Nephi had already been printed. Moroni is an add-on (Chapter 18).

The Issue of Mosiah Priority: The Problem of the Retained Pages

When a major disruption in one's plan occurs, such as the loss of the 116 pages, the recovery effort might not happen smoothly. This can partly arise out of some effort to disguise one's real intent or problem. There can be some puzzling statements. Take for example D&C 10:

> 41. Therefore, you shall translate the engravings which are on the plates of Nephi, down even till you come to the reign of king Benjamin, or until you come to that which you have translated, which you have retained;
> 42. And behold, you shall publish it as the record of Nephi…

What is the purpose of verse 41? Ostensibly it is to indicate how far to translate the plates of the replacement text. But we know that the small plates of Nephi had been completed, filled up by Amaleki just before his death, at the end of the Book of Omni (1:30). What was published as the translation of these plates extended right to the last line. There should have been no need to indicate how far to translate them. So then, what is the author really saying?

Furthermore, we cannot even know for sure that there were any pages retained. Note that 116 is evenly divisible by four, and therefore the purloined pages may have been two or three gatherings (such as two of ten sheets each and one of nine sheets). This would be how Smith knew how many pages had gone missing. It could be that an additional gathering had been begun, and it constituted the pages retained. It could also be that the work completed to that point had not fully filled up the last lost gathering and nothing was retained. Even if there were retained pages, we have to be careful about assuming that they contained any reference to Mosiah or king Benjamin. We do not know this.

Adding to the puzzle, the dating of Section 10 is disputed. When first published, in the *Book of Commandments* (BC 9,1833), the date given was May, 1829. In a study by Max H. Parkin we read:

> the 1828 date has not always been the one used for the revelation in Section 10. In fact, this date was not used until early in our present [20th] century. In all manuscripts of the revelations ... and in all published appearances of it during the Prophet's lifetime and for more than half a century after his death, this revelation bore the date May 1829... The first time that the revelation was ever dated summer 1828 was in 1902 in the first printing of volume 1 of the [History of the Church], and then in the new edition of the [D&C] that followed....[264]

These dates are in the heading introducing the revelations, not in the text. Moreover, we read in the first verse that Martin Harris is referred to as a "wicked man." Yet by May of 1829, he was back in Smith's good graces. This, and other issues, may be resolved by seeing BC 9 (D&C 10) as a composite: "the revelation, therefore, did not take its written form as we have it until 1829. The arguments listed above and others for both dates might be appropriate in their rightful places."[265]

There are a couple of possible explanations for the assertion of retained pages. First, if the Mosiah draft was produced by someone in Manchester, perhaps it was feared that this had been suspected. This assertion would give assurance that Mosiah had been begun in Harmony before the pages even went missing. Second, and perhaps more probable, this may have been extra insurance against an attack from whomever might have the purloined pages. Even with their new strategy, the worst case scenario would be for the pages to be produced totally intact after the new bible had been printed, with a carefully forged 117th page with

---

[264] Max H. Parkin, "Dating D&C 10," *Mormon History Association Newsletter* 45 (November 1980), 24. Max H. Parkin, "A Preliminary Analysis of the Dating of Section 10," in the *Seventh Annual Sydney B. Sperry Symposium: The Doctrine and Covenants* (Provo, UT: Brigham Young University, 1979), 68-84.

[265] Parkin, "A Preliminary Analysis of the Dating of Section 10."

content incompatible with the published text. If these subversives thought that pages had been retained, they might not attempt it. If they did, this verse laid the groundwork for the BOM authors to produce "retained" pages to refute the attack.

The Issue of Mosiah Priority: Words of Mormon

Other important verses on this subject are in Words of Mormon. In verse three we learn that Mormon discovered the replacement text after abridging the large plates of Nephi down to Amaleki, i.e. after completing the text of the lost 116 pages. He did not discover them after he had completed his entire BOM abridgment.

> 3. ...after I had made an abridgment from the **plates of Nephi**, down to the reign of this king Benjamin, of whom Amaleki spake, I searched among the records which had been delivered into my hands, and I found **these plates**, which contained this small account of the prophets, from Jacob down to the reign of this king Benjamin, and also many of the words of Nephi. (bolding added)

Here, the large plates are called the plates of Nephi, his initial set. After this reference to the prophecies of the replacement text (the small plates, i.e. "these plates"), he turns to the fulfillment of many of the prophecies up to his day (i.e. the events from Mosiah on), which he will record to finish his abridgment of the plates of Nephi (mentioned in verse three, i.e. the large plates, the abridgment of which he resumes).

> 4 And the things which are upon **these plates** [the small plates] pleasing me, because of the prophecies of the coming of Christ; and my fathers knowing that many of them have been fulfilled; yea, and I also know that as many things as have been prophesied concerning us down to this day have been fulfilled, and as many as go beyond this day must surely come to pass—
> 5 Wherefore, I chose these things [the fulfillment of the prophecies in the small plates], to finish my record upon them, which remainder of my record I shall take from the **plates of Nephi** [the large plates]; and I cannot write the hundredth part of the things of my people. (bolding added)

He then again mentions the replacement text (plates with prophesyings and revelations), which he intends to put with the remainder of his record.

> 6 But behold, I shall take **these plates**, which contain these prophesyings and revelations, and put them **with** the remainder of my record, for they are choice unto me; and I know they will be choice unto my brethren. (bolding added)

Mormon states that the small plates will be put *with*, not *at the end of* his record. Although at this point he should not have known it, he will be slain in one of the great battles at Cumorah and will not even be able to finish his own record. His son Moroni completed it for him (Mormon 8-9). And even if he had, this would not place the plates after Moroni.

Another argument that has been adduced in support of the Mosiah priority position is founded in a comment once attributed to Joseph Smith in his 1839 history, that in the process of translation they had come across a reference to the promise that there would be three witnesses to the gold plates, and that upon seeing this, Oliver Cowdery, David Whitmer and Martin Harris begged Smith to seek of the Lord on their behalf that they could be the three. Shortly after doing so, they were shown the plates. There is a reference in this passage to 2 Nephi 11 (see 2 Nephi 27:12 in the current LDS chapter divisions), seemingly linking the translation (or composition) of Nephi to this late event. However, in his edition of this history, Jessee points out in a note that this reference is an insertion in pencil in a different hand.[266] It is not Joseph Smith. Unfortunately for the Nephi posteriority position, the calling of three witnesses is also mentioned in Ether 5:4, near the end of the *Book of Mormon*. To the extent that this story has any historicity, it could be the translation or composition of the passage in Ether that gave rise to this trio's desire to be the three witnesses.[267] Also, references of this sort could have been added in the process of editing the drafts, after some discussion: "Should we say it here, or perhaps there? Better yet, let's say it in both places." Finally, Smith's histories were composed to create an official history.

Another argument in support of the Mosiah priority position has to do with child baptism. In a letter from Oliver to Hyrum Smith, dated 14 June 1829, he wrote, "he commandeth all men every where to repent and

---

[266] Jessee, *Papers of Joseph Smith*, I:295.

[267] For a major analysis of this issue, made in support of Mosiah priority, see Brent Lee Metcalfe, "The Priority of Mosiah: A Prelude to *Book of Mormon* Exegesis," in Brent Lee Metcalfe, ed., *New Approaches to the* Book of Mormon, 395-444.

~~not only~~ [be] baptized and not only men but women [and] children which have arrived to the years of accountibility (sic)."[268] This has been argued to be drawn from Moroni 8:20: "he that saith that little children need baptism denieth the mercies of Christ," and therefore evidence that Moroni was written prior to that date. However, a similar view is already expressed in Mosiah 3:18: "the infant perisheth not that dieth in his infancy." More likely, this was the personal view of both Cowdery and Smith, shared by many others at the time. Infant mortality was high, many dying unbaptized. In 1810, Ephraim Smith lived only eleven days, and in 1823 Alvin Smith died without the benefit of baptism by the restored priesthood authority.

Metcalfe's Style Shift: *Wherefore/Therefore* and Mosiah Priority

In a study of the Mosiah priority position, Brent Metcalfe reviewed the principal arguments. His seminal contribution has been in analysis of style.[269] He presented a table of the incidence of the words *whosoever* and *whoso* from an unpublished paper by Glen Foster, Jr.,[270] in each of the BOM books having at least one of the words in the pair (i.e. in ten books). He also presented a table of the incidence of the words *wherefore* and *therefore* in each of all fifteen BOM books, drawing from data from John L. Hilton and Kenneth D. Jenkins.[271] He observed that *whosoever* dominates in Mosiah, Alma, and Helaman, but becomes about equal in 3 Nephi, and shifts to *whoso* in Mormon, Ether, Moroni, 1 Nephi, 2 Nephi and Jacob. He observed a similar but more marked phenomenon for *therefore*, which dominates in Mosiah, Alma, Helaman and 3 Nephi, while *wherefore* dominates in Moroni, 1 Nephi, 2 Nephi Jacob and Enos through Words of Mormon. He displayed his data in both the traditional order of the books, and in an order beginning with Mosiah, having 1 Nephi through Words of Mormon following Moroni (the Mosiah priority order). In the latter order, he noted what appeared to be a developmental

---

[268] Oliver Cowdery letter to Hyrum Smith dated 14/06/1829, in Vogel, *Early Mormon Documents*, II:403.
[269] Metcalfe, "The Priority of Mosiah," 404-17.
[270] Arthur Glen Foster, Jr. "The Plates of Jacob: An Analysis of the Replacement to the Lost Manuscript of the *Book of Mormon*," (privately circulated, 1983).
[271] John L. Hilton and Kenneth D. Jenkins, "Vocabulary and Numerical Count of all Words from the King James Old Testament, New Testament and the 1830 *Book of Mormon*," *Preliminary Report*. (Provo, UT: FARMS, n.d.)

shift of style of a single author/translator (Joseph Smith), from *therefore* to *wherefore* and from *whosoever* to *whoso*. Since a clear pattern emerged only when the books were placed in Mosiah priority order, he concluded that Mosiah represented the earlier stylistic preference, and Moroni the later preference, which was continued in 1 Nephi. So the data, as presented, clearly supported Mosiah priority in the order of the production of the BOM text.

I undertook to replicate this study. For this purpose, and for all my work producing the results displayed in tables 29 and 30, I used an 1830 edition of the *Book of Mormon* that had been prepared in electronic format using the current LDS chapter-verse divisions.[272]

Although these data, so presented, are very striking, the procedure is fatally flawed, largely because the BOM books vary so much in length, and the data were not standardized for this variable. Alma has 85,073 words, Moroni only 6,142 and Jarom 733. The problem seems obvious, but can be exampled in this manner. Assume that you and I engage in a bit of friendly gambling. We will throw a single indian-head nickel. Every time I get a head, you owe me a dollar, and vice versa. So after a hundred throws, on average neither of us should be out more than a dollar or two, if the nickel is honest. But here is the catch. For every throw you get, I get ten. On average, for every dollar I owe you, you will owe me ten. Well, no one in Vegas would play such a game, not even the most well lubricated at 3 AM. Putting the gross tally of 1 Nephi on an equal basis with Alma is just this sort of game.

A simple way to standardize for length is to calculate incidence per 5,000 words. But there is another factor. The major premise of the argument is that these word pairs are functional equivalents. So when the author needs a word with the function of *wherefore/therefore* or *whoso/whosoever*, which of the two words does he choose? As it turns out, *wherefore* has two meanings. It occurs twice with interrogative meaning, once in 1 Nephi and once in 2 Nephi. Since these do not correspond semantically to *therefore*, they need to be omitted from the count. Of far greater import, the BOM uses another expression corresponding to *whoso* and *whosoever*. This is *he that* (occurring in alternate forms, lumped together here: *he that, him that, they that* and

---

[272] "The 1830 *Book of Mormon* Text," accessed at https://carm.org/1830-book-of-mormon on 12/02/2016. In addition to the current chapter-verse divisions, this text also has the original 1830 chapter divisions.

them that). Due to the strong preference for using the word *that* in the BOM, we find *he that* rather than *he who*, which at least visually corresponds better to *who so*. In BOM parlance, when the writer needed a word with this meaning/function, he could have chosen *whoso*, *whosoever* or he *that*. The interchangeability of these in actual BOM usage is illustrated in the following passages:

> And now, whoso readeth, let him understand; he that hath the scriptures, let him search them (3 Nephi 10:14)

> whoso shall hide up treasures in the earth shall find them again no more and he that hideth not up his treasures unto me, cursed is he, and also the treasure (Helaman 13:18-19)

He that can also be used with a referent, in which case it is not indefinite and so not equivalent to *whoso* or *whosoever*. When this occurs, it cannot be added to the tally for this research. Moreover, in addition to *whosoever*, it is necessary to also count *whomsoever*. In Table 30 the data for *therefore, wherefore, whoso, whosoever* and *he that* are presented, standardized on a base of 5,000 words (see Chapter 16).

So far, we have two variables, the standardized incidence of each word in each book, and each book's length. Proceeding with the *therefore/wherefore* comparison, we express each value in the graph in terms of its percent of the largest column total. The largest incidence per 5,000 words of *therefore* and *wherefore* added together is in 2 Nephi. It is 1.49 + 33.61 = 35.1 (Table 30). Being the largest, it is made the base for comparison. Dividing the 2 Nephi column total (35.1) by the base (35.1) yields unity (1). All graphs in this chapter and Chapter 16 are set to unity in this manner. Dividing the incidence of *therefore* per 5000 words in 2 Nephi (1.49) by the base (35.1) yields .04245 or 4.25% of unity. The same operation for *wherefore* is 33.61/35.1=.95754 or 95.75% of unity. The column for 2 Nephi in the graph is divided into these proportions. All other values from the table were divided as well by 35.1 to get the values (percentages of unity) used to construct Figure 16. As a result, the *therefore* segment of 1 Nephi represents both its percent of the maximum incidence (unity), as indicated above, and its percent of the total incidence of the 1 Nephi bar. The width of the bar indicates the length of the book, in total number of words. The same is done for the *whoso/whosoever/he that* triad.

Figure 16. Distribution of *Therefore* & *Wherefore*

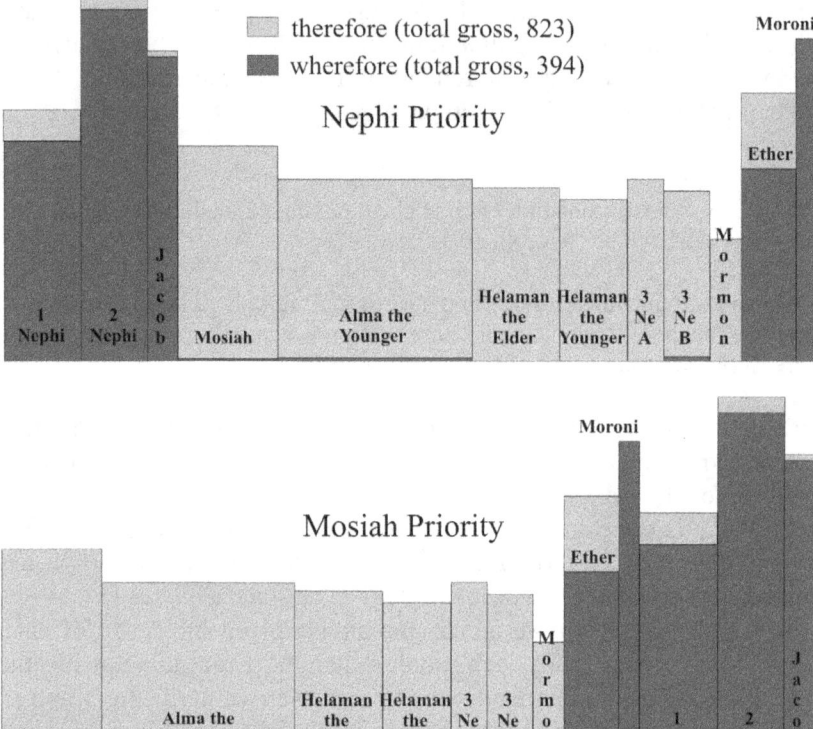

Note that the figures listed in tables 29 and 30 can be converted to the original gross scores by multiplying by the number of words in the book (from Table 30) and dividing by 5,000. In 2 Nephi, the standardized incidence for *therefore* is 1.49. So, (1.49x20,084)/5,000=5.985. Round to the nearest whole number to get the original tally: 6.

In both Figure 16 and Figure 17, the upper graph is in Nephi priority order and the lower graph is in Mosiah priority. As can be seen in Figure 16, there is some observable similarity between 1 Nephi and Moroni. Based on this alone, the latter appears to belong to the Nephi group. But overall, the data do not evidence a steady shift in stylistic preference from *therefore* to *wherefore* in either order.

Figure 17. Distribution of *Whoso, Whosoever* and *He That*

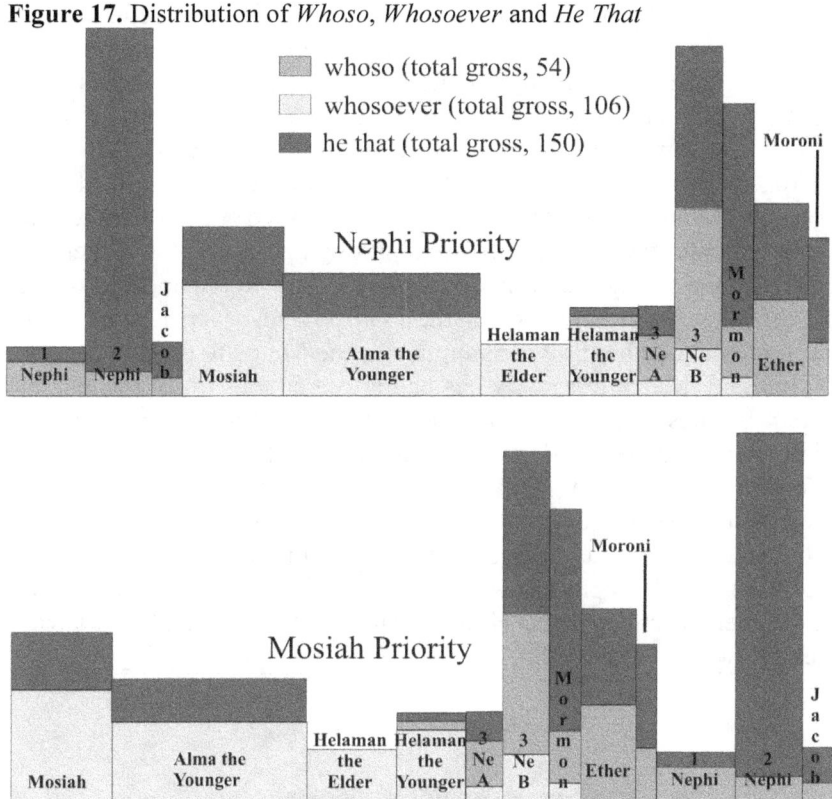

In Figure 17, Metcalfe's *whosoever* and *whoso* are listed below *he that* to facilitate inspecting for a pattern for just these two. In this case we find minimal similarity between 1 Nephi and Moroni in the *whosoever*, *whoso* and *he that* group, and no indication of a gradual shift in style. Note the striking difference within the traditional Book of Alma, i.e. between Alma the Younger and Helaman the Elder. There is also a striking difference within traditional 3 Nephi, between 3 Nephi A and 3 Nephi B.

The Metcalf thesis holds that after it became necessary to replace the Book of Lehi, Smith had no idea what to do about the loss of the 116 pages. Not wanting to lose time, he continued where he left off, with Mosiah, and continued all the way to the end of Moroni, by which time he had the traditional answer worked out based on a parallel set of plates for the time period that Lehi had covered. At that point, he was ready to tackle 1 Nephi. During this period of composition, his preference for *therefore* or *wherefore* was one way when Joseph Smith began work on Mosiah, but shifted gradually to the opposite preference as his work progressed. The same happened with his preference for *whosoever* and *whoso*. Using gross numbers, his data, supported this. But when standardized for book size, we see that there is no gradual shift of style. The books Mosiah through Mormon show a strong preference for *therefore*, while the books 1 Nephi through Jacob, plus Ether and Moroni, show a strong preference for *wherefore*. 1 Nephi and Moroni are quite different with respect to the *whoso/whosoever/he that* triad. Overall, the data do not provide support for the Metcalfe thesis.

This said, Metcalfe's study has had a tremendous impact in *Book of Mormon* Studies, being interpreted to be hard-data support for the Mosiah priority thesis, and one assumes indirectly leading to the *after that* (etc.) research below, and my own study of the distribution of *that* clauses. But when the data are standardized for book length, which is fundamental in such data analysis, then the significance of both of these studies is reversed. Nephi and Alma are so different that the studies now must be seen to support the Hilton result, that Nephi and Alma were written by two different authors.

Observations

Let us assemble what we know.

First, the "small plates of Nephi" must be understood to mean the small plates that he had made from gold, not plates entirely written by him. Although he did write most of that text, his successors continued their records on the same plates.

Second, the small plates of Nephi, were mostly written in the first several decades in the New World, and so must have been written in the Egyptian of the Brass Plates, i.e. Late Egyptian or Demotic.

Third, the small plates of Nephi were filled up by Amaleki with his contribution to the Mosiah/Benjamin history. Smith was to translate these in their entirety, and needed no instruction for how far to translate.

Fourth, Mormon's portion of the Mosiah/Benjamin story in his abridgment is drawn from the large plates as a continuation of Amaleki's account on the small plates.

Fifth, what had been chapter one in the original Mosiah draft was reassigned, part to Omni and part to Words of Mormon. These two parts gave rise to the chapter numbers of Omni [Chapter first] and Words of Mormon [2.d I], making the original second chapter of Mosiah [I.II]. This, and the misnumbering from chapter eight on, shows Smith was reading from a draft that was so highly developed that it was already divided into numbered chapters, a draft however that had not been updated.

Sixth, Mormon says he placed the small plates of Nephi *with* not necessarily *after* his own record, which he was unable to complete. Even placing them after Mormon's abridgment does not locate them after Moroni.

Chapter 16

BOM Authorship: Sequential or Collaborative?

So far we have identified two fundamental considerations for research into the authorship of the BOM narrative. The most important source material is ms *O* (supplemented by ms *P* when necessary). These documents are absolutely contemporary with the process under examination, and contain important clues. They totally trump comments made years (sometimes decades) later by persons active in developing and projecting the official history. Above all, the fact that ms *O* displays relatively few substantive edits requires the conclusion that it was produced by Joseph Smith reading from drafts while Oliver Cowdery (mostly) wrote ms *O*. The analysis of the beginning of 2 Nephi, and the reassignment of the original draft Chapter One of Mosiah to Omni and Words of Mormon, has shown that these two drafts, at least, were so finished that they had already been divided into numbered chapters. The second fundamental consideration is the segmental character of the BOM narrative. The layout is made up of records of different recorders, producing books that are in some cases stand-alone works. This feature is ideal for a degree of division of labor, and the possibility of two or more initial drafts being produced at roughly the same time.

The orthodox LDS position, the Spalding-Rigdon argument and both the Nephi priority and Mosiah priority approaches all have one thing in common. They assume that the production of the BOM books was done sequentially, one book after another in the order found in the published *Book of Mormon*. Sequential composition may have been rarely questioned because this is the way the BOM has come down to us, and how most researchers (LDS scholars and most BOM critics alike) have always seen it ever since Junior Sunday School. In practice, it is treated, perhaps subconsciously, as being axiomatic. Furthermore, apart from Hilton's wordprint results, multiple authorship has been only rarely considered, although for him Nephite protagonists were the authors, Nephi, Mormon and Moroni, even when analyzing the English text.

Quantitative content analysis has usually avoided the distinctive thematic words and expressions in the BOM. We will examine both ends of the spectrum.

The Distribution of Distinctive and/or Thematic Words and Phrases

The wordprint technique used by Larsen, Rencher and Layton, and further elaborated by Hilton, is based on data considered to be noncontextual. These and other quantitative studies attempt to be independent of the subject matter of the sample texts. When noncontextual data are not used, studies are based on a data selection process that in some way homogenizes and/or sanitizes the data. Unfortunately, all of these produce rather sterile quantitative results. Even while recognizing the technical rationale and merits of this approach, it might prove interesting to make a foray in the opposite direction, just to leave no stone unturned. The first study presented here surveys thematic words and phrases, which do admittedly produce distributions that are influenced by context. One advantage is that they have an intrinsic interest for the reader. The issue of validity is only partly addressed by insisting that even large differences are only suggestive. Even so, every author in some sense choses or creates his or her own context. Arguably, eliminating it removes at least some evidence of authorship.

For this study, forty-three words and phrases were chosen. Each BOM book was searched to determine the incidence of each word or phrase, and the results tabulated. The gross numbers are meaningless, due to the different length of the books. For example, 1 Nephi is 23,517 words in length, Jarom only 733 and Alma 85,073. This last, divided into its two constituent parts, yields Alma the Younger with 58,519 words and Helaman the Elder with 26,554. To enable meaningful comparisons, the tallied figures were put on a base of 5,000 words. Each total was multiplied by 5,000, and the product was divided by the number of words in the book. Most books have at least 5,000 words. The results for the smaller books are inherently unreliable. Small populations are characterized by data instability because the occurrence of one or two cases can be a mere matter of chance. The results of this study are displayed in Table 29 for all books, but only the larger books are included in the analysis. In the table, only they have been standardized for book size on a base of 5,000 words. The data for the smaller books are gross tallies placed in parentheses. These are Enos through Words of Mormon plus 4 Nephi. The remaining books are sufficient to identify distribution trends and/or anomalies. The data are presented in Table 29, roughly grouped by theme.

Table 29. Distribution of Thematic Words and Expressions (per 5000 words)

Expression	NE1	NE2	JC	EN	JR	OM	WM
write/wrote/written	8.7	14	6	(1)	(8)	(11)	(5)
read (present, past, past participle)	2.8	3.5	1.1	0	0	0	0
seen and heard	.2	.2	0	0	0	0	0
Murmur	4.0	1.0	0	0	0	0	0
Confound	1.5	.7	.5	0	0	(1)	0
own due time	.4	.5	0	(1)	0	0	0
in the flesh	.4	3.2	.5	0	0	0	0
fruit of the (his, my, etc.) loins	0	4.5	.5	0	0	0	0
seed (descendants: my, his, etc.)	11	9.5	1.6	0	0	(1)	0
covenant people	.4	1.2	0	0	0	0	0
gentiles	11	7.2	0	0	0	0	0
children of men	5	8.7	.5	0	(1)	0	0
Israel	11	11	3.3	0	0	(2)	0
Zion	.64	2.74	0	0	0	0	0
House of Israel	7.4	5.5	2.7	0	0	0	0
Jerusalem (2 are Lamanite Jerusalem)	8.3	4.7	2.7	(1)	0	(2)	0
Land of Promise	2.8	1	.5	0	0	0	0
Jew	7	9	1.6	0	0	(1)	0
God of Israel	1	.25	0	0	0	0	0
Holy One of Israel	1.7	5.5	0	0	0	(2)	0
Lord of hosts/Lord God of hosts	0	1.7	3.3	0	0	0	0
Messiah	2.3	4.2	0	0	(1)	0	0
Redeemer	2.1	2	0	(1)	0	0	0
Savior	.9	.5	0	0	0	0	0
condescension	.4	.5	.5	0	0	0	0
baptize, baptism	1.49	3.49	0	0	0	0	0
lake of fire	0	1	1.6	0	0	0	0
Seer	0	1.5	0	0	0	0	0
plan of redemption/salvation	0	0	.5	0	(1)	0	0
Good shepherd	0	0	0	0	0	0	0
high priesthood	0	0	0	0	0	0	0
holy order of God/order of God	0	.25	0	0	0	0	0
lawyers	0	0	0	0	0	0	0
fort/fortify/fortification	0	.5	.5	0	(1)	0	0
Soldier	0	0	0	0	0	0	0
Stronghold	0	0	0	0	0	0	0
weapons of war	0	0	0	0	(1)	0	0
Treasure	0	.75	0	0	0	0	0
retain/retained/retaining	0	0	.5	0	0	0	0
Sabbath day	0	0	0	0	(1)	0	0
Forever	1.7	7.5	1.6	0	0	0	0
begat	.4	0	0	0	0	0	0
New Jerusalem	0	0	0	0	0	0	0

16. BOM Authorship: Sequential or Collaborative 361

Entries Are Incidence per 5,000 Words

MO	AL	ALY	HEE	HEY	3NE	3NA	3NB	4NE	MR	ET	MN
2.6	1.6	1.2	2.4	2.2	9.5	4.6	13	(1)	12	9	17
1.8	.3	.3	.4	.5	.4	.5	.4	0	1.1	.9	1.6
0	0	0	0	0	.2	0	.4	0	.5	.6	0
.5	.3	.3	.4	0	.2	0	.4	0	0	0	0
.3	.2	.3	0	.5	0	0	0	0	0	2.4	.8
0	0	0	0	0	.4	.5	.4	0	.5	.6	0
0	.1	.1	0	0	.4	0	.7	0	0	.9	0
0	0	0	0	0	0	0	0	0	0	0	0
1.2	1.1	1.5	.2	.2	2	1.8	2.2	0	1.6	1.8	0
0	0	0	0	0	0	0	0	0	1.6	0	0
0	0	0	0	0	0	0	11.5	0	5.3	3.3	0
3	.9	.9	.9	1.2	.8	.5	1.1	(1)	1.1	2.7	12.2
.5	.1	.1	0	.2	8.7	2.8	13	(1)	6.4	1.5	.8
.66	0	0	0	0	.20	0	.36	0	0	0	.81
0	0	0	0	0	7.5	2.8	11	(1)	5.8	1.5	.8
2.1	.9	1.3	.2	2.2	4.4	4.1	4.7	(1)	1.1	2.7	.8
0	.06	.09	0	0	0	0	0	0	0	.9	0
0	.2	.3	0	0	1	0	1.8	(1)	2.7	.3	0
0	0	0	0	0	.2	0	.4	0	0	0	0
0	0	0	0	0	0	0	0	0	0	0	0
0	0	0	0	.7	0	0	0	0	0	0	0
.17	0	0	0	.2	0	0	0	0	0	0	0
.7	.4	.4	.2	.7	.6	.9	.4	0	0	0	.8
.2	0	0	0	0	.2	.5	0	0	1.6	0	.8
0	0	0	0	0	0	0	0	0	0	0	0
3.31	1.18	1.45	.56	1.96	8.68	2.75	13.34	(1)	2.65	.90	17.91
.2	.1	.2	0	0	0	0	0	0	0	0	0
.8	0	0	0	0	0	0	0	0	0	0	0
0	1.1	1.5	0	0	0	0	0	0	0	0	0
0	.4	.6	0	.2	0	0	0	0	0	0	0
0	.5	.7	0	0	0	0	0	0	0	0	0
0	.9	1.2	.2	.2	0	0	0	0	0	.3	0
0	.8	1.1	0	0	1	2.3	0	0	0	0	0
0	1.5	0	4.9	.5	.4	.9	0	0	2.1	0	0
0	.4	.4	.4	0	0	0	0	0	0	0	0
0	.8	0	2.4	.2	.2	.5	0	0	.5	0	0
.2	2.2	1.4	4.1	.5	.2	.5	0	0	1.1	.6	0
0	0	0	0	3.2	0	0	0	0	.5	.3	0
.7	2.2	2	2.8	.7	.2	.5	0	0	.5	0	.8
.7	0	0	0	0	0	0	0	0	0	0	0
1.5	1.7	2.4	.2	1.0	.2	0	.4	0	2.1	.6	4.9
0	0	0	0	0	0	0	0	0	0	12.4	0
0	0	0	0	0	.6	0	1.1	0	0	2.7	0

To determine the book word totals, an MS Word file was created for each book. Then words not part of the text itself were laboriously deleted, including page headings, such the "The Book of Mormon," the word "chapter" and any number accompanying it, and even verse designations, such as 7:32. The longer KJV inclusions were also deleted, but not the paraphrases. MS Word then provided the word count.

The cells with relatively higher values have been shaded to facilitate the visual identification of patterns. The most interesting initial observation is the fact that entries with higher values for the Nephi books (1 Nephi through Jacob) often have relatively low values for the Alma-Helaman group, and vice versa. For example, note the first group, made up of words that characterize what one might call BOM English: *behold*, *yea* and *wo* (Table 30). Mosiah appears to go its own way, at times more similar to the Nephi group, and at times similar to the Alma group. The shading in the table suggests general agreement with Hilton's conclusion that Nephi and Alma were written by two different authors. We can understand that Nephi would have more occurrences of Israel, Zion, House of Israel, Jerusalem, Jew, Messiah and Redeemer, but what can explain the dearth of these words in Alma the Younger, Helaman the Elder and even Moroni? The branch of Israel in America and the gathering of Israel in the latter days are central themes of the BOM *raison d'être* throughout.

The Distribution of Strategies and Habits of English Usage

Because the *Book of Mormon* was written in English, the features of this language should give us some avenue to investigate authorship. The formation of sentences can be highly complex. The simple sentence (Dick likes Jane), even amplified by a second clause with a coordinating conjunction (Dick likes Jane and she tolerates him), can be fleshed out with adjectives and adverbs. Additionally, meaning is added by the use of subordinating conjunctions. One website lists over 35 of them. Although many occur in the *Book of Mormon*, by far the most common is *that*. In fact, if you open up 1 Nephi in MS Word and search on *that*, each match will be highlighted, and the page will light up like a Christmas tree. If this special effect is not enough, search on *and*. Even though ancient Egyptian did not even have a word for *and*, the BOM is seriously addicted to this coordinating conjunction.

That is not only polysemous but multifunctional. It can be a simple pronoun (That is good), a demonstrative adjective (That man is my uncle), or a conjunctive relative pronoun (The man that you see is my uncle). It can introduce an adverbial subordinate clause, as in "The general sent a division to the river bank that the enemy might not cross." In this case it indicates the objective or purpose of the action in the main clause, but it can also indicate degree or even consequence of an action. At times it is used with another word, such as *insomuch that*. Furthermore, it can introduce a noun clause, which is especially common as the direct object of a verb: "I know that it is true." The same clause can also function as the subject: "That it is true has not been questioned." Finally, it can serve as a type of predicate complement, as in "Should it be that you repent, then..."

In addition to clauses, English makes use of an arsenal of phrases. A direct object *that* clause can be replaced by a pronoun plus an infinitive phrase: "I know that it is a lie," or "I know it to be a lie." It can replace a *that* clause of objective, as in "He went to town to buy a pony," rather than "that he might buy a pony." BOM English tends to prefer the option with *that*. Perhaps the authors thought it sounded more formal.

A gerund (verbal noun) can replace an infinitive phrase, as in "To be or not to be" as opposed to "Being or not being, that is the question." (OK, I like Shakespeare's version better too.) The *-ing* ending has been very productive in English. In addition to what might be its primary function to form the continuous tense ("John is riding his horse."), it can be a gerund phrase: "Bareback riding that horse is dangerous." It can also be a participial phrase of accompanying circumstance: "Yankee Doodle came to town, riding on a pony." In some books of the BOM it is used to introduce a main clause, at the head of a sentence: "Knowing your love for her, I did not repeat the rumor."

None of this is intended to teach English to my readers, who probably know the language better than I. This revue is intended to highlight the extent of English complexity, and the fact that it offers considerable choice in how to frame a sentence. This being the case we are led to wonder to what extent speakers develop individualized strategies and habits in both speaking and writing, and to what extent preferences might be found in various BOM books. If so, is this lens capable of sufficient resolution to enable us to discriminate one author from another? Or is it too crude, leaving us peering through a glass darkly. The strategy of this chapter is to identify English language features that can be identified and therefore tallied by a computer full-text search, to produce data sets for each book so we can inspect the resulting distributions for patterns and/or anomalies.

Figure 18. Distribution of Phrases with Superfluous *That*

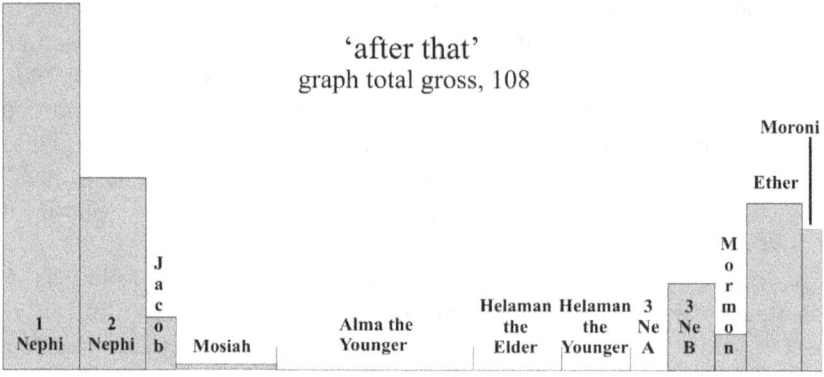

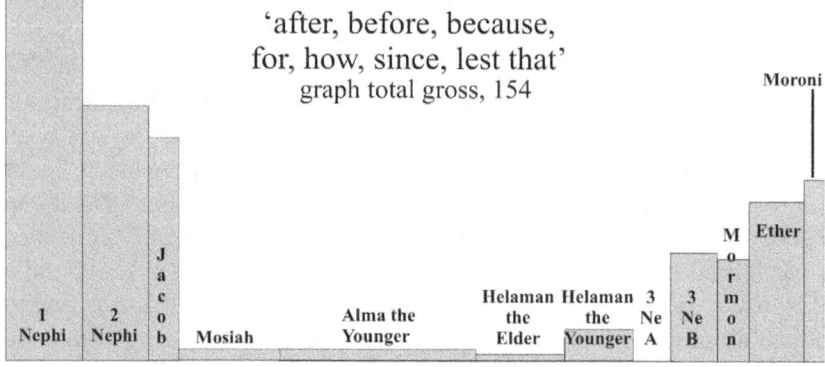

The Distribution of Superfluous *That* Phrases

Superfluous *that* refers to cases where *that* is not needed, and even wrong. Perhaps it is added because the speaker feels that it is more formal. Or he feels that an adverb needs it to make it a subordinating adverb. *Before* can be used as an adverbial preposition, as in "I did it before the bell." *That* is erroneously added when used to introduce a subordinate clause, as in "I did it before that the bell rang."

There is a difference between using *that* too much in composition, and superfluous *that*. An example of the usage of this phrase is: "After that the king came, we attacked." The better sentence would be "After the king came, we attacked." My study lumps together the incidence of a number of such phrases, although my raw data list them individually. They are: *after that, before that, because that, for that, how that, since that* and *lest that*. The data for *after that* and for this group of phrases aggregated are in Table 30, and presented in the graphs of Figure 18.

Although there is a somewhat acute difference between Moroni and 1 Nephi, it is far more radical between Nephi-Jacob and Mosiah through 3 Nephi A. Here again, the results are consistent with the Hilton results indicating that Nephi and Alma were done by different authors. They are consistent as well with the study of Moon et al., which indicated that Nephi and Mormon were also done by two separate authors. Note again the difference within traditional 3 Nephi, between 3 Nephi A and 3 Nephi B. For this however, one must bear in mind the radical content difference of 3 Nephi B (the ministry of Christ to the Nephites).

The Distribution of *That* Clauses

As stated above, *that* is polysemous. In the *Book of Mormon*, it is also ubiquitous. This does not mean that treating a serious case of *that* overabundance is most properly addressed by simply omitting *that* in some instances, or replacing it in others. Bryan A. Garner gives an example of editing out *thats* using a published passage with five *thats* in as many lines. The resulting passage has only one and is strikingly better. In the process, the original was seriously reworded but said the same thing.[273] However, our purpose here is not to improve the BOM text. It is to provide a procedure that enables us to distinguish the various types of *that* clauses, in order to tally them and examine their distribution.

The project presented here began by creating a key-word-in-context document for each BOM book. *That* is the key-word. Each book was copied into its own MS Word document, minus large Biblical inclusions if present (eg., *1 Nephi.docx*). The search function was used to manually examine every *that* in the book. Every one qualified for this project was copied into a key-word-in-context document for that book (eg., *that clauses 1 Nephi.docx*). In each case, *that* introduces a clause. Each entry

---

[273] Bryan A. Garner, *A Dictionary of Modern American Usage* (Oxford: Oxford University Press, 1998), 649.

Table 30. Grammatical Element Distribution

Element	NE1	NE2	JC	EN	JR	OM	WM
Therefore	2.98	1.49	.55	0	0	0	0
Wherefore	21.05	33.61	29.03	(6)	(3)	(6)	(4)
Whoso	1.06	.50	.55	0	0	0	0
whosoever	0	0	0	0	0	0	0
he (him, they, them) that	.43	10.71	1.10	0	0	0	0
Behold	19	3.8	7.7	0	0	0	0
Hearken	2.8	5.48	3.2	0	0	(2)	0
Yea	23	7	14.2	(1)	(2)	(4)	(2)
Wo	.6	5.7	1.1	0	0	0	0
Verily	0	.25	0	0	0	0	0
Whereby	.43	.50	0	0	0	0	0
Thereby	0	0	0	0	0	0	0
Inasmuch as	1.1	2.5	0	0	(1)	(1)	0
Moreover	0	0	0	0	0	0	0
Rather	0	.25	0	0	0	0	0
Whether	0	0	0	0	0	0	0
Notwithstanding	.43	2.24	2.19	0	0	0	0
Durst	.9	0	0	0	0	0	0
Unto	85	99	90	(22)	(7)	(12)	(3)
like unto	4.04	5.23	6.03	(1)	0	0	0
Thence	0	0	0	0	0	0	0
And	320	261	300	(89)	(56)	(98)	(49)
infinitive phrase as verbal complement	18.92	20.91	34.51	(7)	(5)	(4)	(2)
infinitive phrase as potential that clause	11.69	8.96	9.86	(2)	(2)	(4)	(4)
for to + infinitive	0	0	0	0	0	0	0
participial phrase	17.65	7.72	14.79	(10)	(5)	(7)	(4)
that thereby	0	0	0	0	0	0	0
relative pronoun *that*	8.08	25.89	10.96	(1)	0	(4)	0
redundant *that*	1.06	.75	2.74	(1)	0	0	0
after that	10.84	5.73	1.64	(1)	0	0	0
after (before, because, for, how) *that*	13.18	7.97	8.22	(3)	0	(1)	0
insomuch that	4.46	.25	2.74	0	0	(1)	0
that of objective, purpose, consequence	15.10	19.92	39.99	(4)	(1)	(1)	(3)
adverbial subordinate *that* clauses	35.08	29.63	53.14	(7)	(1)	(3)	(3)
would that	1.49	1.99	0	0	0	(2)	0
suffer that	1.28	0.75	1.64	0	0	(1)	0
cause that	.43	.75	.55	0	0	(1)	0
suppose that	2.13	1.99	2.74	0	0	0	(1)
see that	4.89	.75	2.74	(1)	0	0	0
know that	11.91	10.46	8.22	(3)	0	(1)	(3)
command that	3.61	5.48	2.19	0	(1)	(1)	0

Note: Small books are not standardized on a base of 5,000. The figures in parentheses are gross tallies for these books.

16. BOM Authorship: Sequential or Collaborative   367

Entries Are Incidence per 5,000 Words

MO	AL	ALY	HEE	HEY	3NE	3NA	3NB	4NE	MR	ET	MN
20.34	16.93	17.09	16.57	15.47	16.55	17.44	15.86	(5)	11.68	7.23	0
.17	.18	.26	0	0	.20	0	.36	0	0	18.39	30.93
0	0	0	0	.25	3.03	1.38	4.33	0	1.59	3.01	1.63
3.47	2.057	2.307	1.506	2.21	1.01	.46	1.44	0	.53	0	0
1.82	.94	1.37	0	.250	3.23	.92	5.05	0	6.90	3.01	3.26
.5	.9	1.1	.4	1.5	.4	0	.7	0	.5	1.2	0
1.16	.88	.85	.94	3.68	1.21	.46	1.80	0	.53	.60	0
22	31	31	36	41	13	19	9	(10)	16	7.5	5.7
.8	.2	.3	0	3.7	2.2	1.8	2.5	0	1.1	.3	4.9
.17	.24	.17	.38	0	9.49	.46	16.58	0	0	0	0
1.49	.12	.17	0	.49	.61	0	1.08	0	1.59	.60	.81
3.64	.53	.77	0	.49	.20	0	.36	0	0	.90	0
0	.7	.9	.4	.5	0	0	0	0	0	.3	0
1.32	.24	.34	0	.49	0	0	0	0	0	0	0
.5	1.2	1.5	.8	.5	.4	.46	.36	0	1.1	0	0
.7	1.6	2	.8	1	1.4	0	2.5	0	1.6	0	.8
.66	1.23	.85	2.07	2.46	1.41	2.29	.72	(3)	2.12	.30	1.63
.5	1.4	1	2	2.7	.6	.5	.7	0	0	0	0
44	56	70	27	76	94	49	129	(10)	61	69	94
.33	.41	.17	.94	.98	.81	.92	.72	(2)	.53	3.62	6.51
0	.4	.5	0	.7	.2	0	.4	0	0	.3	0
326	274	275	272	329	332	356	311	(182)	329	353	276
38.37	48.25	45.28	58.00	40.22	34.12	50.94	20.91	(21)	43.52	34.36	43.96
15.38	18.81	16.83	23.16	14.98	11.51	16.06	7.93	(3)	10.62	11.15	13.84
.33	.53	.68	.19	.49	.20	0	.36	0	0	.30	0
32.25	24.10	26.32	19.21	15.71	11.31	18.36	5.77	(5)	13.27	10.85	19.54
3.47	.47	.68	0	.49	.20	0	.36	0	0	.90	0
20.67	9.70	11.79	5.08	6.87	15.55	12.39	18.02	(2)	16.99	11.76	17.91
3.14	2.18	2.14	2.26	.98	1..41	.92	1.80	0	0	1.51	1.63
.17	0	0	0	0	1.41	0	2.52	0	1.06	4.82	4.07
.66	.35	.43	.19	.98	1.62	0	2.88	0	2.12	5.12	5.70
0	3.41	1.20	8.29	11.29	4.64	8.26	1.80	(4)	4.25	1.81	0
22.82	19.28	22.47	12.24	16.45	16.76	11.93	20.55	(1)	15.92	18.09	25.24
25.63	25.04	25.63	23.73	30.93	26.85	25.70	27.76	(5)	24.42	27.13	30.93
2.81	2.00	2.56	.75	1.96	1.41	0	2.52	(1)	1.59	2.41	.81
2.81	1.29	1.28	1.32	1.23	.20	0	.36	0	1.06	1.81	0
7.44	3.23	1.97	6.03	3.44	2.02	3.21	1.08	0	.53	2.11	0
0	3.64	2.82	5.46	1.72	1.21	1.84	.72	0	2.12	0	1.63
.99	5.64	6.07	4.71	9.33	1.01	.46	1.44	0	1.59	3.01	.81
2.65	6.35	7.78	3.20	4.91	4.24	5.05	3.60	(2)	10.62	7.23	7.33
4.47	2.35	2.48	2.07	.74	9.69	2.75	15.14	0	1.06	3.32	0

Book totals: NE1: 23,517; NE2: 20,084; JC: 9,127; EN, 1,166; JR, 733; OM, 1,401; WM: 857; MO: 30,233; AL: 85,073; ALY: 58,519; HEE: 26,554; HEY: 20,366; 3NE: 24,766; 3NA: 10,895; 3NB: 13,871; 4NE: 1,924; MR: 9,820; ET: 16,587; MN: 6,142.

begins with a chapter-verse identifier (e.g., 7:26). This is followed by the word *that* with enough text before and after it to provide context. On a second pass, each occurrence was assigned a code indicating the type of *that* clause. One category was when it introduces a direct object clause, in which case separate codes were used for each verb involved, such as "to know that" or "to expect that." Another code was used for a redundant *that*. In addition to the cases studied in the previous section, it sometimes occurs when the introduction "And it came to pass that..." is followed by a subordinate clause, followed by a second *that* to continue the sentence, as in "And it came to pass that, when the king came, that we greeted him." Delete the second *that*. When introducing an adverbial clause, the code indicates the nature of the clause. An example: "The general sent a division to the river bank that the enemy might not cross." In this case, the code would indicate an adverbial *that* clause, with the function of showing the objective of the action of the verb.

This work was done in such detail that the total number of codes came to 195. The detail was done to enhance the chance of discovering anything of interest, or perhaps even importance. This tedious work was done for the entire BOM. Searches were done for each code in each book to get its total incidence by type. It was found in the end that usually the most interesting results emerged when codes were grouped by meaningful criteria, and then the categories collapsed. These results are reported in Table 30, standardized in terms of incidence per 5,000 words. The figures in parentheses are gross tallies for the small books.

That clauses include superfluous *that* studied above, *that* introducing a direct object clause of a verb, *that* serving as a verbal complement for a verb such as "to be" (Should it be that you repent...), or adverbial *that* clauses (defined above). These are arguably much more significant than so-called "patterns" of noncontextual words, or vocabulary thought to be of thematic interest or of greater complexity. *That* clauses are among the most basic building blocks of the English language. They are used subconsciously. One does not modify, embellish or disguise something that escapes one's awareness. The figures in this chapter show that the BOM books reflect differences in *that*-clause habits. They vary in incidence. Some expressions number less than 100 in the BOM text. Others number in the hundreds, and even well beyond a thousand. This is especially true of major categories, such as all adverbial *that* clauses, and all direct-object *that* clauses. The total number of clauses or phrases in a table is given in the figure, where "gross" means that the incidence is the original tally unstandardized for book size.

Figure 19. Distribution of Adverbial & Direct Object *That* Clauses

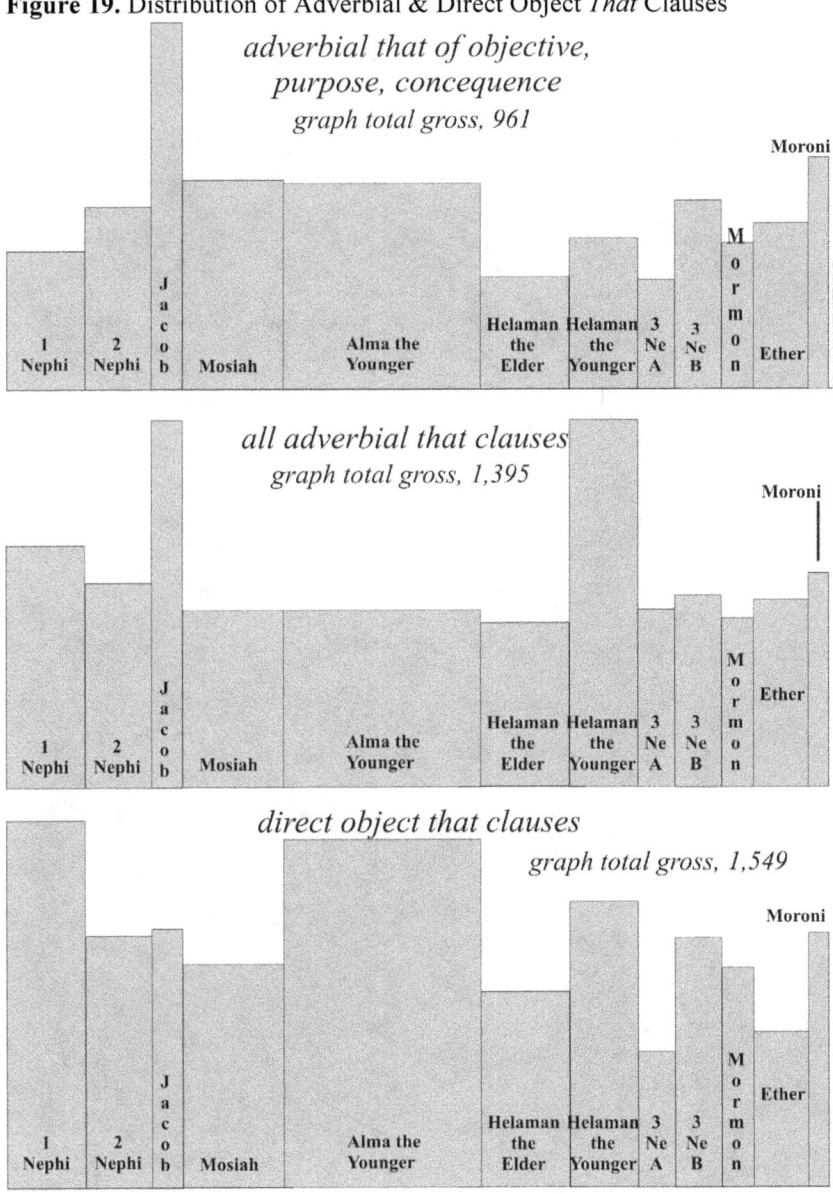

The two most salient observations are that very often the Nephi group differs sharply from Alma, while Mosiah often differs markedly from both.

Figure 20. Distribution of *Relative, Redundant and Insomuch That*

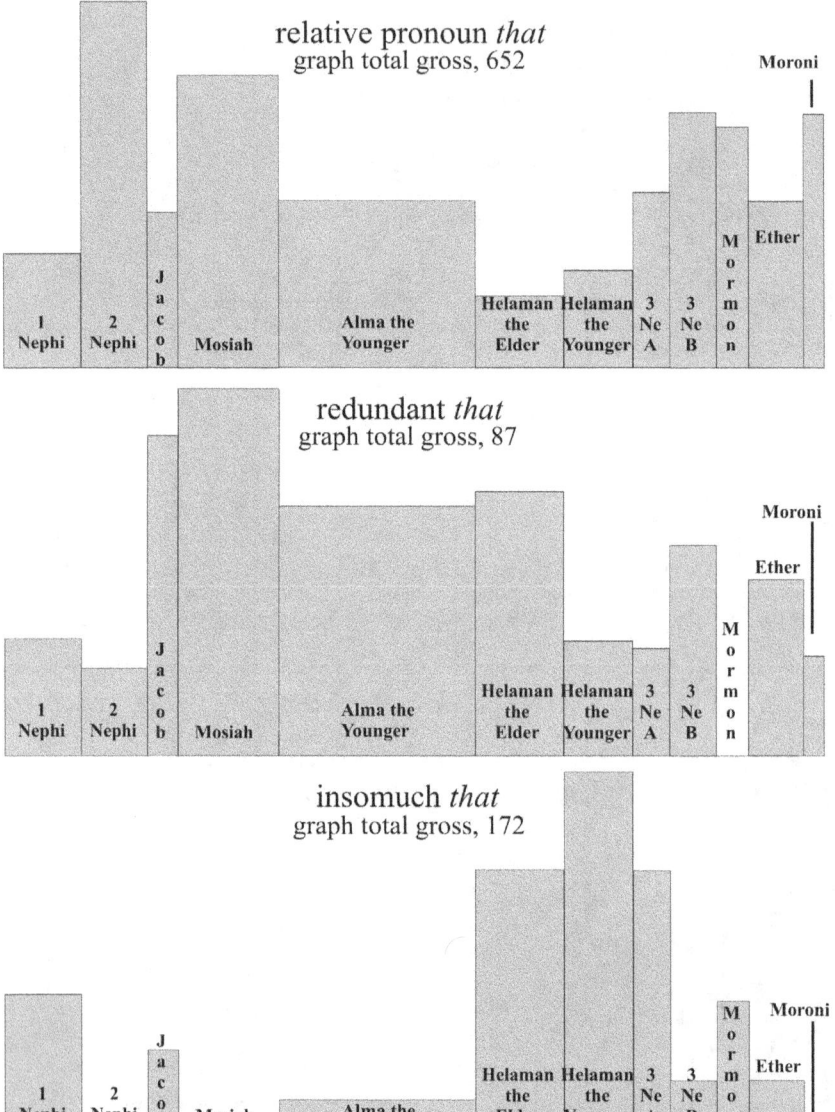

16. BOM Authorship: Sequential or Collaborative   371

Figure 21. Distribution of *Would That*, *Suffer That* & *Cause That*

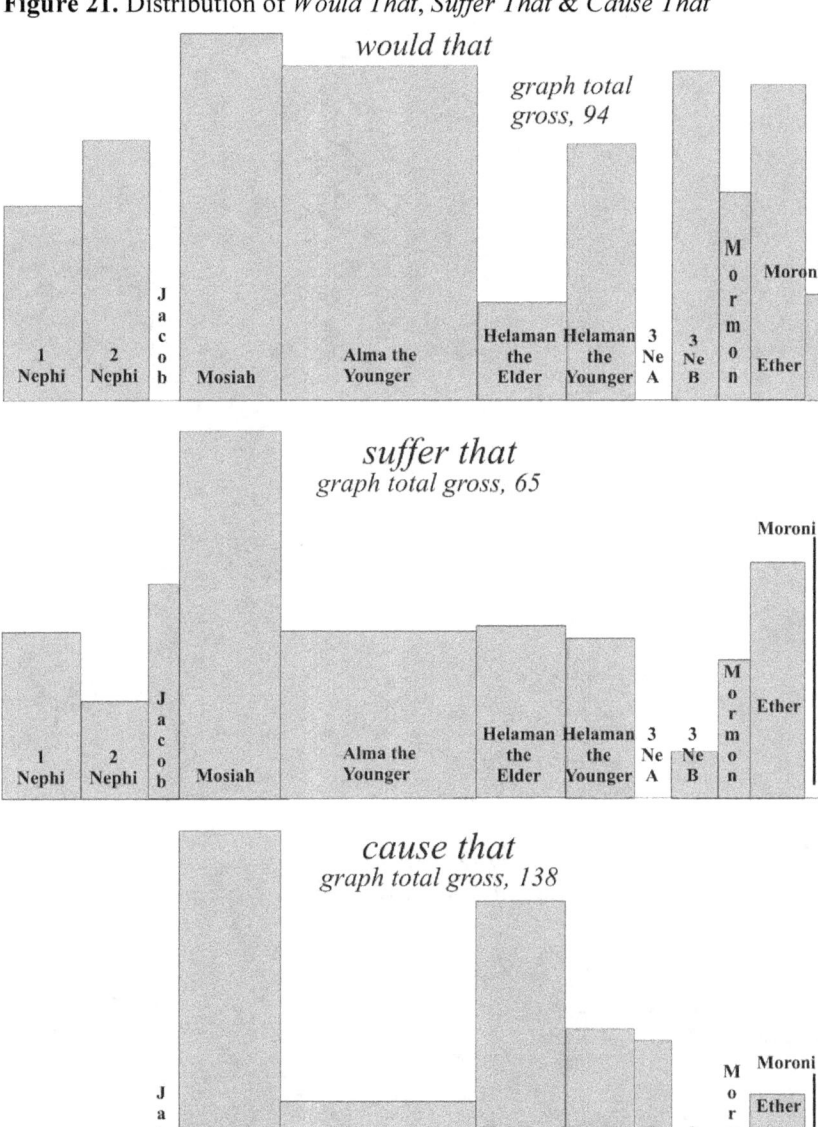

372 Mormon Genesis

Figure 22. Distribution of *Suppose That, See That & Know That*

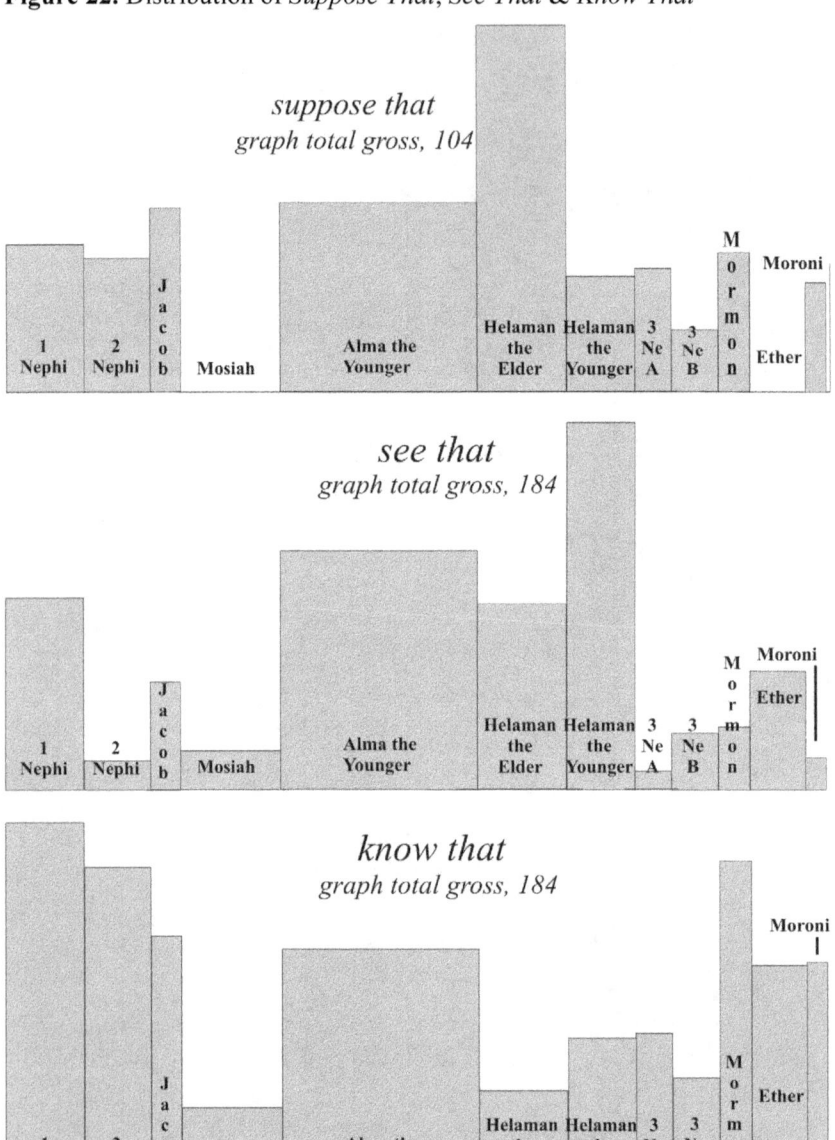

Figure 23. Distribution of *Command That* and *That Thereby*

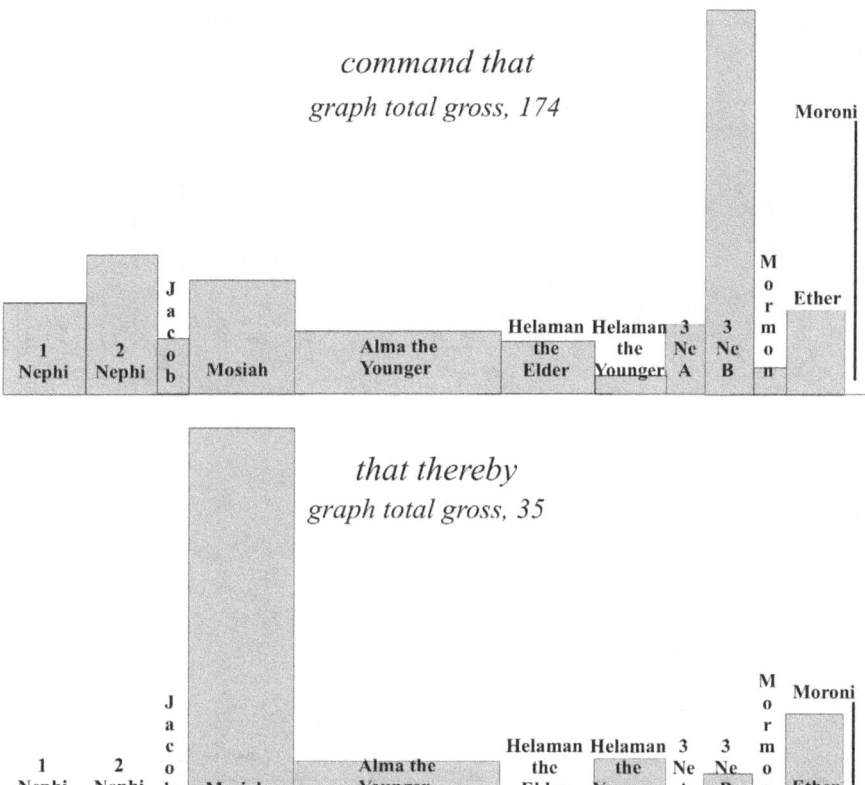

The distributions with significant to severe differences of magnitude between Nephi and Alma (et. al.) include figures 18 (*after that, after/before* [etc.] *that*); 19 (*adverbial that*, although to a lesser degree); 20 (relative *that*, redundant *that* & *insomuch that*); 21 (*would that* & *cause that*); 22 (*know that*), 23 (*that thereby*) and 24 (*like unto*). Words such as *would that, suffer that* and *cause that* are as distinctive of BOM English as *behold, yea* and *it came to pass*. These results are consistent with those of Hilton. Furthermore, Mosiah emerges from the pack, and is distinguished from both Nephi and Alma in figures 17 (*whoso/whosoever/he that*); 20 (relative *that*, redundant *that* & *insomuch that*); 21 (*suffer that* & *cause that*); 22 (*suppose that, see that* & *know that*) and 23 (*that thereby* & *unto*). The radical differences observed between 3 Nephi A and 3 Nephi B are largely a function of content.

Figure 24. Distribution of *Unto* and *Like Unto*

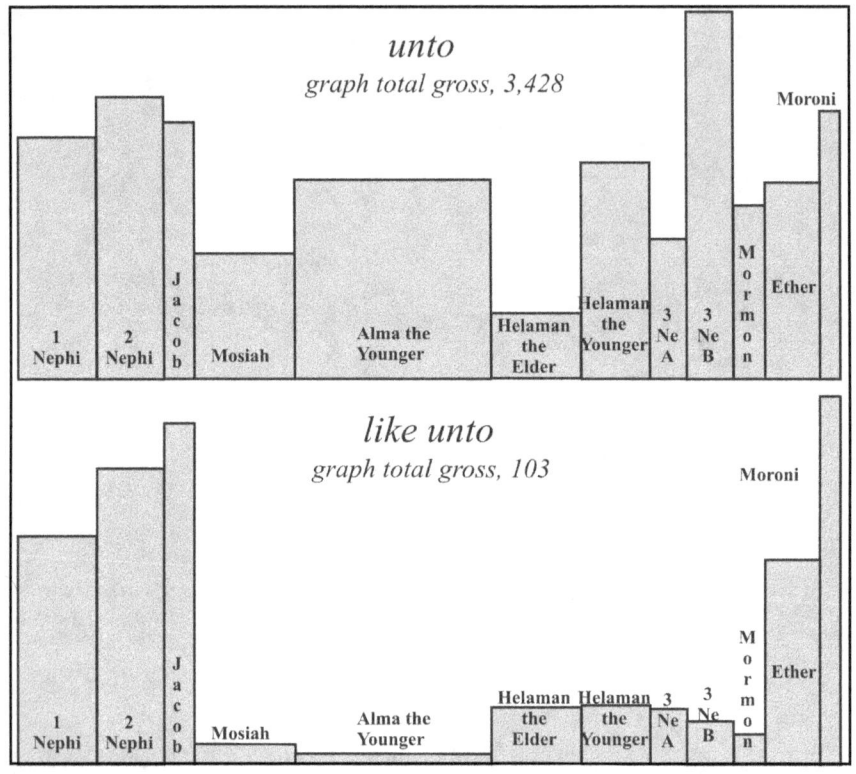

Note that in 3 Nephi B, Jesus does a lot more commanding than in the gospels. Also the two books that make up Alma, Alma the Younger and Helaman the Elder show very interesting differences in several distributions.

The Distribution of Participial, Infinitive and Gerund Phrases

In English, some of the basic phrases are participial phrases, infinitive phrases and gerund phrases. Without these, and subordinate clauses introduced by *that*, it is difficult to compose anything but the simplest text. The phrases can be used as an alternative to *that* clauses. An example of a participial phrase is, "Knowing him so well, I did not believe a word he said." An infinitive phrase can replace a direct object *that* clause, such as, "I know him to be just" instead of "I know that he is just." When such phrases occur, potentially a *that* clause could have been used. An example of a gerund phrase is, "Giving alms to the poor is commendable." Since these are among the most basic building blocks of the English language, they are amply represented in all of the books.

Computer searches were performed to acquire virtually all of these phrases in the BOM text. A search on the preposition *to* not only turned up all of the infinitive phrases, but resulted in many irrelevant "hits" that had to be waded through, such as *together*, *today*, *unto*, and simply *to* used as a preposition. *To* is not part of the infinitive, and an infinitive with *to* is already an infinitive phrase, although nearly all included here have complements, such as "to give him compensation." An infinitive phrase can replace a direct-object *that* clause in combination with a pronoun, such as in "I know him to be reliable." It can also be a subject, such as in "To drive at night requires good night vision." It can replace an adverbial *that* clause of objective, such as in "the general sent a division to the river bank to prevent the enemy from crossing."

Both gerund and participial phrases were rounded up by searching on *-ing*. Once again it was necessary to wade through irrelevant hits, such as *king* and *thing*. Every effort was made to be comprehensive. However, participles that have become fully fledged nouns and were used as such were not included, such as *blessing*. For example, *blessing* would not be counted in the sentence "He gave her a blessing." But it would be counted in the sentence "Blessing the sick, he spoke these words." Likewise it would be counted in the sentence "Blessing the sick is a common practice." Nor were they included when they were used to form the continuous tense, such as in "He was riding his horse that day." Another example of one that could qualify is, "I saw mountains tumbling into pieces." This replaces "that were tumbling into pieces." Past participial phrases were not included.

376 Mormon Genesis

Figure 25. Distribution of Infinitive and Participial Phrases

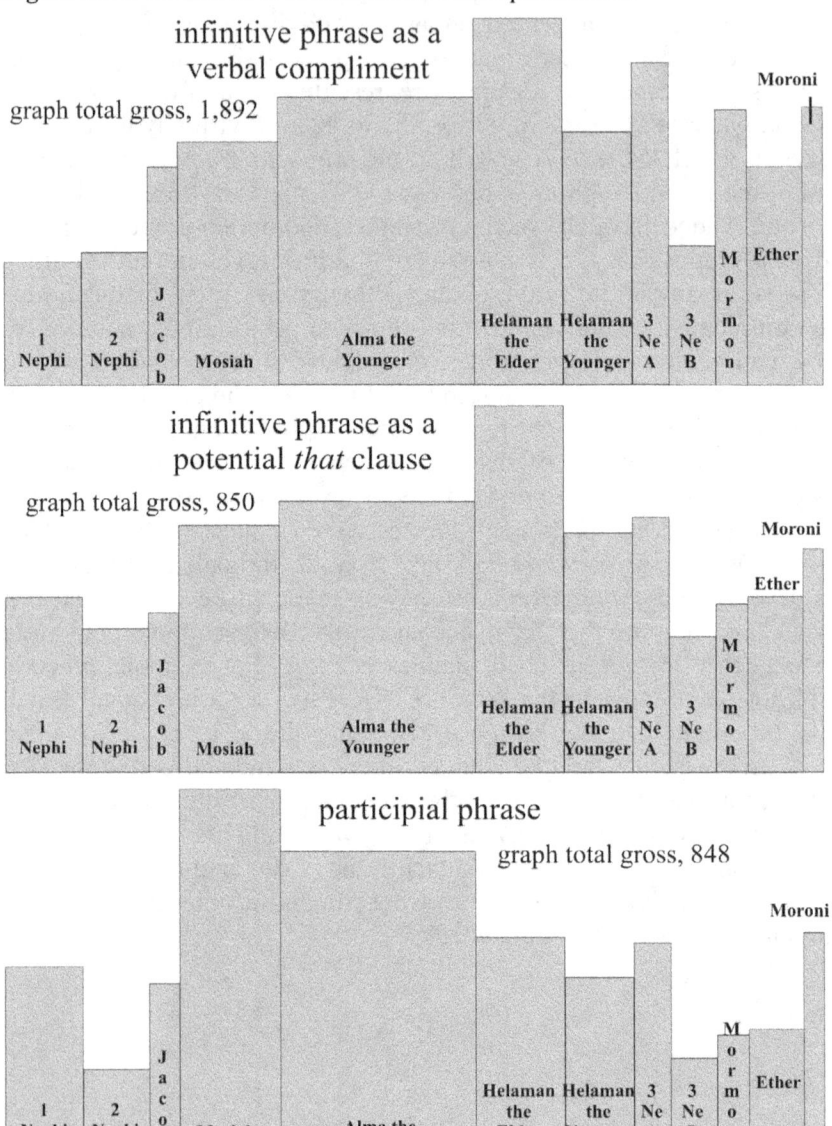

16. BOM Authorship: Sequential or Collaborative 377

Figure 26. Distribution of *Behold, Begin* (Plus Infinitive) & *for to*

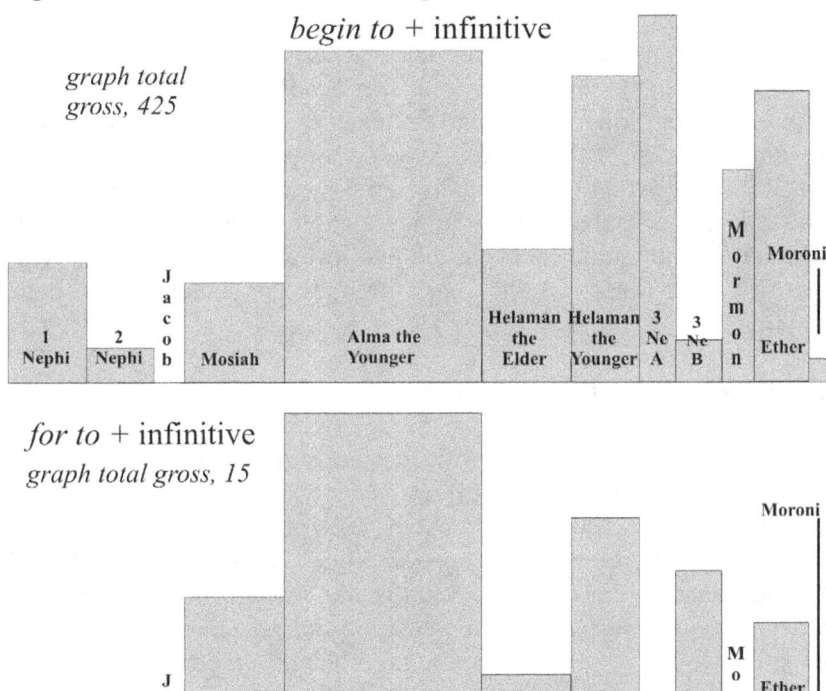

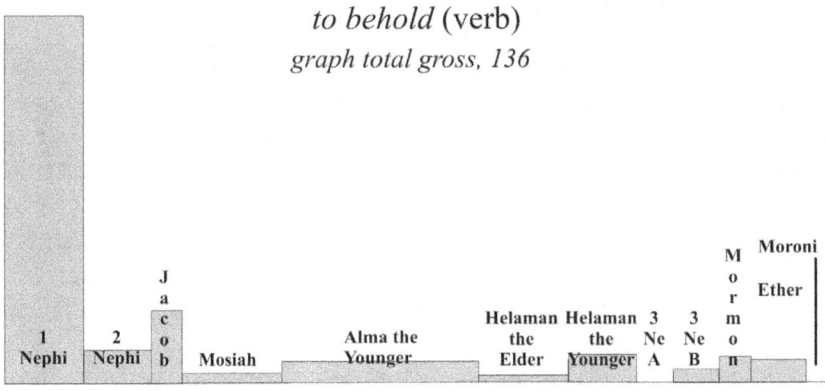

Once again we observe important differences between Nephi and Alma. Note figures 25 (infinitive phrases as a verbal complement, infinitive phrases as potential that clauses & participial phrases), and 26 (*begin to*, *for to* + infinitive, and *to behold*). The three phrase distributions are striking in that total frequencies range from 848 to 1892, these being the total of the graphs, but also to the best of my ability the whole BOM text. Alma is larger than Nephi by a factor ranging between 1.4 and 2.4. Of particular note is the fact that Helaman the Elder is quite a bit larger than any other book in the two infinitive distributions. What makes this important is the high frequencies making up these distributions.

Note: Verbs in Transition

The verb "to want" is not used with the meaning "to desire." The verb "to like" expressing positive affect is not used. The verb "will" expressing desire is used rarely, as in 1 Nephi 18:10 ("we will not that…"). "I want you to…" is expressed either with the verb "to desire" or "I would that ye…" This is especially the case in Mosiah and Alma (Figure 21). These verbs were in transition during the period of BOM composition with respect to semantic content and/or usage. Their presence or absence in the BOM may reflect a preference for the older rather than "modern" usage.

Nephi-Mosiah Simultaneity?

When considering a scenario of two or more authors, Smith and Cowdery come to mind. So it is important to note that on three occasions, when Cowdery was copying ms 𝓟, he inadvertently wrote *whosoever*,[274] and then corrected it to *whoso*. Only one of these cases is present in the extant portion of MS 𝓞. It reads *whoso* (Ether 10:6). A second case must also have read *whoso* in MS 𝓞, since it occurs in the same verse. This is evidence that the natural usage in his idiolect was *whosoever*. It is also the preference found in Mosiah through Helaman the Younger. Of the two, Smith and Cowdery, the latter may be to some degree associated with that group. An opposite scenario seems to have obtained in the case of *for to* (meaning *to*, i.e. *in order to*). In ms 𝓟 there

---

[274] Skousen, *History of the Text of the* Book of Mormon. *Part Two,* 1248-49.

were 15 instances of *for to*, two in Mosiah, nine in Alma, two in Helaman, one in 3 Nephi and one in Ether. None occurs in the Nephi group. Joseph Smith marked nine for the deletion of *for* in ms P (*for* to), removed four for the 1837 printing, and missed two. Apparently this usage may not have been prominent in Smith's idiolect.[275]

It is virtually certain that Smith Jr. did the first draft of Nephi. First of all, in addition to the foregoing observation, he had already covered this ground in writing the Book of Lehi, so the basic outline would not have been new to him. Second, during all of his post-1830 life, he was determined to produce his inspired version of the Bible. This was an extension of the work he had already begun when producing the Isaiah inclusions for the Book of Nephi. In addition to this, we have the evidence in BC 3 (D&C 4:1, dated February 1829) and 1 Nephi 14:7:

> Now behold, a marvelous work is about to come forth among the children of men (BC)

> For the time cometh, saith the Lamb of God, that I will work a great and a marvelous work among the children of men (1 Nephi)

The similarity in wording cannot be coincidental: "a [great and] marvelous work," paired with "among the children of men." We are left only to wonder which came first. If it were Nephi, we would have to assume that at least 1 Nephi through chapter 14 was already drafted by the time of the visit of Smith's father and brother Samuel in February 1829. More probably, the revelation on the occasion of their visit came first, as a confirmation of the decision they had arrived at, to embark on a far grander project than the mission to the Lamanites mentioned in BC 2 (D&C 3:19-20).

Once the Smiths and Cowdery had charted the recast of the gold record into a gold bible, Cowdery could have gone straight to work at father Smith's direction on a draft of Alma in Manchester. Someone else could have been drafting Mosiah, possibly Hyrum, keeping the work on these two key books close to home, i.e. father Smith. Joe Jr. would not have been broadsided in February. As early as the visit of his parents to Harmony in the September previous, father and son could have reviewed possibilities and arrived at initial options for a new course. During the February visit, Samuel worked as his scribe, with their father present.

---

[275] Skousen, *History of the Text of the* Book of Mormon. *Part One*, 310-13.

After their departure, Emma provided scribal service, until some time in March, when he issued a revelation ordering him to stop (D&C 5:34). This was most probably a previous agreement that at a certain point it would be advisable to wait for Cowdery's arrival to see what he would bring from Manchester. When these two got to work on April 7, their first task was to review each other's work, each making proposals for the other's writing, making notes directly on their drafts and adding, deleting and substituting pages. This may have taken April and part of May, before beginning work on ms $\mathcal{O}$. Smith's sudden and irrepressible additions would make it impossible to determine before starting a new page in ms $\mathcal{O}$ how much of the draft might fit, and what to write on the page content line before the page was completed. So three separate authors may have drafted Nephi, Mosiah and Alma more or less simultaneously.

The discussion so far presented gives rise to the following fundamental observations:

    1. The fact that the extant portion of ms $\mathcal{O}$ is relatively free of substantive edits requires the conclusion that it was produced by Smith reading from drafts for Cowdery to write.

    2. The chapter number confusion at the beginning of 2 Nephi and especially Mosiah (throughout, but including Omni and Words of Mormon) shows that the drafts at least for these two books were so highly developed that they already had numbered chapters.

    3. The analysis of the distribution of Hilton's wordprint patterns, and also of some of the key grammatical building blocks of the English language, provides strong evidence that Nephi and Alma were not originally drafted by the same person. There is even some evidence for at least one other drafter, for Mosiah.

    4. The layout of the BOM narrative was made up of highly segmental divisions, enabling two or more books to be drafted at the same time.

    5. Evidence for more-or-less simultaneous, multiple authorship liberates the analysis of the *Book of Mormon* production process from the constraints of sequential composition.

Chapter 17

Project Completion: Smith's A Team & Their Milieu

The traditional claim asserts that a second account, from a different set of plates, covering the period of the lost Book of Lehi was needed because the enemies of the restoration would change the text of the stolen pages in an effort to show that Smith, claiming divine assistance, was unable to produce a replacement text in the same words. The Smiths were no fools. They knew very well that the ink-on-paper stolen pages could not be altered to mount any such attack. If Joe Jr. could have reproduced Lehi word for word as it had been, there could have been no problem. This was not an option. Yet, a replacement text was needed. What will be the rational for it? Resolving this issue took an undetermined amount of time. Days? Weeks? By the time Joe Jr. returned home from Manchester, or his parent's visit in September? Or during the first month or two after that, in deliberation between Cowdery and Smith Sr.? Probably it was after Smith's July 1828 revelation, since it contains no trace of this strategy. As clever as it was, I expect that the time to come up with the solution was relatively short. As options were considered, sharp minds were available to cut the Gordian knot expeditiously. After all, they had the gospels before them, four tellings of the same story in different words. It is as simple as that.

In the process, they could seize this opportunity to set out on a more ambitious course. The solution chosen was to produce a very different book, as a group project, and in the form of a new bible rather than a history. Perhaps in late 1828, and no later than the following February, drafts may have already been undertaken for the Nephi replacement text, as well as Alma and possibly Mosiah. In his son's absence, father Smith mobilized new talent to supplement the considerable talents of Joseph Smith Jr. Just as the idea of gold plates as treasure to be translated existed in a culture predisposed to believe in treasure and seer stone scryers, this new project would also take place in a culture almost made to order.

Predispositions in Early 19th-Century New England

A study by a former professor at Brigham Young University, D. Michael Quinn,[276] presents an exhaustive and well-documented analysis of these predispositions. They include a culture in which many claimed to have received visions of angels or God and Jesus Christ. Many also believed in witchcraft. As we saw in Chapter 1, a belief was alive and well among many that the Indians were of Hebrew origin and were to be gathered to the fold of the Lord in the latter days.

Of note is the conversion experience of David Brainerd, active in the Second Great Awakening, and also considered by some to be an apostle to the Indians. His account was published in twenty-five editions from 1745 to 1835: "My soul rejoiced with joy unspeakable to see such a God, such a glorious divine Being."[277] Elias Smith recounted a vision he had in the woods, published in New Hampshire in 1816: "While in this situation, a light appeared to shine from heaven. ... My mind seemed to rise in that light to the throne of God and the Lamb."[278] The *Wayne Sentinel* of Palmyra (22 October 1823) published an article titled "Remarkable VISION and REVELATION, as seen and received by Asa Wild of Amsterdam [NY]." Wild said, "I dreamed Christ descended from the firmament, in a glare of brightness exceeding ten fold the brilliancy of the meridian Sun, and that he came to me, saying: 'I commission you to go and tell mankind that I am come; and bid every man to shout victory.'" From January to March of 1825, Wild, a Universalist minister, preached in Palmyra. Joseph Smith Sr. was at one time attending Universalist meetings. In the 1790's, a Billy Hibbard in Norway, New York, claimed a vision, saying, "as I looked up I saw heaven open, and Jesus at the right hand of God, and the Heavenly hosts surrounding the throne, adoring the Father and Son in the most sublime strains."[279] Benjamin Abbott published a narrative that went through thirteen printings, including New York editions in 1805 and 1813, in which he remembered "and at that instant I awoke , and saw, by faith, the Lord Jesus Christ standing by me, with his arms extended wide, saying to me,

---

[276] Quinn, *Early Mormonism and the Magic World View*.
[277] Quinn, *ibid*, 14.
[278] Quinn, *ibid*, 14.
[279] B[illy] Hibbard, *Memoirs* ... (New York: 1825), in Quinn, *ibid*, 15.

'I died for you.'"[280] In 1815, Norris Stearns published a vision in which he saw "a small gleam of light in the room, above the brightness of the sun," and two personages; "One was God, my Maker, almost in bodily shape like a man. His face was, as it were a flame of fire … Below him stood Jesus Christ my redeemer, in perfect shape like a man—His face was not ablaze, but had the countenance of fire, being bright and shining."[281] These are just examples, just experiences that managed to get into print. The many editions of these publications indicate the great interest at the time. Even without reading any of them, it is certain that faith-building mentions were made of visionary experiences by the preachers of this religious awakening.

The Smiths had been exposed to the idea that the Indians were of Israelite origin. H. Michael Marquardt notes, "After they moved to their Manchester farm, the Smith family received the *Wayne Sentinel*." On one occasion, Joseph Sr. placed an advertisement in this paper.[282] The newspaper ran a series by Mordecai M. Noah on the Hebrew origins of the Indians. He wrote, "If the tribes could be brought together, could be made sensible of their origin, could be civilized, and restored to their long lost brethren, what joy to our people, what glory to our God, how clearly have the prophecies been fulfilled, how certain our dispersion, how miraculous our preservation, how providential our deliverance."[283]

Perspective: Pseudepigrapha and Other Deceptions

Pseudepigrapha are works composed by one person, but ascribed by the author to another. This is usually done because the author absolutely knows that he has some important knowledge that needs to be taught to those who are able to understand it, but also knows that if issued to the world under his own name, it would not be accepted or read, and even in some cases, the author may fear retribution. There are over forty works of Old Testament Pseudepigrapha. There are also a number of works of

---

[280] Benjamin Abbott, *The experience and gospel labours of the Rev. Benjamin Abbott: to which is annexed a narrative of his life and death, by John Ffirth*, (Philadelphia: pr. by Solomon 1801, W. Conrad, for Ezekiel Cooper, 1801). Benjamin Abbott was an itinerant minister of the Methodist Episcopal Church in New Jersey, 1732-1796. For the quote here, v. Quinn, *ibid*, 15.
[281] Quinn, *ibid*, 15.
[282] Marquardt, *Rise of Mormonism*, 22-23.
[283] *Wayne Sentinel*, 11 October, 1825.

New Testament Pseudepigrapha, such as the *Gospel according to Mary* and the *Gospel according to Judas*. A late work, the *Gospel according to Barnabas*, apparently written by a convert to Islam in Italy, was written to prefigure the coming of Muhammad. Presumably, the author labored to bring Catholics into the true faith of Islam. Some pseudepigrapha made it into the Bible. Most scholars divide Isaiah into two, and even three parts (1st, 2nd & 3rd Isaiah), only the first being accepted as mostly the work of Isaiah himself. Many scholars accept that several of the epistles of Paul were not written by the man himself. The four canonical gospels do not fall into this category, for although they were not written by Matthew, Mark, Luke and John, they do not claim to have been, the titles saying the Gospel *according to* Matthew, etc., the probable author being a student of the apostle. There are also pseudepigrapha posing as classical, nonreligious works.

Pseudepigrapha may be written to influence the theology of an established religion, but they are not generally written for personal gain (no large print runs or best sellers back then, and the author must remain unknown), or to establish a new religion. In this sense, the Smith pseudepigrapha are unusually ambitious.

Some more recent pseudepigrapha, and similar impostures, have been exposed and studied. One such work is a presumed epic by Ossian, a Gaelic bard contrived by Scott James Macpherson in the 1770's, a legend with Irish heroes that Macpherson said were part of Scottish heritage, angering the Irish. He even developed a sufficiently credible old Gaelic text that many experts were fooled for years, and even today there are a few die-hards who adhere to this Gaelic Homer.

A non-textual work is the infamous Piltdown man. It was fabricated from a medieval human skull, a 500-year-old lower jaw of a Sarawak orangutan and fossilized chimpanzee teeth. The identity of the author of this hoax has not been identified, although there are some interesting candidates. It is thought that it was done by someone who wanted to provide the missing link for the evidence for human evolution. He was a bit too impatient. Little did he know that not just one, but a whole series of fossil links would be discovered legitimately.

A fascinating literary example is the works of the presumed Patience Worth, allegedly a spirit contacted by Pearl Lenore Curran (1883–1937). This otherworldly symbiotic relationship produced several novels, poetry and prose that Pearl Curran claimed were delivered to her through channeling the spirit, Patience Worth. Literary critic William

Marion Reedy considered *The Sorry Tale* to be a new classic of world literature. The Joint Committee of Literary Arts of New York listed Patience Worth as one of the outstanding authors of 1918. That year's edition of *The Anthology of Magazine Verse and Year Book of American Poetry* honored her by printing the complete text of five of her poems, along with other leading poets of the day. Some used her example as evidence for life after death. Eventually the enthusiasm for her work abated, and she slid into oblivion. Curan's supporters typically exaggerated her humble origins as proof that she could not have done this work herself (as in the case of Jesus, Muhammad and Joseph Smith).

A work more closely paralleling that of the BOM authors is *Walam Olum* of Samuel Constantine Rafinesque. A fascinating polymath, born in the outskirts of Constantinople (Istanbul), and self-educated in Paris, he pursued a distinguished and productive career in US academia in the first half of the 19th century, identifying various species of the Americas, and surveying pre-Columbian earthworks of North America. He claimed that a medical doctor, Dr. Ward, had received an Indian document written on strips of birch bark. Rafinesque obtained the strips and claimed to translate them, rendering a single character into a whole phrase or sentence. He claimed to have lost the strips, but fortunately had made a complete transcription of the original texts. Made up of 183 verses, it is supposed to be the tribal chronicle of the Lenni Lenape (Delaware Indians), reporting their migration from Asia to Alaska, and then on down to the eastern United States. The work was taken very seriously by scholars of the 19th century. During the 20th century it has been critically analyzed and the overwhelming consensus now rejects it, although it remains unclear whether the otherwise distinguished Rafinesque created a hoax, or was himself the victim of a fraud, or, perhaps, sincerely fabricated a text and translation to evidence what he was so sure must really have happened.[284]

---

[284] *Walam Olum, or Red Score. The Migration Legend of the Lenni Lenape or Delaware Indians*, including a transcription and ostensible translation of *Walam Olum* by C. (Constantine) S. (Samuel) Rafinesque, with studies by various authors, (Indianapolis: Indiana Historical Society, 1954).

The Necromancer's Magic Book and the Rodsman's Hazel

During much of the 1820's, an able and very active necromancer, Luman Walters (c. 1788-1860), who apparently had lived a bit in Europe, plied his trade in the region of Palmyra and Manchester. He had an itinerant lifestyle, going about with all of "the trappings of a medieval magician— 'magic stone,' 'stuffed toad,' 'rusty sword' used for drawing magic circles on the ground [i.e. where to dig], esoteric books written in Latin from which he read various incantations, and a flair for the dramatic."[285] In 1818 he escaped from jail in Hopkinton, New Hampshire, where he had been sentenced for breaking a hundred-year-old law against the occult practices of his occupation. Subsequently he moved to Pultneyville/Sodus, a town only about seventeen miles from Palmyra, which Vogel estimates to have been several hours on horseback. His activities are rather well recorded in local papers and by witnesses, including a colorful description by Brigham Young who had known him.[286] Lorenzo Saunders reported, albeit decades after the fact, that Willard Chase told him that he and Alvin Smith had dug for treasure under Walters' direction, once on the Chase property, and again on that of justice of the peace Abner Cole.[287] Some accounts indicate that Walters had a relationship with both Joseph Sr. and Jr.[288] Additionally, Vogel suggests that it was after he left the area that Joseph Smith Jr. undertook to fill the necromantic void left in his wake,[289] a view also expressed in an 1830 newspaper.[290]

Apart from treasure hunting, there are some parallels between his practices and the early history of Joseph Smith. Walters' use of a magic book could have suggested finding treasure in the form of a book. The use of a sword to mark off a magic circle has a parallel in the relic of the sword of Laban. The role of necromancy, charming a custodian spirit, which was part of Walters' routine, may have led to the idea that a spirit guarded the gold plates, and that the custodian spirit of an ancient American would appear to guide the one chosen to find them. Even early

---

[285] Vogel, *Joseph Smith, The Making of a Prophet* (Salt Lake City: Signature Books, 2004), 37 & 583, note 14.
[286] Quinn, *Early Mormonism and the Magic World View*, 120. See 119-32.
[287] Vogel, *Joseph Smith*, 37.
[288] Quinn, *Early Mormonism and the Magic World View*, 118.
[289] Vogel, *Joseph Smith*, 38.
[290] Quinn, *Early Mormonism and the Magic World View*, 118.

17. Project Completion: Smith's A Team & Their Milieu 387

Mormons sometimes referred to the plates as a treasure.[291] Altogether, these ideas were part of the general milieu of the Smiths, Cowdery and the Whitmers.

In the same timeframe that this necromancer was active in the Smiths' neighborhood, a prominent rodsman, Justus Winchell, kept his hazel divining rod in good practice. One can be forgiven for thinking of a magic wand in this connection, since in one common rodsman role he would have been known as a water witch. Martin Quinn has investigated in detail his connections and possible mentor relationship with both Joseph Smith Sr. and William Cowdery.[292] Joseph Smith's use of a seer stone was never hidden, so this practice has generally not been a problem for LDS scholars, even in extension to others involved in the BOM project. The use of a divining rod is altogether another matter. Ground zero for this issue is none other than Smith Jr. and Cowdery. In a revelation in the *Book of Commandments*, the Lord says to Oliver Cowdery, "for you have another gift, which is the gift of working with the rod: behold, it has told you things: behold, there is no other power save God, that can cause this rod of nature, to work in your hands..." (BC 7). God's words were revised for the D&C, so that the gift became "the gift of Aaron," with other rewording to eliminate any reference to Cowdery's use of the rod, and especially any notion that it had divine approval. Since Smith's original revelation shows approval, then he too must have approved of the practice initially, even if he was not himself a rodsman. Evidence indicates that both Joseph Jr. and Oliver got their background in the occult from their father, with some influence from Justus Winchell.[293] In addition to seer stones and hazel rods (at least in the case of Oliver, Joseph Smith Sr. and William Cowdery), other paraphernalia of the Smiths in the 1820's included lamens (magic parchments), an engraved silver magic talisman and a family dagger "inscribed with the astrological symbol of Mars, the magic 'sigil' (or 'seal') for the 'intelligence' of Mars" and a name of the OT deity in Hebrew letters: *Adonay*."[294] The dagger was used like Winchell's sword to draw magic circles in treasure hunting. Note that the hazel divining rod was used to get information, as well as for treasure hunting.

---

[291] Vogel, *Joseph Smith*, 139, 160-64 & 168.
[292] Quinn, *Early Mormonism and the Magic World View*, 119-133.
[293] *Ibid*, 121-32.
[294] *Ibid*, 66-7, 102-05.

The Heritage and Family of Joseph Smith

The early nineteenth-century religious scene was not monolithic. There were many who opposed practices related to magic or the occult, among the clergy of the more established religions, and in various social circles. Even so, the Smiths and Cowderys were not highly unusual in their milieu. The negative image of the Smiths portrayed in Howe's *Mormonism Unvailed* is undeserved. They were hardworking people descended from rather recent prosperous progenitors active in civic affairs, but who had fallen on hard times. This can be seen in the paternal lines of both Joseph Smith Sr. and Lucy Mack (Smith).

Table 31. The Paternal Line of Joseph Smith Jr.

162?	Robert Smith was born in England (possibly Kirton, Lincolnshire).
1638	He came to Massachusetts at about age 12.
1656	He married the daughter of Thomas French, & later bought 280 acres in Rowley (aka Boxford, MA).
1666	Samuel Smith was born, son of Robert Smith (Rowley, Essex, MA). He came to hold public office, and is listed with the title of "Gentleman."
1673	Active in civic affairs, he signed a petition to the General Court.
1693	He died leaving an estate valued at 189 pounds.
1707	He married Rebecca Curtis.
1714	Samuel Jr. was born in Topsfield, MA, son of Samuel Smith. He was active in public affairs, served six terms in the legislature, and twelve terms as selectman.
1744	Asael (Asahel; the grandfather of Joseph Smith Jr.) was born in Topsfield, Essex, MA.
1768	Jesse Smith was born in Topsfield, Essex, MA.
1771	July 12, 1771, Joseph Smith Sr. was born.
1772	March 8, 1772, Jesse, Priscilla and Joseph were baptized in the Topsfield Congregational Church.
1773	Asael was chairman of the Tea Committee at Topsfield, which sustained the action of the Boston Tea Party.
1774	He was elected to the Ipswich Convention and the First Provincial Congress in Massachusetts.
1775	Captain Asael Smith, marched on the Alarm, April 19.
1776	He enlisted in Colonel Joshua Wingate's Regiment for service in the Revolutionary War.
1779	1779-1786, he served as town clerk of Derryfield (Manchester, NH). His son Silas Smith was born.
1781	John Smith was born.

(Table 31 continued)

1786	Asael was listed as a cooper.
1791	Asael sold his lands to settle his father's debts incurred partly due to neglect of private affairs and partly due to economic crisis associated with the Revolutionary War. He rented a dairy farm.
1791	He acquired land in Tunbridge, VT.
1792	Jesse married Hannah Peabody in Middleton, Essex, MA.
1793	Asael began to serve frequently as a selectman of Tunbridge, VT.
1797	He moderated a meeting to establish one of the early Universalist Societies in Vermont. (submitted in Tunbridge, VT)
18??	Sometime between 1811 & 1820 Asael moved to Stockholm, NY.
1829	Jesse Smith was residing in Stockholm, St. Lawrence, NY.
1830	Asael died in Stockholm, St. Lawrence, NY.

Smith's maternal forebears had suffered a gradual decline in fortune. Still, we note that his grandmother Lydia taught school. His father learned to read and write. All were hardworking. Even Asael, Joseph Smith's grandfather, was very active throughout his life.

Table 32. The Maternal Line of Joseph Smith Jr.

1669	John Mack came to Massachusetts and settled in Salisbury. He was born in Inverness, Scotland, descended from a line of clergymen.
1697	Ebenezer Mack was born. He inherited his father's large property in Lyme, Connecticut. He married Hannah Huntley, a teacher for thirty years. He suffered financial misfortunes.
1732	Solomon Mack was born in Lyme, Connecticut. Due to his father's financial problems, he was indentured.
1755	Enlisted in the French and Indian War, he fought in the battle of Halfway Brook.
1756	Solomon bought a farm in Connecticut and added to it in 1758.
1759	Solomon married Lydia Gates, schoolteacher and member of the Congregational Church. She taught him to read and write along with their children, but he resisted her religious instruction.
1761	He and Lydia acquire 100 acres in a wilderness at Marlow, New Hampshire.
1767	He was elected deer reeve (game warden).
1775	Lucy Mack, born in Gilsum, Cheshire, NH.
1796	Solomon's daughter Lucy married Joseph Smith Sr.
1810	At age 77 & seriously ill, he became religious.
1820	Solomon died nearly 88 years old.
1856	Lucy Mack Smith, died 14 May in Nauvoo, Il.

Joseph Smith Sr.'s children had fewer opportunities for education as the family fortunes declined. Hyrum was the best off in this regard, being sent to Moor's Academy, which had been moved to Hanover, and re-established as Dartmouth College. Even so, current research indicates that Joe Jr.'s education, as irregular as it may have been, was better than formerly characterized.[295]

Table 33. The Birth Family of Joseph Smith Jr.

1771	Joseph Smith Sr. was born in Topsfield, MA.
1775	Lucy Mack (Smith) was born in Gilsum, NH.
1779	Apparently residing in Derryfield (Manchester), NH, since his father served as town clerk of Derryfield during this period.
1796	Joseph Sr. and Lucy married in Tunbridge, VT.
1797	He, along with his father Asael Smith and brother Jesse Smith, joined with others to state that they had formed a society and "wish to be known by the Name or forme of universalists." (Tunbridge, VT)
1797	An infant was born to Lucy and Joseph Sr., but did not survive.
1798	Alvin was born, first child of Joseph & Lucy. (Tunbridge, VT)
1800	Hyrum was born, their second child. (Tunbridge, VT)
1803	Sophronia was born (Tunbridge, VT). About this time Lucy attended church at several denominations, including the Methodists. Her husband attended at her request, seriously angering his father Asael, who insisted that he read the *Age of Reason* by Thomas Paine.
1805	Joseph Smith Jr. was born, 23 December, in Sharon, VT. The Smiths moved back to Tunbridge, Vermont, having lived previously in Tunbridge, Royalton and Sharon, where Joseph Sr. farmed summers and taught school winters.
1808	Samuel was born in Tunbridge. Soon after the Smiths moved to Royalton, Vermont. There, Joseph Sr. went to school on Dewey Hill and was taught by Deacon Jonathan Rinney
1810	Ephraim was born, but died 11 days after his birth. (Royalton, VT)
1811	William was born in Royalton, VT. The family moved to Lebanon, New Hampshire. Hyrum was sent to Moor's Academy in Hanover, and the others to a common school nearby. Joseph Smith Sr. had what Lucy called his first vision.
1812	Catherine was born. (Lebanon, NH)
1813	In the winter of 1812-13 the children were afflicted with typhoid fever. All survived, but Joseph Jr. suffered an abscess in his shoulder and pain in his leg. Hyrum cared for him, and braced his afflicted leg,

---

[295] William Davis, "Reassessing Joseph Smith Jr.'s Formal Education," *Dialogue: A Journal of Mormon Thought* 49, no. 4 (Winter 2016):1-58.

(Table 33 continued)

	one of the events in a lifelong devotion to his younger brother. Eventually, an operation was performed to remove afflicted parts of the bone without anesthesia. Joseph was on crutches for about three years, and had a slight limp for life.
1814	Having become essentially penniless, the Smiths moved to Norwich, Vermont, farming perhaps as squatters. Due to a series of cold winters, their crops failed.
1816	Don Carlos was born in Norwich, VT. The Smith family moved to Palmyra in northwest New York.
1820	Joseph Smith Sr. had his seventh and last vision in 1819 or 1820, according to his wife.
1821	Lucy was born in Palmyra, NY.
1823	Alvin Smith died of mercury poisoning from a calomel treatment for bilious colic.
1824?	1824-25: The possible time when Lucy, Hyrum, Samuel and Sophronia joined the Presbyterian Church. Joseph Sr. & Jr. did not.
1825	November 1, Joseph Smith Sr. & Jr. sign the "Articles of Agreement" with Josiah Stowell and others to share in any gold or silver mine found "at a certain place in Pennsylvania near a Wm. Hale's."
1826	Hyrum married Jerusha Barden.
1828	Since about September of this year, Lucy, Hyrum and Samuel stopped attending the Presbyterian Church. Concerned, on March 3, 1830, a Presbyterian committee was assigned to visit them and report.
1831	Samuel went on a mission to Kirtland, Ohio. This was followed by proselytism in Missouri, Indiana, Connecticut, Massachusetts, Rhode Island, Maine and New York.
1834	Samuel married Mary Bailey. He was appointed as one of 12 members of the High Council of the Church.

Joseph Smith Sr. (1771-1840)

Born in Topsfield, Massachusetts, he moved with his parents to Tunbridge, Vermont, where he met his wife, Lucy Mack Smith. They were married there in 1796. After a failed business venture, and being forced to sell their farm and become tenant farmers, they moved from Norwich (in the Tunbridge area) to Palmyra in upstate New York (Joseph Smith Sr. in late 1816, and his family in early 1817). Apart from farming and business, he was also a cooper like his father, a schoolteacher, a seer stone scryer and rodsman. Rural coopers often made their own hoops. Unlike his wife, Lucy, who was searching for a church for her family, he was not comfortable with organized religion. The principal exception to this was his interest in Universalism. Nonetheless, he claimed seven visions, five of which were quoted by his wife in some detail, showing the degree to which his visions were taken seriously, at least at home. In Royalton, Vermont, he went to school on Dewey Hill and was taught by Deacon Jonathan Rinney.

It is clear that Joseph Smith Jr. was influenced by his father in these regards. One important question is the extent to which the father played a leading role in his son's efforts to produce a new scripture and church. The *Book of Mormon* begins with the divine command to emigrate from Jerusalem, coming to the family patriarch, Lehi, although his son Nephi is by far the chief protagonist. Lehi descends from Joseph; Smith Sr. and Jr. are both named Joseph. How autobiographical is this?[296]

Another important issue concerns the family relations between William Cowdery, father of Oliver Cowdery, and Joseph Smith Sr. His son and Oliver Cowdery were third cousins. The two families lived for over a decade not much more than fifty miles apart. There are reports that for a time Joseph Smith Sr. resided in Poultney, Vermont, and that both he and William Cowdery were involved in the rodsmen religious movement of Nathaniel Wood in Middletown. This came to a head in an infamous incident called the Wood Scrape. Whether they, either one or both, were involved in this cannot be proved, and the assertion has been challenged.[297] The fact that William's son, Oliver, was a rodsman raises the possibility that his father was as well. Family relations between the Smiths and Cowderys are also rendered probable by the fact that in the late 1820's, Hyrum got Oliver Cowdery appointed as a teacher, and the latter took up residence in the home of Joseph Sr. This does not happen casually.[298]

His son, Hyrum, was a member of the Masonic Lodge in Palmyra, and was listed as a member of the Mount Moriah Masonic Lodge No. 112 for the period June 1827 to June 1828. Joseph Smith Jr. later became a Freemason. About 1830, Joseph Smith Sr. with his son Don Carlos, visited Smith family relatives in Stockholm and Potsdam, St. Lawrence, NY, to announce the message of Mormonism. In 1833 he was ordained the first Church Patriarch, and in 1836 he and his brother John Smith

---

[296] For insight into this issue, see Dan Vogel, *Joseph Smith*, 2004), 698.
[297] Quinn, *Early Mormonism and the Magic World View*, 121 (see 121-30).
[298] Quinn, 34-39.

went on a mission for three months to the branches of the Eastern States.[299] John became Presiding Patriarch under Brigham Young.

Joseph Smith Jr. Begins His Mission

Joseph Smith's education was sporadic due to demands made on him to help support his birth family. His account is that he studied reading, writing and arithmetic. We know that he owned a book titled *First Lines in Arithmetic, For the Use of Young Scholars* and the *Sacred Geography or a Description of the Places Mentioned in the Old and New Testament* (1824) by Thomas T. Smiley. It is safe to assume that he had access to other books in the Smith household. Although he initially started off slowly, his progress improved greatly once his father began teaching his children at home.[300] William Davis has taken a new look at Joseph Jr.'s education, and concluded regarding his school attendance during his family's time in Royalton, VT, that, "prior to Joseph's departure from Royalton, he may well have obtained as much formal education as historians tend to attribute to his entire lifetime, if not more."[301]

After moving to West Lebanon, VT, Joseph Jr. suffered a serious illness requiring surgery to remove a large abscess on a leg. Although this clearly had an impact on his formal education, it was not without some possible positive consequence. Smith's mother wrote that his uncle Jesse Smith took him to convalesce for a bit at his home in Salem. This is not proven, but it seems unlikely that she would have written this if at least some trip to Salem had not happened.[302] Michael Marquardt points out that there is nothing in Jesse's ledger book to evidence such a visit.[303] William Davis, in his study of Joseph's education, writes,

> Joseph's trip to Salem, of whatever length and whenever it actually took place, would have offered its own form of practical education. Salem was a major port city of trade: merchant ships brought exotic cargo from all over the world, and its bustling shops were packed with a rich panoply of merchandise and patrons. Yet, such excitement would have been counterbalanced by a hostile British navy patrolling along the seacoast,

---

[299] *History of the Church*, 2:446.
[300] Marquardt, *Rise of Mormonism*, 21.
[301] Davis, "Reassessing Joseph Smith Jr.'s Formal Education," 17.
[302] Lucy Smith, in Anderson, *Lucy's Book*, 310.
[303] H. Michael Marquardt, personal communication.

seizing ships, impressing sailors, and threatening invasion.

Regarding this possible visit, see also Vogel and Hill.[304] Davis further suggests that in the last part of the family's time in West Lebanon, while recuperating on crutches from his illness he might have attended school, since he would not have been able to engage in heavy labor.[305] He argues that the lack of specific documentary evidence should not outweigh Lucy Smith's declared commitment to education. After the arrival of the Smith's in Palmyra, and then in Manchester, there is more evidence of at least some school attendance. Jacob E. Terry of East Palmyra was a classmate with Joseph. In the Parshall Terry family history, reviewing dates in her memory Jacob's sister wrote, "this would indicate that Joseph Smith attended school immediately after his arrival at Palmyra sometime during the winter of 1816–1817."[306] Marquardt adds to the picture, stating that "Smith, though almost twenty years old, enrolled in school in the Bainbridge, New York area while he was working for Josiah Stowell during the winter of 1825-26. While being examined before Justice Albert Neely on March 20, 1826, Smith testified that he had been 'going to school.'"[307]

Another source of education in the Smith home was the *Palmyra Register and Herald*, and later the *Wayne Sentinel*. In these sources the Smiths had available the article on the Hebrew origins of the Indians by Mordecai M. Noah, and the visions of Asa Wild, who claimed that the existing churches were in error, as well as coverage of other religious events in the area. The above evidence must be considered in the context of anti-Mormon efforts to demean Joseph Jr. as an illiterate country bumpkin, and a concerted Smith-Cowdery effort to control the early history of the Church, which also involved depicting the founding prophet as being decidedly unable to produce the *Book of Mormon*.

Although we cannot take the sequencing as proven, Lucy Mack Smith, Joseph's mother, wrote that after her son had started talking about the visit of an angel, but before he claimed to have gotten the gold plates, he was a great story teller:

---

[304] Vogel, *Joseph Smith*, 18. Donna Hill, *Joseph Smith, the First Mormon* (Salt Lake City: Signature Books, 1999 [1977]), 36.
[305] *Ibid*, 17-22.
[306] Davis, "Reassessing Joseph Smith Jr.'s Formal Education," 24.
[307] *Ibid*, 22.

During our evening conversations, Joseph would occasionally give us some of the most amusing recitals that could be imagined. He would describe the ancient inhabitants of this continent, their dress, mode of travelling, and the animals upon which they rode; their cities, their buildings, with every particular; their mode of warfare; and also their religious worship. This he would do with as much ease, seemingly, as if he had spent his whole life with them.[308]

Smith attended Methodist training to be an exhorter (in Palmyra, and again in Harmony, Pennsylvania). Orsamus Turner, a Palmyra *Register* newspaper apprentice, reported, "after catching a spark of Methodism in the camp meeting, away down in the woods, on the Vienna road, he was a very passable exhorter in evening meetings."[309] The importance of this effort goes beyond the training received; becoming an exhorter was the first step to becoming a Methodist minister. At least the possibility of a career in religion was on the table. He also attended a debating club in Palmyra, where he made positive impressions.[310] We do not know if Joseph Smith's considerable ability at extemporaneous dictation was totally natural, or if it was at least partly acquired in these two training experiences. Itinerant preachers often used the extemporaneous style, which became highly prized in the second half of the nineteenth century, and was used on occasion even by the renowned Reverend C. H. Spurgeon, whose massive sermon collection is still studied today. Finally, like the rest of Joseph's family, he was able to make use of the family Bible, which he was apparently quite fond of studying.

As early as July 1828, he began receiving regular revelations worded in the first person, i.e., that of the Lord (D&C 5:1). After 1830, it was not uncommon for these to be received in the presence of his scribe, who wrote down the Lord's words issuing from Smith's mouth. Two of his scribes have left us a description of Smith's ability to perform extemporaneously (although considerable preparation may have gone into each session). Scribe William E. McLellin wrote:

---

[308] Lucy Smith, in Anderson, ed., *Lucy's Book*, 345.
[309] O[rsamus] Turner, *History of the Pioneer Settlement*, 214, 400; quoted here from Marquardt, *Rise of Mormonism*, 30.
[310] Marquardt, *Rise of Mormonism*, 31.

> I, as scribe, have written revelations from the mouth of both the Revelators, Joseph Smith and David Whitmer. And I have been present many times when others wrote for Joseph; therefore I speak as one having experience. The scribe seats himself at a desk or table, with pen, ink and paper. The subject of enquiry being understood, the Prophet and Revelator enquires of God. He spiritually sees, hears and feels, and then speaks as he is moved upon by the Holy Ghost, the 'thus saith the Lord,' sentence after sentence, and waits for his amanuenses to write and then read aloud each sentence. Thus they proceed until the revelator says Amen, at the close of what is then communicated.[311]

Parley P. Pratt gave virtually the same account, and said, "...I was present to witness the dictation of several communications of several pages each."[312] This said, let us bear in mind that Smith's dictation was done in small bits. He dictated, then waited (reflected) while his scribe finished writing, and then dictated again. These texts were later edited.

Smith received more education than has usually been thought, was fascinated from the start with the American Indians, capable of extemporaneously entertaining his family as a young man with detailed stories about them, capable of articulating extemporaneous revelations several pages in length, and articulate enough to impress as a Methodist exhorter, although at a neophyte level. In the mid-18th century, Jonathan Edwards became concerned regarding the activities of exhorters. On the issue of reversals in church progress, he assigned blame:

> far more to the unrestrained zeal of a considerable number of misguided men—some of them preachers of the gospel, and others lay exhorters—who, intending to take Mr. Whitefield as the model, travelled from place to place, preaching and exhorting wheresoever they could collect an audience...and whenever they judged a minister, or a majority of the church, destitute of piety—which they usually did, not on account of their false principles or their irreligious life, but for the want of an ardour and zeal equal to their own—advised, in one case, the whole church to withdraw from the minister...[313]

---

[311] William E. McLellin, ed., *The Ensign of Liberty* (1, August, 1849), 98.
[312] Parley P. Pratt, *Autobiography of Parley P. Pratt*, edited by his son, Parley P. Pratt (Salt Lake City: Deseret Book Company, 1934), 48. Edition quoted, 1994.
[313] Sereno E. Dwight, "Memoirs of Jonathan Edwards," in *Works of Jonathan Edwards*, I:lxxi.

England had similar problems. By 1746, the status of "exhorter" was formalized. The Minutes of the 1746 Methodist Conference contain the following resolution:

> 1. Let none exhort in any of our Societies, without a note of recommendation from the Assistant. 2. Let every exhorter see that this is renewed yearly. 3. Let every Assistant rigorously insist upon this.[314]

In New England this note came to be known as an exhorter's license.

> By 1778 the term exhorter appeared often without explanation. We can assume that the office of exhorter was a commonly known part of the Methodist working system by this time and no explanation was needed. At the Conference held at Kent County, Delaware, beginning April 28, 1779, a rule recorded in the Minutes states that "every exhorter and local preacher go by the directions of the assistants where, and only where, they shall appoint." On April 24, 1780, when the northern Conference met in Lovely Lane Chapel in Baltimore, Question 10 noted that every local preacher and exhorter should have a license, to be renewed quarterly, after examination, and that none should "presume to speak in public without taking a note."[315]

Smith had not gotten a license, and had not even become a Methodist. Any action on his part in the role of exhorter would have drawn fire form the clergy. Rather than knuckle under to Methodist rules and theology, he went his own way, determined to preach on his own terms. Later in his life, the view of Smith's authority that he wished others to accept is expressed in one of his revelations: "…my [the Lord's] word…whether by my own voice, or by the voice of my servants, it is the same." (D&C 1:38) Even so, once received, Smith's sacred texts were not set in concrete. They were edited, not just for typos, but at times for substantive content. Smith could be somewhat cavalier regarding his relationship to God. In a letter seeking to ingratiate himself to General Smith, Major-General James Arlington Bennet wrote, "You know,

---

[314] *Minutes of the Methodist Conferences from the first held in London by the late Rev. John Wesley, A.M. in the Year 1744* (London: Methodist Conference Office, 1812), 1: 30.

[315] Rev. Robert A. Sisler, Newburg Charge, District Director on Lay Speaking "History of Lay Speaking" (http://www.angelfire.com/biz/SELLC/history.html, accessed 14/04/2017).

Mahomet had his '*right-hand man.*" Smith's reply did not mince words, saying, "I combat the errors of ages; I meet the violence of mobs; I cope with illegal proceedings from executive authority; I cut the Gordian knot of powers; and I solve mathematical problems of Universities: WITH TRUTH, *diamond truth, and God is my 'right-hand man.*'"[316] It is not always possible to know how seriously he took his own words. In a letter to Oliver Cowdery in October, 1829, he wrote, "two of our most formidable persacutors (*sic*) are now under censure and are cited to a triyal (*sic*) in the church for crimes which if true are worse than all the Gold Book business."[317]

Smith Sr. had his 7th vision in 1819 and shortly afterward Joseph Jr. became agitated regarding the then ongoing religious awakening.

Joseph Smith's First Vision

After his father had experienced seven vivid dreams or visions, and apparently either at about the same time or shortly after the seventh, Joseph Smith Jr. claimed to also have had a vision, in some ways similar to those mentioned above. We will never know the actual year this happened, or the specific content. The first full account is found in Smith's 1832 history, about a decade after the event, and at a time when the concept of an official history was emerging. There was a need to tell the story of his early life in terms more religious than his reputation as a scryer, and foreshadowing the mission that would become his destiny. He claimed that he was sixteen at the time.[318] Giving this earliest account priority, and since he was born on 23 December 1805, 1821 is possible, but 1822 more probable. The text follows:

> while in ‹the› attitude of calling upon the Lord ‹in the 16th year of my age› a pillar of ~~fire~~ light above the brightness of sun at noon day come down from above and rested upon me and I was filled with the spirit of god and the ‹Lord› opened the heavens upon me and I saw the Lord and he spake

---

[316] Joseph Smith, letter to James Arlington Bennet dated 13 November 1843, *History of the Church*, 6:78. It was also published in Henry Mayhew & Charles MacKay, *The Mormons: or Latter-day Saints* (London: Office of the National Illustrated Library, 1851), 119.

[317] Joseph Smith, letter to Oliver Cowdery dated 22 October 1829, in Vogel, *Early Mormon Documents*, II:7.

[318] Joseph Smith, "History, 1832," in Vogel, *Early Mormon Documents*, I:28.

unto me saying Joseph ‹my son› thy sins are forgiven thee. go thy way walk in my statutes and keep my commandments behold I am the Lord of glory I was crucifyed (sic) for the world that all those who believe on my name may have Eternal life behold the world lieth in sin ~~and~~ at this time and none doeth good no not one they have turned aside from the gospel and keep not ‹my› commandments they draw near to me with their lips while their hearts are far from me and my anger is kindling against the inhabitants of the earth to visit them according to th[e]ir ungodliness ...[319]

In Joseph Smith's *History of the Church*, he wrote in 1838-39:

Just at this moment of great alarm I saw a pillar ‹of› light exactly over my head above the brightness of the sun, which descended ~~gracefully~~ gradually until it fell upon me. It no sooner appeared than I found myself delivered from the enemy which held me bound. When the light rested upon me I saw two personages (whose brightness and glory defy all description) standing above me in the air. One of ‹them› spake unto me calling me by name and said "This is my beloved son. Hear him."... No sooner therefore did I get possession of myself as to be able to speak, than I asked the personages who stood above me in the light, which of all the sects was right... I was answered that I must join none of them, for they were all wrong, and the Personage who addressed me said that all their creeds were an abomination in his sight, that those professors were all corrupt, that "they draw near to me with their lips but their hearts are far from me, They teach for doctrines the commandments of men, having a form of Godliness but they deny the power thereof."[320] [Cf. Isaiah 29:13; Matthew 15:8; and 2 Nephi 27:25.]

This is the third of Smith's accounts, and currently the official one.[321] All accounts were written a decade or more after the presumed event. Already we see an evolution in the story. The first account only mentions Jesus Christ, while the official version features God the Father

---

[319] Dean C. Jessee, *The Personal Writings of Joseph Smith*, 6.

[320] Jessee, *Personal Writings of Joseph Smith*, 199-200. Jessee, *Papers of Joseph Smith*, I:265-66 & 272-73. Milton V. Backman, Jr., *Joseph Smith's First Vision; Confirming Evidences and Contemporary Accounts, Second Edition, Revised and Enlarged* (Salt Lake City: Bookcraft, 1980), 160-63. The text was possibly dictated in 1838, but the ms reporting it was begun in 1839.

[321] The 1838-39 account; for all three, and a study of them, see Backman, Jr., *Joseph Smith's First Vision*; & Dean C. Jessee, *The Early Accounts of Joseph Smith's First Vision* (Sandy, UT: Mormon Miscellaneous [reprint series],1984).

and God the Son as two anthropomorphic deities, presumably reflecting the move from a period of monotheism toward the emergence of LDS polytheist Christianity. It is God the Father who addresses Smith.

In the account of 1832 he states, "by searching the scriptures I found that mand ‹mankind› did not come unto the Lord but that they had apostatised [sic]." The message he reports that he received from Christ does not mention the churches of the day. It was more far-reaching and severe, condemning all mankind: "the world lieth in sin ~~and~~ at this time and none doeth good no not one they have turned aside from the gospel…" Christ's "anger is kindling against the inhabitants of the earth." The absence of any order to not join any of the churches is consistent with Smith's entering into training as a Methodist exhorter, and even practicing as one on a neophyte level. Furthermore, several members of his family to whom he was close and over whom his religious persona held a certain sway, his mother, brothers Hyrum and Samuel and sister Sophronia continued to be practicing Presbyterians up to September of 1828. By contrast, this is clearly inconsistent with the harsh language directed at the churches in the third dated version of his First Vision, and the admonition not to join any of them. It militates against a date for this portion of his experience prior to 1828. The message of apostasy was first ramped up in the *Book of Mormon* where an angel shows Nephi the "great and abominable church" and declares that there are but two churches, the church of God and the church of the devil (1 Nephi 14:9-10). This message is closer to that of the 1838-39 account of the First Vision.

A strong disdain for the churches of his day was alive and well in the region, a view shared by Joseph Sr. This disdain, passed on to his son, was probably the first manifestation of this declaration. It was first made a revealed doctrine in the *Book of Mormon*, with God condemning all of the churches of his day, and ratcheted up considerably in the First Vision account of 1832, condemning all mankind. In the 1838-39 account it was walked back again to just a condemnation of the churches.

Just as a gold history became a gold bible, and a guardian messenger eventually became the angel Moroni, so too a vision of Christ became a vision of God the Father and God the Son in anthropomorphic form in the 1838-39 vision, consistent with the emergence of LDS Christian polytheism. Similarly, Smith's aversion towards these churches acquired from his father first became expressed in terms of the "great and abominable church" in the *Book of Mormon* (1 Nephi 14:9), then a condemnation of all mankind in the 1832 recital of the First Vision, and then the declaration in the 1838-39 version just condemning the churches, declaring that "all their creeds were an abomination in his sight," coupled with a command to not join any of them. All of this shows the fluidity of Joseph Smith's assertions over time.[322]

Hyrum Smith: Elder Brother, Confidant & Collaborator

Hyrum was five years older than Joseph. After the death of his eldest brother Alvin, Hyrum assumed an important place in the life of his younger brother. He was sent to Moor's Academy (Moor's Indian Charity School), which had been established by Eleazar Wheelock in 1754 to educate Native Americans to become preachers of the gospel to their own people. In 1770 it was moved to Hanover, New Hampshire, where it was re-established as Dartmouth College. Hyrum's education there was possibly at the level of secondary education. There, he must have heard a great deal about missions to convert Native Americans, or, in those days, simply the Indians. He moved to Manchester, Ontario Co., New York in 1825 and was there when the entire Smith family was living in their log home after June 1829. He married Jerusha Barden on 2 November 1826 at Manchester. In 1827 he was initiated into Freemasonry (Mount Moriah Masonic Lodge No. 112).

Hyrum's role in the BOM project began early. According to his mother Lucy, early in 1828 he accompanied Martin Harris to Harmony to begin his work as Joseph's scribe, before Martin's mission to show characters said to be from the gold plates to learned scholars, including Charles Anthon.[323] In May of 1829, he visited Joseph and Oliver in Harmony ostensibly to check on how the translation was coming along.[324] During this visit he may already have informed them that David Whitmer would come. In a letter of 14/06/1829, Oliver Cowdery was already urging Hyrum, "Stir up the minds of our friends against the time we come unto you, that thus they may be willing to take upon them the name of Christ..."[325] On 17/06/1829 his uncle Jesse wrote him accusing

---

[322] For perspective on this transition, see Brant Gardner, The Gift and the Power (Sandy, UT: Greg Kofford Books, 2011).
[323] Lucy Smith, in Anderson, *Lucy's Book*, 402.
[324] Marquardt, *Rise of Mormonism*, 86.
[325] Oliver Cowdery, letter to Hyrum Smith dated 14 June 1829, in Vogel, *Early Mormon Documents*, II:403.

that, "Uncle Jesse did, and still does think the whole pretended discovery, not a very deep, but a very clear and foolish deception, a very great wickedness…"[326] After they completed their stay at the home of Peter Whitmer Sr. to finish up ms 𝒪, Oliver resided with Hyrum Smith, apparently with the rest of the Smith family, while he worked on ms 𝒫. He was one of the Eight Witnesses who claimed to have viewed, hefted and handled the gold plates. It was he who brought the first gathering of ms 𝒫 to the printer for publication, and he brought other gatherings along with Cowdery and Harris. He was thus to some degree a collaborator as early as work on the Book of Lehi, was urged to engage in preparatory proselytism while Cowdery was in Fayette, and worked in a facilitator role all the way through to the publication of the *Book of Mormon*. If Mosiah is the product of a third drafter, he is a probable candidate.

Joseph Smith Sr. Seizes the Moment

We will never fully know the role of father Smith in the early history of the BOM project, prior to the time when his son was collaborating with Martin Harris on a history translated from the gold plates. For his son, he was a role model as a visionary, and their relationship was close in the business of scrying for gold. The problem with using the seer stone or the rod to find gold is that one rarely found anything of much value. The virtue of finding the gold plates is that one can make the claim while being commanded to not show the find to detractors. Perhaps the father sat back and observed as his son's claims started to gain traction in their community. At some point, he may have begun to get a glimmer of how one could develop this emerging phenomenon into something much bigger than a history that might not even sell. Unfortunately, the transition from treasure hunting to gold plates to a gold bible is lost in a void of contemporary records, and a fog of official account obfuscation.

As a result of his actions resulting in the loss of the 116 pages, Joseph Jr. claimed to have lost his gift for a spell (D&C 3):

---

[326] Jesse Smith in a letter to Hyrum Smith dated 17 June 1829, in Vogel, *ibid*, I:552.

> 12. And when thou deliveredst up that which God had given thee sight and power to translate, thou deliveredst up that which was sacred into the hands of a wicked man,
> 13. Who has set at naught the counsels of God, and has broken the most sacred promises which were made before God, and has depended upon his own judgment and boasted in his own wisdom.
> 14. And this is the reason that thou hast lost thy privileges for a season—

It is clear from this that there was a cessation of work on the BOM text for an unknown period of time. In his 1832 history, Smith wrote:

> ... wherefore the plates was taken from me by the power of God and I was not able to obtain them for a season and it came to pass after much humility and affliction of soul I obtained them again when Lord appeared unto a young man by the name of Oliver Cowdry (*sic*) and showed unto him the plates in a vision[327]

We do not know when Cowdery had this vision, but most probably it would be in the fall of 1828. In his 1838-39 history, he claimed that in July of 1828 a heavenly messenger took "the plates and the Urim and Thummin (*sic*)" away, but gave them back after a few days.[328] After tarrying with his parents for a while, he repaired to Harmony, Pennsylvania, to work on his farm, out of necessity to support his family:

> I did not however go immediately to translating, but went to laboring with my hands upon a small farm which I had purchased of my wife's father, in order to provide for my family.[329]

This suspension of his gift decreed by his heavenly father may have actually been advice to suspend work for a while, advice from his biological father, whom he respected tremendously, to the point of making him the first patriarch of the Church, and the heir to what was to be claimed to be the highest priesthood, the Patriarchal Priesthood. His need to work his farm might reflect the strained relations with Harris and the very good possibility that for a while Martin was not forthcoming with money. His parents visited him in September of 1828 at which time they probably reviewed their options to replace the Book of Lehi.

---

[327] Joseph Smith, 1832 history, in *Papers of Joseph Smith*, I:10.
[328] *Ibid*, 1838-39 History, 1:287. Smith's comment regarding D&C 3.
[329] *Ibid*, 288.

When Joseph Smith arrived at the Smith home in Manchester in mid-summer of 1828, he must have been justifiably proud of his work thus far. The loss of the 116 pages clearly came as a blow. But this loss did not necessarily mean abandoning his overall concept of what his project should be about. It is reasonable to assume that a radically new approach would probably not have come from him. In Harmony he was largely isolated from those who would become major players. The eventual cast of characters reads almost like a reunion of seer stone scryers. Joseph Sr., his son Joseph Jr., Oliver Cowdery, David Whitmer, Jacob Whitmer and Hiram Page were all scryers.[330] Since the next major steps took place in the Manchester-Palmyra area, it must have been father Smith who stepped up to the challenge. His eldest son, Hyrum, was a trustee of the local school, and so responsible for hiring teachers. Lyman Cowdery applied, but after being accepted, he found he had to pursue some other option, and recommended his brother Oliver, who was hired. For a while, he boarded in the Smith home in Manchester. During that period, in the fall of 1828, Joe Sr. was able to recruit Oliver to the project. This was done in the absence of his son, who was a hundred miles to the south.

Oliver Cowdery had been a friend of David Whitmer. It makes sense that he would have played a role, with Smith Sr., in recruiting him, with his father, Peter Whitmer Sr. not far behind. In just months, Whitmer Sr.'s sons, Jacob, Peter Jr. and John, as well as David's brother-in-law, Hiram Page, all followed suit. Arrangements were made for David Whitmer to go to Harmony and get Joseph Jr. and Oliver to the home of Peter Whitmer Sr. in upstate New York to complete the *Book of Mormon* (most probably, its draft). This too must have been at father Smith's initiative. Smith Jr. had been in Harmony nine months, and Cowdery since April 5. Harmony-Manchester communications being what they were, certainly Smith Jr. did not recruit the Whitmers, and neither one could have arranged for the move to the Whitmer home. Joseph reported that the Whitmer family was very helpful from the moment they arrived.[331] Moreover, it was during his father's visit in February 1829 that his son issued a revelation for him, announcing that "a marvelous work is about to come forth." This may have been an

---

[330] Jessee, *Papers of Joseph Smith*, I: 322–23; D. Michael Quinn, *Early Mormonism and the Magic World View*, 239–40, 247–48.

[331] Joseph Smith, "History, 1839," in Vogel, *Early Mormon Documents*, I:80.

expression of his concurrence with a grander project for a new bible already explored in Manchester. Also at that time he may have been apprised of the addition of Cowdery and David Whitmer to the project. Clearly, he welcomed the addition of both. Starting with Oliver Cowdery, and then in collaboration with him, his father's recruits accounted for two of the three witnesses to the gold plates and five of the eight witnesses, essentially all in the absence of Joe Jr. The Whitmer addition is particularly noteworthy. They met Joseph Smith in early June and progressed to being witnesses of the plates, in less than a month!

Two of Joseph Sr.'s sons were especially close to Joseph Jr. and present in the Manchester-Palmyra area for participation in the project, Hyrum and Samuel. Their role was at times largely as facilitators. Samuel accompanied his father to visit Joseph in February of 1829. During this February visit he served as scribe for the first draft of the Nephi replacement text prior to Cowdery's arrival. Later, he accompanied Cowdery to Harmony. Hyrum accompanied Harris to Harmony to begin his scribal duties there, and visited Joseph and Oliver in May of 1829, ostensibly to check on how the translation was coming. Apart from brother William, in one capacity or another, the whole Smith family was involved in the project.

Enter Oliver Cowdery

Perhaps because Oliver Cowdery was deliberately kept in the background as scribe, his life was never the object of scrutiny to the extent that was the case of Joseph Smith, and so was never so well documented. Even though his paternal line goes back to illustrious origins, once in the New World his forebears became less so.

Table 34. Heritage and Family of Oliver Cowdery

1602	Deacon William Cowdery was born in Weymouth, England, descendant of the family of Lord Cowdery, of Cowdery Castle at Midhurst, England.
1630	Deacon William Cowdery came to America & settled first in Essex, then Reading, Massachusetts.
1630?	Nathaniel Sr. was sired by Deacon William Cowdery (in England?).
1657	Samuel Sr. was sired by Nathaniel Sr. in Reading, Middlesex, MA
1691	Nathaniel Sr. was sired by Samuel Sr. in Reading, Middlesex, MA

(Table 34 continued)

1737	William Sr. was sired by Nathaniel Sr.
1765	William Jr. was born in East Haddam, Connecticut.
1768	Rebecca Fuller was born. She became the wife of William Jr.
1777	The Vermont Constitution enjoined the legislature the duty of establishing schools in each town at public expense, a factor that made it probable that Oliver received essential education.
1787	A Congregational Church was established and William Sr. became one of four deacons. In 1792 the pastor died and the deacons took turns for many years reading the sermons of Jonathan Edwards. Oliver was raised Congregationalist.
1788	Oliver's eldest brother Warren was born.
1792	He was appointed Surveyor of Highways (and again in 1803).
1802	Oliver's brother Lyman was born. He became a lawyer, served as a probate judge and served in the state legislature.
1806	Oliver Cowdery was born of William Jr. and Rebecca in Wells Township, Vermont. John Fuller was the grandfather of Rebecca and John Fuller's brother. Shubael was the great-grandfather of Lucy Mack.
1816	Warren Cowdery moved to Freedom, New York
1818	Warren Cowdery became a commissioner of Ontario County, New York.
1824	Warren became the first postmaster in Freedom, New York
1825	In about 1825-1828 Oliver Cowdery clerked in a store (Jensen, LDS Biographical Encyclopedia, 1:246)
1828	Taught school in the fall of 1828 and winter of 1829.
1829	In April he was made cotranslator with Joseph Smith. Later, but still in April, he was demoted to translator (D&C 9)
1829	He wrote most of ms O and P, where we observe that his work was superior to the other scribes.
1831	He was appointed in a revelation to assist printer William Phelps in printing the revelations, "to copy, and to correct, and to select."

Oliver's birth family shows well above average accomplishment. Father William Cowdery was for a time Inspector of Roads (or Surveyor of Highways) at Wells, Vermont.[332] His eldest brother studied to become a physician and became a commissioner of Ontario County, while his brother Lyman became a lawyer, served as a probate judge and a

---

[332] Larry E. Morris, "Oliver Cowdery's Vermont Years and the Origins of Mormonism," *BYU Studies* 39:1 (2000), 106-129.

representative in the state legislature. Oliver Cowdery clerked in a store and taught school before 1829. He may have worked at a couple of newspapers, possibly as an editor. Regarding his assistance to Gilbert in printing the *Book of Mormon*, he wrote to Joseph Smith in December 1829, "it may look rather strange to you to find that I have so soon become a printer and you may cast in your mind what I shall become next."[333] Following up by later assisting Church printer William Phelps, he acquired the printer's art sufficiently that in 1835 he could take on a nephew as an apprentice.[334] We do not know when he began reading law, but he was able to establish a law practice (twice) after leaving the Mormons.

As stated above, in the fall of 1828, Hyrum Smith, a member of the School Board of Trustees of Manchester, Ontario, New York, hired Oliver as a teacher. Moving to the Manchester area, he took up residence at the Joseph Smith Sr. home. It is generally said that at this time, Cowdery learned of the gold plates. Knowing that his son's gold-plates project was at a standstill, it may be more accurate to say that Father Smith saw an opportunity to recruit sorely needed fresh and better educated talent. With the original manuscript out of the picture, there was the opportunity to start *de novo*.

The official version of this history states that on 5 April 1829, Samuel Harrison Smith and Oliver Cowdery showed up on the latter's distant cousin Joseph's doorstep, and the two met for the first time. Incredibly, already on April 7, Cowdery was made Joseph's scribe for the project, and then a cotranslator for a short while. Joseph the scryer and Oliver the rodsman were colleagues in the occult, and respected each other's gifts. It was later claimed that in mid May of 1829, Joseph and Oliver were ordained by John the Baptist to the Aaronic Priesthood. Then Joseph baptized Oliver, followed by Joseph's baptism at the hands of Oliver.[335] Referring to this messenger as John the Baptist, Smith wrote that he, "descended in a cloud of light, and having laid his hands upon us, he ordained us..."[336] Cowdery described this experience as being

---

[333] Oliver Cowdery, letter to Joseph Smith dated 28 December 1829, in Vogel, *Early Mormon Documents*, II:408.

[334] Oliver Cowdery, in a letter of Oliver to Warren Cowdery dated 15/10/1835, in Stanley R. Gunn, *Oliver Cowdery, Second Elder and Scribe* (Salt Lake City: Bookcraft, 1962), 17.

[335] Marquardt, Rise of Mormonism, 85, 221.

[336] Joseph Smith, "History, 1839," in Vogel, *Early Mormon Documents*, I:75.

"while we were in the heavenly vision."[337] Prior to their ordination, he seems to describe some sort of theophany: "and we were rapt in the vision of the Almighty!" His description of the angel sent to ordain them uses deliberate wording that goes beyond a visionary experience:

> On a sudden, as from the midst of eternity, the voice of the Redeemer Spake peace to us, while the vail was parted and the angel of God came down clothed with glory...and while all men were resting upon uncertainty, as a general mass, our eyes beheld—our ears heard...with what surprise we must have bowed...when we received under his hand the holy priesthood..."[338]

By 1835 it was claimed that a bit later they were visited by and communed with Peter, James and John (D&C, 27:7, 8 & 12-13). Apart from being favored by a vision of the Almighty, these events go beyond the language of being in vision: "our eyes beheld—our ears heard." This, and other concrete aspects of their claim, such as the laying on of the hands of John the Baptist, the Baptism by immersion and the apostolic visitation, make it clear that Oliver Cowdery was already a total confederate. His supposed sudden appearance on Smith's doorstep on April 5 indicates that he had been recruited, briefed and probably even already put to work by Joseph Smith Sr.

As will be pointed out, from this time on, the work takes on a more organized and professional aspect. Oliver Cowdery was a friend of the Whitmers. In December 1832, he married Elizabeth Ann Whitmer, whom he had baptized on 18 April 1830. Joseph Smith Sr. was also in contact with David Whitmer, whom he had quite possibly known for some time. At least the groundwork for the arrangement for Joseph Jr. and Oliver to complete the *Book of Mormon* in the extended family home of Peter Whitmer Sr. must have been through the joint efforts of Cowdery and Smith Sr., although the latter probably secured it after Oliver's move to Harmony. Near the beginning of June, David Whitmer arrived at Joseph Jr.'s home in Harmony, Pennsylvania, and took him, Emma Smith and Oliver back to the Peter Whitmer Sr. farm in Fayette

---

[337] Oliver Cowdery in an introduction to blessings, 09/1835, in Vogel, Early Mormon Documents, II:453.
[338] Oliver Cowdery, a letter to W. W. Phelps dated 07/09/1834, in Vogel, *Early Mormon Documents*, II:420-21.

17. Project Completion: Smith's A Team & Their Milieu   409

Township, Seneca County, New York, where they completed the translation (possibly just the first drafts).

Ms *O* was clearly made from prior drafts (Chapter 12). We have already seen considerable stylistic evidence that Nephi, Alma and possibly even Mosiah were written be different authors (Chapter 16). I think that evidence shows that Smith did the Nephi draft. Cowdery may have been the drafter of Alma.

As remarkable as his immediate appointment as scribe was, it is nothing compared to Cowdery's further elevation a bit later (still in April) to cotranslator, along-side Joseph. "And, behold, I grant unto you a gift, if you desire of me, to translate, even as my servant Joseph." (D&C 6:25 & 8:3-4) *A cotranslator was a coauthor.* Bear in mind that in principle they are starting the *Book of Mormon* all over again. So how is it that Smith would make Cowdery a coauthor? It makes sense if Oliver arrived in the company of Samuel with a draft text in hand that he had already produced, and so had expectations of being more than just a scribe, and had Smith family support for the same.

Even more curious is the wording of the revelation that reduced his role in producing the BOM to scribe rather than translator (D&C 9:1):

> Behold, I say unto you, my son, that because you did not translate according to that which you desired of me, and did commence again to write for my servant, Joseph Smith, Jun, even so I would that ye should continue until you have finished this record, which I have entrusted unto him.

Here again we have a statement that makes no sense, and leaves us wondering what the subtext might be. In this revelation he is promised that he may yet translate other records. But what was the reason for this demotion? How is this a meaningful justification: "because you did not translate according to that which you desired of me, and did commence again to write for my servant, Joseph…"? How does this rather brief service to his distant cousin make him ineligible to translate? As a justification, it is a lame excuse. But is that all it is? At first blush, one might presume that Joseph realized that Oliver's elevation to his own level might nurture a future competitor. But the wording of the justification suggests a different, or perhaps additional reason. Especially in view of Cowdery's talents and experience, even as a schoolteacher, it was necessary to avoid the appearance that this duo was in fact in collaboration. The Smith family strategy had been to keep everyone else in the background to give credence to the claim that since the BOM could not have been written by Joseph Smith, it can only have come from a divinely assisted translation of the gold plates. Just issuing a revelation saying Cowdery did not contribute substantively would draw attention to what might appear to be a suspicious denial of what was really happening. A more clever approach was to make him a translator, and then revoke that status with a justification that asserts that he had not translated so far, and never would translate on this project. Otherwise, this justification for his demotion makes no sense.

We know that Emma and Samuel had been writing for Joseph before Cowdery's arrival, and that their work does not appear in ms $\mathcal{O}$. In addition to this evidence that Cowdery may have already been drafting while in Manchester, it seems that Joseph too was working on another draft prior to April 5 (probably Nephi).

Furthermore, Oliver was perfectly capable of finding his own way to Joseph's small farm in Harmony. It may be that father Smith sent his son Samuel along with him to assure a smooth transition to collaboration between the distant cousins. Samuel's role needs to be further investigated. He also accompanied his father to visit Joseph Jr. in February, when he wrote for him.

On the occasion of Smith Sr.'s visit in February, an imminent "marvelous work" was announced. Two months later, with Cowdery onboard, the project for a new bible was coupled with steps to establish a new church. Only about five weeks after his arrival at Harmony, he and Smith claimed to have received both the authority to baptize, and a valid baptism. The claim of a restored priesthood clearly indicates an intention to establish a true church. The role of a revelation claimed to have been received in June 1829 by Cowdery, and its church establishment passages, will be examined below in the context of the somewhat belated addition of the Book of Moroni.

The possibility of drafting in Manchester is strongly supported by the time factor. Due to the nearly edit-free condition of ms $\mathcal{O}$, it is certain that at least the major books were first done in the form of initial drafts that had to be worked into highly developed drafts. Between April 5 and even September, there just is not enough time to produce the work first in fully developed drafts, with considerable investigation into the scriptures and other issues, and then to produce ms $\mathcal{O}$. Logistically, the timeline works much better if we assume drafting done in both Manchester and Harmony prior to April. The evidence of at least two, but possibly three drafters indicates that in addition to Joseph Smith, one or two others were involved. One of these must certainly be Oliver Cowdery. A third might well be Hyrum Smith, although Joseph Sr. cannot be ruled out.

The text composed by Joseph Jr. and Martin Harris was not designed to be a new bible. The plan to address the loss of Lehi by starting over and producing a New World bible was complemented by plans to restore all things in preparation for the gathering of both branches of Israel, and therefore the restoration of the true church of Christ. If this far grander project, this departure from the Book of Lehi history of the Indians, was already formulated in Manchester, it probably emerged from collaboration between one or more Smiths plus Cowdery.

The Witnesses

When the *Book of Mormon* was published, two testimonials were appended at the end, the testimony of the Three Witnesses, and the testimony of the Eight Witnesses. Many Mormons, who have serious doubts about the *Book of Mormon*, find that they cannot reject it due to these witnesses, whose veracity they fully, or in some cases, begrudgingly accept. The testimonies are as follows:

The Testimony of the Three Witnesses

Be it known unto all nations, kindreds, tongues, and people, unto whom this work shall come, that we, through the grace of God the Father, and our Lord Jesus Chris, have seen the plates which contain this record, which is a record of the people of Nephi, and also of the Lamanites, his brethren, and also of the people of Jared, which came from the tower of which hath been spoken; and we also know that they have been translated by the gift and power of God, for his voice hath declared it unto us; wherefore we know of a surety, that the work is true. And we also testify that we have seen the engravings which are upon the plates; and they have been shewn unto us by the power of God, and not of man. And we declare with words of soberness, that an Angel of God came down from heaven, and he brought and laid before our eyes, that we beheld and saw the plates, and the engravings thereon; and we know that it is by the grace of God the Father, and our Lord Jesus Chris, that we beheld and bear record that these things are true; and it is marvelous in our eyes; Nevertheless, the voice of the Lord commanded us that we should bear record of it; wherefore, to be obedient unto the commandments of God, we bear testimony of these things. — And we know that if we are faithful in

(Three witnesses continued)

> Christ, we shall rid our garments of the blood of all men, and be found spotless before the judgement (sic) seat of Christ, and shall dwell with him eternally in the heavens. And the honor be to the Father, and to the Son, and to the Holy Ghost, which is one God. Amen.
>
> Oliver Cowdery
David Whitmer
Martin Harris

> ### The Testimony of the Eight Witnesses
>
> Be it known unto all nations, kindreds, tongues, and peoples unto whom this work shall come, that Joseph Smith, Jr. the Author and Proprietor of this work, has shewn unto us the plates of which hath been spoken, which have the appearance of gold; and as many of the leaves as the said Smith has translated, we did handle with our hands; and we also saw the engravings thereon, all of which has the appearance of ancient work, and of curious workmanship. And this we bear record, with words of soberness, that the said Smith has shewn unto us, for we have seen and hefted, and know of a surety, that the said Smith has got the plates of which we have spoken. And we give our names unto the world, to witness unto the world that which we have seen: and we lie not, God bearing witness of it.
>
> | Christian Whitmer, | Hiram Page |
> |---|---|
> | Jacob Whitmer, | Joseph Smith, Sen. |
> | Peter Whitmer, Jr. | Hyrum Smith |
> | John Whitmer, | Samuel H. Smith. |

Three observations can be made immediately. First, the eleven witnesses are three Smiths (plus Joseph Jr. and Oliver Cowdery, a distant relative of the Smiths), and four Whitmers (plus Hiram Page, the brother-in-law of David Whitmer). Martin Harris was the odd man out, being the only one not related to either one of these two families. He was also the only one of the leading figures who was not a scryer.

Second, the Three Witnesses saw the plates by the "power of God, and not of man," meaning that they had been visited by an angel for that purpose, and so were in effect called by God. According to Smith, the event took place in a wood near the Whitmer home. An angel came twice, once with Smith, Cowdery and Whitmer present, and again with Smith and Harris present. Of the first visitation, Smith recounted:

> ...we beheld a light above us in the air of exceeding brightness. Behold, an angel stood before us; In his hands he held the plates which we had been praying for these to have a view of: he turned over the leaves one by one, so that we could see them and discover the engravings thereon distinctly. He addressed himself to David Whitmer and said, 'David, blessed is the Lord and he that keeps his commandments.' Immediately afterwards, we heard a voice from out of the bright light above us saying, 'The plates have been revealed by the power of God, and they have been translated by the power of God; the translation of them which you have seen is correct, and I command you to bear record of what you now see and hear.'

Minutes later, in another part of the woods, Smith and Harris had the same visitation and saw and heard the same things, according to Smith.[339]

Third, the visionary character of the language of the experience of the three witnesses led to attempts by interviewers to suggest that they had not really actually seen the plates. What escapes attention is the fact that such language is totally absent from the testimony of the eight witnesses. They all simply claimed that Joseph Smith showed them the plates, which they hefted and digitally handled. There is no indication that this was a visionary experience. The three could not have had a lesser experience.

In 1881, after having been excommunicated and having founded his own church, which also used the *Book of Mormon*, David Whitmer wrote that this angel was dressed in white, and that

> They were shown to us in this way. Joseph and Oliver and I were sitting on a log, when we were overshadowed by a light more glorious than that of the sun...there appeared as it were, a table with many records or plates upon it, besides the plates of the *Book of Mormon*, also the Sword of Laban, the directors [Liahona?].[340]

---

[339] *Times and Seasons* 3, (1 Sept. 1842), 897-98.

[340] *Kansas City Journal*, June 5, 1881, p. 1 (in Milton V. Backman, Jr., *Eyewitness Accounts of the Restoration* (Salt Lake City: Deseret Book Company, 1986), 232.

Apart from this experience, Oliver Cowdery stated at a Church conference, that during the translation process at the Whitmer home, "I beheld with my eye and handled with my hands the gold plates from which it was translated. I also beheld the Interpreters."[341]

Martin Harris claimed, "Joseph Smith was the first to handle the... tablets of gold... and I... the second. At one time... [I held] the plates on my knee an hour and a half, whilest (sic) in conversation with Joseph, when we went to bury them in the woods, that the enemy might not obtain them... There was also found in the chest [used for the plates] the Urim and Thummim..."[342]

Other statements of Oliver Cowdery and Martin Harris were reported by persons other than themselves, but agree in substance with Whitmer's account.[343] What they claimed to have seen and heard placed them on a higher level than the eight witnesses, who were shown the plates by a mere mortal, and so were called through Joseph Smith.

The experience of the eight witnesses is described as having taken place at Manchester either one or a few days later. John Whitmer wrote that these eight "are the men to whom Joseph Smith, Junior, showed the plates."[344] They claimed to have handled them with their hands. When the translation was complete, the angel returned and collected the plates from Smith.

The testimonies of these twelve (including Joseph) are important since they are contemporary with the publication of the book. Other testimonies were made much later.

A Mr. Alvah Beeman (Beman/Beaman, a rodsman) helped to modify a box for glass panes. Harris reported that when he helped to put the plates in the box "he heard them jink."[345] Joseph B. Noble, his son-in-law, wrote that Beeman "was permited (sic) to handle the plates with a thin cloth hovering over them."[346]

---

[341] Reuben Miller, Journal (October 21, 1848), LDS Church History Library); Marquardt, *Rise of Mormonism*, 126; and *Millennial Star* 21 (August 20, 1859), 544.

[342] *Iowa State Register*, August 16, 1870. See Backman, *Eyewitness Accounts*, 128 & 225-7.

[343] Backman, *ibid*, 156.

[344] John Whitmer's History, 25, in Backman, *ibid*, 161.

[345] *Tiffany's Monthly* 5 (Aug. 1859) 167. See Marquardt, *Rise of Mormonism*, 58.

[346] Joseph B. Noble, Journal, LDS archives, in Marquardt, *ibid*, 58n45.

As pointed out above, this hefting would not have been possible if they were actually made of gold or even tumbaga. Either they hefted something else that felt like plates through a thin cloth, or their testimonies are suspect.

In addition to handling the plates through a tow frock, Mother Lucy Smith stated that, after returning from the hill, he placed [the Urim and Thummim]

> into my hands, and upon examination, [I] found that it consisted of two smooth three-cornered diamonds set in glass, and the glasses were set in silver bows, which were connected with each other in much the same way as old fashioned spectacles...
>
> Soon after this, he came in from work, one afternoon, and... handed me the breastplate spoken of in his history.
>
> It was wrapped in a thin muslin handkerchief, so thin that I could see the glistening metal, and ascertain its proportions without any difficulty.
>
> It was concave on one side, and convex on the other, and extended from the neck downwards, as far as the centre of the stomach of a man of extraordinary size. It had four straps of the same material, for the purposes of fastening it to the breast, two of which ran back to go over the shoulders, and the other two were designed to fasten to the hips. They were just the width of two of my fingers, (for I measured them,) and they had holes in the end of them, to be convenient for fastening.[347]

Emma Smith stated further that during the translation

> ...the plates often lay on the [table in our home], without any attempt at concealment, wrapped in a small linen tablecloth, which I had given him [Joseph Smith] to fold them in. I once felt... the plates, as they thus lay on the table, tracing their outline and shape. They seemed to be pliable like thick paper, and would rustle with a metallic sound when the edges were moved by the thumb, as one does sometimes thumb the edges of the

---

[347] Lucy Smith, *Biographical Sketches of Joseph Smith the Prophet and His Progenitors for Many Generations* (Liverpool: published for Orson Pratt and S. W. Richards, 1853) 101, 106-7; Backman, *Eye Witness Accounts*, 73-74.

book... I did not attempt to handle the plates, other than [through the linen cloth][348]

Here follows a review of the testimonies:

Table 35. Claimed Experiences of Persons Purported to Be Witnesses

Name	What They Claimed to Have Seen or Heard
Joseph Smith, Jr.	saw gold plates, Urim & Thummim, breastplate, sword, God the Father, the Son, angel Moroni, John the Baptist, Peter, James & John. heard the voice of all of the above. laying on of hands of John for the Aaronic priesthood. same by Peter, James & John for the Melchizedek priesthood.
Oliver Cowdery	saw gold plates, Urim & Thummim, breastplate, sword, angel Moroni, John the Baptist, Peter, James & John. saw the plates & Urim & Thummim. heard the voice all of the above. laying on of hands of John for the Aaronic priesthood. same by Peter, James & John for the Melchizedek priesthood.
Martin Harris	saw gold plates, Urim & Thummim, breastplate, sword, angel Moroni. hefted the plates in Smith's home under a cloth. held the plates on his knee an hour and a half. may have seen the Urim and Thummim in the chest. heard the angel's voice.
David Whitmer	saw gold plates, Urim & Thummim, breastplate, sword, angel Moroni. heard the angel's voice.
Joseph Smith Sr.	handled and hefted the plates at the Smith home in a frock. saw, handled and hefted the plates in the woods.
Samuel Smith	handled and hefted the plates at the Smith home in a frock. saw, handled and hefted the plates in the woods.
Hyrum Smith	handled and hefted the plates at the Smith home. saw, handled and hefted the plates in the woods.
Peter Whitmer Sr.	saw, handled and hefted the plates in the woods.
John Whitmer	saw, handled and hefted the plates in the woods.
Christian Whitmer	saw, handled and hefted the plates in the woods.

---

[348] Emma Smith, statement to her son, Joseph Smith III, February 4-10, 1879, cited in *The Saint' Herald* 26 (October 1, 1879), 289-90; in Backman, *Eye Witness Accounts*, 107.

(Table 35 continued)

Jacob Whitmer	saw, handled and hefted the plates in the woods
Hiram Page	saw, handled and hefted the plates in the woods.
William Smith	handled and hefted the plates at the Smith home in a frock.
Lucy Smith	handled and hefted the plates, examined the breastplate, all under a thin cloth, allowing her to see them. handled and examined the Urim & Thummim.
Emma Smith	saw and handled the plates under a cloth.
Alvah Beeman	helped put the covered plates in the glass-box, according to Lucy.
Lucy Harris	handled & hefted the plates under a cloth according to her husband.
Harris' daughter	handled & hefted the plates under a cloth according to her father.

The account of Smith and Cowdery regarding their ordination by John the Baptist and Peter, James and John, clearly indicates that Cowdery was a total confederate. Martin Harris' claim regarding the visitation, plus his claim to have held the plates on his knee, shows that he too was confederate.

Clearly the twelve witnesses (including Joseph Jr.) were all confederate. Their claims, plus the level of their involvement in the early history of the church and its scriptures, all indicate this. In the case of others, some sort of plates or heavy object wrapped up in linen or a tow cloth pillowcase could have given rise to their experience, such as that of Alvah Beeman, Mrs. Harris and her daughter who are not directly quoted as having given a testimony.

In addition to the claims made by the Smiths, Cowdery, Harris and the Whitmers, perhaps the most clear indication of their being confederates is what we must conclude from the loss of the 116 pages, the story of the small plates of Nephi to recover from that blow, and the subsequent development of a New World bible. No Smith, nor Harris or Cowdery, nor any Whitmer could have failed to realize almost immediately that there was absolutely zero possibility that the stolen ink-on-paper pages could be modified to be used to compare and refute a word-for-word replacement text of the Book of Lehi. They therefore knew very well that there never had been any gold plates, and that Joseph

Jr. was not translating an ancient record. They could however have agreed with the general historical outline as something close to what must have happened, and they may have agreed that the doctrinal teachings in the BOM narrative were in some measure inspired.

The Witnesses: Demise and Apostasy

Within fifteen years of the publication of the *Book of Mormon*, all twelve witnesses to the gold plates had been murdered, had died of natural causes or had left the Church. The two remaining ties to the period prior to 1830 were Lucy Mack Smith and Emma Hale Smith. Neither of these accepted Brigham Young as a valid successor to Joseph Smith. The entire Smith family had been virtually eradicated from the Mormon movement.

Table 36. Death and Apostasy among the Witnesses

Natural Deaths
1835 Christian Whitmer died.
1836 Peter Whitmer Jr. died.
1840 Joseph Smith Sr. died.
1844 Samuel Smith died (cause of death then called of a "bilious fever").
Excommunication
1837 Martin Harris was excommunicated (died 1875)
1838 Oliver Cowdery was excommunicated (died 1850).
1838 David Whitmer was excommunicated (died 1888)
1838 Jacob Whitmer was excommunicated (died 1856)
1838 Hiram Page was excommunicated (died 1852)
1845 William Smith was excommunicated after disputes with B. Young.
Murder Victims
1844 Joseph and Hyrum Smith murdered.
The Last Ones Standing
1856 Lucy Mack Smith, wavered between moving to Utah and joining the Strang group, but stayed in Nauvoo with her daughters & Emma Smith.
1879 Emma Smith died, a member of the Reorganized Church of Jesus Christ of Latter Day Saints.

17. Project Completion: Smith's A Team & Their Milieu 419

Any Confessions?

Due to the central importance of the statements of those claiming to have seen, hefted or handled the plates and the associated BOM relics, the LDS establishment has controlled the spin on the issue. It is framed in terms of whether or not they ever *denied their testimonies*. In any normal investigatory situation, one would frame the issue in terms of whether or not any ever *confessed*. This is of great importance, because it is axiomatic in criminology that "there are no guilty men in prison;" many found guilty with the most clear forensic evidence continue to insist on their innocence. Confession is the last thing we would expect.

A theological backdrop exists to the issue of confession: Mormons do not shrive. They have no concept of dying unshriven.

There were several reasons for the witnesses to remain loyal. First, people are concerned about what their family, wife, children and grandchildren would say. They do not want to cast themselves in a light that would impair the family's standing in the community. Far better to be remembered as a man of God that a fraud.

Second, there came into existence a vigilante group, self-styled the Danites, who roughed up dissidents who took actions to undermine the church, roughed them up, or worse. The greater one's prominence, the more apostasy is tantamount to persecuting the Church. To know that the LDS establishment could pose a threat, we need only recollect the passage in Smith's polygamy revelation, where presumably God speaks, saying: "But if she [Emma Smith] will not abide this commandment [polygamy] she shall be destroyed, saith the Lord." Emma waited until Joseph was dead, and Brigham Young and his followers were at a safe distance in Utah, before she began to publicly maintain that to her knowledge her husband had never taken any wife but her. This has been shown to be patently untrue, and itself shows how people say what they must to survive. In her case, she and her son, Joseph Smith III were being welcomed by the dissident saints who stayed behind, and never had adopted polygamy. Still, the revelation itself, and her later claim, show she was not in agreement with polygamy, but was made to keep her mouth shut, at least at many venues.

Third, there was another motivation to maintain one's testimony: the agendas that most of these men nurtured. Shortly after the *Book of Mormon* was published, Hiram Page made his move. He used his seer stone and received some revelations. Joseph clearly detected the rivalry, and instructed Oliver Cowdery to inform brother Hiram that his revelation had come from Satan. Oliver succeeded in this, and Page withdrew his claim. In the conference of the new church, the assembly voted unanimously that only Joseph could receive revelation for the Church. Others, such as David Whitmer, attempted to become the prophet, seer and revelator, at the head of the presidency of the Church, in the aftermath of Smith's murder, and when that failed he established his own congregation also based on the *Book of Mormon*. Martin Harris and Warren Parrish in Kirtland attempted the formation of a new church, the Church of Christ, to take over from Smith.

The Saints have gone to great effort to track the lives of the witnesses, take subsequent testimonies and claim that they can show that not one of them ever denied his testimony, even on his deathbed. This has been disputed, to some degree, but any denial that can be alleged is not unequivocal. At times, it was reported by a journalist, and the media liked nothing better than to elicit such a denial. When this happened, the person making the denial issued a statement to the effect that he had been misquoted. There were no outright confessions.

Lucy Smith: Devoted Mother, Biographer and Propagandist

Even though her son Joseph had himself written a history of the church, with considerable autobiographical detail, Lucy felt called to write her own, a family history. By the time she began this project, near the end of 1844, her husband and sons Joseph, Hyrum and Samuel were all in their graves. All of the other male participants in the original BOM project had left the Church. She was the principal tie to the key pre-1830 period of LDS history, and the font to which many looked for its historical detail. She was undoubtedly aware of her situation, and the unique opportunity that it offered her. In a letter to her son William dated 23 June 1845, she wrote:

> People are often inquiring of me the particulars of Joseph's getting the plates, seeing the angels at first, and many other things which Joseph never wrote or published. I have told over many things pertaining to these matters to different persons to gratify their curiosity, indeed have almost destroyed my lungs giving these recitals to those who felt anxious to hear

them. I have now concluded to write down every particular as far as possible...³⁴⁹

Her description of contact with the plates was very conservative, her description of her investigation of the breastplate of Laban involved much more detail, and her assertion that she held and examined the Urim and Thummim was without restraint. These claims leave very little room for doubt that she was a principal confederate with the rest of her family in the BOM project. This is not surprising, in that, like her husband and son, she too apparently had used a seer stone (as did other women, such as Sarah [Sally] Chase), and had an interest in and apparently knowledge of New England magic (although the references are late).³⁵⁰

Her book was first published in 1853. Due to its positive treatment of her son William, it was suppressed by Brigham Young, who urged the Saints to burn any copy they could get their hands on. Later, the LDS authorities produced "corrected" (expurgated) versions.

By the time of its composition, she was sixty-nine years old and writing about events that happened at least a quarter of a century earlier. We are unable to know to what extent her participation in the early development of the official account of events had merged with her memory, and to what extent she was still consciously functioning as a proponent of the family's official line. One of the difficulties faced by anyone attempting to acquire the facts regarding this period in LDS history is the fact that Joseph Smith and Oliver Cowdery began a conscious effort to control knowledge re the particulars predating 1830, and most other information is either anti-Mormon, or in the form of reminiscences of very late date, or both.

Oliver Cowdery: You Can Run, but You Cannot Hide

The challenge that both Whitmer and Cowdery mounted to Joseph Smith was partly due to different views on church organization and Smith's supremacy. It is also clear that they all had their own agendas. This was known early to Smith. Although made a cotranslator (coauthor) in April

---

[349] Lucy Mack Smith, a letter to her son William Smith dated 23/01/1845, as quoted by Richard L. Anderson, "Circumstantial Confirmation of the First Vision through Reminiscences, *BYU Studies* 9:3 (Spring, 1969), 9.
[350] Quinn, *Early Mormonism and the Magic World View* (re both Lucy & Sally), 42. For Lucy & magic, see Quinn's index listings under Lucy Mack Smith.

of 1829, Smith soon demoted Cowdery to just scribe. Subsequent to this, he claimed to have received a revelation for church establishment. This is treated in the next chapter. He was commanded, in one of Smith's revelations, "Therefore be diligent; stand by my servant Joseph, faithfully, in whatsoever difficult circumstances he may be for the word's sake." (D&C 6:18) He was promised a reward for doing so.

After leaving the Church, he attempted to put his whole Mormon experience behind him. He began to practice law in Tiffin, Ohio. There, he became a civic and political leader. Perhaps it was for political advantage that he joined the Methodist church, apparently keeping his past under wraps. He served as secretary in 1844, and edited the local Democratic newspaper until it was learned that he was one of the *Book of Mormon* witnesses. Demoted to assistant editor, in 1846, Cowdery was nominated as his district's Democratic Party candidate for the state senate, but was defeated apparently due to his Mormon background. After founding his own religion, James Jesse Strang called upon the Saints to gather in Voree, Wisconsin. William Cowdery became associated with the Strangites, and in 1847, Oliver and Lyman moved to Elkhorn, Wisconsin, about 12 miles away from Strang's base in Voree. He entered law practice with his brother, became co-editor of the *Walworth County Democrat* and, in 1848, ran for state assemblyman. His Mormon ties were again revealed and he was defeated. Finding that he could not escape his Mormon past, he requested to return to the Church. In 1848 he was rebaptized by Orson Hyde of the LDS Quorum of the Twelve. Due to his financial situation, and health problems, he decided not to attempt the trip to the Utah Territory, and in 1850 he died in David Whitmer's home in Richmond, Missouri.

Martin Harris: The Disgruntled Investor

Initially, Martin Harris' vested interest was largely financial. He was the bankroll for the project. He gave Smith money to help get the *Book of Mormon* written, and in order to get the funds to publish it he had to mortgage part of his farm. In 1837, dissension arose in Kirtland over the failure of the Kirtland Safety Society bank. Having lost nearly everything, he was no longer needed. After he joined with Warren Parrish in the formation of a new church, the Church of Christ, the LDS leadership excommunicated him for his opposition to Smith.

After Joseph Smith's death, he joined the Strangites, a church, at one point fairly successful, founded by James Strang, who claimed to be Smith's successor. They too accepted the *Book of Mormon*. Strang claimed to have translated *The Book of the Law of the Lord* from the Brass Plates of Laban. Followers of the Strangites also included Cowdery's father, William, his brother, Lyman, and initially, most of Joseph Smith's surviving family, including William Smith, Lucy Mack Smith and three of Joseph's sisters. By 1847 he had left the Strangites, and went on to join with other Mormon offshoots: the Whitmerites of David Whitmer, the Gladdenites founded by Gladden Bishop and the Williamites, who held that Joseph's younger brother William, was the true successor. In 1856 his second wife, Caroline, left to join with the Utah Mormons, and Harris eked out a living as a sort of guide, giving tours to the Kirtland temple.

His financial situation continued to deteriorate and in 1870, at age 87, his son in Utah prevailed upon Brigham Young to allow his father to return to the fold. Friends had to give him $200 to pay for his fare. Throughout his religious peregrinations, each group's commitment to the *Book of Mormon* required that he hold to his testimony re the gold plates.

David Whitmer: Waiting in the Wings

David Whitmer's father moved to Waterloo, New York, in 1809, and then to Fayette, New York, after 1827. We have very little reliable information regarding his conversion to the BOM project. He said that in 1828 he "stopped with one Oliver Cowdery" while on a business trip in Palmyra. This sounds like they already knew each other. Lucy Smith recalled, "the only acquaintance which existed between the Smith and Whitmer families, was that formed by Mr. Smith and myself when on our way from Manchester to Pennsylvania to visit Joseph, at which time we stopped with David over night, and gave him a brief history of the Record."[351] Lucy's usage of "stop with" means "stay with," a meaning made clear by adding "over night." If Whitmer also meant to say he "stayed with" Oliver, this may have been at the Smith's home, depending on the date. If so, then we can understand how it was they in turn stayed in the Whitmer home. It may be that these people had more contact with each other than they were letting on.

---

[351] Lucy Smith in Anderson, *Lucy's Book*, 449-50.

These two founding families had a great deal in common. They were visionary families, largely disaffected with the organized churches of their day and what was being called priestcraft, and they were very motivated by an immutable sense of family loyalty. Consequently, no matter what influence Cowdery had with David Whitmer, it was essential for the family head, Peter Sr., to be mobilized as well. The visit of the Smith elders to his home in February 1829 may have been key. David was baptized on 3 June 1829, about as soon as Cowdery and Smith had unpacked. His brother John Whitmer was also baptized in that June, but Peter Sr., Peter Jr., Christian, Jacob and Hiram Page were not baptized until April 1830. Clearly when Joseph Jr. arrived he did not disappoint. All of these Whitmers save Peter Sr. were chosen to be witnesses of the plates. He promptly received revelations to David (D&C 14), John (D&C 15) and Peter Jr. (D&C 16). To arrive at an understanding of the mentality of both of these families, it is necessary to investigate how two seemingly incompatible dimensions could comfortably coexist, to wit, some sort of spirituality along with a somewhat opportunistic and less-than-honest facility with asserting truth. Less than four weeks after meeting Joseph, six members of this family were comfortable with a testimony that they had viewed the plates, and five averring no accompanying visionary dimension.

In addition to David's association with Smith and Cowdery during the composition of the BOM, and his claims as one of the three witnesses, he was appointed church president in Zion (Missouri). It is clear that he considered himself to be a prophet, no less than Joseph Smith. William E. McLellin, after leaving the Church, served as Whitmer's scribe to record at least one revelation, and referred to "both the Revelators, Joseph Smith and David Whitmer."[352] It is probable that he saw in the incipient movement an opportunity for himself.

But it was *early* Mormonism that was his idea of the church in true Christianity, and not the theocracy that it was becoming. He and the Prophet, Seer and Revelator were on a collision course, leading to the dissolution of the church presidency in Missouri. A group of elders of the Church, who had established themselves in Caldwell County, Missouri, were warned regarding action by an extralegal enforcement group, and told to get out of the county. Being among those warned, Oliver Cowdery, David Whitmer and John Whitmer fled. Cowdery and the

---

[352] William E. McLellin, ed., *The Ensign of Liberty* (August, 1849), 98.

Whitmers were excommunicated and left the Church on 12 April 1838. After Joseph Smith's murder, David Whitmer asserted that he had been ordained to be his successor. When this initiative was unsuccessful, he founded the Church of Christ (Whitmerite). Oliver Cowdery, Martin Harris, Hiram Page and John Whitmer all were members at one time or another. This church survived after Whitmer's death until the 1960's. It too was based on the *Book of Mormon*, and so would require a continuation of the assertions of the witnesses involved.

When Joseph Smith returned to his wife in Harmony late in the summer of 1828, the BOM project was in shambles. At that time, in his first recorded revelation, he described the "very purpose" of the plates to be to bring the 19th-century Lamanites to a knowledge of who they were, and to embrace the gospel of Christ. Only seven months later, on the occasion of the visit of his father and Samuel to Harmony in February1829, he issued a revelation for his father announcing an imminent marvelous work to take place among the children of men. From July 1828 he remained there until he and Cowdery moved to the home of Peter Whitmer Sr. at the beginning of June 1829, where he found himself welcomed to the helm of a project team nucleus that he had not built. The recruitment of Cowdery and the Whitmer family happened in his absence. Smith Jr. attempted to arrogate to himself some credit in his 1839 history, writing, "Shortly after ~~my having~~ commencing to translate, I became acquainted with ~~the f~~ Mr Peter Whitmer ~~Senr~~ of ⟨Fayette⟩ Seneca County, New York, and also with ⟨some of⟩ his family."[353] It is unclear what sort of "acquaintance" this could have been being a hundred miles away. The two parties who are known to have had discussions with the Whitmers regarding the gold plates are Cowdery and the Smiths, Joseph Sr. and Lucy. By the time that Joseph and Oliver arrived in Fayette, the whole Whitmer family welcomed them. Only about three weeks after their arrival, David Whitmer became one of the three witnesses, while Joseph showed the plates to the eight witnesses, including Christian, Jacob, Peter Jr., John and Hiram. Most of the family was largely onboard by the time Joseph Jr. arrived, at which time, Joe Sr. at age 58 resumed his supporter role, and lived to enjoy the status of First Patriarch of the Church.

---

[353] Joseph Smith, 1839 history, in Vogel, *Early Mormon Documents*, I:79.

Chapter 18

Project Completion: Nephi to Mormon, & Moroni

The original BOM manuscript is a clean document with various corrections of scribal errors and minimal substantive changes. It is not possible for anyone to have composed it extemporaneously while dictating it to a scribe. In view of the archaeological verdict, the only viable alternative is that it was dictated from drafts that later were unceremoniously cremated in the family hearth. This manuscript has page numbers in the hand of individual scribes, indicating that the pagination was not done later.[354] Since the extant material begins with 1 Nephi 2:2, only slightly more than the first chapter being missing, it is therefore clear that ms *O* began with Nephi. It would be wonderful if we had contemporary documents to study its development, but few relevant materials are available (v. Appendix 5). Most of early Mormon history must be reconstructed from late and often secondary documents, some of them the product of early LDS leaders engaged in controlling the history of the movement, some others by pious believers, and others produced by anti-Mormons. Even though Joseph Smith's historical compositions are a good example of the first of these, he mentions a useful detail in his 1832 history. He wrote that prior to the coming of Oliver Cowdery to Harmony, on 5 April 1829, "now my wife had written some for me to translate and also my brother Samuel."[355] At the latest, Smith had resumed work by February, 1829 when Samuel came.

Table 37. The *Book of Mormon* Remake: Some Events and Dates

Date	Event
06/1828	Martin Harris took the 116 pages to his farm.
15/06/1828	Date on the tombstone of Joseph and Emma's son who died the day of his birth.
06/1828	The 116 pages in Harris's custody went missing.
Late 06/1828	Smith arrived in Manchester & learned of the loss of Lehi.

---

[354] Skousen, *The Original Manuscript of the* Book of Mormon, 33.
[355] Jessee, *Personal Writings of Joseph Smith*, 640, n14: "Neither the handwriting of Emma Hale Smith nor of Samuel H. Smith appears on the surviving pages of the original *Book of Mormon* manuscript."

(Table 37 continued)

Mid 07/1828	Smith returned to Harmony, having stayed with his parents for a spell.
08/1828	Smith began farming to support his family.
08-09/1828	Joseph Sr. and Lucy visited Joseph in Harmony.
09/1828	Joseph Sr. and Lucy returned to Manchester to find Samuel Harrison Smith and his wife sick. (Lucy's Book, 431)
11/09/1828	Joseph Sr. obtained medicine for Samuel ("Boy Harrison" as recorded in doctor Cains Robinsons's daybook), possibly documenting the date of the Smiths' return from Harmony to Manchester. (Vogel, *Joseph Smith*, 3:439)
09 or 10/1828	Lyman Cowdery visited Hyrum seeking a teaching position in Palmyra. A meeting of the school trustees agreed to hire him, but the next day Lyman presented Oliver to be hired in his place and this was accepted.
10/1828	Initially Oliver resided with the Smiths. Shortly after beginning school he became aware of the BOM project. The date of his recruitment is unknown but it was possibly in mid fall.
Fall of 1828	David Whitmer "stops with" Cowdery.
Early 1829	Emma may have begun writing for her husband.
February, 1829	Joseph Sr. & Lucy stayed over night at Whitmer home.
February, 1829	Joseph Sr. and Samuel visited Joseph Jr. and Emma in Harmony. Samuel served as scribe for an unknown period of time (as the date of his return to Manchester is unknown).
February/March	For some unknown period, Emma wrote for her husband.
5/04/1829	Oliver Cowdery and Samuel Smith arrived in Harmony.
c. April 7, 1829	Oliver became Smith's scribe.
April, 1829	Oliver was made a translator (coauthor).
April, 1829	Oliver was demoted to just scribe.
15 May 1829	Baptism of Joseph and Oliver and restoration of priesthood.
May 1829	Samuel visited Harmony and was baptized. Then returned.
May 1829	Hyrum visited Harmony to check on progress.
May 1829	Joseph Knight Sr. came and brought them provisions.
C. 1 June 1829	David Whitmer arrived to take Joseph and Oliver to the home of his father, Peter Whitmer Sr. in Waterloo to complete the translation. Lucy reports that he drove his wagon 135 miles in 2 days.
Early June, 29	Once the work had begun in the Whitmer home, John Whitmer also began writing for Joseph.
June, 1829	Baptism of Hyrum Smith, David Whitmer and Peter Whitmer Jr.

(Table 37 continued)

11/06/1829	*Book of Mormon* Copyright is issued. (The text on the BOM title page appears on the copyright. Vogel, *Joseph Smith*, 3:461-63.)
Mid June, 29	Grandin asked Gilbert to estimate the cost of the proposed BOM printing project, and for that purpose, pages of the ms were brought to him & an estimate that there would be about 500 pages. These would have to have been ms $\mathcal{O}$ pages.
June, 1829	Smith ordained Oliver an elder, & Oliver ordained Joseph.
June, 1829	Cowdery drafted a revelation he claimed to have received containing important church establishment passages. Some of these were incorporated in 3 Nephi & D&C 18.
June, 1829	Contract with Grandin to print 5000 copies for 3000 dollars.
26/06/1829	Grandin announced intention to print the *Book of Mormon*.
June, 1829	An angel showed the plates to Oliver Cowdery, Martin Harris and David Whitmer with Joseph. Later, Joseph showed the plates to the eight witnesses.
Beginning of July	The whole Smith family moved into the log cabin, including Peter Whitmer Jr. and presumably Oliver Cowdery. (Lucy)
August, 1829	Hyrum brought the first gathering of ms $\mathcal{P}$ to Gilbert. Initially, Joseph collected it each night, but after a few days he trusted Gilbert with it.
04/10/1829	Joseph Smith arrived back in Harmony. (Smith-Cowdery letter)
06/11/1829	The new type had not arrived, so the printing was going rather slowly. (Cowdery-Smith letter)
27/12/1829	The earliest Sunday that Hyrum and Oliver could have discovered Abner Cole publishing extracts from the *Book of Mormon*. (Vogel, *Joseph Smith*, 480)
28/12/1829	Cowdery-Smith letter alluding to the coming of Joseph Sr. [regarding Cole]. Lucy reports he went and came right back with his son in spite of the freezing weather.
End of December	Joseph Sr. in Harmony to fetch his son to deal with Cole?
02/01/1830	Abner Cole's *The Reflector* published the first installment of the *Book of Mormon* (1:1-2:3).
13/01/1830	Cole's second installment from the BOM.
16/01/1830	Agreement signed by Smith Sr. and witnessed by Cowdery re the compensation due to Harris for covering BOM printing. Joseph Jr. was probably in Harmony.
19/01/1830	Smith appeared in court in Pennsylvania over debt to Durfee.
22/01/1830	Cole's third installment from the BOM.

(Table 37 continued)

Late January 1830	Smith is in Manchester to deal with Cole. It appears that the dispute was eventually settled by some sort of arbitration. (*Lucy's Book*, 475) Possibly Grandin settled it.
Early 02/1830	Late sources say Smith received a revelation for a delegation to go to Kingston, Ontario, to sell the BOM copyright. Smith would have been in Manchester to set this up, & Whitmer recalled Smith was there when they returned. Lucy wrote he returned because Grandin had stopped printing fearing nonpayment. Gilbert later denied this.
19/03/1830	*Wayne Sentinel* announced the BOM would soon be ready.
26/03/1830	*Wayne Sentinel* announced the BOM was available.
26/03/1830	Smith was in Manchester when the book was published.

It became clear in the stylistic study of the BOM text that different authors must have drafted Nephi and Alma. Furthermore, the analysis of a number of distributions yielded evidence that yet a third person may have drafted Mosiah. It makes sense that Smith would be the drafter of Nephi. He had already covered the same ground when he did the missing Book of Lehi. And his later extensive effort to produce a "corrected" version of the entire Bible is consistent with the work done to edit Isaiah for inclusion in Nephi. In the entire extant material of ms $\mathcal{O}$, there are only two scribes apart from Cowdery, both in Nephi, and neither is Emma or Samuel. Smith's reference to their work done prior to Oliver's arrival most probably refers to work on a draft, most probably of Nephi. Moreover, Alma addresses issues of church and court organization, separation of church and state, the legal profession and theological and legalistic disputation. All of this is consistent with Cowdery's interest in these issues, his later legal practice in two towns and efforts to enter politics.

From Initial Drafts to Completed Drafts, to Ms $\mathcal{O}$, to Ms $\mathcal{P}$

Two days after Cowdery's arrival he was made Smith's scribe, even though according to statements made later by both, neither had ever laid eyes on the other before then. Not long after that, he was promoted to translator alongside Joseph Smith, making him coauthor. Although this development is nothing less than astounding, it is probable that Smith's father had apprised him of the advisability of this promotion during his visit to Harmony in February. It appears that this did not happen at

Joseph's initiative, but Oliver's. "I [Jesus] grant unto you a gift if you desire of me." (D&C 6, dated April) Later the same month, this status was revoked with a promise that he might translate other records at a future time. (D&C 9) This meteoric elevation would make sense if Cowdery had a justifiable claim to be a translator (coauthor), one at once recognized by Smith, because in fact while in Manchester he had already begun to draft, most probably the Book of Alma the Younger. Also in Manchester, a third author may have been drafting Mosiah. This draft too could have been brought to Harmony by Cowdery, or if not, then by Hyrum who visited in May ostensibly to check on how the work was coming. If Oliver and his friend Hyrum were drafting these two works, they could have conferred with each other to assure consistency and the transition from one to the other. Content-wise, they are almost totally independent works with respect to Nephi-Jacob.

The production of the BOM drafts most probably resembled that of the Book of Moses, undertaken shortly after the 1830 publication of the new bible: "This included a complete rewriting of the early chapters of Genesis, which was then followed in the editorial process by a number of interlinear inserts and deletions. In some instances, additional material was written on small pieces of paper and pinned to the manuscript at places needing still further correction."[356] The BOM drafts are of two types. Reference to pre-April drafts is to first drafts, which may already contain some edits, although relatively few, the emphasis being on composition. We can refer to these drafts as mss^i, the initial drafts. Apart from possibly finishing up whatever drafts they had been working on, the first job of Smith and Cowdery was to review initial drafts and make corrections, additions and deletions. We can refer to the completed drafts as mss^c. Thus there would be a Nephi^i (initial draft of Nephi) followed by a Nephi^c (the completed draft of Nephi), a Mosiah^i and Mosiah^c, and so on. Once a complete draft was done, the initial draft no longer existed, just as upon the emergence of the adult the youth no longer exists. We have a good example of what the mss^c looked like in the extant highly edited draft of the *Book of Moses*. At some point it became clear that the mss^c were so messy and cumbersome that a prospective printer would need a cleaned-up copy. Enter ms ⵔ, initially undertaken to serve as the printer's copy. It was only after Nephi^c (the two Nephis being a single book at that time) was done that it was possible to begin ms ⵔ, possibly

---

[356] Matthews, "How We Got the Book of Moses."

as early as May 1829, but possibly as late as very early in June, at the home of Peter Whitmer Sr. in Waterloo, NY. A certain identification of the two unidentified scribes in Nephi will evidence both the date and location of its commencement. The scribal service of the two unidentified scribes in 1 Nephi occasionally freed up Cowdery to work on drafts. That we are dealing with dictation is clear, at least in much of the text, from errors, such as writing 'no' for 'know' (1 Nephi 10:8), an easy error for someone taking dictation. It is clear that there was a hierarchy among scribes. Cowdery might proof and correct an unidentified scribe, or one unidentified scribe might proof another. But only Cowdery proofed Cowdery's work. From the Book of Alma on, Cowdery was the sole scribe, with the exception of Alma 45:22, inexplicably in the hand of Joseph Smith Jr.

Approximately on June first, David Whitmer arrived in Harmony with a two-horse wagon and took Joseph and Oliver to the home of his father, Peter Whitmer Sr.[357] Lucy Smith relates that to transport the gold plates he was instructed that, "he should commit them into the hands of an angel, for safety, and after arriving at Mr. Whitmer's, the angel would meet him in the garden, and deliver them up again into his hands."[358] She assures us that this worked just fine.

Although Cowdery's arrival on 5 April is generally taken to be a hard date, the first truly hard date is 6 April 1829, the date of the contract for Smith to buy land from Isaac Hale, drawn up and witnessed by Oliver Cowdery. The next hard date is 11 June 1829 when the copyright was issued for the *Book of Mormon*. The requirement to obtain a copyright at that time was to provide the title of the work, and a description. It was not required to submit a manuscript. The description submitted, which appears on the copyright document, is the same as the description that has always appeared on the title page of the printed editions. It is signed by R. R. Lansing, Clerk of the United States District Court for the Northern District of New York.[359] Smith claimed that the title page text "is a literal translation, taken from the very last leaf, on the left hand side of the collection or book of plates..."[360] If the designation "left side"

---

[357] Smith, 1839 History, in Jessee, *Papers of Joseph Smith*, I:293-4; and in Vogel, *Early Mormon Documents*, I:79-80.
[358] Lucy Smith in Anderson, *Lucy's Book*, 450.
[359] Vogel, *Early Mormon Documents* (Salt Lake City: Signature Books, 2000), III:462-3.
[360] Smith, 1839 History, in Vogel, *Early Mormon Documents*, I:91.

refers to its location when the last plate had been turned, then it indicates that he visualized the plates, bound with rings, to turn from right to left like an English book, which would normally mean that he saw reformed Egyptian as being written from left to right. This is not impossible. Egyptians also wrote boustrophedon texts.

While the translation was ongoing, Smith approached E. B. Grandin to publish the *Book of Mormon*. We learn from the printer/typesetter John H. Gilbert that Grandin press accepted only on their second application.[361] On 26 June, Grandin announced in the *Wayne Sentinel* his intention to publish it when the translation is complete.[362] This would indicate that at that date, the translation was still ongoing. The first 28 pages (25 printed pages of 1 Nephi) were delivered to the printer, John H. Gilbert, who wrote that the printing was begun in August and completed in March, 1830.[363] Twenty-eight pages is seven sheets, folded in half to form gatherings (the equivalent of book signatures). This seems to be misremembered, since the first gathering of ms 𝒪 is 24 pages (six sheets).

A composition completion date in late June is supported by David Whitmer, who stated in 1881, that, "The translation at my father's occupied about a month, that is from June 1 to July 1, 1829."[364] At the time of this statement, more than fifty years after the event, he was President of The Church of Christ (Whitmerite), and 76 years old. This completion date is further buttressed by a revelation dated June 1829 stating, "and he [Smith] has translated the book." (D&C 17:6) Note too that Lucy Smith wrote that at the completion of the translation, the whole team had a completion celebration at Waterloo (Fayette). One can imagine that a libation or two was poured on that occasion, when also they read some passages.[365] Her account has to be received with some caution, since she indicated that the copyright was received after that.

---

[361] John H. Gilbert, "Memorandum, made by John H. Gilbert Esq, Sept 8th, 1892, Palmyra, N. Y.," Palmyra King's Daughters Free Library, Palmyra, NY; Vogel, *Early Mormon Documents*, II:542-8. It is in Wilfred C. Wood, *Joseph Smith Begins His Work*. Book of Mormon *1830 First Edition, Reproduced from Uncut Sheets* (Salt Lake City: Deseret News Press, 1958).
[362] Dan Vogel, *Joseph Smith*, 469.
[363] John H. Gilbert, "Memorandum.
[364] David Whitmer, to the *Kansas City Journal*, 5 June 1881; see Backman, *Eyewitness Accounts*, 124.
[365] Lucy Harris, Lucy's Book, 451-52.

But if Smith and Cowdery closed up shop at Waterloo on or just after the end of June, her account supports an end-of-June completion date.

However, this is only the completion of the translation, i.e. the mss^i. It is here that we encounter two very interesting phenomena. First, Smith had begun his career as a modern-day Moses with the first of his officially dated recorded revelations in July 1828. From February 1829 there ensued a flurry of revelations, ending with the last of 1829 dated in June.[366] With regard to recorded revelations, from July 1829 to March 1830, for eight months, silence reigned supreme. Second, Lucy reports that after the witnesses had viewed the plates, the contract was signed with Grandin Press and the copyright was received. She then skips to her son's return to Pennsylvania.[367] In a letter to Cowdery he wrote that he arrived in Harmony on 4 October 1829.[368] For three months, July-September, the translator and his scribe went off the radar.

It was apparently after closing up shop in Waterloo that Smith decided that it was necessary to produce an even cleaner copy of ms O, which had replaced the drafts and was presented to the world as the "original" done by Cowdery as Smith translated. This second copy would become ms P, which could also serve as a backup. He clearly remembered the fate of the purloined 116 pages. Once bitten, twice shy.

Most probably, during these ninety days after the celebration party, the remaining mss^i were edited to completion. Smith and Cowdery continued to copy the mss^c into ms O. This copy work was cut in half by two working on it. Smith would study through the next group of words and phrases in the edited mess, and dictate a brief passage as edited. Cowdery would write it. While he wrote, Smith would be preparing in his mind the next group of words and phrases and when Cowdery was ready he dictated that bit. If Cowdery were working alone, he would have had to do Smith's bit before writing. Working together, Cowdery wrote more or less nonstop. The principal obstacle to completing ms O

---

[366] There are indications that Smith did claim to have had operational revelations that have never been printed. Lucy wrote that he received a commandment regarding the preparation of ms P and associated issues. Lucy Smith, in Anderson, *Lucy's Book*, 459. Possibly in January of 1830 it appears that Smith claimed a revelation that the copyright could be sold in Canada for a large sum. See Marquardt, *Rise of Mormonism*, 93-94.

[367] *Ibid*, 451-59.

[368] Joseph Smith's letter to Oliver Cowdery of 22 October 1829, in the LDS Church Archives, reproduced in Vogel, *Early Mormon Documents*, I:7.

was the need now for Cowdery to work alone on copying it into ms 𝒫 to get the first gathering to the printer in late August. While he did this, Smith could have been busy producing the last of the mss^c.

Obviously there had been a sense of urgency to get the text done, as is seen by the fact that the period from Christ's departure, about year 34, to when Moroni buried the plates, about 421, was covered in only thirty-nine pages. This is only 8% of the text (not counting the Jaredite account) to cover almost 40% of the *Book of Mormon* (Nephite) time span. This same period also has fewer people in the chain of transmission of Nephite records, i.e. the number of generations, thereby requiring radically longer generation spans, again showing haste. Likewise, few new personal and city names are introduced. A likely source of this urgency was largely to get on with the next stage of the project, i.e. the establishment of the Church. They may also have had some fear of getting behind the printer's schedule, even though printing was at that time slow, as we see in a letter from Cowdery to Smith dated 6/11/1829 when he wrote, "the printing goes rather slow yet as the type founder has been sick but we expect that the type will be in…"[369] Given the type issue, it is probable that Cowdery did not have to provide the second gathering prior to mid October.

Cousin Rivalry: Oliver Cowdery's Revelation

Sometime in 1829 Cowdery penned "A commandment from God unto Oliver [Cowdery] how he should build up his church & the manner thereof." It ended with the words "A true copy of the articles of the Church of Christ."[370] The designation "Church of Christ" occurs in Mosiah, 3 Nephi B, 4 Nephi and Moroni. Around 70% of the text consists of passages found in 3 Nephi, Moroni and D&C 18, including, in order: a call to the world to repent (D&C 18:6, 9); procedures and the prayer for baptism (3 Nephi 11:23-27); the BOM monotheistic Trinity (3 Nephi 11:27); the procedures and prayer to ordain priests and teachers (Moroni 3:2-4); the procedures and blessing for the bread (Moroni 4:2-3); the procedures and blessing for the wine (Moroni 5:1-2); the order to not administer the sacrament to the unworthy, but to minister unto them (3 Nephi 18:28-33); frequent church meetings (3 Nephi 18:22); speaking

---

[369] Vogel, *Early Mormon Documents*, II:405-06.
[370] Vogel, *Early Mormon Documents*, II:409-412.

one to another regarding one's spiritual progress (Moroni 6:5) and that only the name of Jesus Christ can save (D&C 18:23-25).

Some LDS and even secular scholars have regarded this to be a Cowdery plagiarism. He simply rounded up all of these passages, cobbled them together, and attempted to foist them off as his own revelation.[371] This view gives us a puerile and even somewhat comical image of Cowdery the man. Did he think that no one would notice?

In the extant text, at the end of the revelation, he wrote in the first person asserting his authority to write these things, declaring:

> And now if I have not authority to write these things judge ye behold ye shall know that I have authority when you & I shall be brought to stand before the judgment seat of God. Now may [the grace] of God the Father & our Lord Jesus Christ be & abide with you all & xxx save you eternally in his kingdom through the Infinite atonement which is in Jesus Christ Amen—Behold I am Oliver. I am an Apostle of Jesus Christ by the will of God the Father & the Lord Jesus Christ. Behold I have written the things which he hath commanded me for behold his word was unto me as a burning fire shut up in my bones & I was weary with forbearing & I could forbear no longer Amen. (cf. Jeremiah 20:9)[372]

An approximate timeframe for BC 15 (D&C 18) is clearly indicated by an equally curious letter from Cowdery to Hyrum dated 14 June 1829 with similar and even some identical wording found in the revelation (D&C 18:9-13).[373] The revelation must have issued at a proximate date, although we do not know what redaction changes might have occurred before or when it was recorded in the BC, or even the degree of collaboration between Smith and Cowdery, even in the original formulation of the revelation. Assuming that these passages originated in the revelation, if D&C 18 refers to Cowdery's revelation, then the date of the latter may have been in the first week of June.

Even so, we are faced here with a question of the chicken and the egg. Did D&C 18 preceded Cowdery's revelation? Section 18:1-5 appears to me to be unambiguous

---

[371] For a secular view quite different from my own, see Vogel, *Joseph Smith*, 406-7; Vogel, *Early Mormon Documents*, II:409-12.
[372] Vogel, *Early Mormon Documents*, II:412.
[373] Vogel, Early *Mormon Documents*, II:402-3.

1. Now, behold, because of the thing which you, my servant Oliver Cowdery, have desired to know of me, I give unto you these words:
2 Behold, I have manifested unto you, by my Spirit in many instances, that the things which you have written are true; wherefore you know that they are true.
3 And if you know that they are true, behold, I give unto you a commandment, that you rely upon the things which are written;
4 For in them are all things written concerning the foundation of my church, my gospel, and my rock.
5 Wherefore, if you shall build up my a church, upon the foundation of my gospel and my rock, the gates of hell shall not prevail against you.

Some have interpreted "the things which are [which you have] written" to refer to passages in the *Book of Mormon*, particularly 3 Nephi and Moroni. This is not certain. The content of Cowdery's revelation perfectly corresponds to verses 4-5. The wording in D&C 18:5, "if you shall build up my church," corresponds to the wording in his revelation, "how he should build up the church..." There is no need to read the BOM into this passage, instead of Cowdery's revelation. It makes no sense to hold that "rely upon the things which are written" refers to the BOM and D&C 18 rather than his revelation, since they are one and the same, in most cases word for word. Moreover, Cowdery's text is a well-framed and properly written document. Even though *whoso* and *whosoever* both occur (one time each), *therefore* occurs five times, while *wherefore* does not occur. Apart from a possible coining of the word *covetiousness*, there is no misspelled word. By contrast, Smith in his 1832 history was even then unable to write a paragraph without several misspelled words. Since there are only two candidates, I have no hesitation accepting the authorship as Cowdery's.

An alternate characterization of Cowdery's revelation, as a draft, can be found in the *Encyclopedia of Latter-day Saint History*, which states[374] that "it appears from Cowdery's draft that Joseph Smith and Oliver Cowdery were formulating the documents [sections 20 & 22] throughout 1829." Two points are key: 1) Cowdery's defiant assertion of his authority may not have been part of his original document, and 2) we do not know the redaction history of D&C 18.

---

[374] Arnold K. Garr, Donald Q. Cannon & Richard O. Cowan, "Articles and Covenants, The," *Encyclopedia of Latter-Day Saint History* (Salt Lake City: Deseret Book Company, 2000), 52.

If Cowdery's revelation preceded D&C 18, then its date would be in the first week of June. Cowdery had been told that he could not translate the plates, but was promised that he could translate other records. Considering himself an apostle, presumably he too could receive revelation. His view of the true church (and that of the Whitmers) was apostolical, to wit, that of the Twelve Apostles. Only Matthew (16:18) makes Peter the rock upon which Jesus would build his church. Among the Twelve, there was no papal figure, not even James the brother of Jesus who may have headed the Jerusalem church. Gospels now in the canonical NT are attributed to various apostles. With the church prior to "the great apostasy" as his model, Cowdery felt he had every right to be a revelator equal to Smith, who took Moses as his model. In that dispensation, none other than Moses received revelation for Israel.

Although this revelation may have been nothing more than yet another draft made for Smith and himself to draw upon in their work, it is possible that it was a well-calculated strategic move on Cowdery's part. The timing was right. They had just arrived at the Whitmers, among Cowdery's friends and allies to be. Although top dog in principle, Smith was sociopolitically the new kid on the block. At this delicate juncture, he could not afford to alienate Cowdery, or worse, wage war against him. But Cowdery also had his own vulnerability. Smith enjoyed the full support of his family. The bridge between them was Hyrum, to whom Joseph looked up, and already a friend of Cowdery.

Although compromise became the name of the game, Joseph Smith showed that he was a past master at playing it. First, he accepted this text as a true revelation. (D&C 18:2&3) Second, he responded to his colleague's appropriation of the title "apostle" by making it official, extending it to David Whitmer as well, and putting them in charge of selecting the twelve, making it clear that they would be but two of a number of apostles. Although this commission may have already been included in what was to become D&C 18 as early as June 1829, at the time of the Church's first conference of 9/06/1830, they had not yet made their selection. Quinn writes, "Eight days before the church's organization, evangelical preacher David Marks met the Whitmer witnesses to the *Book of Mormon* who 'further stated, that twelve apostles were to be appointed, who would soon confirm their mission by miracles.'"[375] At the time of this first conference, five had been specifically called apostles, Joseph Smith, Oliver Cowdery, David Whitmer, John Whitmer and Ziba Peterson. It seems clear that two others, Peter Whitmer and Samuel H. Smith, had the designation "apostle" included in their elder license.[376] The title was used for other charismatic apostles, and even evangelical apostles (missionaries). In 1835 Smith instructed the three witnesses (thereby adding Martin Harris) to select the Quorum of the Twelve. It did not include Joseph Smith, nor the three witnesses. The only Smith was William. Since in June 1829 the church was not even in existence, Smith's commission to Cowdery and Whitmer may have been primarily to indicate what was to come, and even Cowdery might have begun to wonder if it would be wise for every one once selected to be able to receive revelation for the Church just because he was an apostle.

David Whitmer was fully aware of Cowdery's revelation. We learn from Smith that when the Articles and Covenants, based partly on Cowdery's revelation, added wording requiring tests of faith before being accepted for baptism (BC 34/D&C 20:37), Cowdery told Smith that the verse was erroneous and added, "I command you in the name of God to erase those words, that no priestcraft be amongst us."[377] To his dismay, Smith found that initially the whole Whitmer family sided with Cowdery, although Smith prevailed in the end.[378] He won this skirmish, but the battle went on. One of the most basic cleavages in early Mormon practice was the conflict between Smith's tendency towards theocratic hierarchy on the one hand, and opposition to it by Cowdery, the Whitmers and their supporters. This conflict festered at first, but came to a head when these two were excommunicated, the Salt Sermon was pronounced and they fled for their lives. That Cowdery's revelation played a role in the early period of this development can be seen by the fact that in late 1833 or very early 1834, LDS dissident Ezra Booth sent a letter to Eber D. Howe quoting from Cowdery's fiery defence of his

---

[375] Quinn, *The Mormon Hierarchy: Origins of Power* (Salt Lake City: Signature Books, 1994), 11. His source is David Marks statement, 29 Mar. 1830, in his *The Life of David Marks, To the 26th Year of His Age* (Limerick, ME: Office of the Morning Star, 1831), 340.
[376] Ibid, 11-13.
[377] Smith, 1839 History, in Vogel, *Early Mormon Documents*, I:128.
[378] Ibid, I:129.

authority to write his revelation.[379] At least to some degree, its text was in circulation, and now at least, armed with Cowdery's fiery declaration of authority. Perhaps this is why the extant text assures that it is a true copy. There may have been others. Alternatively, perhaps Cowdery made himself a copy expecting the original to wind up among Smith's papers.

Having given Cowdery much of what he wanted, Smith's third move in the game was to make the revelation into a source document. The first step was to incorporate the sections on baptism, the godhead and the treatment of persons unworthy of the sacrament into the text of 3 Nephi, which would still have been in the draft editorial stage. As the BOM project neared completion, it was decided that the passages for the ordination of priests and the procedures and wording for the blessing of the bread and wine should be added to the BOM text as well. With other material added to D&C 18, Smith was able to accommodate Cowdery with none of his text going out as his revelation. Checkmate.

The Moroni Addition

When Gilbert worked to set the type for a gathering of ms P, he occasionally marked on it capitalization and punctuation. In addition, he made take marks. These are a sort of check mark to indicate where a stick of type left off so he could begin his next stick at that point. He also sometimes undid the string binding the gathering so he could lay the sheets out to work more quickly. More rarely, he even cut the pages apart along the fold line. Skousen has informed us that four gatherings, numbers 16 through 19, lack all of these marks and cuts. The puzzle thickens when we learn that the marks are present on gatherings 20 and 21 of ms P. There is no evidence that Gilbert ever saw ms P gatherings 16-19. Because the corresponding ms O gatherings do bear his marks, it is clear that they were provided to him instead of ms P. Skousen's explanation for this is that Cowdery had fallen behind in his copying. His solution was a division of labor. Beginning with 3 Nephi 19:25 (just after the beginning of gathering 18), scribe number two copied ms O gatherings into P as they came back from the printer. Thus freed up, Cowdery jumped ahead to copy Ether into P beginning on the first page of a new gathering, number 20. This is indicated by the fact that Mormon ends on the last page of ms P gathering 19, where it occupies only eleven

---

[379] Howe, *Mormonism Unvailed*, 303.

lines. The remainder of the page (27 lines) was left blank. This had never happened between books prior to this point. It had to happen here because when Cowdery jumped ahead he had no way of knowing where Mormon would end.[380] Gathering 20 seems to have been calculated to be sufficient for the Book of Ether, but it was not, and its last 18 verses had to begin gathering 21. These filled the first page and Moroni began at the top of page two. This explanation is perfect from the LDS perspective, which imposes the constraint of the traditional book sequence with Moroni at the end.

This order is so ingrained in most scholars, LDS and otherwise, that the alternative is rarely considered. The far more normal sequence would be for the *Book of Mormon* to be completed before Ether, a separate record of a different people. This would have been in accordance with the text of the copyright submission of June 11, which has subsequently appeared on the BOM title page. Ether is listed separately, even at the head of the second paragraph. It is highly incongruous for Ether to be sandwiched in between two books of the Nephite record. Indeed, if Moroni existed when Cowdery jumped ahead, he could have jumped ahead to Moroni to begin copying it at the head of a new gathering, to let the Book of Mormon end where it might and rely on the printer to ignore the empty part of the last page of gathering 19. This is, after all, what was done by jumping ahead to Ether. Fixing the formatting irregularity was left to the printer.

Cowdery could well have fallen behind in copying. Just as Smith had to return to Harmony to provide for his family, Cowdery too had to make a living. We have almost no information on what he did. It is possible that Grandin Press was in need of assistance. Lucy Smith wrote that at the time that "rabble, and a party of restless religionists" met to oppose work on the new bible, "Oliver and a young man by the name of Robinson were printing…"[381] We recall that in December 1829 he wrote to Smith, "it may look rather strange to you to find that I have so soon become a printer and you may cast in your mind what I shall become

---

[380] Skousen, *Printer's Manuscript of the* Book of Mormon, I:46. For photos of ms P, see Ronald K. Esplin & Matthew J. Grow, gen. eds., *The Joseph Smith Papers*, vol. 3, pt. 2 (Salt Lake City: The Church Historian's Press, 2015).
[381] Lucy Smith, in Anderson, *Lucy's Book*, 460.

next."[382] Several years later he worked as a printer and was able to take on an apprentice. Perhaps this work slowed down his copying.

Clearly, the authors did not plan on Moroni recording very much of the Nephite record. It is the book of Mormon, after all. When he took over briefly as a record-keeper, referring to things his deceased father had written, he complained, "I would write it also if I had room upon the plates, but I have not; and ore [gold] I have none." (Mormon 8:5) Note that Mormon had taken all the records of the Nephites, plus those of Jared with their translation, plus the relics, from the hill Shim about 375 CE, and was killed in 400 CE. For all of this period he was the commander of all of the Nephite forces as they were driven from there to Cumorah, when, after a prolonged military retreat with occasional pitched battles, the Nephites suffered their final defeat. Remarkably, it is during this time that he did his entire share of the BOM narrative, from Words of Mormon to Mormon 7:10. One can understand that the BOM authors would not also have had him abridge the plates of Ether. Rather, this was assigned to Moroni. We have to assume that he had calculated that there was still enough room on the gold plates for that.

The text of the end of Mormon, Chapter 9, clearly ends the *Book of Mormon*:

> 35. And these things are written that we may rid our garments of the blood of our brethren, who have dwindled in unbelief.
> 36. And behold, these things which we have desired concerning our brethren, yea, even their restoration to the knowledge of Christ, are according to the prayers of all the saints who have dwelt in the land.
> 37. And may the Lord Jesus Christ grant that their prayers may be answered according to their faith; and may God the Father remember the covenant which he hath made with the house of Israel; and may he bless them forever, through faith on the name of Jesus Christ. Amen.

It is accordingly late in the Jaredite narrative that we find Moroni's personal farewell speech to both the gentiles and his own people. He begins, "And now I, Moroni, bid farewell unto the Gentiles, yea, and also unto my brethren whom I love, until we shall meet before the judgment-seat of Christ…" (Ether 12:38) He adds, "And only a few have I written, because of my weakness in writing." (12:40)

---

[382] Oliver Cowdery, letter to Joseph Smith dated 28/12/1829, in Vogel, *Early Mormon Documents*, II:407

The BOM authors were well aware that Moroni had signed off when they decided to add an additional book to their work, and penned the first verse of Moroni: "Now I, Moroni, after having made an end of abridging the account of the people of Jared, I had supposed not to have written more." He repeats, "Wherefore, I write a few more things, contrary to that which I had supposed; for I had supposed not to have written any more." (1:4) This evidence demonstrates that originally the *Book of Mormon* ended with Mormon. His death in 400 CE marked an even 1000 years, the Nephite millennium. They intended the Book of Ether to be a separate record that would be appended to the end of the *Book of Mormon*. Then, as the completion of the printing was drawing nigh, they decided to add the Book of Moroni. But while it was still in the draft editorial stage, the printer finished Mormon. To avoid a delay it was necessary to provide him with gathering 20, Ether, unavoidably sandwiching it into the Nephite record.

The question is, "Why write Moroni at all?"

Moroni is an inseparable part of the story of Cowdery's revelation. Its author essentially says somewhat lamely that since the Lamanites have not yet killed me, I will write more. By its own admission, it is an add-on. Moroni has a lot in common with Words of Mormon. Each has a functional text that needed to be inserted, and each adds additional material to disguise the real reason for the work. The second part of chapter one of the Mosiah draft was added to Words of Mormon, to disguise the real purpose of explaining the existence of the small plates of Nephi. In the case of Moroni, the functional material is the church establishment verses, which were-intended to be disguised by the addition of three epistles of Mormon to his son, and then yet another farewell. Moroni specifically refers to his abridgment of Ether indicating that he was following up on his Jaredite account. If Moroni had existed when Cowdery had to jump ahead in his copying, it would have made more sense to jump ahead to Moroni. And if it did not exist, then it drew from Cowdery's revelation, and not the other way around.

The Cowdery material added into 3 Nephi did not sufficiently dampen his ambitions for his revelation. These two cousins had worked cheek by jowl for months, each needing the other. Undoubtedly issues between them were settled in extensive discussion, and in this case they arrived at an additional and somewhat belated compromise, perhaps brokered by Hyrum. They agreed that additional material would be inserted into the BOM by adding a new book, Moroni. There was something in this deal for both. The remaining substantive part of the revelation would be recognized but would not go out in Smith's name. The Bible wraps up with epistles, so why not the BOM. The first of these Mormon epistles was on the theme of faith, hope and charity, a good Pauline topic and totally neutral. But Mormon's second epistle gave Smith the opportunity to more fully develop his view against the need to baptize children prior to the age of accountability. Cowdery was keenly aware of the importance of this issue to Joseph, in view of the death of his first-born son in the first hours of his life; of Alvin, his eldest brother in 1823 and Ephraim Smith, who died after only eleven days in this world in 1810. Smith would welcome this opportunity to inveigh against this doctrine of the Whore of All the Earth.

The coming together of the two is further indicated in BC 24 (D&C 20:2-3), an overtly collaborative work that further elaborated aspects of the organization of the Church. It comprises commandments "given to Joseph the seer who was called of God & ordained an Apostle of Jesus Christ an Elder of the Church & also to Oliver who was also called of God an Apostle of Jesus Christ an Elder of the Church & ordained under his hand." Although this already gave pride of place to Smith over Cowdery, he was not satisfied with it. In the D&C version, Smith's designation, "an elder," was changed to "the first elder," and Cowdery's was changed to "the second elder."

Meanwhile, in Palmyra, Abner Cole, the editor of *The Reflector*, was using Grandin press nights to print his paper. This gave him access to the printed pages of the BOM text printed so far. Around late December he promised his readers that his newspaper would print the new Gold Bible, giving them the chance to read some of it without buying a copy, and thereby avoid putting money into the Smiths' coffers. On 2 January he published 1 Nephi 1:1-2:3. Two more installments appeared, on the 13th and 22nd. Joseph Smith Sr. apparently rushed off to Harmony to fetch Joseph to deal with Cole. It is generally thought that Joseph Jr.'s return was delayed so that he could appear in court on 19 January regarding a debt owed to Lemuel Durfee.[383] If Smith departed Harmony the next day, he could have arrived at Manchester on 24

---

[383] "Nathan Pierce Docket Book," in Vogel, *Early Mormon Documents*, III:491-92.

January. There is also evidence that he was in Manchester in early February when, it is said, he had a revelation to sell his copyright in Kingston, Ontario, Canada. This failed, but Whitmer recalled that Smith was in Manchester when the party arrived back. These events brought Smith back in touch with Cowdery, and at that time they could have arrived at the Moroni compromise.

Time was not an issue. The printing was not completed until 26 March 1830. Ms *P* has a total of 453 pages not including Moroni. If we allow 5.5 months up to an estimated completion date for Ether (half of August, half of September and October to mid February), then the rate of copying into ms *P* would be eighty-two pages a month. Moroni occupies a bit less than ten ms pages. This could be done easily in less than one week in late February or early March. Before the printer got to this new, small and last gathering, they also had to produce an initial draft and a completed draft of Moroni. Then the latter had to be copied into ms *O*, and then into ms *P*. In a pinch, ms *P* could have been done first, and ms *O* updated later.

The above derives from key observations. First, there must have been antecedent drafts. Second, there must have been at least two drafters, but quite possibly three. Third, if there were three, one or two must have worked up north, in Manchester. Fourth, there is evidence that drafting commenced prior to the arrival of Cowdery in Harmony. Fifth, for the completion of ms *O*, the translator and his scribe had nearly two months at Joseph Jr.'s home, one month in Fayette and three months in Manchester. Sixth, not only does Mosiah display stylistic distributions different from the rest of the BOM books, but Moroni was not even thought of until Nephi had been printed. With work already done prior to April 5 there was plenty of time for the project. The dates to complete ms *O* to the end of Mormon plus Ether are from some time in May (or as late as the first of June) to the end of September (or even before), or to early March 1830 if we include Moroni.

Getting the Job Done

From June on, events happened expeditiously. Martin Harris secured the contract with Grandin Press for publication. In a memorandum made by the printer and typesetter John H. Gilbert dated 8 September 1892 we read:

> When the printer was ready to commence work, Harris was notified, and Hyrum Smith brought the first installment of manuscript, of 24 pages, closely written on common foolscap paper—he had it under his vest, and vest and coat closely buttoned over it. At night Smith came and got the manuscript, and with the same precaution carried it away. The next morning with the same watchfulness, he brought it again, and at night took it away…
>
> Martin Harris, Hyrum Smith and Oliver Cowdery were very frequent visitors to the office during the printing of the Mormon Bible. The manuscript was supposed to be in the handwriting of Cowdery. Every Chapter, if I remember correctly, was one solid paragraph, without a punctuation mark, from beginning to end.
>
> Names of persons and places were generally capitalized, but sentences had no end. The character for short &, was used almost invariably where the word and, occurred, except at the end of a chapter. I punctuated it to make it read as I supposed the Author intended, and but very little punctuation was altered. …
>
> The work was commenced in August 1829, and finished in March 1830,—seven months. …
>
> Joseph Smith, Jr. had nothing to do whatever with the printing or furnishing copy for the printers, being but once in the office during the printing of the Bible, and then not over 15 or 20 minutes.[384]

Stephen S. Harding also reported on Smith's visit to the printer, placing him in Manchester in August.[385] While the printer was working on typesetting, Oliver Cowdery was hard at work making a printer's copy. Material was taken to the printer as the copying was completed. On 19 March 1830, the *Wayne Sentinel* announced that the BOM would be available the following week. It later confirmed that it was available at Palmyra's bookstore on 26 March. Joseph Knight Sr. picked up Joseph Smith Jr. from Manchester to take him to Palmyra. Some books were

---

[384] Gilbert, "Memorandum."
[385] Stephen S. Harding, statement to Thomas Gregg, in Vogel, *Early Mormon Documents*, III:161.

ready but most still needed to be bound.[386] This segment of Joseph Smith's career was finished, and the business of building a community of believers was to begin.

This new bible did not have to compete for the Nobel Prize for literature; indeed, Mark Twain, who was no friend of the Mormons, called it "chloroform in print."[387] Even so, it has won a place in the history of the United States of America. It not only served well as a platform for a new world religion, but has been the backbone of its sustainability over time. Its community of believers went on to play an important role in settling the American West.

---

[386] Vogel, *Joseph Smith*, 486.
[387] Mark Twain, *Roughing It* (Hartford: American Publishing Co., 1872), 58-59.

Chapter 19

Church, Power and the Promised Land

When the *Book of Mormon* was published, the Smiths may have thought: "done at last." But it was just the beginning. Very early on, the founders, and probably many of the new adherents, hoped for a place reserved for them, much like Lehi's promised land. In December of 1830, Smith received a revelation that the whole church should move to Ohio. (D&C 37:1-3) This choice to gather the Saints was probably a response to the fact that on 29 October, 1830, a group of missionaries sent to preach to the Indians in Missouri, arrived at Kirtland, Ohio, where they preached and baptized numerous converts. These most notably included a major pillar of early Church development, Sidney Rigdon (8 Nov. 1830), the former preacher of yet another early Church leader, Parley P. Pratt (himself baptized c. 1 Sept. 1830, in Seneca Lake, New York, by Oliver Cowdery). In January of 1831, Smith moved his family to Kirtland. Over half of the revelations in the *Book of Commandments* would be received there. Soon after Smith's arrival, revelatory instructions were given regarding Church organization.

Only about six months later, in June, a Church conference was held, and shortly after that, a fateful instruction was received that the next conference would be held in Missouri, on the border of the territory of the Lamanites (D&C 52). Smith and an exploratory party arrived in St. Louis, Missouri on 1 July1831, and on 20 July a revelation was received that a temple would be built west of Independence (D&C 57). The site for this temple was chosen, and on 3 Aug. 1831, Smith laid a cornerstone as an expression of their determination that this building would be built. Plans for the city were developed, including a number of temples, for different purposes. In August of 1831, a commandment instructed Sidney Rigdon to write a description of this new land, a type of prospectus to convince Saints to embrace it, and to donate funds for the temple (D&C 58). These plans were overtaken by events on the ground. Many non-Mormon citizens of Missouri were bitterly opposed to the Mormons, and on 20 July 1833, citizens of Jackson County met at the courthouse in Independence and made a request for the Mormons to leave the county. In essence, they were "warned out," a time-honored New England practice to keep out persons deemed "undesirable." When this request was refused, a mob destroyed the printing house. The original temple lot is currently owned by the Church of Christ (temple lot), and most of the greater temple lot is owned by the Community of Christ. The LDS Church has dedicated temples in the area, one in St. Louis in 1997 and a second one in Kansas City in 2012.

Plan B: On 1 June 1833, a revelation was received for the establishment of a temple in Kirtland, "which house I [the Lord] design to endow those whom I have chosen with power from on high..." (D&C 95:8) In a sense, for a while the Church would have two centers, one in Kirtland, Ohio, and the other in Missouri, where members of the Church continued to live in several counties, and later developed a center in a place that came to be called Far West, in a somewhat less inhabited area. The Missouri center persisted for the church largely as an intention. This dream was forcibly put on hold when, in 1838, Missouri Governor Lilburn W. Boggs issued an executive order (the infamous extermination order) for the removal of the Mormons from the state.

In May of 1839, the Saints made their first land purchases at Commerce, Illinois, on the east bank of the Mississippi River. In August, Smith renamed the new settlement Nauvoo, and in December the state of Illinois granted the Nauvoo Charter, which provided for the creation of a University of Nauvoo and the Nauvoo Legion. It grew rapidly and in only five years rivaled Chicago in population. Work began on the Nauvoo temple in March 1841, and in December Smith opened his Red Brick Store. On 15 March 1842 the Nauvoo Masonic Lodge was formed, and two days later a female Relief Society. Joseph Smith, President, Prophet, Seer and Revelator, became the Mayor of Nauvoo, and Lieutenant-General of the Nauvoo Legion. In August 1843 the Smith family moved into the Mansion House, which was partly a hotel.

Joseph Smith had arrived. But it was not to last. Opposition to him, within the Church, and to the Church itself, from apostates (then called dissidents) and non-Mormons, became acute once again. On 27 June 1844, Joseph and his brother Hyrum were murdered at Carthage Jail, where they were being held for trial, presumably with protection.

That empty land, like the promised land that Lehi's people inherited, had still not been found. LDS Church President, Wilford Woodruff reported that Smith himself had prophesied that "There will be tens of thousands of Latter-day Saints who will be gathered in the Rocky

Mountains..."[388] This report however was remembered long after the event.

Smith's death resulted in a major succession crisis. On 8 August 1844, the Church voted to sustain the Quorum of the Twelve (apostles) to take the lead as guardians of the Church, assisted by Sidney Rigdon and Amasa Lyman as counselors, as they had been to the First Presidency. Brigham Young was effectively the leader of the Twelve, possibly even before Rigdon's exit from the scene. After a period of contention, and efforts of several claimants, on 27 December 1847, in Kanesville, Iowa, he, Willard Richards and Heber C. Kimball, were sustained as the new First Presidency, and Brigham Young was recognized as the new President, Prophet, Seer and Revelator. The Smith family era was over. Emma Smith, with her son Joseph Smith III, remained in Illinois, and in 1860 the latter became the head of the Reorganized Church of Jesus Christ of Latter Day Saints (RLDS, now the Community of Christ). On 14 January 1847, Brigham Young received his only revelation published in the *Doctrine and Covenants*, the plan of organization for the migration further west. Those who had the means were to load as much as possible into covered wagons and depart for a land not yet revealed. Lying sick in his wagon, on the outskirts of what is now Salt Lake City, he looked over the land lying at the foot of the Wasatch Mountains, and said, "This is the place."

A second group was to follow using handcarts. They could not arrange to depart until early fall, and requested that they be permitted to wait until spring. Young apparently feared that even more would join the ranks of the dissenters, and commanded that they depart immediately promising that the Lord would provide a mild winter for their journey. Unfortunately, the winter was hard, and many perished. But once they had arrived, the Mormons finally occupied a land that was largely unpopulated and sufficiently remote that they would be able to develop their religion and society in security. This would be about as close as they would get to having a land reserved just for them.

---

[388] Wilford Woodruff, *Sixty-Eighth Annual Conference of the Church of Jesus Christ of Latter-day Saints. Full Report of the Discourses* (Salt Lake City: April 1898), 57.

Proselytism: Mormonism on the Rise

From the earliest days after the establishment of the Church, Joseph Smith demonstrated an amazing ability to delegate authority. Within just six months after baptism, individuals who would become early Mormon leaders were entrusted with important duties, and even sent off on distant missions to preach Mormonism. This practice required controls. First, they were often sent off in groups of two or more. Second, they were, of course, preaching the *Book of Mormon*, which itself contained a message, and was ineluctably associated with Smith himself. Third, a document called the *Articles and Covenants*, developed during 1829, but read and unanimously accepted by the first conference of the Church on 9 June 1830, served as a formal statement of beliefs, and a source that could be used for developing sermons. Fourth, a number of Biblical scriptures were identified that missionaries could use to support the claims of Mormonism. Proselyting was strenuously promoted from the beginning.

In a sense, the first missionary work began when Smith recruited Martin Harris to work with him on a translation of the gold plates, and also when Joseph Smith Sr. recruited Oliver Cowdery to the cause, and they recruited David Whitmer. On 6 April 1830, Oliver Cowdery was designated "the first preacher of this church." (D&C 21:12) He preached in Fayette, New York, organized that branch of the Church, and baptized six converts.[389] Officially, the first missionary is said to have been Joseph's brother, Samuel, who was sent, with copies of the *Book of Mormon*, to preach the Restoration. Subsequently, he acquired a reputation for his missionary activities. On one mission, with Orson Hyde, he traveled on foot from Ohio to Maine. In 1830, almost immediately after the founding of the Church, Oliver Cowdery, Peter Whitmer Jr., Parley P. Pratt and Ziba Peterson were sent out to convert the Lamanites. Although they did not report Indian baptisms, they arrived in Kirtland, Ohio, on 29 October 1830, where they baptized 127 people, according to Pratt.[390] Over time, this nucleus expanded, and their success may have led to the decision to locate the Church in Kirtland. In 1837, a delegation of the Quorum of the Twelve Apostles, including

---

[389] Marquardt, *The Rise of Mormonism*, 135.
[390] Parley P. Pratt, in Parley P. Pratt, Jr., ed., *Autobiography of Parley P. Pratt* (Salt Lake City: Deseret Book Company, 1938, 1985), 36.

Orson Hyde and Heber C. Kimball, were sent to preach in England, where they met with considerable success. In 1843, Smith sent missionaries to the Society Islands in French Polynesia, presumably to convert the descendants of the Nephites taken there by Hagoth (Alma 63:5-8). In principle, every member is charged with a missionary responsibility with respect to their friends and acquaintances, and many early converts resulted from the efforts of ordinary members.

An examination of the conversion of some of the key early leaders of this new community shows that Smith was primarily involved in the development of the Church, its organization, rites and theology. Spreading the message of the Restoration, also a top priority, had to be left largely to the missionaries.

Convert	Instrumental Person	Comment
Martin Harris	Joseph Smith	Smith worked for him.
Oliver Cowdery	Joseph Smith Sr.	Cowdery roomed in Smith home.
David Whitmer	Cowdery & Smith Sr.	Cowdery had known him.
Parley P. Pratt	Hyrum Smith	Hyrum Smith (baptized by Cowdery).
Sidney Rigdon	Pratt/Cowdery/others	Cowdery & missionary colleagues.
F. G. Williams	Cowdery & colleagues	He was Kirtland Justice of the Peace.
W. E. McLellin	D. Whitmer/Hyrum Smith	First heard Whitmer preach.
John Corrill	Cowdery & colleagues	He gave the missionaries lodging.
Orson Hyde	Sidney Rigdon	Rigdon had known him earlier.
Brigham Young	Joseph Smith	Young sought him out.

Security, Persecution and Slander

Joseph Smith's earliest expression of security concerns focused on home intrusion activities of persons who believed he had found gold plates, and who wished to steal them. When Egbert B. Grandin, editor of the *Wayne Sentinel*, was first approached to publish the *Book of Mormon*, he refused, but later agreed to it when it was made clear that it would be published elsewhere if he did not publish it. On about 1 July 1830, Smith was again arrested for disorderly conduct, based on the same event for which he had been examined in 1826. This was essentially harassment and he was acquitted. Shortly after this, he was arrested again and brought to a court only six miles away, for the same event. This charge was not sustained. Joseph took up residence in the home of John Johnson in Hiram, Ohio. During this time violent opposition developed towards him, and 24 March 1832 he was attacked by a mob and tarred and feathered. As though this were not bad enough, a story was circulated that Smith had been caught in intimate relations with Johnson's daughter, that her irate brother complained, and that this mob (apparently the one that did in fact tar and feather Joseph), attempted to castrate him for his crime.[391] In fact, the girl's parents and brother had converted to Mormonism and remained active members until 1837, when they joined a group of apostates. They did, however, return to the Church. The story appears to be an example of the calumny suffered by not only the prophet but also many ordinary adherents to the new faith.

This missionary work was oriented to more than just conversions. The members were urged to gather to the Church center, initially in Kirtland, Ohio, but which was eventually to be in Jackson County (Independence) Missouri, Zion, the place for the establishment of the New Jerusalem. As the converts increased the Mormon community in Missouri increased. Mormon determination to claim the land of their inheritance, and their plans to convert the Indians, were threatening to the already established citizenry, who were also subject to motivations of bigotry. As a result, Missouri became the site of the most severe persecution. Following the destruction of the Phelps printing house, the Mormons continued to settle in Missouri, motivated by a desire to "gather to Zion." A non-Mormon, Jacob Haun, had established a mill on Shoal Creek, Haun's Mill. Although only a few Mormon families resided in this small settlement, over 750 LDS families resided in the adjoining area. On 30 October 1838, around 200 men attacked the settlement. Fifteen Latter-day Saints died as a result of this attack. Although it may be that this massacre was not a result of Governor Boggs' Mormon extermination/removal order, violence and opposition to the Saints resulted in the expulsion of over 10,000 Mormons.

Creating a Church: Organization and Control

Joseph Smith was successful in attracting many able, energetic and ambitious people, whom he appointed to serious positions in his Church. From the start, he was aware of the possibility that there could be an effort to wrest the movement away from him. His ace was, of course, his

---

[391] "History of Luke Johnson," *Deseret News*, 19 May 1858.

19. Church, Power and the Promised Land 453

key connection to the founding scripture. Short of his untimely demise, or clear fall from grace as a fallen prophet, the *Book of Mormon* underpinned his position, at least to a large degree.

As noted above, the three witnesses were apparently interested in being listed as having seen the gold plates by the power of God, and not at the hand of Joseph Smith like the other eight witnesses, setting themselves apart as having a special connection with the divine. Oliver Cowdery revealed a desire to elevate his role when he tried to become a cotranslator along with Joseph. A revelation was received regarding Cowdery (April, 1829), wherein the Lord said, "And, behold, I grant unto you a gift, if you desire of me, to translate, even as my servant Joseph." (D&C6:25) A second revelation, also in April, says, "And that you may know the mysteries of God, and that you may translate and receive knowledge from all those ancient records which have been hid up, that are sacred;.." (D&C 8:11) But in a subsequent revelation, he was deprived of this power: "Be patient, my son, for it is wisdom in me, and it is not expedient that you should translate at this present time." Cowdery, claiming to be an apostle, also claimed to have received a revelation for the establishment of the new church. As we have seen, Smith had to foil this effort to be on a par with the prophet. It is improbable that Cowdery's role in producing the *Book of Mormon* had changed. Rather, Smith understood that it was not in his interest for Cowdery to become, as it were, an equal to himself. And Cowdery was made to understand that the chances of the new scripture being accepted were far greater if there were no hint of collaboration in its composition. Potential converts should be left to conclude that Smith, farm boy that he was, could never have written the *Book of Mormon*, just as Jesus is depicted as impressing the learned in the temple as a young boy, and Muhammad was always said to have been illiterate.

The first emergence of hierarchy was already there: Smith who translated by the gift of God, Smith and Cowdery who received the priesthood from John the Baptist personally and became the first elders, David Whitmer and Harris who were called to be shown the plates by the power of God, and those who were shown the plates by Joseph Smith. With the instruction given in D&C 20 for the selection of the twelve, the top of the hierarchy became Smith, and then Cowdery, with David Whitmer actually or nearly on the same level.

The express rational for the entire enterprise was the Restoration of All Things (D&C 27:6 & 86:10) prior to the coming of Christ. A minimal idea of what this would entail is already made clear in the *Book of Mormon*. The true church will bear the name of Christ. (3 Nephi 27:5-8) Nephi "did consecrate Jacob and Joseph, that they should be priests and teachers over the land of my people." (2 Nephi 5:26; cf. Jacob 1:18) A church was established by Alma at the waters of Mormon, "And they were called the church of God, or the church of Christ, from that time forward." (Mosiah 18:17) He established another "in the land of Sidom, and consecrated priests and teachers in the land, to baptize..." (Alma 15:13) He preached about the high priesthood of Melchizedek. (Alma 13:14-18) The procedures and prayer for baptism was given in 3 Nephi 11:23-27. The Book of Moroni makes a rather jarring break from the characteristic *Book of Mormon* language, and delineates church institutions and rites "that perhaps they may be of worth unto my brethren, the Lamanites, in some future day..." (Moroni 1:4) These passages were taken from a revelation received by Oliver Cowdery in June and inserted into Moroni, which was added later on so they could appear as part of the BOM. They included the procedures and prayer for the ordination of priests and teachers, and the blessing of the Sacrament (Holy Communion). Even the wording of the prayers to bless the bread and wine is given. Although this did not yet constitute an ecclesiastical hierarchy, it shows that the issues of Church organization and rites were being thought out even before the new bible saw the light of day. The intention was clear: as soon as the *Book of Mormon* was printed, the foundation of the new church could begin.

The Church was organized on 6 April 1830, and a revelation received that day began with the words, "Behold, there shall be kept a record among you." (D&C 21:1) Oliver Cowdery was assigned to write the Church history, but after he was sent to Missouri, John Whitmer became the first historian in his place, in March of 1831. After Cowdery's return five months later, he, Whitmer and Phelps (Church printer) were assigned to prepare the Church revelations and print them in Missouri. The production of a Church history, which was at that point essentially the history of Joseph Smith, was considered so important that Smith himself put pen to paper and produced a personal account between 20 July and 27 November 1832.[392] He wrote another account in 1838-

---

[392] Dean C. Jessee, *Personal Writings of Joseph Smith*, 3-14.

39.[393] On 1 March 1842, he provided a historical sketch, upon request, to a Chicago editor, John Wentworth.[394]

In 1834-35, in consultation with Joseph to some extent, Cowdery published a history of the Church in its publication, *Messenger and Advocate*. This account does not agree with the later official version in some important details.

Smith's managerial style could be called management by revelation. For this reason, the collection of his revelations in the current *Doctrine and Covenants* contains considerable detail regarding Church history. As a result, this had to be carefully edited, and was subject to change over time. Cowdery worked with Smith on the preparation of the first publication of revelations, called the *Book of Commandments*. He was also either the editor, or on the editorial board, of early Church publications, such as the *Evening and the Morning Star*, the *Messenger and Advocate*, and the *Northern Times*. In this capacity he could also monitor the messages of the Church over time. An example of the problems that he could face is treated by Marquardt: "*The Evening and the Morning Star* [printed originally by Phelps in Missouri], reprinted in Kirtland between January and June 1835 under the title *Evening and Morning Star*, altered the texts, deleted previously published material, and inserted editorial comments by Cowdery."[395] An important Cowdery editorial comment reads: "On the revelations we merely say, that we were not a little surprised to find the previous print so different from the original."[396] In other words, the original used in Missouri for the *Book of Commandments* was not the original used in Kirtland for the D&C, and Cowdery felt he might be blamed.

For the occasion of the organization meeting of the Church, a different sort of revelation was presented to the membership, a collaborative effort of Smith and Cowdery regarding details of church organization. In his 1839 history, Smith introduced it by saying, "We obtained of him [Jesus Christ] the following, by the spirit of prophecy and revelation..."[397] The text is not in the divine first person, but in the first person plural. Smith and Cowdery are referred to as "an Apostle of

---

[393] Jessee, *ibid*, 196-211.

[394] Jessee, *ibid*, 212-220.

[395] Marquardt, *Rise of Mormonism*, 175.

[396] *Idem*.

[397] Joseph Smith's 1839 history, in Vogel, *Early Mormon Documents*, I:90.

Jesus Christ an elder of the Church."[398] Smith was called of God and ordained, while Cowdery was just called of God. This is stated in the past tense, indicating that they claimed that they had already been called to that status. Perhaps Cowdery was ordained by Smith, since there is no other referent for the pronoun in the phrase "under his hand." It is interesting to note that in the later D&C 20 version, Smith became "the first elder of this Church," and Cowdery "the second elder of this church."

The revelation describes the manner of baptism (20:37); the duties of the elders, priests, teachers, deacons, and members of the church of Christ (20:38-67); and the duties of the members after they are received by baptism (20:68-84). Another revelation gives the position of Joseph Smith: "...thou shalt be called a seer, a translator, a prophet, an apostle of Jesus Christ, an elder of the church through the will of God the Father, and the grace of your Lord Jesus Christ." Oliver Cowdery was again called an apostle, and "the first preacher of this church unto the church, and before the world..." (21:10-12)

Another issue is the emergence of the status of apostle. It is no easy matter to separate the statuses of "apostle" and "elder" at this early date. The study of the evolution of the authority to receive revelation, and of various statuses and positions, has been difficult due to a lack of sufficient contemporary information, and statements made by those who left the Church, the dissenters. For men such as David Whitmer and William E. McLellin, these issues were points of contention in their war with Joseph Smith and the Mormon establishment.

Already prior to 6 April 1830, both Smith and Cowdery had been ordained to be apostles. Church tradition has held that this was under the hands of Peter, James and John, but early references to support this are not found. As for Smith's statuses indicated in his long title, the revelation states: "Wherefore it behooveth me that he shall be ordained by you, Oliver Cowdery mine apostle..." (D&C 21:10) Since the ordination by John the Baptist on 15 May 1829 was by the laying on of hands, and the ordination to be an apostle, and first and second elders, was "under his hand," it seems reasonable to conclude that Cowdery's ordination of Smith to be seer, translator, prophet, and apostle was also by the laying on of hands. Cowdery had already been referred to as an

---

[398] D&C, 20:2-3; cf. the text in the Zebedee Coltrin Journal, in Marquardt, *Joseph Smith Revelations*, 63.

apostle in his revelation received *circa* June 1829, and both he and David Whitmer were called apostles in D&C 18.

Given the central role of revelation in the management of the church, establishing both doctrine and ritual, as well as the authority and power relations between the leaders of the Church, it quickly became obvious that the authority to receive revelation should be defined. In September of 1830, *Book of Mormon* witness Hiram Page claimed to have received revelations by means of his seer stone pertaining to the "upbuilding of Zion." This set off alarms. A revelation came, addressing the issue (D&C 28):

> 1. Behold, I say unto thee, Oliver, that it shall be given unto thee that thou shalt be heard by the church in all things whatsoever thou shalt teach them by the Comforter, concerning the revelations and commandments which I have given.
> 2. But, behold, verily, verily, I say unto thee, no one shall be appointed to receive commandments and revelations in this church excepting my servant Joseph Smith, Jun., for he receiveth them even as Moses.
> 11. And again thou [Oliver] shalt take thy brother, Hiram Page, between him and thee alone, and tell him that those things which he hath written from that stone are not of me and that Satan deceiveth him...

Smith had taken two steps to cut off this threat. First, he made it perfectly clear that although someone such as Cowdery could be guided by the Comforter to understand and teach what had already been received, only Smith could receive doctrine and commandments, including directives, for the Church. Second, he used the talents of Cowdery to get Page to retract his revelation, while remaining in the faith. Cowdery enforced the rule that limited himself as well.

This did not end there. A few months later a woman named Hubble claimed to be a prophetess, to have received a number of revelations, and to be a teacher to the Church.[399] After providing a number of examples of the problem, Elder George A. Smith said, "There was a prevalent spirit all through the early history of this church, which prompted the Elders to suppose that they knew more than the Prophet. Elders would tell you that

---

[399] *History of the Church,* 1:154n.

the Prophet was going wrong."[400] This situation prompted a second revelation, which went even further. Smith devised a strategy to undermine efforts to displace him (D&C 43):

> 3. And this ye shall know assuredly, that there is none other appointed unto you to receive commandments and revelations until he be taken, if he abide in me.
> 4. But verily, verily, I say unto you, that none else shall be appointed unto this gift except it be through him, for if it be taken from him, he shall not have power except to appoint another in his stead...

In other words, even if Joseph should be found to be a fallen prophet, he would have the one remaining power: to designate his successor. This is not simply a matter of theology. It is a matter of authority, and ultimately power within the emerging organization. Smith did not establish the Church to stand by and allow recent converts, or even one of the eleven witnesses, arguably the least of them at that, to determine its organization or theology.

In the *Book of Mormon*, during the mission of Jesus Christ in the New World, he established his church, and selected twelve disciples. It is interesting that these were not called apostles. Most probably this was due to a concern that some latter-day converts may have felt that there could only be the twelve they were already familiar with. Apart from this change in title, their role was the same. By June 14, 1829, a revelation commanded: "And now, behold, I give unto you Oliver Cowdery, and also unto David Whitmer, that you shall search out the Twelve who shall have the desires of which I have spoken" (D&C 18:37). Irrespective of title or role, it was decided already, long before the publication of the new scripture, that there would be twelve. This traditional number is already evident in Smith plus the eleven witnesses. During the first few years, sources refer to a number of persons as apostles, although it is not clear what is meant on each occasion.[401] The most we can say for sure is that with reference to apostleship as a fundamental component of Church organization, as early as 14 June 1829 there were to be twelve, and on 14 February 1835, in Kirtland, Ohio, Cowdery, Whitmer and Harris, the

---

[400] *Journal of Discourses,* (Liverpool: B. Young, 1867) 11:7. Edition cited, Photo Lithographic Reprint (Los Angeles: Gartner Printing & Litho Co., 1956).
[401] D. Michael Quinn, *Mormon Hierarchy*, 7-14.

original three witnesses, chose twelve men to be ordained as apostles.[402] These included: John F. Boynton, Orson Hyde, Luke S. Johnson, Lyman E. Johnson, Heber C. Kimball, Thomas B. Marsh, William E. McLellin, David W. Patten, Orson Pratt, Parley P. Pratt, William Smith and Brigham Young. William Smith is the only blood relative (brother) of Joseph Smith; and no witness to the gold plates was included.

In the New Testament, the term "apostle" was not restricted to the twelve disciples of Christ. Those Twelve, however, became a special group very early in Christian custom and theology. However, they were scattered about, and never were able to function as a body. So too in Mormonism, even this Quorum of Twelve Apostles did not occupy the same position that they have today. Certainly Smith, the three witnesses, probably the eight as well, and other early leaders, such as Sidney Rigdon, did not see themselves as being reduced by their exclusion from the group.

The essence of authority in Mormonism is priesthood. The earliest printed reference to priesthood is in the *Book of Mormon* itself, which refers to Melchizedek as "having exercised mighty faith, and received the office of the high priesthood according to the holy order of God..." (Alma 13:18) The account of the visitation of John the Baptist to Smith and Cowdery does not find its way into print until Cowdery's October, 1834 history.[403] Baptisms were happening prior to the publication of the *Book of Mormon*, so it would appear that there was some event that served as the basis for this authority. Early references to priesthood refer to the high priesthood, probably taken from the *Book of Mormon* passage above. Two distinct priesthoods, the high priesthood (of Melchizedek) and the lesser priesthood (of Aaron, the Aaronic or Levitical priesthood) were explained in 22-23 September 1832: "Abraham received the Priesthood from Melchizedek... and the Lord confirmed a priesthood also upon Aaron and his seed..." Due to the sins of Israel, "therefore he [the Lord] took Moses out of their midst and the holy Priesthood also, and the lesser Priesthood continued, which Priesthood holdeth the keys of ministering of angels and the preparatory gospel,.. which [priesthood] the Lord caused to continue with the house of Aaron among the children of Israel..." (D&C 84:14, 18, 25-27)

---

[402] Kirtland Council Minute Book, 147, 149. See Marquardt, *Rise of Mormonism*, 231-32.
[403] Quinn, *Mormon Hierarchy*, 15.

Yet a third priesthood had emerged by 1834, the patriarchal priesthood, which came to be limited to the bestowal and sealing of patriarchal blessings. A significant aspect is that it is by blood. Joseph Smith claimed to have it by birth (D&C 86:8-9).[404] No ordination or laying on of hands was needed. This implies that his bloodline goes back to the ancient patriarchs. In this sense, it served to add to Smith's status. In 1834, Joseph Smith Sr. was ordained Presiding Patriarch. Others are ordained to be patriarchs without having this hereditary priesthood. The duties of the Presiding Patriarch (Patriarch of the Church) have varied over time. Until 1942 he supervised, presided over, and sometimes ordained local patriarchs.[405]

Finally, the LDS doctrine of "keys" is an important adjunct to the concept of priesthood. The keys are powers to perform specific acts; they direct the use of priesthood. In current Mormon belief, Smith and Cowdery not only received the Melchizedek priesthood from Peter, James and John, but also the keys to the apostolic office. An account of events in the summer of 1832, told in an autobiographical work of Philo Dibble, is at least illustrative of the role of keys in the power struggle:

> On invitation of Father [John] Johnson, of Hiram, Joseph removed his family to his home, to translate the New Testament. This was in the year 1831.
>
> At this time Sidney Rigdon was left to preside at Kirtland and frequently preached to us. Upon one occasion he said the keys of the kingdom were taken from us. On hearing this, many of his hearers wept, and when some one undertook to dismiss the meeting by prayer he said praying would do them no good, and the meeting broke up in confusion.
>
> Brother Hyrum [Smith] came to my house the next morning and told me all about it, and said it was false, and that the keys of the kingdom were still with us. He wanted my carriage and horses to go to the town of Hiram and bring Joseph. The word went abroad among the people immediately that Sidney [Rigdon] was going to expose "Mormonism."

---

[404] *Ibid*, 32-34.
[405] Arnold K. Garr, Donald Q. Cannon & Richard O. Cowan, *Encyclopedia of Latter-day Saint History* (Salt Lake City: Deseret Book Company, 2011), 899.

19. Church, Power and the Promised Land

Joseph came up to Kirtland a few days afterwards and held a meeting in a large barn. Nearly all the inhabitants of Kirtland turned out to hear him. The barn was filled with people, and others, unable to get inside, stood around the door as far as they could hear.

Joseph arose in our midst and spoke in mighty power, saying: "I can contend with wicked men and devils--yes with angels. No power can pluck those keys from me, except the power that gave them to me; that was Peter, James and John. But for what Sidney [Rigdon] has done, the devil shall handle him as one man handles another."[406]

Smith had to act, but ever so carefully. Rigdon had brought with him into the church former members of his Baptist congregation who were loyal to him. Initially, he disfellowshipped Rigdon (6 July 1832), but on the next day he rebuked him again and stripped him of the high priesthood. After receiving an expression of repentance, Smith reordained him to the high priesthood (28 July 1832).[407]

The ecclesiastical administrative divisions in the Church developed slowly. Initially, Smith referred to Kirtland as a stake in Zion, a metaphor based on the stakes of a tent (cf. Isaiah 33:20 & 54:2). Another was the stake in Missouri. The Nauvoo stake was composed of wards. In modern Mormonism, these correspond roughly to a parish (ward) and a diocese (stake). In Nauvoo, the divisions were more administrative. Each ward, once established, was headed by a lay bishop, whose duties tended to be temporal, administering to the needs of the members, and mobilizing them for projects, such as work on the temple. Each stake was also headed by a bishop, initially Newel K. Whitney for Ohio, and Edward Partridge for Missouri (Zion). John Corrill and Isaac Morley were ordained as assistants to Bishop Partridge. Both were ordained to the position (1831), but the positions lacked definition. They were to collect donations, essentially for the poor, but the residue should be stored, and used to purchase land for the church or construction projects. They should also investigate those who sin, for if they do not repent they "shall be cast out of the church." (D&C 42:31-37) Jurisdictional issues arose, largely as Bishop Partridge interpreted his authority very broadly,

---

[406] Philo Dibble in "Early Scenes in Church History," *Four Faith Promoting Classics* (Salt Lake City: Bookcraft, 1968), pp. 79-80.
[407] Quinn, Mormon Hierarchy, 42.

to the point of challenging Smith's ecclesiastical supremacy. A revelation rebuked and warned Partridge. (D&C 58: 14-15)

In November of 1831 Smith issued a divine clarification:

> 65. Wherefore, it must needs be that one be appointed, of the High Priesthood, to preside over the Priesthood; and he shall be called President of the High Priesthood of the Church.
> 66. Or in other words, the presiding High Priest over the High Priesthood of the Church.
> 67. From the same comes the administering of ordinances and blessings upon the church, by the laying on of the hands.
> 68. Wherefore, the office of a bishop is not equal unto it; for the office of a bishop is in administering all temporal things[408]

Five weeks after being ordained to that office by Sidney Rigdon, Smith chose counselors to assist him in the Presidency of the High Priesthood, later changed to the First Presidency of the Church. Out of this incident, Smith not only limited and defined the office of Bishop, but also added another title, making it perfectly clear that he presided over all priesthood in the Church.

When the First Presidency was established, Sidney Rigdon (a former minister), and Jesse Gause (a relatively recent convert), were chosen as Smith's counselors in this office. These selections were made under an unlucky star. Ordained 8 March 1832, Gause was excommunicated 3 December 1832, following Smith's actions to reign in Sidney Rigdon. On 5 January 1833, Frederick G. Williams was appointed a counselor to Smith. Back in favor, Sidney Rigdon was made first counselor "to preside over the Church in the abscence (sic) of brother Joseph."[409] On 5 December 1834, Smith ordained Cowdery as Assistant President of the High Priesthood, placing him over Rigdon and Williams, administratively.

Having presented his mission as the Restoration of All Things, and not wanting to leave anything out, Smith established a quorum of seventies, like the seventy elders of Israel (Numbers 11:16) and the seventy to announce the gospel. (Luke 10:1-17) He began choosing them on 28 February 1835. Proselytism was the essence of their calling, but

---

[408] Received in a revelation of November 1831, but inserted into D&C 107:65-68. See Quinn, *Mormon Hierarchy*, 39-40 & 70-71.

[409] Dean C. Jessee, *Personal Writings of Joseph Smith*, 34.

over time, the institution has been reinvented a number of times. The fact that they are sometimes called apostles comes from their calling to travel out to preach (evangelical apostles), apostle originally meaning one who has been sent forth, an emissary. The Seventies, whether they actually numbered seventy or fewer, were presided over by seven drawn from their midst. Beginning in 1835, the seven Presidents of the Seventy were included in the Church General Authorities.

Church hierarchy came to be the President of the Church, the two Counselors to the President (these three being the First Presidency), the Quorum of the Twelve Apostles, the Presidents of the Seventy, and the Presiding Bishopric.

Hierarchy, Incipient Theocracy, Opposition, and Resolution

As all of this was developing, considerable discontent developed on the part of two groups, those who had initially felt strongly that the churches had become far too bureaucratic and cherished the principle of a clear separation of church and state, and those who leaned toward hierarchy. In addition to the bureaucratic development in Mormonism, there emerged an inherent theocratic tendency. The Church was established as a precursor for the Second Coming, and Christ's reign on earth. That would be a world government, it would be totally theocratic under the Kingship of Christ, and church and state would be one and the same. Joseph Smith tended to see himself as a new Moses, while for Cowdery and the Whitmers, the appropriate model was Christ's Twelve Apostles with a high degree of autonomy in their revelation-guided ministries.

In September of 1837, Smith personally announced that "Oliver Cowdery has been in transgression, but as he is now chosen as one of the presidents or counselors, I trust that he will humble himself and magnify his calling..."[410] The truth of the charge cannot be ascertained. But it is known that Cowdery had become increasingly interested in politics. Furthermore, he, David and John Whitmer, and W. W. Phelps sold their land in Missouri at a time when some prominent Saints felt that doing so showed a lack of faith in the prospects of Jackson County becoming the gathering place for Zion. They were seen by some to be property speculators. The Whitmers and Phelps were then the presidency in

---

[410] Gunn, *Oliver Cowdery*, 141.

Missouri. They were replaced by Thomas B. Marsh and David W. Patten. The former gave an account in his autobiography.[411]

> Sometime in the winter, George M. Hinkle, John Murdock and some others came to my house, and suggested the importance of calling a meeting to take into consideration the manner that W. [William] W. Phelps and David and John Whitmer had disposed of the money which I had borrowed in the Tennessee and Kentucky Branches in 1836. Accordingly, a meeting was called February 5th, 1838, and the conduct of the Presidency in Zion investigated. The Church would not sustain said presidency, but appointed myself and Brother D. [David] W. Patten presidents, pro tem., until Joseph Smith would arrive. We also reorganized the Church in Zion, placing every officer in his proper place. Joseph arrived in Far West, March 14th, and approved of the course we had pursued.

On 30 January 1838, Cowdery, David and John Whitmer, W. W. Phelps, Frederick G. Williams, Jacob Whitmer and Lyman E. Johnson, met in the home of Oliver Cowdery in Far West, to discuss the "state of said church and the manner in which some of the authorities of the same have for a time past, and are still endeavoring to unite ecclesiastical and civil authority, and force men under pretense of incurring the displeasure of heaven to use their earthly substance contrary to their own interest and privilege..."[412] The new presidency proceeded to try Cowdery and the Whitmers, and they were cut off from the Church. They and Cowdery protested that this council was illegitimate.

On 14 March 1838, Smith arrived in Far West, but even with his presence things grew no better. Nine formal charges were drawn up against Oliver Cowdery, including a charge that he had accused Joseph Smith of adultery. When he failed (refused) to attend the hearing, he was excommunicated on 12 April 1838. Since Martin Harris had joined the Kirtland apostates and the church of Warren Parrish, all of the Three Witnesses had left the Church, and all of the Eight Witnesses excepting the three Smiths. Joseph and his family had a whole new team.

---

[411] Thomas B. Marsh, "History of Thomas Baldwin Marsh [by himself]," *The Latter-day Saints' Millennial Star* 26 (1864), 359-60, 375-76, 390- 92, 406.
[412] Huntington Library Letters, no. 90, in Gunn, *Oliver Cowdery*, 149-50.

Creating a Church: Ritual

There is evidence that Cowdery's nemesis was Sidney Rigdon. Smith's attention now turned to establishing the rites of a new religion, and Rigdon, a former minister, probably had ideas along these lines. On at least one occasion, he simply inquired about an issue and asked the prophet to inquire of the Lord about it. It is possible that in this manner he was able to introduce many of his ideas. Smith was a collaborator, and was probably not adverse to input of this nature, put in the right manner, privately, and from the right person. This is not to say that Smith was himself devoid of ideas in these matters.

The announced mission for a latter-day prophet was the Restoration of All Things. The initial rites of the nascent church were largely limited to baptism by immersion, the gift of the Holy Ghost, the Sacrament (Holy Communion) and ordination to receive the priesthood by the laying on of hands. Another component important in Mormon worship is music. Emma Smith collected hymns for an LDS hymnal, published in 1836.[413] A very talented convert, Eliza R. Snow, composed two hymns for Emma's collection, and many others later. In various contexts, Mormons exhibited the Gift of Tongues, and occasionally burst into song in Tongues.

1. Washings and Anointing. The beginning of ritual innovation was with the founding of the School of the Prophets, commanded in revelation 3 January 1833 (D&C 88:127). The first meeting, 23 January 1833, was in the upper room of the Newel K. Whitney store. Joseph Smith presided, and all present participated in the first practice of a ritual washing of the feet, also as commanded (D&C 88):

> 138. And ye shall not receive any among you in this school save he is clean from the blood of this generation;
> 139. And he shall be received by the ordinance of the washing of feet, for unto this end was the ordinance of the washing of feet instituted.
> 140. And again, the ordinance of washing feet is to be administered by the president, or presiding elder of the church.

---

[413] Emma Smith, ed., *A Collection of Sacred Hymns for the Church of the Latter Day Saints*, Selected by Emma Smith (Kirtland, OH: F. G. Williams & Co., 1836). The title page says 1835 but it was printed in 1836.

141. It is to be commenced with prayer; and after partaking of bread and wine, he is to gird himself according to the pattern given in the thirteenth chapter of John's testimony concerning me. Amen.

The official account reads:

> On the 23rd of January, we again assembled in conference; when, after much speaking, singing, praying, and praising God, all in tongues, we proceeded to the washing of feet... Each Elder washed his own feet first, after which I girded myself with a towel and washed the feet of all of them, wiping them with the towel with which I was girded... Having continued all day in fasting and prayer, and ordinances, we closed by partaking of the Lord's supper. I blessed the bread and wine in the name of the Lord, when we all ate and drank, and were filled; then we sang a hymn, and the meeting adjourned."[414]

The Lord's Supper was described by Zebedee Coltrin:

> ... warm bread to break easy was provided, and broken into pieces as large as my fist, and each person had a glass of wine and sat and ate the bread and drank the wine; and Joseph said that was the way that Jesus and his disciples partook of the bread and wine; and this was the order of the church anciently..."[415]

2. Sealing. One account refers to a consequence of the ordinance, saying, "they were cleansed and sealed up unto eternal life..."[416] The concept of sealing is at times very specific, indicating that whatever was bound on earth is sealed in the hereafter, for all eternity. The term is found in a *Book of Mormon* paraphrase (Helaman 10:7) of Matthew 16:19:

> *Matthew*: And I will give unto thee the keys of the kingdom of heaven: and whatsoever thou shalt bind on earth shall be bound in heaven: and whatsoever thou shalt loose on earth shall be loosed in heaven.

---

[414] Smith, *History of the Church*, 1:323.
[415] In David John Buerger, *The Mysteries of Godliness. A History of Mormon Temple Worship* (Salt Lake City: Signature Books, 1994), 9.
[416] Buerger, *Mysteries of Godliness*, 8)

19. Church, Power and the Promised Land

Helaman: Behold, I give unto you power, that whatsoever ye shall seal on earth shall be sealed in heaven; and whatsoever ye shall loose on earth shall be loosed in heaven;

Smith had promised a great blessing to come, the endowment (D&C 105):

12. For behold, I have prepared a great endowment and blessing to be poured out upon them [elders of the Lord].
33. Verily, I say unto you, it is expedient in me that the first elders of my church should receive their endowment from on high in my house, which I have commanded to be built unto my name in the land of Kirtland.

Anticipating the Kirtland Temple's completion, on 21 January 1836 Smith and brethren met in the attic of the printing office. They washed their bodies in pure water and perfumed their bodies and heads. They then went to the unfinished temple where Joseph met with the Presidency and proceeded to anoint their heads with oil. They anointed the Patriarch (Joseph Smith Sr.) and invoked blessings upon him. Blessings were also invoked upon the Prophet. The Bishop of Kirtland and the Bishop of Zion (Missouri) were brought in with their counselors for their anointing, followed by the counselors of Kirtland and Zion. The next day more anointing ordinances were performed, for the Council of the Twelve, the Presidency of the Seventies, and members of the high councils of Kirtland and Missouri. The meeting was concluded with President Sidney Rigdon invoking the benediction of heaven upon the Lord's anointed. When his benediction was done, he instructed all to shout: "Hosannah, Blessed be the name of the Most High God."[417] These anointings were the first temple sealing ordinances.

The Kirtland Temple was dedicated on 27 March 1836. Each person coming for the event was asked to donate what he could to help pay the debts the Church had incurred. Joseph Smith gave the dedication prayer, followed by a short prayer by Sidney Rigdon. This time the whole congregation, apparently by instruction, raised both hands and shouted: "Hosannah! Hosannah! Hosannah to God and the Lamb. Amen! Amen."

---

[417]Buerger, *Mysteries of Godliness*, 12-17; Devery S. Anderson & Gary James Bergera, eds., *Joseph Smith's Quorum of the Anointed, 1842-1845, a Documentary History* (Salt Lake City: Signature Books, 2005), xvi-xvii.

It was estimated that 1,000 attended and they contributed $963.[418] On 30 March 1836, about 300 of the Church's male elite came to the temple for a washing ordinance and solemn ceremony. Donations were again requested.

Due to intense persecution in Kirtland, serious financial difficulties, and considerable apostasy, the Saints abandoned this center of the Church, and moved out, first to Missouri, and then to Commerce, Illinois, the new LDS center renamed Nauvoo. John Taylor, a future President of the Church, converted only in 1836, stopped in Kirtland in late 1839 to get his endowment (17 November). Most Saints had by then gone west.

3. Temple Ceremony. In Nauvoo Smith undertook to go further in the Restoration of All Things, by restoring the ceremony in Solomon's temple. He had drawn from Biblical texts for much of his work so far. In this case, he needed to seek a text that did not make it into the Bible. Its only survival, as he might have seen it, was the Masonic ceremony. Smith's brother Hyrum had been a Mason. To get access to the ritual, Smith managed to get a Masonic lodge created in Nauvoo. It eventually became one of the largest lodges in the nation, all Mormon. Like any other enactment, the ceremony has a script. Smith and his colleagues apparently reasoned that like the Bible itself, it had been modified and corrupted. But it could serve as a base to arrive at a correct ceremony, with divine help.

On 16 February 1832, Joseph Smith and Sidney Rigdon received a vision in which heaven was clarified as being divided into three kingdoms. The highest is the Celestial Kingdom, the lowest is the Telestial Kingdom, and in between is the Terrestrial Kingdom. Even the lowest is described in glowing terms, and the vast majority of mankind will go to one of these three. This vision is merged with Masonic lore to produce the Mormon temple ceremony. "On 4 and 5 May, forty-nine days after his Masonic initiation, Smith introduced the new endowment ceremony to trusted friends in the upper story of his Red Brick Store."[419]

The temple ceremony is enacted. First come the washing and anointing. A separate area for this existed for each gender. It appears that in the Nauvoo temple there were large basins to wash the entire body. Everyone donned a loose garment for modesty. Then came the

---

[418] Marquardt, *Rise of Mormonism*, 253-54.
[419] Buerger, *Mysteries of Godliness*, 52.

19. Church, Power and the Promised Land 469

anointings. When ready, the participants (later called patrons) went through the progress of mankind: creation (in the creation room), the Garden of Eden and the fall of Adam and Eve (in the garden room) and the dreary world (in the Telestial room), where:

> ...after the man has proved himself faithful he receives the first signs and tokens of the Melchizedek priesthood and an additional charge. Here also he vouches for the conduct of his companion. They are then left to prove themselves faithful, after which they are admitted into the terrestrial kingdom, where at the alter (sic) they receive an additional charge and the second token of the Melchizedek Priesthood and also the key word on the five points of fellowship.
>
> There are words given with every token and the new name is given in the preparation room when they receive their washing and annointing (sic).
>
> After [having] received all the tokens and words and signs they are led to the vail (sic) where they give each to Eloheem through the vail (sic) and are then admitted into the Celestial Room...
>
> ...Heber C. Kimball acting as Eloheem, George A. Smith as Jehovah, Orson Hyde as Michael, W.W. Phelps as the serpent.[420]

The Masonic elements of the ceremony, and temple design, are:

> 1. The three Mormon hand grips correspond to the Masonic grip of the Entered Apprentice, the pass-grip of the Fellow Craft, and the pass-grip of the Master Mason.
> 2. The Mormon penalty enactments (one for having one's throat cut, one for having one's breast split open, and one for being disemboweled) are the Masonic sign and Due-Guard enactments.
> 3. Both have the five points of fellowship: inside of right foot of one to same of the other, knee to knee, chest to chest, and mouth to each other's right ear.
> 4. In the Mormon temple, this embrace through the veil is with the patron's left arm through the mark of the compass and the Lord's left arm through the mark of the square. The compass and square are the primary Masonic symbols.
> 5. The beehive, representing industriousness.

---

[420] William Clayton, in George D. Smith, ed., *An Intimate Chronicle: The Journals of William Clayton* (Salt Lake City: Signature Books, 1972), 205-208.

6. The all-seeing eye.

Although today's Saints are sometimes disturbed by the Masonic elements in the temple ceremony, this was not the case in Nauvoo, where so many were Masons. Heber C. Kimball and Franklin D. Richards called the ceremony "true Masonry."[421]

Both ceremonies, Mormon and Masonic, have a strong emphasis on secrecy. This is the role of the penalties. For the first penalty, the officiator says "The execution of the penalty is represented by placing the thumb under the left ear, the palm of the hand down, and by drawing the thumb quickly across the throat to the right ear, and dropping the hand to the side." This enacts having one's throat cut. If John is the person going through the ritual, then he says, "I, John, covenant that I will never reveal the First Token of the Aaronic Priesthood, with its accompanying name, sign and penalty. Rather than do so, I would suffer [patrons all place right thumbs under left ears as described above] my life [patrons all draw thumbs across throats to right ears] to be taken [patrons all drop right hands down to sides]."

The second penalty, as described above, represents the chest being split apart. So John would say, "I, John, covenant that I will never reveal the Second Token of the Aaronic Priesthood, with its accompanying name, sign and penalty. Rather than do so, I would suffer [right hand to left breast] my life [draws hand across chest to right breast] to be taken [drops hands to side]." For the third penalty, representing being disemboweled, John would say, "I covenant in the name of the Son that I will never reveal the First Token of the Melchizedek Priesthood or Sign of the Nail, with its accompanying name, sign, and penalty. Rather than do so, I would suffer my life [patrons all draw the right thumb quickly across their body] to be taken [patrons all drop both hands to their sides]." Before passing through the veil into the Celestial Kingdom, the participants are instructed in the true order of prayer. As part of this, all again make the three signs, and the three penalties.

The temple ceremonies have evolved. They were updated in 1984, and again in 1990. These penalties have been disturbing to some members, and it was decided that they had outlived their usefulness. So in the 1990 revision, they were dropped.[422]

---

[421] See Buerger, *Mysteries of Godliness*, 56-58.
[422] Buerger, *The Mysteries of Godliness*, 120. For the temple ceremony c. 1980, see Chuck Sackett, *What's Going on in There? The Verbatim Text of the*

19. Church, Power and the Promised Land 471

4. Baptism for the Dead. One application of the sealing power of the High (Melchizedek) Priesthood is baptism for the dead. This is a creative institution that addressed a vexing problem that had disturbed Christians from the beginning. One of the NT red-letter passages (i.e., presumably stated by Jesus himself) declares, "Except a man be born of water and of the Spirit, he cannot enter into the kingdom of God." (John 3:5) This gave rise to speculation as to the eternal fate of infants who die without baptism, righteous persons who die having never heard the gospel message, and even pre-Christian prophets such as Abraham and Moses. For centuries, the Roman church held that such individuals go to a special place called limbo, sometimes located in Hell, and at times said to be an appendage between Heaven and Hell. This also led to infant baptism. Given the high rate of infant mortality, it was always advisable to have a priest on hand at childbirth to baptize the infant while it still breathed. In France, a young priest made the news for getting his girlfriend pregnant and when her condition became obvious, slitting her throat in a dark alleyway, ripping open her womb, baptizing the unborn infant, and then killing it. This shows how a deeply-rooted doctrine such as this can grip the mind of even the most deranged.

The Smith family was put into an extended mourning when Smith's elder brother Alvin died. The *Book of Mormon* states, "he that knoweth not good from evil is blameless..." (Alma 29:5) As early as September, 1830, a revelation stated (D&C 29:46-47):

> 46. But behold, I say unto you, that little children are redeemed from the foundation of the world through mine Only Begotten;
> 47. Wherefore, they cannot sin, for power is not given unto Satan to tempt little children until they begin to become accountable before me.

On 21 January 1836, on the occasion of the first washings in Kirtland, Smith reported a vision of which he said:

> I saw father Adam, and Abraham and Michael and my father and mother, my brother Alvin that has long since slept, and marveled how it was that he had obtained ~~this~~ an inheritance ‹in› that Kingdom, seeing that he had

---

Mormon Temple Rituals Annotated and Explained by a Former Temple Worker (Thousand Oaks, CA: Sword of the Shepherd Ministries, ND).

departed this life, before the Lord ‹had› set his hand to gather Israel ‹the second time› and had not been baptized for the remission of sins...[423]

An answer to this dilemma came from an interpretation of a verse by the Apostle Paul. Since Smith was so very collaborative, it is not possible to know who actually noticed this verse, but by this time, former minister Sidney Rigdon was Smith's most prominent collaborator in theological matters. Prior to his conversion to Mormonism, as a Campbellite he had been opposed to infant baptism. Arguing in defense of the doctrine of resurrection, Paul wrote, "Else what shall they do which are baptized for the dead, if the dead rise not at all? why are they then baptized for the dead?" (1 Corinthians 15:29) A light went on in someone's head, and the answer came: Of course, baptism for the dead, by proxy. A major institution was born.

The ordinance was established by revelation on 19 January 1841 (D&C 124:29-35), but the practice was already under way. The first occurrence of this baptism was on 13 August 1840, when Smith baptized a widow, Jane Nyman, in the Mississippi River for her deceased son.[424] Once the Nauvoo temple was completed, baptism for the dead was to be limited to the temple, as directed in revelation.

Today, typically, busloads of Mormon youth arrive at a temple, are gowned in baptismal clothes and stand in line next to a large baptismal font. The first is led down into the water, and a temple worker stands next to the youth, says the baptismal prayer, using the name of a deceased, and dunks the kid. As soon as the baptizee gets his or her breath, the prayer is repeated again with another name, and the kid is dunked. This is done several times, sometimes until the kid is gasping for air (we joked about it in the bus on the way home), and another is led into the font, until the whole group have performed this service for God and the deceased. In Nauvoo, it is probable that this was done primarily or even solely with adults. This work will be done for the many for whom there are no records after Christ comes.

After death, the spirits of the dead go to a spirit world where they have anthropomorphic spirit bodies, live in a social situation, subject to many concerns and opportunities to sin, with many preaching various doctrines. Each person who has ever lived will get a meaningful opportunity to hear and accept or reject the true gospel of Christ, aka

---

[423] Jessee, *Personal Writings of Joseph Smith*, 146.
[424] Garr, Cannon & Cowan, *Encyclopedia of Latter-day Saint History*, 76.

Mormonism. If the deceased is converted in this spirit world, and accepts his or her proxy baptism, then, and only then, is it validated. At the base of this practice is the doctrine that baptism cannot be done in the spirit world because it can only be done in the flesh.

The LDS church has accepted a mission to baptize all who have ever lived. No baptism, or any other proxy temple ordinance, is done without proper records of the birth and death of the individual. The Church has spent a huge amount of resources and effort to obtain the records needed. In particular, they have approached governments and institutions that have such records, offering to microfilm them, and give a copy of the microfilm to that institution. Since these records are often poorly archived and endangered, this offer is welcomed. In a huge cavern carved into the granite heart of the Wasatch mountain range, a climate-controlled repository has been made to store all the records. The LDS genealogical society has a large well-equipped center to digitalize all records and work out genealogical relationships. They produce the evidence-based forms used in the temples. In an effort to reach out to persons who— Who knows?— could be interested in Mormonism as a religion, they open their doors to researchers worldwide, so that these records can be used in research totally unrelated to the Mormon mission. This is an instance where Mormon doctrine, dedication and resources have yielded collateral benefits for the gentiles.

5. Celestial Marriage and Polygamy. Celestial marriage also arises from a NT passage. In another red-letter verse, Jesus says, "For when they shall rise from the dead, they neither marry, nor are given in marriage; but are as the angels which are in heaven." (Mark 12:25) This might appear to mean that upon death, families are dissolved. Not a happy thought for those who are very family oriented, nor for devoted couples. The LDS interpretation is that this is literally true in the case put to Jesus, but that a marriage performed and sealed for all time and eternity in a temple of God would be valid in the hereafter (D&C 132, recorded 12 July 1843). Marriages performed by a church minister, justice of the peace, by contracting parties in Islam or by a shaman, are all equally valid for this life. Only Mormon celestial marriages are forever.

This ordinance was revealed in the same revelation that established polygamy, dated July 12, 1843. (D&C 132:61-62) Marquardt has documented a list of 17 single women who were sealed to Joseph Smith.

The oldest at the time of marriage was Rhoda Richards, 58. The youngest was Helen Mar Kimball, 14. Most were between 17 and 30 years of age. Although we do not know how much time passed between the receipt/drafting of the revelation and the date it was recorded, it is interesting to note that Louisa Beeman's sealing date was 5 April 1841, more than two years earlier. Two other sealings occurred a year before the recording date of the revelation. Three widows are also listed as sealed to Joseph Smith, two of them being in 1842. Whatever the actual date of the revelation, it is certain that the practice was kept secret for up to two years.[425]

In addition to these, Marquardt lists eight women, married to other men, who were sealed to Joseph Smith. Minimally, this means that they would be his in the next life. We have no way of knowing what contact Smith had with them in this life. Since a higher degree of glory in the Celestial Kingdom is possible to couples that are sealed than those who are not, this may be a matter of women deemed worthy of being sealed, but who are married to men who are not deemed worthy. These women may have sought an avenue to exaltation in the next life within the order of celestial marriage.

The practice of polygamy was from the start a point of major dissension among the Saints. Cowdery's stance has been debated. Many if not most converts came from conservative Christian backgrounds. They would be aware of the *Book of Mormon*'s condemnation of both polygamy and concubinage (Ether 10:5& Jacob 1:15):

> *Ether.* And it came to pass that Riplakish did not do that which was right in the sight of the Lord, for he did have many wives and concubines, and did lay that upon men's shoulders which was grievous to be borne
>
> *Jacob.* And now it came to pass that the people of Nephi, under the reign of the second king, began to grow hard in their hearts, and indulge themselves somewhat in wicked practices, such as like unto David of old desiring many wives and concubines, and also Solomon, his son.

For true believers, the answer to this was not hard to come by. Riplakish undoubtedly took many wives outside the "new and everlasting covenant." In fact, this condemnation of the practice probably represents the view of the scripture's authors earlier in their career.

---

[425] Marquardt, *Rise of Mormonism*, 342-3.

19. Church, Power and the Promised Land

In Utah, Brigham Young and his polygamous establishment put pressure on prominent men to take a second wife, partly to improve the image of the institution. In her famous and history-making book, *Tell It All, the Story of a Life's Experience in Mormonism* (1875), Fanny Stenhouse wrote of the pressure to take a second wife placed on her husband, T. B. Stenhouse, a productive contributor to the *New York Herald* and, as editor of the *Salt Lake Telegraph*, a founder of real journalism in Utah. Recounting what a trial it was for them both, and her own experience, she wrote:

> Brigham Young performed the ceremony. He sat at the end of the altar and we three knelt down—my husband on one side and Miss Pratt and myself on the other. Speaking to me, Brigham Young asked: "Are you willing to give this woman to your husband to be his lawful wife for time and for all eternity? If you are you will signify it by placing her right hand within the right hand of your husband.
>
> I did so; but what words can describe my feelings! The anguish of a whole lifetime was crowded into that one single moment. The painful meaning of those words, "for all eternity" withered my soul...

Ultimately, she and her husband left the Church. She wrote her book. Between 1874 and 1888, it was reprinted thirteen times, including once in Spanish. It has been republished numerous times ever since, including once in an American feminist series. After leaving the Church, she urged Congress to outlaw polygamy (already outlawed in most if not all states at the time), and the Federal law doing so was partly due to her efforts. This law has been challenged twice on grounds of being a violation of constitutionally protected freedom of religion, and the U. S. Supreme Court has upheld the law on grounds of being in the public interest.

Fanny Stenhouse wrote in her book about the observations young women would have growing up,

> They would notice the neglect which wives endured even from good husbands; they would see a man leaving the wife of his youth, the mother of his children, and careless of the cruel wrong he did her, leave her in lonely sorrow while he was spending his time in love-making with some young girl who might have been his daughter. They would see a wife crushing out from her heart the holiest impulses which God had implanted

there, striving to destroy all affection for him whose dearest treasure that affection should have been...[426]

Polygamy was practiced only through a temple sealing, which means that it had to be authorized. This gave the hierarchy power over access to women beyond one's first wife. If an elder took a second wife outside of the temple sealing framework, he was tried for adultery.

Joseph Smith was accused of having two illicit relationships while in Kirtland. The first involved a young woman working in the Smith home. There is little information about this alleged affair. The second regards Fanny Alger. There is more information regarding this charge, but conflicting information. Whatever is the case, two things are certain. First, Smith had a strong penchant for women. And second, in his celestial marriage/polygamy revelation, the strong assertion of divine approval for concubinage was gratuitous, if it was not intended to extend the license of a prophet even further.

Creating a Church: Theology

Although the new scriptures and institutions of Mormonism examined thus far already set it apart as being unique within the Christian world, it is ultimately its theology that makes it truly a new religion, rather than just a further elaboration of a Christian faith that had come over from Europe. What was to come is not obvious in the *Book of Mormon*. Like religionists in New England at the time, it argues against atheism (Alma 30:28) and agnosticism (Alma 30:48 & 54:21). About 47 BCE Alma urges his son: "cross yourself in all these things... Oh, remember, and take it upon you and cross yourself in these things." (Alma 39:9)

It is not altogether clear when the first vision story first contained the description of God the Father and the Son appearing to Joseph Smith, in human form, and as two separate divine beings, but this may be the earliest appearance of that doctrine. Perhaps it was after the *Book of Mormon* was written, which seems wedded to the doctrine that the Father and Son are one God. The Lord shows himself to the brother of Jared (at the time of the Tower of Babel), in full human form, and says (Ether 3):

---

[426] Mrs. T. B. H. Stenhouse, *Tell It All: The Story of a Life's Experience in Mormonism. An Autobiography* (Hartford: Worthington & Co., 1874), 381.

19. Church, Power and the Promised Land

14. Behold, I am he who was prepared from the foundation of the world to redeem my people. Behold, I am Jesus Chris. I am the father and the Son. In me shall all mankind have light, and that eternally, even they who shall believe on my name; and they shall become my sons and my daughters.
16. Behold, this body, which ye now behold, is the body of my spirit; and man have I created after the body of my spirit...

The Nephite prophet Abinadi says (Mosiah 15):

1. God himself shall come down among the children of men, and shall redeem his people,
2. And because he dwelleth in flesh he shall be called the Son of God, and having subjected the flesh to the will of the Father, being the Father and the Son—
3. The Father, because he was conceived by the power of God; and the Son, because of the flesh; thus becoming the Father and Son—
4. And they are one God, yea, the very Eternal Father of heaven and of earth.

When adducing NT scriptural support, LDS polytheist theology bases itself partly on the statement of Paul (1 Corinthians 8):

5. For though there be that are called gods, whether in heaven or in earth (as there be gods many, and lords many,)
6. But to us, there is but one God, the Father, of whom are all things, and we in him; and one Lord Jesus Christ, by whom are all things, and we by him.

On 20 March 1839, a revelation came, saying: "According to that which was ordained in the midst of the Council of the Eternal God of all other gods before this world was..." (D&C 121:32) An authoritative LDS reference, *Mormon Doctrine*, by Bruce R. McConkie, says:

> Three separate personages—Father, Son, and Holy Ghost—comprise the Godhead. As each of these persons is a God, it is evident, from this standpoint alone, that a *plurality of Gods* exists. To us, speaking in the proper finite sense, these three are the only Gods we worship. But in addition there is an infinite number of holy personages, drawn from worlds without number, who have passed on to exaltation and are thus gods.[427]

---

[427] McConkie, *Mormon Doctrine*, 576-77.

Mormonism thus has the distinction of being the only polytheist branch of Christianity. The term polytheism is further delimited by the fact that these three are organized, along with all other gods that may be from this creation, and the angels, and the priesthood holders of the Church, in one priesthood, with God the Father at the head. The three are totally separate. Each of the two, God the Father and God the Son, has his own material anthropomorphic body. Yet while acting in the priesthood along with the Holy Ghost the three are functionally unitary. Admittedly this is a bit novel, but far easier to grasp than the mystery of the three-in-one Trinity. Mormons address all prayers to Our Father or Our Father in Heaven, and close all prayers "In the name of Jesus Christ, Amen." They believe that Jesus, God the Son, died on the cross for the remission of the sins of mankind, and they commemorate this every Sunday with the rite of the sacrament, partaking of bread and water (rather than wine).

That LDS theology was in flux very early on is seen in the *Book of Moses*, where we read: "For I, the Lord God, created all things, of which I have spoken, spiritually, before they were naturally upon the face of the earth." Mormons believe that they lived in a preexistence prior to being born into a carnal body. Just as Jesus appeared to the brother of Jared as a spirit body, but of human form, humans also were of human form in the preexistence. There they had free will, and the capacity to do right and wrong. So each human being is born here already having an achievement record made in the preexistence.

The Book of Abraham is rooted into LDS theology, guaranteeing its place in the canon. How to harmonize it with the Egyptian papyri is for Mormon scholars and apologists to figure out. In it, God speaks to Abraham, saying (Abraham 3):

> 18. ...if there be two spirits, and one shall be more intelligent than the other, yet these two spirits, notwithstanding one is more intelligent than the other, have no beginning; they existed before, they shall have no end, they shall exist after, for they are gnolaum, or eternal.
> 19. ...These two facts do exist, that there are two spirits, one being more intelligent than the others; there shall be another more intelligent than they; I am the Lord thy God, I am more intelligent than they all.
> 21. I dwell in the midst of them all... for I rule in the heavens above, and in the earth beneath, in all wisdom and prudence, over all the intelligences thine eyes have seen from the beginning; I came down in the beginning in the midst of all the intelligences thou has seen.

> 22. Now the Lord had shown unto me, Abraham, the intelligences that were organized before the world was; and among all these there were many of the noble and great ones;
> 3:23. And God saw these souls that they were good, and he stood in the midst of them, and said: These I will make my rulers; for he stood among those that were spirits, and he saw that they were good; and he said unto me: Abraham, thou art one of them; thou wast chosen before thou wast born.

This was anticipated, at least to some degree, in the Doctrine and Covenants 93:

> 29, Man was also in the beginning with God. Intelligence, or the light of truth, was not created or made, neither indeed can be.
> 30. All truth is independent in that sphere in which God has placed it, to act for itself, as all intelligence also; otherwise there is no existence.
> 31. Behold, here is the agency of man, and here is the condemnation of man; because that which was from the beginning is plainly manifest unto them, and they receive not the light.

The interpretation of these BOA verses separates the terms intelligences and souls or spirits. Verse 22, where Abraham saw that the intelligences had been organized, marks a transition from the intelligence stage to the spirit stage. This is generally taken to mean that the intelligences are coeternal with God, that they are clothed with a body of refined matter in human form to become spirits, and then acquire a corporeal body on earth, which will be the third component, in an incorruptible form, of the resurrected person. This is Mormonism's own three-in-one doctrine. Thus the problem of the origin of good and evil is partially solved. Since the intelligence was never created by God, He is not responsible for its evil. This does not solve the problem of why bad things happen to good people. Like others, Mormons usually say that it must be part of God's plan, somehow.

This is further explained in Mormon theology by the concept of the family unit in the hereafter. As we have seen, the LDS concept of Heaven is that it is tripartite, mirrored in the structure and ceremony of the temple. A Mormon couple that has been sealed together for time and eternity are eligible for the Celestial Kingdom. If judged worthy, they can enter on the path to become gods and goddesses. This most exalted status is not immediate. LDS theology has the concept of eternal progression. Over time they can progress to the point that they can achieve this degree of exaltation. A god-and-goddess couple produce spirit children. This is normally thought of as an increate intelligence entering into the spirit body as it develops. LDS who have a testimony of the truth of Mormonism but are not sufficiently valiant to be worthy of the Celestial Kingdom can be eligible for the Terrestrial Kingdom, as well as righteous persons who have not accepted the gospel in circumstances that would qualify for the Celestial Kingdom. Those who have failed to acquire a testimony or have denied a testimony once received have to go to the lowest, the Telestial Kingdom. Most who have ever lived will go there. This also includes murderers, thieves and all sorts of really bad guys, since Mormonism sends very few to Hell. Even so, persons in the Telestial Kingdom differ in glory. A Mormon worthy of the Celestial Kingdom, but who is not married, or whose spouse did not make it, can still go to that Kingdom, but would be an angel or servant (divine functionary) in that exalted place. All who do not make it to the Celestial Kingdom have their family ties severed. Family only exists in the Celestial Kingdom.

All of this leads to issues. Occasionally, in a gathering of Saints, two or three present might get into these issues and attempt to theorize. Others will shift nervously, until, often, someone will say, "Hey, don't you think we're going off the deep end here?" At least at this point, Mormonism does not have what one can truly call speculative theology. The normal position is that they have all the knowledge that is presently needed for their salvation, and if they need to know more, it will be revealed in due time.

Worship

Ironically, in spite of the complexities of LDS priesthood and rites, worship is rather simple, to the point that a Protestant attending a Mormon Sunday service would not feel seriously out of place. Initially, Smith's first priority was to build a temple. Normal worship was in the homes of the faithful. Persecution and the need to relocate every few years made it difficult to establish meeting houses, now universally called chapels. Although the iconic Mormon temple in Salt Lake City exhibits some remarkable architecture, subsequent temples, although often imposing, are simpler. They, and the chapels, have been criticized by some members as being an architectural style that a fellow missionary companion of mine once dubbed *Mormon mediocre*. For their temples, an elevated location is sought, if possible, a location where the public cannot escape noticing it. None is more representative of this tendency than the Washington, D.C. temple, which seems to suddenly appear, larger than life, to commuters on the beltway. Sunday worship and other Church activities are in the chapels, while the temples are reserved for temple ordinances.

Mormon chapels usually have no images other than a traditional painting of a rather blondish Jesus. Perhaps he took his Father's side? There is no absolute prohibition on images. A large statue of Jesus greets people at the Temple Square Visitors Center. The angel Moroni, sounding his trump, graces the top of the Salt Lake Temple, and is the image used, instead of a cross, on U.S. military gravestones. The cross is totally absent. Mormons see it as a symbol of torture, an instrument of Satanic forces; but for the most part, it is simply felt to be inappropriate, even bad taste.

Sunday meetings include Sunday School, Sacrament Meeting, and meetings for the priesthood and Relief Society. Meeting, details of Mormon worship, and the progression of members from cradle to temple, will be treated in Chapter 23.

Mormons Do Not Shrive

Each Latter-day Saint is personally responsible for his behavior, and misbehavior. Just like mainstream Christianity, in LDS theology, Jesus made the infinite sacrifice for the sins of all mankind. The remission of sin is dependent on repentance and not backsliding with respect to the same sin. There is no confessional in an LDS chapel or temple. The elders cannot grant absolution for a sin, much less across the board. Death is just one more event on the way towards the last judgment. After death, all people pass over into a spirit world, a world in many ways similar to the world prior to death. The spirits are material beings, and each individual retains his or her own traits prior to death, including strengths and weaknesses. Virtue, evil, adherence to the true religion, or to the church of Satan, good deeds, sin, all these continue. In all, right up to the last judgment, each person must face the Judge, personally. There is no intercession, no acquisition of special favor on one's behalf from a saint or any other being. Mormons do not shrive; there are no last rites. There is no fear of dying unshriven.

Are Mormons Christians?

This has been a vexing issue. Presidential candidate Mitt Romney attempted to finesse it. His statement was an example of LDS dissimulation. This is not to say that he lied, or that Mormons are not Christians. It simply means that one should tell the truth, but not necessarily the whole truth. Ultimately the issue is theological, which is the study of God. Theology defines the divine, it draws lines, and establishes cutoff points or boundaries.

If what is meant is "Do Mormons worship Jesus?" the answer is a resounding "Yes."

If what is meant is "Do Mormons accept Jesus as their personal Redeemer?" the answer is a resounding "Yes."

But is Jesus Christ in the traditional churches the same Jesus Christ in the LDS faith. In traditional Christian theology, Jesus is God. Father and Son are One God in the absolute sense. Even though their God can and did take on flesh, to better relate to His human creation, that was just a garment, not His essence or real being. For many if not all, this God is omnipotent, omniscient and omnipresent. For the Mormons, Jesus Christ is the Only Begotten Son of God, in the literal biological sense, in the flesh. They do not accept the doctrine of Virgin Birth, or even a Virginal Conception. God did not create all things, but organized them. He did not even create the ultimate being within each of us, the intelligences, which are increate, and coeternal with God. LDS theological speculation is comfortable with the proposition that the law of eternal progression means that even the Supreme God, Elohim, is still progressing, at least in some sense. It is for each Christian faith to determine for itself where to draw the line. But there is a very strong logical case that the deity of traditional Christianity is not the LDS deity. Jesus is not God, but a god, and just the number-two god at that. Prayer is not offered to Jesus (much less the Virgin Mary). So it is quite reasonable to answer the question in the negative: strictly speaking, for the traditional churches, Mormons cannot be Christians.

It might be hoped that in this modern, ecumenical age, Christian charity can bridge this chasm. But if so, the LDS Church, and its Saints, have not led the way. In the *Book of Mormon*, all churches except the one true Church (Mormonism) are, collectively, the Whore of all the Earth mentioned in the *Book of Revelations* (although for John of Patmos, this phrase probably referred to the Roman Empire and its power establishment). There are variations in the wording of Joseph Smith's accounts of his first vision. But typical of his later characterizations of the churches of his day, the answer from Jesus was:

> I was answered that I must join none of them, for they were all wrong, and the Personage who addressed me said that all their Creeds were an abomination in his sight, that those professors were all corrupt, that "they draw near to me with their lips but their hearts are far from me; They teach for doctrines the commandments of men, having a form of Godliness but they deny the power thereof."[428]

Although the LDS position has remained essentially unchanged, the tone of its expression has softened. Ultimately, the Church and its Saints hold that all other churches are in error, and the Church of Jesus Christ of Latter-day Saints alone is recognized by God; it alone has the true priesthood, and can offer the valid baptism for the remission of sins, and salvation and exaltation in the next life. This position is absolute, clear and foundational. The Church has remained aloof from ecumenism, and is not an appropriate participant in any serious ecumenical gathering.

Financial Foundations

For much of Joseph Smith's career, his church was strapped for cash. Converts were generally not overly prosperous, and due to the call to gather, first to Kirtland, then to Missouri (Zion) and then to Nauvoo, they had to abandon or sell much of what they had, sometimes even an ancestral farm, and relocate, and relocate, and relocate, all the while facing persecution. We must always remember that there are two histories of Mormonism, the history of the founders and subsequent establishment, and the history of the membership, their trials and tribulations, and of their small triumphs and joys.

Money was a problem in early nineteenth-century America in general. By the end of 1780, the Continental bills, or continentals, were worth no more than one fortieth of their face value. Benjamin Franklin declared that they had in effect acted as a tax to pay for the war of secession from the British crown. The issuance of the United States

---

[428] This is the 1938 account. For all three, and a study of them, see Backman, *Joseph Smith's First Vision*; and Jessee, *Early Accounts of Joseph Smith's First Vision*.

dollar coin was in 1792, and the first one-dollar note was printed in 1863. Street-savvy Americans preferred coins to bills. A bill was by definition a promissory note. Paper money was issued by banks and private entities until 1861. It has been estimated that as many as 8,000 entities had issued paper instruments up to that point. Smith was not about to get his hands on coins in the quantities that he needed, and paper money was in any case not stable. This situation created ideal circumstances, or temptation, to create one's own money.

In 1836 Smith and some colleagues applied to the Ohio State Legislature for a charter to establish the Kirtland Society Bank. Sure of their success, Cowdery went to Philadelphia to get plates engraved for the notes. The plates arrived, but the charter was refused. After appealing, and failing, they organized a Stock Industrial Company, the Kirtland Safety Society Anti-Banking Company. Printing was commenced with the same plates, and rubber-stamped ANTI-BANKING COMPANY over the word BANK. These notes were illegal, and rejected by creditors in New York, Pittsburgh and Cleveland, where large amounts of merchandise had been purchased on credit. The Kirtland Society failed, apparently in conjunction with a financial crisis in the country in general, although Smith promised that someday the notes would be as good as gold. Smith (Society cashier) and Rigdon (President) were arrested and in October 1837 were tried and convicted in a jury trial. They were each fined $1,000 plus court charges. After announcing their intention to appeal, they both fled the state.[429]

Also in Kirtland, the Church established a United Firm. This was a society for what the LDS more usually term the United Order, a voluntary society of members who would hold their property in common. But funds were desperately needed to construct the Kirtland Temple, and finance a paramilitary group called Zion's Camp. On 5 December 1833, Smith wrote "our means are already exhausted, and we are deeply in debt, and know of no means whereby we shall be able to extricate ourselves."[430] Although the United Firm was set up as a member's cooperative, it was used as collateral to raise funds. It is not certain to what extent the members had been apprised of this. On 11 January 1834, Smith and his associates prayed "that the Lord would provide, in the

---

[429] Sheridan L. McGarry, "Mormon Money," reprinted from *The Numismatist*, 1962, 3-4; Van Wagoner, *Sidney Rigdon*, 178-87.
[430] Smith, *History of the Church*, 1:450; Marquardt, *Rise of Mormonism*, 227.

order of his Providence, the bishop of this Church with means sufficient to discharge every debt that the Firm owes, in due season, that the Church may not be braught (sic) into disrepute, and the saints be afflicted by the hands of their enemies."[431] The United Firm was dissolved in 1834. By 1835, the identities of the United Firm officers were obscured by pseudonyms. The 1835 edition of the Doctrine and Covenants reads:

> And again, let my servant Ahashdah [Newel K. Whitney] have appointed unto him, the houses and lot where he now resides, and the lot and building on which the Ozondah [store] stands; and also the lot which is on the corner south of the Ozondah; and also the lot on which the Shule [ashery] is situated: And all this I [the Lord] have appointed unto my servant Ahashdah, for his stewardship, for a blessing upon him and his seed after him, for the benefit of the Ozondah of my order [Firm], which I have established for my stake in the land of Shinehah [Kirtland]; yea, verily this is the stewardship which I have appointed unto my servant Ahashdah; even this whole Ozondah establishment, him and his agent, and his seed after him...[432]

These maneuvers appear to have been to frustrate the Firm's creditors. Estimates of United Firm debts range from $102,300 (the more probable end of the range) to as high as $150,000. When the Firm was dissolved, Rigdon received the home in which he was living, and a tannery for his future financial support.[433]

Along with the Firm, Smith and Rigdon's incomes came also from the Literary Firm, established to print the *Doctrine and Covenants*, *Book of Mormon* and several periodicals. There were plans also to publish Smith and Rigdon's revision of the Bible. Due to high operating expenses and low sales, the Firm collapsed, with debts, early in 1834.[434]

These financial failures, and legal difficulties, were the main reasons for the flight of Smith and Rigdon, but it was also due to rising mob violence, and perhaps the even sharper reaction of some very unhappy members and apostates, some of whom had been thrown into financial ruin. Even so, in Far West, tithing was introduced (D&C 119).

---

[431] Joseph Smith, Journal, January 11, 1834, in Marquardt, *Rise of Mormonism*, 139.
[432] D&C:98:7 (1835); see Marquardt, *Rise of Mormonism*, 256-57.
[433] Van Wagoner, *Sidney Rigdon*, 178-79.
[434] Van Wagoner, *ibid*, 177-78.

Once in Nauvoo, many ambitious projects were undertaken, including the new temple. Among the buildings undertaken was a hotel, the Nauvoo House. To cover this expense, the Mormons issued stock. The first series, a $50 certificate, was crudely printed. The second series, $50 and $100 certificates were much more professionally done. The first was transferrable by endorsement, and probably the second as well. In 1843, there was also a city scrip. In Smith's Journal History he recorded, "I burned twenty-three dollars of city scrip, and while it was burning, said, 'so may all unsound and uncurrent money go down!'"[435]

Once Brigham Young and the Saints were in Utah, financial institutions and instruments of exchange multiplied, much as they did across the United States, since the whole country was in need of stable instruments of exchange. Initially, and in practice for a large part of the second half of the nineteenth century, barter, payment in kind, was common. Brigham Young obtained authority to issue hand-written notes, but this turned out to be woefully inadequate. Certificates could be issued against goods in the Bishop's Storehouse that kept tithing. John Kay obtained the equipment needed to mint gold coins. Gold was procured from California, and Kay succeeded on his second attempt at minting. Young made a trip to the Mississippi and returned with a limited supply of U.S. coins, but they soon disappeared. Bad money drives out good. Gold obtained by the Church was used to back G.S.L. (Great Salt Lake) notes, which bore the private seal of the Twelve Apostles. Other notes were issued by The Drovers Bank, the Deseret Currency Association, Deseret University Bank, Holladay & Halsey, Great Salt Lake City Corporation, and The Salt Lake City National Bank of Utah. There were also merchandise-due bills issued by mercantile institutions, including the Zion's Cooperative Mercantile Institution. Currency and minting ended in Utah as a ready supply of stable U.S. coins and currency became available.

There is no doubt that the Church, from the start, was struggling with an experimental and unstable monetary situation in the U.S. in general. It is also true that its projects far outstripped the real wealth available, and schemes to circumvent this problem were destined to doom, at the expense of many members. Although Mormonism was in principle a lay church, the burgeoning hierarchy meant a number of full-time personnel who needed an income, and it is safe to assume that

---

[435] *History of the Church*, 5:288; McGarry, "Mormon Money," 5-6.

higher officers expected a bit more. Funds were made available when needed, and land and business establishments were assigned to some. The situation at the top can be seen by the fact that one of the inheritance problems of Emma Smith, Joseph's legal widow, was the extreme commingling of Church finances with his own. In addition to all of the other causes for tension and even apostasy, Smith and Rigdon's financial schemes, especially in Kirtland, were a major irritant.

Theocracy and the Power to Coerce

Politically, the *Book of Mormon* strongly reflects concerns in the time of Joseph Smith in New England. "Nevertheless, the Nephites were inspired by a better cause for they were not fighting for monarchy, nor power but they were fighting for their home and their liberties..." (Alma 43:45) Some were called "king-men, for they were desirous that the law should be altered in a manner to overthrow the free government and to establish a king over the land." (Alma 51:5) Alma "selected a wise man who was among the elders of the church, and gave him power according to the voice of the people, that he might have power to enact laws according to the laws which had been given... Now Alma did not grant unto him the office of being high priest over the church, but he retained the office of high priest unto himself..." (Alma 4:16-18) "Now I would that ye should understand that the word of God was liberal unto all, that none were deprived of the privilege of assembling themselves together to hear the word of God." (Alma 6:5) "And whatsoever nation shall uphold such secret combinations, to get power and gain, until they shall spread over the nation, behold, they shall be destroyed..." (Ether 8:22)

In spite of this, theocracy seems to be inherent in Mormonism. It sees the Church as a precursor to the government of Christ on earth. Jesus will be King, authority will be priesthood, and raising one's hand will be to sustain and express allegiance. Of course no religion is a democracy. But the early history of the Church took place in situations where the functions of state tended to be performed, for a while, by the Church. And along with state power comes enforcement, the power to coerce.

Coercion does not necessarily mean the use of force. Ritual can be used to intimidate, as in the case of the Mormon temple marriage ceremony. Until the 1990 revision, married women receiving their endowments in the temple were required to take an oath of obedience to their husbands:

> *Elohim*: We will put the sisters under covenant to obey the law of their husbands. Sister, arise.
> [Female patrons stand as instructed.]
> *Elohim*: Each of you bring your right arm to the square. You and each of you solemnly covenant and promise before God, angels and these witnesses at this altar that you will each observe and keep the law of your husband, and abide by his council in righteousness. Each of you bow your head and say yes.
> *Women:* Yes

Similarly, regardless of whether Smith had any improper contact with the wives of other men whom he sealed to himself for time and eternity, this act must have been experienced by the other men as an exercise of male dominance. Compare this with the exercise of sexual privilege over the wives of male followers to establish dominance in some cults of the twentieth century.

Church councils also could threaten disfellowship and excommunication, a threat that many took seriously, and could silence considerable criticism and opposition.

Violence was first encountered at the hands of persecuting mobs. Americans at the time, like now, often owned arms. When mobs threatened one's home, it was wise to keep weapons close by. Mormons responded to defend themselves, and their forces acquired a role in internal enforcement as well. D. Michael Quinn has put together an impressive table of Mormon Security Forces, and their external and internal functions. Much of the following is based on his work.[436]

---

[436] Quinn, *Mormon Hierarchy*, 467-478.

On 6 August 1833, "Smith announced a revelation authorizing Mormons to wage theocratic war when attacked by 'enemies' a fourth time." (D&C 98:39-48) On 4 November 1833, David Whitmer, presiding in Missouri, "led a counterattack against a Missouri mob, killing two anti-Mormons at the 'Battle of Blue River.' This was in response to the fourth attack, as allowed by the revelation."[437] A revelation was received on 24 February 1834 commanding "God's 'friends' to 'avenge me of mine enemies.' [D&C 103] The Kirtland High Council appointed Smith as commander-in-chief of the Armies of Israel." Within, dissenters are to "be 'cast out and trodden under the foot of men' by 'my friends.'"[438] Through 1834-37, Joseph Smith's "Lifeguards" provided internal and external security.[439]

Smith had promised the gathering to Zion in Independence Missouri, and even gave a date for the next conference. To respond to the events of the summer of 1833, Smith organized the first Mormon military force in the summer of 1834, called Zion's Camp, and led it to Missouri to put this project back on track. Smith had to negotiate peace, without achieving his objectives. Zion's Camp became the basis for selecting the Quorum of the Twelve and the Seventy in 1835.[440]

On 24 September 1835, by revelation, the Kirtland High Council appointed Joseph Smith as "head" of the Church's "War Department."[441] The Ohio Army of Israel existed in Kirtland from 1835 into 1837. On 7 November 1836, an official ultimatum was issued by twelve general authorities, including the First Presidency, and fifty-nine others, warning Kirtland's non-Mormon Justice-of-the-Peace to "depart forthwith out of Kirtland."[442] In December of 1837, Smith's Lifeguards went into apostasy, and Brigham Young carried weapons as an ad hoc bodyguard for the Prophet. On 22 December 1837, armed dissenters (former-Mormons) seized the temple and forced Brigham Young to flee the Kirtland headquarters for his life, followed three weeks later by the First Presidency. By December 1837, the Missouri Army of Israel was formed in Caldwell County, Missouri.[443]

---

[437] Quinn, *ibid*, 470.
[438] *Idem*.
[439] *Idem*.
[440] Quinn, *Idem*.
[441] *Idem*.
[442] Quinn, *ibid*, 471.
[443] *Idem*.

During this period, the infamous Danites came into existence. It was drawn from members of Zion's Camp, Smith's Lifeguards, the Ohio Army of Israel and the Missouri Army of Israel. This group clearly felt that the problems of the Saints came from without and within. On 3 July 1837, the ground was broken for a temple at Far West. On 4 July 1838, Sidney Rigdon gave an oration in which he said:

> We therefore, take all men to record this day, that we proclaim our liberty on this day, as did our fathers. And we pledge this day to one another, our fortunes, our lives, and our sacred honors, to be delivered from the persecutions which we have had to endure, for the last nine years, or nearly that.[444]

George W. Robinson, that same month, wrote of the Danites:

> Thus far, according to the ‹Revelat[or]r› order of the Danites, we have a company of Danites in these times, to put to right physically that which is not right, and to cleanse the Church of verry (sic) great evils which hath hitherto existed among us inasmuch as they cannot be put to right by teachings & persuasyons (sic), This company or a part of them exhibited on the fourth day of July They come up to consecrate, by companies of tens, commanded by their captain over ten.[445]

One estimate of the eventual number of the Danites is 800-1,000. Quinn gives a list of many of them.[446] The formation of these forces to enable the Mormons to establish their Zion in Missouri caused great concern among the citizens of Missouri, and prompted Governor Boggs to issue his Mormon extermination/removal order.

With the collapse of LDS projects in Kirtland, the de facto center became Far West, Missouri. By this time, and with Smith preoccupied in Kirtland, a number of principal LDS leaders had developed a personal history in "Zion."

Their story began in October 1830, when Oliver Cowdery, Parley P. Pratt, Peter Whitmer, Jr., and Ziba Peterson were called to undertake a

---

[444] Oration Delivered by Mr. S. Rigdon, on the 4th of July, 1838 (Far West: Printed at the Journal Office, 1838), 8, 12. See Marquardt, *Rise of Mormonism*, 284-85.
[445] *Scriptory Book of Joseph Smith*, 60-61, in Marquardt, *Rise of Mormonism*, 286-87.
[446] Quinn, *Mormon Hierarchy*, 479-85.

mission to the "Lamanites." They reached Independence, Missouri, early in the year 1831. Cowdery returned to Kirtland but in November 1831, he and John Whitmer were sent to Independence with the revelations to be published there by William W. Phelps. During Joseph Smith's second visit to Missouri (in 1832), Oliver was appointed one of the high priests to preside over the members in the gathering place. When conflict with Missourians developed in July of 1833, he was sent as a messenger to inform the First Presidency at Kirtland. When Smith marched with Zion's Camp to Missouri in May of 1834, Sidney Rigdon and Oliver were left in charge of the Church at Kirtland. By early 1838 he had returned to Far West, Missouri.

On July 7, 1834, Smith ordained Whitmer to be the president of the church in Missouri and possibly his own successor. He served in that capacity with his brother John Whitmer and William W. Phelps as his counsellors, from then until 1838. They and their fellows virtually founded the town of Far West.

Joseph Smith and family arrived there in March of 1838. Cowdery and the Whitmers openly confronted Smith regarding his failure to separate church and state. Cowdery accused Smith of immoral behavior. After failing to appear in his defense, he was excommunicated on 12 April 1838. David Whitmer was excommunicated the day after, his brother John on 10 March 1838, and William W. Phelps on 17 March 1838. From September 1837 through May 1838, the excommunicated included two of the Church Presidency, the three of the Presidency at Far West, four of the Quorum of the Twelve Apostles and six of the *Book of Mormon* witnesses.[447] In addition to the fact that there were important issues at stake, the purge left the Smiths and Rigdon in firm control.

Excommunication was not sufficient. On 17 June 1838, Sidney Rigdon delivered his "salt" sermon, described by John Corrill as follows:

> President Rigden ⟨Rigdon⟩ delivered from the pulpit what I call the salt sermon; "If the salt have lost its savour, it is thenceforth good for nothing, but to be cast out and trodden under the feet of men," was his text, and although he did not call names in his sermon, yet it was plainly understood that he meant the dissenters, or those who denied the faith, ought to be cast

---

[447]Marquardt, *Rise of Mormonism*, 282.

out, and literally trodden under foot. He, indirectly, accused some of them with crime.[448]

Two days later, Oliver Cowdery, David Whitmer, John Whitmer, Apostle Lyman E. Johnson, and Mormon printer/editor William W. Phelps fled Missouri for their lives in response to a written death threat signed by eighty-three Saints, including the Danite chief Sampson Avard, two members of the First Presidency, and eight other Danites.[449] The letter reads as follows:

> ...for out of the county you shall go, and no power shall save you. And you shall have three days after you receive this communication to you, including twenty-four hours in each day, for you to depart with your families peaceably; which you may do undisturbed by any person; but in that time, if you do not depart, we will use the means in our power to cause you to depart; for go you shall... and vengeance sleepeth not, neither does it slumber; and unless you heed us this time, and attend to our request, it will overtake you at an hour when you do not expect, and at a day when you do not look for it; and for you there shall be no escape; for there is but one decree for you, which is depart, depart, or a more fatal calamity shall befall you.[450]

Joseph Smith and Criminal Justice in Missouri

The history of conflict between the Mormon settlers and Missouri residents tested Smith's judgment as a leader and statesman. The successful relocation to Commerce, Illinois, and its transformation to an impressive and viable community, shows that he had options. A simple revelation could have been received stating that because Satan had turned the hearts of enemies in Zion against the work of the Lord, and as in the case of Israel wandering in the desert, the plan of the Lord was for a temporary settlement in peace elsewhere until the time was ripe, thereby sparing innocent lives. The success of Brigham Young later to direct the Saints to undertake a massive move to the Rockies also shows that

---

[448] John Corrill, *A Brief History of the Church of Christ of Latter Day Saints*, 30; quoted in Marquardt, *Ibid*, 283.

[449] Marquardt, *ibid*; Quinn, *Mormon Hierarchy*, 472.

[450] *Document Containing the Correspondence, Orders &C. in Relation to the Disturbances with the Mormons; and the Evidence Given before the Hon. Austin A. King, Judge of the Fifth Judicial Circuit of the State of Missouri* (1841: Fayette, MO, Office of the Boob's Lick Democrat), 103.

alternatives existed. Perhaps inspired by the success of the holy warriors in the *Book of Mormon*, Joseph chose a less peaceful course.

During June to October 1838, the Mormon-Missourian conflict developed into what Missouri historians have dubbed the Mormon war. During this time, the Danites were "under the general command of Secretary of War Joseph Smith."[451]

On August 8: Smith led an armed group of over a hundred and surrounded the home of Justice of the Peace Adam Black, who had been elected Judge only two days earlier.

August 10: Based on a sworn statement from William P. Peniston, Judge King issued a warrant for the arrest of Smith and Lyman Wight. (August 28, Judge Black gave his sworn statement of the events.) Sheriff William Morgan attempted to arrest Wight, but arrived at Wight's home only to find Wight was protected by an armed force of about 100 men.

Around August 16: Daviess County Sheriff Morgan, accompanied by Judge Josiah Morin, went to serve a warrant on Smith in Far West. Smith refused to return to Daviess County.

September 7: Judge Austin Augustus King conducted a hearing and found sufficient evidence to send the case to a grand jury. Smith was released on a $500 bond.

November 2: After the surrender of Mormon forces, Smith was surrendered to authorities, arrested and imprisoned in the jail at Liberty, Missouri.

November 12: Judge King found "probable cause to believe that Joseph Smith, Jr., Lyman Wight, Hyram (sic) Smith, Alexander McRay & Caleb Baldwin are guilty of Overt acts of Treason in Daviess County." Smith and other Mormons continued to be held at Liberty Jail (MO).

April 11, 1839: Smith was indicted by grand jury on the charge of treason.

April 16: Smith and his companions escaped (were permitted to escape?) while they were being escorted to Boone County. Smith fled across the border to Illinois.[452]

---

[451] Quinn, *Mormon Hierarchy*, 472.
[452] "Joseph Smith and the criminal justice system," Wikipedia, 20 October 2015.

Security and Enforcement in Nauvoo

During 1839-1844, Joseph Smith's Lifeguards were in place in Nauvoo, with former Danites, including a former Danite captain.[453] During the period 1839-1843, ad hoc enforcers, former Danites, undertook internal and external security.

The Nauvoo Legion was organized for external security, but included former Danites and members of Smith's ceremonial Lifeguards.[454] The needs of internal and external security were also met by Nauvoo's constables, including a Danite officer. During 1843-46, the Nauvoo police undertook external and internal security duties, including acting as bodyguards for Joseph Smith until his murder in 1844, and for Brigham Young as of August, 1844. The officers were former Danites, and most policemen were Danites.[455] Adolescents and preadolescents were organized into the Nauvoo Whistling & Whittling Brigade, primarily for non-Mormon targets.

On 7 June 1844, the *Nauvoo Expositor*, a four-page newspaper, was issued. Although expressing faith in the Bible and *Book of Mormon*, it criticized Joseph Smith. It contained a list of fifteen resolutions relating to Church abuses. The doctrines of spiritual wives and polytheism were rejected. At a time when Illinois was reviewing its decision to issue the Nauvoo Charter, it called for the repeal of the Charter. On June 8, the Nauvoo City Council met to discuss the *Expositor*. On June 10, Joseph Smith commanded the city marshal to destroy the press. William Clayton reported, "The City council passed a resolution declaring the Printing press on the hill a 'nuisance' and ordered it destroyed if not moved in 3 hours notice. The police gathered at the Temple about sundown and after organizing proceeded to the office and demolished the press & scattered the Type."[456]

Following Smith's death, there were various attempts against dissenters and traitors. In the period 1845-46, the Nauvoo Whistling & Whittling Brigade, now aged 17 to 56, targeted mainly dissidents. On 3 April 1845, Brigham Young praised the Nauvoo police for beating "a man almost to death in the Temple." On 14 September 1845, the Nauvoo

---

[453] *Idem.*
[454] Quinn, *ibid*, 473.
[455] Quinn, *ibid*, 474.
[456] William Clayton Journal, entry for June 10, 1844; Marquardt, *Rise of Mormonism*, 387-89.

police "had to flog" dissenters for trying to attend an open-air "business meeting" of the Church.[457]

Security and Enforcement in Brigham Young's Utah Territory

In Utah, up to 1870, "Ad hoc enforcers (former Danites, non-Danites and some trusted Mormon criminals on specific assignments against anti-Mormons and apostates)" continued activities, called variously "'minute Men,' or 'Be'-boys,' or 'Brigham's Boys'."[458] Brigham Young had undertaken to establish his own country in Utah Territory.

The main group of Mormons, with Brigham Young, arrived in the Salt Lake valley on 24 July 1847. Apparently anticipating Young's ambitions, three years later the U. S. Congress created the Utah Territory (9 September 1850). This act of Congress set up the territory political structure, including the office of Territorial Governor (appointed every four years), the Utah Territorial Assembly (representatives chosen annually), and a Utah judiciary, including a Supreme Court, District Courts, Probate Courts and a Justice of the Peace. On 9 February 1851, Brigham Young was inaugurated the first governor, and was appointed for two terms (appointed by Fillmore and Pierce). No sooner had the Mormons gotten across the plains and Rockies, and arrived in their new Zion, than the Federal government stepped in and, in a sense, took it over, created Federal institutions, and sent in Federal officers. The reaction on the part of some was violent. Shortly after Young's appointment, a number of Federal appointees left their posts, some claiming that they were fleeing for their lives. An Associate Justice, William W. Drummond was especially influential, and reported that the Mormons recognize no authority but the priesthood. Their reports convinced the White House that the Mormons were revolting against the United State government. Events led to the "Utah War." Alfred Cumming accompanied Albert Sidney Johnston's expedition to put down the rebellion. Brigham Young issued a call to arms:

Proclamation by the Governor. "Citizens of Utah—We are invaded by a hostile force who are evidently assailing us to accomplish our overthrow and destruction ... Therefore I, Brigham Young, Governor and Superintendent for Indian Affairs for the Territory of Utah ... forbid all armed forces, of every description, from coming into this Territory under any pretence [sic] whatever

---

[457] Quinn, *ibid*, 476.
[458] Quinn, *ibid*, 477.

... That all the forces in said Territory hold themselves in readiness to march at a moment's notice, to repel any and all such invasion ... Martial law is hereby declared to exist in this Territory, from and after the Publication of this Proclamation...fifteenth day of September, A.D. Eighteen hundred and fifty seven...,"[459]

President James Buchanan decided to appoint a new governor; initially, prospective appointees refused the honor. Finally, Alfred Cumming was appointed, and Buchanan sent a military force of 2,500 to create a post in Utah, in support of the governor. Cumming arrived in the territory in November, 1857. After considerable military developments on both sides, both decided that a peaceful settlement was the best option. Buchanan's terms were that the Mormons should submit to federal laws, and in exchange, amnesties were offered. Young accepted; but he was never again appointed governor. His loss of government office probably did not represent a significant decrease in his effective power and influence in Utah. Still, Utah was under *de facto* military occupation.

The times were changing, and eventually the Mormons sought statehood. In the process, the Utah territory was whittled down to a fraction of its maximum size, polygamy was outlawed, and Utah achieved statehood in 1896. The contrast between Utah, and its two neighbors, Wyoming and Colorado, is remarkable. While Utah was still practicing polygamy, Wyoming became the first state to give women the vote, and the first state to have a woman governor, while Colorado was the second.

Joseph Smith: Loose Cannon, or Mission Accomplished?

After destroying the *Nauvoo Expositor*, Smith and a number of colleagues were charged at Carthage, Illinois, with instigating a riot in destroying the *Expositor*. Rather than submit to the sheriff who came to arrest them, he secured a writ from the Nauvoo court; he, Hyrum Smith, John Taylor, William W. Phelps and others were tried and acquitted on June 17 by Daniel H. Wells, a non-Mormon judge in Nauvoo, who was friendly to the Mormons. This provoked an angry reaction among his

---

[459] Text in a Sotheby Park Bernet Inc. auction notice: *Highly Important American Historical Documents, Autograph Letters & Manuscripts. The Property of the Elsie O. & Philip D. Lang Foundation, Part Two* (New York: Cosmos Press, 1978), item 585.

opponents, and thousands gathered to take up arms. On June 18, Smith called up the Nauvoo Legion, nearly 5,000 strong when in full force.

As the Saints were digging in, Governor Thomas Ford decided to visit the scene himself. At Carthage he found the forces against the Mormons to be formidable, and on 21 June he sent a letter to Smith asking that representatives come to Carthage to inform him. Smith immediately prepared statements which he sent to Ford with John M. Bernhisel and John Taylor. These delegates were given a message from Ford, in which he stated that the Mormons had violated freedom of the press, freedom from search and seizure without due process, and the division of powers, i.e., the legislative and judicial powers. He requested that Smith surrender for trial.

On 23 June, Joseph, Hyrum, Willard Richards and Orrin Porter Rockwell crossed the Mississippi to take refuge among friends. When word of his flight spread through Nauvoo, the reaction of the Mormons was confusion and dissension. Some accused him of cowardice, to flee in their hour of need. His wife Emma wrote a letter urging his return. When word of this reached Joseph, reportedly he said, "If my life is of no value to my friends, it is of none to myself," and he returned. Most probably he had had time to reflect. Apparently there was a price on his head, and Missouri was full of people ready to hunt him down, even without the offer of a bounty. He must have realized that he had no chance on the run.

He returned, and upon the order of Major General Jonathan Dunham he disbanded the Nauvoo Legion, and surrendered at Carthage. Those charged appeared at a hearing before Robert F. Smith, a justice of the Peace who was also Captain of the Carthage Greys and anti-Mormon. He charged them with riot in destroying the *Nauvoo Expositor,* released them on bond of five hundred dollars each to appear at the next term of the circuit court. That evening at their hotel they were served with a mittimus signed by Robert F. Smith to hold Joseph, Hyrum, and Apostles John Taylor and Willard Richards in jail until they could be tried for treason. They protested this new charge, but to no avail. They were put in Carthage jail, where Joseph and Hyrum were killed by the mob on 27 June 1844.

Joseph Smith had made serious miscalculations. The first was his response to the events in Missouri in the summer of 1833. He could have resorted to plan B, yet another location, with a metaphor of the children of Israel wandering in the wilderness, waiting for the time to be right to enter into the land of promise. Instead, he decided to pursue plan A with a military force, Zion's Camp, and accompany it to Missouri. Although a peaceful stalemate was arrived at in 1834, the military option was prepared, and its use in response to subsequent persecution of Mormons resulted in the Mormon War in Missouri. Even when the court system falls short of justice, by any American law, then or now, raising a military force to seek justice outside of the legal order, resulting in injury and death, has to lead to capital charges.

But Smith was ensconced in Nauvoo, outside of Missouri jurisdiction, and protected by the Nauvoo legion, the Nauvoo police, his bodyguards and the Danites. His next miscalculation was the destruction of the *Nauvoo Expositor* press. He might rather have stood his ground theologically against his distractors, while possibly pursuing other legal action. As Ford explained to him, a legal response to the *Expositor* had to follow due process. Ignoring this enabled his enemies to press charges for violation of Illinois law, and gave them the opportunity to extricate him from Nauvoo.

The next miscalculation was to urge Ford to take a detachment to protect Nauvoo. His concern for his family and his community of believers is understandable. But the armed focus was then on him, in Carthage, where he was staying in a hotel, on bail. Ford's absence and the removal of one of his detachments created ideal circumstances for an anti-Mormon judge to prefer an outstanding Missouri charge of treason, and to jail him to await trial. The many Missouri vigilantes experienced no resistance in their attack.

His death was totally traumatic to the Mormons in Nauvoo. Sidney Rigdon, having already attempted a failed coup to take over the movement, quickly played his cards, but was not accepted as the successor. He left to found his own church and was excommunicated. A second claimant, James Jesse Strang, claimed that Joseph had appointed him in a letter, but his claim was not accepted. He too left and established the "Strangites," and was excommunicated. At the urging of Apostle William E. McClellin, David Whitmer made his claim, but unsuccessfully. In 1847, Joseph's brother William announced that he was the legitimate successor by right of descent. His church lasted only a few years. On August 8, 1844, the Saints sustained the Quorum of the Twelve Apostles, with Brigham Young, as their leaders. Young then worked both with the Twelve and the Quorum of the Anointed, adding twenty new members to its rolls. He opened up the temple ceremony to

19. Church, Power and the Promised Land

all worthy members, which helped to weld the members into a cohesive community and prevent their scattering. Before the westward exodus, he directed the endowment of some 5,615 Saints.[460] His succession was gradual. Having built a following among Church leaders and the general membership, he organized a new First Presidency and was sustained as President, Prophet, Seer and Revelator on 27 December 1847.

Joseph Smith apparently saw his mission in terms of family, and of creating a dynasty. More and more, it was family that he trusted. After the excommunication of Cowdery and the Whitmers, the only witnesses to the *Book of Mormon* left standing were the Smiths. By the time of his death, forty-four percent of the members of the Quorum of the Anointed were related to Smith, either by blood or marriage.[461] Although his virility is not in question, it may be that his interest in polygamy was largely due to a desire to have more progeny, or, as Mormons like to say, to build his kingdom. Ironically, of his nine known children by Emma, five died before the age of two, and DNA research has not so far verified claims of offspring from polygamous wives.Smith's priesthood doctrine follows suite. Judaism, Christianity and Islam trace themselves back to Abraham, and are called the Abrahamic religions by many scholars. Smith picked up on the fact that Abraham paid his tithing to Melchizedek. Surely he must have had a very high authority. The next towering figure is Moses. Smith's revelation likens him to this leader, who spoke with God and received the Pentateuch, replete with laws and rituals, and instructions on who gets what. Smith clearly reasoned that it was not Moses who could not enter the Promised Land, but his priesthood, due to Israel's sin in worshipping the golden calf. The priesthood that did enter was that which became hereditary among the Levites, and must have come into the land of their inheritance with Aaron. Hence there were two, the Melchizedek and Aaronic (Levitical) priesthoods. But these had been restored by visitations, of John the Baptist and Peter, James and John. Surely, a hereditary priesthood would not need this. It would be by birth. Smith decided that this must be the Patriarchal priesthood, the highest of all. He and his family had it by birth. He made his father the Church Patriarch, and Joseph Smith Sr. was given a very special blessing in the first anointing in Kirtland. After his

---

[460] Garr, Cannon & Cowan, *Encyclopedia of Latter-day Saint History*, 1377.
[461] Anderson and Bergera, *Smith's Quorum of the Anointed* (Salt Lake City: Signature Books, 2005), xxx.

father's death, seven other members of the Smith family have held this office. When the office was filled by someone not of the Smith family, he was designated "Acting Presiding Patriarch." In 1979, when Presiding Patriarch Eldred G. Smith was released, no successor was appointed, effectively ending the office. Smith's strategy to assure the continuance of his family in the top echelons of the Church had come to an end.

Smith had three main collaborators, each in a different sphere. Oliver Cowdery was essential for the production of the *Book of Mormon*, and the early elaboration of Church rites and hierarchy. Sidney Rigdon played his role in the development of ritual and theology. And according to some accounts, Smith's closest collaborator in celestial marriage and spiritual wives was Brigham Young. By 1845, Joseph Smith had been murdered, and his two principal associates, Oliver Cowdery and Sidney Rigdon, had been excommunicated. Harris and Cowdery eventually returned to the fold in their last years of life, sick and with nowhere else to go. For all practical purposes, the Mormons under Brigham Young for the first time had no one at the helm that had created the religion they believed in so firmly. Young began to pack the Quorum of the Anointed with polygamists, many of them spiritual wives.[462] He knew that his control over this privilege was a juicy plum to attract capable men, and cement their loyalty.

For many, Joseph Smith had become a wildcard. His financial ventures had ruined many. His theology was getting more and more extreme, in the view of many. His personal life seemed out of control, although it was always rubber-stamped by the divine. And his conduct of external security affairs, and reliance on violence inside and out, exposed the members to insecurity.

Brigham Young, although the polygamist par excellence, had not been involved in the theological and organizational developments. He seems to have been a stalwart supporter of the prophet while he lived. Once in Utah, he understood very well that the Church had enough theology, ritual and organization. Under his iron-fisted leadership, the Church could enter into a period of consolidation, in virtual isolation.

---

[462] Quinn, *Mormon Hierarchy*, 176, 398-402.

Chapter 20

Private Initiatives to Develop a Mormon Culture

Thus far we have looked at the institutions, rites and beliefs put in place by LDS leaders. But the Mormon society and culture of today have also been created by private efforts. Some of these were later adopted by the LDS Church establishment. Others have remained independent, and to a significant extent virtually secular. This happened after the Mormons established themselves in Utah, and increasingly as outside, often secular influences at first penetrated and then overwhelmed the insulation enjoyed by this Rocky Mountain Zion.

Dimensions of Insulation

When the LDS settled in the Utah Territory, they began a period of great insulation from the non-LDS world. Although the Federal presence was felt, they were the dominant force in society, economy, politics and culture. Initially, the principal non-LDS penetration was due to the location of the Wasatch front on the way west, especially to the California gold rush. As the Mormons made their valley a more desirable place to live, with economic opportunities, non-Mormon settlers came. They were supplemented by dissenters from the Mormon community. The next big intrusion was brought about by the transcontinental railroad. The ceremony for driving in the last spike, joining the east and west of the United States, was held on May 10, 1869 on Promontory Summit, Utah. Its completion dramatically reduced the traffic on the California and Oregon trails. Although it did swing down towards Salt Lake City, it actually passed through Ogden, Utah. Eventually, a spur connected it to Salt Lake City, Provo, Juab and Frisco. For decades, the LDS homeland was right on the American RR highway across the country. Later, the Utahns strove to make their capital an air travel hub.

An example of the role of Utah ambitions in change in the Mormon heartland is the partial relaxation of its famous (infamous) liquor laws in order to accommodate the 2002 Winter Olympics. When no disasters were caused by this measure, a degree of relaxation was made permanent. This is the sort of compromise required by the desire to be somehow "in the world, but not of the world."[463]

Demography and Economy

The more the LDS worked to create a prosperous and desirable place to live, the more they drew outsiders. In Utah, they remain the majority religion.

Table 38. Religion Statistics Profile of Salt Lake County, Utah

Religion	2010 Total	2010 %
Church of Jesus Christ of Latter-day Saints	610,846	59.3
Catholic	84,342	8.2
Evangelical Protestant	27,497	2.7
Mainline Protestant	12,789	1.2
Orthodox	5,352	0.5
Black Protestant	1,302	0.1
Other	11,961	1.2
None	275,566	2.7
Total	1,029,655	100

Source: *U. S. Religion Census: Religious Congregations & Membership Study*. Dale E. Jones, et al., Association of Statisticians of American Religious Bodies, 2012.

The population of Utah is estimated to be 62.1% Mormon, and recently this proportion has held fairly constant.[464]

Population growth has been accompanied by the development of employments that differ radically from those available during the nineteenth century:

Table 39. Utah Employment by Industry Sector, 2014

Industry Sector	Average Employment
Agriculture, Forestry, Fishing & Hunting	5,261
Mining	12,168
Utilities	6,105

---

[463] Bill Kerig, "What's Up with Utah Liquor Laws?" (*USA Today*, 29/10/2003).
[464] Matt Canham, "Census: Share of Utah's Mormon Residents Holds Steady" (Salt Lake: *The Salt Lake Tribune*, April 17, 2012).

(Table 39 continued)

Construction	79,769
Manufacturing	120,691
Wholesale Trade	48,648
Retail Trade	152,275
Transportation and Warehousing	59,223
Information	34,631
Finance and Insurance	57,534
Real Estate and Rental and Leasing	18,273
Professional, Scientific & Technical Services	83,220
Management of Companies and Enterprises	19,903
Admin., Support, Waste Mgmt., Remediation	82,778
Education Services	151,565
Health Care and Social Assistance	151,388
Arts, Entertainment, and Recreation	26,618
Accommodation and Food Services	108,198
Other Services (except Public Admin.)	38,001
Public Administration	77,024
Unclassified Establishment	75

These employments have required much more education, and education often in specialized fields. The LDS establishment has both embraced and mistrusted this development.

State/Secular Education

Since the Saints entered Utah, they have worked at establishing educational institutions, but have not ranked in, or even near the top ten states. All in all, most citizens of Utah are being exposed to the ideas and information that a secondary education affords, and a significant proportion have imbibed from the fonts of post-secondary learning. Even so, educational achievement has been found lagging behind.

These changes prompted the development of institutions to define and defend a distinctly Mormon way of life: a Mormon culture.

University of Utah: The John Pack family used their humble home to host social and educational events. This was the embryo from which the University of Utah would spring. Brigham Young organized a board of regents to establish a university. In 1850, they established the University of Deseret, named after the provisional State of Deseret. In spite of the leadership of well-educated Orson Spencer, it closed in 1853 due to lack of funds, and was reestablished under the direction of David O. Calder in 1867, followed by Orson Spencer. Under the leadership of John R. Park, president from 1869-92, it was developed into a modern university. In 1892 the name was changed to the University of Utah. Upon his death, Park bequeathed his entire fortune to it. The University of Deseret is considered the first university west of the Mississippi, and, as the University of Utah, it has become the flagship institution in the university system of Utah.

Utah State University: In 1888 a bill was passed to establish the Agricultural College of Utah in Logan. Its expansion into non-agricultural fields was opposed by interests in Salt Lake City, which were slowly overcome, and in 1957 it became the Utah State University of Agriculture and Applied Science, which was shortened to Utah State University, with full university status.

The Utah System of Higher Education has grown to also include Weber State University, Southern Utah University, Snow College, Dixie State University, USU Eastern, Utah Valley University, Salt Lake Community College, and Utah College of Applied Technology.

There are a number of private universities and colleges in Utah. These include, Brigham Young University, Westminster College (established in 1875 as the Salt Lake Collegiate Institute) and Stevens Henager College (with campuses in Ogden, Logan and Murray, and its College of Business in Provo).

Enrollment in primary and secondary education in Utah was 598,832 in 2012. Utah is ranked average (between the top ten and bottom ten) in all performance indicators. Even so, in 2008-2009, only 80% finished high school, and 59% went on to college. The graduation rate for associate and certificate students in 2009 was 36% (in the top ten), whereas the graduation rate for bachelor students was average at 60%.[465] Members of the population 25 years old or older with a bachelor's degree or higher was 29% in the period 2009-2013.[466]

In 2013, the Utah state budget for education per student was rock bottom, at $6,555. However, this needs to be adjusted a bit due to the relatively low cost structure in Utah, including both wages and prices. Even so, it is not clear that such an adjustment would change the picture

---

[465] See the National Center for Education Statistics and the Integrated Postsecondary Education Data System.
[466] US Census, Quick Facts

greatly. Furthermore, Utah ranks no. 44 in educational achievement, as reported by The States Project.[467] Although, the establishment of educational institutions and awarding of degrees only partially reflect a people's commitment to education, one has to wonder if there is a certain ambivalence to exposing one's youth to too much information.

The Church of Jesus Christ of Latter-day Saints has responded to the perceived threat that is posed by its youth spending so many hours of their formative years being taught, well—"Who knows what?" by, well—"Who knows whom?" In the seventies, I heard the U (University of Utah) called "those atheists on the hill."

Mormon Education to Enable Orthodox and Reverent Learning

The LDS Seminaries. On the elementary level, the Church established its Seminary system. This is an LDS religious studies system of schools, often located adjacent to public schools, and in some cases landscaped as though they were part of them. In Utah, and some adjacent states, where the LDS Church has sufficient influence over the public system, there is a time release program, to work a seminary course into the public school schedule so that the student does not have to spend extra "school time." An LDS school counselor in the public system at times allows him- or herself to suggest to the student to consider taking a seminary course. There is a seminary Graduation Diploma for the completion of all four courses of study: *Book of Mormon, Doctrine and Covenants* and Church History, New Testament, and Old Testament. Naturally, the Biblical courses will include and interpret the passages that the Church uses to support the *Book of Mormon* and its Nephite narrative.

In 1912 the first seminary class was held in a private home near Granite High School in Salt Lake City. Granite allowed a time-release system to enable students to attend during school hours.

Statistical information from the Seminaries and Institutes of Religion Annual Report for 2013, released recently by The Church of Jesus Christ of Latter-day Saints, reveals the growing internationalism of the seminary program. Of the 391,680 LDS seminary students, nearly half (186,996) live outside the United States. While there are more

---

[467] The States Project, Nonpartisan Reporting on the State of Our States, a joint venture of Harvard University's Institute of Politics at the Kennedy School, the University of Pennsylvania's Fels Institute of Government, and the American Education Foundation.

seminary students in the United States (204,684) than in any other single nation, countries like Mexico (28,299), Brazil (22,655), Peru (17,969) and the Philippines (16,791) boast rapidly growing LDS populations, and, not coincidentally, growing numbers of seminary students. Seminaries are also taking hold in nations like Nigeria (3,115), Ghana (2,511) and the Democratic Republic of the Congo (1,943), where LDS influence is relatively new. The vast majority of LDS seminary students (240,227) participate in early morning religious education programs held before school in local church buildings and, sometimes, in the homes of church members. The next-biggest number of students (126,176) participate in time-release programs. The remaining 25,277 seminary students participate in home study programs.[468]

The LDS Institutes. The LDS Institutes are a system on the college level, with an inviting institute building convenient to and seemingly almost part of a university campus. This development took place in Moscow, Idaho, with two independent grass-roots efforts. First, the concept was promoted by logging magnate William C. Geddes, and his daughters Norma and Zola. He eventually prevailed upon the LDS establishment through his friendship with Preston Nibley, including the agreement of the First Presidency. Second, two LDS members on the faculty of the University of Idaho, William J. Wilde and George L. Luke, prevailed upon the University and then the State Board of Education and Board of Regents to allow an LDS Institute of Religion to be established adjacent to the university. A nonmember professor of German proposed that the building be called the Latter-day Saint Institute of Religion at Moscow, Idaho, and this was accepted.[469]

The courses of study include the Cornerstone courses (Jesus Christ and the Everlasting Gospel; Foundation of the Restoration; The Eternal Family; and Teaching and Doctrine of the *Book of Mormon*) and the elective courses (Old Testament; New Testament; *Book of Mormon*; *Doctrine and Covenants*, *Pearl of Great Price*; Gospel Teaching and Learning; Church History in the Fulness (sic) of Times; and others). Fourteen credits are required to graduate: eight Cornerstone course credits and six primary or secondary elective course credits. To make these studies accessible to members outside of the formal system, in

---

[468] Joseph Walker, "LDS seminary enrollment reaches all-time high" (Salt Lake City: *Deseret News*, April 24 2013)

[469] Dennis A. Wright, "The Beginnings of the First LDS Institute of Religion at Moscow, Idaho" (mormonhistoricsites.org, accessed 19 December 2015).

1992, an expanded Institute program was inaugurated by requiring that at least one institute course be taught, often by a volunteer, in each stake. Including those studying in stake institutes, in 2015 there were 52,236 enrolled.[470]

Today the seminary and institute programs teach over 700,000 students in 143 different countries through the efforts of nearly 50,000 full-time, part-time, and volunteer teachers and administrators.[471]

The LDS University System. In 1862, Warren Dusenberry established a school in Provo, Utah, paying the building rent and making the school desks himself. In 1869, he and his brother established a second school in the Lewis Building in Provo. When the student body reached 300, the school became the Timpanogos Branch of the University of Deseret. The accepted founding date of Brigham Young University is October 16, 1875, when President Young personally purchased the Lewis Building. He tore the school off the University of Deseret and christened it Brigham Young Academy.[472] The Church also set up other academies. Some eventually evolved into colleges or universities, including

Brigham Young Academy (founded 1875), now Brigham Young University;

Salt Lake Stake Academy (founded 1886), spawning LDS Business College;

Bannock Stake Academy (founded 1888), now Brigham Young University–Idaho;

Church College of Hawaii (1955), now Brigham Young University–Hawaii

In 2015, BYU was considered to be the largest religious university in the United States, and the third largest private university, with around 30,000 students on campus. Since many students and even professors, have returned from lay missions abroad, the university is highly multilingual. In addition to its sister campuses in Idaho and Hawaii, it operates two satellite campuses, in Salt Lake City and Jerusalem.

---

[470] Information accessed from seminary.lds.org.
[471] Information accessed from seminary.lds.org ("History of Seminary").
[472] "History of Brigham Young University" (wikipedia.org accessed on 19 December 2015).

A major issue among both students and faculty has been academic freedom: A statement issued by BYU in 1992 stated its position, saying in part:

> At Brigham Young University, faculty and students are enjoined to "seek learning . . . by study and also by faith" (D&C 88:118). This integration of truth lies at the heart of BYU's institutional mission. As a religiously distinctive university, BYU opens up a space in the academic world in which its faculty and students can pursue knowledge in light of the restored gospel as taught by The Church of Jesus Christ of Latter-day Saints. For those who have embraced the gospel, BYU offers an especially rich and full kind of academic freedom. To seek knowledge in the light of revealed truth is, for believers, to be free indeed. ("Statement on Academic Freedom at BYU" (Provo: BYU. September 14, 1992.)

In addition to operating on a principle of orthodox and reverent learning and research, BYU implements an honor code, governing dress, behavior (sexual propriety and clean speech), and consumables (no alcohol, coffee or tea in the dorms, or drugs). Clearly students are not monitored for tithe paying; but the situation is less clear for professors. For the faculty, certainly one's tithing status is known (10% before taxes). One expects that being a non-tithe-payer is not career-enhancing.

LDS students must take two hours of religion classes per term to graduate. An association of non-LDS students (NLDSA) has apparently succeeded in getting a special section of the required *Book of Mormon* course for non-LDS students. This was sought by the students to avoid occasional friction with LDS students.

Although BYU prefers to have LDS professors when equally qualified, non-LDS professors exist, especially in nonsensitive fields, such as chemistry. On non-LDS persons at BYU, see an article by Jeff Call.[473]

The Neal A. Maxwell Institute for Religious Scholarship focuses on a select number of sacred and religious texts and the traditions within which they are situated. In support of its apologetics, and to compete for the minds and hearts of even its own students, it established the Religious Studies Center, in support of religious education. The model that it strives to emulate is the late Hugh Nibley, who would be the

---

[473] Jeff Call, "Religious freedom: What's BYU life like for non-LDS professors, students?" (Salt Lake City: *Deseret News*, Nov. 21 1999).

patron saint for such activity if Mormonism had such a thing. On its website as of October, 2015, it published the following: "Hugh Winder Nibley (1910–2005) was a professor at Brigham Young University and an apologist for The Church of Jesus Christ of Latter-day Saints...At the request of Apostle John A. Widtsoe, he became a professor at Brigham Young University in 1946, teaching history, languages, and religion." A set of Nibley's collected works has appeared in around eighteen volumes. His importance in the defense of Mormonism is immense.

The Institute has the following initiatives:

The Center for the Preservation of Ancient Religious Texts (Syriac literature, the Dead Sea Scrolls, and other ancient texts) was established in 2001, and renamed the *Neil A. Maxwell Institute for Religious Scholarship* in 2006.

The Laura F. Willes Center for Book of Mormon Studies was the brainchild of Mark H. Willes, businessman and former CEO of Times-Mirror. Commenting on the establishment of the Center, Elder Dallin H. Oakes of the Quorum of the Twelve Apostles said, "It's a remarkable combination to have the resources, the inspiration of what to do with them and the faith to do it..."[474]

The Middle Eastern Texts Initiative works to produce bilingual editions of important Jewish, Christian, and Islamic texts.

The William (Bill) Gay Research Chair for scholarship in fields of study related to ancient scriptures. It publishes the *Journal of Book of Mormon Studies, Studies in the Bible and Antiquity,* and the *Mormon Studies Review*. One of its foci is Egyptology and *The Book of Abraham*.

The New World Archaeological Foundation (NWAF) was founded in 1952, and although Thomas Stuart Ferguson, an LDS apologist, was one of the founders (along with Alfred V. Kidder and Gordon Willey), it was not initially a Mormon institution. It was founded to support archaeological research in Pre-Colombian Mesoamerica. Although initially incorporated in California as a private institution, it began receiving money from the LDS Church, and in 1961 the Church made it a part of BYU, with the mission of pursuing New World archaeology, without relating findings to the *Book of Mormon*. Researchers include non-Mormon scholars.

---

[474] "BYU Announces Formation of Laura F. Willes Center for *Book of Mormon* Studies" (News Release, news.byu.edu, accessed 19 December 1915).

The Foundation for Ancient Research and Mormon Studies (FARMS), organized by John W. Welch in 1979 in California, began as a relatively informal group of LDS academics devoted to, or seeking a career in research using mostly ancient materials to address issues posed by the Mormon canon or relevant aspects in the history of religion. In 1997 it was asked to become a BYU organization by none other than the fifteenth President, Prophet, Seer and Revelator of the LDS Church, Gordon B. Hinckley, and in 2006, the group was absorbed into the Neal A. Maxwell Institute for Religious Scholarship. So it too was drawn safely under the wing of the LDS establishment at BYU.

The fact that there is a significant degree of overlap between these organizations is largely due to the fact that they generally began as separate private organizations, became dependent on LDS funding, and were eventually taken over by the Church.

LDS Publishing. The first LDS publication was of course the *Book of Mormon*, but was contracted out. In 1832, William W. Phelps began publication of the first official Church organ, *The Evening and the Morning Star* (1832-34), in Independence, Missouri, and Kirtland, Ohio. In 1833, he began printing the *Book of Commandments*, but a mob destroyed his press. Some printed pages were saved, and a small number of partial copies are still extant. The Church organ was replaced by the *Latter Day Saints Messenger and Advocate* (1834-37), which was followed by several others, each the Church organ in its day: the *Elder's Journal* (1837-38), the *Times and Seasons* (1839-46) and others. The *Improvement Era* was the official Church magazine from 1897 to 1970, when it was replaced by the *Ensign* (1971 to the present). There has also been a series of Church publications for targeted groups, such as the youth and members abroad.

Private Publishing. The first professional LDS publishing company independent of the Church was George Q. Cannon and Sons. It consisted of both a publishing facility and a bookstore. Cannon sold the bookstore to the LDS Church in 1900. It became the Deseret News Bookstore, which was replaced by the Deseret Book Company.

The Relief Society. In Nauvoo in 1842, a number of LDS women decided that they would be able to contribute to those working on the construction of the Nauvoo Temple, and to alleviate the suffering of the poor among them by forming a benevolent society. A constitution was drawn up and presented to Joseph Smith, who approved of the idea in principle, decided that the constitution was not needed, and organized the women into a benevolent society under the priesthood, in some sense parallel to it, but lacking anything resembling priesthood authority. The women performed valuable charitable work, but soon addressed their own issues. In particular, Emma, the prophet's first (and in her opinion, only) wife used the organization to express opposition to polygamy. Her husband intervened, and promptly dissolved the society in 1844. It was in the year prior to this that a revelation stated that "if she [Emma] will not abide this commandment [polygamy] she shall be destroyed." (D&C 132:54)

After the move to the Utah Territory, many women continued to perform charity work informally. Eliza R. Snow, secretary of the organization in Nauvoo, brought her notes with her to Utah and used them to teach women. Brigham Young called for them to assist destitute Indians in the area, and in 1854 an Indian Relief Society was formed. Over time, various wards began organizing women's relief societies. In 1867 Brigham Young called for the organization of relief societies in every ward. In 1880, Snow was formally sustained as the first President of the Relief Society in Utah. By the turn of the century, these society meetings included religious education for the women. In 1902 stakes began using lesson outlines. Additional instruction was provided in 1914 in the *Relief Society Bulletin*, renamed the *Relief Society Magazine* in the following year. Although charitable work continues, the role of female education in the doctrines and culture of the Church was becoming prominent. Eventually, the societies were more formally organized, with Relief Society presidencies at the ward and stake level, all under a Relief Society Presidency for the entire Church. Today, the Relief Society is headquartered in the very attractive Relief Society Building in Salt Lake City. The fact that it is the only Church organization to have its own building, separate from the Church Offices Building, can be taken as a positive distinction, or a step to distinguish it from the priesthood, which continues to be a men-only institution.

The LDS Welfare Program had a long and complex development, prior to the formal establishment of the program in 1935 by Harold B. Lee (inaugurated in 1936 by David O. McKay). Some early converts had collectivist beliefs, possibly prompting the phenomenon of the United Order in Church history. Emma Smith and other women took the first initiative in founding the Relief Society. When Brigham Young was attempting to establish a grain storage program for the Church, he eventually asked Emmeline Wells to organize it. Her efforts were quite successful. She went further, and in 1919 established six-week training programs, including assistance to wards and stakes to help women find employment. Later, when the great depression struck, assistance efforts first developed, at least as early as 1933, by various wards and stakes, i.e. on the community level. It was as a continuation of this long development, in recognition of the need with the nation in depression, and to extend and systematize on a Church-wide level, that the program was established formally. When this happened, a founding principle was work. Bishops administering the program were to find some sort of work for members receiving aid as compensation, and to get them back to regular employment.[475]

The LDS Primary Organization was established initially in 1878 by Aurelia Spencer Rogers, mother of twelve at age 44, in Farmington, Utah. She promoted her program within the Relief Society, and Eliza R. Snow acted as a de facto Primary director. Established Church-wide in 1880, it worked to promote the moral and religious education of young boys, initially, and young girls, age 4-14.[476]

The LDS Fast Offerings Program was apparently established in Kirtland, Ohio, by Joseph Smith.[477] Members are asked to calculate the money saved by fasting one day, and donate it to the Fast Offerings Program to assist the poor. Originally, members were to fast once a month, on Thursday. In the nineteenth century Mormon miners in England were given an exception and allowed to fast on Sunday, a practice that spread to the rest of the Church.[478]

The Young Men's Mutual Improvement Association (YMMIA) and the *Young Women* organization had several precursors, reflecting the Church's interest in developing the faith and energies of young LDS members. Although the Young Gentlemen's and Young Ladies' Relief Society, established by Joseph Smith, may be considered a precursor, its goals were a bit different, and it did not continue. In 1854 LDS Apostle Lorenzo Snow established the Polysophical Society as an organization

---

[475] "Emmeline Wells—Welfare Edition" (ldswomenshistory.blogspot.com: 16 March 2015. "Development of the Church Welfare Program" (historyofmormonism.com: accessed 20 December 2015)

[476] "History of Primary" (lds.org: accessed 20 December 2015). "Primary (LDS Church)" (en.wikipedia.org: accessed 20 December 2015).

[477] Brigham Young, *Journal of Discourses* (12:115). "Fast Sunday" (en.wikipedia.org: accessed 20 December 2015).

[478] "Fast Sunday" (en.wikipedia.org: accessed 20 December 2015).

for young men to acquire some knowledge of various branches of human learning. In 1869, out of concern that young LDS women were dressing and speaking inappropriately, Brigham Young established the Young Ladies' Department of the Cooperative Retrenchment Association. This was renamed the Young Ladies' National Mutual Improvement Association in 1877. As an equivalent to it for young men, Brigham Young organized the Young Men's Mutual Improvement Association in 1875. This eventually developed into the Aaronic Priesthood MIA, while the young women's organization became Young Women.

The Word of Wisdom is not an organization, but Mormons are so identified by it, by themselves and others, that it has to be included. The temperance movement in the U.S. dates to the 1820's. Similarly, opposition to tobacco goes back as far as Pope Urban VII, and tobacco was at times outlawed in various European countries.[479] American temperance reformers began to recommend coffee as a substitute for alcohol. In 1830, Congress removed a burdensome duty on coffee, and immediately the sales of alcohol suffered. Even so, some reformers, such as Sylvester Graham and William A. Alcott preached against all stimulants.[480] It is reasonable to assume that various opinions were present among the early converts to Mormonism, and that Joseph Smith found himself caught between both sides. His position was awkward, since some members liked their drink. The reply was an effort to please both sides. It came as a *word of wisdom*: "not by commandment or constraint, but by revelation and the word of wisdom." (D&C 89:2) It addressed alcohol and tobacco specifically, but was vague on what might be interpreted to be coffee and tea, the "hot drinks." (D&C 89:9) Over time, the LDS themselves leaned towards a more prohibitive stance, and eventually coffee and tea were included as hot drinks. Once both were found to contain the stimulant caffeine, many LDS privately extended the prohibition to include the colas. This, however, has never been made Church policy, as is evidenced by the fact that drinking colas is not a bar to a temple recommend. This phenomenon is indicative of the zeal (or the overzealousness?) of some, and the role of grass roots campaigning in shaping what became the Word of Wisdom, and perhaps the issuing of the revelation in the first place. If so, it is a good example of the ability

---

[479] "Tobacco Control" (en.wikipedia.org: accessed 20 December 2015).
[480] "The Word of Wisdom. D&C 89." (history.lds.org: accessed on 20 December 2015).

of Joseph Smith to accommodate various sides in negotiating treacherous waters.

The Mormon Tabernacle Choir is world-famous. Music had been important to the LDS from the beginning. Emma Smith collected the hymns for the first Mormon hymnal, published in 1836, with two hymns composed by Eliza R. Snow. In 1849, John Parry and about 100 other Welsh converts to Mormonism sailed from Liverpool and journeyed to the Utah Territory. At the October 1849 general conference he conducted a group of 85 Welsh converts in singing several songs. After the conference, Brigham Young asked him to organize a church choir. Parry was the conductor of the new choir until 1854, when he was followed by George Edward Percy Careless, who is credited with improving its musical quality. The famous Mormon Tabernacle building was completed in 1867, and acquired one of the most elaborate organs in the world, with 11,623 pipes. It became the home of the new choir. In 1873, having over 300 members, the Mormon Tabernacle Choir sang at the Church's October general conference.

Theater in Zion

LDS theater got a jump start in 1842 with the conversion of Thomas A. Lyne, an accomplished professional actor. He put on a number of plays in Nauvoo, including "Pizarro," in which he cast none other than Brigham Young as the Peruvian priest. He left Nauvoo, and Mormonism, but moved to Salt Lake City some twenty years later. There he continued his thespian career, and died a "gentile" at eighty four. When asked regarding his regret for having cast Brigham Young as a Peruvian priest, he replied "Why don't you see John, he's been playing the character with great success ever since."[481]

Circa 1850, the Musical and Dramatic Club (later, Deseret Dramatic Organization) was organized, based largely on the members of the Nauvoo Brass Band, led by the lefty fiddler William Pitt. An amusement hall was built at Warm Springs, which was replaced by the Social Hall in 1852. Later, Brigham Young had the historic Social Hall built in a more convenient location, and the original became a roadside tavern for a

---

[481] John S. Lindsay, *The Mormons and the Theatre, or The History of Theatricals in Utah with Reminiscences and Comments, Humorous and Critical* (Salt Lake City: Century Printing, 1905), 7.

while, run by Jesse C. Little. Due to the limitations of the Social Hall, Brigham Young subsequently ordered the construction of the Salt Lake Theatre.

In the wake of the "Mormon War," Sargent R. C. White (Dick White) organized the Camp Floyd Theatre to entertain the troops. Due to the scarcity of women at the camp, efforts were made to recruit from the LDS community, producing predictable suspicion and friction.

Circa 1860, a new company was organized, the Mechanic's Dramatic Association, headed by the Social Hall comedian Phil Margets. A member, Harry Bowring, had begun the construction of a home, and even before its completion this new company began staging plays in part of it. It was dubbed "Bowring's Theatre," becoming the first place to be called a theater in Salt Lake. Earlier, a place for outdoor worship, the Bowery, hosted some productions, but due to its primary religious function, could not be called a theater. On 6 March 1862, the Salt Lake Theatre was completed. Its grand opening was a free invitation-only event with invitation extended by Brigham Young to LDS Church authorities and their families, as well as those of state, county and municipal officers, and even the construction workers who had built the theater. The evening began with a dedicatory prayer, with President Young presiding. The theater had been planned by William H. Folsom, the same architect that had proven himself in the execution of the Tabernacle,.

Brigham Young delivered an address giving the objective of the theater as harmless amusement for the edification of the Saints. There should be no tragedies as they had suffered enough tragedy, and no non-Mormon actors. Lyne resurfaced in a production in Denver and was persuaded to undertake tutoring the LDS actors. He soon was staging and acting in more classical works. Although no longer committed to the LDS faith, President young welcomed him back on board theatrically. Thus the ban on gentile actors fell by the wayside.

The Salt Lake Theater soon became a cultural oasis in the Rocky Mountain wilderness. Brigham Young loved dancing, and theater of the "desirable" kind. His material support in the form of venues and some financial compensation to Lyne was important. But the initiatives to get theater going in the first place, and to form theatrical companies, arose from among the Saints acting apart from any official Church capacity.

One might be tempted to say that this legacy has been overtaken and overwhelmed by the silver screen, then by TV and finally by digital

DVD and online entertainment, from the best in family fare to hardcore. Right. But wrong. Utah remains a dynamic center for the live performing arts of every sort. The following is not comprehensive, but makes the point.

Table 40. Utah Performing Arts, 2016-17

Capital Theatre (Utah Opera Company, plus theatrical and musical productions, including JazzSLC)
Abravanel Hall (home of the Utah Symphony Orchestra)
The Jessie Eccles Quinney Ballet Centre (center for Ballet West)
Odyssey Dance Theatre (theatrical dance, Salt Lake)
Simmons Pioneer Theatre (Home to the Pioneer Theatre Company)
Kingsbury Hall (performing arts, Salt Lake)
Rose Wagner Performing Arts Center (Pygmalion Theatre Company, SLC)
The George S. and Dolores Dore Eccles Theatre (Broadway, concerts, Salt Lake)
The State Room (live music, Salt Lake)
Jazz and Blues SLC (Salt Lake)
Laughing Stock (live comedy, Salt Lake City)
Wiseguys Comedy Club (live comedy, Salt Lake & Ogden)
Sundance Film Festival (Park City)
The Eccles Center (state-of-the-art theater, Park City)
Jim Santy Auditorium (film, Park City)
Eccles Conference Center & Peery's Egyptian Theater (Ogden)
SCERA Center for the Arts (Orem)
Hale Center Theater (live theater, Orem and West Valley)
Centerpoint Legacy Theater (Davis Center for the Performing Arts)
Echo Theater (performing arts, Provo)
Covey Center for the Arts (Provo)
Desert Star Playhouse (musical comedy, Murray, UT)
The Utah Shakespeare Festival (Cedar City, Shakespeare & modern theater)
The Tuacahn complex (St. George, amphitheatre)

The theatrical arts are important. They act as a sort of mirror, in which we see ourselves, and our society. One ought not wonder that religion has used drama to such an extent, nor that Brigham Young was concerned about its content. It cannot help but be in competition with religion.

Overview: Private Initiatives in Creating Mormon Culture

The following table reviews the principal institutions and those who laid the groundwork inherited by the twenty-first century.

Table 41. Initiators of Institutions in the Mormon Heartland

Institution	Early Initiator
University of Utah	The John Pack family
LDS Seminaries	Private home in Granite school district
LDS Institutes	William C. Geddes; William J. Wilde and George L. Luke
Brigham Young University	Warren Dusenberry
Neil A. Maxwell Institute	BYU initiative
The Laura F. Willes Center for *Book of Mormon* Studies	Mark Willes
BYU religious publications	With funding from William (Bill) Gay
New World Archaeological Foundation	Thomas Stuart Ferguson, Alfred V. Kidder and Gordon Willey
The Foundation for Ancient Research and Mormon Studies	John W. Welch
LDS periodicals	LDS Church
Deseret Book Company	George Q. Cannon
The Relief Society	Emma Smith; LDS women working independently; Eliza R. Snow
Church Welfare Program	Brigham Young; Emmeline Wells
LDS Primary Organization	Aurelia Spencer Rogers
Fast Offerings Program	Joseph Smith
Mutual Improvement Organization	Brigham Young
The Word of Wisdom	Joseph Smith & grass roots zeal
Mormon Tabernacle Choir	Emma Smith (hymnal); John Parry
Theater in Zion	Lyne, Pitt, Margets, Bowring, Young

We can see from this table the prominence of LDS individuals in the development of these key institutions. During the first century of the LDS in their Rocky Mountain Zion, an extensive network of institutions had been created for this garden of saints, to plant, nurture and prune them from cradle to grave, to assure their proper Mormon faith and behavior. In many cases, their efforts were embraced by the Church, although the Relief Society had a rocky road, at first.

Whatever one might think of the founders of Mormonism, and of some of its rite and certain aspects of its theology, we must not lose sight of the fact that in their "land of our inheritance," the Mormon people themselves created the distinctive institutions, which work together like a grand symphony, to produce a continuous celebration of their life and toils, and their hopes, aspirations and virtues.

Chapter 21

Secular Issues and LDS Apologetics

Secular Progress in Knowledge Relevant to LDS Claims

Another dimension of insulation, with respect to one's beliefs, is the degree to which disconfirming information exists at all, and the degree that it can impinge upon the minds of individuals.[482] From 1850 through the first half of the twentieth century, many Mormon writers clearly felt that there was no real writing in pre-Columbian America, and that their *Book of Mormon* was the best guide to interpreting the monuments. This has been a natural continuation of the Smith-Cowdery strategy of reserving historical detail for the New World, where certain information regarding such an early period would never be available to test the BOM narrative. The idea that the ruins of the Maya were available for anyone to make a case to support an agenda has been beautifully studied in *Romancing the Maya* by Tripp Evans.[483] Speaking of "a period in the age of the world of which all history is silent," and "ruins utterly barren of all record of their own history," but being sure that the *Book of Mormon* is a true history, John Taylor, yet to become the third LDS prophet, seer and revelator, asserted confidently in 1851 re the Mesoamerican glyphs:

> For not only do we find the characters so common to all the ruins of Central America, but tracing them back, without as yet knowing precisely their import, we reach by progressive though receding steps a period when they were identical with and purely the Egyptian hieroglyphs easily deciphered and as easily understood.[484]

The process of deciphering the Mayan glyphs got off to a slow start. The documentation of the many Mayan written materials, and their

---

[482] For a systematic study of these factors, see A. Chris Eccel, *Egypt, Islam and Social Change: Al-Azhar in Conflict and Accommodation* (Berlin: Schwartz Verlag, 1984).
[483] Tripp Evans, *Romancing the Maya, Mexican Antiquity in the American Imagination, 1820-1915* (Austin: University of Texas Press, 2004).
[484] John Taylor, "The Discovery of Ancient Ruins in Northern California" (Salt Lake City: *The Millennial Star of the Latter-day Saints*, vol. XIII, 1851), 93-95.

publication to produce a corpus in a clear scholarly format (photographs plus hand-drawn monographs), was slow, as was the decipherment of the Mayan writing system so that these many texts could be read. From the archaeological, epigraphic and linguistic point of view, LDS insulation from the facts that pre-Columbian civilizations had left behind lasted for over 150 years, from 1830 to at least 1980. The history of Mayan decipherment is summarized in the following table.

Table 42. Decipherment of Mayan Writing

1519	Cortez at Cozumel; several screen-fold Mayan books are sent back to Spain.
1561	Diego de Landa has a Mayan friar to help him list the Mayan characters with their Spanish equivalents. He mistakenly thought the Maya used and alphabet, whereas they used a syllabary.
1562	Diego de Landa burned all the Mayan books he could find. Only four screen-fold books are known to have survived.
1785	Jose Calderon discovers Palenque.
1810	Five pages of the Dresden codex are published in Paris in a massive volume on the Americas.
18??	Constantine Samuel Rafinesque deciphers some elements of the Mayan numbering system. This is the first decipherment of any Mayan writing.
1862	Brasseur de Bourbourg finds the description of the Maya written by Diego de Landa. He used it to attempt a translation of the Madrid manuscript, but produced a text that bore no similarity to what this manuscript actually says.
1881	Alfred Percival Maudslay begins photographing monuments and inscriptions, producing the first accurate corpus of written Mayan.
1880	Ernst Förstemann, in Dresden, discovers that the Maya invented the concept of zero, and a base-20 counting system; they used rows to record numbers, a ones row (up to 19), a 20's row, a 400's row, an 8,000's row, etc., much like our system of a one's column, a tens column, etc. They carried over from row to row, just as we carry over from column to column. He also succeeded in working out the Mayan calendar. He used Diego de Landa's notes on the Mayan months, with the Mayan month names written in the Spanish alphabet to be able to read Month glyphs in Mayan. He discovered the Mayan beginning point of the calendar thousands of years ago, the Mayan date of creation. Using Maudslay's photographs, he found that this creation date was used throughout the Mayan world.
1880's	American agricultural scientist Cyrus Thomas discovered that the Maya used a syllabary to write, not an alphabet, and worked out some characters correctly.
1892	German Mayanist Eduard Seler attacks Thomas' discovery, and Thomas abandons his efforts. Seler held that the glyphs were pictorial rather than phonological.
1905	A Nevada newspaper man, Joseph Goodman, worked out the correlation between the Mayan dates and the Gregorian calendar. Now Mayan monuments would be dated by their inscriptions.

(Table 42 continued)

1900's	In the 1930's through about 1970, Eric Thompson of the Carnegie Foundation catalogues Mayan glyphs, assigning to each a T number. The vast majority could not be read. Unfortunately, Thompson dominated Mayan inscription studies, & held that the Maya did not write, but used symbols in a vague manner for priests, gods & their high mysteries. Tatiana Proskouriakoff of the Peabody Museum identifies the glyphs for birth, ascension to the throne and death. With this she worked out the dynastic succession of Piedras Negras, showing that the Maya wrote their history. The meaning of these glyphs was clear, but she still could not read them in Mayan.
1952	Russian linguist Yuri Knorosov recognized that the characters in the work of Diego de Landa are a partial syllabary, in which, instead of a character for b, there are separate characters of bi, bu, ba, bo, be, and so on, for all the consonant-vowel combinations of the Mayan language. In addition, the system uses pictorial signs, logograms, where a single sign represents a whole word, as in the Chinese writing system. He knew that some other languages uses both phonological characters, and logograms, such as ancient Egyptian. In both Mayan and Egyptian, a word can be represented by a single logogram, or spelled out phonologically.
1953	Anti-Communist Eric Thompson attacked Knorosov's work. This, & the fact that it was in Russian, caused his work to be ignored in the West.
1955	Michael Coe and his Russian-born wife Sophi, discovered a copy of Knorosov's work in Merida, Mexico, and begin collaboration with Knorosov. Sophi Coe translates his papers into English. Unfortunately, Eric Thompson's view dominated, and Knorosov remained isolated behind the iron curtain.
1959	Heinrich Berlin identifies city "emblem" glyphs that recorded the names of Mayan cities. Geography could now be identified in the inscriptions, although these glyphs could not be read in Mayan.
1968	Heinrich Berlin identified the glyphs for four rulers at Palenque.
1970's	Merle Robertson founded the Pre-Columbian Art Research Institute.
1973	She organized a mesa redonda, round table, the first Mayanist conference. Scholarly collaboration begins. During this conference, Peter Mathews, Linda Schele and Floyd Lounsbury picked up where Heinrich Berlin left off, and worked out 200 years of the Palenque dynasty, including six rulers, Lord Hanab Pakal and his five successors.
1974	At a conference at the Dumbarton Oaks research library, using the rubbings from the Hanab Pakal sarcophagus, this ruler's ancestors were added to the Palenque dynasty list, finally covering 400 years, beginning in the late 4th century. Subsequently, similar work was done for other Mayan cities.
1970s	Although a minimum of eighty syllabic signs would be needed to write all of Mayan sounds, by the 1980's fewer than thirty could be read with confidence.

(Table 42 continued)

1980	The recognition that the relationship of classical Mayan to modern Mayan is a bit like that of Chaucer to modern English has been extremely useful in achieving a better understanding of the Mayan inscriptional language. This contribution has been much like Champollion's knowledge of Coptic (Egyptian), which he used to decipher ancient Egyptian, once he realized that Coptic was simply the latest development of the former. Since there are some thirty Mayan languages, dictionaries have been written specific to individual languages. An example specific to Yucatec Maya is Diccionario maya Cordemex: maya-español, español-maya, by Alfredo Barrera Vásquez ((Mérida, Yucatán, México: Ediciones Cordemex, 1980); see other works by Juan Ramón Bastarrachea Manzano and William Brito Sansores.
1985	David Stuart discovered that the Maya used more than one sign for the same sound, much like in English ch can be represented by ch and by t (as in "nature"), and s can be represented by s and by c (as in "cistern"). This opened up a flood gate for the identification of syllabic signs.
Even though there is still much work to be done, by thirty years later, thousands of inscriptions on stone and ceramics have been transcribed, and very adequate translations have been made of many of them.	

The greater access to essential facts afforded by the ability to read ancient texts has had an impact among LDS information and scholarly elites. This has been seen in the case of the decipherment of Egyptian, which enabled LDS scholars to know that the so-called Abraham papyri are burial documents, and not the text of a scripture penned by Abraham. So too, the decipherment of the impressive Mayan writing system, and the translation of many monumental inscriptions, have enabled scholars to know that Central America cannot have been the setting for a Nephite/Lamanite civilization.

Mormon Apologetics

The word *apologist* does not mean *apologizing*. It comes from Greek, *apo* and *logos*, discourse in response to or against, in other words, a verbal defense, and in religious affairs, it is the defense of the faith: no apology needed, or intended, thank you very much.

LDS leadership are concerned about the exodus from the Church on the part of its best educated, its intelligentsia. If not stemmed, over the mid to long term, it can have a deleterious effect on the makeup of the Church, and on what it will become in the future, as it continues to reinvent itself.

A comment made in this regard by David A. Palmer has considerable poignancy: "The Church of Jesus Christ of Latter-day Saints has no official position on *Book of Mormon* geography. In fact, the Church sponsored New World Archaeological Foundation (NWAF), which for two decades has been conducting excavations in the state of Chiapas, Mexico, has steered away from direct *Book of Mormon* studies."[485] Many suspect that the real mission of the NWAF is to conduct valid research, so that the Church can point to its archaeologists and say, "See. They are experts, and they still believe."

This can be a powerful message, but the strategy can backfire. An example is that of self-taught archaeologist Thomas Stuart Ferguson, the principal founder and first president of the NWAF, coauthor (with Milton R. Hunter) of *Ancient America and the Book of Mormon*, author of *One Fold, One Shepherd* (1958), popular Mormon apologist lecturer, and occasional author of articles published in LDS periodicals. Posthumously, he is on the cover of *The Messiah in Ancient America*, along with Bruce W. Warren, although Ferguson's coauthorship has been challenged, and he has not spoken from the grave. A sympathetic account of his life journey has been written by Stan Larson, who details Ferguson's gradual loss of faith, and struggle with what to do about it.[486] In 1961, the NWAF was reorganized, and a new Archaeological Committee was created to supervise it. The then Prophet, Seer, Revelator & President of the Church, David O. McKay appointed Howard W. Hunter, the youngest member of the Quorum of the Twelve Apostles of the Church as Chairman, while Ferguson was demoted to secretary. Presumably, it was at this point that it was decided, at the highest level, to erect a firewall between the *Book of Mormon* and New World archaeology. Ferguson knew that major breakthroughs were happening in New World, especially Mesoamerican archaeology, in the form of more numerous and exhaustive excavations, but especially the decipherment of the Mayan glyphs. Initially he must have expected that the *Book of Mormon* would be vindicated, and, like the role of the Bible in the archaeology of Palestine, it would become a textual source that even non-LDS researchers would have to consult. When it turned out to be just the opposite, Ferguson was unable to repress his growing doubts.

---

[485] David A. Palmer, *In Search of Cumorah*, 19.
[486] Stan Larson, *Quest for the Gold Plates, Thomas Stuart Ferguson's Archaeological Search for the* Book of Mormon (Salt Lake City: Freethinker Press, 1996).

Larson analyzes Ferguson's correspondence, and finds that eventually he decided that God does not get involved in any of the religions. On 9 February 1976, Ferguson wrote to Harold W. Lawrence and his wife, who were also suffering a crisis of faith:

> Why not say the right things and keep your membership in the great fraternity [the LDS Church], enjoying the good things you like and discarding the ones you can't swallow (and keeping your mouths shut)? Hypocritical? Maybe. But perhaps a realistic way of dealing with a very difficult problem. There is lots left in the Church to enjoy—and thousands of members have done, and are doing, what I suggest you consider doing.[487]

Over time, Church officials have adopted a systematic strategy. It can be illustrated in a study of its reaction to *The Book of Abraham* crisis. At first, it seemed to think that it could just simply acquire the papyri and let them disappear in the vaults at Brigham Young University. Their finder, Dr. Aziz Suryal Atiya, Founder and Director of the Middle East Studies Center at the University of Utah, made an announcement to the press regarding his find. This news hit like a thunderbolt among the Church leadership and intelligentsia. Among the latter were the editors of an unofficial periodical, *Dialogue a Journal of Mormon Thought*, who pressured the Church to enable scholarly access to the papyri. The Church responded, publishing them in large format, full and clear photos, in its principal official organ the *Improvement Era*. *Dialogue* responded by getting top Egyptologists to analyze and translate them, within the context of their history since their acquisition by Joseph Smith, and Smith's *Egyptian Alphabet and Grammar*, as well.

Apologetics in the Official Church Organ. Prior to this event, the Church had used its official magazine, *The Improvement Era*, as a tool for apologetics, focusing primarily on what it considered to be material that supported the *Book of Mormon*. After acquiring the Joseph Smith (Abraham) papyri, the focus shifted almost entirely to *The Book of Abraham*. But its approach to Church-wide apologetics has changed.

The Improvement Era was the official magazine of the Church until January of 1971 (although other Church magazines were being published, for special audiences), when it was replaced by *Ensign*. From 1950 through 1966, an amazing amount of space was dedicated to

---

[487] Larson, *Quest for the Gold Plates*, 161.

support the *Book of Mormon*. Late in 1966 information was had that Dr. Aziz Atiyah, founder of the Middle East Center at the University of Utah, may have found the long lost Joseph Smith papyri. During the entire year of 1967, the *Era* did not publish a single thing on LDS apologetics. It is clear that this news had disrupted the normal conduct of information dissemination to the membership, as the LDS establishment attempted to determine what to make of this news, what positive or negative potential it might have.

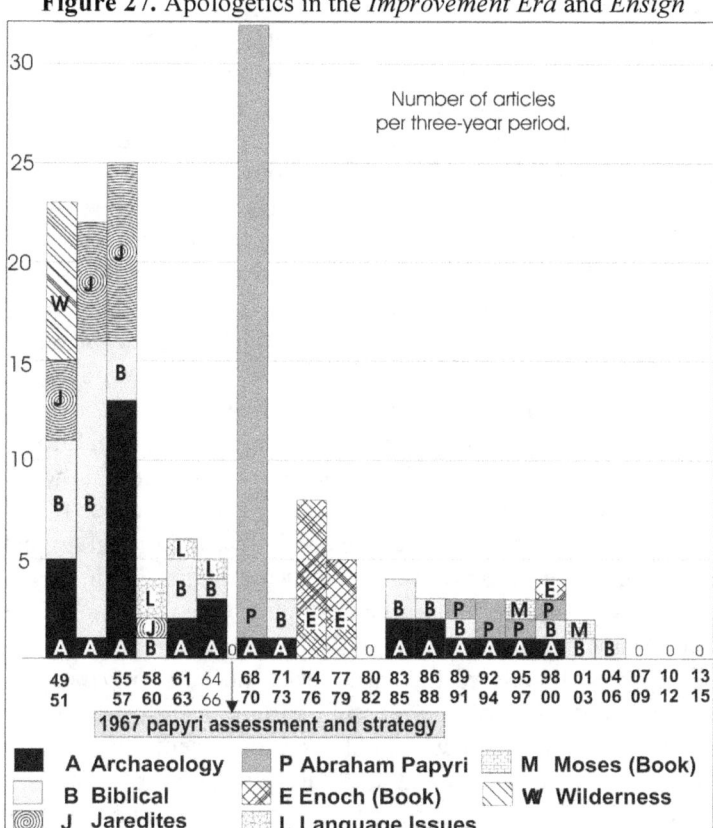

Figure 27. Apologetics in the *Improvement Era* and *Ensign*

In January of 1968, the Church announced the find in the *Era*, and in February it published the papyri in clear photos. The stance would be that *The Book of Abraham* had nothing to fear, and beginning with the January Issue, the LDS Apologist in Chief, Hugh Nibley, began a serialized work to address the issue: "A New Look at the *Pearl of Great Price*: Part 1, Challenge and Response." It is interesting that the title avoids a reference to *The Book of Abraham*, to give the impression that there is no need for a special focus on this *cause célèbre* that had all of Mormon intelligentsia asking the same question: Will this text translate into *The Book of Abraham*, and prove Joseph Smith to be a prophet, or will it turn out to be something quite other than what he and the Church had claimed. For a while, the Church published a number of articles about Abraham and the papyri. Then, silence, at which point the *Era* died. A coincidence? No way to know.

The *Ensign* would take a far different approach to apologetics. It had become clear to Church leadership that most members had no idea that a problem even existed, and that carrying on a defense in their official organs simply called attention re the problem to the great many who were living in blissful ignorance. From this time on, or to some extent even before, the Church was aware that it had a variety of audiences, and that its messages needed to be tailored for each one. It has since used its official organs more to educate regarding the cardinal points of the faith, and as faith-building tools. At the same time, it has established studies centers (the Religious Studies Center and the Neal A. Maxwell Institute for Religious Scholarship), and promotes apologetics by appropriate scholars. Individuals, who have become aware of the problems faced by Mormon scriptures, and/or controversial doctrines or events in Mormon history, can be discretely directed to these works. Figure 27 shows the abrupt change of policy, and the degree to which the *Ensign* was made largely into an exclusively devotional magazine to build the faith, and address daily issues of the Saints, including old age, temple marriage, unemployment and how to deal with a loved one "suffering" from "same-sex attraction."

The articles listed in the last three decades in the categories "archaeology" and "papyri" are mostly a diluted form of apologetics. For a while an occasional series was published to present a sort of survey of what BYU researchers were doing, and how their work supported Mormonism. Three or four research efforts were surveyed in a single short article, such that it was not possible to go into much detail. This approach was discontinued, but the items have been included in Figure 27, overstating the apologetics present in the last three decades. For a list of all the articles gleaned for this graph, see Appendix 4.

A Bible in Search of a Geographical Setting

Table 43. Summary of BOM Cartography Efforts

Abstract	Mesoamerica	South America	Great Lakes
	Joseph Smith (1842)		
		O. Pratt, 1872	
		Comer/Maeser, 1880	
		Reynolds, 1888	
	Cluff, 1901		
	Holmes, 1903		
	Palfrey, 1903		
	Shook, 1910	Knisley, 1909	
	Smith, 1911		
	Hills, 1917		
	Young, 1921	Ricks, 1921	
	Ivins, 1921		
	Roberts, c. 1922, c. 1927		
	Driggs, 1928		
Layton, 1938			
Washburn/Washburn, 39			
	Ferguson, 1947		
	Farnsworth, 1947		
	Wilde, 1947		
	Birrell, 1948		
	McGavin/Bean, 1948		
	Stout, 1950		
	Hansen, 1951		
	Hunter, 1956, 1970		
	Ferguson, 1958	Dixon, 1957	
	Reynolds/Sjodahl, 1957		
Hammond, 1959	Hammond, 1959		
	Davila, 1961		
	Jakeman, 1963		
	DeLong-Steede-Simmons 1977	Priddis, 1975	
		Le Poidevin, 1977	
	Cheesman, 1978		
	Ellsworth, 1980		
	Palmer, 1981		Holley, 1983
	Sorenson, 1985		
Nielsen, 1987	Hauck, 1988	Kocherhans, 1989	Curtis, 1988
	Peay, 1993		
	Hansen, 1997		Aston, 1998
	Welch/Welch, 1999		
	Sutton, 2001		Olive, 2000
			Goble/May 2002
	Calderwood, 2005		
	Diane Wirth, 2007		
	Lund, 2007		
	Allen & Allen, 2008		
	Johnson, et. al., 2008	Potter, 2009	Coon, 2009
		Conway, 2012	Meldrum, 2011
			Neville, 2015

The BOM setting problem is reflected in some book titles:

The Lost Lands of the Book of Mormon; Where O Where is the Book of Mormon? An Ancient American Setting for the Book of Mormon; In Search of Cumorah; Cumorah—Where?

The pattern we see in Figure 27 finds a parallel in Table 43, which reflects the penetration of the realities of Mesoamerican archaeology into the circle of LDS scholars wrestling with the issue of locating a plausible setting for the BOM history (See Chapter 3). The Mesoamerican setting now has competition. As LDS scholars became increasingly aware of its problems, they began seeking a new piece of real estate for the BOM narrative. Only time will tell to what extent the new views can prevail, being so at odds with the *Book of Mormon* itself.

John L. Sorenson has been one of the more ambitious apologists, whose magnum opus brings together the results of his life's work.[488] To his credit, he accepts the BOM geographical references for what they are, although he locates the narrow neck of land at Coatzacoalcos, across the Isthmus of Tehuantepec, even though the march across from sea to sea there would take a minimum of four days, and probably longer. This places virtually the entire BOM history in Mexico. Those interested in a massive effort to champion this view should study this work, but do beware of a certain point of contention between him and some of his colleagues. He locates the Cumorah, where Mormon, Moroni and the Nephite armies were finally destroyed, at Tuxtla in south-east Mexico, only about eighty miles north-west of Coatzacoalcos. Presumably Joseph Smith dug up his plates from a different Cumorah.

A large part of this book proceeds by topic, and seeks similarities between the Maya and the BOM in such things as warfare and language. The more concrete part of the book is in the chapter "Material Culture." He frankly concedes, "we cannot hope to find a single integral set of correspondences between Old World and Mesoamerican civilizations, especially in their material culture." This work fudges the facts quite a lot. For example, he refers to the Hohokam civilization, their irrigation, and the presence of a species of barley. In fact, the plant in question is *Hordeum pusillum*, or little barley, a grass that was gathered for its tiny seeds. Their diet depended largely on the cultivation of corn, just like

---

[488] Sorenson, *Mormon's Codex*.

their neighbors. Little barley derives most probably from a plant in South America, not from the Middle East. Sorenson's presentation is misleading. More puzzling is his reference to an Akkadian word for 'barley' or 'grain', *še'u*, which he relates to a name of a food in the BOM, *sheum* (Mosiah 9:9). Although he gives great elaboration, he neglects to mention that in the BOM *sheum* occurs in a list that also includes barley, and so is clearly not barley. Now things are getting even more misleading. He uses similar arguments to finesse other items on the BOM archaeological item list (Table 1), such as cattle, sheep, goats and horses. While suggesting that archaeology has barely scratched the surface and future exploration may yet discover the Nephite farm animals, his last refuge is to suggest that the BOM animal names may have referred to other similar animals native to Central America, such as 'horse' really meaning 'deer.'

His treatment of construction focuses on the use of cement and brick, rather than stone structures. The bottom line is that although Mayan construction used such materials, he can point to no site that is a Nephite, Lamanite or Jaredite site, and no trace of the mighty Nephite capital, Zarahemla, or any of the many other BOM cities.

Metallurgy focuses largely on iron and steel, where he refers to various ferrous items found, and suggests that Pre-Columbian peoples may have worked natural iron into useful objects, including some of steel. Natural iron can refer to chunks from volcanic activity, but mostly to iron meteorites. These could indeed have been heated and hammered into various shapes, although it is hard to imagine using this material to produce a fine sword, let alone enough swords to arm the millions of combatants in the BOM. It is iron smelting that is the issue, not chance discoveries of ferrous meteorites.

The scientific validity of this work is not the issue. Its importance lies in its success in strengthening the faith of a believing readership. For us, it makes two contributions. First, it shows that after a lifetime of gathering information, he has not been able to successfully address the items in the archaeological item list. Finally, although he places the Nephites in the heartland of the Maya, Olmec, and others, he shows no sign of being aware of the biggest archaeological problem of all: the failure of the BOM narrative to mention any people other than its Jaredites, Nephites, Lamanites, Mulekites and Zoramites.

Archaeology: Just Horsing Around?

The articles designated under the rubric of "archaeology" in Figure 27 represents the situation but poorly. There are no excavation reports, or articles that analyze the finds of excavations, no attempt to label any site or artifact as being Nephite, or deriving from Nephite/Lamanite civilization. One example, however, invites us to exercise some caution regarding those articles labeled "Archaeology." In the 12/1955 issue of the *Improvement Era*, in a serialized work titled "Archaeology and the *Book of Mormon*," Milton R Hunter published a photo that he claimed to be an image of a horse carved in stone on a panel at Chichen Itza[489]:

Figure 28. The Temple of the Panels of Reliefs: Hunter vs. Others[490]

Source: photo by Otto Done   Source: Church of Christ Temple Lot

Hunter's photo on the left clearly has been heavily retouched. To me, this jollied-up version looks very much like a European. It is not clear who touched up the photo. A similar photo, also retouched, appeared in the book form of this series, in 1956.[491] Since it too was taken by Otto Done, both photos were probably taken on the same visit to the monument near the end of 1954. Several photos have appeared online, all resembling the photo on the right from the Church of Christ (Temple Lot). Hunter's project photographer is the likely candidate for the photo modification. Even so, Hunter himself, a member of the Church's Council of the

---

[489] *Improvement Era*, December 1955.
[490] Otto Done (photographer), "Archaeology and the *Book of Mormon*, VII," *Improvement Era* (December, 1955), 899. Church of Christ Temple Lot, accessed online 19/04/2017 at: https://images.search.yahoo.com (photo sourced to http:// www.cocsermons.net.
[491] Milton R. Hunter, *Archaeology and the* Book of Mormon (Salt Lake City: Deseret Book Company, 1956), 6.

Seventies, could not have not known that it had been done. We do not know why Hunter went back to an unretouched photo fifteen years later.[492] We do know that the site had become a must-see for LDS tourists to the "Land of Zarahemla" and BYU students on study tours. Hunter had possibly been made aware of their disappointment when they saw the real thing. In any case, these photos reveal the degree to which it was acceptable to someone of his position to enhance the evidence of the "truth" for the greater glory of the cause. This bas-relief has not survived in the artifact repertoire of later apologists.

As for the animal in the image, its identification is complicated by the fact that the images on this temple's panels feature a number of legendary animals. So a correct identification may be some animal that does not even exist. Note that the retouched photo made the feet look like the human is walking to the left, and the face was retouched from the back of the man's head gear. In the original, the human and animal are walking in the same direction. Also, the head of the animal has been modified, with a heftier lower jaw, making it resemble a horse a bit more. The head only comes up a bit higher than the human's navel. The neck does not rise up like that of a horse, but extends out like a big cat. Although the tail of a horse can extend out at full gallop, it hangs down when it is standing or walking. The tail is more appropriate for a big cat. My money is on some animal, perhaps real, perhaps mythical, of a more feline nature.

Hugh Winder Nibley, Apologist in Chief.

The book that firmly established Nibley, and launched his career in LDS apologetics, was *Lehi in the Desert*, although the BOM narrative itself states that Nephi's account of Lehi's travel in the wilderness lacks detail. His method can be illustrated by the following assertions: 1) Lehi possessed precious things not manufactured in Jerusalem (the BOM does not say this); 2) Lehi had close ties with Sidon (the BOM does not say this); 3) Lehi lived on an estate in the country (the BOM say he lived in Jerusalem all his days); and 4) Lehi was "something of an expert in vine, olive, fig and honey culture" (the BOM does not say this). He concludes, "so there can be little doubt of the nature of his business with Egypt." In

---

[492] Milton R. Hunter, *Great Civilizations and the* Book of Mormon (Salt Lake City: Bookcraft, 1970), 197.

fact, the BOM does not say that he had any business with Egypt. This whole sequence is fanciful and deliberately misleading.[493] In addition to effectively rewriting his only source for Lehi, i.e. the *Book of Mormon*, he searches a huge body of early, mostly out of date secondary literature about the Middle East to glean occasional statements, some of them paraphrased, to develop his analysis and to project erudition.

Nibley's works have not impressed the experts in any of the fields of Middle East scholarship, but they were not intended to do so. His elixir so expertly compounded is served to those whose great faith in the *Book of Mormon* is only matched by their great thirst for scholarly evidence to support it. Its success is virtually guaranteed.

Although Nibley had in the past defended *The Book of Abraham*, and its translation from the papyri, when the actual Egyptian document in question surfaced, he changed his argument. After providing the Egyptian text, transliteration and translation by Egyptologists, he states: "Though as correct and literal as we can make it, the translation in the preceding chapter is not a translation. It is nonsense."[494] He looks at the method of Joseph Smith in translating the gold plates, where phrases and sentences appeared before him, and, implying that something like that obtained in his translation of the papyri, he states: "Plainly, this peculiar type of translation depends on getting in the spirit and is not to be accomplished by intellectual effort alone."[495] It appears that his view is that while working on the papyri, the text of *The Book of Abraham* was revealed to him. He concludes: "If 'it mattereth not' by what imponderable method Joseph Smith produced his translations, as long as he came up with the right answers, it matters even less from what particular edition of what particular text he was translating. It is enough at present to know that the prophet was translating from real books of Abraham, Moses, Enoch, Mosiah and Zenos..."[496] This is a neat argument. But this effort to divorce *The Book of Abraham* from the

---

[493] Hugh Nibley, *Lehi in the Desert & the World of the Jaredites* (Salt Lake City: Bookcraft, 1952/1980), 12.
[494] Hugh Nibley, *The Message of the Joseph Smith Papyri, An Egyptian Egyptian Endowment*. Second Edition, edited by John Gee & Michael D. Rhodes (Salt Lake City: Deseret Book Company, 2005), 52.
[495] Nibley, Message of the Joseph Smith Papyri, 58.
[496] Nibley, Message of the Joseph Smith Papyri, 65.

papyrus ignores the fact that Abraham himself claims to have written the book himself. Writing in the first person, he refers to his own illustration, Facsimile Number 1 found in the Smith papyrus, which has actually turned out to be a Breathing Permit of the Book of the Dead.

Just when the Church was still engaged in the crisis caused by the discovery of the Joseph Smith papyri, Nibley began his series in *Ensign* on the *Book of Enoch*. The timing of the publication of this study served as a diversion from the Abraham issue. The *Book of Enoch* is a pseudepigraphic (falsely attributed) work, composed by various authors, some of it perhaps as early as 300 BCE, and some as late as the first century BCE. It is found in what appears to be its full text, at least as it existed by the first century CE, only in Geez (classical Ethiopic), and is recognized as canonical only in the Ethiopian Orthodox Church.

The details in Genesis make Enoch an ideal figure to be a Pseudepigraphal author. His life lay between Adam and Noah, and the OT says that he walked with God, and then "he was not, for God took him." In view of the fact that there are so many apocryphal works, it would be strange if Enoch had been left out.

The *Book of Moses*, presented to the world by Joseph Smith, Oliver Cowdery and Sidney Rigdon about a year after the publication of the *Book of Mormon*, contains an elaborated account of Enoch. When I acquired Nibley's treatment,[497] I was already familiar with the Ethiopic text of *Enoch*, and fragments in Greek and Aramaic. So I was expecting to find a presentation in two columns, one having "the book of Moses version says," and the other having "the Book of Enoch says." The conclusion would be that Smith and Cowdery did not have the *Book of Enoch*, and could not have produced these parallels. So the *Book of Moses* must have been received by revelation.

In Nibley's first comparison, the *Moses* Enoch weeps and is embittered by the vision of the destruction of man in the great deluge, but in the Ethiopic Enoch, the opposite happens, as it is Noah who cries out to his grandfather Enoch with a bitter voice, and Enoch consoles him. In the second pairing, in the Enoch account of the *Book of Moses*, Methuselah prophesies that all the kingdoms of the earth shall spring from his own loins through Noah, while in a Greek fragment of Enoch

---

[497] Hugh Nibley, *Enoch the Prophet* (Salt Lake City: Deseret Book Company, 1986). This volume contains two separate compositions: "Enoch the Prophet and His World," and "A Strange Thing in the Land."

106:16 it is Enoch who speaks, simply foretelling that Noah and his three sons will be saved from the deluge. A couple of comparisons follow with considerable text and occasional similarities, all being predictable from the account given subsequently in the OT, including the divine promise to never again destroy the earth in a deluge.

Having hardly begun his book about Enoch, Nibley turns to making pairings mostly from other apocryphal books, including *Bet ham-Midrash*, *The Secrets of Enoch*, the Ethiopic *Book of Mysteries*, an Egyptian ritual text Papyrus Salt, The *Apocalypse of Abraham*, the *Combat of Adam and Eve*, the *Zohar*, the *Apocalypse of Adam*, the *Miracles of Jesus*, *Berayta*, the *Apocryphon of John*, the *Book of Adam*, the *Apocalypse of Elijah*, Origen, Clement of Alexandria, Jubilees, and other post-Biblical materials. Even though not one of these works can be considered a sacred scripture, Nibley asserts that each one has its kernels of divine inspiration, or flashes of memory from a more ancient source. When gleaned and properly arrayed, one can glimpse a mosaic of a vision that is present as well in the *Book of Moses*, both drawn from the same Divine Source. Since Nibley's guide to sift the very rare most precious kernels from the chaff is the *Book of Moses* itself, there is a degree of similarity, albeit vague, between it and the mosaic thus produced. No surprise here.

In *Lehi in the Desert* he took an assertive posture, attempting to present evidence for the authenticity of the *Book of Mormon*. When *The Book of Abraham* crisis happened, he was forced into a defensive posture. In both works, he took refuge in the hazy world of scholarly esoterica, never addressing the real issue, the archaeological verdict of the New World, for which, after all, the BOM narrative is supposed to be a historical record.

In Search of a Hebrew BOM Text

The hypothesis underlying Hebrew language arguments in the context of the BOM text is that BOM English displays certain peculiarities or abnormalities that can be explained by features, usually syntax, characteristic of Hebrew. The principal LDS researcher in this endeavor is my old friend and missionary colleague John Tvedtnes.[498]

---

[498] John Tvedtnes, "Hebraisms in the *Book of Mormon*," transcript downloaded from the FARMS website.

The principal hurdle for this hypothesis is the hypothesis itself, inasmuch as the plates were supposed to have been written in reformed Egyptian, not Hebrew at all. So why should one even expect to find influences from a Hebrew text on the gold plates? Usually this problem is not mentioned, but, for the reader who might think of it independently, a solution is devised. Tvedtnes' solution is to suggest that we do not really know what language was on the plates, and that the phrase "reformed Egyptian" might simply mean that Hebrew was written with Egyptian characters, presumably logograms, to compress it, and thereby reduce the number of plates required, gold being in short supply (Mormon 9:32). In the very next verse, Mormon clearly states, "And if our plates had been sufficiently large we should have written in Hebrew..." Clearly, there was no Hebrew text on the gold plates, and the hypothesis is disconfirmed from the start. Still, giving Tvedtnes the benefit of the doubt, and assuming that somehow the influence of Hebrew morphology and syntax had found its way into Mormon's Egyptian, I will deal with his arguments on an "as though" basis.

One argument is that the BOM text uses phrases with *of* when normal English would prefer an adjectival noun.[499] He explains the Hebrew (and more broadly, the Semitic) construct state, as being two adjacent nouns, where the second is either possessive, or an adjectival modifier of the first, such as *house king* meaning *house of the king*, or *book brass* (my example), meaning *book of brass*. English would prefer *king's house* and *brass book* (a phrase used here, since it is not clear what word the OT might have use for *plates* to say *plates of brass*). In fact, English is perfectly at home with *house of the king* and even *plates of brass*.

Note that in the phrase *book brass* there is no word meaning *of*. In fact, the second noun is analogous to an adjective. Hebrew, like many other languages, prefers to place attributives after their noun, such as *man big* (*'īš gādōl*) instead of *big man*. In the adjectival construct state, the two nouns are better understood as being a primary noun followed by an attributive, in this case an adjectival noun, rather than reading *of* into the phrase when no such word is actually there.

---

[499] Tvedtnes, "Hebraisms," 3.

An additional problem is that Hebrew actually has a word used to express the English preposition *of* in just such a context: *men* (usually meaning *from* but also used to mean *of* much like *von* in German). Just as an English writer, wishing to stress the substance from which the book was made, might quite deliberately choose to say *book of brass*, Hebrew can say *sēfer men nəḥošet* (*book of brass*) instead of *sēfer nəḥošet*. So this argument falls, first because English is comfortable with the *of* phrases quoted by Tvedtnes, and because Hebrew can choose between an adjectival construct state comparable to *brass book* and a phrase using *men* directly equivalent to English *book of brass*.

A similar argument is made with regard to the phrase *of me* rather than *my*, or *of him* instead of *his*, both found in the BOM: "hear the words of me" (Jacob 5:2; cf. 2 Nephi 10:8) and "how unsearchable are the depths of the mysteries of him" (Jacob 4:8; cf. 2 Nephi 9:25 & Moroni 8:20). Here again we do not find in Hebrew any word meaning *of*. This is provided by Tvedtnes. When Hebrew affixes a pronoun to the end of a noun, it becomes a possessive pronoun. Here again, Hebrew syntax places an attributive after its noun. The suffixed pronoun means *my* and *his* respectively, and follows its noun. The BOM *of me* and *of him* is just quaint idiolectic English, having nothing to do with Hebrew. If we were really seeing a Hebrew influence here, we would also find such-and-such *of you* or *of them* as well.

Another example is what Tvedtnes calls a compound preposition, but is actually a preposition-noun phrase used in Hebrew, *by the hand of* or *by the mouth of* (the Lord, your enemies, etc.). An example is Mosiah 17:18, "Ye shall be taken by the hand of your enemies." Actually, such Hebrew phrases had entered into the English language, especially in religious writings, a phenomenon that produced a significant effect on the creation of modern English. Indeed, in the 1611 edition of the KJV, the translators wrote that they had completed it "through the good hand of the Lord upon us." Compare 1 Nephi 3:20 "spoken by the mouth of all the prophets" with "by the mouth of his true prophet Jeremiah" in the sermon "An Exhortation to Those Who Love Righteousness" by George Whitefield.

A true compound preposition is *mil-li-pnē* (*from+to* [before]+*face* [countenance, presence]). This phrase is translated literally: "from before," as in Exodus 14:19: "from before their face." A reader of the Bible would certainly know the phrase, and just add a noun complement ('presence,' etc.). [Rabbinical Hebrew would render it *mil-li-fnē*.]

A certain amount of Hebrew influence in BOM English is expectable for two reasons: A) the English language in general has absorbed considerable Hebrew influence due to the influence of the very literal KJV translation, and B) a person who has read extensively in the Bible will have even more of these Hebrew expressions and syntax at his command. This is sufficient to explain the observations made by the proponents of this hypothesis, which is itself refuted by the BOM text cited above: the plates were not even in Hebrew.

BOM Names and LDS Apologetics

Make no mistake. The apologist studies BOM names with reference to Hebrew for only one reason: to find support for the authenticity of the *Book of Mormon*. It is hard work. My good friend, John Tvedtnes, has spent much of his adult life honing his Hebrew and engaged in this quest.

Hebrew names, and Semitic names in general, often bear the name of a deity; they are theophoric (god-bearing). Sometimes the divine name is understood, such as in the name Joshua, which means "he (Yahweh) shall help." In very ancient times, the name Yahweh could be pronounced, but over time the Hebrews began to feel that it was too holy for human utterance. In English, it is sometimes called the pentagram, since it has five letters. But it still needed to be incorporated into names. To do this, the divine name was shortened, or otherwise modified. A longer form, almost Yahweh, is *–yahū* as in Netanyahu, "Yahweh has given." Note that Hebrew names are often sentences. Using *–yahū* instead of Yahweh is a bit like saying "Gosh!" rather than "God!" This can be further shortened to *–yah/-iah*. A totally different word can also do the trick. *Shem* is the ordinary word meaning *name*. But in some contexts, it means the divine name, Yahweh, and can be used with this meaning without incurring divine wrath. The shortening of a name, for example Jeff rather than Jeffrey, is called hypocorism, and such a name is a hypocoristicon. On the other hand, names that are not theophoric do exist, such as Deborah, honey bee. This does not mean 'honey bee of Yahweh.' Just honey bee.

Like all Semitic languages, Hebrew is based on triliteral roots, i.e. roots consisting of three consonants. Each triad has a base meaning, and specific words are formed by configuring the root consonants, with vowels, prefixes and postfixes, to produce standard forms. One cannot reconfigure at will for fun or effect. The very ability of the language to convey the desired meaning requires respecting the integrity of the forms. For this reason, all Semitic languages, after thousands of years of development, still have some of the same forms and have resisted change to a remarkable degree.

The study to be examined here is perhaps the principal one on the subject, coauthored by John Tvedtnes, John Gee and Matthew Roper (herein referred to as Tvedtnes et al.).[500] The central argument of the apologist is that a BOM name, not found in the OT, has been found in a Hebrew inscription. Joseph Smith et al. could not have known of this non-Biblical name, so its occurrence in the BOM text provides evidence that the *Book of Mormon* is a translation of an ancient record. The best evidence would be a BOM name that is not similar to any name in the OT, such as Shiz, or Zoram. Next to that would be a name that is similar to one that is found in the OT, but a distinguishing feature of the BOM name is present in the name in an inscription. The valid inclusion of a name actually found in the OT would require very special justification, and is even less impressive.

Table 44. Assertion that BOM Names Occur in Hebrew Inscriptions

Names Not Found in the Old Testament in Any Form
Abish (Claim: Abish is the name of a Lamanite woman. In ancient Hebrew inscriptions it is written *'bš'*. The final ' is an abbreviation of the theophoric element *'Yahweh'* found in other such names.) <u>Comment</u>: It is not certain that the final ' is a theophoric element for Yahweh since the root *'bš* does not exist in Hebrew, and therefore it is unlikely that it is the base for the hypocoristic ending. Avigad/Sas do not venture an interpretation, but they and Röllig suggest it is a variant of *'byšw'*.[501] As in similar names, the first element of two may be *'b* (*'by*, father). The fact that it also occurs in Egypt adds nothing to the issue. The meaning in the BOM is unknown. Note that Hebrew names do not begin with a vowel; in the initial position, a vowel can be preceded by either *aleph* (') or *'ayin* ('). As a result, BOM Abish could be

---

[500] John Tvedtnes, John Gee and Matthew Roper, "*Book of Mormon* Names Attested in Ancient Hebrew Inscriptions," *Journal of* Book of Mormon *Studies*, 9/1/2000.
[501] Nahman Avigad, *Corpus of West Semitic Stamp Seals, revised and completed by Benjamin Sass*, herein referenced as Avigad/Sass (Jerusalem: Ketterpress, 1997), 66 & 476; Wolfgang Röllig, "Siegel und Gewichte," in Johannes Renz and Wofgang Röllig, *Handbuch der Althebräischen Epigraphik*, 4 vols. (Darmstadt: Wissenschftliche Buchgesellschaft, 1995 & 2003), II/2, 120.

(Table 44 continued)

'abiš or *'abiš*. Tvedtnes et al. fail to alert the reader to the fact that the inscription reads *'bš' ben Uri'el*, "Abisha son of Uri'el." It is a man's name, and inappropriate for a Lamanite woman.

Aha (Claim: This is *'ḥ'* from the root for brother with a hypocoristic ' standing for Yahweh, thereby meaning "brother of Yahweh," similar to the Biblical name *'aḥīyāh(u)*, of the same meaning.) Comment: The root for "brother" (*'ḥ*) has an alternative form (*'ḥy*) and the second is typically used to append suffixes. This is seen in *'aḥī-yāh(u)*. The final ' in the inscription is a Hebrew consonant that is pronounced (as it still is in modern Arabic). We are invited to assume that the final *a* in Aha corresponds to this hypocoristic ending. Furthermore, the English letter *h* could be one of two letters in Hebrew: *h* and *ḥ*. In addition to its presence in some Hebrew inscriptions, it is also attested in a Moabite inscription written in Canaanite letters. In both of these languages, it is improbable that the final ' represents the Hebrew deity. Note too that Steve Smoot argues that this name is ancient Egyptian (see below). It is not possible to know that BOM Aha is the same name attested in these inscriptions.

Himni (Claim: This is attested as *ḥmn* on two Hebrew seals. The final *i* of the BOM name is a gentilic ending: *of ḥmn*.) Comment: Again we are asked to believe that English *h* in Himni is Hebrew *ḥ* rather than Hebrew *h*. Avigad/Sass find it difficult to determine what the name might have been, proposing *'ḥmn* (with aphaeresis), or *ḥammon* (either a hypocoristicon or a noun meaning 'hot spring'). Furthermore, the so-called gentilic *i* is not attested in the inscription. There is no BOM toponym or personal name for which this could be a gentilic (such as *Hemen [eg., gezer*, a name of a place, Gezer, becoming *gizrī*, someone from Gezer]. It is not clear that Himni is even attested in an inscription.

Luram (Claim: A seal, dated c. 720 BCE, and found at Hamath, north Syria, bears the name *'dn lrm*, Lord of *lrm*.) Comment: The name hails from Hamath (Syria) at a time when it had been for some time an Aramaean center. It also had Hittite and Assyrian influences. The name also occurs on a brick at the same site followed by *skn byt mlkh* (steward of the king's house).[502] The terminal *h* on *mlk* is the Aramaic emphatic affix functioning in lieu of a definite article, and identifying this inscription as being Old Aramaic. Avigad/Sass vocalize the name *'adanluram* with no indication

---

[502] Avigad/*Sass*, 285. For *skn byt mlkh* see J. Hoftijzer and K. Jongeling, *Dictionary of the North-West Semitic Inscriptions* (E.J. Brill: Leiden, 1995), 2:786.

(Table 44 continued)

where it should be divided (i.e. *luram* may not be a word unit). If *lrm* is a word, it is an unknown place name, not a personal name. Above all, there is no reason to assume that it is even Hebrew.

Names Similar to Old Testament Names

Ammonihah (Claim: The ending -*ihah* is a hypocoristicon for Yahweh, and therefore it is fair to claim that this name is attested as '*mnyhw* and '*mnwyhw*.)
Comment: Only LDS apologists give -*ihah* this meaning. Doing so is ad hoc, and without merit since it does not readily work with other BOM names, such as Cumenihah, Moronihah, Mathonihah and Zemnariha. Ammon is in the OT, but Ammonihah is not attested in Hebrew.

Chemosh (Claim: The name has been found on seals as a personal name.)
Comment: All of the occurrences are on Moabite seals, as the name of the Moabite deity Kemosh.[503] It is found in Numbers 21:29; Judges 11:24; 1 Kings 11:7, 33; 2 Kings 23:13; and Jeremiah 48:7, 13 and 46. The BOM authors simply changed the vowel. It is not surprising that it should show up in the BOM, which does occasionally switch good and evil, such as by making Noah a wicked king. No evidence for the BOM here.

Hagoth (Claim: It is attested in an Ammonite seal as *hgt*. The Ammonites wrote and spoke the same language as the Hebrews.) Comment: This is not a seal of the Hebrews. Although Hebrew and Ammonite are increasingly considered to be dialects, they are different cultures and have some different names. There is no Hebrew root *hgt* or *ḥgt*. Playing with possibilities, treating *h* as a preformative, or *t* as an affix, would be purely speculative. One notes that Tvedtnes et al. rigorously provide references, but strangely none is provided for this seal. I have not found it in the works edited by Aufrecht,[504] Renz/Röllig or Avigad/Sass. Furthermore, the BOM name could have been quite readily modified from Biblical Haggith (2 Samuel 3:4, etc.).

Isabel (Claim: It is now attested *yzbl* in an inscription that might be Phoenician.) Comment: It is not clear what this spelling has to do with the BOM name, since initial *i* would be preceded by aleph (' thereby reading '*zbl* or '*yzbl*), not *y*. In fact, Isabel is the proper rendition of Jezebel in the

---

[503] Avigad/Sass, 508.
[504] Walter E. Aufrecht, *A Corpus of Ammonite Inscriptions* (Lewiston, NY: The Edwin Mellen Press, 1989).

(Table 44 continued)

> OT. Why not take credit for that? The seal has Egyptian influences, including a winged solar disk and a winged sphinx holding the ankh sign. The owner's gender is uncertain.[505] What is known is that the English name Isabel, derived from Elizabeth, has been extremely popular. It cannot have been a great leap to associate it with the Jezebel of the Bible. As such, it was appropriate that she be a harlot, a temptress, and of all places, at Siron (cf. the ancient Greek siren, temptress of sailors, and when borrowed in English, simply a temptress). Surely the extra-Biblical source for this name is clear. *Yzbl* is apparently Phoenician.
>
> **Jarom** (Claim: The form *yrm* [rather than Biblical *ywrm*] is now attested. This is considered to be a hypocoristic form of Jeremiah). <u>Comment</u>: The name *yrm* is listed by Avigad/Sass and vocalized Yarim (*Yarīm*).[506] As a hypocoristic form of Jeremiah, it is not clear that it would be vocalized Jarom. The hypocoristicon *yrm* (from *rwm*: He [the deity] exalts, or is exalted) recurs in Phoenician. And since Joram occurs frequently in the OT, it is most probably the source of BOM Jarom. The relevance of this inscription is ambiguous.
>
> **Josh** (Claim: The form *y'š* has been attested. This should be vocalized *jōš* and considered to be the hypocoristic form of Josiah [*jōšiyyāhu*]). <u>Comment</u>: Avigad/Sass indicate that the verbal root is *'wš*, and that the name should be vocalized *yo'aš* (Joash), a name that occurs many times in Judges and 1 and 2 Kings. The vocalization is not indicated in the inscription. The aleph (glottal stop) is a root letter, not a device to indicate a vowel. If it were, aleph would normally represent *ā*. In any case, Josh, as an English shorter form for Joshua, may be as far as we have to look for this BOM name.
>
> **Mathoni/Mathonihah** (Claim: This is the BOM form for Mattaniah [Hebrew *mtnyhw*], with the theophoric hypocoristicon *-ihah* on the second one.) <u>Comment</u>: This is not possible, because the root is *ntn*. This standard Hebrew form has a preformative *m* and a *t* infix:
>
> m-vowel-**nt**-vowel-**t**-vowel-**n** (bolding the root).
>
> The consonant *n* is absolutely weak in Hebrew, Aramaic and even Akkadian. When directly before *t* (and many other consonants) as in this

---

[505] Avigad/Sass, 375.
[506] Avigad/Sass, 112.

(Table 44 continued)

case, the first *n* of the root combines with *t*, in this case becoming *tt* (*Mantaniah ▶ Mattaniah). The root means "to give" and the noun produced by this form (*mattān*) means "gift" (understood to be "gift of the deity"). In this doubled form, *t* never aspirates, i.e. *tt* cannot become *th*. Since Mattan and Mattaniah are both frequent in the OT, and are common Hebrew names, the fact that they are found at Lachish and Elephantine is superfluous. So why are these inscriptional sources referenced at all, when they occur so often in the OT? We can only speculate as to whether this name was derived by the BOM authors from Mattaniah, or more probably from Matthew, since BOM Mathoni and Mathonihah were two of the twelve disciples (apostles) chosen by Jesus when he visited the Nephites after his resurrection.

Muloki (Claim: This appears on a bulla found in the City of David, as *mlky*. It
is a hypocoristicon for *mlkyhw* [king Yahweh]. The objection that the vocalization of Mulok makes it inappropriate to be a hypocoristicon is not valid, since vowel changes do happen in such cases.) Comment: Vowel changes are not random changes. Tvedtnes et al. cite Baruch for Berechiah, Nahum for Nehemiah, Shallum for Shelmiah, and Zaccur for Zechariah. Note that in all of these cases, the *u* is in the second syllable. This is a standard form for passives. So Berechiah means "Yahweh has blessed," and Baruch means "blessed" (by Yahweh, understood). This makes sense as a short form, a hypocoristicon. Mulok is not even a Hebrew form at all and makes no sense as a base for a hypocoristicon. What can be said in a positive vein is that this inscription at least has terminal *y* that corresponds to the final *i* of Muloki. On the other hand, the BOM already has Mulek, which it claims to be a son of Zedekiah (while the OT says his sons were killed), and frequently makes modifications of existing names as a means of name generation. It occurs as Melech in 1 Chronicles 8:35, 9:41, etc. (*mlk*, where *ch* is aspirated *k*). Note, *mlkyhw* is *malkīyāhū* meaning "my king is Yahweh."

Sam (Claim: The name šəmū'ēl is comprised of *šem* ['name'] and *'ēl* [(of) El], i.e. god. The name *šem* can be *śem* in inscriptional Hebrew, because the letters š and ś are written with the same character in the Hebrew of the inscriptions. In old Hebrew ś was pronounced variably, including *s*. So the name can be *sam*) Comment: It is implied that the first consonant of the name in the inscription was pronounced *s*. Evidence from Old South Arabian (OSA) and Hebrew indicates that there was an "extra" sibilant in Proto-Semitic, in addition to *s*, *z* and *š*. In Hebrew it is transliterated as *ś*. At some point, the pronunciation of *ś* was totally forgotten, and the convention

(Table 44 continued)

developed to pronounce it the same as *s* as a matter of convenience. Since Hebrew already had a letter for *s* (*samech*), it is improbable that there would be two letters for the same sound. The assertion that *ś* was at an early date pronounced *s* is unevidenced.

In any case, this word, *šm* (not *śm*), occurs on a rather small signet seal. The surface is divided into upper and lower registers by a horizontal line. Above the line is the name of the signet owner, *'ḥyhw* (*Aḥīyāhū*). Below the line we find *šm*.[507] It is common to place a patronymic below the line, such as "son of ..." Because space is lacking, the word *ben* (son of) was not written. So *šm* is Shem (son of Noah in Genesis). The name therefore is *Aḥīyāhū* (*ben*) *Shem*.

The assertion that ש is ש, and pronounced *s* is purely to argue that they have found Sam in inscriptional Hebrew, independent of the proper name "Samuel" (which is written with *ś*). The objective is to counter the common observation that the BOM authors erroneously used the English nickname Sam, the English short form for Samuel, which should not be in the BOM.

Sariah (Claim: The name of the wife of Lehi has been found in an inscription as *śryh*. This is *śār* + the theophoric ending *–yā*, meaning "prince of Yahweh." It is attested at Elephantine as a woman's name.) Comment: The name in the OT is vocalized *śərāyā*, "one who contends for Yahweh, warrior of Yahweh" or "Yahweh has contended" (for his people). It is found in Jeremiah 36:26; 40:8; 51:59, 61; and 52:24; and 2 Samuel 8:17, spelled Seraiah in the KJV. There, *śərāyā* is a man's name. At Elephantine *śryh* is a woman's name. The experts on this, Porten and Lund, vocalize it also as *śərāyā*, KJV *serāiā* (*śərā* being the third person masculine of the root *śry*, "to contend") not *śaryā/saryā* (*śar* being a primitive noun meaning "person of note, commander, governor, prince").[508]

Lehi is to become the patriarch of a numerous people, much like Abraham, whose wife had two names, originally Sarai, and then Sarah. To enhance Lehi's persona as patriarch, his wife is given a name similar to that of Abraham, combining the two, Sarai+Sarah=Sariah (pronounced in English Sarayah). When dictated to the scribe, *ay* was written with the letter *i* in keeping with the English convention. The English letter *i* is an abbreviation for *ay* (as in "Aye, aye, Sir!"). As a result, inadvertently, a name was given her that is phonologically nearly the same as Seraiah, a man's name. The very important vowel *a* distinguishes Sariah from Seraiah. It would be spelled in an unvocalized text the same as the OT name. If it is

---

[507] Avigad/Sass, 69.
[508] Bezalel Porten and Jerome A. Lund, *Aramaic Documents from Egypt: A Key-Word-in-Context Concordance* (Winona Lake: Eisenbrauns, 2002), p. 416.

(Table 44 continued)

> a blend of Sarai and Sarah, it is not the same name, and is not the name in the Elephantine inscription. In any case, the Hebrew-origin residents in Elephantine, in the furthest south reaches of Egypt, apparently mercenaries, had unorthodox religious traditions and wrote Aramaic. If we grant that it is Seraiah, then at most the contribution only provides a case where it can be a woman's name.

Overall, this analysis finds that Tvedtnes et al. have not found any non-Biblical BOM names that are unambiguously attested in Hebrew inscriptional materials. Even if we admit that Sariah is an exception to this, it is a dictational version of a name common in one of the favorite books of the BOM authors, Jeremiah. This is by no means the end. Avigad/Sass, in a large folio-size book, and double columns, have 64 pages of West Semitic names. More material is being constantly discovered, and more names. More claims will be made of BOM names in Hebrew inscriptions. It's in the cards. Even so, the study analyzed here is a very successful work, in that the authors' apologist colleagues have cited it as strong evidence, if not proof for the authenticity of the *Book of Mormon*. Most Mormons never see the study itself, but just references to it. Very few have the background to assess it.

Seeking Egyptian Names in the *Book of Mormon*

The BOM authors had no knowledge of Egyptian, and so there should be no Egyptian names in the *Book of Mormon*, right? Well, it is not as simple as that. After all, Brigham Young had a Chinese name right? Young and Yong? Bishop Lee as well, right? Well, it is not as simple as that.

The first step in this inquiry is to assemble from the BOM text the possible candidates, for analysis. Such a list (below) has been compiled by Steve Smoot, who has cast his net rather broadly, and made use of a wide range of phonological shifts.[509] The next step here is to divide the names by categories relevant to the research. The first of these is names found in the Bible, which therefore should not be included as Egyptian names, or at least as Egyptian names unavailable to the BOM authors.

---

[509] Steve Smoot, "Authentic Egyptian Names in the *Book of Mormon*," posted on americantestament.com and accessed on 28 Feb 2016.

Table 45. Assertion that Egyptian Names Occur in the BOM

Ammon
Ammon (Genesis 19:38, & many other passages)
Aminadab/Amminadab (Matthew 1:4)

The second group relates BOM names to Egyptian transliterations of Semitic place names, or names of governors outside of Egypt. Egypt never had an administration outside of Palestine. These men were not Egyptians, but locals left in place or established by the Pharaoh after a military campaign, as resident governors, like Zedekiah, established in Jerusalem by Nebuchadnezzar, Herod established by Rome in Jerusalem and Cleopatra established by Caesar in Alexandria, all having their local names.

Ammonihah (Claim: *Ammuni-ra*, prince of Beyrut under Egyptian rule author of letters EA 141-43 of the Amarna Letters, in Akkadian.)
Cezoram (Claim: *Chiziri*, governor of a Syrian city under Egyptian rule.)
Giddonah (claim: *Dji-dw-na*, the Egyptian name for Sidon.) <u>Comment</u>: Actually, it is the local Semitic name transliterated into Egyptian.
Zenock, in BOM text, an ancient Hebrew prophet (Claim: *Zenekh*, Egyptian proper name; once a serpent-god.) <u>Comment</u>: The BOM attributes Zenock to the
Israelite world, not the Americas, and not part of BOM naming. Why would he have an Egyptian name? And one of a serpent-god?.

The third group consists of names matched with Egyptian names or words that are superficially similar, and involve interpretation via sound shifts or metathesis (change in the order of consonants).

Gidgiddoni and Gidgiddonah (Claim: djed-djhwt-iw-f-ankh/djed-djhwti-iw-s-ankh, meaning "Thoth hath said: he shall live," and "Thoth hath said: she shall live," respectively. So the Nephite names mean "Thoth hath said I shall live," and "Thoth hath said: we shall live," respectively.)
Gimgimno (Claim: *Kenkeme*, an Egyptian city [+ *-no* assumed to mean city], cf. *Kipkip*, seat of the Egyptian dynasty in Nubia.)
Helaman (Claim: *Her-amon*. Smoot: "in the presence of Amon," as in the Egyptian proper name *Heri-i-her-imn*. Semitic *l* is always written *r* in Egyptian, which has no *l*. Conversely, the Egyptian *r* is often written *l* in Semitic languages.) <u>Comment</u>: Since Semitic has both *l* and *r* there is no reason for this. Both Egyptian and Hebrew have *r*, so Hebrew would have Heraman. This claim arbitrarily divides Helaman into two words.
Korihor (Claim: *Kherihor/Khurhor*/etc., great high priest of Ammon who seized the throne of Egypt at Thebes, c. 1085 B.C.) <u>Comment</u>: *k* and *kh* are very different consonants, involving a shift).

(Table 45 continued)

> **Manti** (Claim: *Manti*, Semitic form of an Egyptian proper name, e.g., *Manti-mankhi*, a prince in Upper Egypt c. 650 B.C. It is a late form of Month, god of Hermonthis.) <u>Comment</u>: That it is a Semitic form of an Egyptian name is also Smoot's claim.).
> **Morianton** (Claim: *Meriaton/Meriamon*, names of Egyptian princes, "Beloved of Aton" and "Beloved of Amon," respectively.) Comment: Smoot ignores the *n* and vowel difference.
> **Nephi** (Claim: *Nehi/Nehri*, famous Egyptian noblemen. *Nfy* was the name of an Egyptian captain. Since BOM insists on 'ph,' Nephi is closer to Nihpi, original name of the god Pa-nepi, which may even have been Nephi.)
> **Paanchi** (Claim: *Paanchi*, a) chief high priest of Amon, and b) ruler of the south who conquered all of Egypt and was high priest of Amon at Thebes.) Comment: Smoot takes the liberty of changing the *kh* of Paankhi to *ch*, two very different consonants. Indeed, it is not clear what consonant *ch* might represent in Egyptian. The name of the ruler was formerly transliterated as *Piankhhi*, but is now Piye. However, the ruler of Nubia who conquered Egypt was Piankh or Payankh. The *i* is important, as is indicated in the latter transliteration.
> **Pahoran** (Claim: *Pa-hura* (The Syrian), commissioner of Egypt at Byblos.
> **Pacumeni** (Claim: *Pakamen*, meaning "blind man.")
> **Pachus** (Claim: Pa-ks/Pach-qs, personal name. Cf. Pa-ches-i, "he is praised.") <u>Comment</u>: what is this *ch*?
> **Sam** (Claim: *Sam Tawi* [uniter of the lands], title taken by the brother of Nehri upon mounting the throne.) Comment: this name is just the first element of a title (phrase), not attested as standing alone as a name.
> **Zemnarihah** (Claim: *Zmn-ha-re*, Egyptian proper name.)
> **Zeniff** (Claim: *Znb, Snb*, elements in Egyptian proper names, cf. *Senep-ta*.)
>
> *The fourth group* consists of three names with straightforward phonological correspondence with Egyptian names.
>
> **Aha** (claim: *Aha* [warrior], a name of the second Pharaoh.)
> **Hem** (claim: *Hem* [servant], as in the title Hem tp n 'Imn, "chief servant of Ammon" held by the high priest of Thebes.)
> **Himni** (claim: *Hmn*, a name of the Egyptian hawk-god, symbol of the emperor.) Note that Egyptian has three consonants that can be represented by English *h*: *h*, *ḥ* and *ḫ*. So even in these names, the similarity is superficial.

Having Fun with Names

To evaluate the previous section, it is important to distinguish between "finding an Egyptian name in the BOM" and "finding a BOM name that is similar to an Egyptian name, word or phrase." This can be illustrated with a comparison between English and Chinese names.

As can be seen below, Brigham Young, Bishop Lee and Lehi all have Chinese names. Well, of course, they do not. They have names that are phonologically similar to Chinese names.

Anne: An (tranquil, peace)
Dillon: Delun (virtuous order)
Fay: Fai (initial beginning)
Huey: Hui (clever)
June: Jun (to be truthful)
King: Kang (hale, healthy)/
           Keung (cosmos)/
           Qing (to be clear, greenish blue)
Lee: Li (strong, powerful)

Lee-Ann: Lian (lovely willow)
Lehi: Li-hai (strong-sea)
Lynne: Lin (forest, gem)
May: Mei (gorgeous)
Shanny: Shan (moderate)
Singer: Song (strong, powerful)
Sue: Su (unadorned; respectful)
Young: Yong (courageous harmonious)

Japanese in the BOM Narrative

We tighten up a comparison when we limit the names to a defined corpus, such as those in the BOM, rather from a whole language, such as English. Consider the following:

Cumom	Kumon/Kumom	Mosiah	Masuyo
Cumorah	Kimura	Ogath	Ogata/Ogita
Himni	Hamano	Omer	Omori
Kib	Kaiba, Chiba	Onidah	Onida
Kish	Kish[i]	Sam	Asami
Korihor	Kurihara	Seth	Saito, Sato
Kumen	Kimura	Shim, Shum	Shin
Minon	Mino	Shiz, shez	Shizu, Shizuka
Mocum	Megumi/Mikami	Shum	Shun

Of course there is no Japanese in the BOM. But a diligent search can make it appear to be the case.

The Problem with Names

The study of names is called onomastics. There are scholars who specialize in the onomastics of a particular language or dialect, such as Akkadian or Palmyrene Aramaic. Their results are often tentative. When comparing a noun, verb or adjective in one language to the same in another, usually there are two components, the phonological component, and the semantic component. Both are usually known in both languages. When the semantic component is not known, there is usually at least some context that can narrow it down. This is less true when the word occurs in a short inscription, such as those carved into stone in Arabia, which are at times not much more than "So-and-so did such-and-such." In the case of proper names in these short inscriptions, the semantic component is often not known, and at times not even the language. For these, the results of onomastic research are often especially tentative.

An example of these difficulties is Jerusalem. *Rušalim* in the Execration texts of the Middle Kingdom of Egypt (c. 2000 BCE) is considered to be Jerusalem. It is *Urušalim* or *Urusalim* in the Amarna letters of Abdi-Heba (1330's BCE). It is also called *bēt šalem*, "House of Shalem." The element *uru* meaning "city" came into Akkadian from Sumerian. The element *šalim/salim* comes either from a very common Semitic root having to do with peace, or from the name of the Canaanite deity of the setting sun, dusk. It means "The City of Shalem (God of Peace, or God of the Dusk, with Underworld connotations)."

As for personal names, consider Moses. The OT narrative implies that it comes from Hebrew, and would mean "drawn out of" the water (Exodus 2:10). This is considered a folk-etymology. Grammatically, the name would be an active participle, not passive, and it assumes that the Egyptian princess knew Hebrew. It has been argued that it comes from an Egyptian verb "to sire" and is theophoric, like the name of the pharaoh Thutmose (Thut-mose), "Born of Thoth," but with the name of the god omitted. In the end, there is no consensus on the etymology, or even the language of the name of this very important figure in the Israelite, and later Jewish religion and history.

Like Moses, most of the BOM names have no known semantic element. Even the phonological correspondence to Hebrew or Egyptian is ambiguous, since the same English letter can correspond to more than one Hebrew of Egyptian letter. In such a case, one has great freedom to relate many BOM names to one or more in inscriptional Hebrew, or to one or more of the very many names in ancient Egyptian onomastics, or even to Chinese (*Li-hai*) or to Japanese (*Shiz^u*). So what do the results mean? Not very much.

Chiasmus, *Parallelismus Membrorum, Māshal*, & Poetry

There has been a significant amount of LDS literary analysis of the *Book of Mormon*, partly to improve its reputation among those few in the world of literature who have actually read it, but mostly to find in it literary forms that could prove it to be an authentic translation of an ancient work of pre-Columbian Israelite origin. While tastes can and do vary, and good taste is at least significantly a reflection of cultural norms, it is clear that these scholars venerate the object of their study, and see it through the eyes of faith, as indeed the Church urges them to do.[510] Even so, there can be no doubt that it has a valid place in the history of religion. As a work of literature, I would suggest that it has a parallel in the history of art. Some museums of art have a collection of naïve art, where the word "naïve" is not intended as a pejorative. Some individuals have followed their creative inspirations totally without any formal training, and often without proper materials. Some worked in remote rural areas, and others in an urban ghetto. Yet they produced works that have museum-quality merit, within their own genre. Similarly, even though the archaeological verdict is clear, the BOM is worthy of study for what it is.

Every culture has distinctive literary and public speaking patterns or devices. Take for example the classical drama of ancient Greece. The stichomythia (dialogue) with short statements, back and forth, in the language of the day in Attica, was balanced by periodical long passages sung/chanted by the chorus, in deliberately archaic forms and language. This is not found, to my knowledge, as an indigenous dramatic form, in other drama (barring imitations). More germane to our investigation is Old Testament poetry, and literary forms such as the *māšāl, parallelismus membrorum* and chiastic constructions.

---

[510] James T. Duke, *The Literary Masterpiece Called the* Book of Mormon (Springville, UT: Cedar Fort, 2003). Note too, Angela M. Crowell, *Hebrew Poetry in the* Book of Mormon (Zarahemla Research Foundation, published online, restoredcovenant.org)

Poetry

It is axiomatic that poetry was more important and generally more appreciated in the past than today. Ancient cultures of the circum-Mediterranean basin valued poetry. Perhaps the best of classical Arab literature was composed by the pre-Islamic poets. Tribes competed to recruit famous poets to their side, and feared that they would support the cause of an enemy tribe. Poetry competitions occurred in Arabia's Sūq 'Ukāẓ and the ancient Greek Olympics. The poetry of the Old Testament shows that the Hebrews were not outdone by their neighbors.

Hebrew has both rhymed and unrhymed poetry. It often has accented-syllable rhythm much more than quantitative rhythm. Parallelism (*parallelismus membrorum*) is often used in poetry, but not always. Various genres exist. A common one is the dirge (*kinot*) comprising the entire Book of Lamentations. The rhythm of this form is marked by the fact that a longer line is followed by a shorter one. Another technique is anadiplosis, where the end of one phrase is the beginning of another:

> they came not to the help of the Lord,
> to the help of the Lord against the mighty (Judges 5:23)
>
> From whence shall my help come?
> My help cometh from the Lord (Psalm 121:1b-2a, R. V.).

Alphabetical acrostics are also found, where the first letter of each line occurs in the ordinary order of the alphabet. This has been found in the poetry of other cultures in the region. In addition to the dirge, we also find the psalm and the drama (Job). The Book of Ecclesiastes has a strong poetic quality. An oracle can come in poetry, as in the oracle of Balaam (Numbers 24).

Another distinct type is the taunt song. A shorter reference is in Habakkuk 2:6:

> Shall not all these take up a parable against him,
> and a taunting riddle against him, and say:
> "Woe to him that increaseth that which is not his! how long?
> and that ladeth himself with many pledges!"

Many who have read the *Book of Mormon* many times will probably say that it has no poetry. In fact, one can certainly identify passages that remind one of the Bible, which it took as its model. The BOM authors were not just imbued with Biblical material, but with the verses of numerous Bible-inspired hymns. Poetic style was no stranger to them. BOM poetic passages include Mosiah 2:13-17, Mormon 4:26, 1 Nephi 6:25-26 and others. LDS writers have called one long passage the Psalm of Nephi (2 Nephi 4:15-35). An ambitious analysis of it is that of Stephen Sondrup, my debate partner at East High in Salt Lake City, fellow graduate student at Harvard, and later, a professor at BYU. He is as qualified as they come in European-language comparative literature. In a footnote, he comments, "Although Professor Sperry may be right in his unsubstantiated argument that 'this is a true psalm in both form and ideas,' he seems to have misunderstood the basic poetic structure of this passage, at least insofar as his arrangement of lines and stanzas allows inference."[511] Sondrup adds, "The question to be discussed with reference to these verses is not whether they are a psalm in the biblical sense of the term but rather the nature and extent of their poetic qualities..." With all due respect, however, I have found it difficult to detect clear instances of chiastic constructions, and whatever couplets could be interpreted as instances of *parallelismus membrorum* are far more vague than those found in the Old Testament. The interested or skeptical reader should check out this study personally.

Parallelismus Membrorum

This technique has been discussed above, in the section on the Isaiah inclusions in the *Book of Mormon*. An example adduced from the *Book of Mormon* (1 Nephi 1:14) has been compared with Psalm 34:3.

For his soul did rejoice,
and his whole heart was filled.   BOM

0 magnify the Lord with me,
and let us exalt his name together.   Palms

---

[511] Stephen P. Sondrup, "The Psalm of Nephi: A Lyric Reading," *BYU Studies* (Provo, UT: Brigham Young University, 21:3, 1981), 357. See page 358, & footnote no. 4.

What is more distinctly characteristic of the Old Testament is when an actual series of these pairs is used. It is then that we have a fully developed pattern for a poetic work. An example is found in a taunt song (in this case, one of prophetic character, and hence tantamount to a curse) in Isaiah raised against the king of Babylon (Isaiah 14):

12. For the day of the Lord of hosts shall be upon
    every one that is **proud and lofty**
    and upon every one that is **lifted up** and he shall be made low:
13. And upon all the **cedars of Lebanon** that are high and lifted up
    and upon all the **oaks of Bāshan**
14. And upon all the **high mountains**
    and upon all the **hills that are lifted up**
15. And upon every **high tower**
    and upon every **fenced wall**

To be fair to Isaiah, we must add here that in some cases a single Hebrew word has been rendered by two or three English words, or even a subordinate clause, which disturbs the force of this device in translation. I am unaware of veritable taunt songs in the *Book of Mormon*, or of a series of paired verses using *parallelismus membrorum*. Note that just as the OT uses a specific term for dirge (*kinot*), it has a specific phrase for raising a taunt song against someone: *nāśā māšāl*: to raise up a similitude against… In this passage, the Lord commands Isaiah to do so.

Chiasmus.

He used this rhetorical device to create the impression of logic,
To bestow the appearance of reason, he employed this figure of speech.

A simple form of a chiasmus is JFK's statement

Ask not what your country can do for you
But ask what you can do for your country.

The basic form has two members, each with two elements. The two in the second member must be essentially the same as the two in the first member, but in reverse order: AB-BA. In this one from JFK, they are "country" "you" – "you" "country". This can happen in ordinary speech without having any knowledge of rhetoric. It often happens that some A and some B will be repeated in the next breath, and one naturally mentions first the one that was mentioned last in the first member, simply because it is the most fresh in one's mind. But, at some point in cultural history, persons interested in using language to the best effect noticed that stating a sentence in this manner could be very effective. Some writers or speakers got the habit of doing it, it entered into the culture, and the Greeks gave it a name: *chiasmus*. For them, the ideal form could not repeat the same words, as in my example above: "rhetorical device" "figure of speech" – "impression of logic" "appearance of reason". There are various types of chiasmus, and some are a bit complex. But they should not be so complex that they escape the notice of the reader or listener. If it does, the effect would be lost. So, did JFK know about chiasmus, and use it deliberately, as a master of rhetoric? More likely, having heard it from time to time, he spontaneously produced a chiastic sentence as a result of his natural speaking ability. I once noticed an example in my college physics textbook, probably just because it sounded good to the author.

It has been asserted that ancient writers, among some ancient cultures, the Hebrews, Greeks and the Romans, used chiasmus more than modern English writers. This may well be the case. But to my knowledge, no one has ever done quantified research to prove that it is so. Some fun examples are:

> Your manuscript is both good and original; but the part that is good is not original, and the part that is original is not good.
> (Samuel Johnson)

> Do I love you because you're beautiful?
> Or are you beautiful because I love you?
> (Oscar Hammerstein II

> You can take it out of the country,
> but you can't take the country out of it.
> (slogan for Salem cigarettes, 1960s)

> Someone once said that the difference between William James and Henry James was that the former was a psychologist who wrote like a novelist while the latter was a novelist who wrote like a psychologist.
> (Archibald Henderson, "Aspects of Contemporary Fiction," *The Arena*, July 1906)

All of this is relevant inasmuch as some LDS apologists have claimed to have found a significant amount of chiasmus in the *Book of Mormon*, and argue that this shows that it is a translation of an ancient source, rather than a modern English composition. In particular, it would show that the BOM narrative was written by individuals schooled in a pre-Colombian Hebrew literary tradition.

Chiastic analysis necessarily poses the problem of how similar wording has to be, and how much one can delete that is deemed irrelevant, without being guilty of cherry-picking just that which fits. A good example of this issue in the study of Biblical chiasmus is a passage claimed to be chiastic in Joshua 1:5-9, where the proposed chiastic elements have been underlined:

A <u>as I was with Moses, [so] I will be with thee</u>: I will not fail thee, nor forsake thee.
    B <u>Be strong and of a good courage</u>: for unto this people shalt thou divide for an inheritance the land, which I sware unto their fathers to give them. Only be thou strong and very courageous,
        C <u>that thou mayest observe to do according to all the law</u>, which Moses my servant commanded thee: turn not from it [to] the right hand or [to] the left, <u>that thou mayest prosper</u> whithersoever thou goest.
            D <u>This book of the law shall not depart out of thy mouth</u>;
            D <u>but thou shalt meditate therein day and night</u>
        C <u>that thou mayest observe to do according to all that is written therein</u>: for then shalt thou make thy way prosperous, and <u>then thou shalt have good success</u>.
    B Have not I commanded thee? <u>Be strong and of a good courage</u>; be not afraid, neither be thou dismayed:
A <u>for the LORD thy God [is] with thee</u> whithersoever thou goest.

Calling this a true chiasmus is quite a stretch, but instances of chiasmus do occur in the BOM narrative (although matched elements repeat the same words). One is found in Jacob (3:12):

By the power of his word
man came upon the face of the earth;
which earth was created
By the power of his word.

Note also (1 Nephi 21:1):

    A   Hearken,
    B   O ye house of Israel,
    C   All ye that are broken off and are driven out
    D   Because of the wickedness of the pastors of my people;
    C'   Yea, all ye that are broken off, that are scattered abroad,
    B'   Who are of my people, O house of Israel.
    A'   Listen, O isles, unto me, and hearken ye people from far

Here, D is not a pair. Furthermore, chapter 21 is an Isaiah inclusion (chapter 49) and the last line above is from Isaiah. The more verbiage in a long text, the more raw material one has to "discover" a chiasmus. One proceeds to identify elements in a passage, and then scans down the page until roughly similar mates occur, but in reverse order. Consider for example the chiastic analysis of John Welch of Alma 36.[512] The bolded words are those that Welch extracts to construct his chiasmus. In other words, delete the words not bolded, and you will have his published chiasmus. He did not alert his reader to the large amount of text that had to be eliminated in the process. Instead, this is left for one to discover by reading Alma 36 for oneself. When thus displayed, A should equal A, B should equal B, and so on.

A **My son, give ear to my words**;
  B for I swear unto you, that inasmuch as ye shall **keep the commandments** of God **[and] ye shall prosper in the land**.
    C I would that ye should **do as I have done**,
      D **in remembering the captivity of our fathers**; for they were in ***bondage***,
        E and none could deliver them except it was the God of Abraham, and the God of Isaac, and the God of Jacob; and **he surely did deliver them** in their afflictions.
          F And now, O my son Helaman, behold, thou art in thy youth, and therefore, I beseech of thee that thou wilt hear my words and learn of me; for I do know that whosoever shall put their **trust in God**
            G shall be **supported in their trials, and** their **troubles, and** their **afflictions**, and shall be lifted up at the last day.
              H And I would not that ye think that **I know [this not] of myself** — not of

---

[512] John W. Welch, "Chiasmus in the *Book of Mormon*," in John W. Welch, ed., *Chiasmus in Antiquity* (Provo, UT: Research Press [The Foundation for Ancient Research and Mormon Studies—F.A.R.M.S.], 1981), 206. See also H. Clay Gorton, *A New Witness for Christ. Chiastic Structures in the* Book of Mormon (Bountiful, UT: Horizon Publishers, 1997).

the temporal but of the spiritual, not of the carnal mind but of God.
I Now, behold, I say unto you, if I had not been **born of God** I should not have known these things; but God has, by the mouth of his holy angel, made these things known unto me, not of any worthiness of myself.
J For I went about with the sons of Mosiah, **seeking to destroy the church of God**; but behold, God sent his holy angel to stop us by the way. And behold, he spake unto us, as it were the voice of thunder, and the whole earth did tremble beneath our feet; and we all fell to the earth, for the fear of the Lord came upon us. But behold, the voice said unto me: Arise. And I arose and stood up, and beheld the angel. And he said unto me: If thou wilt of thyself be destroyed, seek no more to destroy the church of God.
K. And it came to pass that I fell to the earth; and it was for the space of three days and three nights that I could not open my mouth, neither had I the use of my limbs [**my limbs were paralyzed**] And the angel spake more things unto me, which were heard by my brethren, but I did not hear them; for when I heard the words — If thou wilt be destroyed of destroyed of Thyself, seek no more to destroy the church of God — of God — I was struck with such great fear and amazement lest perhaps I should be destroyed, that I fell to the earth and did hear no more. But I was racked with eternal torment, for my soul was harrowed up to the greatest degree and racked with all my sins. Yea, I did remember all my sins and iniquities, for which I was tormented with the pains of hell; yea, I saw that I had rebelled against my God, and that I had not kept his holy commandments.
L Yea, and I had murdered many of his children, or rather led them away unto destruction; yea, and in fine so great had been my iniquities, that the very thought of coming into the presence of my God did rack my soul with inexpressible horror. [**Fear of the PRESENCE OF GOD**] Oh, thought I, that I could be banished and become extinct both soul and body, that I might not be brought to stand in the presence of my God, to be judged of my deeds.
M And now, for three days and for three nights was I racked, even with the **pains of a damned soul**. And it came to pass that as I was thus racked with torment, while I was harrowed up by the memory of my many sins,
N behold, **I remembered** also to have heard my father prophesy unto the people concerning the coming of **one Jesus Christ, a Son of God**, to atone for the sins of the world.
N Now, as my mind caught hold upon this thought, *I cried* within my heart: O **Jesus**, thou **Son of God**, have mercy on me, who am in the gall of bitterness, and am encircled about by the everlasting chains of death.
M And now, behold, when I thought this, I could remember my pains no more; yea, I was harrowed up by the memory of my sins no more. And oh, what joy, and what marvelous light I did behold; yea, my soul was filled with **joy as exceeding as was my pain**! Yea, I say unto you, my son, that there could be nothing so exquisite and so bitter as were my pains. Yea, and again I say unto you, my son, that on the other hand, there can be nothing so exquisite and sweet as was my joy.
L Yea, methought [sic] I saw, even as our father Lehi saw, God sitting upon his throne, surrounded with numberless concourses of angels, in the attitude of singing and praising their God; yea, and my soul did long to be there. [**Long to be in the PRESENCE OF GOD**]
K But behold, **my limbs did receive their strength again**, and I stood upon

>   ~~my feet, and did manifest unto the people that I had been born of God.~~
> J ~~Yea, and from that time even until now, I have~~ **labored** ~~without ceasing,~~ **that I might bring souls unto repentance**; ~~that I might bring them to taste of the exceeding joy of which I did taste; that they might also be born of God, and be filled with the Holy Ghost. Yea, and now behold, O my son, the Lord doth give me exceedingly great joy in the fruit of my labors;~~
>   I ~~For because of the word which he has imparted unto me, behold, many have Been~~ **born of God**, ~~and have tasted as I have tasted, and have seen eye to eye as I have seen;~~
>   H ~~therefore they do know of these things of which I have spoken, as I do know;~~ ~~and~~ **the knowledge which I have is of God**.
>   G ~~And I have been~~ **supported under trials and troubles** ~~of every kind, yea,~~ **and** ~~in all manner of~~ **afflictions**; ~~yea, God has delivered me from prison, and from bonds, and from death;~~
>   F ~~yea, and I do put my~~ **trust in him**,
>   E **and he will still deliver me**.
>   D ~~And I know that he will raise me up at the last day, to dwell with him in glory; yea, and I will praise him forever, for he has brought our fathers out of~~ **Egypt**, ~~and he has swallowed up the Egyptians in the Red Sea; and he led them by his power into the promised land; yea, and he has delivered them out of bondage and~~ **captivity** ~~from time to time. Yea, and he has also brought our fathers out of the land of Jerusalem; and he has also, by his everlasting power, delivered them out of bondage and captivity, from time to time even down to the present day; and I have always retained in remembrance their captivity; yea, and ye also ought to retain in remembrance, as I have done, their captivity.~~
>   C ~~But behold, my son, this is not all; for ye ought to~~ **know as I do know**,
>   B ~~that inasmuch as ye shall~~ **keep the commandments of God ye shall prosper in the land**; ~~and ye ought to know also, that inasmuch as ye will not keep the commandments of God ye shall be cut off from his presence.~~
> A **Now this is according to his word**.

He allows himself to call this "a rigorous chiastic pattern."[513] His extractions, displayed in chiastic format, may very well impress some. To me, it is obvious that he has picked the best of the low-hanging cherries from a very large tree to achieve his objective.

If you have to tease a chiastic structure from a forest of verbiage, its rhetorical efficacy for the listener or reader will be minimal or nonexistent. True chiasmus is a rhetorical tool. If it is lost in complexity, and cannot function as a chiasmus, it is just not a chiasmus. Note that occasionally he was unable to find the words he needed for the mates. So instead he matched passages with similar meaning, and inserted words in

---

[513] Welch, Chiasmus in Antiquity, 206. See also Duane L. Christensen, *World Biblical Commentary* (Dallas, TX: Word Books, 1991), xli; and Yehuda Radday "Chiasmus in Hebrew Biblical Narrative", in John W. Welch, ed., *Chiasmus in Antiquity* (Provo, UT: Research Press [The Foundation for Ancient Research and Mormon Studies—F.A.R.M.S.], 1981), 50-76.,

square brackets so his reader would not fail to notice them (as in the two "L" mates).

When faced with the fact that chiasmus occurs not only in English literature, but even in popular culture, we have to ask whether any of this rises to the level of passing the "So what?" test. It certainly cannot override the archaeological verdict, although it has been used effectively by apologists to buttress the faith of some.

Summary

Although passages do occur in the *Book of Mormon* that qualify as poetry, they are worked into the text (which also happens in the OT); but there are no separate works consisting of poetry; and no dirges or psalms such as those found in the Old Testament (unless one accepts 2 Nephi 4:15-35 as a psalm). The poetry, being in English, cannot reveal Hebrew or Egyptian elements of rhyme or rhythm, or acrostic patterns. Chiasmus does occur, although the degree to which true chiastic passages occur has been exaggerated. There are even some instances of *parallelismus membrorum*, but no sustained chains of paired elements. There is no clear instance of a taunt song, nor especially any instance of the Lord commanding a prophet to take up a similitude (*nāśā māšāl*), nor any poetic oracle such as the oracle of Balaam. The elements that do occur are not absent in English language and literature. There is nothing surprising for BOM authors, steeped in Biblical reading and imbued with religious hymns drawn from Biblical passages and themes. Indeed, Joseph Smith, before working on the BOM project, was a member of a debate club, and worked to be a Methodist exhorter in two different states. Finally, the bottom line, as always, is that no manner of literary analysis can trump the archaeological verdict.

Lehi's Arabia

The study that most Mormons associate with this topic is *Lehi in the Desert* by Hugh Nibley.[514] This is the work that established his career in LDS apologetics. Various details in First Nephi were marshaled and claimed to be geographically or culturally correct, such as the fact that

---

[514] Hugh Nibley, "Lehi in the Desert" (*Improvement Era*, issues 1950/1-6, 9-10); Hugh Nibley, *Lehi in the Desert & the World of the Jaredites*.

Lehi dwelled in a tent on route, or that when returning from the Red Sea to Jerusalem Nephi is said to go up to Jerusalem. This latter phrase is typical of Hebrew usage in reference to persons traveling from parts of Palestine, and especially from the Mediterranean, the Jordan river and the Dead Sea to Jerusalem, which is uphill. But it may be less applicable when traversing the varied terrain from the Red Sea, depending on the route. In any case, one can also say, in English, "Well, I went up to Chicago." This is not alien to English.

Others have referred to the Lihyani civilization as having been converted to the "true" Christian faith by Lehi, based on a superficial similarity between the names Lehi and Lihyani. This is a pure invention, being neither evidenced in archaeology nor mentioned in the BOM.

Some have been impressed by the fact that when Ishmael died in the desert, he was buried in "the place which was called Nahom." In Hebrew, this could refer to "mourning" or "growling, groaning," depending on which h (h or ḥ) one wishes to assign to it. There has been some LDS writing about it, in defense of the BOM text. Following BOM practice, we find that Lehi names a river after his eldest son, Laman (1 Nephi 2:8: "he called the name of the river Laman"). It flows in the Valley of Lemuel, clearly named after his second son. A camp site was also named by the party, (1 Nephi16:13): "we did call the name of the place Shazer"). The land where they dwelled to build their ship was also named by the group (1 Nephi 17:5: "the land which we called Bountiful"), as was the Indian Ocean (1 Nephi 17:5: "the Sea, which we called Irreantum, which being interpreted, is, many waters"). Contrary to this practice, Nahom is "the place which was called Nahom." The implication is that it already existed, and was not named because of mourning for Lehi. In any case, it is inevitable to find references to places, peoples, tribes or clans with a name with n at the beginning, m at the end, and one of three possible consonants in the middle, in Hebrew, Arabic, Old South Arabian (four languages) or considerable Arabian inscriptional material deriving from various languages. Moreover, it is not hard to get a general idea of where the BOM Nahom should be found. The party traveled southeast along the Red Sea, from Laman to Shazer, to the camp where Nephi broke his bow, to Nahom. There, they took a course to the east. Most probably this would be near Abha, or if further south, then it would be near Hudaydah in Yemen. On the other hand, this issue should not even arise, since most probably the BOM Nahom was taken from the KJV Book of Nahum.

Location! Location! Location!

The entire Nephite millennium is set in the New World. Yet, the overwhelming majority of apologist work studies the BOM text in the light of Biblical and other Near East texts, languages, history and culture, to the nearly total exclusion of the Americas.

It is much like a story of Joha, an Arab folk hero. He is searching in the street in front of his doorstep when a neighbor asks:

"Joha, have you lost something."
❖ "Yes, the key to my house."
"I'll help you find it. Did you lose it around here?"
❖ "No, I lost it in my bedroom."
"So, why are you looking for it in the street?"
❖ "The light is better here."

Chapter 22

Fragmentation and Consequent Conflict

Although we normally think of defense of the faith in terms of critics of Mormonism, and in some cases, anti-Mormons, much of the Church's concern has historically centered on challenges to its own orthodoxy posed by dissidents and persons from within the broader Mormon movement. Already before Joseph Smith was murdered, his movement had begun to experience a schismatic tendency. This was partly due to the fact that some of the original founders had their own agendas from the beginning, and were "waiting in the wings," so to speak. The earliest of these include Hiram Page, who claimed to receive revelations from his seer stone, and Sidney Rigdon's attempt to wrest the leadership from Joseph Smith. Later, those who broke away founded their own versions of Mormonism. Those that operate today can create ambiguity and confusion regarding the epithet "Mormon" among outsiders, and even "LDS" in contrast with "RLDS" and "FLDS."

Churches That Separated in Joseph Smith's Lifetime

The Pure Church of Christ was the first group to split off from the LDS community. Organized in 1831 by Wycam Clark, Northrop Sweet and others in Kirtland, it never numbered more than a few members and lasted only a short time. Smith himself attempted to convince them that their spiritual experiences were a deception, but failed.

Other ventures resulted in small groups breaking away, although none of them survived. In 1832, the Independent Church was formed by a little-known person called Hoton. It rejected both Smith and the *Book of Mormon*. In 1836, Ezra Booth also made a clean break with the Mormon movement, eventually establishing his own Church of Christ. In 1837-38, Warren Parrish formed another Church of Christ, teaching that Joseph Smith was a fallen prophet, and rejecting the *Book of Mormon*. William Chubby, in the late 1830's, established yet another Church of Christ to bring the restored gospel to African Americans. In 1839, Isaac Russell broke with Smith, teaching that the Saints should not leave Missouri. He founded the Alston Church. George M. Hinkle was excommunicated 17 March 1839 and organized The Church of Jesus Christ, the Bride, the Lamb's Wife, 24 June 1840, at Moscow, Muscatine Co., Iowa Territory.[515] In 1844, William Law became the president of the True Church of Jesus Christ of Latter Day Saints. It opposed polygamy, published the *Nauvoo Expositor* and brought charges against Smith for the destruction of the press.

Churches Resulting from Bids to Succeed Joseph Smith

After the death of Joseph Smith, Sidney Rigdon, Smith's First Counselor, who had been ordained by Smith as a prophet, seer and revelator, began his move to be the successor. By 1847, he had been outflanked by Brigham Young, and Rigdon relocated to his old stomping grounds, Pittsburg, Pennsylvania, where he established what was claimed to be the true organization of the Church. There, Ebenezer Robinson, who had founded and published the *Times and Seasons*, began publishing the *Latter-day Saints Advocate and Messenger*, which accused Young of usurping the presidency out of expectation that Rigdon would end the practice of polygamy. Ultimately, the group held that Smith himself had become a fallen prophet when he began the practice. Rigdon began to gather the eastern branches of the Church, and succeeded in attracting important former leaders, including the First Presidency, John C. Bennett and William Law, as well as the former Apostle William E. McLellin. On April 6, 1845, at a General Conference in Pittsburg, Rigdon was sustained as president of the Church, along with a new quorum of twelve apostles. That fall, Rigdon attempted to relocate his group to what he called "Adventure Farm" in the area of Greencastle, Pennsylvania, to join together in a communitarian life. Like other United Order experiments, this soon failed, and Rigdon abandoned his flock.

During this period, Rigdonite apostles William E. McLellin and Benjamin Winchester gave up on Rigdon's leadership and joined with David Whitmer, whom they sustained as President of the Church under the name of the Church of Christ (Whitmerite). William Bickerton had refused to relocate to Adventure Farm, and severing his ties to the church, he initially remained in Monongahela, Pennsylvania. He began to

---

[515] "George M. Hinkle," josephsmithpapers.org (accessed 21 March 2017).

preach in a branch of the LDS Church in Elizabeth, Pennsylvania. After receiving from Brigham Young a directive that he must teach polygamy, he disassociated himself from the LDS Church and in May 1851 a branch of the church was organized under his leadership, the LDS Church in West Elizabeth. There he began meeting with other believers whom he had converted to the faith, and formally organized them into The Church of Jesus Christ (Bickertonite) in 1862. In 1907, a doctrinal dispute about life in the millennium resulted in about half of the Bickertonites to split off and form the Reorganized Church of Jesus Christ (Bickertonite). In 1914, James Caldwell split with the original Bickertonites over whether the First Presidency was a valid form of leadership for the Church. They formed the Primitive Church of Jesus Christ (Bickertonite) and these were later joined by the Reorganized Church of Jesus Christ (Bickertonite). Both splinter groups are now defunct, but the original Bickertonite church still existed in the second decade of the 21st century.

Another claimant to succession to Joseph Smith was James Strang, the multitalented preacher, lawyer, amateur scientist, local newspaper editor (*Randolph Herald*), *New York Tribune* correspondent, county Postmaster and politician (member of the Michigan House of Representatives). When his bid failed, he founded his own organization, the Church of Jesus Christ of Latter-day Saints (Strangite), in Voree, Wisconsin. A polygamist, he claimed to have received numerous revelations, and most notably, to have found centuries-old brass plates, the last testament of Rajah Manchou of Vorito, which he translated with the Urim and Thummim as the *Voree Record*, a text containing long lost spiritual wisdom. He also claimed to have translated the Brass Plates of Laban, which he published as *The Book of the Law of the Lord*. Based thereon, he claimed that all prophets since the beginning of time were kings, and that he, as the prophet of the current true church, was also to be a king. On July 8, 1850, he was crowned by his counselor and Prime Minister, George J. Adams, an actor, and ruled as a king, ritually at least, for six years. In 1856, two disgruntled Strangites assassinated him.

Joseph Smith's brother William was excommunicated by Brigham Young and his Quorum of the Twelve Apostles in 1845. After a short period with the Strangites, in 1847 he announced he was the legitimate president of the LDS Church, arguing that lineal succession gave him the right to the presidency. His church lasted only a few years.

The principal claimant by lineal succession was the murdered prophet's eldest surviving son, Joseph Smith III. He was only eleven years old at the time of the succession crisis. Many of the Smiths looked to James Strang as successor, but Smith's widow Emma remained aloof. Strang's open practice of polygamy in 1849 alienated him from her even further. Smith III engaged in studies and practiced law. Increasingly, the Saints remaining in Illinois and thereabouts, strongly opposed to Brigham Young as a usurper, began to call for the establishment of a new church organization. In 1860, the Church of Jesus Christ of Latter Day Saints (changed in 1872 to the Reorganized Church of Jesus Christ of Latter Day Saints, the RLDS Church) was founded with Joseph Smith III as its prophet. In 2001 the name was changed again to the Community of Christ. Although the *Book of Mormon* is part of its canon, *The Book of Abraham* is not. Over time, it has grown closer to mainstream Protestantism (with a version of the Revised Common Lectionary) but differs in several ways, including its belief that the church must have a prophet at its head, and in continuing revelation from God. It has around a quarter of a million members, and a presence in fifty countries. At least ten sects have split off from it, most of them small, and still in existence.

In the twentieth century, succession in the LDS Church seems to have been routinized. The senior member of the Quorum of the Twelve Apostles becomes the new Church President.

Churches That Split over the Suspension of Polygamy

Although the LDS Church was coming under attack for its doctrine of polygamy, it turned out that the Manifesto of 1890 (the Woodruff Manifesto) resulted in even more fragmentation. The then Prophet, Seer, Revelator and President of the Church of Jesus Christ of Latter-day Saints, Wilford Woodruff, issued a manifesto containing the following:

> Inasmuch as laws have been enacted by Congress forbidding plural marriages, which laws have been pronounced constitutional by the court of last resort, I hereby declare my intention to submit to those laws, to use my influence with the members of the Church over which I preside to have

22. Fragmentation and Consequent Conflict

them do likewise. There is nothing in my teachings to the Church or in those of my associates, during the time specified, which can be reasonably construed to inculcate or encourage polygamy; and when any Elder of the Church has used language which appeared to convey such teaching, he has been promptly reproved. And I now publicly declare that my advice to the Latter-day Saints is to refrain from contracting any marriage forbidden by the law of the land.

The issue is not just a desire to practice polygamy. By the time of the Manifesto, many polygamous families already existed. Woodruff himself had at least nine wives. The status of these people, the wives, and especially the children, was ambiguous, leaving many potentially vulnerable. The Church saw fit to accommodate their very real needs as they slipped into the polygamy underground. Accusations circulated that the Church tolerated the solemnization of polygamous unions if done in Mexico, Canada or on the high seas, resulting on 6 April 1904 in a second manifesto issued by Church President Joseph F. Smith.

In the 1920's, a courier and guard for polygamous leaders underground, Lorin C. Woolley, established the Council of Friends (the Priesthood Council), in Salt Lake City, and the Short Creek Community in what is now Colorado City, Arizona. Many if not most later fundamentalist polygamous groups claim their descent from the Council of Friends. After Woolley's death in 1934, and the death of his second elder J. Leslie Broadbent six months later, John Y. Barlow lead the group until his death in 1949. He was followed by Joseph White Musser, who met with opposition due to his condemnation of underaged and arranged marriages, and his appointment of Rulon C. Allred as an apostle and his successor. Upon his death in 1954, the Short Creek community rejected Allred's leadership, who then founded the Apostolic United Brethren. The leadership of what was to become the Fundamentalist Church of Jesus Christ of Latter-Day Saints passed to Leroy S. Johnson. Many if not most of the Short Creek fundamentalists continued to consider themselves LDS Mormons, believing that the Church was simply wrong with respect to polygamy. It may be that the formal establishment of the FLDS movement as a church happened with Rulon Jeffs succession after Johnson's death in 1986.

Another group splintering off from the Council of Friends is the Latter Day Church of Christ (the Kingston clan, or the Davis County Cooperative Society), founded in Utah by Elden Kingston in 1935.

The Apostolic United Brethren has undergone additional splintering. An unusual development was the establishment of the Church of Jesus Christ in Solemn Assembly, founded by Alex Joseph. In association with this church, he and some associates formed the Confederate Nations of Israel, a sort of umbrella nondenominational organization that even accepted atheists. It has been estimated that perhaps as many as one fourth of its members practice polygamy.

Another somewhat aberrant offshoot of the Apostolic United Brethren is the Church of the New Covenant in Christ founded by John W. Bryant. One does not know how much to trust the testimony of a former wife, but according to her, he converted the temple rites into sexual orgies and free love.

The Righteous Branch of the Church of Jesus Christ of Latter-day Saints is another offshoot of the Apostolic United Brethren. It is claimed that its founder, Gerald Peterson Sr., is the rightful successor to Rulon C. Allred and Spencer W. Kimball. Peterson claimed that God, Jesus, Allred and others favored him with visitations.

There have also been groups that have split off from the FLDS. The Centennial Park group (the Second Ward group), led by Marion Hammon and Alma Timpson, broke off from Leroy S. Johnson over issues of presiding priesthood authority. The Church of Jesus Christ of Latter-day Saints and the Kingdom of God (the Naylor group, or Third Ward), in turn, was formed by Frank Naylor and Ivan Neilsen of the Centennial Park group, also over the issue of leadership. Finally, in 2003, when FLDS leader Warren Jeffs excommunicated Winston Blackmore, dividing the Bountiful community in two, the latter founded the Church of Jesus Christ (Original Doctrine), Inc. (also called the Blackmore/Bountiful Community).

Other polygamist sects have divided directly off of the Church of Jesus Christ of Latter-day Saints. In the 1920's, Alma Dayer LeBaron Sr. began his work, establishing a group that gave rise to other LeBaron-led groups. He was the grandson of Benjamin F. Johnson, a close associate of Joseph Smith, and a member of the Council of Fifty. To escape legal consequences, he made his headquarters in Colonia LeBaron, Chihuahua, Mexico. Although a polygamist, he had seven sons with Maud McDonald: Benjamin Teasdale, Ross Wesley, Alma Dayer Jr., Floren, Verlan, Joel F. and Ervil. In 1955, Joel F. established the Church of the Firstborn of the Fullness of Times, in Colonia LeBaron. In the same year, Ross Wesley established a branch in Salt Lake City, but within months he broke with his brothers and established his own church, the Church of the Firstborn. He taught that he had been sent to prepare the way for an Indian prophet, the One Mighty and Strong. In 1972, Ervil split with Joel F. He ordered him killed, as well as Rulon C. Allred, founder of the Apostolic United Brethren. He was extradited to the U.S. and sentenced to life in prison. The exact status of the LeBaron group (any of them), is currently unknown.

In 1968, Robert C. Crossfield published the *Book of Onias*, which criticized LDS Church leaders, for which he was excommunicated. He joined the Mormon fundamentalists in Creston, British Columbia, Canada, and through contacts there, he founded the School of the Prophets in 1982. The Provo, Utah, School of the Prophets became notorious because Ron and Dan Lafferty, convicted for the murder of their brother's wife and infant daughter, had served as two of his six counselors in 1984.

In 1994, the True and Living Church of Jesus Christ of Saints of the Last Days was founded by James D. Harmston, without lineage from Woolley or LeBaron. More exotic is the Church of the Firstborn and the General Assembly of Heaven, founded in 2001, in Magna, Utah, by Terrill R. Dalton. He claimed to be the Holy Ghost and Father of Jesus.

Schismatic Secularism: the Godbeites

William S. Godbe, and other LDS merchants, felt that the LDS Church needed to be reformed, and that the chief obstacle to reform was Brigham Young's control in affairs secular. In 1868, they began seeking changes in the Prophet's economic control and policies, and published their positions in *Utah Magazine*, which became the *Salt Lake Tribune*. Godbe and several of his colleagues were excommunicated in the following year. He responded by establishing the Church of Zion in

1870, and became increasingly anti-Mormon over time. He sought his fortune in silver mining, which eventually petered out. He was also active in the Utah political scene.

Schisms and Lifestyle: the Gay Mormons

New times bring new issues. In 1969, David-Edward Desmond founded the United Order Family of Christ for young gay men (18 to 30). The members were to hold everything in common, in an effort to live in accordance with the United Order, an LDS form of Christian communalism in which everyone would deed (consecrate) his or her property to the Church. Eventually, efforts to apply it were abandoned under Joseph Smith. However, various individual communities attempted it, including the famous Orderville, Utah, established at the direction of Brigham Young in 1875. This was the most successful of a number of such communities in Utah. Although it became prosperous, its United Order system lasted only about ten years. The United Order Family of Christ lasted only about four or five years, as far as one can determine. This may have been for several reasons, including problems arising from the United Order system itself, or from the lifestyle of the members with the accompanying lack of legitimacy in the community at large, or from the age limits.

In 1985, Antonio A. Feliz established the Restoration Church of Jesus Christ in Los Angeles, CA. The majority of the members were LGBT (Lesbian, Gay, Bisexual, Transgender), although others were welcome to join. Antonio Feliz, a former LDS bishop, had served as the Director of (LDS) Church Welfare in the Andean Region (now the South America West Area). In addition to the standard LDS scriptures, they believe in a collection of their own revelations, the *Hidden Treasures and Promises*. Although focused on meeting the spiritual needs of their LGBT membership, they also opened their doors to equal participation of women in general. Both men and women could be called of God, by prophecy, and given authority by the laying on of hands, to teach the gospel and administer its rites. Pamela J. Calkins was the first woman to be ordained to the priesthood. Feliz went on record as being willing to perform polygamous homosexual marriages if requested to do so. The Church was disbanded in 2010.[516]

A Few of the Utah Offshoots

There are many other offshoots of the LDS in Utah. One of the more colorful is the Church of the Potter Christ, founded in 1857 by Arnold Potter who claimed to be a messiah. He and a small group of followers settled in Council Bluffs. In 1872, he announced the time of his ascent into heaven. He rode a donkey to the edge of the bluffs and leapt off, intending to ascend, but instead, fell to his death.

In 1861, Joseph Morris founded the Church of the Firstborn (Morrisite). Having claimed a revelation that he was the Seventh Angel of the Book of Revelations, he wrote Brigham Young seeking recognition, but received no reply. In 1860 he began attracting followers, and was excommunicated, at which point he founded the Church of Jesus Christ of Saints of the Most High. This was not a move that would go unnoticed in Brigham Young's Utah Territory. In 1861, he and his followers began to fear for their security. He gathered them to Kingston (Kington) Fort, which lay abandoned on the Weber River, near present-day Ogden, Utah. Reportedly the group reached 300 in number. They arrived with items of property, including livestock. In 1862, when food in the fort became scarce, individuals were allowed to leave with the property they had brought with them. Soon the accusation was made that some were leaving with better stock or tools than they had brought in. Three, William Jones, John Jensen and Lars C. Geertsen swore revenge for unfair reckoning, and seized a load of wheat on route to the Kaysville mills. The Morrisites sent out a band that captured the wheat and the three men, to be held for judgment when Christ came. Eventually the situation escalated, and the Utah territorial militia was sent, resulting in what has been called the Morrisite War. When it was over, seven Morrisites were convicted of murder and 66 convicted of resisting arrest, although three days later all were pardoned by the new territorial governor Stephen S. Harding. The Morrisites scattered, but many

---

[516] *List of Saints in the Latter Day Saints Movement* (A Wikipedia ebook, accessed 21 July 2015 [Creative Commons Attribution-Share Alike]), 85.

gathered in Deer Lodge County, Montana, under the leadership of George Williams, who claimed to be Morris' rightful successor and the Prophet Cainan. He claimed to have received many revelations. One of these revealed that Deer Lodge County would be the site of the Second Coming of Christ. He also authored St. Anne's Hill Record, which he claimed to have translated from an ancient record. After Williams died in 1882, the group fragmented, and disbanded in 1969.

Mormon-Related Crime

When Mormons sing "Whose on the Lord's side, who?" some might interpret it with broad suspicion. The Utah LDS Church must not only look right and left, for attacks from outside, but behind their back as well, for the next pretender to prophecy, from within.

Whenever a crime involves a Latter-day Saint, or member of a Mormon breakaway group, and is sufficiently sensational that it gets into the mass media, there will be suggestions and innuendos that somehow it is related to Mormon belief. The Mormon bomber and the Jodi Arias murder cases were typical of this phenomenon. More sober analysts bear in mind that there have been numerous cases involving Catholics, Muslims, Hindus and other groups that garner similar attention. Some people in every group do commit crimes, and much of human behavior is at least in some way related to their cultural background. The interpretation of that relationship is often subjective and or tendentious. Nothing new or strange here.

A more pertinent analysis with respect to our topic focuses on two types of cases: first, criminal attacks on the leaders of a group, perpetrated by members, and particularly leaders of a rival group; and second, criminal acts perpetrated by leaders or members in the leadership of a group victimizing members of that group in the name of religion.

The Legacy of Theocracy and Violence in the First Decades

It seems clear that the initial adoption of violence on the part of Mormons, including Joseph Smith, was defensive. When persecution developed in Kirtland, the faithful, like many Americans, tended to possess at least one firearm at home. Joseph Smith probably feared more from the dissidents than from non-Mormons. Already in Kirtland, he found it necessary to have an armed bodyguard, the famous Orrin Porter

22. Fragmentation and Consequent Conflict

Rockwell. This latter served also as bodyguard to Brigham Young and was reputed to have killed many men. Reportedly he once said, "I never killed anyone who didn't need killing."

The first major adoption of the use of force to achieve the Mormon plan was Zion's Camp, a paramilitary group organized by Joseph Smith in Kirtland, in obedience to a revelation of divine will (D&C 103):

> 15. Behold, I say unto you, the redemption of Zion must needs come by power;
> 16. Therefore, I will raise up unto my people a man, who shall lead them like as Moses led the children of Israel
> 17. For ye are the children of Israel, and of the seed of Abraham, and ye must needs be led out of bondage by power, and with a stretched-out arm
> 18. And as your fathers were led at the first, even so shall the redemption of Zion be.
> 22. Therefore let my servant Joseph Smith, Jun, say unto the strength of my house, my young men and the middle aged—Gather yourselves together unto the land of Zion, upon the land which I have bought with money that has been consecrated unto me.
> 25 And whomsoever ye curse, I will curse, and ye shall avenge me of mine enemies.

Smith had been divinely instructed that a New Jerusalem would be built in America, in Jackson County, Missouri, and that a City of Zion should be established there. This became known as the Mormon people's "land of our inheritance," and was rightfully theirs by divine decree. When their initial attempt met with opposition from the Missourians, who had no intention of just standing by while Mormon heretics dominated the land that they had settled, Smith initially engaged attorneys to pursue the matter in the courts and with the governor. Perhaps in response to this, more severe Missourian opposition occurred, destroying some homes and the Church printing shop, and forcing the Mormons out. It is then that Smith received this order from on high, and in compliance he organized Zion's Camp. Around two hundred marched with Smith to redeem Zion. When they arrived, initially, attempts were made to negotiate. As these attempts broke down, cholera broke out, and Smith disbanded Zion's Camp. Most returned to Kirtland, seven had died, and some criticized Smith for not fighting. This should have been the first indication to him that creating a paramilitary force is easier than controlling it, or leading it to victory.[517]

Toward the end of 1836, Lilburn William Boggs, the new Missouri Governor, undertook to arrive at a solution to the Mormon issue, and designated Caldwell County for Mormon settlement. Already, in August, W. W. Phelps and John Whitmer had founded the town of Far West within the boundaries of that county, although many Mormons continued to live in Clay County. Anti-Mormon violence developed, including the infamous attack called the Haun's Mill massacre, on 30 October 1838.

Joseph Smith arrived in Far West on 14 March 1838, and it became the headquarters of the Mormon movement. Already in June of 1838, Mormons in Far West had formed the Danites (aka fraternal organization of the Danites, Daughter of Zion, Revelator Order of the Danites) in Far West. Although it seems clear that it was not founded by Joseph Smith, he openly lent it his support and prestige, if not formal priesthood authority. On July 4 of the same year, Mormons celebrated their own Declaration of Independence, and cornerstones were laid for a temple. As part of the celebrations, Joseph Smith and the First Presidency of the Church, along with the Danite commanders, exhibited with the company in a parade. It should be noted that this was not a Missouri militia, but a paramilitary group commanded in Far West, with loose connections to the First Presidency. Its mandate was not clearly defined, but the way it was understood by many is perhaps best reflected in the speech on this occasion of Sidney Rigdon, a member of the First Presidency:

> We take God and the holy angels to witness this day, that we warn all men in the name of Jesus Christ, to come on us no more forever, for from this hour, we will bear it no more, our rights shall no more be trampled on with impunity. The man or the set of men, who attempt it, does it at the expense of their lives. And that mob that comes on us to disturb us; it shall be between us and them a war of extermination, for we will follow them, till the last drop of their blood is spilled, or else they will have to exterminate us; for we will carry the seat of war to their own houses, and their own

---

[517] For information regarding the conflict in Missouri, see Stephen C. LeSueur, *The 1838 Mormon War in Missouri* (Columbia, MO: University of Missouri Press, 1987).

families, and our party or the other shall be utterly destroyed, —Remember it then all MEN.[518]

Subsequently, conflict escalated between vigilante groups across Missouri and Mormons, usually characterized in terms of justifiable vengeance by both sides. These incidents included the expulsion of Mormons from De Witt, a largely vacant town settled by non-Mormons, but virtually purchased entirely by the Church; as well as the looting and destruction of Mormon homes, and the trashing of Gallatin by the Danites when efforts were made to prevent Mormons from voting on 6 August 1838. On 18 October, the Caldwell County (Mormon) militia leader Colonel George M. Hinkle and his men, along with elements of the Danites, and Church leaders including Joseph Smith, marched under arms on Gallatin, Millport and Grindstone Fork. The inhabitants fled before them, and the Mormons plundered the properties and burned homes and stores. This was followed during the next few days by LDS vigilantes led by Lyman Wight attacking and plundering farms. On October 24, the Mormons won the Battle of Crooked River against a state militia, although they took heavier casualties. Missouri vigilantes reacted in large numbers driving Mormons to Far West and Adam-Ondi-Ahman. On 27 October, having received exaggerated reports of the battle, Governor Lilburn Boggs issued Missouri Executive Order 44, his infamous order to General John B. Clark, in LDS history called the extermination order. It said "The Mormons must be treated as enemies, and must be exterminated or driven from the state if necessary for the public peace." Far West was besieged, and Clark issued his terms: surrender of the LDS leadership. Smith and his counselors surrendered. Legal proceedings were begun against him and others for treason, but during a prison transfer, Smith escaped and fled the state. By the spring of 1839, nearly all of perhaps as many as 10,000 Mormons had fled Missouri.

Sidney Rigdon's salt sermon, the issuance of an order to the Danites for action against dissidents and the flight of Oliver Cowdery and David Whitmer from Far West, Missouri, show that the Danite mission was very much to cleanse the community within, as much as to counter external attack. The continuation of Danite activity in the Utah territory

---

[518] *Oration Delivered by Mr. S. Rigdon, on the 4th of July, 1838* (Far West: printed at the Journal Office, 1838), 8, 12. Quoted from Marquardt, *Rise of Mormonism*, 284-5.

under Brigham Young cannot be gone into here, but clearly a legacy had been born.

Once the Saints had established themselves in Nauvoo, Illinois, Missouri continued demanding Smith's extradition, and crossborder conflicts continued between the Danites and Missouri vigilantes. Smith was most probably neither really in control of the passions for revenge among some of the Saints, nor paramilitary operations. But his decision to resort to extralegal means to destroy the *Nauvoo Expositor* press evidences his contempt for civil law when it did not meet his needs. By the time of his own murder, a long legacy had been established, with convenient supporting revelations, and the backdrop of wars of extermination in the keystone scripture, the *Book of Mormon*. Mormonism had been born in an environment of bigotry, theocratic law and tragic violence.

Church-related Incidents of Violence in the Utah Territory

Ambiguity arises when the relationship of criminal acts to Church officers is unclear. One case, involving the Utah LDS, is the Mountain Meadows massacre, consisting of attacks on the Baker–Fancher emigrant wagon train, at Mountain Meadows in southern Utah, 7-11 September 1857, resulting in the mass slaughter of most in the party (largely from Arkansas) by members of the Utah Territorial Militia (officially, the Nauvoo Legion) from the Iron County district, together with some Paiute Native Americans. Apparently they created a mock Indian attack. After a siege, under the pretense of a white flag, the militiamen convinced the emigrants that they would lead them out in safety. Once out of their makeshift fortifications, the militiamen cut them down. About 120 were killed, men, women and children. There were seventeen child survivors, who apparently were placed in families to be raised as orphans. The event took place during the tensions arising from what has been called the Utah War. Legal proceedings were interrupted by the Civil War, but nine indictments issued in 1874, and only one individual was actually tried: Bishop John D. Lee. After his conviction, he was executed on 23 March 1877. Since then, anti-Mormons, Mormon critics, and the Church with its formidable apologetic capability, have produced numerous studies of how this tragedy happened.

Much has been written as well about the Morrisite war of 1862. In fear for their lives as a dissident group on Brigham Young's turf, they gathered in a fort near what is now Ogden, Utah. After the Morrisites had recaptured a wagon of their wheat and the Morrisite dissidents who had seized it, events led to a request from Chief Justice John F. Kinney to the acting governor to activate the territorial militia (i.e. the Nauvoo Legion) as a posse comitatus to arrest the Morrisite leaders. The Nauvoo Legion was commanded by Robert T. Burton, a prominent Mormon, and one of the principal officers in the Nauvoo Legion. He served as a member of the presiding bishopric of The Church of Jesus Christ of Latter Day Saints from 1874 until his death. One has to wonder whether he felt his authority as commander in this operation came primarily from the territorial governor, or Brigham Young. After "Morris' fort" had been surrounded with militiamen and cannon, the order was given for the besieged to surrender in thirty minutes. Morris was no more in the mood to compromise than Burton. He managed to receive a revelation that the militia would be destroyed. With the Morrisites gathered to hear this message from on high, the half hour expired, and Burton ordered two warning cannon shots. One ball bounced across the ground, and killed a woman, while another was seriously wounded. When some Morrisites returned fire, militia member Jared Smith was killed. The militia entered the fort. At that point, it is not clear what transpired, but Burton shot and killed Morris. In the following melee two women were killed, Morris' counselor John Banks was mortally wounded, and ninety-nine men were taken prisoner. Although seven Morrisites were convicted of second-degree murder, and 66 of resistance, all were pardoned by a new territorial governor, Stephen S. Harding.

On a lighter note, let us revisit the case of Arnold Potter (Potter Christ). While in Council Bluffs, in 1872, his followers were very few. It appears that these few, or a few of these few, were the only witnesses to his attempted ascension on the edge of the bluffs; they claimed that he leapt from his donkey and fell to his death rather than ascending to heaven. Was he really that crazy? Or, whether he went there willingly or not, when push came to shove, did push come to shove?

Assassination and Murder in and among Mormon Splinter Groups

The murders among and by the members of the LeBaron clan amounted to a veritable crime wave. On 20 August 1972, Joel LeBaron was shot in the head by one of his brother Ervil's followers. Ervil was tried and convicted in Mexico for Joel's murder, but this was overturned on a technicality, or possibly a bribe. Ervil's followers subsequently raided Los Molinos in an effort to kill another brother, Verlan LeBaron, who happened to be in Nicaragua. The town was destroyed and two men were killed. In April of 1975, Ervil ordered the killing of Bob Simons, and in 1977 the killing of Rulon C. Allred, leader of the Apostolic United Brethren. His 13th wife, Rena Chynoweth, carried out the murder with Ramona Marston. Rena confessed in her memoir, *The Blood Covenant* (1990). Ervil also targeted his supporters. His 10th wife, Vonda White, was convicted and sentenced to life in prison for the murder of Dean Grover Vest, one of LeBaron's henchmen, who had attempted to leave the church. Vonda White is also said to have killed Noemi Zarate Chynoweth, the plural wife of Ervil's father-in-law; she had been critical of Ervil's practices. Ervil LeBaron has also been linked to the death of his own 17-year-old daughter Rebecca, who was pregnant with her second child and hoped to leave the group. It is alleged that his stepson Eddie Marston and brother-in-law Duane Chynoweth strangled her in April 1977.

On 1 June 1979, Ervil LeBaron was apprehended by police in Mexico and extradited to the United States, where he was convicted of having ordered Allred's death. In 1980 he was sentenced to life imprisonment at the Utah State Prison in Draper, Utah, where he died on 16 August 1981. Ervil's brother Verlan (whom Ervil had tried to murder) died in an auto accident in Mexico City two days after Ervil's body was discovered in his cell. Family members suspect that this was not a coincidence.

While in prison, Ervil wrote a 400-page "bible" known as *The Book of the New Covenants*, which included a commandment to kill disobedient church members who were included in a hit list written by LeBaron. Three of the murders were carried out simultaneously on 27 June 1988, at 4:00 PM (the 4:00 PM murders). Duane Chynoweth, one of LeBaron's former followers, was shot and killed with his 8-year-old daughter while running errands. Eddie Marston, one of LeBaron's stepsons and former thugs, was killed in the same manner. Mark Chynoweth, a father of 6, was shot multiple times in his office in Houston, Texas. Five (of seven) of the killers were found guilty of murder. One other, Cynthia LeBaron, testified against her siblings and was granted immunity. The final suspect, Jacqueline LeBaron, was captured by the FBI in May 2010. On 16 June 2011, Jacqueline LeBaron pled guilty to conspiracy to obstruct religious beliefs and faced a 5-year maximum sentence in a future sentencing hearing. On 14 December 2012, she was released from federal custody several months earlier than her original sentence. It has been estimated that more than 25 people were killed as a result of LeBaron's prison-cell orders.

A notably gruesome case is that of cult leader and self-proclaimed prophet Jeffrey Don Lundgren, who was raised in the Reorganized Church of Jesus Christ of Latter Day Saints. For a while he was a lay minister for the RLDS, and then a volunteer tour guide at the Mormon Temple in Kirtland, Ohio. Claiming to have moved to Kirtland because O-H-I-O is chiastic (?), he applied his own version of literary chiasmus to the interpretation of scripture, and began attracting followers. After being dismissed by the RLDS in 1988, Lundgren formed his own sect, with himself as prophet. A plan to take over the Kirtland Temple was aborted when a dissident went to the police. Lundgren called his followers to move to Kirtland, and said that on 3 May, his birthday (no specific year), the Second Coming would happen at the Kirtland Temple. Having already practiced systematic mind control over his closest followers, he began to teach that in order to see God, followers had to kill a family of five, an act which he called "pruning the garden." For this purpose, he targeted the family of Dennis Avery, whom he distrusted. A burial pit was dug by several male followers in a barn, and one by one all five members of the Avery family were led in and killed, starting with the father. He was followed by his wife, then his 15 year-old daughter Trina, 13 year-old Becky and 6 year-old Karen. He then led followers to West Virginia, abandoned them there, and went to California, disillusioned. Nine months after the murders, on a tip, the police dug up the bodies. After several appeals, Lundgren was executed on 24 October 2006.

In another case, inspired by a desire to practice Polygamy, a woman and her infant child were "slaughtered" in compliance with a command from on high. Dan Lafferty, 36, a prosperous chiropractor in Provo, had run for county sheriff and served as an elder in his church. His older brother, Ronald, 43, was a member of the city council in Highland, Utah. After excommunication from the LDS Church, they joined a splinter sect, the School of the Prophets, and in March of 1984 served for a month as counselors in Provo, Utah. Brenda, the wife of their brother Allen had opposed her husband's joining this faith. Ron blamed her for encouraging his own wife to oppose her husband's intention to practice polygamy, and to leave him.

In the same year, brother Ron claimed he had a revelation from God: "Thus sayeth the Lord unto my servants the prophets. It is my will and commandment that ye remove the following individuals in order that my work might go forward for they truly have become obstacles in my path and I will not allow my work to be stopped. First, thy brother's wife, Brenda, and her baby, then Chloe Low and then Richard Stowe. And it is my will that they be removed in rapid succession and that an example be made of them in order that others might see the fate of those who fight against the true saints of God." Chloe Low was a former Relief Society President who had supported Dan's wife, and Richard Stowe was the Stake President who had presided over his excommunication from the LDS Church.

Dan Lafferty, with his brother Ronald, wielding a consecrated "slaughter weapon," a 10-inch boning knife, beat Brenda unconscious, strangled her with a vacuum cord and slashed her throat as his brother held her by her long blond hair. Then Dan Lafferty went to Erica's crib and cut the infant's tiny neck "to the spine." The brothers, unable to find the other two people on the list, Low and Stowe, who were on vacation, fled Utah for Nevada shortly after the murders. This case inspired the book *Under the Banner of Heaven*.

Rape under Religious Cover

A very different example is that of Warren Jeffs, the prophet of the Fundamentalist Church of Jesus Christ of Latter-day Saints. When he acceded to the head of the FLDS, he followed his father Rulon, who has been estimated to have had between 70 and 75 wives. Dissident members have claimed that Warren had as many as 70 wives. The State of Utah charged him with arranging marriages with underage girls, and the State of Arizona charged him with eight additional counts, including incest and sexual conduct with minors. He has been accused by three male nephews of sodomy when they were children, including the accusation of Brent Jeffs in a lawsuit, and Clyne Jeffs, who committed suicide after making his accusation. He is serving time for two felony counts of sexual assault on minors.

Jeffs did not engage in this activity totally without some claim to authority from prior high-level example. Polygamy was introduced by

Joseph Smith, who took Helen Mar Kimball to wife when she was only fourteen years old. Words attributed to her in 1881[519] claim that Joseph said, "If you will take this step, it will ensure your eternal salvation & exaltation and that of your father's household & all of your kindred." Although the term "spiritual wife" may have been used in some cases, and in the presence of some company, it is not known to have been used in this case. This term seems to have been used as a euphemism, possibly to make the proposition sound better to the woman in question, but also as a source of ambiguity to blunt criticism of the practice. Smith had been accused of sexual relations with Fanny Alger as well.[520] Furthermore, he had sealed several wives of other men to himself for the next life, a clear exercise of asserting male dominance.[521] When the revelation on polygamy came, it said concubinage was in accordance with divine will in the cases of Abraham and two kings, David and Solomon. This inclusion would be gratuitous if it were not intended to give Smith cover for his behavior. Although the proper age for marriage may have been younger at the time, there can be no doubt that in today's laws, marrying a girl only fourteen years old would bring a charge of statutory rape today. For us, the important observation is that the practice of the prophet can be used today to justify behavior such as that found among the FLDS.

The population dynamics of polygamy in a small community are also interesting. When the practice is common among enough of the men, and many of them take several wives, the gender ratio has to be significantly female. Reports from some young men who left the Jeffs' community indicate that potential young male competitors were pressured to leave. This produced a gender balance that allowed the polygamy privilege among older men.

Another potential obstacle to the desire for wives among the older men is the possibility that prospective brides might not accept. Although many attribute their taking young girls as brides to a prurient interest in sex with the under-aged, the practice is also a strategy. At that age, the

---

[519] *Helen Mar Kimball Autobiography*, March 30, 1881, LDS Church History Library, as cited in Jeni Broberg Holzapfel and Richard Neitzel Holzapfel, *A Woman's View: Helen Mar Whitney's Reminiscences of Early Church History*, (Salt Lake City: Bookcraft [Religious Studies Center, BYU], 1997), 482-86. See also Marquardt, *Rise of Mormonism*, 342, 374.
[520] Marquardt, *Rise of Mormonism*, 274-77.
[521] Marquardt, *ibid*, 343.

girls are more tractable, and once married and pregnant, their fate is sealed.

In a more recent case, Terrill Dalton, 45, leader of the Church of the Firstborn and the General Assembly of Heaven was convicted of two counts of rape, a first-degree felony, for having sex with his own then 15-year-old daughter. Dalton claimed that he had had a revelation saying that he is "the Holy Ghost and Father of Jesus." His First Counselor Geody Harman, 38, often referred to as "God in the flesh," who also had sex with her, was sentenced to probation in a plea deal to convict Dalton. The rapes occurred in 2005. Dalton's daughter testified that she was promised she would receive blessings if she had sex with the two men and felt extreme pressure from her father and those in his church to comply.

Incest and Inbreeding in Mormon Communities

Brigham Young pursued a policy of settling the LDS (Utah) territory by calling families to establish communities in remote places. These developed for some time as very small isolated agricultural towns. The policy may be one of the contributing factors to the phenomenon of inbreeding among Mormons. Various professional research projects have used Utah data to better understand the effects of inbreeding. "Utah DNA is being used for an international study that seeks to identify chromosomes linked to diseases like asthma and diabetes… 'Utah's contribution to genetics has been enormous,' said Dr. Mark S. Guyer, a division director at the National Human Genome Research Institute in Maryland."[522]

In splinter groups, inbreeding is especially serious. First-cousin procreation in the US usually involves a first-cousin relationship along only one line of descent. But in these small inbred groups, nearly everyone is related to nearly everyone else, so that the first-cousin relationship can be multiple, along several lines of descent. Among the FLDS, this has resulted in infants born with Fumarase Deficiency, "an enzyme irregularity that causes severe mental retardation, epileptic

---

[522] Kirk Johnson, "By Accident, Utah is Proving an Ideal Genetic Laboratory," in *The New York Times* (July 31, 2004).

seizures and other cruel effects that leave children nearly helpless and unable to take care of themselves."[523]

Some inbreeding is unfortunately a result of incest relations. A student at the University of Utah told me in 1971 that her father was also her mother's father. An LDS teenage friend of mine in Green River, Wyoming, told me that he knew that his father was sleeping with his teenage cousin in the room next to his own. The doctrine of polygamy may also be a contributing factor, as it can exercise the mind of young males in the community. When I was twelve I was told the following rhyme by a 14 year-old LDS friend, about a Mormon President, John Taylor, Prophet, Seer and Revelator, who had at least seven wives and thirty-four children:

> My name is John Taylor,
> My prick is a whaler,
> My balls weight ninety-eight pounds.
> If you know any ladies
> Who want to have babies,
> Please tell them John Taylor's in town.

Clearly this was not invented by a young Wyoming boy. Its origin may have been from antipolygamy Mormons, but more probably by some in praise of their polygamous president's virility. In any case, it illustrates how polygamy can impress the mind with sexual fantasies among males as they grow up Mormon. Among a very small part of the population, this can lead to an interest in polygamous groups, or much more rarely, lead to sexual crimes.

American Christian traditions more in touch with their Puritan roots might be at least mildly surprised at LDS attitudes towards sex. In the old Salt Lake Mission Home, when being prepared for my mission to France, we were urged, by the Mission Home President's wife, to remain morally clean in the following terms. In the next life, marriage exists only in the Celestial Kingdom between married couples. On your mission, an illicit sexual episode may involve only fifteen minutes of pleasure. So in exchange for this bit of pleasure, you will sacrifice an eternity of marital sexual bliss. No one in his or her right mind would do this. We all, elders and sisters alike, listened with solemn attention. So, will those who do

---

[523] John Hollenhorst, "Birth defect is plaguing children in FLDS towns, in the *Deseret News* (9 February 2006).

not make it even have sexual organs? As an example in the degrees of latitude one finds in this discussion, and sense of humor, Bishop Mike T. Young stated on mormonmatters.org that those who fail to achieve salvation at the level of the highest degree of glory in the Celestial Kingdom

> will be turned into a Terrestrial-Telestial Kingdom Smoothie (TK Smoothies). I like to imagine these lesser kingdoms as the Barbie and Ken Kingdoms. Everyone walking around and looking beautiful and perfect for eternity, but having a smooth under-carriage like Barbie and Ken.[524]

The reference is to the famous Barbie dolls. In a similar humorous vein, to make fun of Brigham Young's excessive polygamy, one occasionally hears his name pronounced "Bring'em young."

Most members of the mainstream LDS Church only think about splinter apostate groups when media reports seem to give their own faith a bad reputation. And yet, the evidence shows that it is not impossible that a member of one's own family could become involved, or even go so far as to establish a new group. Ward bishops have to be on the lookout for signs that a member might be moving in that direction, especially among young missionary candidates. This concern, on a more official level, is evidenced by the fact that one must now give assurance of no association or sympathy with an apostate group in order to get an LDS temple recommend.

---

[524] Bishop Mike T. Young, in an answer to the question "Are we going to be Eunuchs after this life?" (accessed from mormonmatters.org on 16/1/2017).

Chapter 23

Quest for Exaltation in a Secular Society

Salvationist religion basically teaches that certain secrets, rituals or authority are needed to assure the believer's wellbeing beyond the grave, and usually for eternity. This is normally at least a moderately sophisticated system of belief, beyond the charms, incantations and potions of the shaman. The earliest well documented and developed example is the religion of the ancient Egyptians, where the deceased's heart is weighed against the feather of justice. Just to get to that point, rituals and secret knowledge were required.

LDS doctrine is an interesting example. Its three realms in heaven set the goal posts. To achieve ultimate exaltation, not only is sincere conversion required, the acquisition of a testimony, but baptism, the gift of the Holy Ghost, the temple rites and temple marriage. For males, this process includes progress through the priesthood ranks to become an elder in the Church. For all, a life in compliance with LDS teachings, including payment of a full tithe, or nearly so, goes a long way toward exaltation. What makes this somewhat unique, and most effective, is that actually achieving the highest salvation, in the Celestial Kingdom, cannot be done flying solo. It requires a marriage for all time and eternity. Members are exalted as a couple. The singles in that kingdom can at best aspire to be mere angels, in support roles to the deities.

If the parents of an LDS family do not make it to this exalted station, their family ties are severed. Families, in the next life, are composed only of those of the earthly family who measured up, as couples. Although those at the highest level can visit friends and former relatives below them, children or parents who did not get into the Celestial Kingdom cannot go to a higher kingdom for a visit. There develops a major gulf between oneself and some of those most beloved on earth. In this life, in practice, many individuals experience these teachings with the same acute sense of reality as anything else in their life. The threat that a member of the family might reject the *Book of Mormon* and leave the faith can produce severe strain between family members, and overwhelming pressure to conform.

With the birth of universalist religion, in Christianity and later Islam, criteria became faith-based. For the ancient Egyptians, as for the

Israelites, religion was largely ethnicity-based. With the universalism of Christianity, membership was often a result of conversion. Faith in the teachings of the new religion was essential for its success, growth and sustainability. It became the cardinal requirement for salvation. As Paul wrote in Ephesians 2:

> 8. For by grace are ye saved through faith; and that not of yourselves: it is the gift of God:
> 9 Not of works, lest any man should boast.

LDS theology takes this about as far as possible. A Mormon who lives sufficiently righteously can be exalted, i.e. saved in the Celestial Kingdom. A person who has lived equally righteously, who has had a chance to accept Mormonism but did not, can only be saved in the Terrestrial Kingdom. And the believer who has had a testimony of the authenticity of the *Book of Mormon* and of the election of Joseph Smith, who subsequently leaves Mormonism, can only hope to be saved in the Telestial Kingdom, even if his life was led on a plain equal to the other two with respect to works. The difference is essentially faith, expressed in terms of being in tune with the spirit. At times this is thought of as rejecting the promptings of the spirit, but at times it seems to be almost a special capacity. In any case, accepting Mormonism, obviously meaning acceptance of the *Book of Mormon* and the prophethood of Joseph Smith, is paramount, and the absolute *sine qua non*.

On the Other Hand

It is commonly said that the Bible is the most sold and least read book in the history of the world. Mormons have a far larger library of sacred texts. Very few have read the entire Bible or *Book of Mormon*, not to mention *The Book of Abraham* or the *Book of Moses*, and perhaps least of all the *Doctrine and Covenants*. One suspects that if they do not read their scriptures, most certainly do not read books about them.

Even in scriptural religions, even in literate societies, most believers experience their religion almost exclusively aurally, visually and ritually. There are a very limited number of verses that are commonly read from the pulpit, or given musical expression. These, for the worshipper, are the scriptures. *Qur'an*, in Arabic, means recitation, and the text of the *Qur'an* is experienced in Qur'anic recitations, done by reciters, famous for their beautiful voices, and in Qur'anic Arabic, that is poorly understood by most Arabs, and not understood at all by Turks, Iranians, Pakistanis, Indians, Malaysians and Indonesians.

Mormons are very similar to the non-Mormons in their town or city. Most range from working class to upper-middle class. Most important to them is their family, home and the employments that make these possible and secure. They enjoy sports, music, mass media and a range of social activities. Some members of the community have fallen away totally, and are dubbed apostates. Others do not practice, and drink, smoke, or both, and are called Jack-Mormons. Although it is notoriously difficult to assess religious participation, generally studies have indicated that those who attend church once a week reach at least 40% among the LDS. These are active Mormons. Within their ranks are those who are the tithe-payers, and even fewer, those who are deemed worthy to receive and have received a temple recommend, allowing them to participate for two years in temple work for the dead.

Tithing is important to the Church. I have heard exhortations to the young to work hard to succeed, for the more prosperous you are, the more you pay to the Church, and the more you can contribute to the building up of the Kingdom of God. The great and ever growing wealth of the Mormon Church is not just due to those who pay their ten percent, calculated before taxes, but because, as a lay church, it can keep its expenses to a minimum. Today, the Church is so large that there is a large administrative group that have full-time jobs with compensation. Its universities also are very expensive. But nearly all clergy receive no pay at all; in fact, they have regular jobs and pay tithing to the Church. For a large religious establishment, it doesn't get better than that.

Tithing and the performance of other duties are also important as what LDS leaders call the "law" of sacrifice. People who sacrifice for a belief become more firmly attached and devoted to it. To leave implies, at least subconsciously, that one has been a fool, and has paid a large sum of money for nothing. The Church has reached a point where demanding this level of sacrifice actually strengthens the group.

Socialization into the LDS Community: From Cradle to Temple

LDS children come into the world sinless, although presumably every human being has some sort of behavior record acquired in the preexistence. Soon after the child's birth, it is given a "name and a blessing" in accordance with the revelation in D&C 20:70. This rite is performed by a holder of the Melchizedek priesthood, a relative of the child if possible, and often the father. Usually, that individual and one or several others do it, standing in a circle before the congregation, usually in a sacrament meeting. Giving the name in public serves to introduce this new member of the community, and bestows blessings for the child's health and wellbeing in this life. It is not required for salvation, and is not a rite of passage, properly speaking, inasmuch as the infant is unaware of what is going on.

Attendance at Sunday meetings in the chapel begins early, often even as a babe in arms. Starting already at eighteen months (through age two), this new LDS member can, optionally, attend a special Sunday School nursery program in the Primary program. This is offered largely to enable both parents to attend Sunday School classes together unencumbered by toddlers. The program is also focused on the child, being conducted with the use of a manual, and a simple lesson each Sunday, emphasizing being loved by Jesus, etc.

Normal Primary classes begin at age three (through eleven) with proper classes, taught from a manual produced for the purpose. Depending on ward size, and local preferences, this group can be broken down variously. One common option is two groups, ages 3-7 and ages 8-11, each with a manual appropriate to the age spread.

The second rite that a young member will usually experience is the sacrament (communion). Initially, the sacrament used bread and wine. In one account of Joseph Smith and his upper leadership, they took the sacrament with a piece of bread the size of a fist, and a glass of wine, each. Later, the bread became the size of a quarter, and is always ordinary bread. After the prohibition on alcohol, water was substituted for wine. Although the sacrament is to renew one's baptismal covenants, young children are allowed to partake, in preparation for those covenants. This helps to instill in them the habit of weekly participation in the sacrament meeting. They have never known life without it.

The first major rituals in a young member's life are baptism, always by full immersion, and the gift of the Holy Ghost by the laying on of hands. Eight is considered to be the age of accountability, and so children are typically baptized shortly after their eighth birthday. This is monitored by the bishopric. Shortly before that date, brothers and sisters in positions of authority will engage the parents, singly and together as circumstances permit, often as they mingle before or after a Sunday

School or Sacrament meeting, or at a home teaching session, and comment with a nice smile, "Isn't Jack's (or Jill's) birthday coming up? Let us know when to arrange for the baptism." Such comments are spontaneous and well received by active members (and less active members as well). The baptismal rate of children of members, whatever their status in the Church, is very high.

Primary for the 8-11 group is for baptized members. Although in a small ward, they can be treated as a group, alternatively, special classes for each birth-year cohort can be organized, each with a special manual. Since members are typically baptized shortly after their eighth birthday, the first year focuses on baptism and issues associated with this new status, including instruction for the age of accountability. The others usually involve learning about the LDS canon: *Book of Mormon*, *Doctrine and Covenants*, *Pearl of Great Price*, Old Testament and New Testament. All texts are age-graded, and present faith-building stories, not scriptural technicalities, although some verse memorization can be included.

It is between eight and eleven that members are first asked to stand before their age peers, some of their best friends, and deliver a short talk. This does not just give early training in public speaking, and build self-confidence. Without even realizing it, they are already publicly committing themselves to Mormonism, something that they will have the occasion to do from time to time throughout the rest of their lives. Once a month, as adults, sacrament meeting will be a testimony meeting, and as "moved by the spirit," they will stand and tell how their faith has been made even stronger by some recent event. The welds that this experience strengthens are first made well before puberty.

At age twelve, all changes. It is then that the sexes are separated, and the males receive the priesthood. The Aaronic priesthood is the lesser one, and at age twelve young boys are ordained deacons, the lowest rung, followed by the teachers, ordained at age fourteen, and the priests, ordained at age sixteen. It is at age eighteen that the worthy can receive the Melchizedek priesthood, and be ordained an elder in the Church. From this time on, all boys with the priesthood attend priesthood classes.

These age designations are a later development. Originally, even deacons were adults, and all D&C passages are either age-irrelevant or assume that the deacon is an adult. An example is D&C 84:11:

And behold, the high priests should travel, and also the elders, and also the lesser priests; but the deacons and teachers should be appointed to watch over the church, to be standing ministers unto the church.

Presumably, God can modify details such as age as befits the times and seasons.

In March of 1980, a consolidated Sunday meeting schedule was established with Sacrament Meeting, followed or preceded by Sunday School, and then priesthood, Relief Society or Young Women meetings, all within a three-hour time span. Before that, Sacrament meeting tended to be in the afternoon, breaking up the whole day. Presumably, the new schedule was designed to increase attendance at all three, with instructions that Sunday afternoons should be spent in family activities. Many prior to 1980 partook of the sacrament in Sunday School, and skipped Sacrament meeting to enjoy the afternoon, or slept in and attended only Sacrament meeting. In the new schedule, the sacrament is passed in the Sacrament meeting (c. 70 minutes), the Sunday School meetings are for religious education and to build faith (c. 40 minutes) and the special classes are focused on the roles of the groups that attend: Melchizedek priesthood meeting for adult men, Aaronic priesthood meeting for the male youth, Relief Society meeting for adult women, and Young Women meeting for the female youth.

Although the programs for all youth are to teach church scripture and doctrine, to assist in the acquisition of a testimony that Joseph Smith was a prophet and that the *Book of Mormon* is true, and to prepare oneself to eventually be married in the temple for all time and eternity, the program for young men has an additional focus: preparation and encouragement to go on a mission for the church. Although there are also sister missionaries, they are a small minority, and young women do not receive instruction specifically oriented to sending out sisters to spread the LDS faith.

Another rite, not needed for salvation, and occurring often during one's teenage years, is receiving a patriarchal blessing. These blessings usually involve various promises regarding what one might become in this life or the next, but conditioned upon one's worthiness. They are generally intended to be inspirational, and are received at times as being aspirational.

Another rite is to receive one's temple endowment. Missionaries have all received the Melchizedek priesthood (age eighteen or older) and go through the temple for their endowments prior to going to the mission field. The endowment ceremony begins with washing and anointing; it is intended to prepare the individual to become a king or queen, and a priest or priestess, in the next life, i.e. in the Celestial Kingdom. Upon application, other worthy members may receive their endowments. Many receive their endowments when they marry in the temple. All must receive a temple recommend.

> The interview for a temple recommend is conducted privately between the bishop and the Church member concerned. Here the member is asked searching questions about his or her personal conduct, worthiness, and loyalty to the Church and its officers. The person must certify that he or she is morally clean and is keeping the Word of Wisdom, paying a full tithing, living in harmony with the teachings of the Church, and not maintaining any affiliation or sympathy with apostate groups.[525]

Affiliation or sympathy with apostate groups never came up in the interviews I had in the 1960's. The word of wisdom includes abstention from alcohol, tobacco, coffee and tea. So far, it does not include soft drinks with caffeine.

The final rite is temple marriage. Persons who have received their endowments are married in one of the small sealing rooms in the temple for that purpose. This is a sealing for time and all eternity. But it is conditioned on the worthiness of both parties. Those who are worthy will continue to be a married couple in the Celestial Kingdom.

There is nothing equivalent to the last rites in Catholicism. Mormons do not shrive. Nor do chapels have a confessional.

Members of the Aaronic priesthood also attend the Young Men's Mutual Improvement Association weekly meeting. Scouting has long been integrated into this Church auxiliary. The awards include a Faith in God Award, On My Honor Youth Award and On My Honor Adult Award. My own experience may be pertinent here, although it dates to the 1950's. I began scouting in what I personally call a "real" scout pack. We did all of the scouting things, including plenty of Wyoming rough-country camping and survival skills. Then, upon my parents' urging, I switched to LDS YMMIA, where we did some knot tying, and got additional religious instruction. At present, the program's idea of

---

[525] The Church of Jesus Chris of Latter-day Saints, "Preparing to Enter the Holy Temple" (lds.org/manual/preparing-to-enter-the-holy-temple).

camping consists mostly of annual or biannual men's camps, organized by the ward or stake. Is it unfair to say that it is a bit like a safari where the African experts have arranged five-star tents with hot and cold running water for the Western "explorer"?

A parallel auxiliary exists, the Young Women. The participants are age graded. A girl (Young Woman) is a Beehive (age 12-13), a Mia Maid (14-15) and a Laurel (16-17).

> Beehives today learn to work together in cooperation and harmony as they strengthen their faith in Jesus Christ and prepare to stand for truth and righteousness. This is a time to 'arise and shine forth' (D&C 115:5)... Mia Maids today learn about love, faith, and purity as they strengthen their testimony and accept and act upon the Young Women values... Laurels today are finishing their preparation to make and keep sacred covenants and receive the ordinances of the temple.[526]

One would not be far from the mark to understand the whole process to mean, "to prepare for marriage in the temple." The Church has a Girls Camp independent of the Girls Scouts of America, which has not been embraced due to its progressive feminist stands.

By coopting the scouting program into its YMMIA, and shunning the Girls Scouting Association altogether, the Church makes significant progress towards its goal of insulating its youth from the world of the "gentiles." It cannot protect them from the public school system, but tries to offset it as much as possible with its seminary and institute systems. When missionaries are sent out, they too are protected, first by being sent out in pairs and rarely out of each other's sight, and by the injunction, "You have been sent to teach, not to be taught." A missionary should be able to detect that a contact is not progressing in the lesson program, and wants to teach the missionaries. At that point, it is time to politely excuse oneself, and move on to someone "whom the spirit has prepared."

The LDS infant at the beginning of this presentation thus has the first two decades of his or her life more or less programmed. In this respect, there is little difference between being baptized at birth and at age eight. The situation of males is especially interesting. At the tender age of twelve, a boy will become a low-level member of the LDS lay clergy. Progression up to teacher and priest is pretty much automatic.

---

[526] The Church of Jesus Christ of Latter-day Saints, "Young Women Classes and Symbols" (lds.org/young-women/personal-progress)

Few teenage boys will be precocious and assertive enough to desire to escape the process, much less do it. The issue often is not religion proper, but a desire to please parents in a close family. At twelve, one does not say, "Sorry dad, but I really do not want to be a deacon." Furthermore, one's best friend often is already a deacon. Right? Even as a teen, when I fancied myself an atheist, I stayed with the program. Not wanting to waste my time, in college I accompanied my parents to church and studied New Testament syntax, in Greek, with a neighbor giving a very predictable talk in the background. Already in high school, my stake president and bishop visited us, together, and warned my parents that my Sunday School teacher could not compete with me, and if I did not stop teaching atheism in her class, I would be barred from coming to church. I did my best to make my parents happy, or at least spare them embarrassment.

Some drop-off might happen in the progression to elder, and then temple marriage. The boys will have gone to work or to university, or both, and some of them will no longer reside at home. The LDS university and institute systems are only a partial solution. But the Church has made every effort to bridge this gap, from about age seventeen to elder, and temple marriage. At that point, the cycle begins all over. Cradle to temple.

The Appeal of LDS Theology

Many Latter-day Saints are especially attached to the promises made to them, if they are worthy, promises of becoming kings and queens for eternity, gods and goddesses over their own kingdoms. Who would not be attracted? Far from fearing death, or trembling at the thought of judgment day, many are confident of their election, filled with faith, and hopeful for their future, as described by Orson Pratt, in a biographical sketch qua encomium for his assassinated brother Parley P. Pratt, in 1857:

> O, how pleasant is the death of a righteous person! He lays down his body with the sure and certain hope of coming forth from the tomb in the morning of the first resurrection, to reign as a mighty King and Prince of

the Most High God, to sit enthroned in eternal glory, ruling with power and dominion for ever and ever.[527]

In this status, they will continue to enjoy the presence of the worthy members of their family and enjoy righteous conjugal bliss to engender the spirits to populate future creations.

The Anguish of Apostasy

Once a young man and a young woman have completed this part of their journey, and leave the temple, man and wife, potentially forever, they have not just wed each other, but the couple have become wedded to a doctrine at once potentially beautiful, and potentially dreadful.

In Mormonism, the highest level of salvation, as kings and queens in the Celestial Kingdom, can only be achieved as a couple. One's eternal future now is in the hands of the other, as much as oneself. Depending on one's minimal definition of heaven, it can get more complicated. For when the children enter the picture, and the parent-child bonding happens, for many heaven can be unimaginable without them as well. But for an entire family unit to achieve this highest Celestial glory, each member of an often large Mormon family, and their spouses, must be worthy. There can be considerable pressure on each to measure up.

To complete the picture, Mormons who have not measured up sufficiently to enter the Celestial Kingdom will potentially go to the next kingdom down, the Terrestrial Kingdom. These are they "who have testimonies of Christ and the divinity of the great latter-day work and who are not valiant, but who are instead lukewarm in their devotion to the Church and to righteousness."[528] The key to this is that they have testimonies. Apparently, if Mormons do not even meet this criterion, they must go to the lowest kingdom. Furthermore, even though persons in a higher kingdom can visit those below, those below cannot visit someone in a higher kingdom. The potential fate of a family thus split asunder for all of eternity can be dreadful to contemplate.

---

[527] Orson Pratt, "Biographical Sketch of Parley P. Pratt," extracted from the *Millennial Star*, July 4, 1857, in an appendix to Parley P. Pratt, Jr., ed., *Autobiography of Parley P. Pratt*, 419.
[528] McConkie, *Mormon Doctrine*, 784.

This is bad enough when individuals just did not measure up. But it is totally different in the case of apostasy. In such a situation, the breakup is happening due to a deliberate act of the apostate, or so it is perceived. The believing spouse sees the other as jeopardizing his or her chances for the highest Celestial salvation, the chance to be a king or queen for all eternity. The parent sees the rebellious child as rejecting the family, and destroying the entire material and emotional parental investment. The child sees the recalcitrant parent as willfully inflicting pain and suffering. Throughout it all, harsh and hurtful words are spoken, words one might later regret, but which cannot be taken back, or truly expunged. A father might say, "Think what a serious terrible decision you are making!" And the mother, "How can you do this to me?"

A similar anguish is experienced by the family member departing from the faith. This begins with self-doubt. What if in fact Mormonism is somehow true, and I am wrong? What if I am risking my eternal soul, just because I dare to evaluate the evidence by scientific rather than spiritual criteria, and go by my own assessment, against the authority of the Church, and so many LDS scholars defending the *Book of Mormon*? And even if I am right, is Mormonism more wrong than the others? Can I justify the pain and suffering I am causing, just to insist on my own views?

A lot depends on the personalities, and perhaps the wisdom, of the family members. In some cases, the believers stand rigid and unbending. In others, they give priority to family unity, at least for the time available on this earth, and every effort is made to extend love and understanding to the apostate member. Much also depends on the personality of the apostate. Some become proselytes for their new cause. What if the case involves an older or adult sibling influencing a younger one, a minor? From the perspective of the believing family members, this can be truly the last straw. Others who have lost their faith are able to walk away from Mormonism with considerable ease, and move on with their lives. Others drop out of society, psychologically paralyzed, sometimes for years. A very few even commit suicide.

There are people who work to help those who are going through this struggle. One example is the website exmormon.com. It states its mission as follows: "Recovery from Mormonism. A site for those who are questioning their faith in the Mormon Church and for those who need support as they transition their lives to a normal life. We are not affiliated with any religion and we do not advocate any religion."

Another cross to be born, all the way around, is the belief that one cannot truly be leaving the faith because there is information that makes belief impossible. Apostasy happens because the apostate is seriously attracted to some secret sin, usually a sexual sin. This ignoble motivation has undermined his or her faith. When a close acquaintance abandoned his mission, he had a discussion with a Church leader, who, at some point asked, "Brother, are you a homosexual? If so, we should talk about it. The Church can work with you on this problem." My very hetero friend had to restrain a chuckle.

Thou Shalt Be Happy

Life as a Mormon at times reminded me of the story of the Communist rally, where the speaker says, "Comrades, when the revolution comes, we will all eat strawberries and cream." A voice from the rear says, "But comrade, I don't like strawberries and cream." The speaker replies, "Comrade, when the revolution comes, you will eat strawberries and cream, and you will like it!"

One might think that apostasy is primarily motivated by one's inability to believe, for whatever reason (weak in faith? possessing disconfirming information?). Some would have us believe that it is due to a deviant lifestyle. But often enough, the same thing that keeps some members in the Church, alienates others. As one former Mormon wrote:

> I can't think of a more unbearable organization to suffer social anxiety in. I have a form of social phobia and grew up in a very Mormon involved family. Speaking in church made me seriously ill. I remember the Saturday before I was assigned to give a talk in sacrament meeting as a child. I was crossing the street and the thought hit me that maybe I would be hit by a car and not have to speak tomorrow. I hated and dreaded bishop interviews. They were so awkward and invasive. My face would turn red and I would sweat with embarrassment even as an adult. All of the forced fake friendships and socializing drove me nuts. Visiting teaching was a nightmare especially while visiting less actives. Wow and the mission experience as someone with social anxiety might as well have been hell. I lasted 6 months before I couldn't handle it anymore and went home. I was told by my parents I just couldn't hack it.[529]

---

[529] Posted by turnonthelights on exmormon.com (accessed 5 November 2015)

The cultural dogma is that Mormonism, if lived properly, brings happiness. So, it follows, that if you are not happy, you are not living Mormonism properly. One feels pressure to be cheerful. Perhaps this is in keeping with the Western song, "Oh give me a home...where seldom is heard a discouraging word." Without elaborating further, the point here is that some find Mormon society a bit suffocating. Perhaps for some, it is a bit like a bow-only Japanese trying to socialize with bear-hug Russians.

The Plight of Willful Women

As one might expect, with family being at the center of Mormon theology, and families being historically larger than the American average, the role of women centers on the home, supporting their husband's priesthood calling, and raising children in and committed to the faith. Numerous articles in the now defunct *Improvement Era*, and today's *Ensign*, drive this message home. Any suggestion that women might someday hold the priesthood is a nonstarter in Mormonism.

Polygamy is indicative of the place given to women in the Church. Although today, the LDS Church will proclaim loud and clear that it no longer solemnizes plural marriages, and will excommunicate members who live in a polygamous marriage, the truth is never really told. The doctrine was never changed; rather, its practice was suspended in favor of a decision to obey the law of the land. Even this happened when the law of the land was enforced by the courts. The law was challenged, all the way to the Supreme Court in a Utah case, and again in an Idaho case. In both decisions, almost word for word the same, the Court upheld the law, against the constitutional guarantee of separation of church and state on the grounds that the practice of polygamy had provoked social unrest, and abolishing it was in the public good.

The practice of LDS dissimulation, discussed above, means that one must tell the truth, but not necessarily the whole truth. The doctrine regarding polygamy has never been changed, and it is fully expected that all of the many wives of Joseph Smith and Brigham Young (followed by others) will be theirs for eternity, if they are worthy.

It is also the case that plural marriages are indeed solemnized in the LDS temples. If a man, say at age forty, loses his wife, sealed to him in the temple, he may remarry again in the temple, with the expectation that he will have both wives in the next life, if all are worthy. In 2002, as a

U.S. diplomat at the US embassy in Algiers, I brought a retired federal judge of the ninth circuit (in California) to Algeria for a program on judicial reform. At a dinner given by the Minister of Justice in his honor, our host brought up polygamy, since many educated Muslims know that, like them, Mormons believe in polygamy, and he had found out that our federal judge was a Mormon. I commented that in present-day LDS practice, a second wife can still be sealed to a man if his first wife has died, even though she too had been sealed to him. The judge spoke up with a glowing face and bright smile, "Oh yes! That is my case. My dearly beloved first wife died, and my second wife has also been sealed to me. I fully expect to have both wives in the next life." His second wife sat at his side, silent, but smiling nicely.

The same revelation that created the "new and everlasting covenant" of temple marriage, also approved both polygamy, and in certain cases, concubinage (D&C 132).

> 37. Abraham received concubines, and they bore him children; and it was accounted unto him for righteousness; ...
> 38. David also received many wives and concubines, and also Solomon and Moses my servants... and in nothing did they sin...

Joseph Smith's first wife, Emma, did not approve, and militated against the practice, even publicly, in the newly formed relief society. Her husband was not to be opposed in this:

> 52. And let mine handmaid Emma Smith [Joseph Smith's first wife], receive all those that have been given unto my servant Joseph, and who are virtuous and pure before me...
> 54. But if she will not abide this commandment she shall be destroyed, saith the Lord

The Relief Society was suspended. When Smith was murdered, she remained in Illinois, and maintained that she was Joseph's only wife, resting comfortably in the realm of plausible denial, possibly considering his other women to be nothing more than mistresses. She may have had a less polite word for them.

For those LDS women who do the math, the situation will get worse in the next life. For one thing, it is always possible that when all the loose ends are taken care of during the millennium of Christ's rule on earth, some worthy women might get their chance for the highest glory by being sealed to a worthy man, even if he already has a worthy wife. A monogamous couple could end up polygamous, for eternity.

Even worse, according to LDS doctrine, the gods and goddesses procreate, eternally, producing spirit children, who are born in human form with material, albeit more refined bodies. As kings and queens, they will create and populate new planets, adding to the many mansions of the Father that Jesus referred to in the New Testament. Last century, there was little knowledge of the size of the population of this planet, and no way to imagine that it would reach seven billion in the first decade of the third millennium CE. For the procreation needed to populate just one planet, a goddess would have to bear billions of spirit children. Life for eternity for her would be as a mass-production baby machine. Resurrected bodies would have to have amazing memories, to remember the name and face of each child. One wonders, "Does she also have to nurse them?"

Some women, who have done the math, tolerate the situation by not thinking about it too much, with the admonition that we really do not know all that there is to know about the hereafter, and that this whole discussion is "going a tad off the deep end." But an LDS woman can be excused for finding all of the above a bit overwhelming.

Some urge change, while remaining in the faith. An example is a group called Young Mormon Feminists. On their website, they assert that they are young, they are Mormon and they are feminists.[530]

Like feminists in other denominations, LDS feminists have demanded the priesthood, and bolster their position by references to prophetesses in the Bible. The Church has at its disposal a strong reply, within the givens of its theology. Indeed, prophetesses have existed, and can exist today. All members are urged to pray and seek guidance in their lives. Women can receive a divine answer in the form of inspiration, or perhaps even a revelation. But they cannot receive revelations for the Church. And a prophetess does not have the priesthood. Even Joseph Smith had several important revelations, and became a prophet, even before receiving the Aaronic priesthood. This has not satisfied the women, who note that there is actually no passage in the Bible or the Mormon canon saying explicitly that women cannot have the priesthood. For a long time, persons of African descent could not hold the priesthood, but when the time was right (expedient), this doctrine and

---

[530] As of my last access of youngmormonfeminists.org (16/1/2017).

practice were changed. Certainly by now the time must have come for women too.

Where Have All the Apostates Gone?

A subject worthy of investigation, about which little is known, is what happens to the apostates. Some of course found breakaway sects, but even these continue to believe in the *Book of Mormon* and Joseph Smith. Others have founded Christian, essentially Protestant congregations for former Mormons, rejecting the Mormon scriptures and prophets. Others have founded groups to serve former Mormons, and those who are no longer satisfied by the LDS faith. An example of this is Jerald and Sandra Tanner, and their Utah Lighthouse Ministry. They affirm their faith in Christianity, author books arguing against Mormon claims and operate a bookstore to make such literature available in the Salt Lake City area, and beyond. A host of others also have undertaken to research Mormon history and produce books and articles based on their research.

My own hypothesis is that most pass through a stage first where they decide that even if Mormonism is not literally true, it is as good as anything else out there. This stage can last a while. Eventually, a few become total atheists, while most either continue to be Christians, but never actually joining another denomination, or believe only in the existence of a higher power. Most probably do not change formally to a competing denomination. This would be a good topic for one, or more likely several PhD dissertations.

Probably only a small proportion of apostates have actually sought to have their names removed from the rolls, i.e. excommunication. This step is a very serious matter for Church officials. It does occur from time to time. After my sister Jodi's requested-by-self excommunication, she felt relieved, and glad that home teachers would no longer be coming to her door, but resented that the elders who came for the process behaved as though they held authority over her in some sort of tribunal.

Cultural Mormons

The LDS Church is near the top of the list with respect to church attendance. Gallop polling done in 2002-2005 found that the percent of attendance once/week or nearly once/week was 68% (Church of Christ), 67% (LDS Church), 65% (Pentecostal), 61% (Protestant, other), 61%

(Southern Baptist), 56% (other Baptist), and others on down to 45% (Catholic) and 44% (for both the Methodists, and the Presbyterians). These figures are based on 11,000 interviews.[531] If about 70% of LDS members on the books are active weekly or almost, it would appear that some practice occasionally, but perhaps as many as 20% are essentially nonpracticing. Some of these are persons who no longer consider themselves Mormon. With respect to those who have lost their faith, we do not know how many fit the category Fergusen referred to in his advice to a friend:

> Why not say the right things and keep your membership in the great fraternity [the LDS Church], enjoying the good things you like and discarding the ones you can't swallow (and keeping your mouths shut)? Hypocritical? Maybe. But perhaps a realistic way of dealing with a very difficult problem. There is lots left in the Church to enjoy—and thousands of members have done, and are doing, what I suggest you consider doing.

Some who attend regularly may not believe, but are cultural Mormons. My guess is that today's Latter-day Saints are a very diverse group, in many ways.

And Then There Is Joseph Smith

I am decidedly not qualified to do a professional psychoanalysis or other similar evaluation of Joseph Smith, the man. But one can identify some points that must be born in mind in forming an informed personal opinion. First, he obviously was imbued with belief in concepts from the occult, including curses and guardian spirits of treasure that could appear to a person to reveal its location. Second, he believed that some people can and do receive inspired dreams and even apparitions, such as those reported in the papers, but especially those of his father. Third, as a scryer, he believed that he personally had a gift to gain access to hidden knowledge and treasure. Fourth, according to his mother, at an early age he became fascinated by the ancient inhabitants of the land, and their "degenerate" descendants, the Indians. His brother Hyrum had attended a school established to convert these native Americans. Fifth, like his father, he was critical of the religions of his day. Sixth, even so, he was a

---

[531] Gallup, in Frank Newport, "Mormons, Evangelical Protestants, Baptists Top Church Attendance List" (14 April 2006).

religious person who read the Bible and clearly entertained the possibility of a career in religion, as indicated by his having sought out the opportunity to train to be a Methodist exhorter, and to actually perform as such. Seventh, I see no reason to doubt that he had had some sort of dream experiences, either at night or while micro-sleeping, with content that he remembered and interpreted differently over time. Eighth, through his debate training and by natural ability, he was able to acquire a reputation as a scryer and, eventually, for having acquired gold in the form of an ancient record. Some found him to be very convincing.

Even so, it is clear that one cannot believe sincerely that one has and handles gold plates, the Urim and Thummim spectacles, and the sword and breastplate of Laban, month after month, when none of these things exists. He must have had a keen awareness of the implications of composing and penning words from God Himself, and then editing and changing those words when convenient. So too, his substantial modification of the Egyptian papyri to fabricate Facsimiles nos. 1 & 2 for his fictional *Book of Abraham* required careful and studied deception.

As we attempt to peep into the world of purveyors of the divine, things become a bit murky. Parables are an example. Did the prodigal son really exist, or his father and brethren? How important is it that the story be true? One might think that it is the meaning that counts, and that the parable is just a way of teaching. Perhaps the purpose of the parable is not even that. When Christ's disciples asked about a parable, he replied:

> And he said, Unto you it is given to know the mysteries of the kingdom of God: but to others in parables; that seeing they might not see, and hearing they might not understand. (Luke 8:10)

This verse has been grist for the exegetical mills for 2,000 years.

Social Psychology has studied techniques of guilt neutralization. Most perpetrators find ways to justify their actions. We are face to face here with the possibility that the gold plates came to be used as an effective vehicle to present an inspired but rough outline of Pre-Columbian history filled with fictional events that were essentially the *sort of thing that they felt must certainly have happened*. By far the more important thing was the exhortations, sermons, theological explanations and religious disputations that fleshed out this historical skeleton. They constituted an exposition of the Gospel of Jesus that far excelled the errors of the religions of their day, which they roundly despised.

The role of the gold plates reminds me of a passage that I will paraphrase from *Stealing Heaven*, a fanciful historical and biographical film of the forbidden love of Peter Abélard and Héloïse. She accuses her rich guardian uncle of selling bogus Christian relics, often for very high prices. He retorts, "My dear, I lack the expertise to know if they are true or bogus, but I do know that they strengthen the faith of many in the Gospel of Lord Jesus, and if I realize a profit in this service to Our Lord, I see no harm in that."

Alternatively, Smith may have started with a very dark view of the existing churches. Perhaps all churches are no more than Man reaching out to God. He may have thought, "I can produce one better than those, while rendering a great service to the Lord by bringing the Indians to His Gospel." Perhaps he believed that whatever idea came to him, it came from the Spirit, just as ancient Greek poets gave credit to their muses.

But his work went well beyond abstract theology and worship. All through his career, he made representations to his followers, and gave them commands from on high, that put their assets at risk, and brought financial ruin, eventually including decisions that inevitably would result in injury and loss of life among both his loyal followers and his enemies. Also, contrary to the apostolic orientations of his earliest colleagues, and puritanical mores in his *Book of Mormon*, he used priesthood and ritual to build a hierarchy giving himself a position modeled after that of Moses, and a marital life modeled after Solomon. Moreover, contrary to the BOM text, he eventually created the only example of Christian polytheism.

Joseph Smith was a man of signal ability, inexhaustible energy and striking creativity. But by the time of his burial, his movement was stripped of the Smiths, Whitmers, Cowdery, Rigdon and Harris. A much more pragmatic leadership retained almost all of Smith's foundational legacy, while consolidating his scriptural community in the cocoon-like isolation of the Utah Territory.

A Scriptural Community like No Other

In the beginning of the current era, the Christian community was based on the "good news," the story of Jesus, and doctrines of the New Testament. Over time, this community subdivided into various communities, each still holding to the Good Book as the anchor of their faith. There have been many detractors. They could assail some details, such as the idea that sickness is caused by demon possession, but nothing sufficiently substantial to shake the foundations of Christianity.

Only the *Book of Mormon* posits an entire and distinct civilization of an Israelite people, spanning a full millennium, replete with details of language, tools, architecture, fauna and flora, all being demonstrably alien to the continents where they are situated. The challenge that this poses to its scriptural community is qualitatively different. This scripture offers more and different research opportunities within the canons of empirical research methods.

Against all odds, the farm boy from upstate New York, and his collaborators, built a viable scriptural community that attracted believers in the thousands by 1844. Immediately after the official organization of the Church, he sent new converts out only a few months or less in their new faith, armed with a copy of their gold bible, a copy of the Articles and Covenants and a preacher's license. This bold, sometimes rash use of delegation of authority at times backfired, but mostly it reaped a bounteous crop of new members. Since then, there has been nothing but progress. True, in most countries of the world, the percent LDS is less than 1%. Church records indicate that as of about 2015, for the United States it is 2%. No European country, nor any Asian country reaches 1%. In North/Central America, only El Salvador reaches 2%, although Honduras is 1.93%. In South America, two countries are over 3%, Chile and Uruguay. However, in Oceania, Tonga is nearly 60% Mormon, Samoa 39%, American Samoa 30%, the Cook Islands 19%, Kiribati 17% and the Marshall Islands 10%. New Zealand is 2.5%, while Australia and Papua New Guinea are under 1%.[532] The higher percentages in Oceania are concentrated in countries with small populations. They reflect the strong missionary commitment to this region, based on the LDS belief that the BOM voyages of Hagoth brought a Nephite population to those

---

[532] From *Wikipedia*, "The Church of Jesus Christ of Latter-day Saints membership statistics" (accessed 16/1/2017).

"isles of the sea." Joseph Smith himself sent a mission to the Society Islands in 1843. In any case, Mormonism has become a global faith.

However, we do not know the "health" of these LDS communities abroad. In mid-summer of 1963, Henry D. Moyle Jr., President of the French East Mission, called an emergency mission conference in Marseille to find a solution to the problem of recent converts dropping quickly into inactivity. Well over half of the converts so far that year were already inactive. In some cases, missionaries anxious to get a baptism had glossed over the word of wisdom, or the law of tithing. In other cases, when a good-looking baptizing elder was transferred to another city, the young woman or women he had converted lost interest in her new faith. At the time, it was said among us there that it was easier to convert the French than the Germans, but more of the latter remained converted. The above statistics are based largely on church records. We cannot know how many converts still consider themselves to be Mormon.

In the same timeframe, members abroad successfully brought the LDS authorities to understand that the commitment of converts was undermined by the emphasis on temple endowments coupled with the absence of any temple in their country. Many and perhaps most could not afford to travel to the nearest temple. Again demonstrating the Church's ability to innovate, President Gordon B. Hinckley inaugurated a program of mini temples in 1998 when there were only 51 temples. By 2017, about 180 temples were on the LDS roster, most of them completed and others announced.

Even after nearly two centuries, the LDS community remains as strong as ever. Certainly it is more united than it was in the crisis years at Kirtland. But there is evidence that secular challenges have taken a certain toll. For three years, from 2000 through 2002, the number of full-time missionaries was over 60,000, reaching 61,638 in 2002 (.53% of membership). The following year, this number fell to 56,237, and the next year to 51,067. One wonders if this was partly the effect of a reaction to the terrorist attack on the Twin Towers in New York City. It took some time for the numbers to recover. On 31/12/2010 the number was only 52,225 (.37% of membership).[533] The Church had begun a campaign to encourage members to serve, but with inadequate results. Then, a new strategy was adopted. It had always been possible for retired

---

[533] Annual statistical reports in *Ensign*.

couples to serve, but many were in difficult financial circumstances, and a long period of service was daunting. The authorities announced "As of September 1, 2011, couples may serve for 6, 12, 18, or 23 months. In addition, a housing cap of $1,400 (US) per month will be established." The response was impressive. By 31/12/2012 the number jumped to 58,990, and reached 85,147 by 31/12/2014 (.55% of membership). This is slightly higher than before the decline as a percent of membership, a decade earlier. Knowing that even then, many who were willing to serve were unable, the Church instituted the program of Church-Service Missionaries, who serve many hours working with the full-time missionaries, performing other tasks to free them up to focus solely on proselytism. The number of this new cadre reached 30,404 in 31/12/2014. This reaction to the situation shows the creativity of the Church, and its ability to mobilize its flock. But we must bear in mind that much of the jump in full-time missionaries came from the ranks of retirees. Clearly there still in 2014 there must have been a decline in the number of the traditional young missionaries as a percent of church membership. The issue of retaining the commitment of LDS young men must remain a concern for the leadership.

There is another potential area of concern. The LDS Church is no more forthcoming regarding its finances than other denominations. But it may be that tithe paying might take a bit of a hit even before attendance. If a significant number of members pay as they are able, and reduce that from twelve months a year to ten, the Church not only takes a financial hit, but has an indicator of another area of secular impact. The focus would be on two groups: first, church-going folk who have decided that even if Mormonism is not the only true church, it is as good as anything else out there; and second, cultural Mormons. These may be susceptible to the notion that there can be no serious consequence in the next life if one were to pay ten percent less, or even as little as six months out of twelve. The Church has significant expenses, including the operation of its university system, and maintenance of many temples and thousands of chapels worldwide. Many of its assets are non-revenue-producing. On the other hand, it may well be that the Church could take as much as a ten percent hit and still continue all of its programs without a decrease in its net worth adjusted for inflation. If so, this decrease may not be so much a concern for its finances, as for the spiritual health of its members.

23. Quest for Exaltation in a Secular Society

The LDS Church has demonstrated the effectiveness of creating a ritual and participatory cocoon to get a large part of each generation from cradle to temple. Most of this capability has developed apace with and in response to exposure to disconfirming information. But, unlike the traditional Christian denominations, the LDS community is based on a scripture that is empirically testable and does not pass the tests. It is inevitable that archaeological and other realities will march on as well, and become increasingly well known and understood. Increasing awareness of the archaeological verdict will provide friction eroding gains in the LDS base and robbing it of some of its best and brightest, thereby impeding its advancement. Even so, the Church will undoubtedly thrive for the foreseeable future.

Appendices

Appendix 1. Additional Analysis of BOM-KJ Variants

Changes in Number

There are cases where a *Book of Mormon* variant finds agreement in the manuscripts, but, alas, no agreement of significance. A good example is the case where there is a change in number, such as "The men raised their hand" and "The men raised their hands." The number in these cases is optional. The following are the cases that found some agreement where there is a change from singular to plural (where the italics are original in the King James):

Variants in Number: Singular to Plural

(Agreement is listed in parentheses: H=Hebrew; D=Dead Sea Scrolls; G=Greek; S=Syriac (Aramaic); T=Targumim (Aramaic); L=Latin; E=Ethiopic; C=Coptic; A=Arabic. The sources are listed in Bibliography 1.)

Exodus20:5:	visiting the iniquity of the fathers upon the children	(GSTY)
Mosiah 13:13	visiting the iniquities of the fathers upon the children	
Exodus 20:5:	unto the third and fourth *generation*	(S)
Mosiah 13:13	unto the third and fourth generations	
Isaiah 3:8:	their tongue and their doings *are* against the Lord	(GSC)
2 Nephi 13:8:	their tongues and their doings are against the Lord	
Isaiah 3:9:	Woe unto their soul!	(LA)
2 Nephi 13:9:	Woe unto their souls,	
Isaiah 5:24:	their blossom shall go up as dust	(A?)
2 Nephi 15:24:	their blossoms shall go up as dust	
Isaiah 9:9:	the inhabitant of Samaria	(GSLC)
2 Nephi 19:9:	the inhabitants of Samaria	
Isaiah 13:4:	the Lord of hosts mustereth the host of the battle	(S)
2 Nephi 23:4:	the Lord of Hosts mustereth the hosts of the battle	
Isaiah 13:18	their eye shall not spare children	(GSTCA)
2 Nephi 23:18:	their eyes shall not spare children	

Isaiah 14:21; 2 Nephi 24:21:	for the iniquity of their fathers for the iniquities of their fathers	(GTSCA)
Isaiah 14:32: 2 Nephi 24:32:	What shall *one* then answer the messengers of the nation? What shall then answer the messengers of the nations?	(GSTLC)
Isaiah 29:13: 2 Nephi 27:25:	have removed their heart far from me have removed their hearts far from me	(A)
Isaiah 49:6: 1 Nephi 21:6:	my salvation unto the end of the earth my salvation unto the ends of the earth	(GSTA)
Isaiah 51:11: 2 Nephi 8:11:	*shall be* upon their head shall be upon their heads	(DSTL)
Isaiah 53:6: Mosiah 14:6:	hath laid on him the iniquity of us all hath laid on him the iniquities of us all	(GSTLCA)
Isaiah 53:8: Mosiah 14:8:	for the transgression of my people for the transgressions of my people	(GSLC)
Isaiah 53:12: Mosiah 14:12	the sin of many the sins of many	(DGSTLC)
Malachi 3:14: 3 Nephi 24:14:	we have kept his ordinance we have kept his ordinances	(GSTLC)

In Isaiah 49:6 above, the word for 'end' means the furthest point, not the end of times, and so here there is no difference in meaning.

In the legend for the table above, "H=Hebrew" was listed *pro forma*. As can be seen, there is no agreement in the original language, Hebrew. This is typical of agreement in general, when it happens. The other sources are translations, and so by definition, changed. As in all translation, some change happens either because the receiving language requires it grammatically, or prefers it. And in some cases, it is idiolectical, i.e., according to what the translator feels sounds better, his personal speech habit.

Variants in Number: Singular to Plural

(Agreement is listed in parentheses: H=Hebrew; D=Dead Sea Scrolls; G=Greek; S=Syriac (Aramaic); T=Targumim (Aramaic); L=Latin; E=Ethiopic; C=Coptic; A=Arabic. The sources are listed in Bibliography 1.)

Exodus 20:3:	Thou shalt have no other gods before me.	(T)
Mosiah 12:35:	Thou shalt have no other God before me.	
Isaiah 13:22	her days shall not be prolonged	(T)
2 Nephi 23:22	her day shall not be prolonged	
Isaiah 48:18	O that thou hadst hearkened to my commandments	(S)
1 Nephi 20:18	O that thou hadst hearkened to my commandment	
Isaiah 51:5	mine arms shall judge the people	(GLSA)
2 Nephi 8:5	mine arm shall judge the people	
Isaiah 53:3	we hid as it were *our* faces from him	(H[?]GLA)
Mosiah 14:3	we hid as it were our face from him	
Matthew 3:10	the axe is laid unto the root of the trees	(SL)
Alma 5:52	the ax is laid at the root of the tree	

In the Isaiah 53:3 case, above, the agreement in Hebrew is marked with a question mark because the word for face in Hebrew is *pânîm*, which is plural in form, but most usually singular in meaning. Whether it is singular or plural in meaning is determined purely by context, as in this case, where the meaning is plural. But in English, it makes no difference.

In all other cases, the agreement occurs in translations of the original language, just as is the case in the group where the change was from singular to plural.

Variants Involving Verbs

The largest group is those that exhibit a change in tense:

Variants with a Change in Tense

(Agreement is listed in parentheses: H=Hebrew; D=Dead Sea Scrolls; G=Greek; S=Syriac (Aramaic); T=Targumim (Aramaic); L=Latin; E=Ethiopic; C=Coptic; A=Arabic. The sources are listed in Bibliography 1.)

Isaiah 2:12	For the day of the Lord of Hosts shall be upon	(TA)
2 Nephi 12:12	For the day of the Lord of Hosts soon cometh upon	
Isaiah 3:6	a man shall take hold of his brother...*saying*	(A)
2 Nephi 13:6	a man shall take hold of his brother...and shall say	

Isaiah 9:7	Of the increase of *his* government and peace *there shall be* no end	(GSA)
2 Nephi 19:7	Of the increase of government and peace there is no end	
Isaiah 14:16	They that see thee shall narrowly look upon thee, and consider thee, saying	(GSA)
2 Nephi 24:16	They that see thee shall narrowly look upon thee, and shall consider the, and shall say	
Malachi 3:7	But ye said, Wherein shall we return?	(TCA)
3 Nephi 24:7	But ye say, Wherein shall we return?	
Matthew 3:10	every tree which bringeth not forth good fruit is hewn down	(SLCA)
Alma 5:52	every tree that bringeth not forth good fruit shall be hewn down	
Matthew 5:13	but if the salt have lost his savour	(SL)
3 Nephi 12:13	but if the salt shall lose its savor	
Matthew 5:25	and thou be cast into prison	(GL)
3 Nephi 12:25	and thou shalt be cast into prison	
Matthew 6:2	Therefore when thou doest *thine* alms	(LC)
	Therefore, when ye shall do your alms	

Minor Changes

Forty-five of the variants that find agreement in at least some ancient text are simply the addition of the word 'and.' In four cases, the word 'and' is deleted. In one verse, 'till' is substituted by 'and,' and in another 'but' is substituted by 'and.' In three cases 'that' (conjunction) is added, where it is optional. In one verse, 'according' is changed to 'according as' with no meaning change. Two variants enjoy agreement where 'wherefore' is changed from interrogative to declarative, but the punctuation was largely done by the typesetter. 'Behold' and 'yea' are deleted with slight meaning change, and find agreement in translations. In three verses, the deletion of optional repetitions of 'for' found agreement in some translations, and the addition of optional additions of 'with' also found some agreement, all being cases where there was no meaning change. In two cases, added prepositional phrases ('of them' and 'unto them') found some agreement in translations, but meaning was not changed. Optional, almost pleonastic, pronouns were added in two cases: 'that' changed to 'they that' and 'that' changed to 'she that.'

Appendix 2. Mistranslation in the King James Version of Isaiah

Additional Mistranslations or Weak Translations in the KJ	
HM: the Hebrew Masoretic text Q: the Great Isaiah Scroll found at Qumran =Q designates orthographic differences to HM T: the Aramaic Targum of Jonathan (Yonatan, Sperber edition) S: the Greek Septuagint (edited by Rahlfs) Editions and Dictionaries: All are listed in the bibliographies. Transliteration: In keeping with the early date of Isaiah, b, g, d, k, p & t are not aspirated after vowels.	
Text at Issue with Chapter & Verse	Translation & Comments
2:6: thou hast foresaken thy people HM: $n\bar{a}ta\check{s}t\hat{a}$ (=Q) T: $^{\ni a}r\bar{e}^y\ \check{s}\partial baqt\bar{u}n\ da\d{h}lat\ taqq\bar{\imath}p\bar{a}\ da\text{-}h^aw\bar{a}\ p\bar{a}r\bar{\imath}q\ lak\bar{o}n$ S: ἀνῆκεν	HM: you have uprooted your people (literally, to pluck out, uproot; but here the implication is to uproot and cast out like a weed) T: you have forsaken the fear of the (All) Mighty, who was your redeemer S: he foresook
2:6b: they please thomselves (in the children of strangers) HM: $ya\acute{s}p\hat{\imath}q\hat{u}$ (=Q) T: $b\text{-}nim\bar{u}s\bar{e}^y\ {}^{\varsigma}am\partial may\bar{a}\ {}^{\ni}azl\bar{\imath}n$ S: τέκνα πολλὰ ἀλλόφυλα ἐγενήθη αὐτοῖς	HM: they clap (hands with the children of strangers; like us shaking hands, to make deals [the verb literally means "to clap"]) T: (you) have gone with the laws of the nations (gentiles) S: they have had many foreign children
2:19: to shake terribly the earth HM: $la\text{-}{}^{\varsigma a}r\hat{o}\d{s}\ h\bar{a}\text{-}{}^{\ni}\bar{a}re\d{s}$ (=Q) T: $l\partial\text{-}mitbar\ ra\check{s}\check{s}\bar{\imath}^{\varsigma}\bar{e}^y\ {}^{\ni}\bar{\imath}r^{\varsigma}\bar{a}$ S: θραῦσαι τὴν γῆν	HM: the verb means "to fear" & "to terrify"; one might conjecture that it could mean "to tremble in fear" and so translate this passage as "to make the earth tremble in fear" T: to shatter the wicked of the earth S: to shatter the earth
§ **3:3**: the cunning artificer HM: $\d{h}^akam\ \d{h}^ir\bar{a}\check{s}\hat{\imath}m$ (=Q) T: $s\bar{\imath}b$ S: σοφὸν ἀρχιτέκτονα	HM: one skilled in magic, a magician (this may be a gloss to explain the following phrase) T: scholar, senior scholar S: skilled master-builder

3:3: the eloquent orator	
HM: *nəbôn lāḥaš* (=Q)	HM: the verb means to utter, probably whisper (incantations against snakes, etc.; so the phrase is "the expert in incantation")
T: *sōklatān bə-ʿēʸṣā*	T: one intelligent in counsel
S: συνετὸν ἀκροατήν	S: intelligent listener
3:7: a healer	
HM: *ḥōbēš* (=Q)	HM: the verb means "to bind, saddle, imprison", and here, apparently "to bridle", hence "to govern", so that the active participle means "a governor", and is in parallel construction with "ruler"
T: *rēʸš*	T: head, chief
S: ἀρχηγός	T: head, chief
3:8: Jerusalem is ruined	
HM: *kāšəlâ yərûšālaʸim* (=Q)	HM: the verb means "to stumble, stagger as to fall" so the phrase means "Jerusalem has stumbled" and is in parallel construction with "Judah is fallen"
T: *ʾitqīlū yātəbēʸ yərūšalām*	T: those dwelling in Jerusalem have stumbled
S: ἀνεῖται Ιερσυσαλημ	S: Jerusalem is ruined
3:8: to provoke the eyes of his glory	
HM: *l-amrôt ʿênê kəbôdô* (=Q)	HM: the verbal root means "to be rebellious", and here the better translation is "to defy the eyes of his glory"
T: *margəzīn qədām yəqārēʸh*	T: who provoke anger before his dignity
S: ἐταπεινώθη ἡ δόξα αὐτῶν	S: their glory has been brought low
3:18: cauls	
HM: *šəbîsîm* (Q has š/ś instead of s)	HM: a sunburst worn as a hair ornament
T: *šəbīsayā*	T: woman's head decoration, head band
S: κοσύμβους	S: tassels, fringes
3:18: round tires like the moon	
HM: *šahᵃrônîm* (=Q)	HM: small crescent hair ornaments (the word is a diminutive form)
T: *sibkayā*	T: net, hair net
S: μηνίσκους	S: crescent-shaped ornament
3:19: chains	
HM: *nitîpôt* (Q reads *nṭpwt*)	HM: pendants (possibly ear pendants (the variant in Q is orthographic)
T: *ʿinqayā*	T: neck; neck ornament
S: κάθεμα	S: necklace
3:19: muflers	
HM: *rəʿālôt* (=Q)	HM: veils (possibly with an eye slit)
T: *hᵃnisnəsayā*	T: veils
S: τὸν κόσμον τοῦ προσώπου αὐτῶν	S: their face ornamentation

3:20: bonnets HM: *pəʾērîm* (=Q) T: *kəlīlayā* S: τὴν σύνθεσιν τοῦ κόσμου τῆς δόξης	HM: a turban headwrap worn by women T: crown, bridal crown, women's headdress S: the set of decoration of glory
3:20: headbands HM: *qiššurîm* (=Q) T: *qūlmazməsayā* S: ἐμπλόκιον	HM: bands or breast-sashes worn by women T: hair ornament (or curling pins?) S: hair clasp (or wreath)
3:20: tablets HM: *bottê han-nepeš* (=Q) T: *qədāšayā* S: τοὺς δακτυλίους	HM: scent bottles (*bottê*, pl. of "house" is used to mean containers, + *nepeš*, breath; vapor, scent) T: ear or nose rings S: finger rings, signet rings
3:20: earrings HM: *ləḥāšîm* (=Q) T: *ḥᵃlītāyā* S: ἐνώτια	HM: ornamental amulets T: necklace S: earrings (note: S has two items more than HM & T but these seem to match best)
3:22: crisping pins HM: *hā-ḥᵃrîṭîm* (=Q) T: *maḥakayā* (variant: *maḥaṭṭayā*) S: διαφανῆ Λακωνικά	HM: purses T: *maḥakayā*: girdles or breast holders (the variant: pins, needles (for sewing, or decoration) S: a type of Laconian shear (transparent) garment
3:23: glasses HM: *gilyônîm* (Q reads: *glywnym*) T: *maḥzəyātā* S: βύσσινα	HM: either a papyrus item, fine garment made of papyrus, or a transparent or reflective accessory, a type of ornamental mirror (the reading in Q is orthographic) T: mirrors S: fine linen (clothing)
3:23: hoods HM: *ṣənîpôt* (=Q) T: *kitrayā* S: βύσσον	HM: headband, head wrap, women's turban (verbal root means "to wind around") T: crown, fine headdress S: fine linen (with gold and blue interwoven)
3:24: stomacher HM: *pətîgîl* (=Q) T: *məhalləkān bə-gēʸwāh* S: τοῦ χιτῶνος τοῦ μεσοπορφύρου	HM: a fine garment or chest band? T: (instead of) walking in pride S: tunic mixed with purple

5:2: he fenced it	
HM: wa-yʿazzēqahû (=Q)	HM: Semitic evidence indicates that it means "he hoed it, dug up the soil"; cf. post-Biblical Hebrew, "to dig up, hoe"
T: qaddēʸštinūn	T: I sanctified them (the translation here borders on exegisis)
S: φραγμὸν περιέθηκα	S: I set a hedge round about
5:5: shall be eaten up	
HM: lə-bāʿēr (=Q)	HM: the root means "to burn", and this form "to kindle"; hence, "it shall be for kindling (for firewood)" (or figuratively, "for plunder")
T: lə-mībazz	T: for plundering
S: εἰς διαρπαγήν	S: for plunder
5:9: shall be desolate	
HM: lə-šammâ yihyû (=Q)	HM: "shall be in ruins ... without inhabitant" (šannâ is used in passages of horrific destruction, often as a divine judgment)
T: lə-ṣādū	T: shall be for desolation
S: εἰς ἔρημον	S: shall be a desert, desolation
5:12: harp	
HM: kinnôr (Q: lacuna)	HM: zither
T: kinnār	T: a string instrument, lute, lyre
S: κιθάρας	S: cithora, lyre
5:12: viol	
HM: nebel (Q: lacuna)	HM: harp
T: nəbal qatrōs	T: a type of lute or lyre (nebel κιθάρας)
S: ψαλτηρου	S: a string instrument, lyre or harp
5:12: pipe	
HM: ḥālîl (Q unclear)	HM: flute
T: ʾᵃbūbā	T: reed; flute, pipe
S: αὐλῶν	S: flute, pipe
5:14: their glory and their multitude and their pomp	
HM: hᵃdārāh wa-hᵃmônāh û-šʾônāh (=Q)	HM: the pronominal suffix is feminine singular for each noun, and seems to refer to Jerusalem; the word the KJ translated as "pomp" (šāʾôn; with the suffix, šəʾônā) means "her roar (of water), tumult (of battle), din (of merrymaking), etc.
T: yaqqīrēʸhōn w-sīgōyēʸhōn wə-ʾitrəgōšāthōn	T: their honorable (men), their multitudes and their tumultuous parties
S: οἱ ἔνδοξοι καὶ οἱ μεγάλοι καὶ οἱ πλούσιοι καὶ οἱ λοιμοὶ αὐτῆς	S: her honorable men, great men, rich men and destroyers (or plague-ridden)

5:24: the flame consumeth the chaff	
HM: $ḥ^ašaš$ $lehābâ$ $yirpe$	HM: the verb means "to grow slack, wither" and is in the masculine, while "flame" is feminine; so the subject is chaff, i.e., "the chaff of [in] the flame withers"
Q: w-ʾš lwhbt yrph	Q: ʾš is probably an error for $ḥ^ašaš$
T: $yitʾakkəlūn$ $kə$-$qaššā$ ba-$ʾe^yššātā$	T: "they shall be consumed like chaff in the fire"
S: κανθήσεται καλάμη ὑπὸ ἄνθρακος πυρός	S: straw is burned under the hot coals of fire
5:24: they have cast away the law of the Lord	
HM: $mā^ʾasû$ $ʾēt$ $tôrat$ $yahwe$ (=Q)	HM: the verb means to reject: "they have rejected the law of Yahweh"
T: $qaṣṣū$ $bə$-$ʾōrāytā$ $də$-ywy	T: they have cut, destroyed, rejected the law of Yahweh
S: οὐ γὰρ ἠθέλησαν τὸν νόμον κυρίου	S: they have not held to the law of the Lord
6:4: the posts of the door	
HM: $ʾammôt$ has-$sippîm$ (=Q)	HM: threshold pivots? ($sippîm$ is the threshold, i.e., a flat stone underlying and supporting the door frame; but the meaning of $ʾammôt$ is still not resolved, except that they are a feature of, or a part associated with, the threshold, possibly the sockets into which the door pivots fit, or the door pivots, or door posts; in any case, the word "threshold" should be part of the translation)
T: $ʾilwāt$ $si^ypē^y$	T: meanings suggessted for $ʾilwāt$ ($allātā$/$ʾalwātā$) include a piece of aloes wood, a wood span, branch, club, and door post; while meanings for $si^ypē^y$ ($sippē^y$) include a stone block, a course of stone blocks, door sill (threshold) and door post; so that put together one has "the door posts of the threshold" or "the posts of the lintel"
S: ὑπέρθυρον	S: the door lintel
6:7: he laid it upon my mouth	
HM: $yaggaʿ$ $ʿal$ (Q: lacuna)	HM: the verb means "to cause to touch" so: "he caused it to touch my mouth"
T: $sədar$ $bə$-	T: "he arranged it by/at my mouth"
S: ἥψατο	S: "he touched it to my mouth"

6:7: thine iniquity is taken away, and thy sin purged HM: *sār ʿawōnekā wə-haṭṭāʾtkā təkuppār* (Q reads *ḥṭʾwtyk*; change to plural, which was understood anyway)	HM: *sār* (to change direction, turn, turn away, go away, cease to exist) is intransitive, and *ʾawōnekā* (your sin) is the subject of the first clause (hence, "your iniquity has gone away"), and *təkuppār* (3rd person feminine imperfect passive) acquired interrelated meanings of "to cover up, hide" and "to wipe off", but the OT meaning became "to cover, but more usually, to atone (hence: "thy sin is atoned")
T: *yiʿdōn ḥōbāk wa-ḥtāʾak yitkapparūn*	T: the analysis here is similar to HM: "your iniquity has passed away (ceased) and your sins have been atoned"
S: ἀφελεῖ τὰς ἀνομίας σου καὶ τὰς ἁμαρτίας σου περικαθαριεῖ	S: "this (the hot coal) shall take away your illicit deeds and cleanse away your sins"
6:13: teil tree HM: *ʾēlâ* (=Q)	HM: terebinth (the KJ teil tree is a contemporary word for the linden tree (Latin *tilia*), which does not grow in the Middle East; but it later became associated with the terebinth as a result of the KJ mistranslation
T: *būṭmā*	T: terebinth (cf. Arabic *buṭm*)
S: τερέβινθος	S: terebinth
7:1: but could not prevail against it HM: *lō yākōl lə-hillāḥēm ʿāleʸhā* (=Q)	HM: the verb is the infinitive of the "n" passive/middle, which occurs c. 165 times in the OT, and is well known, meaning "to wage war, fight", and "enter into battle", the meaning here, since the Assyrian army of Tiglath-pileser attacked Aram (Syria in the KJ), forcing a withdrawal of the Aramaean-Israelite coalition, giving rise to the statement here: "but could not enter into battle against it"
T: *lā yākēʸl la-ʾgāḥā ʿalah*	T: "could not attack it"
S: οὐκ ἠδυνήθησαν πολιορκῆσαι αὐτήν	S: "could not besiege it"
7:4: for the fierce anger of Rēzin with Syria, and of the son of Remaliah HM: *bā-ḥorî-ʾap rəṣîn wa-ʾarām ū-ben-rəmalyāhū* (Q spelling: *ḥorî*)	HM: "for the fierce anger of Rezin and Aram and the son of Remalyahu" ("with" in the KJ is not found)
T: *bi-tqōp rəgaz rəzīn wa-ʾrām ū-bar rəmalyāh*	T: "for the strength of the anger of Rezin and Aram and the son of Remalyah"
S: this phrase is absent from S	S:

7:12. I will not tempt the Lord HM: lō ᵃnasse ʾet-yahweh (Q: lacuna)	HM: "tempt" originally meant "to try, test" and the normal meaning of this verb is to "to test" which makes sense here, and in 19th-21st century English, "I wll not test the Lord" is less misleading
T: lā ᵃnassēʸ qādām yahweh	T: the verb can mean either "to test" or "to seek a sign, omen" and since the introduction of qādām (before) means Yahweh cannot be the direct object, the best translation is: "I will not test by seeking a sign, omen, before Yahweh"
S: οὐ μὴ πειράσω κύριον	S: "I will certainly not test the Lord"
7:19: in the desolate valleys and in the holes of the rocks HM: bə-naḥᵃlê hab-battôt ū-bi-nqîqê has-səlāʿîm (=Q)	HM: battôt (linguistically difficult to associate with bātâ) is a hapax legomenon, and is currently defined as "cliffs, precipices"; and naqîqê means "clefts, cracks"; giving us "in the ravines of the cliffs and the clefts of the rocks"
T: bi-rḥōbēʸ qiryā u-bi-šqīpēʸ kēʸpayā	T: "in the open area (town markets, squares) and in the clefts of rocks"
S: ἐν ταῖς φάραγξι τῆς χώρας καὶ ἐν ταῖς τρώγλαις τῶν πετρῶν	S: "in the ravines of the contryside and the caves of the rocks"
7:19: bushes HM: naḥᵃlōlîm (Q reads: nhlylym)	HM: a hapax legomenon of undetermined meaning, but possibly watering holes, wadis (cf. Arabic nhl)
T: bātēʸ tūšbəḥātā	T: houses of hymns of praise (i.e. of worship, or praised in song?)
S: εἰς πᾶσαν ραγάδα καὶ ἐν παντὶ ξύλῳ	S: in every ravine and every tree
8:19: them that have familiar spirits HM: hā-ʾōbôt (=Q)	HM: ʾōbôt (plural of ʾōb, a spirit of the dead that returns to give an omen or prophecy) related to the Arabic verb ʾwb, to return (One who can call them back from the dead is illustrated in the story of Saul when he consulted the so-called "witch of endor", who was called a baʿᵃlat ʾob, a mistress of an ʾōb, female necromancer; so the correct translation here would be "spirits of necromancy" ["them that have" being absent in HM])
T: biddīn	T: "lying oracles; conjuring" from a root meaning to invent, make things up
S: τοὺς ἀπὸ τῆς γῆς φθνοῦντας	S: "those speaking from the earth" (i.e., the returning spirits)

8:19: wizards	
HM: *yiddəʿōnîm* (=Q)	HM: "soothsayers"; *yiddəʿōnîm* comes from the common verb "to know" and these are the knowers (by supernatural means); whereas wizards are practitioners of magic, sorcerers
T: *zəkūrū*	T: "necromancy, necromantic apparition"
S: ἐγγαστριμύθους	S: "ventriloquists"
8:21: and fret themselves	
HM: *hitqaṣṣap* (=Q)	HM: "and become enraged"; the base form of the verb means "to be angry" and this form means to be absorbed in anger
T: *w-īlōṭ wə-yibzē*	T: "he shall curse and despise"
S: λυπηθήσεσθε	S: "you shall be grieved, vexed"
§ 9:2: shadow of death	
HM: *ṣalmāwet* (=Q)	HM: "gloom" (An ancient folk etymology separated this word into two pieces, *ṣēl* (shadow) and *māwet* (death), although it is always written as one word (even in Q), and Hebrew does not compound; but the word originally would have been pronounced *ṣalmôt*, with the meaning "gloom, darkness.") (cf. Arabic *ẓulm*)
T: *ṭūllēʸ mōtā*	T: "shadow/s of death"
S: σκια θανάτου EDIT A IN SKIA	S: "shadow of death"
9:4: oppressor	
HM: *nōgēś* (=Q)	HM: "slave driver"; the active participle of a verb meaning to spur on a beast of burden, or to use a rod to make slaves or forced labor to pull harder, move faster, etc.
T: *da-hwā maplaḥ bēʸh*	T: "by which he exacted forced labor"
S: ἀπαιτούντων	S: "exactors"
9:7: to order it and to establish it	
HM: *lə-hākîn ʾōtāh ū-l-saʿădāh*	HM: "to establish it and sustain it"
Q: .. *ʾôtô* .. *saʿădû*	Q: changing "it" from feminine to masculine, which does not agree grammatically
T: *lə-atqānā yātah u-l-mibnah*	T: "to establish it and build it"
S: κατορθῶσαι αὐτὴν καὶ ἀντιλαβέθαι αὐτῆς	S: "to set it up and to take firm hold of it (support, help it)"
9:10: we will change them into cedars	
HM: *wa-ʾărāzîm naḥălîp* (=Q)	HM: the verb means to cause one thing to succeed another: "We will make cedars their successors."
T: *wa-d-šappīrīn mi-hōn niqnēʸ*	T: " and we shall obtain more goodly ones than they"
S: ἐκκόψωμεν συκαμίνους καὶ κέδρους καὶ οἰκοδομήσωμεν ἑαυτοῖς πύγον	S: "We should cut down sycomores and cedars and build them a tower."

9:11: join his enemies together	
HM: ʾet ʾōyəbāʸw yəsaksēk (=Q)	HM: "incite his enemies"; a *hapax legomenon* (found in later Hebrew and Ethiopic: v. Koehler & Baumgartner, and Klein)
T: yāt baʿalēʸ dəbābōhi yəʿārar	T: "incite his enemies "
S: τοὺς ἐχθροὺς αὐτῶν διασκεδάσει	S: "shall scatter his enemies"
9:15: ancient	
HM: zāqēn (=Q)	HM: "elder" (This noun comes from a word meaning "beard" and can refer to a male old enough to grow a beard, but also means an elderly male, or an elder, as a leading elite of the community. Here, the verse refers to secular elites, "the elder and honorable man" and the religious elites, "the prophet", and the next verse lumps them together as "the leaders of this people" which indicates that here, zāqēn refers to more than just old men.)
T: sāb	T: "elder"; same comments as above (The word refers to grey hair, and can mean an elderly male, an elder, ancestor, patriarch or scholar
S: πρεσβύτην	S: "elder" (This word means old man, spokesman, and in the New Testament, bishop.)
9:20: snatch on the right hand	
HM: yigzôr ʿāl-yāmîn (=Q)	HM: "shall cut on the right" (right hand; properly, to cut, but "to devour" is suggested as well [in Arabic it means "to cut, slaughter an animal, to butcher"])
T: bazz min dārōmā	T: "he has plundered from the south"
S: ἐκκλινεῖ εἰς τὰ δεξιά	S: "he inclines to the right"
10:1: that write grievousness which they have prescribed	
HM: ū-mkattəbîm ʿāmāl kittēbû	HM: This form of the verb is not found elsewhere in the OT, nor in Post-Biblical Hebrew. "mkattəbîm" is the active partictiple of "kittēbû". The form can mean "to write constatnly" (Koehler & Baumgartner, p. 504). So: "Writing (i.e. when they write), they write toil (or burdensomness) constatnly."
T: kətāb də-lēʸʾū kātəbīn	T: "who write writ of toil (or burdensomness)"
S: γράφοντες γὰρ πονηρίαν γράφουσιν	S: "for writing (for when they write) they write wickedness"
10:2: their prey	
HM: šəlālām (=Q)	HM: "their booty" – the normal word for booty
T: ʿadāyhōn	T: "their booty"
S: ἁρπαγὴν	S: "booty"

10:6: prey	
HM: *baz* (=Q)	HM: "booty"
T: *ʿadāʾā*	T: "spoil"
S: *προνομήν*	S: "booty"
10:31: Madmēnah is removed	
HM: *nādədâ madmēnâ* (=Q)	HM: "Madmēnah has fled (escaped, or is wandering)"
T: *ʾiyttabbarū ʾanāš madmēnā*	T: "the people of Madmēnah are broken"
S: *ἐξέστη Μαδεβηνα*	S: "Madebēna is amazed"
10:31: gather themselves to flee	
HM: *hēʿîzû* (=Q)	HM: "bring (goods, flocks) to safety (or, seek refuge)" (from a root "to take refuge")
T: *gəlō*	T: "have gone into exile [have fled]"
S: not present	S:
11:3: shall make him of quick understanding in the fear of the Lord	
HM: *haʾrîhô bə-yirʾat yahweh* (=Q)	HM: "he shall inspire him with fear of the Lord"; where "inspire (*haʾrîaḥ*) would be denominated from *rûaḥ* (spirit)
T: *wə-yəqārbīnīnēyh lə-daḥlətēyh yahweh*	T: "he will bring him near to his fear of Yahweh"
S: *ἐμπλήσει αὐτὸν πνεῦμα φόβου θεοῦ*	S: "he shall fill him with the spirit of the fear of God"
13:2: shake the hand	
HM: *hānîpû yād* (=Q)	HM: "wave the hand"; the verb means to move a thing back and forth, and, in this case, to wave them through the gates of the nobles (the same verb is used for waving the wave-offering)
T: *ʾanīpū yād*	T: "wave the hand"; same as above
S: *παρακαλεῖτε τῇ χειρί*	S: "call out with the hand"
13:8: sorrows	
HM: *ḥabālîm* (=Q)	HM: "labor pains", used here metaphorically. The context specifies pain, not sorrow.
T: *ḥabālîm*	T: "labor pains"
S: *ὠδῖνες*	S: "labor pains"

13:11: world HM: *tēbēl* (=Q)	HM: "inhabited land." *tēbēl* is often mentioned as only part of the world, and, hearkening back to Genesis, it may refer to the dry land, separated from the waters; best compared with Akkadian *tābalu*, dry land (derived from *'abālu*, "to dry up." While *tēbēl* seems to be derived from *'ābal*, to dry up"); it is interesting to note that it never takes the definite article, being a well established proper noun. It is not the "world." It is just the dry land, or the inhabited land. (*tēbēl* also in 14:17 & 21 refers to the inhabited world.)
T: *də-dāyrīn bə-tēbēl*	T: "those dwelling in the dry land, or inhabited land" *(tēbēl)*
S: οἰκομένη ὅλη	S: "the whole inhabitable land"
13:21: wild beasts ... doleful creatures HM: *ṣīyīm* .. *'ōḥîm* (=Q)	HM: "desert animals"? (related to *ṣīyâ*, a dry place); & "owl" (howling animals?) a name based on the sound made
T: *tāmwʷān ... 'ōḥyān*	T: "desert animals ... eagle owls"
S: θηρία ... ἦχου	S: "wild animals ... sound (howling [beast]?)"
13:21: satyrs HM: *śəʿîrîm* (=Q)	HM: Unclear; taken from the common word for hair. See Koehler & Baumgartner (p. 1341) for a discussion. Possibilities include a desert buck goat, a demon, a satyr, or other hairy animal.
T: *šēʸdīn*	T: "demons"
S: δαιμόνια	S: "demons "
14:12: Lucifer HM: *hêlēl* (=Q:*hylyl*)	HM: "shining one" or "morning star." *hêlēl* is related to Arabic *hilāl* (first moon) and the Hebrew verb from which it derives means "to shine." Although "new moon crescent" is possible, the following phrase, "son of the morning" suggests that it is the morning star. The passage is part of the proverb Isaiah recites about the king of Babylon. This is a deliberately ironic epithet for him, and has nothing to do with the later Christian head demon, the Prince of Darkness. The Latin Vulgate translation is *lucifer*, i.e., light bearer, and this word was personalized to serve theological needs. *hêlēl* is the king of Babylon, not the head devil
T: *zēʸwtān bə-gō bənēʸ 'ᵃnāšā*	T: "resplendant among mankind"
S: ἑωσφόρος	S: "morning star"; bearer of the morning

14:23: pools of water	
HM: ʾagmê māyim (=Q)	HM: "marshes, reed pools" (cf. Syriac ʾegmā and Akkadian agammu)
T: bīṣīn də-mayīn	T: "marshes, swamps of water" [biṣṣīn]
S: πήλου βάραθρον	S: "mud pit"
14:29: cockatrice	
HM: ṣepaʿ (=Q)	HM: "poisonous snake"; a hapax legomenon (v. 11:8)
T: məšīḥā	T: This translation is Messianic exegesis.
S: ἔκγονα ἀσπίδων	S: "offspring of asps"
14:32: shall trust	
HM: yeḥᵉsû (=Q)	HM: "shall take refuge"; a common verb; cf. ḥāsût (refuge)
T: yiḥdōn	T: "shall rejoice"
S: σωθήσονται	S: "shall be saved"
48:3: I shewed them (also 48:6)	
HM: ʾašmîʿēm (=Q)	HM: "I made them heard"
T: bassartīnūn	T: "I announced them"
S: ἀκουστὸν ἐγένετο	S: "they were heard" (hence: known)
48:5: from the beginning	
HM: mē-ʾāz (=Q)	HM: "in advance"; v. 48:3a
T: mib-bə-kēʸn	T: "from there on"
S: πάλαι	S: "of old"
48:5: I shewed	
HM: hišmaʿtîkā (=Q)	HM: "I caused you to hear"
T: bassartāk	T: "I announced to you"
S: ἀκουστόν σοι ἐποίησα	S: "I made them heard unto you"
49:2: polished shaft	
HM: ḥēṣ bārûr (=Q)	HM: "sharpened arrow"
T: gīr bəḥīr	T: "select arrow"
S: βέλος ἐκλεκτόν	S: "select arrow, dart"
49:7: whom man despiseth	
HM: bəzōh nepeš (Q: bəzûy nepeš)	HM: "despised of the soul"; i.e., utterly despised? the Masoretic text is edited, usually to nibze ("despised"), but Q reads bəzûy (also "despised"); nepeš is the normal word for "spirit, soul"
T: not present	T:
S: τὸν φαυλίζοντα τὴν ψυχὴν αὑτοῦ	S: "him lowly valuing his own soul (life?)"
49:8: have I heard thee	
HM: ʿᵃnîtîkā	HM: "have I answered thee"
Q: ʾeʿenkā	Q: "shall I answer thee"
T: məqabbēʸl ṣəlōtkōn	T: "have received (accepted) your prayer"
S: ἐπήκουσά σου	S: "have I listened to you"; with connotation of "heard you with favor"

49:9: high places HM: *šəpāyîm* (Q: *špʾm*) T: *nigdīn* S: τρίβοις	HM: unclear: "clearings"? plains? bare places? the root is špy, and has to do with being swept bare, wiped clean, polished, etc.; no word from this root has to do with being high; the word in Q is unclear, as there is no špʾ root T: " paths, wadis, water courses, steppe" S: "paths"
49:21: am desolate, a captive and removing to and fro HM: *galmûdâ gōlâ wə-sûrâ* (Q: ... *srh*) T: *yəḥīdā galyā u-məṭalṭəlā* S: ἄτεκνα καὶ χήρα	HM: "barren, gone into exile and turned aside" T: "alone, gone into exile and homeless" S: "childless and a widow"
49:24: prey HM: *malkoaḥ* (=Q) T: *ʿaday* S: σκῦλα	HM: "spoils"; the passive imperfect and passive participle of the common verb "to take, seize" are used to say, literally, "shall that which has been seized be taken from the mighty (or, warrior)?" T: "spoil" S: "spoils"
51:11: mourning HM: *ʾanāḥâ* (=Q) T: *tīnnaḥtā* S: στεναγμός	HM: "sighing" or groaning T: "sighing", groaning S: "sighing", groaning
51:14: captive exile HM: *ṣōʿe* (Q: ṣrh) T: *pōrʿānā* S: not present	HM: "captive" There is no word indicating exile. T: "vengeance" S:
51:17: wrung *them out* HM: *māṣît* (=Q) T: *ʾaʿrīt* S: ἐξεκένωσας	HM: "drained [it]" T: "emptied [it] out, drained [it]" S: "emptied [it] out"
51:19: desolation HM: *šōd* (=Q) T: *bizzā* S: πτῶμα	HM: "devastation"; especially destruction through violent action T: "ruin, spoiling" S: "fall (disaster)"

51:22: the Lord, thy Lord	
HM: ᵃdōnayik yahwe (=Q)	HM: "thy Lord Yahweh [Jehovah]" Rabbinical theology made it totally forbidden to pronounce Yahweh, as being too sacred for human lips, and the KJ follows this practice, translating Yahweh as Lord, even when it results in this ridiculous duplication. Since Mormons have no problem rendering it as Jehovah (Yahweh in English) "thy Lord Jehovah" would be preferable here, since it is not clear why a divne translation should follow a later rabbinical practice unkown to Isaiah.
T: rabbōnīk ywy	T: "thy Lord Yahweh" Yahweh is not voweled, indicating that it should not be pronounced.
S: κύριος ὁ θεὸς	S: "the Lord God", translating both words, but avoiding Yahweh

Appendix 3. Scribe Details as Per Manuscript Page of Ms O

Scribe one is Cowdery, while scribes two and three are unidentified, and listed here as scribe² and scribe³. The gatherings are numbered in the order of the page numbers. Line 0 is the page topic heading. The N designation refers to a note below.

Bom Text	Scribe(s)	BOM Text	Scribes
\multicolumn{4}{c}{1 Nephi}			
\multicolumn{4}{c}{*Gathering One*}			
2:2-23	Cowdery (lines 0-54)	8:27-9:4	scribe³ (lines 0-53; N)
2:23-3:18	Scribe³ (line 0) Cowdery (lines 1-13); Scribe² (lines 14-54)	9:4-10:11	scribe³ (lines 0-53; N)
3:18-4:2	scribe³ (line 0); scribe² (lines 1-54)	10:11-11:1	scribe³ (lines 0-53; N)
4:2-20	Cowdery (line 0); scribe² (lines 1-40); Cowdery (41-54)	11:1-18	scribe³ (lines 0-53; N)
4:20-37	scribe³ (lines 0-53)	11:18-32	scribe³ (lines 0-53)
4:38-5:14	scribe³ (lines 0-53)	11:32-12:8	scribe³ (lines 0-53; N)
5:14-7:3	scribe³ (lines 0-53; N)	12:8-23	scribe³ (lines 0-53)
7:3-17	scribe³ (lines 0-53)	13:1-18	scribe² (lines 0-53)
7:17-8:11	scribe³ (lines 0-53; N)	13:18-29	scribe² (lines 0-53; N)
8:11-27	scribe³ (lines 0-53)	13:29-35	scribe² (lines 0-54)
\multicolumn{4}{c}{*Gathering Two*}			
14:11-16	scribe² (lines 0-21)	18:6-18	Cowdery (lines 1-39)
14:23-29	scribe² (lines 0-21)	18:18-19:3	Cowdery (lines 0-39
15:5-15	scribe² (lines 0-39)	19:3-12	Cowdery (lines 1-39)
15:15-25	scribe² (lines 0-39)	19:12-20	Cowdery (lines 0-38; N)
15:25-36	scribe² (lines 1-40; N)	20:1-20	Cowdery (lines 1-39)
15:36-16:14	scribe² (lines 1-39; N)	20:20-21:14	Cowdery (lines 1-39)
16:14-31	Cowdery (lines 1-40)	21:14-:22:4	Cowdery (lines 1-39; N)
16:31-17:5	Cowdery (lines 1-39)	22:4-14	Cowdery (lines 1-39)
17:5-20	Cowdery (lines 1-39)	22:14-26	Cowdery (lines 1-39
17:20-34	Cowdery (lines 1-39)	22:26-**2 Nephi** 1:7	Cowdery (lines 0-38; N)
17:34-48	Cowdery (lines 1-39)	1:8-19	Cowdery (lines 1-39)
17:48-18:6	Cowdery (lines 1-39)	1:19-30	Cowdery (lines 1-39)

(Appendix 3 continued)

2 Nephi³			
Gathering Three			
4:32-35	Cowdery (lines 22-31)	8:6-17	Cowdery (lines 13-35)
5:12-16	Cowdery (lines 22-31)	9:1-2	Cowdery (lines 13-17)
5:22-6:0	Cowdery (lines 13-34; N)	9:12-13	Cowdery (lines 13-17)
6:6-12	Cowdery (lines 13-33)	Nephi 9:25-26	Cowdery (lines 13-18)
6:18-7:9	Cowdery (lines 13-35; N)	9:41-42	Cowdery (lines 13-17)
Gathering Four			
23:1-7	Cowdery (lines 29-39; N)	25:5-8	Cowdery (lines 29-39)
23:22-24:4	Cowdery (lines 29-39)	25:16-18	Cowdery (lines 29-39)
24:21-27	Cowdery (lines 29-39)	25:24-28	Cowdery (lines 29-39)
2 Nephi-Jacob			
Gathering Five			
2 Nephi 33:4-9	Cowdery (lines 31-39)	Jacob 2:25-27	Cowdery (lines 27-29)
Jacob 1:3-7	Cowdery (lines 31-39)	3:5	Cowdery (lines 26-29)
1:18-2:2	Cowdery (lines 29-39)	4:3-5	Cowdery (lines 31-35)
2:11-15	Cowdery (lines 28-39)	4:13-14	Cowdery (lines 31-36)
Jacob-Enos			
Gathering Six			
5:46-48	Cowdery (lines 1-12)	6:11-7:6	Cowdery (lines 1-22; N)
5:57-61	Cowdery (lines 1-12)	7:11-18	Cowdery (lines 0-22; N)
5:69-70	Cowdery (lines 1-3)	7:24-Enos 1:1	Cowdery (lines 0-21; N)
5:77-6:0	Cowdery (lines 1-3; N)	1:9-14	Cowdery (lines 0-21; N)
Alma			
Gathering #?¹ (collected fragments)			
10:31-11:4	Cowdery (lines 6-28)	12:18-24)	Cowdery (lines 5-28)
11:13-23	Cowdery (lines 6-28)	12:26-32)	Cowdery (lines 5-28)
11:26-39	Cowdery (lines 5-28)	12:36-13:4	Cowdery (lines 5-27)
11:42-46)	Cowdery (lines 5-28)	13:7-16	Cowdery (lines 0-27)
Gathering #?² (collected fragments)			
19:3-11	Cowdery (lines 0-28)	19:29-36	Cowdery (lines 0-18)
19:13-19	Cowdery (lines 0-29)	20:5-8	Cowdery (lines 0-5)
19:21-25	Cowdery (lines 0-18)	20:19-22	Cowdery (lines 0-5)
Gathering #?³			
22:22-27	Cowdery (lines 14-32)	43:36-47	Cowdery (lines 0-35)
22:28-34	Cowdery (lines 4-32)	43:47-44:5	Cowdery (lines 0-35)
22:35-23:7	Cowdery (lines 1-31)	44:5-14	Cowdery (lines 0-35)
23:7-24:4	Cowdery (lines 0-35)	44:14-45:2	Cowdery (lines 0-35)

(Appendix 3 continued)

24:5-14	Cowdery (lines 0-35)	45:2-17	Cowdery (lines 0-35)
24:14-23	Cowdery (lines 0-35)	45:17-22	Cowdery (lines 0-17)
24:23-25:5	Cowdery (lines 0-35)	45:22	**Smith** (lines 17-19)
25:5-15	Cowdery (lines 0-35)	45:22	Cowdery (lines 19-35)
25:16-26:11	Cowdery (lines 0-35)	46:6-18	Cowdery (lines 0-35)
26:11-24	Cowdery (lines 0-35)	46:18-28	Cowdery (lines 0-35)
26:24-35	Cowdery (lines 0-35)	46:28-40	Cowdery (lines 0-35)
26:35-27:12	Cowdery (lines 0-35)	46:40-47:10	Cowdery (lines 0-35)
27:12-24	Cowdery (lines 0-35)	47:10-22	Cowdery (lines 0-35)
27:24-28:6	Cowdery (lines 0-35)	47:23-36	Cowdery (lines 0-35)
28:6-29:5	Cowdery (lines 0-35)	47:36-48:11	Cowdery (lines 0-35)
29:5-30:2	Cowdery (lines 0-35)	48:11-23	Cowdery (lines 0-35)
30:2-17	Cowdery (lines 0-35)	48:23-49:9	Cowdery (lines 0-35)
30:17-28	Cowdery (lines 0-35)	49:9-20	Cowdery (lines 0-35)
30:28-42	Cowdery (lines 0-35)	49:20-30	Cowdery (lines 0-35)
30:42-53	Cowdery (lines 0-35)	50:1:12	Cowdery (lines 0-35)
30:53-31:5	Cowdery (lines 0-35)	50:12-26	Cowdery (lines 0-35)
31:5-19	Cowdery (lines 0-35)	50:26-37	Cowdery (lines 0-35; N)
31:19-35	Cowdery (lines 0-35)	50:37-51:8	Cowdery (lines 0-35)
31:35-32:9	Cowdery (lines 0-35)	51:8-19	Cowdery (lines 0-35; N)
32:10-24	Cowdery (lines 0-35)	51:19-31	Cowdery (lines 0-35)
32:24-36)	Cowdery (lines 0-35)	51:31-52:8:	Cowdery (lines 0-35)
32:37-33:5)	Cowdery (lines 0-35)	52:8-17	Cowdery (lines 0-35)
33:5-22)	Cowdery (lines 0-35)	52:17-28	Cowdery (lines 0-35)
33:22-34:12)	Cowdery (lines 0-35)	52:28-53:2	Cowdery (lines 0-35)
34:12-31)	Cowdery (lines 0-35)	53:2-10	Cowdery (lines 0-35)
34:31-41	Cowdery (lines 0-35)	53:10-22	Cowdery (lines 0-35)
35:1-14	Cowdery (lines 0-35)	53:22-54:11	Cowdery (lines 0-35)
35:14-36:10)	Cowdery (lines 0-35)	54:11-24	Cowdery (lines 0-35)
36:10-26	Cowdery (lines 0-35)	54:24-55:15	Cowdery (lines 0-35)
36:26-37:8	Cowdery (lines 0-35)	55:15-28	Cowdery (lines 0-35)
37:8-19	Cowdery (lines 0-35)	55:28-56:8	Cowdery (lines 0-35)
37:19-30	Cowdery (lines 0-35)	56:8-22	Cowdery (lines 0-35)
37:30-43	Cowdery (lines 0-35)	56:22-37	Cowdery (lines 0-35)
37:43-38:8	Cowdery (lines 0-35)	56:38-51	Cowdery (lines 0-35)
38:8-39:7	Cowdery (lines 0-35)	56:51-57:6	Cowdery (lines 0-35)
39:8-40:3	Cowdery (lines 0-35)	57:6-17	Cowdery (lines 0-35)
40:3-15	Cowdery (lines 0-35)	57:17-30	Cowdery (lines 0-35)
40:15-41:2	Cowdery (lines 0-35)	57:30-58:6	Cowdery (lines 0-35)
41:2-14	Cowdery (lines 0-35)	58:6-18	Cowdery (lines 0-35)
41:14-42:13	Cowdery (lines 0-35)	58:18-31	Cowdery (lines 0-35)
42:13-29	Cowdery (lines 0-35)	58:31-59:3	Cowdery (lines 0-35)

(Appendix 3 continued)

42:29-43:10	Cowdery (lines 0-35)	59:3-60:2	Cowdery (lines 0-35)
43:10-22	Cowdery (lines 0-35)	60:5-13	Cowdery (lines 7-35)
43:22-36	Cowdery (lines 0-35)	60:15-22	Cowdery (lines 7-35)

Alma-Helaman
Gathering #?[4]

Alma 61:10-13	Cowdery (lines 11-14)	Helaman 1:5-17	Cowdery (lines 0-35)
62:3:-5	Cowdery (lines 11-14)	1:17-27	Cowdery (lines 0-35)
62:17-18	Cowdery (lines 13-16)	1:27-2:8	Cowdery (lines 0-35)
62:30-31	Cowdery (lines 13-16)	2:8-3:8	Cowdery (lines 0-35)
62:36-49	Cowdery (lines 0-35)	3:8-21	Cowdery (lines 0-35)
62:49-63:11	Cowdery (lines 0-35)		
Alma 63:11-17 & Helaman 1:1-1:5	Cowdery (lines 0-35)		

Helaman-3 Nephi
Gathering #?[5]

Helaman 13:36-14:9	Cowdery (lines 11-35)	3 Nephi 1:10-17	Cowdery (lines 16-35)
14:14-23	Cowdery (lines 11-35)	1:24-29	Cowdery (lines 15-35)
14:29-15:6	Cowdery (lines 11-35)	2:10-12	Cowdery (lines 25-35)
15:9-16:1	Cowdery (lines 11-35)	3:3-7	Cowdery (lines 25-35)
16:4-16	Cowdery (lines 10-35)	3:17-19	Cowdery (lines 32-35)
Helaman 16:20-25 & 3 Nephi 1:1-2	Cowdery (lines 10-35)	4:1-2	Cowdery (lines 32-35)

3 Nephi
Gathering #?[6] (fragments with estimated line numbers)

19:25-28	Cowdery (lines 1-6)	21:10-11	Cowdery (lines 2-5)
20:15-17	Cowdery (lines 1-6)	26:3-6	Cowdery (lines 1-8)
20:37-39	Cowdery (lines 2-5)	27:3-7	Cowdery (lines 1-8)

Ether
Gathering #?[7] (fragments with estimated line numbers)

3:9-10	Cowdery (lines 13-15)	10:30-11:6	Cowdery (lines 2-25)
4:4-5	Cowdery (lines 13-15)	11:20-12:7	Cowdery (lines 2-25)
5:1-6:3	Cowdery (lines 5-25)	12:21-29	Cowdery (lines 1-25)
6:18-27	Cowdery (lines 5-25)	12:41-13:8	Cowdery (lines 2-25)
7:18-24	Cowdery (lines 10-25)	13:20-14:1	Cowdery (lines 2-25)
8:13-19	Cowdery (lines 11-25)	14:15-27	Cowdery (lines 2-25)
9:3-11	Cowdery (lines 10-25)	15:8-17	Cowdery (lines 2-25)
9:26-10:7	Cowdery (lines 2-25)		

NOTES

1 Nephi 5:14-7:3	Line 22 reads "Chapter 2nd".
1 Nephi 7:17-8:11	Cowdery made supralinear edits, adding 'thee' to line 2 and 'me' to line 15.
1 Nephi 8:27-9:4	Unidentified 2 made supralinear edits, adding 'are' to line 21 & 'to' to line 40.
1 Nephi 9:4-10:11	Unidentified 2 made a supralinear edit in line 37, changing 'no' to 'know'; line 10 reads "Chapter 3rd".
1 Nephi 10:11-11:1	Unidentified 2 made supralinear edits, adding 'ed' to 'scatter' in line 4; changing 'now' to 'know'; adding 'to' to 'day' and changing 'co[r]ese' to 'coarse'.
1 Nephi 11:1-18	Cowdery made a supralinear edit, adding 'God' in line 14.
1 Nephi 11:32-12:8	Cowdery made supralinear edits, adding '& it fell' in line 16, and '&' and 'that they rent' in line 37.
1 Nephi 13:18-29	Cowdery made a supralinear edit, adding 'seest' in line 43.
1 Nephi 15:25-36	Cowdery made supralinear edits, adding '&' in lines 9 & 33.
1 Nephi 15:36-16:14	Line 4 ends with "Chapter 5th".
1 Nephi 19:12-20	Line 24 reads "Chapter VI"
1 Nephi 21:14-:22:4	Line 28 ends with "Chapter VII".
1 Nephi 22:26- 2 Nephi 1:7	Cowdery crossed out "Chapter VIII" in line 13 and added a supralinear edit "Chapter I" in line 14. Line 14-16 has the heading for currently found at the beginning of 2 Nephi.
2 Nephi 5:22-6:0	Line 34 ends: "Chapter V".
2 Nephi 7:1-9	Cowdery original to printer ms ( ) changes:
	wherefore when I came (come) there was no man
	I make the (their) rivers a wilderness
	They dieth (die) because of thirst
	he wakeneth (waketh) morning by morning
	he wakeneth (waketh) mine ear
	the Lord God hath opened (appointed) mine ear

This is from a fragment of p. 59 of the "original":

2 Nephi 23:0-7	Line 29 reads "Chapter X".
Jacob 5:77-6:0	Line 3 reads "Chapter IIII"
Jacob 6:11-7:6	Line 5 ends with "Chapter (5)"
Jacob 7:11-18	Line 0 bears page number "112"
Jacob 7:24-Enos 1:1	Line 0 bears page number "113"
Enos 1:9-14	Line 0 bears page number "114"

Appendix 4. Apologetics in the Improvement Era and Ensign

(Era: 1/1951-12/1970; Ensign 1/1971-12/2015)

Years 49-51
"Goldsmiths of Ancient Times," Levi Edgar Young, 49-04. "Anachronisms and the *Book of Mormon*," C. E. Moore, 49/10. "The Sensational Discovery of the Jerusalem Scrolls," Sidney B. Sperry, 49/10.
"Lehi in the Desert," Hugh Nibley, 50/1-6, 9-10. "Was Iron Known in Ancient America?" John A. Widtsoe, 50/3. "The World of the Jaredites," Hugh Nibley, 51/9-12, 52/1-5, 7. "Laman Found", Ariel L. Crowley, 51/2. "America's First Farmers", John Sherman Walker, 50/9.

Years 52-54: "The Anthon Transcript and the Maya Glyphs," Ariel L. Crowley, 52/9. "The Stick of Judah," Hugh Nibley, 53 1-5. "New Approaches to *Book of Mormon* Study," Nibley, 53/11-12, 54/1-3, 5-7. "Hebrew Idioms in *Book of Mormon* Study," Sidney B. Sperry, 54/10.

Years 55-57: "Archaeology and the *Book of Mormon*," Milton R. Hunter, 55/4-5, 7-10, 12. "Archaeology and the *Book of Mormon*," Milton R. Hunter, 56/1, 3-5. "There Were Jaredites," Hugh Nibley, 56/1, 3-5, 6, 9-10, 57/1, 59/7. "The Dead Sea Scrolls and Their Significance for Latter-day Saints," Sidney B Sperry, 57/12.

Years 58-60: "The Dead Sea Scrolls and Their Significance for Latter-day Saints," Sidney B Sperry, 58/1. "The Language of the *Book of Mormon*," James L. Barker, 60/6. "Charles Anthon and the Egyptian Language," Stanley H. Kimball, 60/10.

Years 61-63: "Hebrew Idioms in the Small Plates of Nephi," E. Craig Bramwell, 61/7. "Gold Plates and the *Book of Mormon*," Thomas Stuart Ferguson, 62/4. "The Dead Sea Scrolls" (the *Era*). "The Kinderhook Plates," Welby W. Ricks, 62/9. "The Prophet Said Silk," Maurice W. Cornell, 62/5.

Years 64-66: "Since Cumorah, New Voices from the Dust," Hugh Nibley, 64/10-12, 65/1, 3-4, 6, 8-9, 11, 65/1-4, 6-12. "Were the Golden Plates Made of Tumbaga?" Read H. Putnam, 66/9. "The Stone Box," Paul Cheesman, 66/10.

1967: No apologist articles the whole year, as LDS Church is occupied with the Abraham papyri.

68-70: "Ancient Land of Egypt," Doyl L Green, 68/1. "Egyptian Papyri Rediscovered," Jay M. Todd, 68/1. Publication of the Abraham papyri, 68/2. "A New Look at the Pearl of Great Price," Hugh Nibley, 68/1-12, 69/1-11, 70/1, 3-5. "Sketches on the Papyri Backings," Edgar Lyon, 68/5. "The Lebolo-Chandler Relationship," Jay M. Todd, 68/7. "Ancient Landings in America," John Lear, 70/10. "The *Book of Mormon* as a Mirror of the East," Hugh Nibley, 70/11.

***Ensign* magazine debuts.**

Years 71-73
"Ancient Temples. What Do They Signify?" Hugh Nibley, 72/9.

Years 74-76: "A Strange Thing in the Land: The Return of the Book of Enoch," Hugh Nibley, 75/10, 12. "A Strange Thing in the Land: The Return of the Book of Enoch," Hugh Nibley, 76/2-4, 7, 10, 12.

Years 77-79: "A Strange Thing in the Land: The Return of the Book of Enoch," Hugh Nibley, 77/2-4, 6, 8.

Years 80-82

Years 83-85: "Digging into the *Book of Mormon*," 84/9-10.

Years 86-88: "The Mulekites," Garth A. Wilson, 87/3. "New Developments in *Book of Mormon* Research" (survey of LDS scholars) 88/2. "Chiasmus in Mayan Texts," Allen J. Christensen, 88/10.

Years 89-91: "Recent Research on BOM Studies," 89/06. "Hebrew Lit Patterns in BOM," Donald W. Parry, 89/10. "Where was Abraham's Ur?" Paul Y. Hoskisson, 91/07. Research BOM Update, *Era* feature, 92/04.

Years 92-94: Abraham in Ancient Egyptian, John Gee, 92/07. "News from Antiquity" (Re Abraham), 94/01.

Years 95-97: "The *Book of Mormon*, an Ancient Sacred Record" (Quiché tradition), 95/11. "Wonderful Book of Moses" (& Enoch), Richard D. Draper, 97/02. "*The Book of Abraham*, A Most Remarkable Book" (& papyri story), Andrew Skinner, 97/03.

Years 98-00: "The Abrahamic Covenant," S. Michael Wilcox, 98/01. "Enoch: What Modern Scripture Teaches," Richard D. Draper, 98-01. "The Flood and the Tower of Babel," Donald W. Parry, 98-01. "Mounting Evidence for the B00k of Mormon," Daniel C. Peterson, 00/01.

Years 01-03: "The Origin of Man," The First Presidency (Era, November, 1909), 02/02.

Years 04-06: "The Dead Sea Scrolls and Latter-day Truth," Andrew C. Skinner, 06-02.

Years 07-10: NONE

Years 11-13: NONE

Years 11-15: NONE

Appendix 5. Documents Prior to 1830

Historians in Mormon studies are unable to function without the use of documents written after the events they treat, sometime years and even decades after. Some information they contain reflects a strong orthodox bias due either to official efforts to control history, or due to the piety of the Saints. Other information reflects a strong anti-Mormon bias. I am not aware of any field of research that poses such difficult problems for professional historiography. For the events prior to 1830, ideally one would want primary documents, contemporary or real-time evidence, recorded at or near the time of the event(s) in question. As can be seen below, very little exists.

Brackets are used for the revelations of Joseph Smith because we have no document prior to 1830 to verify when they were actually composed. Even if we assume that all or most are in fact pre-1830, the actual year or time of the year is not documented prior to 1830. These have been culled from Marquardt, *The Joseph Smith Revelations*. Most other materials are from Vogel, *Early Mormon Documents*.

Date	Document
12/11/1799	members of the Anabaptist Society (which Joseph Smith?)
06/12/1797	Universalist Society (Joseph Smith Sr. signature)
15/03/1806	Teacher's note signed by Jos Smith (Joseph Smith Sr.?)
15/10/1807	Petition to Vermont Assembly (signature of Joseph Smith Sr.?)
15/03/1816	Smith Family Warning out of Norwich, VT
19/11/1823	Alvin Smith Gravestone
01/11/1825	Articles of Agreement
27/12/1825	*Wayne Sentinel*, many find treasure (from *Orleans Advocate*)
20/12/1825	Co. records: Durfy buys Smith farm; Smiths tenant-farm it
20/03/1826	Bainbridge (NY) Court records (Joseph Jr's examination) 1826 Albert Neely Bill of Costs 1826 Philip DeZeng Bill of Costs
17/10/1827	*Lyon's Advertiser*, Cowdery unclaimed letters, Arcadia
12/1827-02/1828	Joseph Smith's transcription of characters
(1827 & 1828)	1840 articles of John A. Clark re Harris & Smith (dates questionable)
1827-1828	Return of Mt. Moriah Lodge (04/06/1827-04/06/1828), listing Hyrum Smith, Mason
04/06/1828	Return of Mt. Moriah Lodge # 112, Hyrum, 1827-1828
05/06/1828	Joseph and Emma's deceased infant's gravestone (live birth, died same day)

(Appendix 5 continued)

11/07/1828	*Wayne Sentinel*, Lyman Cowdery unclaimed letters, Palmyra
[07/1828]	BC 2 (D&C 3) on the loss of the 116 pages
06/04/1829	Smith contract to buy land from Hale; Cowdery witness
[02/1829]	BC 3 (D&C 4), a marvelous work
[03/1829]	N. K. W Collection (cf. D&C 5), he hath a gift to translate
[04/1829]	BC 5 (D&C 6), Oliver's gift to translate
[04/1829]	LDS archives (cf. D&C 7), John will tarry until Christ comes
[04/1829]	BC 7 (cf. D&C 8), Cowdery's gift of the rod
[04/1829]	BC 8 (cf. D&C 9), gift to translate taken from Cowdery
[05/1829]	BC 9 (cf. D&C 10), Plates of Nephi, lost pages
[05/1829]	BC 10 (cf. D&C 11) Hyrum's gift
[05/1829]	BC 11 (cf. D&C 12) revelation for Joseph Knight
[early 06/1829]	Cowdery's revelation on church organization
early 06/1829	Title-page BOM description, also submitted for copyright
11/06/1829	*Book of Mormon* copyright
[06/1829]	BC 12 (D&C 14), revelation to David Whitmer
[06/1829]	BC 13 (D&C 15), revelation to John Whitmer
[06/1829]	BC 14 (cf. D&C 16), revelation to Peter Whitmer Jr.
[06/1829]	BC 15 (cf. D&C 18), Oliver & David ordained to ordain priests & instructed to select 12 disciples
[06/1829]	1835 D&C 42 (cf. D&C 17), the 3 witnesses selected
14/06/1829	letter of Oliver Cowdery to Hyrum Smith (begin outreach)
17/06/1829	letter of Jesse Smith to Hyrum Smith
26/06/1829	Wayne Sentinel article re re"gold bible" & its translation
c. 06/1829	Rochester (NY) Gem article re Harris & "gold bible"
c. 06/1829?	Cowdery's revelation (Cowdery: I have written these things…)
c. 06/1829	Testimony of the witnesses
08/1829	*Book of Mormon* preface, prior to commencement of printing
c. 08/1829	Palmyra Freeman article re "gold bible," translation completed and printing will begin (Jonathan Hadley, from Harris?)
27/08/1829	Niagara Courier article re "gold bible" & Smith's characters
29/08/1829	Rochester Dailey Advertiser re "gold bible"
02/09/1829	The Reflector, first BOM extracts printed by a newspaper
05/09/1829	Rochester (NY) Gem, "gold bible," Harris sought a printer
22/09/1829	Painesville Telegraph re "gold bible"
08/10/1829	Smith/Cowdery bible purchased by Cowdery from Grandin's
22/10/1829	letter of Joseph Smith letter to Oliver Cowdery
09/1829-01/1830	Palmyra Reflector notices re the "gold bible"

(Appendix 5 continued)

02/09/1829	Palmyra Reflector, "gold bible" is in press, will appear shortly
06/11/1829	letter of Oliver Cowdery to Joseph Smith (printing slow, type still awaited)
09/11/1829	Cowdery letter to Blatchly
28/12/1829	letter of Oliver Cowdery to Joseph Smith (I've become a printer)
[03/1830]	BC 16 (cf. D&C 19), revelation to Harris: "Pay the printer's debt."

BIBLIOGRAPHIES

Bibliography 1. Biblical Materials (Annotated)

Some of these sources are in languages that cannot be easily transliterated without a special Latin-based transliteration font for the purpose. I have done the transliteration of these titles by using the MS Word symbol insertion function, while mostly trying to stick to the TTF ASCI extended character set.

Old Testament

Hebrew Masoretic

Baer, S., and Fr. Delitsch. *Liber Jesaiae, textum masoreticum accuratissime expressit, e fontibus masorae variae illustravit, notis criticis confirmavit.* Lipsiae: ex Officina Bernhardi Tauchnitz, 1872. The Hebrew text with a small collection of variant readings and Masoretic variations. Latin introduction and notes.

De-Rossi, J. B. *Variae Lectiones Veteris Testamenti.* Parmae: ex Regio Typographeo, 1784, 1786. Collection of Hebrew variant readings complementing the work of Kennicott. Latin introduction and notes.

Goshen-Gottstein. M. H. *The Book of Isaiah.* Hebrew University Bible Project. Jerusalem: Magnes Press, 1995. Hebrew text and large current apparatus, including Masora.

Green, Jay P., editor, translator. *The Interlinear Bible, Hebrew-Greek-English.* Peabody, MA: Hendrickson Publishers, 1986. The Hebrew text of the OT, and the Greek text of the NT, both with a sublinear translation of the Hebrew or Greek, plus a fluent but literal translation at the outside column of large-format pages.

Kennicott, B. *Vetus Testamentum Hebraicum cum Variis Lectionibus* (tomus primus et tomus secundus). Oxonii: e typographeo Clarendoniano, 1776, 1780. Hebrew edited text and perhaps still our largest collection of variant readings, its primary defect being the absence of materials come to light since its appearance. Introduction in Latin, and lists of mss containing each book, in whole or in part.

Kittel, R. *Biblia Hebraica, edidit Rudolf Kittel. Textum Masoreticum curavit Paul Kahle, Editionem Tertiam denue elaboratam ad Finem perduxerunt, editionem septimam auxerunt et emendaverunt A. Alt et O. Eissfeldt.* Stuttgart: Württembergische Bibelanstalt, 1966. Hebrew text, Masora, and good critical apparatus, including variant readings from the Qumran Great Isaiah Scroll.

Elliger, K., & W. Rudolph, eds. *Biblia Hebraica Stuttgartensia.* Masora prepared by G. E. Weil. Stuttgart: Deutsche Bibelgesellschaft, 1997 [1967-77]. Hebrew text, Masora, critical apparatus; a major revision of the Kittel edition. Large apparatus.

Qumran Hebrew

Burrows, M., ed. *The Dead Sea Scrolls of St. Marks Monastery* (Vol. I). J. C. Trever and W. H. Brownlee assisting. New Haven, Connecticut: The American Schools of Oriental Research, 1950. Both photographs of the Great Isaiah Scroll, and the edited text, with an introduction.

De Vaux, R., et al., eds. *Discoveries in the Judean Desert*. Oxford: Clarendon Press, *Vol. I: Qumran Cave I*, by D. Barthélemy and J. T. Milik, 1955; *Vol. II: Les Grottes de Murabba'ât*, par P. Benoit, J. T. Milik et R. de Vaux, 1961; *Vol. III: Lex 'Petites Grottes' de Qumrân* par M. Baillet, J. T. Milik et R. de Vaux, 1962; and *Vol. V: Qumrân Cave 4*, by J. M. Allegro, 1968. Edited fragments and photographic plates from the Qumran caves, with introductions, notes and explanations in English and French.

Habermann, A. M. *Megillôt Midbar Yehûdâ*. Israel: 1959. Hebrew text of Qumran fragments.

Parry, Donald W. and Elisha Qimron. *The Great Isaiah Scroll (1qisa): A New Edition*. Leiden: Brill, 1999. Scroll photos and transliteration on facing large-format pages.

Sukenik, E. L. *The Dead Sea Scrolls of the Hebrew University*. Jerusalem: Magnes Press, The Hebrew University, 1955. *'Oṣar ham-Megillôt hag-Genûzôt*, Jerusalem: Bialik Institute and the Hebrew University, 1954. Hebrew text of Qumran fragments, with an introduction and discussion.

———. *Megillôt Genûzôt, mittôk Genîzâ Qedûmâ še nimṣe'â be-Midbâr Yehûdâ*. Yerušalayim: Môṣâd Bialik, 1948-9. Hebrew text of Qumran fragments.

Samaritan Hebrew

Blayney, B. *Pentateuchos Hebraeo-Samaritanus character Hebraeo-Chaldaico*. Oxonii: ex typographeo Clarendoniano, 1799. Samaritan Hebrew text in Hebrew script and a small critical apparatus. Introduction in Latin.

Bowman, J. "Samaritan Decalogue Inscriptions," *Bulletin of the John Rylands Library*, Vol. 33, No. 1, September. Manchester. A general discussion of the inscriptions, with photographs and transcriptions in Hebrew script.

Sadaqa, A., and R. Sadaqa. *Jewish Version, Samaritan Version, of the Pentateuch, Exodus*. Tel Aviv: 1964. The Samaritan Hebrew text, in Hebrew script, in parallel columns with the Jewish Hebrew text, and differences in large type.

Von Gall, A. F. *Der Hebräische Pentateuch der Samaritaner*. Giessen: Verlag von Alfred Töpelmann, 1918. Samaritan Hebrew text with a relatively thorough critical apparatus. Introduction in German and text in Hebrew script.

Walton, B., ed. Samaritan Pentateuch in *Biblia Sacra Polyglotta Complectentia, cum Apparatu, Appendicibus, Tabulis, Variis Lectionibus, Annotationibus Indicibus*. Londini: imprimebat Thomas Roycroft, 1657. Considered by many to be the greatest of the polyglots.

Greek Septuagint

Brenton, Lancelot *The Septuagint with Apocrypha: Greek and English*. Peabody, MA: Hendrickson Publishers, 2016. Originally published by Samuel Bagster and Sons, London, 1851. The Greek text and an English translation in parallel columns.

Brooke A. E., and N. McLean. *The Old Testament in Greek, according to the text of codex Vaticanus, supplemented from other uncial manuscripts, with a critical apparatus*. Edited by Alan England Brooke and Norman McLean. London: Cambridge University Press, 1917. Greek text and an extensive apparatus, but the work stopped before the prophets.

Holmes, R., and J. Parsons. *Vetus Testamentum Graecum cum Variis Lectionibus, edidit Robertus Holmes, continuavit Jacobus Parsons.* Oxonii: e typographeo Clarendoniano, 1798-1827. Greek text and perhaps still the largest collection of variant readings, but, like Kennicott's Hebrew edition, it lacks readings from subsequently available sources.

Rahlfs, A. *Septuaginta, Id est Vetus Testamentum Graece iuxta LXX interpretes,* edidit Alfred Rahlfs, edition octava. Stuttgart: Württembergische Bibelanstalt, 1965. Greek text with a small but useful critical apparatus and an introduction in German, English and Latin. This is the source used by most scholars today.

Swete, H. B. *The Old Testament in Greek according to the Septuagint,* edited by Henry Barclay Swete. London: Cambridge University Press, 1887. Greek text, a good critical apparatus and a useful introduction in English, including a description of the mss.

Ziegler, J. *Septuaginta Vetus Testamentum Graecum Auctoritate Societatis Literarum Gottingensis,* edidit Joseph Ziegler. Göttingen: Dandenhoect & Ruprecht, 1939. Greek text and two extensive apparatus, including patristic readings. Introduction in German.

Aramaic: Eastern & Western Syriac (Christian Aramaic)

Altschueler, M. *Die Syrische Bibel-Version Peschita im Urtext,* herausgegeben von M. Altschueler, Orbis Antiquitatum. Leipzig und Wien: Verlag "Lumen," 1908. Syriac text of the Pentateuch. No apparatus.

Biblia Sacra juxta Versionem Simplicem quae dicitur Pschitta. Beryti: Typis Typographiae Catholicae, 1951. Three volumes. No apparatus.

Diettrich, G. *Ein Apparatus criticus zur Pešitto zur Propheten Jesaia,* heraus gegeben von G. Diettrich, Beihefte zur Zeitschrift fur die alttestamentliche Wissenschaft. Giessen: Alfred Töpelmann, 1905. No text. Western Syriac, Eastern Syriac and Syrian Patristic sources are used for the apparatus, which is relatively large and carefully done. Introduction in German and the apparatus slightly annotated in Latin.

Lagarde, P. de. *Bibliothecae Syriacae a Paulo de Lagarde collectae quae ad Philologiam Sacram pertinent.* Gottingae: Luederi Horstmann, 1892. Syriac text of the Pentateuch with an apparatus.

Lee, S. *Vetus Testamentum Syriace, recognovit et ad fidem codicum mss. emendavit,* edidit Samuel Lee. Londini: Impensis ejusdem Societatis, impressit R. Watts, 1823. Syriac text, according to the Western Syriac tradition.

Leiden Peshitta Institute. *The Old Testament in Syriac according to the Peshitta Version,* edited by the Peshitta Institute. Leiden: Brill, 1972+. Isaiah is in part 3.1 (1987) and Ezekiel is in part 3.3 (1980). Syriac text and a representative critical apparatus.

[Mausil] *Biblia Sacra juxta Versionem Simplicem quae dicitur Pschitta.* Mausili: Typis Fratrum Praedicatorum, 1887. Syriac text, according to the Eastern Syriac tradition.

Middeldorpf, H. *Codex Syriaco-Heaplaris, Liber Quartus Regum, e codice Parisiensi, Iesaias, Duodecim Prophetae* (et cetera) *e codice Mediolansi,* edidit et commentariis illustravit Henricus Middeldorpf. Berolini: apud Th. Chr. Fr. Enslin, 1835. Syriac text with notes.

[Urmia] *Vetus Testamentum Syriace et Neosyriace*. Urmia: 1852. Syriac text according to the Eastern Syriac tradition.

Walton, B. *Syriac Peshitta in Biblia Sacra Polyglotta Complectentia*. Londini: imprimebat Thomas Roycroft, 1657. Syriac text, according to the Western Syriac tradition.

Aramaic: Targum texts (Palestinian & Babylonian Jewish Aramaic; Samaritan Aramaic)

Berliner, A. *Targum Onkelos*, herausgegeben und erlautert von A. Berliner, text nach editio Sabioneta. Berlin: Gorzelanczyk & Co., 1884. Aramaic text fully pointed.

Brull, A. *Das Samaritanische Targum zur Pentateuch zum erstenmale in Hebraeischer Quadratschrift, nebst einem Anhange textkritischen Inhaltes*, herausgegeben von Adolf Brull. Fankfurt a. M.: Verlag von Wilhelm Eras, 1873. The Samaritan Aramaic text in Hebrew script.

Diez Macho, A. *Neophyti 1, Targum Palestinense Ms. de la Biblioteca Vaticana*, Tomo II, Exodo, Alejandro Diez Macho, Madrid: Consejo Superior de Investigaciones Cientificas, 1970. Aramaic text and a useful apparatus of variant readings, with an introduction in Spanish and translations of the text in Spanish, French and English.

Ginsburger, M. *Das Fragmententhargum (Thargum jeruschalmi zum Pentateuch)* herausgegeben von Moses Ginsburger. Berlin: S. Calvary & Co., 1899. The Aramaic text with German notes.

———. *Pseudo-Jonathan (Thargum Jonathan ben Usiël zum Pentateuch)* herausgegeben von Moses Ginsburger. Hildesheim: Georg Olms Verlag, 1971. The Aramaic text with German notes.

Lagarde, P. de. *Prophetae Chaldaice e fide codicis reuchliniani*. Reproductio phototypica edition 1872. Osnabrück: Otto Zeller, 1967. Aramaic text in unpointed Hebrew script and no apparatus.

———. *Hagiographia Chaldaice*. Reproductio phototypica edition 1873. Osnabrück: Otto Zeller, 1967.

Petermann, H. *Pentateuchus Samaritanus* ad fidem librorum manuscriptorum apud Nablusianos repertorum edidit et variis lectiones adscripsit H. Petermann. Berolini: apud W. Moeser, 1882. The Samaritan Aramaic text in Samaritan script, with variant readings.

Sperber, A. *The Bible in Aramaic Based on Old Manuscripts and Printed Texts*, edited by Alexander Sperber. Leiden: E. J. Brill, 1959. Aramaic text, pointed, with a large systematic critical apparatus and an English introduction. *The Pentateuch* is the Targum Onkelos, and *The Former Prophets* is the Targum Jonathan

Stenning, J. F. *The Targum of Isaiah, edited with a Translation by J. F. Stenning*. Oxford: The Clarendon Press, 1949. Aramaic text with a critical apparatus and an English introduction.

Walton, B. Samaritan Pentateuch in *Biblia Sacra Polyglotta Complectentia*, Londini: imprimebat Thomas Roycroft, 1657. Samaritan Aramaic text in Hebrew script.

Vulgate Latin

Colunga, A., and L. Turrado. *Biblia Sacra iuxta Vulgatem Clementinam nova editio*. Matriti: Biblioteca de Autores Cristianos, 1965. The Latin text but no apparatus.

Gasquet, A., et al. *Biblia Sacra iuxta Latinam Vulgatam Versionem ad Codicum Fidem iussu Pii PP. XI (ejusque successorum) cura et studio Monachorum Abbatiae Sancti Hieronymi praeside (initio) Aidano Gasquet.* Rome: Typis Polyglottis Vaticanis, 1929+. Latin text and three extensive apparatus, certainly the most complete Latin edition, reporting variant readings from both the mss. and the patristic sources.

Vercellone, C. *Variae Lectiones Vulgatae Latinae Bibliorum* editionis quas Carolus Vercellone digessit. Romae: apud Iosephum Spithöver, 1860. Variant readings and notes in Latin, for the Pentateuch.

Weber, R. *Biblia Sacra iuxta Vulgatam Versionem recensuit et brevi apparatu instruxit Robertus Weber*. Stuttgart: Wurttembergische Bibelanstalt, 1969. Latin text, and English introduction with a small apparatus.

Italic (pre-Vulgate) Latin

Marazuela, T. A. *La Vetus Latina Hispana, reconstuccion, sistematizacion y analisis de sus diversos elementos, coordinacion y edicion critica de su texto, studio comparative con los demas elementos de la "vetus latina", los padres y escritores eclesiasticos, los textos griegos y la vulgate por Teofilo Ayuso Narazuela*. Madrid: Consejo Superior de Invesitgaciones Cientificas, Instituto "Francisco Suarez," 1967. The Hispanic Italic (Old Latin) text with variant readings and comparison with Spanish writings and with the patristic fathers, containing the Octateuch.

Sabatier, P. (Sabbathier). *Bibliorum Sacrorum Latinae Versiones Antiquae, Seu Vetus Italica, caeterae quaecunque in codicibuts mss. & antiquorum libris reperiri potuerunt: quae cum Vulgata Latina, & cum textu Graeco comparatuntur, opera & studio D. Petri Sabatier*. Parisiis: apud Franciscum Didot, 1751. The Italic (Old Latin) text and the Vulgate in parallel columns, with a large apparatus of Italic variant readings, those from the mss. being followed by patristic references. A marvelous work.

Sahidic (Southern, i.e., Upper-Egypt) Coptic

Amélineau, E. "Fragments de la Version Thébaine de l'Ecriture (Ancien Testament)," par E. Amélineau, *Recueil de Travaux Relatifs à la Philologie et à l'Archéologie Egyptiennes et Assyriennes*. Paris: Librairie A. Frank, 1887: 101-26. Sahidic text, fragments.

Budge, E. A. W. *Coptic Homilies in the Dialect of Upper Egypt, edited from the Papyrus Codex Oriental 5001 in the British Museum*, by E. A. Wallis Budge. London: The British Museum, 1910. Sahidic text, occasional quotations in Coptic religious literature.

Budge, E. A. W. *Miscellaneous Coptic Texts in the Dialect of Upper Egypt, edited with English translations by E. A. Wallis Budge*. London: British Museum, 1915. Occasional quotations in Coptic religious literature of the Sahidic dialect.

Bybliothecae Pierpont Morgan. *Codices M568 (Morganianus) et Cair. Ham. 1² (Cairensis), Isaias Sahidice, Codices Coptici, photographice expressi*, Tomus III. Romae: 1922. Apparently this is the same as *Codices Coptici photographice expressi / 3, Codex M 568 et Cair. Ham. I²* [et Berol. P. 11966] : Isaias Sahidice. New York: OCLC WorldCat does not list the publisher, 1957. The Sahidic text of Isaiah in a clear clean hand and very legibly photographed, with an index tabulae. The holes in the velum fortunately antedate the writing of the text.

Ciasca, P. A. *Sacrorum Bibliorum Fragmenta Copto-Sahidica Musei Borgiani*, iussu et sumptibus S. Congragationis de Propaganda Fide Studio P. Augustini Ciasca edita. Romae: Typis eiusdem S. Congregationis, 1885-9. Sahidic text, large fragments, with a comparison of the edition of E. Amélineau and notes commented upon in Latin, with references to the Greek text.

Erman, A. "Bruchstücke der oberaegyptischen Uebersetzung des alten Testamentes" von Adolf Erman. *Nachrichten von der Königl. Gesellschaft der Wissenschaften und der Georg-Augusts Universität zu Göttingen*, No. 1-21. pp. 401-27. Göttingen: 1880: 401-27. Sahidic text, fragments with comments.

Hebbelynck, A. "Fragments Inédits de la version copte sahidique d'Isaïe," par Ad. Hebbelynck, *Le Muséon, Revue d'Etudes Orientales*. Tome L. Paris: 1937: 219-23. Sahidic text of fragments with notes.

Kahle, P. E. *Bala'izah, Coptic Texts from Deir el-Bala'izah in Upper Egypt*, edited by Paul E. Kahle, Vol. 1. The Griffith Institute. London: Oxford University Press, 1954: 332-33.

Kasser, R. *Papyrus Bodmer XXIII: Esaïe XLV,1-LXVI,24 en Sahidique*. Rudolphe Kasser, Bibliotheca Bodmeriana, 1965. Sahidic text with a small apparatus; introduction and translation in French.

Laçau, P. "Textes de l'Ancien Testament en Copte Sahidique," par Pierre Laçau. *Recueil de Travaux Relatifs à la Philologie et à l'Archéologie Egyptiennes et Assyriennes*, Nouvelle Série, Tome Septième. Paris: 1901: 103-21. Sahidic text, fragments.

Maspero, G. "Fragments de la Version Thébaine de l'Ancien Testament," *Mémoires Publiés par les Membres de la Mission Archéologique Française au Caire*, Tome sixième, 1er Fascicule. Paris: 1892. Sahidic text, relatively important fragments.

Schleifer, J. "Sahidische Bibel-Fragmente aus dem British Museum zu London, II," von J. Schleifer, *Sitzungsberichte der Kais. Akademie der Wissenschaften in Wien, Philosophisch-Historische Klasse*, 162. Wien: 1909, 1911: Band 6. Abhandlung, 7-21 und 164. Band 6. Abhandlung 33-4. Sahidic text, fragments and comments.

Till, W. *Sahidische Bibelfragmente, Koptische Pergamente Teologischen Inhalts 1*, herausgegeben und bearbeitet von Walter Till. Mitteilungen aus der Papyrussammlung der Nationalbibliothek in Wien. Neue Serie, II. Wien: 1934: Folge, X, 8-10. Sahidic text fragments.

Till, W. C. "Sahidische Fragmente des Alten Testamentes," *Le Muséon, Revue d'Etudes Orientales*, Tome L. Paris: 1937: pp. 219-23. Sahidic text of fragments with notes

Wessely, C. *Griechische und Koptische Texte: Theologischen Inhalts 1*, herausgegeben von Carl Wessely. Studien zur Paleographie und Papyruskunde. Leipzig: Verlag von Eduard Avenarius, 1909: 64-5. Sahidic texts, fragments.

Akhmimic (Middle-Egypt) Coptic

Bouriant, U. "Fragments des Petits Prophètes en Dialecte de Panopolis" par U. Bouriant. *Recueil de Travaux Relatifs à la Philologie et à l'Archéologie Egyptiennes et Assyriennes*, Vol. 19. Paris: 1897: 6. Akhmimic text, fragment.

Till, W. *Die Akhmîmische Version der Zwölf Kleinen Propheten (Codex Rainerianus, Wien)*, herausgegeben mit Einleitung, Anmerkung und Würterverzeichnis von Walter Till. Coptica consilio et impensis institute Rask-Oerstediani edita. Hauniae:

Gyldendalske Boghandel-Nordisk Forlag, 1927. Akhmimic text with notes in German.

Bohairic (Northern, i.e., Lower-Egypt) Coptic

Grossouw, W. *The Coptic Versions of the Minor Prophets, a contribution to the study of the Septuagint*, by Willem Grossouw. Rome: Pontifical Biblical Institute: 1938. No text, but contains variant readings to the Septuagint, the Coptic words (from Akhmimic, Sahidic, Bohairic and Fayyumic sources), being presented in Latin, with a detailed discussion, relating to the Coptic evidence to the Septuagint text (since the Coptic versions are translations of the Septuagint).

Lagarde, P. de. *Der Pentateuch Koptisch*, herausgegeben von Paul de Lagarde. Osnabrück: Otto Zeller, 1967. Bohairic text, the Pentateuch, with a small apparatus.

Tattam, H. *Duodecim Prophetarum Minorum Libros in Lingua Aegyptica Vulgo Coptica Seu Memphitica, Latine* edidit Henricus Tattam. Oxonii: e Typographeo Academico, 1836. Bohairic text with a brief Latin preface and a Latin version.

Tattam, H. *Prophetae Majores in Dialecto Linguae Aegyptiacae Memphitica seu Coptica edidit cum versione Latina Henricus Tattam*, Tomus 1. Oxonii: e Typographeo Academico, 1852. Bohairic text, with a Latin text, which is not to be mistaken for a translation of the Coptic. No apparatus.

Ge'ez (Classical Ethiopic)

Bassano, F. da. *Belûy Kîdân*, edidit Francesco da Bassano. Asmarae: imprimatur Clelestinus Cattaneo, 1926. The Ethiopic Old Testament in four volumes. Ethiopic text and introduction with no apparatus.

Boyd, J. O. *The Octateuch in Ethiopic according to the text of the Paris Codex, with the variants of five other manuscripts*, edited by J. Oscar Boyd, *Bibliotheca Abessinica*, Vol. IV. Leyden: E. J. Brill, 1911. The Ethiopic text with a small apparatus and an English introduction containing a description of the mss.

Dillmann, A. *Biblia Veteris Testamenti Aethiopica, tomus primus, sive Octateuchus Aethiopicus, ad librorum manuscriptorum fidem edidit et apparatu critico instruxit Augustus Dillmann*. Lipsiae: F. C. G. Vogelii, 1853. Ethiopic text with a collection of variant readings and a Latin description of the mss.

Löfgren, O. *Jona, Nahum, Habakuk, Zephanja, Haggai, Sacharja und Maleachi Ätiopisch unter Zugrundelegung des Oxforder Ms. Huntington 625 nach mehreren Handschriften* herausgegeben von Oscar Löfgren. Uppsala: Almqvist & Wiksells, 1930. Ethiopic text with a small apparatus with an introduction in German.

Arabic

Carlyle, J. D., and H. Ford. *The Holy Bible Containing the Old and New Testaments in the Arabic Language*, principally undertaken by J. D. Carlyle and finished by H. Ford. Newcastle-on-Tyne: Sarah Hodgson, 1811-16. Arabic text, no apparatus.

Derenbourg, J. *Version Arabe du Pentateuque de R. Saadia ben Iosef al-Fayyoûmî, revue, corrigée et accompagnée de notes hébraïques, avec quelques fragments de traduction Française d'après l'arabe par J. Derenbourg; Oeuvres Complètes de R.*

Saadia ben Iosef al-Fayyoûmî. Paris: Librairie de la Société Asiatique de l'Ecole des Langues Orientales Vivantes, 1893. Arabic text in Hebrew script, with notes.

Derenbourg, J., and H. Derenbourg. *Version Arabe d'Isaïe de R. Saadia ben Iosef al-Fayyoûmî publié avec des notes hébraïques et une traduction Française d'après l'arabe par Joseph Derenbourg et Hartwig Derenbourg; Oeuvres Complètes de R. Saadia ben Iosef al-Fayyoûmî*. Paris: Librairie de la Société Asiatique de l'Ecole des Langues Orientales Vivantes, 1896. Arabic text in Hebrew script, with notes and a French translation.

'Irâqî, S. B. Y. *Sêfer keter tôrâ han-niqrâ tâg ... sêfer šemôt*. Jerusalem: 1893-4. Pentateuch. Arabic text in Hebrew script of the translation of Saadia Gaon, with no apparatus.

Paulus, H. E. G. R. *Saadiae Phijumensis Versio Iesaiae Arabica cum aliis speciminibus arabico-Biblicis e mss. Bodleiano nunc primum edidit atque ad modum chrestomathiae arabicae Biblicae glossario perpetuo instruxit Henricus Eberh. Gottl. Paulus*. Ienae: apud C. H. Cunonis Haeredes, 1790-1. Arabic text, transliterated from the Hebrew script and partially pointed, though containing many errors (v. emendations in fascicule II), some of which indicate a certain initial innocence of some basic principles of Arabic grammar (cf. 2:16). There are also portions of another Judeo-Arabic ms. in Hebrew script.

Walton, B. Arabic Old Testament, in *Biblia Sacra Polyglotta Complectentia*, Londini: imprimebat Thomas Roycroft, 1657. Arabic text.

New Testament

Greek

Alford, H., and E. F. Harrison. *The Greek Testament with a critically revised text, a digest of various readings, marginal references to verbal and idiomatic usage, prolegomena, and a critical and exegetical commentary by Henry Alford with revision by Everett F. Harrison*. Chicago: Moody Press, 1958. Greek text, a useful apparatus of variant readings, and a detailed description of mss.

Nestle, E. *Novum Testamentum Graece cum apparatu critico curavit Eberhard Nestle, novis curis elaboraverunt Erwin Nestle et Kurt Aland*. Stuttgart: Wüttembergische Bibelanstalt, 1963. Greek text, useful apparatus, and an introduction in German, Latin and English.

Soden, H. F., von. *Die Schriften des Neuen Testaments in ihrer ältesten erreichbaren textgestalt hergestellt auf grund ihrer textgeschichte von Herman Freiherr von Soden*. Göttingen: Vandenhoeck und Ruprecht, 1913. Greek text, large apparatus, German introduction with an analysis of the mss.

Souter, A. *Novum Testamentum Graece textui a retractatoribus anglis adhibito brevem adnotationem criticam subiecit Alexander Souter*. Oxonii: e Typographeo Clarendoniano, 1910. Greek text with a brief apparatus.

Tischendorf, C. *Novum Testamentum Graece ad antiquissimos testes denuo recensuit apparatum criticum omni studio perfectum apposuit commentationem isagogicum praetexuit Constantinus Tischendorf*. Lipsiae: Giesecke & Devrient, 1869. Greek text, useful apparatus, introduction in Latin, and a description of mss.

Tregelles, S. P. *The Greek New Testament, edited from ancient authorities, with their various readings in full, and the Latin version of Jerome, by Samuel Prideaux Tregelles.* London: S. Bagster and Sons, 1857-79. Greek text with a Latin version and a large collection of variant readings that has been criticized for not omitting relatively unimportant details.

Syriac

Bensly, R. L., J. R. Harris and F. C. Burkitt. *The Four Gospels in Syriac Transcribed from the Sinaitic Palimpsest*, by Robert L. Bensly, J. Rendel Harris and F. Crawford Burkitt with an introduction by Agnes Smith Lewis. Cambridge: The University Press, 1894. Syriac text with occasional large lacunae. The text is unpointed.

Bonus, A. *Collatio Codicis Lewisiani Rescripti Evangeliorum Sacrorum Syriacorum cum Codice Curetoniano cui adiectae sunt lectiones e peshitto desumptae, auctore Alberto Bonus.* Oxonii: e Prelo Clarendoniano, 1896. Variant readings in Syriac script explained in Latin and collated in three columns for the three sources stated in the title, plus a small apparatus.

Burkitt, F. C. *Evangelion da-Mepharreshe, the Curetonian Version of the Four Gospels, with the readings of the Sinai Palimpsest and the early Syriac Patristic evidence edited by F. Crawford Burkitt.* Cambridge: The University Press, 1904. Syriac text with an English translation and introduction. The apparatus is useful and is in both Syriac and English.

Cureton, W. *Remains of a Very Ancient Recension of the Four Gospels in Syriac, discovered, edited and translated by William Cureton.* London: John Murray, 1858. A beautiful Syriac text with an English translation. The text is not pointed.

Erizzo, F. M. *Evangeliarium Hierosolymitanum ex codice Vaticano Palaestino deprompsit edidit Latine vertit prolegomenis ac glossario adornavit Comes Franciscus Miniscalchi Erizzo.* Veronae: apud Vicentini et Franchini, 1861. Unpointed Syriac text, replete with gospel quotations, a Latin introduction, and an index to the quotations.

Gwilliam, G. H. *The New Testament in Syriac, edited by G. H. Gwilliam, with the assistance of J. Pinkerton and A. S. Tritton.* London: The British and Foreign Bible Society, 1955. Pointed Syriac text.

Jones, A. R. *Textus Sacrorum Evangeliorum Versionis Simplicis Syriacae juxta Editionem Schaafianam, collates cum duobus ejusdem vetustis codd. mss. in Bibliotheca Bodleiana repositis, nec non cum cod. ms. Commentarii Gregorii Bar-Hebraei ibidem adservato, A. Ricardo Jones.* Oxonii: e Typographeo Clarendoniano, 1805. A list of variant readings, in Syriac script and explained in Latin.

Lee, S. *Prolegomena in Biblia Sacra Polyglotta Bagsteriana, auctore Samuele Lee, et Novum Testamentum Syriacum, Peschito Dictum.* Londini: Sumptibus Samuelis Bagster, 1831. Syriac text with variant readings. The text is fully pointed.

Leusden, J., and C. Schaaf. *Novum Testamentum Syriacum cum versione Latina, cura et studio Johanis Leusden et Caroli Schaaf editum, ad omnes editiones diligenter recensitum, et variis lectionibus, magno labore collectis.* Lugduni Batavorum: apud Joh. Mulleri, 1717. Fully pointed Syriac text with a Latin version and variant readings.

Lewis, A. S. *The Old Syriac Gospels or Evangelion da-Mepharreshe, including the latest additions and emendations, with the variants of the Curetonian text, corroborations from many other mss., and a list of quotations from ancient authors, edited by Agnes Smith Lewis.* London: Williams and Norgate, 1910. Syriac text with a useful apparatus.

Lewis, A. S., and M. S. Gibson. *The Palestinian Syriac Lectionary of the Gospels re-edited from two Sinai mss. and from P. de Lagarde's edition of the "Evangeliarium Hierosolymitarum" by Agnes Smith Lewis and Margaret Dunlop Gibson.* London: Kegan Paul, Trench Trübner & Co., 1899. Unpointed text with apparatus and an index for the gospel quotations.

Pusey, P. E. *Tetraeuangelium Sanctum juxta Simplicem Syrorum Versionem, ad fidem codicum, massorae, editionem denuo recognitum, lectionum supellectilem quam conquisiverat Philippus Edwardus Pusey, auxit, digessit, edidit Georgius Henricus Gwilliam.* Oxonii: e Typographeo Clarendoniano, 1901. Syriac text of the gospels with a relatively large apparatus and an introduction and translation, both in Latin. The text is partially pointed.

Walton, B., ed. Syriac New Testament, in *Biblia Sacra Polyglotta Complectentia.* Londini: imprimebat Thomas Roycroft, 1657. Pointed Syriac text.

White, J. *Sacrorum Evangeliorum Versio Syriaca Philoxeniana ex codd. mss Ridleianis nunc primum edita cum interpretation et annotationibus Josephi White.* Oxonii: e Typographeo Clarendoniano, 1778. Syriac text of the gospels, with notes and a Latin translation. The text is fully pointed.

Vulgate Latin

Colunga, A., and L. Turrado. *Biblia Sacra iuxta Vulgatem Clementinam nova editio.* Matriti: Biblioteca de Autores Cristianos, 1965. The Latin text but no apparatus.

Weber, R. *Biblia Sacra iuxta Vulgatam Versionem recensuit et brevi apparatu instruxit Robertus Weber.* Stuttgart: Wurttembergische Bibelanstalt, 1969. Latin text, and English introduction with a small apparatus.

Wordsworth, J., and H. J. White. *Novum Testamentum Latine secundum editionem Sancti Hieronymi ad codicum manuscriptorum fidem* recensuit Iohannes Wordsworth in operis societatem adsumpto Henrico Iuliano White. Oxonii: e Typographeo Clarendoniano, 1889-1922.

Italic (pre-Vulgate) Latin

Berger, M. S. *Un Ancien Texte Latin des Actes des Apôtres retrouvé dans un manuscript provenant de Perpignan,* par M. Samuel Berger. Paris: Imprimerie Nationale, 1895.

Bruyne, D. de. *Les Fragments de Freising (épitres de S. Paul et épitres catholiques) édités par Donatien de Bruyne, Collectanea Biblica Latina, Vol. V.* Rome: Bibliothèque Vaticane, 1921. Latin text with large lacunae.

Buchanan, E. S. *Euangelium sec. Iohannem, and Actus Discipulorum, both e Cedice Rescripto Tarragonensi, extractum et translatum, per E. S. Buchannan.* New York: Primitive Text Publishing Bureau, 1919.

Buchanan, E. S. *The Four Gospels from the Codex Corbiensis being the first complete edition of the ms., together with fragments of the Catholic Epistles, of the Acts and of the Apocalypse from the Fleury Palimpsest, by E. S. Buchanan, Old-Latin Texts No. V.* Oxford: at the Clarendon Press, 1907.

Buchanan, E. S. *The Four Gospels from the Codex Veronensis (b) being the first complete edition of the Evangeliarium Purpureum, with an introduction descriptive of the ms. by E. S. Buchanan, Old-Latin Biblical Texts No. VI.* Oxford: at the Clarendon Press, 1911.

Jüblicher, A. *Itala, Das Neue Testament in Altlateinischer Uberlieferung nach den Handschriften herausgegeben von Adolf Jüblicher.* Berlin: Walter de Gruyter & Co., 1938-63. Latin text of the Old Latin version with numerous variant readings.

Roensch, H. *Das Neue Testament Tertullian's aus den Schriften des Letzteren Möglichst vollständich reconstruirt mit Einleitungen und Anmerkungen textkritischen und sprachlichen Inhaltes von Herman Roensch.* Leipzig: Fues's Verlag, 1871. Latin text, a presentation of the biblical quotations in Tertullian's works, with a German introduction.

Sabatier, P. (Sabbathier) *Bibliorum Sacrorum Latinae Versiones Antiquae, Seu Vetus Italica, caeterae quaecunque in codicibuts mss. & antiquorum libris reperiri potuerunt: quae cum Vulgata Latina, & cum textu Graeco comparatuntur, opera & studio D. Petri Sabatier.* Parisiis: apud Franciscum Didot, 1751. The Italic (Old Latin) text and the Vulgate in parallel columns, with a large apparatus of Italic variant readings, those from the mss. being followed by patristic references. A marvelous work.

Sanday, W., and C. H. Turner. *Novum Testamentum Sancti Irenaei Episcopi Lugdunensis edited from the mss. with introductions, apparatus, notes and appendices by the late William Sanday and Cuthbert Hamilton Turner, Old Latin Biblical Texts No. VII.* Oxford: at the Clarendon Press, 1922. Latin text with a large collection of variant readings.

Soden, H. F. von. *Das Lateinische Neue Testament in Afrika zur Zeit Cyrians nach bibelhandschriften und väterzeignissen herausgegeben von Hans Freiherr von Soden.* Leipzig: J. C. Hinrichs'sche Buchhandlung, 1909. Latin text with a useful apparatus and a German introduction.

White, H. J. *Portions of the Acts of the Apostles, of the Epistle of St. James and of the First Epistle of St. Peter from the Bobbio Palimpsest (s), edited by Henry J. White, Old=Latin Biblical Texts No. IV.* Oxford: at the Clarendon Press, 1897. Acts III is not present.

White, H. J. *The Four Gospels from the Munich ms. with a fragment from St. John in the Hof-Bibliothek at Vienna, edited by Henry J. White, Old Latin Biblical Texts No. III.* Oxford: at the Clarendon Press, 1888. Latin text with large lacunae.

Wordsworth, J. *The Gospel according to St. Matthew, from the St. Germain ms. with introduction descriptive of the manuscript and five appendices, edited by John Wordsworth, Old-Latin Biblical Texts No. I.* Oxford: at the Clarendon Press, 1883. Latin text with critical notes in Latin.

Wordsworth, J., W. Sanday and H. J. White. *Portions of the Gospels according to St. Mark and St. Matthew from the Bobbio ms together with other fragments of the gospels from six mss, edited by John Wordsworth, W. Sanday and H. J. White, Old-Latin Biblical Texts No. II.* Oxford: at the Clarendon Press, 1886. Latin text and critical notes in Latin.

Sahidic (Southern, i.e., Upper-Egypt) Coptic

Balestri, P. J. *Sacrorum Bibliorum Fragmenta Copto-Sahidica Musei Borgiani, Vol. III, edidit P. J. Balestri.* Romae: e Typographia Polyglotta, 1994. Sahidic Coptic text with useful notes.

Budge, E. A. W. *Coptic Biblical Texts in the Dialect of Upper Egypt* edited by E. A. Wallis Budge. London: The British Museum, 1912. Sahidic text with notes; contains Acts III.

Horner, G. W. *The Coptic Version of the New Testament in the Southern Dialect, otherwise called Theban and Sahidic with introduction, critical apparatus, edited by George William Horner.* Osnabruck: Otto Zeller, 1898-1905. Sahidic Coptic text with a large collection of variant readings, a very literal English translation and an introduction. Reprinted in 1969.

Bohairic (Northern, i.e. Lower-Egypt) Coptic

Girgis, H. et al. *Piǧôm eṯouab tîdiaṯêkê emberi tîhouitî entoi pi"d" eneuangelion (al-ǧuz` al-`awwal, al-bašâ`ir al-`arba`).* Cairo: The Tawfîq Coptic Press, 1935. Bohairic Coptic text of the four gospels with a useful apparatus, a forward in Coptic, and an *explication de texte* in Arabic.

Horner, G. W. *The Coptic Version of the New Testament in the Northern Dialect, otherwise called Memphitic and Bohairic with introduction, critical apparatus and literal English translation, edited by George William Horner.* Osnabruck: Otto Zeller, 1898-1905. Bohairic Coptic text with a large collection of variant readings, a very literal English translation and a detailed description of the mss. Reprinted in 1969.

Kasser, R. *Papyrus Bodmer III: Evangile de Jean et Genèse I-IV,2, en bohairique, édité par Rodolphe Kasser, Corpus Scriptorum Christianorum Orientalium, Scriptores Coptici, Tomus 25.* Louvain: Secretariat du Corpus S. C. O., 1958. Bohairic Coptic text with notes in French.

Lagarde, P. de. *Caterae in Evangelia Aegyptiacae quae supersunt Pauli de Lagarde Studio et sumptibus edita.* Gottingae: Arnoldi Hoyer, 1886. Bohairic Coptic text with an index to the passages, note, and the quotations further located by line at the foot of each page.

Murqus, M., and N. `Azîz. `Inǧîl al Qadîs Murqus bil-luġa al-qibtîya (*Piǧôm eṯouab tîdiaṯêkê emberi, euangelion kata Markon*). Cairo: 1967. Typed Bohairic Coptic text with no apparatus.

Schwartze, M. G. *Quatuor Evangelia in Dialecto Linguae Copticae Memphitica emendavit, adnotationibus criticis et grammaticis, variantibus lectionibus expositis atque texta Coptico cum Graeco comparator instruxit M. G. Schwartze.* Lipsiae: sumptibus Joh. Ambros. Barthii, 1846. Bohairic Coptic text with extensive notes including variant readings.

Ge'ez (Classical Ethiopic)

Platt, T. P. *Novum Testamentum Aethiopice* ad codicum manuscriptorum fidem edidit Thomas Pell Platt. Londini: impressit Ricardus Watts, 1830. Ethiopic text with no apparatus.

Walton, B., ed. Ethiopic New Testament, in *Biblia Sacra Polyglotta Complectentia*. Londini: imprimebat Thomas Roycroft, 1657

Arabic

Lagarde, P. de. *Die Vier Evangelien, Arabisch, aus der Wiener Handschrift herausgegeben von Paul de Lagarde*. Leipzig: G. A. Brockhaus, 1864. Arabic text with a German introduction containing notes to the text.
Walton, B., ed. Arabic New Testament, in *Biblia Sacra Polygotta Complectentia*. Londini: imprimebat Thomas Roycroft, 1657.

Bibliography 2. Lexical and Linguistic Resources

Allen, James P. *Middle Egyptian. An Introduction to the Language and Culture of the Hieroglyphs* (Cambridge: Cambridge University Press, 2000)
American Heritage College Dictionary of the English Language (Boston, New York: Houghton Mifflin Harcourt Publishing Company, Fifth Edition, 2011).
Analytical Greek Lexicon, Harper Brothers, New York, n.d.
E. A. Wallis Budge. *Egyptian Language: Easy Lessons in Egyptian Hieroglyphics*. Mineola, NY: Dover, 1983 [1910].
Clines, David J. A., ed. *The Dictionary of Classical Hebrew* (8 vols.). Sheffield: Sheffield Academic Press, 1993-2011.
Cook, Edward M. *Dictionary of Qumran Aramaic*. Winona Lake, IN: Eisenbrauns, 2015.
———. *A Glossary of Targum Onkelos According to Alexander Sperber's Edition*. Leiden: Brill, 2008.
Crum, W. E. *A Coptic Dictionary* compiled with the help of many scholars. Oxford: at the Clarendon Press, 1939, 1993.
Dalman, Gustav H., *Aramäisch-Neuhebräisches Handwörterbuch zu Targum, Talmud und Midrasch*. Hildesheim, Zürich: Georg Olms Verlag, 1997.
Dillmann, Chr. Fr. Augusti. *Lexicon Linguae Aethiopicae cum Indice Latino*. Osnabrück: Biblio Verlag, 1970.
Gardiner, Alan. *Egyptian Grammar, Being an Introduction to the Study of Hieroglyphs*. London: Oxford University Press, 1973.
Gesenius, Wilhelm. *Handwörterbuch über das Alte Testament*, bearbeitet vom Dr. Frants Buhl. Leipzig: Verlag von F. C. W. Vogel, 1921.
Hava, J. G. *Al-Faraid Arabic-English Dictionary*. Beirut, Lebanon: Catholic Press, 1964.
Hoftijzer J., and K. Jongeling, *Dictionary of the North-West Semitic Inscriptions*. E.J. Brill: Leiden, 1995.
Jastrow, Marcus. *A Dictionary of the Targumim, the Talmud Babli and Yerushalmi, and the Midrashic Literature*. (Two vols. in one, 1943.) Peabody, MA: Hendrickson Publishers, 2005 (4th printing).
Kazimirski, A. de Biberstein. *Dictionnaire Arabe-Français*. 2 vols. Beirut, Lebanon: Librairie du Liban, 1860, reprint, n.d.
Klein, Ernest, *A comprehensive Etymological Dictionary of the Hebrew Language for Readers of English*. Jerusalem: The University of Haifa, Carta, , 1987.
Knisley, Alvin. *Book of Mormon Dictionary*. Independence, MO: Ensign Publishing House, 1909.

Koehler, Ludwig, and Walter Baumgartner. *The Hebrew and Aramaic Lexicon of the Old Testament*. Leiden: E. J. Brill, 1994.

Lane, Edward William. *An Arabic-English Lexicon in Eight Parts*. Beirut, Lebanon: Librairie du Liban, 1863-1893, reprinted 1968.

Levy, Jacob. *Wörterbuch über die Talmudim und Misraschim*. Berlin und Wien: Benjamin Harz Verlag, 1924

Lewis, Charlton T., and Charles Short, *A Latin Dictionary*. Oxford: at the Clarendon Press, 1966.

Leslau, Wolf. *Comparative Dictionary of Geʻez*. Geʻez-English, English-Geʻez. Wiesbaden: Otto Harrassowitz, 1991.

Liddell, Henry George, and Robert Scott, *A Greek-English Lexicon*. Oxford: at the Clarendon Press, 1961

Renz, Johannes, & Wofgang Röllig. *Handbuch der Althebräischen Epigraphik*, 4 vols. Darmstadt: Wissenschftliche Buchgesellschaft, 1995 & 2003.

Lust, J, and E. Eynikel and K. Hauspie, *A Greek-English Lexicon of the Septuagint*. Stuttgart: Deutsche Bibelgesellschaft, 1992.

Sokoloff, Michael, *A Dictionary of Jewish Babylonian Aramaic of the Talmudic and Geonic Periods*. Ramat-Gan, Israel: Bar Ilan University Press, 2002.

———. *A Dictionary of Jewish Palestinian Aramaic*. Ramat-Gan, Israel: Bar Ilan University Press, 1990, 1992.

Sophocles, Evangelinus Apostolides. *Greek Lexicon of the Roman and Byzantine Periods*. Hildesheim, Zürich: Georg Olms Verlag, 2005.

Webster, Noah. *An American Dictionary of the English Language*. New Haven: S. Converse, 1828.

Bibliography 3. *Book of Mormon* Cartography

Allen Joseph Lovell, and Blake Joseph Allen, *Exploring the Lands of the* Book of Mormon, 2nd ed. Orem, UT: *Book of Mormon* Tours and Research Institute, Inc., 2008.

Aston, Duane R. *Return to Cumorah*. Sacramento, CA: American River Publications, 1998/2003.

Birrell, Verla. *The* Book of Mormon *Guide Book*. Salt Lake City: Stevens & Wallis, 1948.

Calderwood, David G. *Voices from the Dust. New Insights into Ancient America.* Austin TX: Historical Publications, Inc. [Print and Bind Direct], 2005.

Cheesman, Paul R. *Early America and the* Book of Mormon, *A photographic Essay of Ancient America*. Salt Lake City: Deseret Book Company, 1972.

———. *These Early Americans*. Salt Lake City: Deseret Book Company, 1974.

———. *The World of the* Book of Mormon. Salt Lake City: Deseret Book Co., 1978.

Cluff (1901) See Joseph Lovell Allen and Blake Joseph Allen, *Exploring the Lands of the* Book of Mormon, 2nd ed. (Orem, UT: *Book of Mormon* Tours and Research Institute, Inc., 2008), 382-83.

Comer, Heber, and Karl G. Maeser.1880. Map published in J. A. and J. N. Washburn, *An Approach to the Study of the* Book of Mormon *Geography*, Provo, Utah, 1939. 212.

Conway, Dayton E. *Where O Where is the* Book of Mormon? CreateSpace Independent Publishing Platform, 2012.

Coon, W. Vincent. *Choice above All Other Lands,* Book of Mormon *Covenant Lands According to the Best Sources* (Salt Lake City: Brit Publishing, 2009.
Curtis, Delbert W. *The Land of the Nephites.* Oren, UT: self-published, 1988.
Davila. "An Account of Our Book of Mormon Lands Tour." Provo, UT: BYU Library, Jan 27th to Feb 16th, 1961.
DeLong-Steede-Simmons model, *FRAA Newsletter* 23 (11 May 1986). "Proposed Book of Mormon Geographical Setting," Wikipedia, accessed 03/19/2017.
Dixon, Riley L. *Just One Cumorah.* Salt Lake city: Bookcraft, 1958.
Driggs, Jean R. *The Palestine of America.* Salt Lake City: no publisher, 1928.
Ellsworth, Robert B. "Lecture Notes on an Interpretation of a Map of Zarahemla and the Land Northward as Described in the *Book of Mormon.*" Ogden, UT: 1980 (referenced in "Proposed *Book of Mormon* Geographical Setting," Wikipedia (accessed 25/02/2017).
Farnsworth, Dewey. *The Americas before Columbus.* El Paso, TX: Farnsworth Publishing Co., 1947.
Farnsworth, Dewey, and Edith Wood Farnsworth. Book of Mormon *Evidences.* Salt Lake City: Deseret Book Company, 1953.
Ferguson, Thomas Stuart. *Cumorah—Where?* Independence, MO: Press of Zion's Printing and Publishing, 1947, 14 & 55.
———. *One Fold and One Shepherd.* San Francisco: Books of California, 1958.
Hammond, Fletcher B. *Geography of the* Book of Mormon. Salt Lake City: Utah Printing Company, 1959.
Hansen. "*Book of Mormon* Geography," *Saints' Herald,* January 8, 1951. "Proposed *Book of Mormon* Geographical Setting," Wikipedia, accessed 03/19/2017.
Hansen, Vaughn E. *Discovering* Book of Mormon *Lands.* Springville, UT: Cedar Fort, 1997.
Hauck, F. Richard. *Deciphering the Geography of the* Book of Mormon. Salt Lake City: Deseret Book Company, 1988.
Hills, Louis Edward. *Geography of Mexico and Central America from from 2234 BC to 421 AD.* Independence, MO: 1917.
Holley, Vernal. Book of Mormon *Authorship: A Closer Look.* Ogden UT: Zenos Publications, 1983. Updated edition, Roy, UT: self published, 1992.
Holmes, Robert. *Geographical Sketches of the* Book of Mormon. LDS Historian's Office, 1903. "Proposed *Book of Mormon* Geographical Settings," Wikipedia, accessed 19/03/2017.
Hunter, Milton R. *Archaeology and the* Book of Mormon. Salt Lake City: Deseret Book Company, 1956.
———. *Great Civilizations and the* Book of Mormon. Salt Lake City: Deseret Book Company, 1970.
———. *Christ in Ancient America.* Salt Lake City: Deseret Book Company, 1972.
Jakeman, M. Wells. "The *Book of Mormon* Civilizations: Their Origins, and Their Development in Space and Time," in Ross T. Christensen, ed., *Progress in Archaeology and Anthropology.* Provo, UT: Brigham Young University, 1963.
Johnson, Daniel, Jared Cooper and Derek Gasser. *An LDS Guide to Mesoamerica.* (Springvile, UT: Cedar Fort, Inc., 2008).
Knisley, Alvin. *Dictionary of All Proper Names in the* Book of Mormon. Independence, MO: Ensign Publishing House, 1909.

Kocherhaus, Arthur J. *Lehi's Isle of Promise*. Fullerton, CA: Et Cetera Graphics and Printing, 1989.

Layton, Lynn C. "An 'Ideal' Book of Mormon Geography," *Improvement Era* 41 (July 1938), 394–395.

Le Poidevin, Cecil George. *Zion, Land of Promise. An Atlas Study of Book of Mormon Geography*. N.P.: by author, 1977.

Lund, John L. *MesoAmerica and the* Book of Mormon. Orem, UT: Granite Publishing & Distribution, 2007.

McGavin E. Cecil, & Willard Bean. *The Geography of the* Book of Mormon (Salt Lake City: Bookcraft, 1948.

Meldrum, Rod L. *Exploring the* Book of Mormon *Heartland Photobook.* New York: Digital Legend Press, 2011.

Neville, Jonathan, *Moroni's America: The North American Setting for the* Book of Mormon (Independent Publishing Platform, 2015)

Nielsen, Harold K. *Mapping the Action Found in the Book of Mormon*. Springville, UT: Cedar Fort, 1987.

Olive, Phyllis Carol. *The Lost Lands of the* Book of Mormon. Springville, UT: Bonneville Books, 2000.

Palfrey, Louise. *The Divinity of the* Book of Mormon *Proven by Archaeology.* Lamoni, IO: Zion's Religio-Literary Society at the Herald Publishing House, 1903.

Palmer, David A. *In Search of Cumorah. New Evidences for the* Book of Mormon *from Ancient Mexico.* Bountiful, UT: Horizon Publishers, 1981.

Peay, E. L. *The Lands of Zarahemla. A* Book of Mormon *Commentary.* (published by the author, 1993.

Potter, George, *Nephi in the Promised Land*, (Springvile, UT: Cedar Fort, Inc., 2009).

Pratt, Orson. "Nephite America—The Day of God's Power—The Shepherd of Israel" in *Journal of Discourses*. February 11, 1872, 14:324-31.

Priddis, Venice. *The Book and the Map, New Insights into* Book of Mormon *Geography.* Salt Lake City: Bookcraft, 1975.

Reynolds, George. *The Story of the* Book of Mormon. Salt Lake City: J. H. Parry, 1888.

Reynolds, George, and Janne M. Sjodahl. Book of Mormon *Geography. The Lands of the Nephites and Jaredites.* Salt Lake City, by author, dist. by Deseret Book Co., 1957.

Ricks, Joel. Only a mention by James E. Talmage in Joseph Trevor Antley, "The Talmage Journals: The Book of Mormon Geography Hearings, 1921," posted July 21, 2012 (withoutend.org/talmage-journals-book-mormon-geography-hearings-1921. See more at: http://www.withoutend.org/talmage-journals-book-mormon-geography-hearings-1921/#sthash.N5nCNQhL.dpuf 1921.

Roberts, B. H. (Brigham Henry). "*Book of Mormon* Difficulties, A Study" and "A *Book of Mormon* Study," both in Brigham D. Madsen, *Studies of the* Book of Mormon. *B. H. Roberts*, 2nd. Edition. Salt Lake City: Signature Books, 1992.

Shook, Chas. A. *Cumorah Revisited.* Cincinnati: Standard Publishing Company, 1910.

Smith, Joseph (?). He may have approved the article in *Times and Seasons*, volume 3, number 23 (1 October 1842).

Smith, Joseph (?). Douglas K. Christensen, "Moroni's 36 Year Trek to New York," (published on Book of Mormon Archaeological Forum: http//:www.Bmaf.org, accessed 24 March 2007). The map in this article is said to have a line of transmission going back to Joseph Smith.

Sorenson, John L. *An Ancient American Setting for the* Book of Mormon. Salt Lake City: Deseret Book Company, 1985.

———. *Mormon's Map* (Provo, UT: The Foundation for Ancient Research and Mormon Studies [F.A.R.M.S], 2000).

———. *Mormon's Codex, an Ancient American Book* (Salt Lake City: Deseret Books, 2013).

Stout, Richard M. *Harmony in* Book of Mormon *Geography*. Boulder City, NV: by author, 1950.

Sutton, Bruce S. *Lehi, Father of Polynesia. Polynesians Are Nephites.* Orem, UT: Hawaiki Publishing, 2001.

Washburn, J. A., and J. N. Washburn. *An Approach to the Study of the* Book of Mormon. Provo, Utah: New Era Publishing Company, 1939.

Washburn, J. Nile. Book of Mormon *Lands and Times.* Bountiful, UT: Horizon Publishers, 1974.

Welch, John W., and J. Gregory Welch. *Charting the* Book of Mormon*: Visual Aids for Personal Study and Teaching* (Provo, UT: Neal A. Maxwell Institute for Religious Scholarship, 1999).

Wilde, Orrin G. *Landmarks of Ancient American People.* N.P.: by author, 1947.

Wirth, Diane. *Decoding Ancient America: A Guide to the Archaeology of the* Book of Mormon. (Springvile, UT: Cedar Fort, Inc., 2007).

Bibliography 4. General References

Abbott, Benjamin. *The experience and gospel labours of the Rev. Benjamin Abbott: to which is annexed a narrative of his life and death, by John Ffirth.* Philadelphia: pr. by Solomon 1801., W. Conrad, for Ezekiel Cooper, 1801.

Adair, James. *The History of the American Indians* (1775). Edited and with an Introduction and Annotations by Kathryn E. Holland Braund. Tuscaloosa: University of Alabama Press, 2005.

Adams, Daniel, with H. (Hazen) Morse, engraver. *School Atlas to Adams Geography.* Boston: Lincoln and Edmonds, 1825.

Allport, Gordon, and Joseph Postman, *Psychology of Rumor.* New York: Henry Holt and Company, 1947.

Allred, Joel M. *Mormonism under the Microscope. "Master, the Tempest is Raging."* Salt Lake City: Mountain Press, 2016.

Anderson, Devery S., & Gary James Bergera, eds. *Joseph Smith's Quorum of the Anointed, 1842-1845, a Documentary History.* Salt Lake City: Signature Books, 2005.

Anderson, Lavina Fielding, ed. *Lucy's Book, A Critical Edition of Lucy Mack Smith's Family Memoir.* Salt Lake City: Signature Books, 2001.

Anderson, Richard Lloyd. *Joseph Smith's New England Heritage.* Salt Lake City: Deseret Book Company, 1971.

———. *Investigating the* Book of Mormon *Witnesses*. Salt Lake City: Deseret Book Company, 1981.

Aufrecht, Walter E. *A Corpus of Ammonite Inscriptions.* Lewiston, NY: The Edwin Mellen Press, 1989.

Avigad, Nahman. *Corpus of West Semitic Stamp Seals, revised and completed by Benjamin Sass.* Herein referenced as Avigad/Sass. Jerusalem: Ketterpress, 1997.

Backman, Milton V. *Eyewitness Accounts of the Restoration.* Salt Lake City: Deseret Book Company, 1986.

———. *Joseph Smth's First Vision; Confirming Evidences and Contemporary Accounts, Second Edition.* Salt Lake City: Deseret Book, 1980.

Bates, Irene M. "Foreword. Lucy Mack Smith—First Mormon Mother," in Anderson, *Lucy's Book.*

Barney, Kevin L., "Reflections on the Documentary Hypothesis" in *Dialogue: A Journal of Mormon Thought,* vol. 33, no. 1, spring 2000.

Bell, Lanny. "The Ancient Egyptian 'Books of Breathings,' the Mormon 'Book of Abraham,' and the Development of Egyptology in America," in Stephen E. Thompson & Peter Der Manuelian, eds., *Egypt and Beyond, Essays Presented to Leonard H. Lesko upon his Retirement.* Providence, RI: Brown University, 2008.

Boudinot, Elias. *Star in the West or a Humble Attempt to Discover the Long Lost Ten Tribes of Israel Preparatory to Their Return to Their Beloved City Jerusalem.* Trenton, NJ: George Sherman, Printer, for D. Fenton, S. Hutchinson and J. Dunham, 1816.

Brennan, Michael, and Rachel Greenstadt, "Practical attacks against authorship recognition techniques," Association for the Advancement of Artificial Intelligence, 2009

Buerger, David John. *The Mysteries of Godliness. A History of Mormon Temple Worship.* Salt Lake City: Signature Books, 1994.

Buttrick, George A. *The Interpreter's Bible.* New York: Abingdon Press, 1956.

Coe, Michael. *Breaking the Mayan Code.* London: Thames & Hudson, 1999.

Cogley, Richard W. *John Eliot's Mission to the Indians before King Philip's War.* Cambridge: Harvard University Press, 1999.

Crawford, Charles. *An Essay on the Propagation of the Gospel in Which There Are Numerous Facts and Arguments Adduced to Prove That Many of the Indians in America Are Descended from the Ten Tribes.* Philadelphia: James Humphreys, 1801.

Davis, William. "Reassessing Joseph Smith Jr.'s Formal Education," *Dialogue: A Journal of Mormon Thought* 49, no. 4 (Winter 2016).

Eccel, A. Chris. *An Analysis of the Distribution of the BOM Variants.* Chicago: unpublished paper, 1972).

———. *Egypt, Islam and Social Change: Al-Azhar in Conflict and Accommodation.* Berlin: Schwartz Verlag, 1984.

Edgell, H. Stewart. *Arabian Deserts, Nature, Origin and Evolution.* New York: Springer Publishing, 2006.

Edwards, Jonathan. *Some Thoughts Concerning the Revival of Religion in New England,* Part II, Sect. II, "The latter-day glory, is probably to begin in America." Boston: Printed and sold by S. Kneeland and T. Green in Queen-street, 1742.

———. *The Works of Jonathan Edwards.* Edinburgh: The Banner of Truth Trust,1990.

Eerdmans Dictionary of the Bible. Grand Rapids: Eerdmans Publishing Company, 2000.

Esplin, Ronald K. & Matthew J. Grow, gen. eds. *The Joseph Smith Papers,* vol. 3, pt. 2. Salt Lake City: The Church Historian's Press, 2015.

Evans, Tripp, *Romancing the Maya, Mexican Antiquity in the American Imagination, 1820-1915.* Austin: University of Texas Press, 2004.

Fortier, John C. "Hobbes and a 'Discourse on Laws': The Perils of Wordprint Analysis," in *The Review of Politics,* vol. 59, no. 04, fall 1997.

Foster, Arthur Glen Jr. "The Plates of Jacob: An Analysis of the Replacement to the Lost Manuscript of the *Book of Mormon*," (privately circulated, 1983).
Gardner, Brant. *The Gift and the Power*. Sandy, UT: Greg Kofford Books, 2011.
Garr, Arnold K., Donald Q. Cannon & Richard O. Cowan, *Encyclopedia of Latter-day Saint History*. Salt Lake City: Deseret Book Company, 2011.
Gilbert, "John H. Memorandum, made by John H. Gilbert Esq, Sept 8th, 1892, Palmyra, N. Y." Palmyra King's Daughters Free Library, Palmyra, NY. It is in Wilfred C. Wood, *Joseph Smith Begins His Work*. Book of Mormon *1830 First Edition*.
Goodman, Felicitas D. *Speaking in Tongues: a Cross-cultural Study of Glossolalia*. Chicago: University of Chicago Press, 1972.
Gookin, Daniel. *Historical Collections of the Indians in New England*. Boston: At the Apollo Press, by Belknan & Hall, 1792. The copy cited is an exact replica from Book Renaisance.
Gorton, H. Clay. *A New Witness for Christ. Chiastic Structures in the* Book of Mormon. Bountiful, UT: Horizon Publishers, 1997.
Gunn, Stanley R. *Oliver Cowdery, Second Elder and Scribe*. Salt Lake City: Bookcraft, 1962.
Hanke, Lewis. *Aristotle and the American Indians: A Study in Race Prejudice in the Modern World*. Mishawaka, IN: Better World Books, 1970.
Heimert, Alan, and Perry Miller, eds. *The Great Awakening*. Indianapolis and New York: The Bobbs-Merrill Company, Inc., 1967, 610.
Hilton, John L., "On Verifying Wordprint Studies: *Book of Mormon* Authorship," in *BYU Studies* 30, no. 3, 1990.
Hilton, John L., and Kenneth D. Jenkins. "Vocabulary and Numerical Count of all Words from the King James Old Testament, New Testament and the 1830 *Book of Mormon*," *Preliminary Report*. Provo, UT: FARMS, n.d.
Holley, Vernal. Book of Mormon *Authorship: A Closer Look*. Ogden UT: Zenos Publications, 1983. Updated edition, Roy, UT: self published, 1992.
Holmes, D. I. "A Stylometric Analysis of Mormon Scripture and Related Texts," in the *Journal of the Royal Statistical Society. Series A (Statistics in Society)*, vol. 155, no. 1 (1992).
Holzapfel, Jeni Broberg, and Richard Neitzel Holzapfel. *A Woman's View: Helen Mar Whitney's Reminiscences of Early Church History*. Salt Lake City: Bookcraft [Religious Studies Center, BYU],
Howard, Richard P. *Restoration Scriptures*. Independence, MO: Herald House, 1969.
Howe, Eber D. *Mormonism Unvailed*. Salt Lake City: Signature Books, 2015.
Huddleston, Lee Eldridge. *Origins of the American Indians, European Concepts, 1492-1729*. Austin: The University of Texas Press, 1967.
Hunter, Milton R. *Archaeology and the* Book of Mormon. Salt Lake City: Deseret Book Company, 1956.
———. *Great Civilizations and the* Book of Mormon. Salt Lake City: Bookcraft, 1970.
Jessee, Dean C. *Papers of Joseph Smith*. Salt Lake City: Deseret Book Company, 1989.
———. *The Personal Writings of Joseph Smith*. Salt Lake City: Deseret Book, 1984.
———. *The Early Accounts of Joseph Smith's First Vision*. Sandy, UT: Mormon Miscellaneous [reprint series], 1984.
———. "The Early Accounts of Joseph Smith's First Vision," *BYU Studies 9 (3): 275–94*. Provo, Utah: Brigham Young University, 1969.

Jockers, Matthew L., Daniela M. Witten and Craig S. Criddle, "Reassessing authorship of the *Book of Mormon* using delta and nearest shrunken centroid classification," *Literary and Linguistic Computing* Advance Access (17 February 2009).
Kendall, Edward Augustus. *Travels Through the Northern Parts of the United States in the Years 1807 and 1808*, 3 vols. New York: I. Riley: 1809.
Kimball, Helen Mar. *Helen Mar Kimball Autobiography*. March 30, 1881, LDS Church History Library.
King, Edward (Lord Kingsborough). *Antiquities of Mexico*. London: R. Havell and Colnaghi, Son & Company, 1831-48.
Kirkham, Francis W. *A New Witness for Christ in America, "The Book of Mormon."* Independence, MO: Press of Zion's Publishing Company, 1951.
Kohn, Hans. *The Idea of Nationalism, a Study in its Origins and Background*. New York: Macmillan, 1944.
Kunich, John C. "Multiply Exceedingly: *Book of Mormon* Population Sizes," in Metcalfe, ed., *New Approaches to the* Book of Mormon. *Explorations in Critical Methodology*. Salt Lake City: Signature Books, 1993.
Larsen, Wayne A., Alvin C. Rencher and Tim Layton, "Who Wrote the *Book of Mormon*? An Analysis of Wordprints," in Noel B. Reynolds, ed., Book of Mormon Authorship. Salt Lake City: Bookcraft, 1982.
Larson, Stan, *Quest for the Gold Plates, Thomas Stuart Ferguson's Archaeological Search for the* Book of Mormon. Salt Lake City: Freethinker Press, 1996.
LeSueur, Stephen C. *The 1838 Mormon War in Missouri*. Columbia, MO: University of Missouri Press, 1987.
Lindsay, John S. *The Mormons and the Theatre, or The History of Theatricals in Utah with Reminiscences and Comments, Humorous and Critical*. Salt Lake City: Century Printing, 1905.
Love, Michael & Jonathan Kaplan, eds., *The Southern Maya in the Late Preclassic: The Rise and Fall of Early Mesoamerican Civilization*. Boulder, CO: University Press of Colorado, 2011.
MacKay, Charles. *Extraordinary Popular Delusions and the Madness of Crowds*. San Bernardino, CA: Pantianos Classics, 2017. First edition: London: Richard Bentley, 1841.
Marquardt, H. Michael. "Joseph Smith's Egyptian Papers: A History," in Robert K. Ritner, *The Joseph Smith Egyptian Papyri, A Complete Edition* (Salt Lake City: Signature Books, 2013), 11-68.
———. *The Joseph Smith Revelations, Text and Commentary*. Salt Lake City: Signature Books, 1999.
———. *The Rise of Mormonism: 1816-1844*. Second Edition, Revised and Enlarged. Maitland, FL: Xulon Press, 2013.
Marquardt, H. Michael, and Wesley P. Walters. *Inventing Mormonism. Tradition and the Historical Record*. Salt Lake City: Smith Research Associates, 1994.
Mather, S. *An Attempt to Shew that America Must be Known to the Ancients*. Boston: J. Kneeland, 1773.
Matthews, Robert J. "How We Got the Book of Moses." Published online at lds.org, accessed 22/01/2017.
Mayhew, Henry. *The Mormons or Latter-day Saints, A Contemporary History*. London: Office of the National Illustrated Library, [1851?]
McConkie, Bruce R. *Mormon Doctrine*. Salt Lake City: Bookcraft, 1966.

McGarry, Sheridan L. "Mormon Money," reprinted from *The Numismatist*, 1962.
Meldrum, Rod L. *Exploring the Book of Mormon Heartland Photobook.* New York: Digital Legend Press, 2011.
Metcalfe, Brent Lee. "The Priority of Mosiah: A Prelude to *Book of Mormon* Exegesis," in Brent Lee Metcalfe, ed., *New Approaches to the Book of Mormon. Explorations in Critical Methodology.*
Metcalfe, Brent Lee, ed. *New Approaches to the Book of Mormon. Explorations in Critical Methodology.* Salt Lake City: Signature Books, 1993.
Moon, Todd K., Peg Howland and Jacob H. Gunther, "Document author classification using Generalized Discriminant Analysis." Proc. Workshop on Text Mining, SIAM, 2006.
Morris, Larry E. "Oliver Cowdery's Vermont Years and the Origins of Mormonism." *BYU Studies* 39:1 (200).
Morton, A. Q., *Literary Detection: How to Prove Authorship and Fraud in Literature and Documents* (New York: Charles Scribner's Sons, 1978)
Nibley, Hugh. *Enoch the Prophet.* Salt Lake City: Deseret Book Company, 1986.
———. *Lehi in the Desert & the World of the Jaredites.* Salt Lake City: Bookcraft, 1952/1980.
———. *The Message of the Joseph Smith Papyri, An Egyptian Egyptian Endowment.* Second Edition, edited by John Gee & Michael D. Rhodes. Salt Lake City: Deseret Book Company, 2005.
Parkin, Max H. "A Preliminary Analysis of the Dating of Section 10." *The Seventh Annual Sidney B. Sperry Symposium: The Doctrine of Covenants.* Provo, UT: Brigham Young University, 1979.
Petersen, Lamar. *Problems in Mormon Text* (Concord, CA: Pacific Publishing Co., no date.
Peterson, H. Donl. *The Story of The Book of Abraham, Mummies, Manuscripts and Mormonism.* Salt Lake City: Deseret Book Company, 1995.
Porten Bezalel, and Jerome A. Lund, *Aramaic Documents from Egypt: A Key-Word-in-Context Concordance.* Winona Lake: Eisenbrauns, 2002.
Pratt, Orson. "Nephite America—The Day of God's Power—The Shepherd of Israel." *Journal of Discourses* (February 11, 1872).
Pratt, Parley P. *Autobiography of Parley P. Pratt,* edited by his son, Parley P. Pratt. Salt Lake City: Deseret Book Company, 1934 (edition quoted, 1994).
Priest, Josiah. *American Antiquities and Discoveries in the West being an Exhibition of the Evidence that an ancient population of partially civilized nations, differing entirely from those of the present Indians, peopled America, many centuries before its discovery by Columbus, and inquiries into their origin.* Albany, NY: Hoffman and White, 1833.
———. *The Wonders of Nature and Providence Displayed.* Albany: published by the author, 1826.
Purchas, Samuel. *Hakluytus Posthumus, or, Purchas his Pilgrimes (a Discourse on Virginia).* Glasgow: James MacLehose & Sons, 1905.
Quinn, D. Michael. *The Mormon Hierarchy: Origins of Power.* Salt Lake City: Signature Books, 1994.
———. *Early Mormonism and the Magic World View.* Salt Lake City: Signature Books, 2nd ed., 1998.

Rafinesque, C. *Ancient History, or Annals of Kentucky; with a Survey of the Ancient Monuments of North America; and a Tabular View of the Principal Languages and Primitive Nations of the Whole Earth.* Frankfort in Kentucky: Printed by the author, 1824.

———. *Atlantic Journal and Friend of Knowledge.* Philadelphia: 1832-33.

———. *A C. S. Rafinesque Anthology.* Edited by Charles E. Boewe. Jefferson, NC: McFarland & Company, 2005.

Redford, Donald B. *The Wars in Syria and Palestine of Thutmose III.* Leiden: Brill, 2003.

Reynolds, Noel B., ed. Book of Mormon *Authorship.* Salt Lake City: Bookcraft, 1982.

Rigdon, John Wickliffe. "The Life and Testimony of Sidney Rigdon," *Dialogue: A Journal of Mormon Thought*, 1:4, 1966.

Ritner, Robert K. *The Joseph Smith Egyptian Papyri, A Complete Edition.* Salt Lake City: Signature Books, 2013.

Roediger III, H.L. "Reconstructive Memory, Psychology of," *International Encyclopedia of the Social & Behavioral Sciences.* Amsterdam: Elsevier B.V., 2001.

Sackett, Chuck. *What's Going on in There? The Verbatim Text of the Mormon Temple Rituals Annotated and Explained by a Former Temple Worker.* Thousand Oaks, CA: Sword of the Shepherd Ministries, ND.

Samarin, William J. *Tongues of Men and Angels: the Religious Language of Pentecostalism.* New York: Macmillan, 1972.

Schaalje, G. Bruce, John L. Hilton and John B. Archer. "Comparative Power of Three Author-Attribution Techniques for Differentiating Authors," *Journal of* Book of Mormon *Studies*, 6/1 (1997).

Schaalje, G. Bruce, Matthew Roper and Gregory L. Snow. "Extended nearest shrunken centroid classification: A new method for open-set authorship attribution of texts of varying sizes," *Literary and Linguistic Computing*, vol. 26, no. 1, 2011.

Shalev, Eran. "'Revive, Renew, and Reestablish': Mordecai Noah's Ararat and the Limits of Biblical Imagination in the Early American Republic," posted on http//:www.americanjewisharchives.org (downloaded 25/03/2017).

Shipps, Jan. *Mormonism: The Story of a New Religious Tradition.* Urbana: University of Illinois Press, 1985.

Simon, Barbara Anne. *Hope of Israel: Presumptive Evidence that the Aborigines of the Western Hemisphere are Descended from the Ten Missing Tribes of Israel.* London: R. B. Seeley, 1829.

———. *The Ten Tribes of Israel Historically Identified with the Aborigines of the Western Hemisphere.* London: R. B. Seeley, 1836.

Skousen, Royal. *The History of the Text of the* Book of Mormon. *Part One, Grammatical Variation.* Provo, UT: The Foundation for Ancient Research and Mormon Studies, 2016.

———. *The History of the Text of the* Book of Mormon. *Part Two, Grammatical Variation.* Provo, UT: The Foundation for Ancient Research and Mormon Studies, 2016.

———. *The Original Manuscript of the* Book of Mormon. *Typographical Facsimile of the Extant Text.* Provo, UT: Foundation for Ancient Research and Mormon Studies, 2001.

———. *The Printer's Manuscript of the* Book of Mormon: *Typographical Facsimile of the Entire Text in Two Parts.* Provo, UT: Foundation for Ancient Research and Mormon Studies, 2001.

Smith, Emma, ed. *A Collection of Sacred Hymns for the Church of the Latter Day Saints.* Selected by Emma Smith. Kirtland, OH: F. G. Williams & Co., 1835.

Smith, Ethan. *View of the Hebrews, Exhibiting the Destruction of Jerusalem...* Poultney, VT: Smith & Shule, 1823.

———. *View of the Hebrews; or the Tribes of Israel in America. Second edition, improved and enlarged.* Poultney, VT: Smith & Shute, 1825 (Edition cited: Salt Lake City: Bookcraft for the Religious Studies Center at Brigham Young University, 1999.)

Smith, George D., ed. *An Intimate Chronicle: The Journals of William Clayton,* Salt Lake City: Signature Books, 1972.

Smith, Joseph. *History of the Church of Jesus Christ of Latter-day Saints.* Salt Lake City: Deseret News, 1902.

Smith, Lucy. *Biographical Sketches of Joseph Smith the Prophet and His Progenitors for Many Generations.* Lamoni, IA: Reorganized Church of Jesus Christ of Latter-day Saints, 1912.

Lucy Mack Smith, in Lavina Fielding Anderson, ed., *Lucy's Book, A Critical Edition of Lucy Mack Smith's Family Memoir.* Salt Lake City: Signature Books, 2001.

Smoot, Steve. "Authentic Egyptian Names in the *Book of Mormon,*" posted on americantestament.com and accessed on 28 Feb 2016.

Sondrup, Stephen P. "The Psalm of Nephi: A Lyric Reading," *BYU Studies* (Provo, UT: Brigham Young University, 21:3, 1981),

Sorenson, John L. *Mormon's Codex, an Ancient American Book.* Salt Lake City: Deseret Books, 2013.

Southerton, Simon G. *Losing a Lost Tribe. Native Americans, DNA and the Mormon Church.* Salt Lake City: Signature Books, 2004.

Spaulding [Spalding], Solomon. *The "Manuscript Found" or "Manuscript Story," of the Late Rev. Solomon Spaulding; from a Verbatim Copy of the Original Now in the Care of Pres. James H. Fairchild, of Oberlin College,* Ohio, *Including Correspondence Touching the Manuscript, Its Preservation and Transmission until It Came into the Hand of the Publisher.* Lamoni, Iowa: The Reorganized Church of Jesus Christ of Latter Day Saints, 1885); *Manuscript Found: The Complete Original.* Provo, UT: BYU Religious Studies Center, 1997.

Sperry, Sidney B. *Our* Book of Mormon. Salt Lake City: Bookcraft, 1950.

Steindorff, George, & Keith C. Seele, *When Egypt Ruled the East.* Chicago: The University of Chicago Press, 1957.

Stenhouse, Mrs. T. B. H. *Tell It All: The Story of a Life's Experience in Mormonism. An Autobiography.* Hartford: Worthington & Co., 1874.

Stephens, John Lloyd. *Incidents of Travel in Central America, Chiapas and Yucatan.* 2 vols. Illustrations by Frederick Catherwood. New York: Harper, 1841.

Sweeney, Marvin A. *Isaiah 1–39: with an introduction to prophetic literature.* Grand Rapids, MI: Eerdmans, 1996.

Sweeney, Marvin A. "The Latter Prophets," in Steven L. McKenzie and M. Patrick Graham. *The Hebrew Bible Today: An Introduction to Critical Issues.* Westminster: John Knox Press, 1998.

Thorowgood, Thomas. (n.d.). *Jews in America, or Probabilities That the Americans Are of That Race.* London: T. Slater, 1650. (Edition cited: 1825 2nd Edition. Provo, UT: Bookcraft for the Religious Studies Center at Brigham Young University, 1996.)

Tvedtnes, John. "Hebraisms in the *Book of Mormon*," transcript downloaded from the FARMS website
———. "Isaiah Variants in the *Book of Mormon*" (1984), transcript accessed at http://publications.mi.byu.edu/people/john-a-tvedtnes/.
Tvedtnes, John, John Gee and Matthew Roper, "*Book of Mormon* Names Attested in Ancient Hebrew Inscriptions," *Journal of* Book of Mormon *Studies*, 9/1/2000.
Van Wagoner, Richard S. *Sidney Rigdon, A Portrait of Religious Excess.* Salt Lake City: Signature Books, 1994.
Vogel, Dan. *Early Mormon Documents.* Salt Lake City: Signature Books (5 vols.), 2007.
———. *Joseph Smith, The Making of a Prophet* .Salt Lake City: Signature Books, 2004.
———. "Preface" to *Mormonism Unvailed* by Eber D. Howe, and "Addenda" to the same. Salt Lake City: Signature Books, 2015.
Walam Olum, or Red Score. The Migration Legend of the Lenni Lenape or Delaware Indians, including a transcription and ostensible translation of *Walam Olum* by C. (Constantine) S. (Samuel) Rafinesque, with studies by various authors. Indianapolis: Indiana Historical Society, 1954.
Walker, John. Walker's *Critical Pronouncing Dictionary, and Expositor of the English Language.* Abridged For the Use of Schools. To Which is Annexed, an Abridgment of Walker's Key to the Pronunciation of Greek, Latin, and Scripture Proper Names. Boston: Lincoln & Edmands, Samuel T. Armstrong, and Charles Ewer, 1823.
Watson, William C. *Dispensationalism before Darby. Seventeenth-Century and Eighteenth-Century English Apocalypticism.* Silverton, OR: Lampion Press, 2015.
Welch, John W. "Chiasmus in the *Book of Mormon*," in John W. Welch, ed., *Chiasmus in Antiquity.* Provo, UT: Research Press [The Foundation for Ancient Research and Mormon Studies—F.A.R.M.S.], 1981.
Williams, Roger. (1643). *A Key into the Language of America.* London: Printed by Gregory Dexter, 1643. (Edition cited, reprint: Bedford, MA: Applewood Books,1936.
Wood, Wilfred C. *Joseph Smith Begins His Work.* Book of Mormon *1830 First Edition, Reproduced from Uncut Sheets.* Salt Lake City: Deseret News Press, 1958.
Worsley, Israel. (1828). *A View of the American Indians.* London: Printed for the author & sold by R. Hunter, 1828; Plymouth: W. W. Arliss. (edition cited: New York: Arno Press reprint, 1971.)

INDEX

116 Purloined pages, 246-47, 258, 285, 289, 381, 403-404, 417; plot to alter them (?), 285
2002 Winter Olympics, 501-502
Abbott, Benjamin, 382
Abyssinia, 255
Abraham ibn Ezra, 96
Adams, George J., 563
Aelius Gallus, expedition of, 255
Adair, James, 6
Adventism, 14
Akkadian, 210
Alcott, William A., 513
Alexandria, 255
Alger, Fanny, 476, 579
Alighieri, Dante, 172
Allport, Gordon, 312
Allred, Rulon C., 565-66, 576
Alston Church, 561
American Zion, 15-16
Americas' isolation, 10-11, 36, 147, 239
Ammaron, 69
Ammon, 64, 138
Anthon, Charles, 215-216, 256, 259, 401
    gives statement to Harris, 281
    informed by Eber D. Howe, 280
    knowledge of Champollion (?), 279
Anti-Semitism, 134-35
apologetics, xiii, 242, 257, 328, 508, 520
apostasy of mankind, 130, 400-401
apostasy, 467, 482-83, 489, 501, 582
    its anguish, 592-94;
    life after Mormonism, 598
    temple recommend, 589
Apostolic United Brethren, 565-567, 576
Arabia, 26, 76, 93, 168, 175, 248-49, 251
    hydrology, 253-54; travek in Arabia,248-52, 254; geography, 249, 252
Arabia Felix, 255, 248
Ararat (proposed Jewish colony), 11
Archaeology
    Archaeological verdict, 41-42, 605
    BOM construction, 27-30
    BOM fortification, 30-32
    claim of a horse bas-relief at Chichen Itza, 530-31
    list of items in the BOM, 17-19
    list of Pre-Columbian sites, 36-41
    the missing cities, 71-73
    the missing texts, 149
Archer, John B., 330
Armies of Israel (LDS), 489
Articles and Covenants, 438, 450, 602
Articles of Agreement, 272, 391
Articles of the Church of Christ, 434
artificial language generation
    speaking in tongues, 145
Assyrians
    bar to Egyptian expansion, 228
    conquer Israel, 132
Atiya, Aziz Suryal, 524-525
Augustus Caesar, 255
Avard, Sampson, 492
Avery, Dennis, 577
Bab al-Mandab, 255
Babylon, 91-96, 118, 132, 165, 171-172, 191, 197, 203, 206, 228, 340, 552
Baldwin, Caleb, 493
Banks, John, 575
baptism procedures, 434
Baptists (Regular Baptists), 321-322
Barden, Jerusha, 391, 401
Barlow, John Y., 565
Bates, Irene M., 291
Battle of Crooked River, 573
Bellamy, Joseph, 14
Beman (Beaman), Alva(h), 267, 414
    Handled & heard the plates, 414
Benedict, Aaron (rolled brass), 277
Bennet, James Arlington, 398
Bennett, John C., 562
Bernhisel, John M., 497
Berlin, Heinrich, 521
Bible & *Book of Mormon*
    "all the ships of the sea," 104-108
    biblia sacra, 94; BOM variants & apologetics, 100; critical editions 94; Dead Sea scrolls, 94, 96, 118; development of canon, 94, 96-99;

Index

graph of distribution of variants, 103; Greek Septuagint, 104; Hebrew *hapax legomena*, 117, 218; Hebrew writing conventions, 106; King James translation, 117-119; Latin Vulgate text, 104, 172; list of BOM inclusions, 100; Masoretic Hebrew text, 104, 118, 124; New Testament intrusions, 126-127; *parallelismus membrorum*, 105-106; table of KJ mistranslations, 119-124; table of longer variants, 112-115; table of shorter variants, 102; targum, 118; Tarshish, 15, 105-108; Translation (KJV), 117; Translations (early), 104; variant analysis, 108-112; variant classification, 101; variant distribution, 101-104;

Bickerton, William, 562-563
Bidamon, Lewis, 293
bishop, 461
Bishop, Gladden, 423
Black, (Judge) Adam, 492
Blackmore, Winston, 566
Boggs, Lilburn W., 448, 452, 490, 497, 572

BOM authorship
  sequential vs. collaborative, 358; simultaneous composition, 301, 358; Spaulding-Rigdon theory, 304

BOM character transcript, 216, 279

BOM geography, THE MAP, 70
  1921 General Authority Book of Mormon Committee, 43
  1820's schoolboy's map, 56
  Alma (valley), 61
  Amulon, 61
  Angola, 69, 168
  Antionum, 58, 62
  Boaz (city), 69
  BOM authors' draft map, 56, 62
  BOM settings
    abstract cartography, 44
    alternative settings, 49-52
    Central America, 47-48, 522
    South America, 45-47
    Trends in LDS views, 527-528;

Bible — BOM Geography (wilderness)
BOM-based cartography, 53
  Brass Plates of Laban, 90-91, 260
  Cluff's Zarahemla Expedition, 43
  Cumorah (hill), xxii, 67-69, 268
  first inheritance (land/place), 57, 60
  fortified east-west line, 54-58, 71
  Gideon (valley), 66
  Gulf of Darien, 62
  Isthmus of Panama, 53, 58, 65, 255
  Jaredite land southward, 63, 68
  Jashon, 69
  Jershon, 62
  Jordan (city), 69
  land among many waters, 64
  (land of) cement houses, 67
  (land of) large bodies of water and many rivers, 50-51, 67
  (land of) many waters, rivers and fountains, 67-69
  Land Desolation, 59-60, 63, 69
  land northward, 54-58, 60, 63-65, 67-68
  land southward, 54-55, 57-60, 63-65, 68-69
  Land of Bountiful, 59-60, 62-63
  Land of David, 69
  Land of Joshua, 69
  land/city of Nephi, 55-62, 64, 78
  land/city of Zarahemla, xxii, 54-55, 57-64, 66, 69, 72, 334, 529
  landfall of Lehi & Mulek, 55, 57
  line Bountiful/Desolation, 54, 58, 60-65, 71
  Manti, 60-62, 66-67
  Melek, 66
  narrow (small) neck of land, 44, 53, 57-60, 63-65, 68-69
  narrow passage (pass), 65-66, 68, 71
  Ramah (Jaredite Cumorah), 68, 166
  sea east, 55, 58, 60, 65
  sea west, 57-58, 60-61, 65
  Shilom, 61
  Shim, 69, 441
  Sidon river, 57, 60, 62, 66-67
  Wilderness: Bountiful (wilderness), 60-63; east wilderness, 59-62; Hermounts (wilderness), 59,

BOM language — *Book of Mormon*
167; narrow strip of.., 59, 60-63
  south wilderness, 59-62, 66
BOM language
  distribution: personal names, 150-52
  English-based word generation, 166
  Linguistic pitfalls, 165-166
  name generation
    from local toponyms (?), 167
    name recurrence, 155
    syllable generation:
      antum, etc. 156
      -hor (ending), 156
      gad/gid names, 156-157
  names with Middle Eastern
    referents, 163-164
  phonology, 152-153
  pseudonyms, 485
  Smith's alias generation, 162-163
  missing Hebrew elements, 157-159
Book of Abraham
  Anubis, 212, 220-221
  Breathing Permit of Hor, 218-220
  canopic jars, 220, 227-228
  Chaldeans (Kaldu), 228, 231
  discovering the papyri, 217-219
  Egyptian administration, 229-230
  facsimile no. 1, 219-222
  facsimile no. 1 fabrication, 221-228
  facsimile no. 2 (hypocephalus), 232
  facsimile no. 3, 237-238
  human sacrifice in Egypt, 231
  hypocephalus fabrication, 232-237
  Improvement Era focus, 524
  Smith's reformed Egyptian; 211
  lion couch scene, 219-221
  Papyrus JS IV, 235
  reformed Egyptian, 210- 211, 259, 522; Coptic, 210; demotic, 210; Gerzean pottery, 210; Hieratic, 210; logograms, 210; Middle Egyptian & Coptic, 211; pyramid of Unas, 210; sign list development, 210
  Ur of Chaldea, 228-230
Book of Commandments
  drafting, 243-244;
  on the angel Moroni, 268

over half received in Kirtland, 447
preparation & printing, 454-455, 490-491, 510
Book of Ether, 238, 335
  Cowdery jumped ahead from Mormon to Ether, 440; plates of Ether abridged by Moroni, 441
  sandwiched between Mormon & Moroni (contrary to plan) to meet copying needs, 440-442
Book of Lehi, 246-247, 256, 262-263, 381, 429
  dictation, 277-278
  King James English, 90, 99-100, 104, 108, 111, 117-118, 175, 260-261
  loss of the 116-page ms of Lehi, 283-284, 288-289
  more detailed than Nephi, 246-247
  pages retained, 347-349
  purpose: for the Indians to believe in the gospel, 246; for the Lamanites to come to a knowledge of "my people," 246, 255
Book of Mormon, xviii, xix-xxi, 98-99, 131-134, 209, 311
  11/06/1829, copyright, 431, 440, 444
  a marvelous work, 246, 263, 292, 379, 404, 410, 425
  a Smith family project, 291, 381
  apologetics in BOM for itself, 334
  arguments for Hebrew influences, 534-544
  BOM names: Hebrew inscriptions, 538-543; Egyptian names, 544-546
  bridging from Nephi to Mosiah, 337
  completion celebration, 432-433
  composition (drafting) completion date, end of August 1829, 432-433
  copies go on sale at Palmyra's bookstore, 445
  drafts, 56, 63, 301, 240, 244-45, 260-261, 294-295, 300-305, 338-339, 342-343, 347, 50, 358, 430
  events & dates of its remake, 426-29;
  opposition to BOM publication, 440

Book of Mormon — **Church of Jesus Christ of Latter-day Saints**

    original ending (end of the "Book of Mormon"), 441
    plagiarism (?), 304, 316, 324-327
    preexistence, 478; free will, 479;
    prebirth election, 478; spirits & intelligences, 478-479
    printing August 1829-26 March 1830, 432, 444-445
    production events & dates, 426-429
    published by Grandin press, 432
    revelation to sell BOM copyright, 444
    segmentation, 333
    Style: chiasmus, 552-557, 577; *parallelismus membrorum*, 551; poetry, 549-550
    title page a literal translation from the gold plates, 431-432
    urgency to complete it, 434
    witchcraft, 266

Book of Moroni
    a late add-on, 439-446; church establishment verses, 334-335, 421, 442-443; reason for adding Moroni, 442-443; Moroni's first farewell, in Ether, 441-442

Book of Moses, 239
    drafts of text still extant, 240, 294, 300, 430
    Enoch, 241-242, 533-534
    God speaking in first person, 241; spiritual creation, 478

Book of Revelations, 97
Book of the Law of the Lord, 423, 563
Book of the New Covenants, 576
Booth, Ezra, 439, 561
Boudinot, Elias, 7
Bowery, 515
Bowring, Harry, 515
"Bowring's Theatre," 515
Boynton, John F., apostle, 459
Brainerd, David, 382
Brass Plates of Laban, 90-91, 95, 97, 99, 145, 212, 216, 253, 258, 422, 563
Brennan, Michael, 332
Broadbent, J. Leslie, 565
Broadhurst, Dale, xvii, 161, 315-316

broadside of gold-plate transcript for *The Prophet* (NY, NY, 1844), 282
Brother of Jared, xxi, 136, 238, 476-478
Bryant, John W., 566
Budge, Sir E. A., 213
Burton, Robert T., 575
Calder, David O., 503-504
Caldwell County, MO, 489, 572
Caldwell, James, 563
California gold rush, 501
Calkins, Pamela J., 568
Camp Floyd Theatre, 515
Campbell, Alexander, 311, 320, 323-324
Campbellism, 319, 322-325, 472
Canaanites, 7, 81, 132, 172, 199, 228, 539
caravans & caravanserai, 93, 251-252
Careless, George Edward Perry, 514
Carthage Greys, 497
Carthage Jail (IL), xx, 448, 496-497
Centennial Park (Second Ward) group, 566
Champollion, 147, 149, 211-212, 214, 279
Charles V, 4
Chase, Willard, 264, 270, 386
Chiapas, Mexico, 523
Chief Red Jacket, 11-12
Christ in America (Mather & others), 11
Christians (Pre-Columbian), xxii, 98-99, 139-144, 334-335
Chubby, William, 561
Church of Christ, 140, 142, 304, 411
Church of Christ (of Ezra Booth), 561
Church of Christ (Rigdonite; Church of Jesus Christ of the Children of Zion), 322, 562
Church of Christ (temple lot), 448
Church of Christ (W. Parrish), 464, 561
Church of Christ Whitmerite 425, 432, 562
Church of Christ (William Chubby), 561
Church of Jesus Christ (Bickertonite), 563
Church of Jesus Christ (Original Doctrine), 566
Church of Jesus Christ in Solemn Assembly, 566
Church of Jesus Christ of Latter-day Saints (Church of Christ), 308
    2015 membership by country, 602; apostle, 97-98, 435, 437-38, 456-59,

finances — rites

486; bishops, 461; church attendance compared, 598-599; Church establishment verses, 434-435, 455-56 Citizens of Jackson County met & requested Saints to leave, (i.e., "to warn them out"), 447; concubinage & the patriarchs, 474; cross, 136, 143, 199, 476, 481; dissimulation, 244, 482, 595; executive order (extermination order) for the removal of the Mormons from Missouri, 448, 452, 490; over 10,000 were expulsed, 452; finances, 467, 483-487:
    city scrip, 486; faith & revenues, 604; money in 19th-century America, 483; stock certificates, 485-486; Utah Territory, 486; tithing (v. infra);
first Church conference (June 1830), 438, 447; First Presidency of Brigham Young, 449; gathering to the Rocky Mountains, 448-449; gathering to Zion in Missouri, 452, 489; hierarchy, 452-463;
militarism:
    Brigham's Boys ('Be'-boys, minute men), 495; Danites, 419, 489-495, 498, 572-574; Justice-of-the-Peace warned out of Kirtland, 489; Ohio Army of Israel, 489; Missouri Army of Israel, 489; Mormon War (Missouri), xxiii, 493, 571-574; Nauvoo constables/police (beating and flogging), 494-495; Nauvoo Legion, 494; Nauvoo Whistling & Whittling Brigade (targeted "dissidents"), 494 Rigdon's proclamation of liberty, 490; Salt Sermon, 438, 491; Smith's Lifeguards, 489-490, 494; Zion's Camp, 31, 484, 490, 491; War Department, 489
mini temples, 603
Missouri mob destroys printing house, 447-448

Missouri-Mormon conflict, 452
Missouri temple announced (D&C 57), 447; cornerstone laid (3 August 1831), 477
move to Kirtland, OH, 447
move to Utah, 449
presidency, succession crisis, 449, 498; Quorum of the Twelve Apostles (interim), 498, 523
Primary Organization, 512, 586
Quorum of the Anointed, 498-499
Quorum of the Twelve Apostles, 422, 438, 449-450, 463, 489, 498, 508
Quorum of the Seventies, 462-463
Relief Society, 510-512, 578
    Indian Relief Society, 511
    religious instruction, 511
Rigdon's prospectus for Missouri temple project, 447
rites
    baptism, 67, 112, 139, 241-242; 257, 351, 407, 410, 434, 438-439, 450, 454, 456, 459, 465, 483, 586-587, 603; infant baptism, 323, 350-51; baptism procedures, 434; baptism for the dead, 470-473 (1st time, 472; and genealogy, 473);
    bearing testimony, 587
    blessing of the bread, 434, 454, 466, 586
    blessing of the wine, 434, 454, 466, 586
    endowment, 466-468, 488, 498-499, 588-589, 603
    Fast Offerings Program, 512
    gift of tongues, 145, 465-466
    Gift of the Holy Ghost, 140, 142, 241-242, 396, 465, 583, 586
    giving a name & a blessing, 585-586
    laying on of hands, 140, 408, 416, 456, 460, 462, 460-465-466, 568, 586
    no shriving, 419, 481, 589

ordination of deacons, 456, 587-588, 591
ordination of elders, 140, 305, 428, 438, 443, 453, 456-458, 465-467, 481, 487, 565, 584, 587-588, 591, 598
ordination of priests & teachers, 434, 454, 587
Patriarchal Blessing, 256, 263, 460, 588
polygamy, 473 condemned in the BOM & Ether, 474; dissension, 474, 562, 564; Fanny Stenhouse, 474; wives of Joseph Smith, 473; Brigham Young, 475
Prayer, 478
sealing, 460, 466-467, 471, 473-476, 589
temple ceremony, 468-470, 498 marriage, 474, 488, 526, 583, 589, 590-591, 596 Masonic ceremony, 468-470; secrecy & penalties, 470; temple recommend, 589
tithing, 486, 499, 508, 583, 585, 589, 603-604
"law" of sacrifice, 585
washing & anointing, 465-469, 471, 589
washing the feet, 465-466
School of the Prophets, 465, 467, 577
second conference announced to be held in Missouri (D&C 52), 447
Seventy, 462-463, 489, 530-531
sexuality, 581-582
Smith's 1831 exploratory party to St. Louis, 447
stakes & wards, 461
theocracy, 487
theology, 476
   appeal of LDS theology, 591; Mormonism & Christianity, 482-483
salvation: exaltation & family, 479, 582-583; kings & queens in the hereafter, 591-592; heaven, 468, 479-480; hell, 480; human beings are tripartite, 479; interim spirit world, 472; salvation & faith, 583-584 salvationist religion, 583; scripture: text vs. perception, 583-585; sexuality, 581-582 speculative theology is limited, 480; Universalist influence, 382, 391, 479-480
United Firm (Order), 162, 484-485
Welfare Program, 511
Women in Mormonism, 595-598
Word of Wisdom, 513, 589
   temperance movement, 513
worship, 480
Young Ladies' Department of the Cooperative Retrenchment Association, 513
Young Men's Mutual Improvement Association (YMMIA), 512, 589; Aaronic Priesthood MIA, 513
Young Women, 512-513, 590
Church of Jesus Christ of Latter-day Saints and the Kingdom of God, 566
Church of Jesus Christ, the Bride, the Lamb's Wife, 562
Church of Jesus Christ of Latter-day Saints (Strangite), 563
Church of Jesus Christ of Saints of the Most High, 569
Church of Potter Christ, 569
Church of Satan, 97, 130, 400
Church of the Firstborn, 567
Church of the Firstborn (Morrisite), 569
Church of the Firstborn and the General Assembly of Heaven, 567, 580
Church of the Firstborn of the Fullness of Times; 567
Church of New Covenant in Christ, 566
Church of Zion, 567-568
Chynoweth, Duane, 576
Chynoweth, Mark, 576
Chynoweth, Noemi Zarate, 576
Chynoweth, Rena, 576

Clapp — Oliver Cowdery

Clapp, Orin (Hurlbut sponsor), 307
Clark, John A. (pastor), 290
Clark, (General) John B., 573
Clark, Wycam, 561
Clay County, MO, 572
Clayton, William, 494
Cluff, Benjamin, 43, 48, 527
Cobb, Mrs., 288
Coe, Michael, 216, 521
Coe, Sophi, 521
Coit, Thomas Winthrop, 281
Cole, Abner, 386, 428-429
    begins printing BOM installments in *The Reflector*, 443
Colonia LeBaron, Mexico, 567
Colorado City, AZ, 565
Coltrin, Zebedee, 466
Columbus, 1
Commerce (Illinois), xxiii, 448
    first Mormon land purchase, 448
Community of Christ (formerly the Reorganized Church of Jesus Christ of Latter Day Saints), xx, 245, 308, 449, 564, 577; ownership of greater temple lot, 448
composition disproportion, 56, 333-335, 434; composition obfuscation attacks, 332; record-keeper terms of service, 83-85; BCE & CE text length, 333-335, 434; number of new proper names, 434
concubinage, 82, 129, 244, 474, 476, 579
Confederate Nations of Israel, 566
Conneaght, 307, 316-317
Conneaut, OH, 305-306, 309, 314, 317
Conneaut Creek/River, 307-308, 316-317
content analysis: distribution of thematic elements, 359-362; distribution of English usage, 362-364, 367-9; stylometry, 329-330
control
    access to plural wives, 476; charismatic election (3 witnesses), 453; controlling Church history, 454 (Smith's personal efforts, 454-455; Cowdery's history, 455); Control of dissidence, 494-496, 573-74; controlling doctrine, 450; controlling the scriptural record, 455; controlling revelation, 457; Cowdery as cotranslator/author, 453; disfellowship & excommunication, 488; the 1837-38 purge, 491; fallen prophet contingency, 458; hierarchy & control, 453; male dominance by marrying other men's wives, 488; management by revelation, 455; Mormon security forces, 488-492; obedience of wives, 488; opposition to bureaucracy, 463-464; personal security, 451; power to coerce, 487-492; priesthood as control, 454-459; Rigdon's salt sermon, 491-492; ritual, 487-488; Smith's Lifeguards, 489, 494; tar & feathering, 311, 452; violent attacks, 452; Zion's Camp, 484, 489, 571
Conversion of the Indians, 4, 246, 450
Coriantumr, 68, 87, 156, 239, 340
Corning, Nathan, 307
Corrill, John, 451, 461, 491-492
Council of Fifty, 566
Council of Friends (Priesthood Council), 565-566
Council of the Twelve, 467
Council of the Fourteen (Valladolid), 4
Cowdery, Lyman, 404, 406, 427; joined the Strangites, 422
Cowdery, Oliver, 56, 74
    05/04/1829 arrival at Harmony, 407, 431
    06/04/1829, drafted & witnessed Smith's contract with Isaac Hale, 431
    07/04/1829, made scribe to write for Joseph, 407, 429
    abilities, 304, 407; accused Joseph Smith of immoral behavior, 491; apostleship, 435; appointed school teacher by Hyrum Smith, 392; appointed one of the high priests to preside in Missouri, 491; Assistant President of the High Priesthood,

462; attempt at a non-Mormon life, 422; authorship, 305, 429-431; baptized by Joseph Smith, 407; bio & family heritage, 405-407; BOM drafting & editing, 301, 378-380; celestial marriage, 473-474; child baptism, 350-351; claim that he & Joseph were ordained by John the Baptist, 407; connection with the Strangites, 422; connection with the Whitmerites, 425; controlling Church history, 454-455; D&C composition & preparation, 454-456; Democratic party candidate in 1846, 422; designated "first preacher of the, church," 450; died in home of David Whitmer, 422; worked as editor of a Democratic newspaper (1845), 422; worked as coeditor of Walworth County Democrat, 422; excommunication (1838), 491; fell behind in copying ms *P*, 439-440; frequent visitor to Grandin press, 445; friend of David Whitmer, 404; got Hiram Page to recant, 419; his revelation, 335, 422, 434-439 [was it a plagiarism (?), 435]; its connection to D&C 18:1-5, 434-435; date, 435-436]; joined the Methodists c. 1844, 422; lawyer (in Tiffin, OH, & Elkhorn, WI), 407, 422; letter to Hyrum Smith (14/06/1829: "stir up the minds"), 350-351, 401; letter from Smith ("the Gold Book business"), 398; made cotranslator (coauthor), 409, 429-430 [reduced to scribe, 409, 430]; main scribe for ms *O*, 294-295; missionary, 450-451, 490; Mosiah Chapter One, 338-339; page headings, 299-300; printer, 407, 440-441; recruited to the BOM project, 407; resided with Joseph Smith Sr. when teaching school, 392, 404, 407; resided with Smith family while working on ms *P*, 402; restoration of the gold plates to Joseph timed with Cowdery's vision of them, 403; returned to the LDS Church, 422; rodsman, 266-67, 392; role in BOM remake, 404; role in recruiting the Whitmers, 408; school teacher in Manchester, 404; seer stone scryer, 404; Smith/Cowdery ordination by Peter, James & John, 408, 417; title changed to "Second Elder," 443; witness to the gold plates, 412-414; worked at Grandin press (?), 440

Cowdery, William, 387, 392, 405, 406 joined the Strangites, 422

Crawford, Charles, 7

Criddle, Craig S., 330-331

Cromwell, Oliver, 2-3

Crossfield, Robert C., 567

Crucifixion Cataclysm, xxii, 45-46, 71, 73-74, 141, 335

Cumming, Alfred, second governor of, the Utah Territory, 495-496

Cunningham, Artemas, 310

Curran, Pearl Lenore, 384-385

Dalton, Terrill R., 567, 580

Dartmouth College, 390, 401

David (king), 131-132, 228

Davidson, Matilda Spalding, 306

Daviess County, MO, 493

Davis, William, 393

de Bourbourg, Brasseur, 520

de Landa, Diego, 216, 520-521

Dead Sea, 251-253

Deseret Book Company, 510

Deseret Dramatic Organization, 514

Desmond, David-Edward, 568

Dialogue. A Journal of Mormon Thought, 524

dissidents, 448

Doctrine and Covenants, 242-245, 330; Church establishment, 434-435, 455-456; editing, 455; pseudonyms, 485

Drummond, William W., 495

Dunham, (Major General) Jonathan, 497

Durfee, Lemuel, 443

Dusenberry, Warren, 507

Eames, Wilberforce, 2

Easty, Mary, 266

ecumenism, 130, 483

Edom — Martin Harris

Edom, 248
Edwards, Jonathan, 15, 173, 181, 207, 396
Elkhorn, WI, 422
Elohim, 482
Ephraim, 132-133, 146, 282
Ethiopic, 90, 104, 108, 216, 226, 533-534
Eusebius, 99
Evans, Tripp, 519
Eliot, John, 5-6
Fairchild, James H., 307
fallen prophet, 453, 458, 461-462
Far West, MO, 448, 464, 485, 490-491, 572
Fayette, NY, 423, 425, 432, 444
    branch organized by Cowdery, 450
Feliz, Antonio A., 568
Ferguson, Thomas Stuart, 49, 509, 517, 523-524, 527, 599, 629
Folsom, William H., 515
Ford, (Governor) Thomas, 497
Förstemann, Ernst, 520
Fortier, John C., 329
Foster (Jr.), Glen, 351
Franklin, Benjamin, 483
Freemasonry, 176, 392, 401, 448, 468-470
Fundamentalist Church of Jesus Christ of Latter-day Saints, 565, 578
Gallus, Aelius, 255
Garden of Eden, xxiii, 163, 469
Gause, Jesse, counselor to Smith, 462
    excommunicated, 462
Geddes, Norma, 506
Geddes, William C., 506
Geddes, Zola, 506
George Q. Cannon & Sons (pub.), 510
Gilbert, John H., 428, 432, 439, 445
Gnosticism, 94, 173
Godbe, William S., 567
Gold plates, xxi-xxii, 14, 46, 101-104, 133, 147, 149, 211-212, 215, 242, 247-248, 268, 259-260, 268, 271-280, 290-291, 381, 386, 402, 417, 431, 441, 535, 601
    brass plates prop (feasible?), 276-277; keeping them safe, 272; location (stone box), 268; pagination right to left, 432; size, 273; Smiths hefted &; handled the plates, under cover, 275; the toad story, 270-271; their weight, 272; transcript of gold plate characters, 216, 277-278, 281-282; featured in a broadside for *The Prophet* (NY, NY), 282; translated by Smith's seer stone, 278; tumbaga plates, 272-274; writing area, 276
gold plates (24 Jaredite plates), 335
Goodman, Felicitas, 145
Goodman, Joseph, 520
Gookin, Daniel, 7
Gould, John, 266
Graham, Sylvester, 513
Grand Island (Niagara River), 11
Grandin, E. B., 428, 432, 451
Grandin press, 432-433, 440, 443-444, 632
Great Awakening (First...), 5-6, 14
Great Awakening (Second...), 6, 14-15, 156, 382
Great Isaiah Scroll, 96, 110, 116, 118, 126
Great Rift, 252
Greenstadt, Rachel, 332
guardian spirits (of treasure), 267-268
Gulf of Aqaba, 250-251, 253-254
Gunther, Jacob H., 329
Hagoth (Alma 63:5-8), 51, 451, 602
Hale, Reuben, 277
Hammon, Marion, 566
Hanke, Lewis, 2
Hanover, NH, 390, 401
hapax legomena, 118, 217
Harding, John, 117
Harding, Stephen S., 445, 569, 575
Harman, Geody, 580
Harmony, Susquehanna Co., PN, 277-278, 379, 401-410, 425-433, 440, 443-444
Harmston, James D., 567
Harris, Caroline, 423
Harris, Lucy
    Hefted & handled the plates under cover, 275
    doubted, 278, 282
    burned the lost 116 pages (?), 287
    stole the lost 116 pages (?), 286-288
Harris, Martin, 215, 246, 256, 271-272
    doubting Thomas or scout? 278-279
    escorted for first visit to Harmony

by Hyrum Smith, 279;
excommunication, 422;
finances BOM project, 279, 403,
422; frequent visitor to Grandin
press, 445; handled & hefted the
plates, 275, 277; his wife & daughter
hefted & handled the plates under
cover, 275; joined the Gladdenites,
423; joined the Strangites, 422;
joined the Whitmerites, 423; joined
the Williamites, 423; joined with
Warren Parrish to found a
breakaway church, 420; Kirtland
Temple guide, 423; loss of the 116-
page ms of Lehi, 283-284; profit
motive, 279, 422; rejoined the Utah
Mormons, 423; scribe for the Book
of Lehi, 277-279, 282; secured BOM
contract, 444; strained relations
with Smith, 403; took the Lehi ms
(116 pages) to his home in upstate
NY, 282-283; visit to Anthon &
Mitchell (Smith's account), 279-281
witness to the gold plates, 412, 414
Harris, Preserved, 288
Haun, Jacob, 452
Haun's mill, 452, 572
Hegra (Al-Hijr, Mada'in Salih), 252
Hibbard, Billy, 382
Higher Criticism, 17, 94-95
Hijaz, 252
Hilton, John, 329-333, 351, 356, 359, 362, 365, 373, 380
Hinkle, George M., 561, 573
Hinckley, Gordon B., 510, 603
Hiram (Canaanite king), 7, 81, 132
Holley, Vernal, 168, 329
Holmes, D. I., 329-331
Hoton, 561
Howard, Nahum, 310
Howe, Eber D., 280-281
letters to Howe and Coit, 280-281; *Mormonism Unvailed*, 306, 307, 310, 314-316; Booth's letter re Cowdery's defense of his revelation, 438-439

Hunter, Milton R., 523, 530-531
Hurlbut, Doctor Philastus
anti-Mormon sponsorship, 307, 311; bio, 306-307; dispute with Joseph Smith, 306, 311; his conversion & excommunication, 305-306; his collected statements, 306, 308-315; ordained an elder, 305; Otsego (Oberlin) Manuscript, 308, 316
Hyde, Orson, 422, 450; acted part of Michael in Nauvoo temple, 469 apostle, 459; missionary, 451
Hyksos, 228
hypocephalus, 232
incest & inbreeding, 580
  fumarase deficiency, 580
Independent Church, 561
Indian Ocean, 248, 252-253, 255, 559
Indians (Native Americans), 2
interpreter (spectacles), 278, 281, 414-415
Isaiah, 95-97, 171-172; BOM variant readings, 99-116; Great Isaiah Scroll, 96-97, 110, 116, 118, 126; Isaiah package, 257-261
Isidore of Seville, 1
Ishmael (BOM), xxi, 76-79, 142, 259, 559
Isles of the Sea, 15, 54, 65, 132-134, 257
Isolation in Utah diminished
  Utah demography, 502
  Utah education, 503-510
    Brigham Young, 503
  Utah employment, 503
  Utah religion, 502
Jackson County/Independence (Missouri), xxiii, 447, 452, 463, 489
Jaredites, xxi, 29, 34, 60, 238-239, 335
  brother of Jared, 476
Jeffs, Brent, 578
Jeffs, Clyne, 578
Jeffs, Rulon, 565, 578
Jeffs, Warren, 578
Jehoiachin, 91-92, 96
Jehoiakim, 91-92
Jehovah, 136, 138, 157-159, 226
Jenkins, Kenneth D., 351
Jeremiah, xxii, 92-93, 132, 151, 262
Jerome (Saint), 1, 99

Jerusalem — LDS religious research

Jerusalem
  sack & exile to Babylon, 91-92
  destruction (walls/temple/palace), 92
  trade routes, 251
  travel of Nephi et al., 253
Jizan, 252
Jockers, Matthew L., 330-332
John of Holywood, 2
John (Revelator vs. the Apostle), 97-99
John the Baptist, 407-408, 417, 453, 456
John the Presbyter, 99
John of Patmos (John the Divine), 99, 130, 482
Johnson, Benjamin F., 566
Johnson, John, 451
Johnson, Leroy S., 565-566
Johnson, Luke S., apostle, 459
Johnson, Lyman E., apostle, 459, 464, 492
Johnston, Albert Sidney, 495
Joseph (Biblical), 132
Joseph (on the Brass Plates), 258
Joseph, Alex, 566
Josephus, Flavius, 1
Juab, UT, 501
Justin Martyr, 99
Kaldu (Chaldeans), 228
Kanesville, Iowa, 449
Kelley, E. L., 287
Kendall, Edward Augustus, 265
Kidder, Alfred V., 509
Kimball, Heber C., 449-450; acted part of Eloheem in the Nauvoo temple, 469-470; apostle, 459
Kimball, Helen Mar, 474, 579
Kimball, Spencer W., 566
King, (Judge) Austin Augustus, 493
King, Edward, 10
Kingdom of Judah, 132
Kingdom of Israel, 132-133, 146
Kingston, Ontario, Canada, 444
Kingston clan, 566
Kingston, Elden, 566
Kinney, John F., 575
Kircher, Athanasius, 212-213
Kirtland (Ohio), xxiii
  departure of the Church, 468; early convert nucleus, 450; High Council, 488-489; seat of the Church, 450
Kirtland Safety Society Bank, 422, 484
Kirtland Temple, 423, 448, 467-468, 484, 577
Knight, Joseph (Sr.), 427, 445
Knorosov, Yuri, 521
Laban, 93, 96-97, 258
  his sword, 26-27, 68, 80-81, 93, 139, 341, 386, 413, 416, 600
Lafferty, Brenda, 577-578
Lafferty, Dan, 567, 577-578
Lafferty, Ronald, 567, 577-578
Lake, Henry, 309, 314
Laman/Lamanites, xxii, 54, 58, 60-62, 68, 93; atheism, 138-139; Lamanite curse, xxii, 14, 134; religion, 137-139; the Great Spirit, 137-138
Lansing, R. R., 431
Larsen, Wayne A., 328-329
Larson, Stan, 523
Las Casas, Bartholomé de, 4
Latin Vulgate, 111, 172
Latter Day Church of Christ (Kingston Clan or Davis County Cooperative Society), 566
Law, William, 562
Lawrence, Harold W., 524
Layton, Tim, 328
LDS canon, xviii-xxi, 303
LDS education:
  academic freedom, 508; Bannock Stake Academy, 507; Brigham Young Academy, 507; Brigham Young University, 328-329, 382, 504, 507, 524; Church College of Hawaii, 507; institutes of religion, 506-507; Salt Lake Stake Academy, 507; seminaries, 505, 507
LDS publishing
  Deseret News Bookstore, 510
  early journals, 510
  Ensign, 510, 524-526
  Improvement Era, 510, 524-525
  Literary Firm (& Phelps press), 485
LDS religious research
  Center for the Preservation of

LDS religious research — missionaries

Ancient Religious Texts, 509; Foundation for Ancient Research and Mormon Studies, 510; Laura F. Willes Center for Book of Mormon Studies, 509; Middle Eastern Texts Initiative, 509; Neal A. Maxwell Institute for Religious Scholarship, 508-510; New World Archaeological Foundation (NWAF), 509, 523; Religious Studies Center, 508, 526; William (Bill) Gay Research Chair, 509
LeBaron, Alma Dayer Jr., 567
LeBaron, Cynthia, 576
LeBaron, Ervil, 567, 576
LeBaron, Jacqueline, 576-577
LeBaron, Joel F., 567, 575-576
LeBaron, Ross Wesley, 567
LeBaron, Verlan, 567, 576
LeBaron Sr., Alma Dayer, 566
Lee, Harold B., 511
Lee, John D. (Bishop), 574
Lehi, xxi, 50, 55-57, 59, 76, 80, 91-93, 95, 146, 261-262; his genealogy, 262
Lehi in the Desert (issues):
  dearth of detail, 255; distance from his camp to Jerusalem, 249-253, 558; genealogy, 147, 247, 256, 258-259, 262; Lehi's camp, 253; Lihyani red herring, 559; Nahom, 559; robbers & tribal warfare, 254-255; the river Laman, 253-254
Lemuel, xxii, 93
Lenni Lenape (Deleware Indians), 385
Liberty Jail (MO), 493
Limhi (king), 62, 64, 75
Little, Jesse C., 515
Lounsbury, Floyd, 521
Lundgren, Jeffrey Don, 577
Lyne, Thomas A., 514-515
logograms, 215
Lost Tribes of Israel, 12, 132
Low, Chloe, 578
Lucifer, 170-172
Luke, George L., 506
Ma'rib, 252, 255
Macpherson, Scott James, 384

Madaba, 252
Madoc, 13
Manasseh, 132, 146, 262
Manasseh ben Israel, 3
Manchester, Ontario County, NY, 268, 278, 283, 290, 348, 379-380, 386, 401, 430
"Manuscript Found," 305, 308, 310, 319
"Manuscript Story," 307-308, 316
Margets, Phil, 515
Marquardt, Michael H., xvii, 127, 176, 217, 243, 270-271, 383, 393-395, 455, 473
Marsh, Thomas B., apostle, 459, 464
Marston, Eddie, 576
Marston, Ramona, 576
Mather, Samuel, 11
Mattaniah, 92
Maudslay, Alfred Percival, 520
Maya, 54, 519, 529
Mayan decipherment, 13, 29, 49, 216-217, 519-523
McConkie, Bruce R., 477
McDonald, Maud, 567
McKay, David O., 511, 523
McLellin, William E., 395, 424, 456, 459, 498, 562; apostle, 459
McRay, Alexander, indicted for treason, 493
Mechanic's Dramatic Association, 515
memory reconstruction, 312-313
Messiah, 132, 190-191
Metcalfe, Brent
  his data actually support Hilton, 354-356; a methodological flaw, 352; overlooking "he that," 352-353; style shift argument, 351-356
Methodism, 395
  Cowdery joined (c. 1844), 422; exhorters, 395-7
  exhorter regulations, 397
methodology
  graphs based on unity, 353
  standardizing for book size, 352
Midian, 248
millennialism, 6, 14-15, 134
Miller, John N., 309, 313-314
Milton, John, 172
missionaries, 450-451

membership by country— Natick

membership by country, 2015, 602; church-service missionaries, 604; controls, 450, 490; convert attrition, 603; dissimulation, 244, 482; missionary trends, 603-604; Quorum of the seventies, 462-463; retired couples serving, 604; speaking in church, 587; sent in groups of two or more, 450; sent to convert Indians in Missouri, 447, 450, 490-491; sent to England, 450-451; sent to the Society Islands in French Polynesia, 451; some early key converts, 451
Mitchill (Mitchell), Samuel L., 279
Moab, 248
monotheism, 131, 136, 400, 412, 434, 482
Moon, Todd K., 329
Moor's Indian Charity School (Moor's Academy), 390, 401
Morgan, (Sheriff) William, 493
Morin, (Judge) Josiah, 493
Morley, Isaac, 461
Mormon (abridger), xx, 68-69, 271, 285 commander of the Nephites, 441
Mormon Tabernacle Choir, 514
Moroni (son of Mormon), xx, 68, 131, 440
Moroni (general), 57
Moroni (angel), 267-270
Morris, Joseph, 569, 575
Morrisite War, 569-570, 575
Morton, Rev. A. Q., 329-30, 332-333
Moscow, ID, 506
Mosiah, 64; relocated the Nephites to a land free of Lehi toponyms, 255
Mosiah priority issue, 343-350
  Mosiah Chapter One, 337-342; the evidence of child baptism, 350-351; D&C 10, 338, 343-348; gathering folds, 345; Ms 𝒪 & the Mosiah priority issue, 301; Nephi-Mosiah simultaneity, 378; page numbers, 346; paper types, 345-346; retained pages, 347-349; the promise for three witnesses, 350; the style shift argument: *whoso/whosoever* & *therefore/wherefore*, 351-356, 378; Words of Mormon, 349-351

Moulton, Joseph W., 9
Mountain Meadows massacre, 574
Moyle Jr., Henry D., 603
ms 𝒪 (original BOM manuscript), 240, 245, 293-303, 380, 402, 406, 409-410, 426, 429-434, 439, 444, 624-627; began with Nephi, 426; book summaries, 301; compared with drafts of the Book of Moses, 430; Cowdery main scribe, 294; dictation, 431, 433-434; English errors, 324; folds, 293, 345; gatherings, 293, 346; hand of Joseph Smith, 294, 431; implications: for BOM composition, 294, 358; implications for Mosiah priority, 345-346; issue of the folds, 345-346; Mosiah, Chapter One, 337-342; Mosiah priority issue, 301; originally the printer's copy, 430 page headings, 295-300, 380; heading utility, 300; page numbering, 346-347, 426; paper types, 345-346; placed in the cornerstone of Nauvoo House, 293; proofing, 431; rate of completion, 444; supplying the printer with 𝒪 instead of 𝒫, 439-440; survival of c. 28%, 293; *whoso* & *whosoever*, 378

ms 𝒫, 289, 295, 301, 337-339, 342-343, 358, 378-379, 402, 429-430, 433-434, 439-440, 444; decision to do it as a backup, 433; printer's marks, 439; Gilbert never saw 𝒫 gatherings *16-19*, 439; Gilbert's description of ms 𝒫, 445; Joseph Jr. not involved in printing, 445; rate of completion, 444; supplying the printer with 𝒪 instead of 𝒫 gatherings *16-19*, 439-440
Mulek/Mulekites, xxii, 34-35, 50, 54, 57, 92
Mulholland, James, 268
Musical and Dramatic Club, 514
Musketaquid Indians, 6
Musser, Joseph White, 565
Najran (Nagran), 252-253
Natick, 6

Native Americans (Indians), xix, xxiii, 4, 5
Nauvoo
    City Counsel, 494; City Marshal, 494; name changed from Commerce, 448; Mayor Joseph Smith, 448; Nauvoo Charter, 448, 494; Smith's Red Brick Store, 448; Nauvoo Brass Band, 514; *Nauvoo Expositor*, 494, 496-497, 562, 574; Nauvoo trial, 496
Nauvoo House, 293, 486
Nauvoo Legion, 31, 448, 496-498, 574
    Lt-General Joseph Smith, 448
Nauvoo Mansion House, 448
    Smith family moved in, August 1843, 448
Nauvoo Masonic Lodge, 448
Nauvoo stakes & wards, 461
Nauvoo Temple, 448, 468, 472, 486, 510
Naylor, Frank, 566
Naylor (Third Ward) group, 566
nearest shrunken centroid (NSC) content analysis, closed set, 330-331; NSC, open set, 331-332
Nebuchadnezzar, 91-92
necromancy, 133, 206, 386
Neilsen, Ivan, 566
Nephi/Nephites, xxii, 17, 54-58, 60-63, 95 cross (symbol & rite), 135-136, 143; language, 145-156; monotheism, 131, 136; religion, 129-136; the missing texts, 148; angel Nephi (?), 268, 271
Nephi (city), xxii, 54-55, 62, 64, 69, 80-81
Neponset Indians, 6
New Jerusalem, 452, 571
Newell, Grandison, 307
Nibley, Hugh Winder, 242, 508-509, 525-526, 531-534; Nibley on Smith's translation method, 532; *Enoch the Prophet*, 533-534
Nibley, Preston, 506
Nicene Creed, xix
Noah, Mordecai Manuel, 11, 383, 394
Noah's Flood (restock fauna), 1, 238-239
Nonantum Indians, 6, 156
Nufud Desert, 254
Nyman, Jane, 472
Oakes, Dallin H., 509

Oberlin College, 306-308
Oberlin Manuscript, 308, 314, 316
    its wrapper, 307-308,, 316-317
    its contents, 318-319
Ogden, UT, 501, 569
Olmecs, 54, 139, 529
Ossian, 384
Otsego County, NY, 308, 319
Otsego Manuscript, 308, 314, 316
    its wrapper, 316-317
    its contents, 318
Pack, John, 503
Page, Hiram
    claimed revelations, 419, 457, 561; connection with the Whitmerites, 425; seer stone scryer, 404; witness to the gold plates, 404-405, 412
Palenque dynasty list, 521
Palmer, David A., 523
Palmyra, NY, 278, 386, 391, 422, 443, 444
Park, John R., 504
Parrish, Warren, 420, 422, 464, 561
Parry, John, 514, 517
Partridge, Edward, bishop, 461
    rebuked, 461-462
Patriarch
    Presiding Patriarch (Patriarch of the Church), 460
Patten, David W., apostle, 459
Patterson & Lambdin, 305, 310, 425
Paul, 134, 258, 334, 443, 472
Peniston, William P., 493
Penn, William, 7
Peterson, Ziba, 438, 450, 490
Peterson, Gerald, Sr., 566
Petra, 252-253, 255
Phelps printing house
    Mob destroyed it, 448, 452
Phelps, William W., 243, 407, 510
    acted part of the serpent in Nauvoo temple, 469; counselor to David Whitmer in Missouri, 490-491; excommunicated (1838), 491; foundation of Far West, 572; *Nauvoo Expositor* trial in Nauvoo, 496
phonological signs, 215, 216

Piltdown man — Sidney Rigdon

Piltdown man, 384
Pitt, William, 514
Pizarro (a play in Nauvoo), 514
plates of Nephi
    large plates, 284-286
        plates of Lehi, 285
        record of Nephi, 262, 286
    small plates, 247, 256-258, 284-286, 302, 338-9, 343, 347, 349-350, 356-357, 381, 417, 442, 629
plot to alter the purloined 116 pages (?), 285
Polygamy, 129, 473, 499-500, 578-580
    concubinage & the patriarchs, 474; Manifesto of 1860, 564; Manifesto of 1904, 565; *Nauvoo Expositor*, 494; polygamy underground, 565; sexuality, 581; spiritual wife, 494, 499-500, 579
Polysophical Society, 512
Polytheism, 136, 400, 476-479
    anthropomorphism, 400, 476
    brother of Jared, 476
    BOM monotheism, 477
        Abinadi, 476-477; LDS orthodoxy, 477; priesthood unity, 477-478; *Nauvoo Expositor*, 494
population
    enabling & limiting, 76, 79-82, 88-89; Jaredite longevity, 86; modeling, 75-78; Nephite longevity, 87; Nephites maximized, 78-79; record-keeper longevity, 86
Post-Biblical Euro-Christian elements
    Biblical interpretation, 170; definition, 169; Freemasonry, 176; influence from hymns, 180; modern issues, 205; theological phrases, 189
Postman, Joseph, 312
Potter, Arnold, 569, 575
Poultney, VT, 392
Pratt, Orson, apostle, 45-46, 241, 459, 591
Pratt, Parley P., 396, 447, 450, 459, 490, 591-592; apostle, 459
Priest, Josiah, 10, 15, 31

Priesthood, 455-463
    Aaronic, restored to Joseph & Oliver by John the Baptist, 407, 459, 499; keys, 460; Melchizedek, 416, 454, 459-460, 468-471, 499, 586-588; ordination of priests & teachers, 434, 454; Patriarchal, 403, 460, 499; women, 568, 595
Primitive Church of Jesus Christ (Bickertonite), 563
"Proclamation for the Jews (M. Noah)," 11
Promontory Summit, 501
Proskouriakoff, Tatiana, 521
Provo, UT, 501, 507, 567, 577
Pseudepigrapha, 383-384, 533
Pultneyville/Sodus, 386
Pure Church of Christ, 561
Queen of Sheba, 252
Quinn, Michael, 267, 382, 387, 437, 488
Rafinesque, Constantine Samuel, 12-13, 385, 520
Rapp, Johan Georg, 15
Rappists (Harmonites), 15
record-keepers, 82-84, 441
record of Nephi, 262, 286, 302, 347
Red Sea, 61, 174-175, 249-253, 254-255
Redford, Donald B., 229-230
Redstone Baptist Association, 322
Rehoboam, 132-133, 146
Relief Society founded in Nauvoo, 448
Rencher, Alvin C., 328
Reorganized Church of Jesus Christ (Bickertonite), 563
Reorganized Church of Jesus Christ of Latter Day Saints (the Community of Christ), xviii, 308, 418, 564; BOM mss, 240; established in 1860, 449
Restoration Church of Jesus Christ, 568
restoration of all things, 14, 453-454, 462, 465, 468
Rice, Lewis L., 307-308, 316
Richards, Franklin D., 470
Richards, Willard, 449, 497
Richmond, MO, 422
Rigdon, Sidney, 304-306, 311, 447, 467
    a prominent Campbellist, 320, 323-324; a very fine English grammarian,

320, 324; Adventure Farm, 562; arrested, tried and convicted in connection with the Kirtland Society Bank, 484; bio, 319-321; circuit preacher, 322; collaboration with Smith, 465; conversion, 447; first counselor to Smith, 462; father-in-law was a tanner, 322; independence speech, 572; infant baptism, 471-472; investigated for heresy, 322; journeyman tanner, 322; minister of the First Baptist Church in Pittsburgh, 321; loss of this position, 322; struggle for a congregation, 322-323; keys of the kingdom taken away, 460, 561 pre-Mormon history, 324-326 rebuked by Joseph Smith, and stripped of the high priesthood, 461; reordained to the high priesthood, 461; succession crisis, 449, 498, 562; tarred and feathered, 311; wife and daughters, 322

Rigdon's Salt Sermon, 438, 491, 573
Righteous Branch of the Church of Jesus Christ of Latter-day Saints, 566
Rinney, Jonathan, 392
River Laman, 253
Roberts, B. H., 268
Robertson, Merle Greene, 521
Robinson (at Grandin press), 440
Robinson, Ebenezer, 562
Robinson, George W., 490
Rockwell, Orrin Porter, 497, 571
rodsmen, 264, 266, 387, 391-392, 407, 414
Roediger, H. L., 313
Roper, Matthew, 331, 538
Rosetta Stone, 147, 211-213, 216
Royalton, VT, 392-393
rumor dynamics, 311-312
Russell, Isaac, 561
Saba (Sheba), 248, 252
Salt Lake City, UT, 449, 486 494, 501, 504-505, 514, 551, 598
Salt Lake Theater, 515
Salt Lake Tribune, 567
Samarin, William J., 145

Satan, 170-174
Saul, 131, 133
Saunders, Benjamin, 311
Saunders, Lorenzo, 287, 386
Schaalje, Bruce, 330-331
Schele, Linda, 521
School of Prophets (Crossfield), 567, 577
scribes:
    contribution to BOM text, 278;
    hierarchy, 431; scribal errors, 293
scriptural community, xviii
Second Coming, 3, 6, 14-16
secret combinations, 177-178
seer stone to translate the gold plates, 278
seer stone scryers, 247, 264-267, 404
Seetzen, Ulrich Jasper, 254
Seler, Eduard, 520
Septuagint, 91, 104-105, 108, 110-111, 114, 116-118, 125, 172
Sepulveda, 4
Shabwa, 252
Shakers, 15
Shakespeare, 169
Sharma, 251-252
Shechem, 132, 146
Shipps, Jan, 291
Shoal Creek, 452
Short Creek Community, 565
Simon, Barbara Anne, 10
Simons, Bob, 576
Skousen, Royal, 289, 293-294, 299, 346
Smith, Alvin, 271, 351, 386, 401, 443, 471
Smith, Don Carlos, 392
Smith, Elias, 382
Smith, Emma, 218, 240, 277-278, 293
    examined the plates through a linen tablecloth, 415; LDS hymnal, 465, 514; letter to Joseph in flight, 497; move to home of Peter Whitmer Sr., 408-409; Relief Society, 511; remained in Illinois, 449, 564; revelation threatened that she must abide by polygamy, 511; scribal work on ms *O*, 294-295, 379
Smith, Ephraim, 351, 443
Smith, Ethan, 8-10, 324
Smith, George A., 457-458, 469

Smith, Hyrum, 267, 401-402
  acted part of Jehovah at the Nauvoo temple, 469
  05/1829 visit to Joseph & Oliver, 401; accompanied Martin Harris on Harris' first trip to Harmony, 401; brought the first gathering of ms *P* to Grandin press, 445; education, 401; flight across the Mississippi, 496-497; frequent visitor to Grandin press, 445; hired Oliver Cowdery to teach school in Manchester, 407; indicted for treason (1838), 493; *Nauvoo Expositor* trial in Nauvoo, 496; letter from Cowdery (14/06/1829:, "stir up the minds"), 350-351, 401; member of Mount Moriah Masonic Lodge No. 112 (1827-1828), 392, 468; member of School Board of Trustees of Manchester, 407; move to Manchester, 401; murdered (with brother Joseph), 448; one of the 8 witnesses to the gold plates, 402 possible drafter of the BOM, 379 practicing Presbyterian, 400; role as facilitator, 405; saw the plates in a frock, 275; witness to the gold plates, 412
Smith, Jared, 575
Smith, Jesse, 393, 401-402
Smith, John, presiding patriarch, 392-393
Smith, Joseph, Jr., 56, 211-212, 304, 599-601; 1826 pretrial examination, 264; 1828 (June or July) visit to his parents, 283; 1829 revelations, 433; 1830, attempts to prosecute him, 264; 1831, move to Kirtland, 447; 1838, moves to Far West, 491; abilities, 304; ability to delegate authority, 450; abscess in his leg, 275, 393; accommodating Oliver Cowdery's revelation, 437-439, 442-443; acquisition of gold plates, 268-270; arrested, tried and convicted in connection with the Kirtland Society Bank, 484; Articles of Agreement, 272; Assassination events, 496-498; attempt to associate himself with the conversion of the Whitmers, 425; author of Nephi, 378-379, 429; baptized by Oliver Cowdery, 407; birth family, 390; blood heir to the Patriarchal priesthood, 460; BOM authorship, 305; BOM remake, 404; appointed commander-in-chief, 489; collaborative accommodation, 513; conflict options in Nauvoo, 492, 497-498; cooper's son, 277; court appearance for a debt owed to Lemuel Durfee, 443; disdain for churches of his day, 400; dynasty, 499; early profit motive, 255; education, 390, 393-394; Egyptian alphabet & grammar, 214-215, 524; escapee (while on route to Boone County, MO, for trial: 1839), 493 exhorter, 256, 395; extemporaneous dictation, 395-396; farmed at Harmony to support his family during fall-winter, 1828-29, 403; fate of the lost 116 pages, 287-288; finished ms *O* draft in home of Peter Whitmer Sr., 402, 432; First Vision, xx, 398-401, 476-477, 483; flight across the Mississippi, 496-497; Freemasonry, 392; "God is my 'right-hand man'," 398; indicted for treason, 493; inspired version of the Bible, 379, 429; letter to Cowdery: "the Gold Book business," 398; loose cannon (?), 496; loss of the 116-page ms of Lehi, 283-284, 403-404, loss of gift for a spell, 402-403; Methodist exhorter, 395; Mosiah Chapter One, 339; murdered (with brother Hyrum), 448; not involved in the printing, 445; plates taken away, then restored, 403; presence in Manchester in August 1829, 445; profit motive, 270-271; Red Brick Store, 448, 468; Relief Society, 510-512; respect for his father, 403; return to Harmony (4/10/1829), 433;

Joseph Smith, Sr. — Matilda Spalding

return to Manchester, c. 23/01/1830, 443-444; revelation to sell BOM copyright, 444; runs carrying the plates, 275; scryer fee, 267; seer stone scryer, 264-267, 404; Secretary of War, 493; sexual accusations, 451-452; speaks for God, 397; tarred and feathered, 311, 452; tombstone of his firstborn, 283; transcript of gold plate characters, 216, 277-278; treasure hunting, 264-265; Urim & Thummim taken away, 344; visit to his parents (1828), 404; Walters, Luman, 386; welcomed by the Whitmers upon his arrival at Peter Whitmer Sr.'s home, 425; witchcraft, 266; wives, 473-474
 prerevelation sealing dates, 473; sealings to other-men's wives, 474; underage, 474
Word of Wisdom, 513
youthful story-teller re Indians, 395

Smith, Joseph, Sr., 74, 266
cooper, 272, 277, 389, 391; arranged David Whitmer's visit to Harmony, and the stay at Peter Whitmer's home to complete the BOM, 404, 423; bio, 388-389; blood heir to the Patriarchal priesthood, 460; disdain for churches of his day, 400; first Church (Presiding) Patriarch, 392, 403, 467; forced to become a tenant farmer, 391; recruiting activity while his son was in Harmony, 379, 381, 402-405; role in the BOM remake, 404; saw the plates in a frock, 275; seer stone scryer, 404; treasure hunting, 267; universalism, 392; his visions, 392; visit to meet Emma's parents, 278; visits after loss of 116 pages, 278, 404, 429; Walters, Luman, 386; witchcraft (enchanting guns), 266; witness to the gold plates, 412

Smith, Joseph III, 449
 succession, 564

Smith, Lucy Mack, 267

account of an angel taking the plates from Harmony to Fayette, 431; bio, 389; biographer, historian, propagandist, 420-421; connection with the Strangites, 423; examined the breastplate of Laban through a thin handkerchief, 415; fate of the lost 116 pages, 286-287; handled the plates, 415; letter to William Smith (1845), 420; practicing Presbyterian, 400; saw & handled the interpreters (urim & thummim), 415; seer stone, 267; visit to meet Emma's parents, 278

Smith, Oliver, 309-310
Smith, Robert F., 497
Smith, Samuel H.
 facilitator role, 405; informally called the first missionary, 450; practicing Presbyterian, 400; saw the gold plates in a frock, 275; scribal work on ms $\mathcal{O}$, 294-295, 379-380; witness to the gold plates, 412
Smith, Samuel (of Boxford), 266
Smith, Sophronia
 practicing Presbyterian, 400
Smith, William
 apostle, 459; connection with the Strangites, 423; excommunication, 563; handled & hefted the gold plates, 275; succession claimant, 498, 563-564
Smith family magic paraphernalia, 387
Smoot, Steve, 539, 544
Snow, Eliza R., composer, 465, 511-512, 514, 517
Snow, Gregory L., 331
Snow, Lorenzo, 512
Social Hall, 514
Solomon, xxiii, 7, 27, 80, 91, 131-133, 146
Sondrup, Stephen, 551
Sophronius of Jerusalem, 99
Sorenson, John L., 29, 527
Southey, Robert, 13
Spalding, John, 306, 309, 314
Spalding, Martha, 306, 309, 314
Spalding, Matilda Sabine (i.e. Davison,

Solomon Spalding — E. W. Vanderhoof

Matilda Sabine Spalding), 305-306, 308, 310, 314
Spalding (Spaulding), Solomon, 13, 304, 307; bio, 305-306, 313-316
Spalding-Rigdon Theory, 13, 304-305
    its premises, 304, 306
    its probability, 325-327, 330-331
spectacles (interpreter), 278, 281, 414-415
Spencer, Orson, 503-504
Sperry, Sidney B., 116, 550
Spurgeon, C. H., 395
Stafford, Cornelius R., 310
State of Deseret, 503
Stearns, Norris, 383
Stenhouse, Fanny, 475
Stenhouse, T. B., 475
Stick of Joseph, 131-134, 282
Stowe, Richard, 578
Stowell, Josiah, 264, 391, 394
Strang, James Jesse, 422, 498, 563
Strangites, 418, 422-423, 498
Stuart, David, 522
stylometry, 329-330
Sumerian, 210, 216, 548
Sweet, Northrop, 561
Synoptic Gospels, 98
Syriac, 109, 111, 229
targum (pl, *targumim*), 90, 111, 116-118, 125
Tarshish, 105-108
Taylor, John, 468
    delegated to Governor Ford, 496; *Nauvoo Expositor* trial in Nauvoo, 496; Central American characters are descended from Egyptian, 519
Thomas, Cyrus, 521
Thompson, Eric, 520
Thorowgood, Thomas, 3-5
Thutmose III, 229
    Campaign to Carchemish, 229-230
Tiffin, OH, 422
Tihama, 249, 252
Timothy, 127, 141, 151
Timpson, Alma, 566
Topsfield, MA, 391
Tower of Babel, xxi, 34, 86-87, 152, 238
transcontinental railroad, 501

treasure hunting ritual, 267, 386-387
True Church of Jesus Christ of Latter Day Saints, 562
True and Living Church of Jesus Christ of Saints of the Last Days, 567
tumbaga, 272-276
    gold-copper formula, 274
Tunbridge, VT, 389-391
Turner, Orsamus, 395
Tvedtnes, John, 110, 116, 534-543
Twain, Mark, 446
Twelve Disciples, 98, 127, 141
Tyre/Sidon, 7, 81, 132
U. S. Congress, 475, 495, 513, 564
United Order, 162, 484, 511, 562, 568
United Order Family of Christ (for young gay men), 568
Universalism, 382, 392
University of Deseret, 503, 507
University of Idaho, 506
University of Nauvoo, 488
University of Utah, 218, 503-505
Urban VII (Pope), 513
Urha, 228-230
Urim & Thummim (interpreter), 278, 344, 403, 414-417, 421, 563, 600
Utah liquor laws, 501-502
Utah Magazine, 567
Utah performing arts, 516
Utah precollege education, 505
Utah State University, 329, 504
Utah Territory, xxiii, 422, 495-496, 514
    Buchanan sent a military force to the Utah territory & established a post in Utah, 495; expedition to put down rebellion, 495; Federal officials flee, 495; martial law, 495; military occupation, 496; Mormon opposition to federal officials, 495; only the priesthood authority is recognized, 495; statehood, 496; Utah War, 495-496, 515; Young's call to arms, 495
Vest, Dean Grover, 576
Vogel, Dan, 278, 310-311, 386, 394
Valladolid, 4
Valley of Lemuel, 77, 252-253, 559
Vanderhoof, E. W., 267

Voree, WI, 422, 563
Voree Record, 563
Wadi Arabah, 59, 251-252
Wadi Hadhramout, 252
Wadi Musa, 252
Walam Olum, 385
Walters, Luman, 386
Ward (Dr.), 385
Warm Springs (site of an amusement hall), 514
Warren, Bruce W., 523
Wasatch Mountains, 449, 473, 501
Waterbury, CN (Brass Town), 277
Waterloo, NY, 423
Welch, John, 510, 517, 555
Wells, (Nauvoo Judge) Daniel H., 496
Wells, Emmeline, 511
Wentworth, John, 455
West Lebanon, VT, 394
Westminster College, 504
Wheelock, Eleazar, 401
White, (Sargent) R. C., 515
White, Vonda, 576
Whitefield, George, 206, 396, 536
Whitmer, Christian
    baptized, April 1830, 424
    witness to the gold plates, 412, 416
Whitmer, David
    apostle, 457; at Harmony, 401, 404; baptized, 03 June 1829, 424; Battle of Blue River, 489; claimed right to succession, 420, 423; established his own church, 420; excommunicated (1838), 491; ordained president of the church in Missouri, 491; prior Whitmer-Smith relations, 423; revelator, 396; seer stone scryer, 404; stopped with Oliver Cowdery (1828), 423; succession claimant, 498; witness to the gold plates, 405
Whitmer, Elizabeth Ann, 408
Whitmer, Jacob
    Baptized, April 1830, 424; Conversion, 404; seer stone scryer, 404; witness to the gold plates, 405, 412
Whitmer, John
    Voree — witnesses to the gold plates
    baptized, June 1829, 424 connection with the Whitmerites, 425; counselor to David Whitmer in Missouri, 491; Excommunicated (1838), 491; foundation of Far West, 572; first Church historian, 454; his conversion, 404; witness to the gold plates, 404, 412
Whitmer, Peter, Jr.
    Baptized (April 1830), 424; his conversion, 404; missionary, 450, 490; witness to the gold plates, 404, 412
Whitmer, Peter, Sr., 402
    Baptized (April 1830), 424; his conversion, 404; completion of ms *O* draft in his home, 404, 408-409; put up the elder Smith (02/1829), 423
Whitney, Bishop Newel K., , 461
    Newel K. Whitney store, 465
Whore of All the Earth, 97, 130, 156, 443, 482-483
Widtsoe, John A., 509
Wight, Lyman
    indicted for treason, 493; vigilante leader, 573
Wild, Asa, 382, 394
Wilde, William J., 506
Wilds, Sarah, 266
Willes, Laura F., 509
Willes, Mark H., 509
Willey, Gordon, 509
Williams, Frederick G., 451, 464
    counselor to Smith, 462
Williams, George, 570
Williams, Roger, 5
Winchell, Justus, 387
Winchester, Benjamin, 562
Winter, Rev. John, 322
witchcraft, 266, 382
witnesses to the gold plates, 411-412, 459
    demise and/or apostasy, 418; no confessions, 418-19; reasons for this, 419; the eight witnesses 412, 414; the three witnesses, 411-412; angelic visitation, 412-413; review of

testimonies, 416
Witten, Daniela M., 330-331
Wood, Nathaniel, 392
Wood Scrape, 392
Woodruff, Wilford, 448
Woodruff Manifesto, 564
Woolley, Lorin C., 565
wordprint content analysis, 328-329, 330, 332, 359
    wordprinting Egyptian (?), 333
Worth, Patience, 384-385
Wright, Aaron, 310, 315-316
Worsley, Israel, 9
Yates, John V., 9
Young, Brigham, xxiii, 386, 393, 423, 507 apostle, 459; bodyguards, 494; call to arms (in Utah), 495; control in affairs secular, 567; first governor of Utah Territory, 495

www.ingramcontent.com/pod-product-compliance
Lightning Source LLC
Chambersburg PA
CBHW071933220426
43662CB00009B/892